THE EMERGENT GIANT

Volume Three of *The Oxford History of the American People* opens with America united after the terrible carnage of the Civil War. It depicts the tremendous release of energy that settled the last frontiers, created an immense industrial system, and ultimately established the United States as the richest and mightiest of world powers. It depicts as well the economic dislocations, the social strife, and the series of foreign wars that were by-products of this power. Closing with John F. Kennedy, whose presidency and whose tragic death symbolized both the greatness of America and its continuing dilemmas, this volume stands as a superb conclusion to a truly great work of American history.

"A splendid book!"—*The New York Times*

"Sparkling, living history, brimming with personality, bright with anecdote . . . the product of America's most fastidious historian. Professor Morison has not merely served up vivid, inspiring impressions. . . . He is precise; he is learned; he imparts to the general reader a knowledge of those dates and deeds, facts and figures, without which talk and writing of 'trends' is meaningless."
—*Saturday Review*

THE
OXFORD HISTORY
OF THE
AMERICAN PEOPLE

Volume Three, *1869-1963*

SAMUEL ELIOT MORISON

A MENTOR BOOK

NEW AMERICAN LIBRARY

A DIVISION OF PENGUIN BOOKS USA INC., NEW YORK
PUBLISHED IN CANADA BY
PENGUIN BOOKS CANADA LIMITED, MARKHAM, ONTARIO

SIGNET, SIGNET CLASSIC, MENTOR, ONYX, PLUME, MERIDIAN
and NAL BOOKS are published *in the United States* by New American Library,
a division of Penguin Books USA Inc., 1633 Broadway,
New York, New York 10019, and *in Canada* by Penguin Books Canada Limited,
2801 John Street, Markham, Ontario L3R 1B4

 MENTOR TRADEMARK REG. U.S. PAT. OFF. AND FOREIGN COUNTRIES
REGISTERED TRADEMARK–MARCA REGISTRADA
HECHO EN WINNIPEG, CANADA

First Mentor Printing, 1972

9 10 11 12 13 14 15 16 17

PRINTED IN CANADA

TO MY BELOVED WIFE

PRISCILLA BARTON MORISON

WHO HAS HELPED ME TO UNDERSTAND

THE MOVING FORCES IN THE HISTORY

OF OUR NATION

I find the great thing in this world is not so much where we stand, as in what direction we are moving. . . . We must sail sometimes with the wind and sometimes against it, — but we must sail, and not drift, nor lie at anchor.

Oliver Wendell Holmes *The Autocrat of the Breakfast Table* (1858)

The role of government and its relationship to the individual has been changed so radically that today government is involved in almost every aspect of our lives.

Political, economic and racial forces have developed which we have not yet learned to understand or control. If we are ever to master these forces, make certain that government will belong to the people, not the people to the government, and provide for the future better than the past, we must somehow learn from the experiences of the past.

Bernard Baruch, presenting his papers to Princeton University, at the age of 93. *The New York Times,* 11 May 1964

Preface

THIS BOOK, in a sense, is a legacy to my countrymen after studying, teaching, and writing the history of the United States for over half a century.

Prospective readers may well ask wherein it may differ in form and content from other American histories of similar length. Politics are not lacking; but my main ambition is to re-create for my readers American ways of living in bygone eras. Here you will find a great deal on social and economic development; horses, ships, popular sports, and pastimes; eating, drinking, and smoking habits. Pugilists will be found cheek-by-jowl with Presidents; rough-necks with reformers, artists with ambassadors. More, proportionally, than in other histories, will be found on sea power, on the colonial period in which basic American principles were established, on the American Indians, and the Caribbean. I am offering fresh, new accounts of the Civil War and the War of Independence. A brief account of the parallel history of Canada, so near and dear to us, yet so unknown in her historical development to most citizens of the United States, has been attempted.

Having lived through several critical eras, dwelt or sojourned in every section of our country, taken part in both world wars, met and talked with almost every President of the United States in the twentieth century, as well as with thousands of men and women active in various pursuits, I have reached some fairly definite opinions about our history. At the same time, I have tried when writing about great controversial issues, such as war and peace and the progressive movement, to relate fairly what each side was trying to accomplish.

Since this is not primarily a textbook, but a history written for my fellow citizens to read and enjoy, footnote references, bibliographies, and other "scholarly apparatus" have been suppressed. Readers may take a certain amount of erudition for granted! Of course nobody, much less myself, can possibly read every printed source and monograph on American history from the beginning through 1964. This is particularly true of social history, comprising ideally, though impossibly, all human activities. Consequently, I have depended for particular subjects on the information and advice of experts, some my colleagues or former pupils, many my friends, but others who were strangers; and it has been most gratifying to find people so generous with their special knowledge. Moreover, having learned from my naval experience the value of oral testimony by participants, I have sought out, talked with, and profited by conversations with many of the civilian and military leaders of the past fifty years. These, excepting a few who wish anonymity, are named in the following section on Acknowledgments.

For many years I have been interested in collecting the popular music of American history, from that of the Indians to the present. The Oxford University Press has given me the opportunity to use some appropriate tags and choruses of these at the ends of appropriate chapters, and more could have been added to the later chapters but for the reluctance of music publishers to part with copyrighted material.

The illustrations have been chosen as much for their artistic appeal as for illustrations in the strict sense. The late Dr. Harold Bowditch helped me to make the point that the English Colonies were not originally democratic, by selecting and delineating coats of arms of colonial founders to which they were entitled, and which they used on bookplates, silver, and in other ways.

One thing has deeply impressed me as I swept through the history of North America — the continuity of American habits, ways, and institutions over a period of three centuries. The seeds or roots of almost everything we have today may be discerned in the English, French, and Spanish colonies as early as 1660. Nobody has better expressed this fundamental unity of American history than George E. Woodberry in his poem "My Country."

> She from old fountains doth new judgment draw,
> Till, word by word, the ancient order swerves
> To the true course more nigh; in every age
> A little she creates, but more preserves.

SAMUEL ELIOT MORISON

44 Brimmer Street
Boston
Christmastide 1964

Preface to the New American Library Edition. The entire text has been reviewed and corrected, in the light of fresh information and of errata noted and sent in by readers. I hope they will continue to do just that! Renewed thanks are due to Miss Antha E. Card for collecting and collating these errata, and to Oxford University Press for its steady cooperation and consideration.

SAMUEL ELIOT MORISON

"Good Hope"
Northeast Harbor, Maine
July 1971

Acknowledgments

MY BELOVED WIFE Priscilla Barton Morison not only encouraged me to write this book but listened critically to the reading of draft chapters, and greatly contributed to my happiness and well being while the work was going on.

General acknowledgments are due to my secretaries during the period of writing, Diana G. Hadgis and Antha E. Card. Miss Card, especially, has helped me by repeatedly checking facts, and by research and suggestions.

To Dr. Sydney V. James, Jr., who for a year helped me by research on the Indians, the Jacksonian period, and other subjects.

To my daughters Emily M. Beck, editor of the latest edition of Bartlett's Familiar Quotations, for looking up and checking quotations, and to Catharine Morison Cooper for research on American music.

To the many naval and military officers and civilians who are mentioned in the prefaces of my earlier books, especially in the fifteen-volume *History of U. S. Naval Operations in World War II.*

To my colleagues at Harvard and other American universities, and at the Universities of Oxford, Paris, and Rome, from whom I have learned very, very much, through friendly conversation and correspondence.[1]

Special Subjects of Acknowledgment

AVIATION: Professors Secor D. Browne and Jerome C. Hunsaker of M.I.T., and Dr. J. Howard Means of Boston.

CANADA: Professor A. R. M. Lower of Queen's University, Professor John J. Conway, formerly of Harvard, and the Honorable William Phillips.

CATHOLIC CHURCH HISTORY: Professor Marshall Smelser of Notre Dame University and Monsignor George Casey of Lexington, Massachusetts.

[1] My Balzan lecture at Rome on "The Experiences and Principles of an Historian" is printed in *Vistas of History* (Knopf, 1964).

COLONIAL PERIOD: Professors Edmund S. Morgan of Yale and Carl Bridenbaugh of Brown; both Professors Schlesinger and the late Perry Miller of Harvard, and the Rev. Arthur Pierce Middleton of Brookfield Center, Connecticut.

CONSERVATION: Mr. Ernest C. Oberholtzer of Ranier, Minnesota, Mr. Edmund Hayes of Portland, Oregon, Mrs. Marguerite Owen of Washington, D.C., and Professor Arthur A. Maass of Harvard.

ECONOMICS, especially the Great Depression: Professors Edward S. Mason of Harvard, Joseph Stancliffe Davis of Stanford, and Adolf A. Berle of Columbia Universities.

FEDERAL CONVENTION: Professor Henry S. Commager of Amherst College.

HORSES AND SPORTS: Mrs. Thomas E. P. Rice of Boston, Mr. Franklin Reynolds of Mount Sterling, Kentucky, Dr. George C. Simpson of the Harvard Museum of Comparative Zoology, and Mr. Colin J. Steuart Thomas of Baltimore.

ILLUSTRATIONS: Addison Gallery of American Art, Andover; American Museum of Natural History; Archives of Canada; Mrs. Bern Anderson of Newport; Atkins Museum of Fine Arts, Kansas City; Mr. David W. Barton; Boston Athenaeum; Boston Museum of Fine Arts; British Museum; Mrs. Richard E. Byrd; Corcoran Gallery, Washington; Mrs. John Duer; the H. F. DuPont Winterthur Museum; Mrs. Frederica F. Emert; the Franklin D. Roosevelt Library; Harvard University; Historical Society of Pennsylvania; Professor M. A. de Wolfe Howe of the Harvard Law School; Mrs. Mabel Ingalls; the John Carter Brown Library; Johns Hopkins University; Karsh of Ottawa; Mrs. Fred C. Kelly; The Mariners Museum, Newport News; Maryland Historical Society; the National Archives and National Gallery of Art, Washington; New-York Historical Society; Pach Brothers of New York; Peabody Museum of Cambridge; Peabody Museum of Salem; Pennsylvania Academy of Fine Arts; Princeton University; the Syracuse Savings Bank; Tennessee Valley Authority; Virginia Chamber of Commerce; United States Navy.

IMMIGRATION: Professor Oscar Handlin of Harvard.

INDIANS AND PRIMITIVE MAN IN AMERICA: Mr. Leonard Ware of the Bureau of Indian Affairs, Department of the Interior; Professor J. Otis Brew of Harvard University and the late Samuel K. Lothrop, curator of Andean Archaeology in the Peabody Museum, Cambridge.

LATIN AMERICA: Professor Roland T. Ely of Rutgers; Colonel Robert D. Heinl Jr. USMC (Ret.); the Honorable Mauricio Obregón of Colombia; the Honorable Aaron S. Brown, American Ambassador to Nicaragua.

MARITIME: Mr. Marion V. Brewington of Peabody Museum, Salem; Professor K. Jack Bauer of Morris Harvey College, Charleston, West Virginia; Rear Admiral Ernest M. Eller, Mr. Jesse R. Thomas, and Mr. Donald R. Martin of the Navy Department; Mrs. John M. Bullard of New Bedford.

MEDICINE: Drs. Paul Dudley White, J. Howard Means, and Sidney Burwell of the Harvard Medical School; Dr. J. Whittington Gorham of New York.

MUSIC AND THE FINE ARTS: Mr. Erich Leinsdorf, conductor of the Boston Symphony Orchestra; Professor G. Wallace Woodworth of Harvard; Mr. George Biddle of New York; Mr. Joseph A. Coletti; the late Maxim Karolik; the several music publishers who have allowed me to quote snatches of their songs.

PSYCHOLOGY: Professor Erik H. Erikson of Harvard.

SUEZ AFFAIRS Marshal of the R.A.F. Sir John Slessor; the Honorable Winthrop Aldrich, former Ambassador to Great Britain.

TEXAS: the late Walter P. Webb and J. Frank Dobie of the University of Texas; Professor Allan Ashcroft of the Texas Agricultural and Mechanical University.

WITCHCRAFT: Miss Esther Forbes of Worcester.

Contents ·

(This volume represents chapters XLV-LXII of the hardcover
edition published by Oxford University Press.)

I   *The Republican Dynasty, 1869–1893*   29

1. The United States, Great Britain, and Canada; 2.
The "Gilded Age"; 3. The Disputed Election and
President Hayes; 4. The Garfield-Arthur Adminis-
tration; 5. Mugwumps, Democrats, and the Second
Harrison

II   *Expansion and Development, 1870–1900*   50

1. Railroads, "Electrics," and Shipping; 2. Indians,
Cattle, and Cowboys; 3. The Farming Country; 4.
Iron and Steel, Big Business and Politics; 5. Canada
Comes of Age

III   *Social and Cultural Developments, 1870–1900*   80

1. The Rise of Organized Labor; 2. The State of Religion; 3. Arts, Letters, and Education; 4. Games,
Sports, and Joining

IV   *The Fecund Eighteen-nineties*   104

1. Populism and Panic; 2. Jim Crow in the South;
3. President Cleveland's Second Term; 4. The Spanish-American War

V   *Theodore Roosevelt, 1901–1909*   130

1. The Progressive Background and "Teddy"; 2.

Consolidation and Reform; 3. Trust and Railway Regulation to 1920; 4. The Big Stick in the Caribbean; 5. Roosevelt and World Politics

VI   *Taft and Wilson 1909–1917*   154
1. Taft Takes Over; 2. Canada and the Caribbean; 3. Insurgents and the Election of 1912; 4. The First Wilson Administration; 5. Woodrow Wilson and Mexico

VII *The First World War: The Neutrality Period, 1914–1917*   174
1. America's Reaction to the War; 2. Neutrality Problems; 3. Preparedness and the Election of 1916; 4. From Wilson's Re-election to War

VIII *The United States in the First World War, 1917–1920*   191
1. Naval Operations; 2. The American Expeditionary Force; 3. The Big Push of 1918; 4. The War at Home; 5. The Peace Conference and the League; 6. The Eclipse of Liberalism

IX   *The Great Change, 1902–1939*   223
1. The Auto and the Ad Men; 2. Aviation, 1903–1960; 3. Immigration; 4. Bootlegging and Other Sports; 5. The Sexual Upheaval; 6. Letters, Arts, and Sciences

X   *Republican Ascendancy, 1921–1933*   259
1. Harding and the "Ohio Gang"; 2. The Republicans and foreign Affairs; 3. Postwar Canada; 4. The Harding Scandals and the Coolidge Administration

XI   *The Hoover Administration, 1929–1933*   280
       1. The Election of 1928;   2. Herbert Hoover and the
       Boom;   3. The 1929 Crash and the Great Depression;
       4. The Accession of Franklin D. Roosevelt

XII   *The New Deal*   299
       1. Roosevelt Himself;   2. The Hundred Days and
       After;   3. Conservation and the TVA;   4. The New
       Deal and Foreign Affairs;   5. The Opposition and
       the Supreme Court;   6. Demagogues and Deviation-
       ists;   7. The Election of 1936

XIII   *The Second Roosevelt Administration,*
          1937–1941   329
       1. The New Deal and Labor;   2. Canada in the De-
       pression;   3. New Deal for Indians and Negroes;   4.
       Conclusion to the New Deal;   5. War in Europe and
       Asia;   6. "Short of War" to Pearl Harbor

XIV   *On the Defensive, 1941–1942*   359
       1. World-wide Disaster;   2. The Strategy and Direc-
       tion of the War;   3. Turn of the Tide;   4. Guadal-
       canal, Papua, and Africa;   5. The U-Boat Mastered,
       Italy Invaded;   6. Leap-Frogging in the Pacific

XV   *Victory, 1944–1945*   389
       1. The Invasion of Europe;   2. The Battle for Leyte
       Gulf;   3. Political Interlude;   4. Victory in Europe;
       5. Victory in the Pacific

XVI   *The Truman Administrations, 1945–1953*   410
       1. The Iron Curtain;   2. Harry's First Term;   3. The

United Nations and the Cold War; 4. China and the Occupation of Japan; 5. The Korean War; 6. The Election of 1952

XVII   *The Eisenhower Administrations, 1953–1961*   448

1. The President and His Domestic Policy; 2. Foreign Relations; 3. The New Free Enterprise; 4. Labor, Automation, and Antarctica

XVIII   *The Kennedy Administration, 1961–1963*   481

1. The Election of 1960; 2. The Cabinet and Domestic Policy; 3. Defense and Foreign Policy; 4. The New Picture and the End

Index   501

List of Illustrations

PLATES BETWEEN PAGES 264 AND 265

Delineations of country life by Winslow Homer:

Milking Time   *Mrs. Frederica F. Emert*
Shoveling Out   Every Saturday, *14 January, 1871*

Post–Civil War architecture and sculpture:

Rogers Group, "Coming to the Parson"
                  From 1889 Catalogue of John Rogers' Groups of Statuary

The Syracuse, New York, Savings Bank, 1875
                                          Courtesy Syracuse Savings Bank

America's Cup:

Finish of the 1870 race off Staten Island. From a painting by
Frederick S. Cozzens
                                                  Mrs. Mabel Ingalls

Volunteer, the 1887 defender. Designed by Edward Burgess. Length
over-all, 106 feet; on waterline, 86 feet; beam 23 feet; sail over
9260 square feet. She won both races off Sandy Hook in September
1887 against cutter *Thistle*.
                      From a photograph in The Paine-Burgess Testimonial

Two great American Thoroughbreds:

Kentucky, by Lexington out of Magnolia, was foaled in 1861. His
owner, Leonard W. Jerome, grandfather of Winston Churchill, is
"holding the ribbons" of the six-horse coach. Jerome Park is in the
background.
                                                  Author's collection

Man O'War, by Fair Play out of Masubah, was foaled in 1917.
Bred by August Belmont at Lexington, Ky. After winning 20 races
out of 21 starts and $250,000 in prizes, he was retired to stud and
sired many of the famous thoroughbreds of the present century.
                                                  Author's collection

William McKinley and Theodore Roosevelt
                                          Pach Brothers, New York

President Wilson and General Pershing
                      From Gerald W. Johnson's Woodrow Wilson.
                      United Press International Photos, N.Y.

Early Aviation:
    A Curtiss Triad A-1 of 1912
    NC-4 arriving Lisbon, May 1919.
                                        U.S. Navy photographs

The "Great Four" of Johns Hopkins, by John Singer Sargent
                            Johns Hopkins School of Medicine

President Franklin Delano Roosevelt
                                        Presented to the author

President Harry S Truman
                                        Presented to the author

William Lyon Mackenzie King
                                        Karsh, Ottawa

Rear Admiral Richard E. Byrd, USN
                            Courtesy of Arnold Bakers, Inc.

TVA's Hiwassee Dam in North Carolina
                                        Courtesy TVA

Senator and Mrs. George W. Norris
                                        Courtesy TVA

President Dwight D. Eisenhower
                                        Karsh, Ottawa

President John F. Kennedy
                                        Karsh, Ottawa

List of Maps

Railroads and Settlement 1865–1900   65

The Caribbean 1898–1934   121

American Participation in the Allied Offensive
    of 1918   201

The Tennessee Valley and the TVA   311

The Pacific Theater of War 1941–1945   372-373

Allied Campaigns in the Mediterranean 1942–1945   384

Invasion of Normandy   391

Liberation of the Philippines 1944–1945   398

The Korean War   434

American Military Bases and Installations outside
    Continental United States   490-491

MAPS BY VAUGHN GRAY

List of Songs

I *Hail, Hail, the Gang's All Here!* 49

Bucks and pols of the Gilded Age roared these simple words to Sullivan's "Come friends who plow the sea," from *The Pirates of Penzance.* It has been the theme song of Republican rallies and conventions for the past fifty years.

From Houghton Library, Harvard College, Wilkins Collection of Sheet Music.

II *The Old Chisholm Trail* 79

The horse's rhythm, the cowboys' calls to their beasts, blend into this most popular song of the Long Trail, which has hundreds of verses.

Arranged by C. M. Cooper, with words remembered by S. E. Morison.

III *A Hot Time in the Old Town Tonight* 129

Composed in 1896 by Theodore Metz, a professional minstrel, while watching a fire in the hamlet of Old Town, Louisiana. It swept the country, became the theme song of the Spanish-American War, and was always played at the appearance of Theodore Roosevelt.

Copyright Edward B. Marks Music Corporation, New York. Used by permission.

IV *I Didn't Raise My Boy To Be a Soldier* 189

This was the most popular song of the neutrality period. New words were written in 1917 starting with, "I'd be proud to be the mother of a soldier," but they never caught on.

Words by Alfred Bryan. Music by Al Piantadosi. Used by permission of Leo Feist, Inc., copyright proprietor.

v *Oh! How I Hate To Get Up in the Morning!* 221

This Irving Berlin work was one of the most popular marching songs of the American soldiers in World War I, as it exactly expressed their sentiments. At the training camps a military band used to march around at about 5:45 a.m., playing it over and over again.

Copyright 1918 Irving Berlin. Copyright Renewed. Reprinted by permission of Irving Berlin Music Corporation.

vi *Of Thee I Sing* 257

The 1931 musical by Ira and George Gershwin made brilliant fun of the politics of that era.

Copyright 1931 by New World Music Corporation. Used by permission.

vii *Camelot* 499

This musical comedy by Lerner and Loewe was beloved by the late President. He and Mrs. Kennedy used often to listen to a record of the lyrics the last thing before going to bed. These concluding bars are a poignant reminder of the "one brief shining moment" when the Kennedys were in the White House.

Reprinted by permission of Alan Jay Lerner.

THE
OXFORD HISTORY
OF THE
AMERICAN PEOPLE

I

The Republican Dynasty

1869-1893

1. *The United States, Great Britain, and Canada*

IT WOULD HAVE BEEN well for Grant's reputation had he retired from public life after his great gesture at Appomattox.
He was unfitted for the presidency by temperament, and less
equipped for it than any predecessor or successor. The simplicity of character which had shielded him from intrigues
during the Civil War exposed him to the wiles of those whose
loyalty to himself he mistook for devotion to the public weal;
he could never understand that a good soldier did not necessarily make an honest public servant. The death in 1869 of his
faithful chief of staff and first war minister, John A. Rawlins,
left him with no intimate adviser, and his choice of cabinet
members fell, with one or two exceptions, on mediocrities. Of
the complex forces that were shaping the United States anew,
he was completely unaware.

"Let us have peace," said Grant, when accepting the Republican nomination for the presidency. But internal peace between North and South, which is what he meant, could not be
obtained by merely wishing it. Grant had been maneuvered,
in part by Southern intransigence, in part by politicians, into
the Radical position; but his doubts about that policy were
voiced in his first inaugural: "I know no method to secure the

repeal of bad or obnoxious laws as effective as their stringent execution." Grant became a fairly consistent supporter of congressional reconstruction.

Foreign affairs, where Grant's innate sense of justice was enforced by a competent secretary of state, Hamilton Fish, show his two administrations in their fairest light. There was much to be done. Seward, by allowing the French (who needed little persuasion) to retire peaceably from Mexico, and by purchasing Alaska from Russia, had eliminated these nations from the American continent. But Earl Russell's peremptory refusal to submit the *Alabama* claims to arbitration prevented any prompt settlement with Great Britain. Postponement of these claims was dangerous. There was a deep feeling of resentment in America that was likely to flare up into war if not satisfied through law. One strong bond, the Canadian reciprocity treaty of 1854, expired in 1866 and was not renewed, largely owing to the rising tide of protectionist policy in the Republican party. When Albert J. Smith, premier of New Brunswick, went to Washington to see what could be done about renewing the treaty, the best offer he could get from the chairman of the ways and means committee was that in return for access to the inshore fisheries of Canada the United States would admit free Canadian firewood, grindstones, old rags, and gypsum.

During the war Canada had been the base for Confederate raids on the United States. The Irish Revolutionary Brotherhood, better known as the Fenians, now took similar liberties from the other side of the border. Two rival Irish Republics were organized in New York City, each with president, cabinet, and general staff in glittering uniforms of green and gold. Each shook down Irish-American businessmen, congressmen, servant girls, and hod carriers, for "loans." Each planned to invade Canada, largely with Irish veterans of the Union army, and hold it as hostage for Irish freedom. In 1866 each Irish Republic of New York attempted to execute its plan. In April an invasion of Campobello, future summer home of Franklin D. Roosevelt, was promptly nipped by federal authorities at Eastport, Maine. But the ensuing howl from the Irish vote, with congressional elections only six months away, frightened President Johnson and his cabinet. Before the attorney general and the secretaries of war and of the navy could decide who should take the onus of stopping him, "General" John O'Neil ferried 1500 armed Irishmen across the Niagara river and raised the green flag on old Fort Erie. Next day (2 June 1866) the Canadian militia gave battle, and fled; but the Fenians, too, fled back to New York where they were arrested and promptly released. Ridiculous and futile as they were, these Fenian forays caused Canada much trouble and expense, for which she was never reimbursed by the United States. And the distrust that they aroused was a leading factor in pushing the Canadian federation movement to its consummation in 1867.

The Dominion of Canada was mainly the product of three forces:—the rise of Canadian nationalism, a desire of British liberals to slough off colonial responsibilities, and the ambition of certain elements in the United States to annex Canada. Both Sumner and Seward adhered to the old Ben Franklin doctrine that a division of North America was "unnatural"; that there could never be lasting peace between Britain and the United States while Canada remained British. Most of the Radical Republicans, and Presidents Johnson and Grant, had the same point of view. Without countenancing aggression against Canada, they hoped that the British provinces would join the American Union voluntarily. They played with a suggestion that Britain hand over all her North American possessions to the United States as payment for the *Alabama* claims. And in Britain an important segment of public opinion, the "little Englanders" or "Manchester school," were bored with Canada and her problems and eager to pull out.

Fortunately it was the Canadians themselves who called the tune in this unharmonious trio. In 1866 Confederationists won the provincial elections in New Brunswick and Nova Scotia, which sent delegates to London to discuss a plan of union with the two Canadas (Quebec and Ontario) and with representatives of the British Parliament. Out of this conference came the British North American Act of 1867, to which Queen Victoria gave her assent, and which established the Dominion of Canada.

Dominion government went into effect 1 July 1867 with Sir John Macdonald, one of its principal architects, as premier. The frame of government was parliamentary, like that of Great Britain. It would have been called the Monarchy of Canada but for fear of offending the United States. Even so, Congress passed a joint resolution to the effect that they "viewed with extreme solicitude" the formation of this Confederation on a monarchical basis, hinting that it contravened the Monroe Doctrine, ignoring the statement in Monroe's original message that "with existing European colonies we have not interfered and will not interfere." President Johnson paid no attention to this piece of bad manners, but neither did he extend the hand of fellowship to Premier Macdonald.

According to the British North American Act the British

government controlled foreign affairs, war and peace, and appointed the governor general of Canada; but in all other essentials the Canadian Parliament was sovereign. It had plenary powers of taxation and the ministry was responsible to it. On paper, the new Canadian federal government enjoyed more power than the one across the border. It not only appointed governors of the member provinces but could disallow acts of provincial legislatures. All residuary powers rested in parliament, not in the provinces or the people, although it was understood that the traditional civil rights of British subjects were still in force. Thus, sovereignty extended from the top down, not from the people up. Warned by the trouble that state rights had made in the United States, provincial rights were, in theory, ruled out in Canada; but that, as we shall see, did not prevent loud cries of outraged localism and the recovery of many powers by the provinces in practice. Canada bought out the Hudson's Bay Company's territorial rights in 1869, adding a big Northwest Territory to the Dominion. British Columbia joined in 1871; and with the entrance of Prince Edward Island two years later, the Dominion of Canada extended north of the United States boundary from sea to sea and to the Arctic Ocean—excluding only Newfoundland which remained a crown colony, and Alaska which Seward had purchased for the United States.

The organization of this Dominion was an achievement equal to that of the Federal Constitution eighty years earlier. The United States now had a northern neighbor of growing power which could no longer be ignored, trifled with, or considered a region for territorial aggrandizement.

President Grant now made a positive contribution to Anglo-American amity by settling the *Alabama* business. After one agreement to submit these claims to arbitration had been rejected by the Senate in 1869, Sir John Rose, finance minister of Canada, staged with Secretary Hamilton Fish a diplomatic play of wooing and yielding that threw dust in the eyes of extremists on both sides. The covenant thus secretly arrived at, the Treaty of Washington of 8 May 1871, provided for submission to arbitration of boundary disputes, the fisheries question, and the *Alabama* claims, and agreed upon rules of neutrality to govern the arbitral tribunal.

In presenting their case to this tribunal at Geneva in December 1871, the United States claimed compensation not only for actual damage inflicted by the Confederate cruisers, but for the numerous transfers of registry occasioned by fear of capture. Hamilton Fish had no intention of pressing these "indirect" claims, but English opinion was outraged by their presentation, and an ill-tempered press discussion ensued. William E. Gladstone, the "Grand Old Man" of British politics, would have withdrawn from the arbitration on that issue had not Charles Francis Adams, the American member, who never forgot that he was a judge, not an advocate, proposed that the Geneva tribunal rule out indirect claims in advance. It was done, and the arbitration proceeded smoothly to its conclusion on 14 September 1872, an award of $15.5 million for depredations committed by C.S.S. *Alabama, Florida,* and *Shenandoah.*

The greater victory was for peace and arbitration. Never before had disputes involving such touchy questions of national honor been submitted to the majority vote of an international tribunal; and England accepted the verdict with good grace. The Treaty of Washington also began a better era in Canadian-American relations. Controversies over the international boundary through Puget Sound, and the rights of American fishermen in Newfoundland waters, were settled peaceably by negotiation and arbitration.

President Grant, by his unwavering support of peaceful methods, showed a quality not unusual in statesmen who know war at first hand. In a later message to a group in Birmingham, England, the soldier President avowed his guiding principle: "Nothing would afford me greater happiness than to know that, as I believe will be the case, at some future day, the nations of the earth will agree upon some sort of congress which will take cognizance of international questions of difficulty and whose decisions will be as binding as the decisions of our Supreme Court are upon us. It is a dream of mine that some such solution may be."

2. *The "Gilded Age"*

In his handling of domestic questions, Grant was the most unfortunate chief magistrate in American history, and the scandals of his administration were only equaled by those of Harding's. In his first administration, the fluctuations of "greenback" currency, a hold-over from Civil War finance, gave some smart operators an opportunity. Uncertainty as to whether Congress would redeem them in gold or keep them in circulation as farmers and debtors wanted, caused their value to fluctuate. In September 1869 two notorious New York stock gamblers, Jay Gould and Jim Fisk, took advantage of this situation to organize a corner in gold; and, with the connivance of persons high in the confidence of the President and the treasury, almost pulled it off. On "Black Friday,"

24 September 1869, the premium on gold rose to 162, and scores of Wall Street brokers faced ruin. The government then dumped $4 million in gold on the market, and the corner collapsed; but Grant was blamed for permitting himself to be enmeshed in the sordid affair. "The worst scandals of the 18th century," wrote Henry Adams, "were relatively harmless by the side of this which smirched executive, judiciary, banks, corporate systems, professions, and people, all the great active forces of society."

Senator James W. Grimes of Iowa wrote to Senator Lyman Trumbull of Illinois in 1870 that the Republican party was "going to the dogs"; that it had become "the most corrupt and debauched political party that has ever existed." This then sounded extravagant; but within ten years it was seen to be true. Weak cabinet appointments, intimacy with New York financiers of bad reputation, failure to obtain any substantial reduction in the wartime customs duties, failure to take even one step toward civil service reform, and the notorious failure in reconstruction, raised opposition to Grant's re-election within his own party.

A Liberal Republican convention met in May 1872 and erected a platform that included withdrawal of garrisons from the South, civil service reform, and the resumption of specie payments. Candidates for the nomination were Salmon P. Chase, whose lust for the presidency increased year by year, Charles Francis Adams the diplomat, and several others. After they had killed each other off, the convention was stampeded for Horace Greeley, and this nomination was endorsed by the Democrats.

As a "headliner," Horace Greeley could not have been bettered. In his thirty years' editorship of the New York *Tribune* he had built it up to be the country's leading newspaper, whose articles and editorials were quoted nationwide. His personal integrity and moral earnestness were unquestioned. But he was also something of a crackpot (recall his needling Lincoln during the war?) and at one time or another he had espoused unpopular causes such as socialism, temperance, spiritism, and women's rights. Greeley made a strong speaking campaign, but the Republicans had the money and the organization; and the average citizen, having to choose between an old soldier whose very name stood for patriotism, and a journalist who had been as often wrong as right, voted for Grant. The President carried all but six states with a popular vote of 3.6 million as against 2.8 million for his opponent. Greeley, exhausted, broken-hearted, and at the age of sixty-one turned out of his editorial chair by the *Tribune's* owner,

Whitelaw Reid, went out of his mind and died before the end of November.

Of the public scandals during Grant's second term, the Credit Mobilier attracted the most attention. This was a company organized by promoters of the Union Pacific in order to divert the profits of railway construction to themselves. Fearing lest Congress intervene, the directors placed large blocks of stock "where they would do the most good"; that is, in the hands of congressmen. Vice President Schuyler Colfax and several Republican senators were also favored. These operations brought the Union Pacific to the verge of bankruptcy but paid the promoters over threefold their investment. After this affair, together with maladministration in several executive departments, had been exposed, the Democrats won the congressional elections of 1874 and plied the muckrake in earnest. A "Whisky Ring" in St. Louis was found to have defrauded the government of millions in taxes, with the collusion of treasury officials and the President's private secretary, General Orville E. Babcock. Despite Grant's honest zeal to "let no guilty man escape," most of them did, Babcock included. Even the Indians, who had little to lose, were victimized; General William W. Belknap, Grant's second-term secretary of war, received a "kickback" of almost $25,000 from the post trader whom he had appointed at Fort Sill. Corruption in the post office and interior departments stopped just short of the President who, though surrounded by crooks, would never believe anything against a friend. Navy yards, regarded by spoilsmen as part of their patronage, were riddled with graft; payrolls were padded before election with the connivance of Grant's navy secretary. Commander Alfred T. Mahan testified in a congressional investigation that a million feet of lumber purchased by the Boston navy yard had simply disappeared, and that the famous yacht *America* had been remodeled for Benjamin F. Butler at the taxpayers' expense.

Until Amendment XVII to the Constitution required popular election, United States senators were chosen by state legislatures, and it was much cheaper to "buy" members than to have to cultivate the entire electorate. Consequently, few reached the Senate without financial support from one or more of the leading "interests," such as railroading, oil, textiles, iron and steel, mining, and sugar refining. Of able senators who made and unmade Presidents, James G. Blaine was easily first; others in the power group who governed the United States until 1910 were Chauncey Depew, Thomas C. Platt, and David B. Hill of New York, William B. Allison of Iowa, Matthew S. Quay of Pennsylvania, Mark Hanna and

Joseph B. Foraker of Ohio, Arthur P. Gorman of Maryland, Nelson W. Aldrich of Rhode Island, and William A. Clark of Montana. These were no faceless puppets of bloated business but men of pungent personality: Depew, perhaps the wittiest impromptu speaker in our history; Blaine, the "Plumed Knight" to his devoted followers; Quay and Foraker, ruthless to political dissidents. All became very rich, some were gentlemen, most were not. No more than any municipal boss are they remembered for any act of generosity or disinterested statesmanship; and their orations, once listened to by enraptured audiences, now seem but sounding brass and tinkling cymbal. But, to do them justice, these men were not simply greedy (though most of them were that); they fancied they were renewing the Hamiltonian policies, binding the great financial and commercial interests to the federal government through mutual favors.

There were still men of integrity in the Senate—Hoar of Massachusetts, Lamar of Georgia, Sherman of Ohio, Trumbull of Illinois, for instance; but nobody of the towering stature of Clay, Calhoun, and Webster. It is also remarkable that all were of colonial or revolutionary stock. The Irish, German, and Italian immigrants of 1830–70 had not yet risen above local and municipal politics.

The federal government was at the summit of a pyramid of corruption in the Northern states: "Boss" Tweed's gang stealing $100 million from New York City; Jim Fisk and Jay Gould looting the Erie Railroad by stock-watering, and their rival, Cornelius Vanderbilt, doing the same, somewhat more respectably, to the New York Central; Collis P. Huntington buying the California legislature and bribing congressmen to promote transcontinental railroad interests; Peter Widener obtaining street railway franchises by bribing aldermen; John D. Rockefeller using strong-arm methods when chicanery failed, to build his Standard Oil empire. These were conspicuous examples in the middle tier of this indecent pyramid, the lower courses of which were built by a sordid alliance between liquor, prostitution, and city police; by the "shell game" at country fairs, "city slickers" selling gold bricks and shares in Boston Common to country bumpkins, and recruiting country girls for prostitution. Well did Mark Twain call this the Gilded Age, for when the gilt wore off one found only base brass; everyone was trying to make a "fast buck." The Civil War, like every other great war, broke down morals, and although Puritan standards for women held up fairly well until after World War I, gambling, heavy drinking, and whoring were prevalent among men of every social class.

Stock speculation, over-rapid expansion of the agricultural West, and a world-wide drop in prices brought on the panic of 1873 and a depression which lasted three years. Before economic recovery took place the centennial of independence was celebrated by the first American world's fair, at Philadelphia. Sidney Lanier symbolized reunion by contributing the words for a Centennial Cantata on a high note of optimism; but James Russell Lowell, who eleven years earlier had sung, "O Beautiful! My Country! Ours once more!" wrote a sarcastic ode on the end products of a century of freedom:

> Show your State Legislatures; show your Rings;
> And challenge Europe to produce such things
> As high officials sitting half in sight
> To share the plunder and to fix things right;
> If that don't fetch her, why you only need
> To show your latest style in martyrs,—Tweed!

And the concerts at the Philadelphia centennial, conducted by Theodore Thomas, were so poorly attended that the sheriff closed them and sold Thomas's music library to pay the performers. Walt Whitman, too, scored the materialism of the age; and even the genial, smiling Longfellow thus expressed his thoughts for 1872 in his *Michael Angelo:*

> Ah, woe is me!
> I hoped to see my country rise to heights
> Of happiness and freedom yet unreached
> By other nations, but the climbing wave
> Pauses, lets go its hold, and slides again
> Back to the common level, with a hoarse
> Death-rattle in its throat. I am too old
> To hope for better days.

3. *The Disputed Election and President Hayes*

Republican defeat seemed certain in 1876 as the Grant administration approached political bankruptcy. The Republican convention nominated Rutherford B. Hayes over James G. Blaine. Hayes, a lawyer old enough to have studied under Joseph Story at Harvard, had won a brigadier's commission under Sheridan and served three terms as governor of Ohio. In that office he became so noted for integrity as to earn the contemptuous nickname "Old Granny" from the professional "pols." He was acceptable to liberal Republicans, and the

Stalwarts, as the Radicals now called themselves, had no alternative to supporting him.

The Democrats, determined to make reform the issue of the campaign, chose Governor Samuel J. Tilden, a wealthy but honest lawyer of Albany Regency background who had exposed the Tweed and similar political rings battening on the canal system of New York. Every paragraph of the Democratic platform began with "Reform is necessary in . . ." and indeed it was. So much dirt was exposed in the campaign of 1876 that it seemed impossible for the Republicans to win again. But "waving the bloody shirt" was still effective. "Every man that shot Union soldiers was a Democrat!" screamed Robert G. Ingersoll, now remembered largely for his militant atheism. "The man that assassinated Lincoln was a Democrat. Soldiers, every scar you have got on your heroic bodies was given you by a Democrat!" Tilden refused to make a vigorous campaign, partly because of bad health, mostly because he did not really want the presidency. Nevertheless, when the first returns came in it seemed that he had won, but the votes of three Southern states and Oregon were doubtful, and without them Tilden had only 184 electoral votes; if the Republicans carried those four states, Hayes would have 185.

From all four disputed states came two sets of electoral votes. In South Carolina, Florida, and Louisiana, still under carpetbag rule, the election boards had thrown out thousands of Democratic votes on the ground of fraud or intimidation. Congress met the problem by setting up an electoral commission of fifteen members, eight Republicans and seven Democrats; from House, Senate, and Supreme Court, "visiting statesmen" were sent to the disputed Southern states; and there seems no doubt that a deal was made by the Republicans with Southern Democratic leaders, by virtue of which, in return for their acquiescence in Hayes's election, they promised on his behalf to withdraw the garrison and to wink at non-enforcement of Amendment XV, guaranteeing civil rights to the freedmen. The bargain was kept on both sides. On 2 March 1877 the electoral commission by a strict party vote rejected the Democratic returns from doubtful states and declared Hayes the winner by a majority of one electoral vote. And virtually no attempt was made by the federal government to enforce Amendment XV until the Franklin D. Roosevelt administration.

Even with the disputed states counted as Republican, Tilden had a plurality of 250,000 votes over Hayes. There is no longer any doubt that this election was "stolen."

Grant spent two years touring Europe, returning in the fall

of 1879 in the hope of being nominated by the Republicans for a third term. The former President and general, who had nothing to live on but income from the gifts of old friends, now formed a brokerage firm with an incompetent partner, and that firm went bankrupt. He was already afflicted with cancer of the throat; but in order to pay his creditors he moved to a small cottage on Mount McGregor, New York, to write his own account of the Civil War. There, suffering intense pain but indomitable to the end, he finished in bed the last page of his great military memoirs on 19 July 1885, four days before death claimed him.

President Hayes appointed a strong cabinet: William Maxwell Evarts, one of the country's greatest lawyers, as secretary of state; Senator John Sherman (principal "fixer" with the Southern Democrats) to the treasury; Carl Schurz, German-American leader, to the interior; and he made the first ex-Confederate cabinet appointment, Senator David M. Key of Tennessee, as postmaster general. The first thing he did about reconstruction was to end the deadlock in South Carolina in favor of Governor Wade Hampton, and his withdrawal of troops from Louisiana allowed the conservatives to take over that state too.

Questions of finance were important in all postwar administrations. The desire of debt-ridden farmers for cheap money was the principal obstacle to redeeming the greenbacks, as big business wanted. Congress, at President Grant's instance, passed an act in January 1875 requiring the treasury four years later to redeem the paper dollars in gold. In protest, farmers organized the Greenback party, pledged to redeem the national debt in depreciated paper, and polled a small vote in the election of 1876. President Hayes insisted that payment of the debt and redemption of paper currency in specie be resumed on 1 January 1879, the date fixed by the Act of 1875. But the Bland-Allison Act for the "free" coinage of silver, an inflationist measure which profited the mining barons of Nevada, was passed over his veto and made mischief later. He took a strong and, on the whole, successful stand against the various acts of congressional usurpation that had taken place under Johnson and Grant, removed some of his predecessor's worst appointees, and began civil service reform. Nevertheless, both houses of Congress went Democratic in 1878, and that party looked forward to a sure-thing election in 1880.

Hayes was an upright, conscientious, and better-than-average President, but the professional politicians of the Republican party disliked him, and his wife's refusal to serve wine at White House dinners brought ridicule from Washington society. He was uneasy in the presidency, and, alone of Presidents since Polk, absolutely refused to be considered for a second term.

4. *The Garfield-Arthur Administration*

In consequence of Hayes's refusal to run in 1880 there was a free-for-all in the Republican convention. Grant's friends entered his name for a third term and he led Blaine for several ballots but could never obtain a majority. On the 36th ballot a liberal "dark horse," General James A. Garfield, ran away from the field. As a sop to the Stalwarts, Chester A. Arthur, a favorite of Roscoe Conkling's Republican machine in New York State, was given the vice presidential nomination. Garfield had a good record in the war and as governor of Ohio, but the Republicans made more of his birth in a log cabin, the last time that that venerable cliché was dragged out. At the same time the "bloody shirt" was buried; this was the first presidential election when reconstruction questions were not seriously discussed. The Democrats, hoping to cash in on military renown, nominated General Winfield Scott Hancock of Pennsylvania, whom Grant considered the best of his corps commanders. As one of the reconstruction "satraps" he had ruled with a moderation that pleased the South. But Hancock, with no experience in politics, made as lame and lazy a campaign as had his namesake General Scott in 1852. His popular vote was only 9500 less than Garfield's, but even with the solid South in his favor he won only 155 electoral votes to Garfield's 214. The Greenback vote of over 300,000 for General James B. Weaver of Iowa, if thrown to Hancock, might well have elected him.

Four months after Garfield's inauguration, while still struggling with questions of patronage, the President was shot by a disappointed office seeker screaming, "I am a Stalwart! Arthur is now President!" After a gallant struggle for life, Garfield died on 19 September 1881, and the Vice President succeeded.

Chester A. Arthur was a prominent lawyer whose sole political position had been that of collector of the port of New York City, to which Grant had appointed him and from which Hayes had tried to remove him. Handsome and affable, a fifty-one-year-old widower, he and his White House hostess, a charming married daughter, gave Washington its only fashionable administration since Tyler's. Champagne returned to White House dinners, and whisky to the sideboard. Whether receiving guests in an East Room reception or dining out with senators, or driving his pair of bay horses in an open landau, Chester A. Arthur was always the gentleman.

Unexpectedly, and to the dismay of his Stalwart supporters, he also became somewhat of a reformer. The manner of Garfield's death gave popular sanction to what the Civil Service Reform League had been advocating for years. Every President since Polk complained of the demands that patronage made on his time, energy, and judgment. Scandal had followed scandal in the civil service; yet the spoils system had been extended even to scrubwomen in the public offices. Rotation in office was never complete, and a large residuum of trained public servants remained in office; but in general the federal service had become permeated with a class of men who were tempted to anticipate future removal by present corruption. Federal officials, regularly assessed for campaign contributions, were expected to spend much of their time in political activity. For the President it was no simple matter of turning out the vanquished and putting in the victors. There were usually several applicants for every vacancy, representing different factions of the party. If the congressional delegation from a state could agree upon federal appointments within their state, the President generally took their advice; but often they disagreed, and by so-called senatorial courtesy no nomination to which the senators from the nominee's state objected, could be confirmed. And the Tenure of Office Act, which limited the presidential power of removal, was not repealed until 1886. Congress, since the Civil War, had so largely eaten into presidential prerogative that the chief executive was by way of becoming a mere figurehead, like the presidents of the Third French Republic. President Garfield, just before the assassin's bullet struck him down, declared, "I'm going to find out whether I am merely a recording clerk for the Senate or chief executive of the United States." The situation was exposed by a book entitled *Congressional Government* published in 1885 by young Professor Woodrow Wilson, who later attained the power to reverse it.

A landmark in civil service reform is a law of 1883 sponsored by "Gentleman George" Pendleton, who had been McClellan's running mate in 1864. This set up a civil service commission to administer a new set of rules, required appointments to be made as the result of open competitive examinations, and forbade political assessments on, or "kickbacks" by, federal officials. These rules were initially applied to some 14,000 positions, about 12 per cent of the total; but the Presidents Cleveland, Wilson, and both Roosevelts made large additions to the merit lists, and in 1940 some 727,000 out of over one million federal employees were in the classified civil service. At the same time, some of the states began to pass civil service laws of their own, but they never went so far as those of the federal government.

It would be idle to pretend that civil service reform fulfilled the expectations of its advocates. Neither the emoluments nor the prestige have been sufficiently high to attract the best men, and too often civil service rules have prevented lazy and incompetent people from being discharged. There has, however, been a great improvement in morale and efficiency; and it was fortunate indeed that the merit principle was adopted before the twentieth century, when administrative expansion greatly enhanced the need for honest and expert service. But a large part of this expansion has not been put under civil service rules; the "pols" still control most of it. Pennsylvania, for instance, had 81,000 jobs at her new governor's disposal in 1963, and only 13,000 were under civil service. The 1962 figures for federal employees in the classified civil service are 1,058,485 out of a total of 2,515,870. Thus, the federal patronage has increased both relatively and absolutely to a height that would have been envied by all nineteenth-century spoilsmen.

James Bryce, visiting the United States in the 1880's to write his *America Commonwealth*, found reformers everywhere fighting corruption and boss rule. Except for civil service reform and the Australian ballot, they accomplished little until the next century. Organized wealth and professional politicians had too strong an interest in keeping things as they were. Periodicals like Godkin's *Nation* and *The Forum*, of which Walter Hines Page became editor in 1890, did much to arouse public opinion and to prepare for the happy day when Theodore Roosevelt became President.

The War of the Pacific of 1879–84, won by Chile against Peru and Bolivia, awakened the United States to the decrepitude of her navy. Twenty years after building the *Monitor* it was inferior to the Chilean navy as well as to that of every principal European country. Not one rifled cannon had been mounted, the capital ships were fourteen small ironclads, mostly monitors, each mounting two 5-inch smooth-bores. After long discussion, Congress on 5 August 1882 authorized the construction of two "steam cruising vessels of war . . . to be constructed of steel of domestic manufacture . . . said vessels to be provided with full sail power and full steam power," and two more in 1883. These were cruisers *Chicago, Atlanta,* and *Boston,* and "dispatch boat" *Dolphin,* which joined the fleet in 1887. That began a new era in American naval history.

5. *Mugwumps, Democrats, and the Second Harrison*

Henry Adams, who had left Cambridge ("a social desert which would have starved a polar bear") for metropolitan Washington, snarled at President Arthur as "a creature for whose skin the romancist ought to go with a carving knife," and sneered at his administration as "the centre for every element of corruption." What Henry Adams found in Washington society is a mystery. His wife wrote that the "moral miasma" was worse than the fogs of "foggy bottom," location of many of the government buildings. There was no opera, little theater, no good university, and only the Smithsonian Institution to attract men of intellect. The legations were staffed with the riffraff of European and South American foreign services. Most of the conversation between men was about who was to get what, or carry which. Apart from a core of old families who had come to the capital in the early years of the Republic, and retired army and navy officers, Washington was a bloated middle-class American town, rootless because few expected to be there long. But Henry Adams, like his creation Mrs. Lightfoot Lee in his novel *Democracy,* wanted to see the wheels go 'round; he was "bent upon getting to the heart of the great American mystery of democracy and government." That, for all his perceptiveness, he never did because nobody in Washington thought about what they were doing; they simply took it for granted. Adams's *Democracy,* nevertheless, is the best mirror of Washington society under Hayes, as Mark Twain's *Gilded Age* is of the Grant administration.

From the viewpoint of the 1960's, Arthur's administration stands up as the best Republican one between Lincoln and Theodore Roosevelt. He had the courage to veto a Chinese exclusion bill which conflicted with a treaty, and a river and harbor bill which was a monument of logrolling and jobbery. This offended the Stalwarts, and the reformers never felt sure of Arthur, so he had no chance to succeed himself in the election of 1884, the most exciting since the Civil War.

The Republicans nominated James G. Blaine, a man of great talents and fascinating personality, long in public life and a leader in party councils. Of all politicians between Henry Clay and Theodore Roosevelt, Blaine had the most devoted personal following; but he had a heavy load to carry.

The principal charge against him was prostitution of the speakership to personal gain. In that connection he had acted as
broker for the bonds of a subsequent bankrupt railroad, the
Little Rock & Fort Smith, and made some $100,000 in the
transaction. When Congress earlier investigated this affair,
Blaine triumphantly vindicated himself. But the reformers
now produced an incriminating letter on the same business by
Blaine, which concluded, "Burn this letter," which the recipient had not done. There is no longer any doubt that Blaine
corruptly profited from his political position. When, as secretary of state for a few months under Garfield and Arthur, he
ordered the American ministers at Lima and Santiago de Chile
to mediate peace in the War of the Pacific, he also instructed
them to include in the settlement the payment of a dubious
claim in which one of his friends was interested. His official
salaries were never enough for his luxurious tastes, and he
had not enough moral stamina to resist temptation. But his
friends would never believe a word against the "Plumed
Knight," as they dubbed this able, charming, sophisticated,
but morally obtuse politician.

Blaine's nomination was more than conscientious Republicans could take. Under the lead of Carl Schurz and George
William Curtis the reform wing of the party "bolted" from the
convention, promised to support any decent nominee of the
Democrats, and proudly assumed the name "Mugwump,"
which was first given them in derision. As bolting is the great
offense in American political ethics, few Mugwumps managed
to resume a public career; younger delegates like Henry Cabot
Lodge and Theodore Roosevelt, who continued to support
Blaine while admitting the worst, had their reward. The
Democrats nominated Grover Cleveland, a self-made man
who as governor of New York had distinguished himself for
firmness and integrity, to the disgust of Tammany Hall. "We
love him for the enemies he has made," said a prominent
Mugwump.

An amusing feature of the 1884 campaign was furnished
by the now aged and disreputable Benjamin F. Butler who
had attended the Democratic convention hoping the presidential "lightning" would strike him. He was, however, nominated
for the presidency by two minor parties, the Antimonopolists
and the Greenbackers. The Republicans paid for Ben Butler
to go on a speaking tour in a private railroad car, hoping he
would take votes from Cleveland; but this attempt backfired
and left the national Republican committee with a pretty bill
to pay for Butler's junket.

As the campaign proceeded, it became noisy and nasty.

Cleveland's supporters were taken aback by his honest admission of the fact that he had fathered an illegitimate child; but, as one of them concluded philosophically, "We should elect Mr. Cleveland to the public office which he is so admirably qualified to fill, and remand Mr. Blaine to the private life which he is so eminently fitted to adorn."

Blaine, profiting by several anti-British orations, had a strong following among Irish-Americans, but lost it at the eleventh hour through the tactless remark of a clerical supporter. In his presence a hapless parson named Burchard described the Democrats as the party of "Rum, Romanism, and Rebellion." At the same time the new Prohibition party's nominee, Governor John P. St. John of the dry state of Kansas, was directing a fiery campaign against Blaine and demon rum from a New York attic. Cleveland carried New York State by a plurality of only 1149; and New York's 36 electoral votes, thanks to St. John's efforts and Burchard's bloopers, won him the presidency.

For a person of such generous bulk, Grover Cleveland was remarkably austere, unbending, and ungenial. Elected at a period when subservience to the popular will was supposed to be the first political virtue, this President remained inflexible in the right as he saw it, modified very slightly his preconceived ideas on any subject, and made little or no attempt to please. He selected a strong cabinet, with Thomas F. Bayard of Delaware secretary of state, and Lucius Quintus Cincinnatus Lamar secretary of the interior, but alienated the Irish vote by appointing a Mugwump, William Crowninshield Endicott, secretary of war instead of Mayor Patrick A. Collins of Boston. Cleveland was a bachelor of forty-eight years upon entering the White House (5 March 1885), but he promptly wooed and won Frances Folsom, a beautiful debutante of half his age— and barely half his weight. An amusing instance of the affectionate irreverence with which Americans regard their chief magistrate occurred on Decoration Day 1886 at a military review before the President. Gilbert and Sullivan's *Mikado* was then the rage; and when the President appeared, the bands struck up "He's going to marry Yum-Yum—*Yum-Yum!*" They were married in the White House three days later, and a very happy marriage it proved to be.

Deserving Democrats, deprived of the sweets of office for twenty-five years, now demanded as clean a sweep as the law would allow—88 per cent clean; virtuous Mugwumps insisted on no sweep at all. Since the Tenure of Office Act had been repealed, the President was free to remove incumbents without senatorial advice and consent; and by the end of his term

Cleveland had replaced nearly every postmaster and about half the other federal officials. The Democrats were not satisfied, and the Mugwumps were not pleased.

Cleveland continued to make enemies. He was rude to the press, resenting its interest in his private affairs. He deeply offended Union veterans—at least so their spokesmen, the G.A.R., insisted—by giving two "rebels," Lamar and Garland, cabinet positions and proposing to return the captured Confederate battle flags to their states. He vetoed hundreds of private pension bills by means of which Congress tried to put deserters, skedadlers, and soldiers dishonorably discharged from the army, on the already bloated pension roll. There was a roar of protest from cattle ranchers when the President nullified their illegal leases of grass lands from the Indians. Congress and the President endeavored to do justice to these wards of the nation in the Dawes Act of 1887, but as we shall see in due course, this made the redskins' situation worse than before. Cleveland endeavored, without success, to stop the "free coinage" of silver under the Bland-Allison Act. Warned not to touch so explosive a subject as the tariff, he nevertheless urged Congress to reduce it. The Interstate Commerce Act of 1887 opened a new volume of federal regulation that is not yet ended; but Cleveland as a protest against this trend vetoed a $10,000 appropriation for distributing seed grain in Texas counties suffering from a drought, declaring, "Federal aid in such cases encourages the expectation of paternal care on the part of the government and weakens the sturdiness of our national character." Nevertheless, American farmers have obtained "paternal care" to the tune of billions of dollars. His administration showed slight positive achievement; but Cleveland dared say "No!" And merely to say "No!" in that era of political favoritism became a prime virtue.

Cleveland was renominated by the Democrats in 1888 without enthusiasm. The Republicans nominated Benjamin Harrison of Indiana, grandson of "Old Tippecanoe," with Levi P. Morton of New York for Vice President. Harrison, an able brigadier general in the Union army, a middle-of-the-road Republican and former senator from Indiana, had such a cold personality that the efforts of Republican politicians to call him "Young Tippecanoe" and wage a rickety-rackety campaign like that of 1840, had to be abandoned. The Republicans carried New York State by 14,000 and again New York was decisive; in the popular vote, however, Cleveland polled a plurality of 100,000.

Harrison made a dignified but ineffective President. With a

Republican majority in both houses,[1] and autocratic Thomas
B. Reed as speaker, the President urged constructive legislation. But Congress was led by men who wanted no legislation
other than raids on the treasury and hold-ups of the consumer.
Senators from the Far West, where silver mining interests
were strong, obtained in return for their support of protection
the Sherman Silver-Purchase Act (1890), increasing the
monthly coinage of that metal by 125 per cent. Manufacturers
who had contributed liberally to the Republican campaign
fund were rewarded by an upward revision of duties, the
McKinley tariff of 1890. Civil service reform languished, although the President promoted it by appointing as civil service
commissioner a young Harvard graduate, amateur historian,
and Western rancher named Theodore Roosevelt. He "brought
a glare of happy publicity" into that office as he did to everything that he undertook.

Harrison's administration might well have been called the
Maine administration. The State of Maine, having attained
prosperity through farming, lumbering, fishing, and wooden
shipbuilding, hatched a clutch of Republican politicians who
occupied key positions in the federal government. Speaker
Reed's private secretary illustrates this by a droll story which
must have happened in 1889.

John Sergeant Wise, a New York financier, was shown
into the Speaker's office.

"Who's running this government, anyway?" he blus-
tered.

"The great and the good, John, of course. Be calm!"
said the Speaker in his Down-East twang, with a twinkle
in his eye.

"Well, the great and the good must all live in Maine,
then. I come up here on business with the secretary of
state—Mr. Blaine of Maine. I call to pay my respects to
the acting vice president—Mr. Frye from Maine. I wish
to consult the leader of the United States Senate—Mr.
Hale from Maine. I would talk over a tariff matter with
the chairman of the ways and means committee—Mr.
Dingley from Maine. There is a naval bill in the house in
which I am greatly interested—Chairman Boutelle from
Maine. I wish an addition to the public building in Richmond—Chairman Milliken from Maine. And here I am

[1] Substantially increased in the Senate by the admission of four new
states: North Dakota, South Dakota, Montana, and Washington, on 22
February 1889. To these were added Wyoming and Idaho in 1890. All
six were then Republican in politics.

in the august presence of the great speaker of the greatest parliamentary body in the world—Mr. Reed from Maine!"

"Yes, John, the great, and the good—and the wise. The country is safe."

And out they went, laughing, to lunch with the Chief Justice of the United States—Mr. Fuller from Maine.

Blaine as secretary of state took up with more zeal than tact the formation of a Pan American Union. But the new McKinley tariff on hides, passed to please the cattle barons of the West, infuriated South Americans and rendered abortive the Pan American Congress that the President summoned to Washington.

The McKinley tariff on manufactures also occasioned a sharp rise in prices, which is probably the main reason for an overturn in the congressional elections of 1890. Only 88 Republicans were returned to the new House, as against 235 Democrats; and the Republican majority in the Senate was reduced to eight unstable votes from the Far West. The same trend continued in the presidential election of 1892. Harrison had alienated many Republican leaders, but it was an accepted principle that if a party did not renominate a President for a second term, it confessed failure. So Harrison won the nomination on the first ballot; and for the same reason Cleveland obtained the Democratic nomination. His running-mate was Adlai E. Stevenson of Illinois, grandfather of the like-named statesman who twice ran against General Eisenhower and became United States representative to the United Nations. The new Populist party with James B. Weaver, a former Greenbacker, as standard bearer, polled over a million votes and carried six states west of the Mississippi; but Cleveland and Stevenson, again supported by the Mugwumps, won a safe majority in the electoral college and polled some 365,000 more votes than Harrison. There was more to this verdict, however, than revulsion from the tariff or disgust at Republican chicanery and corruption. It registered a deep lying unrest that would presently break forth and carry William Jennings Bryan to prominence, Theodore Roosevelt to achievement, and Woodrow Wilson to the presidency.

So, before telling briefly the story of Cleveland's second term, we must survey the winds of change that had been blowing through the nation since reconstruction.

HAIL, HAIL, THE GANG'S ALL HERE

Hail! Hail!___ the gang's all here,___

What the hell do we care, What the hell do we care,

Hail! Hail!___ we're full of cheer,___

What the hell do we care, now!___

II

Expansion and Development

1870-1900

1. Railroads, "Electrics," and Shipping

DURING THE LAST third of the nineteenth century, American society began to reflect the economic transformations that began during the Civil War or earlier, but underwent no profound change such as that which followed a general adoption of the internal combustion engine. There was merely an expansion and extension of the first industrial revolution, marked by the application of machine power, in constantly enlarged units, to new processes and in new regions.

Transportation was the key. There were 35,000 miles of steam railroad in the United States in 1865; more than five times as much in 1900, more than in all Europe. Among inventions which diminished the discomfort of long-distance travel were the Pullman sleeping car, the safety coupler, and the Westinghouse air brake. In the 1870's the refrigerator car, first used to carry freshly slaughtered beef from Chicago to the Eastern cities, was adapted for the carriage of fruit and vegetables, which eventually enabled the products of California to undersell those of Eastern truck gardeners. After the turn of the century the Pennsylvania Railroad built the first all-steel passenger coaches, and the American Locomotive

Company brought out the magnificent Pacific type, which dominated railroading for a quarter-century.

Transcontinental railroads were the most spectacular post-war achievements. The Union Pacific thrust westerly through Nebraska and Wyoming Territory, near the line of the old Oregon and California trails and across the Wasatch Range of the Rockies into the basin of the Great Salt Lake. The Central Pacific, in the meantime, climbed eastward from Sacramento over the difficult grades of the Sierras, then through the arid valleys of Nevada. When the two joined rails with a golden spike near the Great Salt Lake on 10 May 1869, the Union Pacific was regarded as the winner; but the Central Pacific promoters had made enough to enable them to buy the state government of California.

Congress in the meantime had granted charters to three other lines: (1) the Northern Pacific—from Lake Superior across Minnesota, through the Bad Lands of Dakota, up the valley of the Yellowstone, across the continental divide at Bozeman to the headwaters of the Missouri, and by an intricate route through the Rockies to the Columbia river and Portland; (2) the Southern Pacific—from New Orleans across Texas to the Rio Grande, across the *llano estacado* to El Paso, through the territory of the Gadsden Purchase to Los Angeles, and up the San Joaquin valley to San Francisco; (3) the Santa Fe—from Atchison, Kansas, up the Arkansas river to Trinidad, Colorado, across the Raton spur of the Rockies to Santa Fe and Albuquerque, through the country of the Apache and the Navajo parallel to the Grand Canyon of the Colorado, and across the Mojave desert to San Bernardino and San Diego. All three were aided by government land grants—twenty square miles to every mile of track—and by 1884, after numerous bankruptcies and reorganizations, all three had reached the coast. At the same time the Canadian Pacific, aided by even more generous subsidies from the Dominion, was pushing through to the Pacific and reached it on 7 November 1885.

These transcontinental lines were promoted largely with a view to profit, but the peopling of a vast region proved to be their most valuable function. In this respect they performed a work comparable with that of the Virginia Company of 1612 and the Ohio Company of 1785.

At the end of the Civil War the great plains west of eastern Kansas and Nebraska, the high plains, and the Rocky Mountain region, were uninhabited by white men excepting the mining towns in Colorado and Nevada and the Mormon settlements in Utah. Mail coaches of the Overland Stage Line required at least five days to carry passengers and mails from the Missouri river to Denver. Silver ore extracted in Nevada had to be freighted by wagon to San Francisco, thence transported around Cape Horn to the East Coast and Great Britain. Transcontinental railroads pushed out into the plains in advance of settlers, advertised for immigrants in the Eastern states and Europe, transported them at reduced rates to the prairie railhead, and sold them land on credit. Thousands of construction workers became farm hands, obtained free homesteads from the federal government, and bought tools, horses, and cattle with their savings. The termini and junction points of these lines—places like Omaha, Kansas City, Missouri, hard by Independence (old jumping-off place for the Oregon trail), Duluth, the "Zenith City of the Unsalted Seas," Oakland on San Francisco Bay, Portland in Oregon, Seattle and Tacoma in Washington—places non-existent or mere villages before the Civil War, became metropolitan cities in thirty years' time.

Railroading was the biggest business of a big era, and the railway builders were of the mettle that in Europe made Napoleons and Von Moltkes. The Northwest was the domain of James J. Hill, greatest of our railroad builders. St. Paul was a small town on the edge of the frontier when he emigrated thither from eastern Canada just before the Civil War, and Minneapolis a mere village at the St. Anthony falls of the Mississippi. There, the "Twin Cities" were located at the end of a trail which connected Winnipeg with the outside world. In the winter of 1870 Donald A. Smith, the future Lord Strathcona, then resident governor of the Hudson's Bay Company, started south from Winnipeg, and James J. Hill started north from St. Paul, both in dogsleds. They met on the prairie and made camp in a storm, and from that meeting sprang the Canadian Pacific and Great Northern railways.

During the panic of 1873 the St. Paul & Pacific railroad went bankrupt. Hill watched it as a prairie wolf watches a weakening buffalo, and in 1878, in association with Donald Smith and George Stephen (the future Lord Mount Stephen), wrested it from Dutch bondholders by floating new securities.

The day of land grants and federal subsidies was past, and Hill saw that the Great Northern Railway, as he renamed his purchase, could reach the Pacific only by developing the country as it progressed; and that took time. He struck due west across the Dakota plains, sending out branches to people the region and carry wheat to market. In the summer of 1887 his construction made a record stride, 643 miles of grading, bridging, and rail-laying from Minot, North Dakota, to the Great Falls of the Missouri. Two years later, the Rockies yielded their last secret, the Marias pass, to a young engineer, John F. Stevens. In 1893 the trains of the Great Northern reached tidewater at Tacoma. Within ten years Hill acquired partial control of the Northern Pacific Railway, purchased joint control of the Chicago, Burlington & Quincy, connecting his eastern termini with Chicago, and was running steamship lines from Duluth to Buffalo and from Seattle to Japan and China.

The Great Northern, the Northern Pacific, and the Union Pacific (which sent a taproot northwesterly) were responsible for opening the great inland empire between the Cascades and the Rockies, and for an astounding development of the entire Northwest. This once isolated Oregon country, with its rich and varied natural resources, magnificent scenery, and thriving seaports, has become as distinct and self-conscious a section of the Union as New England. The three states into which it was divided—Washington, Oregon, and Idaho—increased in population from 282,000 in 1880 to 2 million in 1910 and 5.3 million in 1960; whilst California, which contained only half a million people when the golden spike was driven in 1869, kept well in front, rising to 15.7 million in 1960. The population of Kansas, Nebraska, and the Dakotas, starting at the same level in 1870, increased sixfold in two decades; Utah and Colorado, where there was a great mining boom in the 'seventies, tripled their population in the same period. Oklahoma and the Indian Territory, where not one white man was enrolled in 1880, had over 2 million palefaces and 55,000 Indians in 1960; and Texas, with the aid of a network of railways, doubled its population of 1.5 million between 1880 and 1900, and by 1960 had almost 10 million people. By 1890 the last serious Indian outbreak had been suppressed, and the surviving redskins confined to reservations; the last great area of public lands had been thrown open to settlement.

There were still great unexplored regions in the Far West in 1865 which the railroad only reached later, if ever. Four men who combined a zest for exploration with skill as naturalists, geologists, and writers were largely responsible for the conservation of some of America's greatest natural wonders. Clarence King, who headed a congressional survey of the region between eastern Colorado and California, published the results in his seven-volume *Exploration of the Fortieth Parallel* (1870–80), which has become a classic. In 1878 King was made head of the newly established United States Geological Survey. He was largely responsible for establishing the wondrous Sequoia National Park in the high Sierras.

John Muir began in 1867 a 1000-mile walk from Wisconsin to the Gulf of Mexico, visited and studied the Yosemite valley and, aided by writing articles in Eastern magazines, labored successfully to have the Yosemite made a national park. Muir was also an apostle of conservation, and it was on the basis of reports by a national forestry commission of which he was a member that President Cleveland, just before the end of his second term, created thirteen forest reserves comprising 21 million acres. The McKinley administration threw most of them back to the loggers, but Muir captured the ear of the public in a series of brilliant articles, and aroused the interest of Theodore Roosevelt in conservation.

John Wesley Powell, who lost an arm at Shiloh and became a professor of geology after the war, led a 900-mile descent of the Colorado river in boats through the Grand Canyon in 1869. He described this and later adventurous surveys in the Southwest in his *Canyons of the Colorado,* and did effective work under King in the Geological Survey; his interest in the Indians found an outlet as head of the Smithsonian's Bureau of Ethnology. Ferdinand V. Hayden, whose career as a soldier and paleontologist paralleled that of Powell, was largely responsible for Congress's creating the Yellowstone National Park in 1872. These four men deserve to be kept in fond remembrance, and not only for their discoveries; they were the lions whose boldness and determination prevented the jackals of exploitation from consuming the whole of America's most glorious natural heritage. But after they died the jackals, armed with the bulldozer, got away with a good part of it, owing, as Bernard DeVoto wrote, to the West's "historic willingness to hold itself cheap and its eagerness to sell out." The end result almost justifies DeVoto's description of the Far West as "the plundered province."

This disappearance of the frontier was hailed by Frederick J. Turner, a great American historian, as the close of a movement that began in 1607; and the Spanish-American War of 1898 was interpreted as the beginning of a new phase of imperialism. After the lapse of years, it is difficult to discern any break in the rhythm of American life in the year 1890. The settlement of the Great West had not then been completed; in areas covering thousands of square miles it had not even begun. The westward movement of population continued. Even outside the national parks and forest reserves there are still areas of virgin wilderness in the Rocky Mountains, the

Sierra Nevada, and the high plains. There has, to be sure, been a gradual assimilation of the West to Eastern modes of living and thinking; but that, too, has been going on since the seventeenth century. Barely two generations separate the male vigor of Bret Harte's *Roaring Camp* and *Poker Flat* (1870) from the insipid society portrayed by Sinclair Lewis's *Main Street* (1920). Yet even today there is a marked difference between East and West. The transcontinental tourist, whether by train or car, as he leaves the settled farms of Dakota or Kansas for the broad sweep of the high plains, has the feeling of a land still young to the white man's tread.

Rail penetration of the far Northwest, improved agricultural machinery, the handling of grain in carload lots, transshipment to lake or ocean steamers by grain elevators, and a new milling process which ground the Northern spring wheat into superfine flour (much too superfine), were factors which combined to move the center of wheat production north and west from Illinois and Iowa into Minnesota, the Dakotas, Montana, Oregon, and the Canadian Northwest. In this new wheat belt the "bonanza" wheat farms, veritable factories for wheat production, were well established by 1890. The wheat crop increased from 152 to 612 million bushels between 1866 and 1891. With the low prices that prevailed after the panic of 1873, this meant disaster to competing farmers in the Middle West and the Eastern states; and, even more completely, to England. The silo which enabled dairy farmers to turn corn into milk, poultry raising, and the breeding of horses and cattle, saved Eastern farming from ruin; but enormous areas within a few hours of the great industrial centers on the Atlantic coast have reverted to forest.

Wool production remained almost constant in this period; and cotton, owing to the dislocation of Southern society, did not attain its high prewar figure until 1878. As the corn belt extended into Kansas and Nebraska, the crop, already 868 million bushels in 1866, passed 2000 million bushels in 1891. The greater part of the corn was converted into meat, cured at thousands of local bacon factories and at the great packing plants in Chicago. And we have yet to record the revolution in meat production which took place between 1865 and 1880.

Richmond, Virginia, has the credit of making the first successful experiment with electric streetcars in 1888, a mode of urban and suburban transportation which reached its zenith around 1920 and has since almost completely disappeared. Other cities at once began replacing horsecars by trolley cars. (Oliver Wendell Holmes saluted the "broomstick train" as the

Salem witches' revenge), or cars that obtained electric power
from underground conduits. Before the end of the century,
interurban electric railways were taking passenger traffic away
from steam railroads, and it was possible to travel from northern New England to the Middle West by "electrics," if one
could spare the time—as few Americans felt they could afford
to do.

Nor did rail have a monopoly of long-distance freight transportation. A large part of the nation's traffic, and all foreign
trade except with Canada and Mexico, was carried by ships,
sail, or steam. This was the heyday of the sternwheeler on the
Mississippi and its tributaries—incidentally producing a galaxy
of songs, such as "Waiting on the Levee . . . for the *Robert E.
Lee,*" a steamboat which beat the *Natchez* in a famous river
race. On the Great Lakes were fleets of ore carriers, tankers,
and grain ships, with a dying fleet of local sailing craft like
the *Jolie Plante* in which poor Marie, fresh-water counterpart
to that golden-haired damsel who perished in Longfellow's
"Wreck of the Hesperus," lost her life. Hard by the "reef of
Norman's Woe" lies the snug haven, Gloucester, home port
for hundreds of sailing fishermen; stubby "bankers" or "hand-
liners" immortalized by Kipling's *Captains Courageous*
(1886), and the tall mackerel seiners, which James B. Con-
nolly described in *Out of Gloucester.* Hundreds of schooners,
two-, three-, and even six-masted, plied between ports of the
Maritime Provinces, the East Coast, the Caribbean, and South
America, carrying fish, coal, lumber, granite, and even general
cargoes in competition with the coastal steamboats. Of these
there were literally hundreds: deep-water runs several times
weekly from New York to Norfolk, Baltimore, Charleston,
Halifax, and New Orleans; night runs of sound steamers to
Hartford, Stonington, New London, and Fall River. Every
evening in Boston, weather permitting, saw departures to
sundry Maine and Nova Scotia ports. Traffic "down east" as
yet had no Cape Cod Canal (completed in 1914), but the inland waterways from Norfolk south were being improved for
tug and barge traffic. By 1894 the Fall River Line's *Puritan*
and *Priscilla,* "queen of all steamboats," were carrying
300,000 passengers annually between New York and New
England. These Long Island Sound lines carried on into the
great depression of the 1930's, when they were killed by the
competition of trucks and the exactions of the Seamen's
Union.

River and coastal traffic had been protected from foreign
competition by navigation laws ever since 1789. But America's
foreign trade had to meet foreign competition, and thereby

suffered. Before the war, two-thirds of the value of American imports and exports had been carried in American-flag ships. By 1870 the proportion had dropped to one-third; and by 1880 to one-sixth. The initial drop has often been ascribed to the depredations of Confederate cruisers; but they could hardly be blamed for the 1870–80 slump. Captain John Codman of Boston testified before a congressional committee in 1882, "We have lost our prestige and experience; we are no longer a maritime nation; our shipowners have been wearied and disgusted; they have gone into other business, forced by their government to abandon their old calling. Our ship-masters, the pride of the ocean in the old packet days, are dead, and they have no successors."

A congressional investigation of 1882 reported that the basic cause of this decline was the superior attraction for American investors of railroads, Western land, manufacturing, and mining, when the merchant navies of several European powers and Japan were earning only 4 or 5 per cent. Congress could have made up the difference by ship subsidies; but Congress, in contrast to its lavish support of transcontinental railroads, let the merchant marine decline nearly to the vanishing point. Almost all the sound, river, and coastal steamers of this era were built of wood, and bad fire hazards they were. Owing to the backwardness of American builders and designers in steel hulls and marine engines, and the laws against placing foreign-built vessels under the American flag, the United States never regained a place in fast transatlantic traffic until after World War II. The American Line, a combine of several, was enabled to compete only by virtue of a special act of Congress allowing it to acquire two foreign-built liners, *City of Paris* and *City of New York*. These two, in 1889–92, were the first to make a transatlantic passage between New York and Queenstown, Ireland, in less than six days. *Deutschland* of the North German Lloyd captured the "blue riband of the Atlantic" in 1900 and held it for seven years, when the ill-fated *Lusitania* made the crossing in less than four days, twenty hours.

Another exception made by Congress after the Civil War was a liberal subsidy of the Pacific Mail Line to carry mail from San Francisco to Hawaii and the Orient. Pacific Mail long held its own in competition with the Canadian Pacific steamship line, and Japan's Toyo Kisen Kaisha. Its 5000-ton, iron-screw steamers *City of Peking* and *City of Tokio*, built at Chester, Pennsylvania, with auxiliary four-masted barque rig, lowered the record from San Francisco to Yokohama to sixteen days. Collis Huntington of the Southern Pacific Railroad got control of this line in 1893, and built five new ships. It carried on until 1915, when killed by a law requiring the Oriental crews to be replaced by Americans.

Despite Captain Codman, the American sailing marine did pretty well. Square-riggers, built largely in Maine or on Puget Sound, officered by Americans and manned by sailors of every nation, race, and color, continued to carry bulk cargoes to European ports, around the Horn to the West Coast, Japan, China, and Hawaii, and around the Cape of Good Hope to Australia and India. As late as 1892 there was more tonnage under the American flag in sail than in steam. In this final phase of deep-water sail, the wooden square-rigger was perfected. "These splendid ships, each with her grace, her glory," as John Masefield wrote, were not so fast as the clippers, but carried more cargo for their size and, with labor-saving devices (but no auxiliary propulsion), were more economical to operate on long voyages than steamers, a large part of whose cargo space had to be given to coal bunkers. Among the famous ships of this era was Donald McKay's last creation, *Glory of the Seas,* launched in 1869, 2000 tons burthen, 240 feet long. In 1875 she hung up a record from San Francisco to Sydney, 35 days, which still stands. The slightly smaller *Grand Admiral,* also built in 1869, carried the black horse flag of the Weld family for 28 years, during which she logged 727,000 miles in 5360 sailing days—an amazing record, considering that many of those days must have been windless. Last full-rigged three-skysail yarder to be built in the United States was *Aryan,* 1939 tons, 248 feet long, designed locally and built on the Kennebec in 1893. Her owners kept her sailing out of sentiment until 1918, long after the competition of steamers had made her unprofitable. The adoption of high-pressure, triple-expansion marine engines in the 1890's, requiring less than one-tenth of the coal per horsepower of the old compound engines, doomed the sailing ship on round-the-world trading routes. They hung on for carrying bulk cargoes on protected coastal routes until the 1930's.

2. Indians, Cattle, and Cowboys

The dismal story of relations between white Americans and the American Indian continued with little change. In contrast to the blacks who were denied their ambition to participate on equal terms in American civilization, the Indians, who desired above all to continue their own way of life, were deprived of hunting grounds which would have made that possible, and were pressured to "settle down" and become "good" farmers and citizens.

Before that pressure could be exerted, the redskins had to be defeated in battle. Indians of the Great Plains and the Rocky Mountains, about 225,000 in number, presented a formidable obstacle to white settlement. The strongest and most warlike were the Sioux, Blackfoot, Crow, Cheyenne, Arapaho, and Nez Percé in the north; the Comanche, Apache, Ute, Kiowa, Southern Cheyenne, and Southern Arapaho in the south and center. Mounted on swift horses, well armed for plains warfare, and living on the herds of buffalo that roamed the open range, these tribes long maintained a stubborn resistance to white penetration of their hunting grounds.

The first serious invasion of these hunting grounds came with the great migration of the 1840's. In 1850 there were approximately 100,000 Indians in California; in 1860 there were barely 35,000 "despoiled by irresistible forces of the land of their fathers; with no country on earth to which they can migrate; in the midst of a people with whom they cannot assimilate," as Congress's committee on Indian affairs reported. The advance of miners into the mountains, the building of transcontinental railroads, and the invasion of the grasslands by cattlemen, threatened every other Indian nation of the West with the same fate. Wanton destruction of the buffalo, indispensable not only for food but for housing, bowstrings, lariats, and fuel; the Colt six-shooter, fearfully efficient in the hands of palefaces, and the spread of white men's diseases among the Indians; all were lethal.

Until 1861 the Indians of the Great Plains had been relatively peaceful, but in that year the invasion of Colorado by thousands of miners, and the advance of white settlers along the upper Mississippi and Missouri, began a series of armed clashes. Sioux of the Dakotas went on the warpath in 1862, devastated the Minnesota frontier, and massacred or captured almost 1000 white people. Retribution was swift and terrible, but for the next 25 years Indian warfare was a constant of Western history. Each new influx of settlers and of railroad gangs who carelessly destroyed the buffalo, drove the redskins to raid settlements in search of food, and to acts of desperation which brought on punitive expeditions by the United States Army. There were some 200 pitched battles between soldiers and Indians in the years 1869–76. The contest was not unequal, for the Indians had become excellent shots. They could attack or flee from the heavy United States cavalry at will, and they were not troubled by logistic problems. Had they been able to unite, they might have tired out the United States (as white resistance to reconstruction was doing in the South); but no Tecumseh, no Prophet appeared. The army could always recruit Indian scouts, and the redskins were defeated piecemeal.

It was not that nobody did anything about it. Congress in 1867 set up an Indian Peace Commission, which included Generals Sherman and Terry, to stop the fighting, and it did that for about two years. This commission recommended an end to the farce of making treaties with Indian nations—there were roughly 370 of them in the archives—and in 1871 Congress did so. General Francis A. Walker (future president of M.I.T.), whom Grant appointed commissioner of Indian affairs that year, did his best to carry out a paternalistic policy. He placed defeated tribes on new reservations, set up schools for their children, and issued rations to those who had no more game; but his best was not good enough. In his report of 1872 he remarked cogently, "Every year's advance of our frontier takes in a territory as large as some of the kingdoms of Europe. We are richer by hundreds of millions, the Indian is poorer by a large part of the little that he has. This growth is bringing imperial greatness to the nation; to the Indian it brings wretchedness, destitution, beggary."

For ten years after the Civil War the Sioux, in particular, fought desperately to preserve their hunting grounds on the Great Plains. In December 1866 Captain William J. Fetterman USA, stationed at Fort Phil Kearny, Wyoming, was ambushed by Red Cloud, and his command of eighty men were killed. Fort Buford, on the Missouri just across the Montana line, was sniped at by Sioux in 1867. The American public was stirred up by a report of a "horrible massacre" there which actually never took place, a report which the commissioner of Indian affairs attributed to "the rapacity and rascality of frontier settlers, whose interests are to bring on a war and supply our armies . . . at exorbitant prices." For several years there were occasional skirmishes with the Sioux, but their knell of doom struck in 1875 when prospectors discovered gold in the Black Hills—"them thar hills"—of South Dakota and founded fabulous Deadwood, where "Wild Bill" Hickok, hero of many a border brawl, died with his boots on. These hills, to the Sioux, were holy ground which the government had promised to retain for them inviolate. For one summer General Sheridan was able to hold back the greedy gold seekers, but in the following spring they broke through. Under Sitting Bull and Crazy Horse the Sioux struck back.

Colonel George A. Custer of the 7th Cavalry, a distinguished veteran of the Civil War who had been fighting Indians off and on for the last nine years, had come to like and respect them. "If I were an Indian," he wrote in an article about an earlier battle with the Sioux, "I would certainly prefer to cast my lot . . . to the free open plains rather than submit to the confined limits of a reservation, there to be the recipients of the blessed benefits of civilization with its vices thrown in." In June 1876 he led a column west from Bismarck to disperse the Sioux and Northern Cheyenne, who had left their Black Hills reservation. On the 25th he found them by the Little Big Horn river in Montana. Rashly, before knowing how many warriors were present, Custer divided the 7th Cavalry into three columns, one of which, his own, was surrounded by some 2500 braves under Crazy Horse. Custer and his entire command of 265 officers and men were killed. Colonel Nelson A. Miles in January 1877 caught up with and defeated Crazy Horse, whose enemies gave him the compliment of calling him "one of the bravest of the brave and one of the subtlest and most capable of captains." Custer became a hero to the boys who grew up in that era, and his bright and joyous figure, his long yellow locks, and trooper's swagger shine through the murk of controversy over who was to blame for the massacre on the Little Big Horn.

More Indians were now driven from their ancient homes. In Montana the Crow and Blackfoot were ejected from their reservations; in Colorado the vast holdings of the Ute were confiscated and opened to settlement. The discovery of gold on the Salmon river in western Idaho precipitated an invasion of the peaceful Nez Percé. They refused to surrender lands guaranteed to them, and the federal government in 1877 decided to drive them out. Chief Joseph struck back, but in vain, and then conducted 200 braves and 600 squaws and papooses on a fighting retreat over 1500 miles of mountain and plain, a memorable feat in the annals of Indian warfare; and for strategic and tactical skill in a class with Marshal Kesselring's Italian campaigns of 1944–45. In the end, when just short of asylum in Canada, Chief Joseph surrendered (5 October 1877), saying, "Hear me, my chiefs. I am tired; my heart is sick and sad. From where the sun now stands I will fight no more, forever." Joseph then devoted himself to the peaceful betterment of his people, part of whom returned to their ancestral lands, and part settled in Oklahoma.

In the Southwest, twenty years of intermittent warfare with various branches of the Apache ended in 1886 with the surrender of their chief Geronimo and the subjugation of his tribe. Geronimo became a Christian convert and lived both to write his autobiography and to take part in the inaugural procession of President Roosevelt in 1905.

In 1881 President Arthur declared, "We have to deal with the appalling fact that though thousands of lives have been sacrificed and hundreds of millions of dollars expended in the attempt to solve the Indian problem, it has until within the past few years seemed scarcely nearer a solution than it was half a century ago." Federal authority over Indian affairs was divided between the war and interior departments, both of which pursued a vacillating and uncertain policy, and each failed to live up to treaty obligations or to protect the Indians on their reservations from white settlers' aggressions. These aggressions often took the form of alienating by fraud and chicanery large areas of Indian lands to railroads and other speculators. One railroad acquired 800,000 acres of Cherokee land in southern Kansas, an operation that the governor of that state denounced as "a cheat and a fraud in every particular," but nothing was done to cancel it, and the railroad resold the lands to settlers at a vast profit. Only the intervention of the secretary of the interior prevented a particularly crass deal whereby the Osage were to sell 8 million acres to a railroad for 20 cents an acre.

American frontiersmen in general still subscribed to their traditional feeling that the only good Indian was a dead Indian; but in the East, churchmen and reformers urged a humane policy toward the nation's wards. Statesmen like Carl Schurz, religious leaders like Bishop Henry B. Whipple, literary figures like Helen Hunt Jackson, whose *Century of Dishonor* (1881) stirred the nation's conscience, were loud in their criticism of the government's treatment of the Indian, and their attitude was effective in bringing about important changes in policy.

Paternalism culminated in the passage of the Dawes Act of 1887, which established the policy of breaking up reservations into individual homesteads. This was an attempt to "civilize" the Indian by folding him into the body politic of the nation. Passage of this law was promoted by Indian Rights and other societies who wished the redskins well; it was based on the "Protestant ethic" premise that ownership of real estate was a moral good, fostering thrift, industry, and providing the spark of energy or ambition that leads to wealth and prestige. But the "do-gooders" overlooked the fact that the Western Indian, by habit and heredity, was a hunter rather than a cultivator; that his ideas of land ownership were communal, not individual; that the last thing he wanted was to become a homesteader. By persuading Indians to be individual land-owners as an alternative to living on government rations on a reservation, pressuring them to try homesteading before they had acquired the technique and values that alone make "the American way of life" viable, the Dawes Act was certain to be a very partial success. It overlooked a trait of the Indian character: that he literally takes "no thought for the morrow," and is easily tempted to sell his birthright to go on a big binge. Thus, it was taken advantage of by landgrabbers and speculators.

The act, in general, provided that the President of the United States should direct that a reservation be broken up when and if he had evidence that the Indians wanted it; then a homestead of 160 acres would be granted to each family, and the unalloted remainder of the reservation would be purchased by the government for sale to white men, the money to be put in trust for the tribe. After allotment began, in 1891, the acreage of Indian reservations was reduced 12 per cent in a single year. Congress then speeded up the process by passing another law which allowed the allottees to lease their lands. That really doomed the system. Indians living on a reservation, lapped about by white men's farms, faced with the alternative of becoming a tribal slum on the prairie or unwilling homesteaders, snapped hungrily at the allotment bait, knowing that individual farms could now be leased, and hoping to live well on the rent. In 1894 it was ascertained that the Omaha and Winnebago in Nebraska had leased lands to a real estate syndicate for 8 to 10 cents an acre, which the syndicate re-leased to white farmers for $1 to $2 an acre, per annum. Out of 140,000 acres allotted by 1898 to these two nations, 112,000 had been leased, mostly illegally, and the wretched lessors were living in squalor on their meager rents, drifting into the towns and cities, unable to fit into the white man's civilization. The Indian allottee did not know what to do with his land. Now for the first time he was subject to state taxes, and if he did not succumb to the temptation to lease, and held his allotment for the required 25 years, he generally sold it as soon as a fee simple patent was issued, squandered the proceeds, and became a pauper. In the half-century after 1887, Indian holdings decreased from 138 to 48 million acres. Indian timberlands, too, were acquired by speculators; the Indian commissioner blandly declared in 1917 that "as the Indian tribes were being liquidated anyway, it was only sensible to liquidate their forest holdings as well." Tribal funds amounting to more than $100 million were diverted from their proper use to meet the costs of the Indian Bureau—including the costs of despoiling the Indians of their lands.

Fortunately for the Five Civilized Tribes, the Dawes Act did not apply to them, or to a few others such as the Osage, Miami, Sauk and Fox who had located in the Indian Territory. These were given special treatment. As punishment for their support of the Confederacy, the Five Civilized Tribes were compelled in 1866 to accept new treaties relinquishing the western half of the Indian Territory, where some twenty tribes from Kansas and Nebraska were settled in thirteen new reservations. Two million acres of this western half, called Oklahoma Territory, were bought from the Indians and thrown open to settlement in 1889, with the consequent land rush which is well described in Edna Ferber's *Cimarron*. It was an extraordinary spectacle, a *reductio ad absurdum* of laissez-faire. Some 12,000 prospective settlers camped along the railroad between the Canadian and Cimarron rivers. Here, wrote an eyewitness, James Morgan, was the chronically moving family in its covered wagon, beaten on a dozen frontiers for half a century but always hopeful that the next would prove a bonanza; Texans who were finding Texas too tame; lawyers and doctors with their diplomas and instruments; gamblers and fancy men; "all the elements of western life—a wonderful mixture of thrift and unthrift, of innocence and guile, of lambs and wolves." Shepherded by United States cavalry, they lined up along the border in wagons, on horseback, and afoot, and at the shot of a pistol, raced to grab one of the 6000 free homestead lots. In many instances these men found the "sooners," those who had jumped the gun, ahead of them; claims staked out had to be defended—or lost—by gunfire, and it took years to straighten out the mess of land titles. Altogether the most inefficient and wasteful way of settling a new country that anyone could have imagined.

The Five Civilized Tribes, who numbered over 51,000 in the census of 1890, were made American citizens in 1901. Allotments under the Dawes Act were now extended to the Cherokee, and the United States Court of Claims awarded $1.1 million to that nation as indemnity for the hardships of their removal in 1838. In 1907 Oklahoma, including Indian Territory, was admitted as a state of the Union, and from that time on the Indians in that state have been not only their own masters, but an element that no politician can ignore.

Hitherto all the world had obtained fresh meat from local butchers; beef could be exported only on the hoof or in pickle. After the Civil War thousands of young Texans came home from army service, to find the grassy plains in the southern part of the state glutted with millions of fat, mature cattle, descendants of the longhorns turned loose by Spaniards a century or more earlier. They were then bringing only $1 to $5 a head, but were worth twenty times as much in the eastern cities. Stretching north through Texas and across the Indian

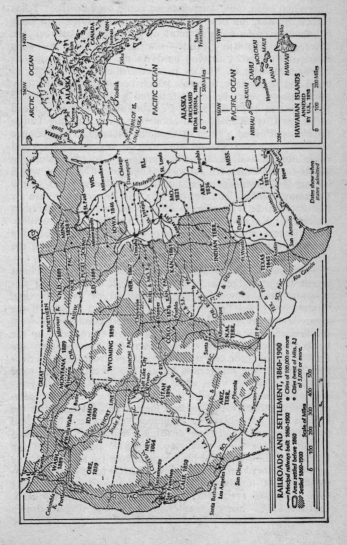

RAILROADS AND SETTLEMENT, 1860–1900

Territory to Kansas, and even into Wyoming, were millions of acres of natural grass which supported the buffalo; but these beasts were rapidly being exterminated by hunters and railroad section gangs, and were practically extinct by 1884. There had been some long-distance cattle droving from Texas before the war, but now the Texans—especially Richard King whose vast ranch covered most of the territory between the Nueces and the Rio Grande—saw an opportunity to reach Eastern markets by driving herds to the western termini of railroads. Joseph G. McCoy persuaded the Kansas Pacific to build out to Abilene, Kansas, which became a famous "cow town" thirty years before it fathered a famous general and President; in 1871 the Santa Fe established another railhead at Dodge City, Kansas, and about the same time the Union Pacific established a third at Ogalalla, Nebraska. The chance discovery that beeves could winter on the Wyoming plains and come out fat and sleek in the spring, led to other shipping points on the Northern railways. Thus, by 1875 there was a belt of free pasturage extending from southern Texas to the Canadian border. The refrigerator car, in common use by that date, made it possible to sell dressed beef, slaughtered at Chicago or Kansas City, in the Eastern centers of population. These factors, with the invention of artificial ice and a canning machine, brought even European markets within reach of the Far West.

This new industry of raising beef cattle on the Great Plains produced the last phase of the Wild West, and the most picturesque development of the ancient art of cattle-droving. Texans, who had ridden from childhood and fought in the Confederate army, and Mexican bucaroos (*vaqueros*) were the first and best cowboys. Every spring they rounded up the herds from eight to ten ranches, identified ownership by the brands, branded the calves, and divided *pro rata* the mavericks and "dogies," the motherless calves. The breeding cattle were set free for another year, while the likely three- and four-year-olds were conducted on the long drive. There were three principal trails, all of which crossed the Indian Territory; but the Indians did not object to palefaces and cattle who passed through instead of settling down; the Cherokee even issued grazier licenses for a small fee. In 1871, peak year of the long drive, some 600,000 head were driven north.

A typical herd on the long drive of 1200 to 1500 miles consisted of 2500 longhorns. This required about twelve cowboys with a *remuda* (remount) of from five to six horses each, controlled by a "horse wrangler," and a "chuck wagon" drawn by mules for the men's food and camp equipment. The cattle walked slowly, making ten to twenty miles a day, swam rivers, and, if properly driven and prevented from stampeding, would even gain weight en route. They were allowed to browse all night, for an hour or two every morning, and again at noon. At the end of the drive the cattle were sold to buyers from Chicago and Kansas City, and the cowboys, after being paid off and "blowing in" most of their wages in the cow town, returned by the same trail.

While the long line of cattle moved slowly, the cowboys were continually riding up and down, urging stragglers along, and on the lookout for raiding "bad men," wild Indians, or prairie-grass fires. They had to continue riding around the herd at night lest it be stampeded by a thunderstorm or by steers simply getting the notion to bolt. The cowboy's high-horned Mexican saddle, lariat, broad-brimmed sombrero, high-heeled boots, and leather "chaps" and six-shooter were perfectly adapted to his work. His bronco—a short-legged, vari-colored mustang of Spanish origin, hardy as a donkey and fleet as an Arab, and which he broke with unnecessary cruelty —made an ideal cow pony. The authentic cowboy was spare of frame, pithy and profane in speech, a superb rider although a bowlegged walker; alert with the sort of courage needed to rope steers, fight cattle rustlers, or stop a stampede; hardworking and enduring, asking no better end than to die with his boots on. His life is recorded in ballads which are now nation-wide favorites. These ballads record the freedom and discipline, the violence and friendship of the Far West; one can almost smell the odor of sun on saddle leather, and of the buffalo-chip fire over which cookie prepared the evening meal; a hard, challenging open-air life that attracted young men, knights of the long trail. The cowboy of the long drive flourished for a brief score of years, fading into legend with the passing of the open range.

By 1885 the range had become too heavily pastured to support the long drive, and was beginning to be crisscrossed by railroads and by the barbed-wire fences of homesteaders. Then came the terrible winter of 1886-87, when thousands of animals perished in the open. Cattle owners began to stake out homestead claims in the names of their employees and to fence off areas to which they had no claim. Almost in a moment cattle and sheep ranches replaced the open range, and the cowboy of the long drive became a domesticated ranch hand.

So much for the cowboy of history. But why did this ephemeral type capture the nation's, almost the world's, imagination rather than the earlier trapper of the Far West, the lumberjack of the northern forests, the river man who rode logs down rapids, or the sailor in blue water? These, too, had their ballads or chanties; their lives were not lacking in beauty, and they too experienced the same violent contrast between long periods of exceedingly hard, dangerous work and brief, bawdy blowouts. One answer is that the cowboy was a horseman, and since the dawn of history the rider has seemed more glamorous than the sailor or footman—witness the gay cavalcade of Athenian knights on the frieze of the Parthenon. And the cowboy was rendered famous by three gifted "tenderfeet" or "dudes,"[1] Eastern college graduates who sojourned briefly in the Far West produced souped-up versions in prose, painting and sculpture of Life in the Raw for the effete East. Frederic Remington, after playing football with Walter Camp at Yale, became a cowboy and rancher in Kansas for about two years but devoted the rest of his life (at New Rochelle, New York) to drawing, painting, and sculpturing cowpunchers, Indians, and trappers in action, partly as illustrations to his own books. Theodore Roosevelt invested half his patrimony in a cattle ranch in the Bad Lands of Dakota Territory in 1883, lived there for less than three years, doing the hardest work and acquiring a taste for the "great open spaces" which produced the Rough Riders of 1898, and fed the Rooseveltian conception of Strenuous Life. "In that land," he wrote in his *Autobiography*, "we led a free and hardy life, with horse and with rifle. . . . We knew toil and hardship and hunger and thirst; and we saw men die violent deaths as they worked among the horses and cattle, or fought in evil feuds with one another; but we felt the beat of hardy life in our veins, and ours was the glory of work and the joy of living."

Roosevelt's love for the Far West was deep and genuine; but the man who contributed most to the cowboy legend was a literary cowboy, Owen Wister, a Philadelphia patrician who reached Wyoming in time to witness the so-called Johnson County War between cattle barons and the homesteaders. Many young Easterners and Englishmen of wealth, eager to combine sportsmanship with profit, had begun cattle-raising in Wyoming, taking advantage of the free open range. Wister found their society, which centered upon the Cheyenne Club, as congenial as that of the Porcellian, although the members

[1] "Tenderfoot" first meant a yard-raised cow turned out on the range; "dude" (pronounced "dood"), a word of unknown origin which appeared around 1881, was first applied to the New York "young men about town" glorified in Richard Harding Davis's *Van Bibber* books, who dressed in the latest London fashion and were caricatured as wearing a monocle and a topper and sucking the handle of a walking stick. In the Far West it meant any well-heeled Easterner, and there it survives in the term "dude ranch."

wore a different costume. It so happened that Johnson County had been thrown open by the Land Office to homesteaders, and many—mostly from the Ozarks—had located there, built barbed-wire fences around their 160-acre lots, and in other ways hindered the operations of the gentlemen who had organized the powerful Wyoming Stock Growers' Association. Wister regarded the "grangers" or "nesters" as the settlers were called locally, as low fellows of the baser sort, and in several short stories, combined in the popular novel *The Virginian* (1902), glorified the cowboy and condoned the murderous onslaughts on homesteaders by the gentlemen's hired killers. Wister created the literary cliché of the gentle cowpuncher who respected virtuous womanhood (and eventually married a schoolteacher from New England), defending the free open life of the range against homesteaders and other bad men who were trying to destroy it. He was the progenitor of standardized "Western" literature, of the rodeos for which horses are trained to buck, and the so-called "horse opera" on radio and in the movies, which have made the fortunes of hundreds of hack and script writers. This distorted image of the American Far West has traveled around the world; small boys in Europe, Asia and Africa are still listening to these impossible tales of the Wild West and sporting imitations of Levi overalls, spurs, Colt revolvers, and "ten-gallon hats."

3. *The Farming Country*

There was no essential change in Northern farm life between the Civil War and the coming of the automobile.[1] From Maine westward through Nebraska and the Dakotas, country folk lived in wooden frame houses such as those depicted by Grant Wood and Grandma Moses. The kitchen served as family living room; the parlor, with horsehair-covered furniture, Prang chromos, and crayon enlargements of family photos on the walls, perhaps a Rogers group on the table, was used mostly for the daughters' courting, and for weddings and funerals. The carpenter who built a farmer's house differentiated it from the barn by putting scroll work under the eaves and by building at the front a porch with carved posts. These houses were heated in winter by cast-iron stoves, lighted by

[1] Alexander Graham Bell invented the telephone in 1876, and Thomas A. Edison the incandescent light bulb in 1879; but it was long before either spread to country districts. In 1885 the Bell Telephone Company had over 134,000 subscribers in the United States as compared with about 13,500 in the United Kingdom; but most of the telephones were in towns and cities.

kerosene lamps and protected from flying insects by iron-meshed screens. The farmer's wife cooked for her own family and the hired hands on a wood or coal stove and hauled or pumped her water from a nearby well, unless she lived in a region where a windmill could do it. Fewer than 10 per cent of American farm houses before 1900 had plumbing; a wooden washtub served for the weekly bath, and the back-house, whose passing James Whitcomb Riley celebrated in a famous unpublished poem, served other basic human needs.

The cow barn, always larger than the house, doubled as horse stable and afforded plenty of storage space for root crops as well as hay; its well-worn floor of wide boards was perfect for country dances. Daily Bible reading and Sunday "goin' to meetin'" were the rule, and much of the farm family's recreation turned around church socials. The farmer did not invite neighbors to dinner—"swapping meals" made no sense to him. The horse served as pet, transportation, and sport to all country-bred Americans, and to many in the cities. It was a poor farmer who hadn't a team of Clydesdales or Percherons for heavy hauling, a fast trotter for his buggy, and a saddle horse or two for his children; nobody walked if he could help it. Breeding horses, raising and training the colts, were part of a farmer's education and afforded him and his children infinite pleasure and profit, especially in horse trading. And it was a rare farmer who did not take the time to go fishing with his boys, or to shoot quail, duck, and partridge; or, if he lived on the edge of the northern wilderness, to hunt deer and moose.

This horse-centered economy created a vast market for hay and feed grains, and supported such handicraft industries as blacksmithing, saddlery, and harness making, and the construction of wagons, carriages, buggies, and sleighs. These were generally lighter than European models, but fashioned to last; beautifully functional, with a different kind of wood for each part, as Dr. Holmes described in "The Wonderful One-Hoss Shay." Winter and snow were a blessing in those days. Roads were tramped down by pooling the community's ox teams as Whittier described in "Snow-Bound," or, later, by great wooden horse-drawn rollers. The farmer and his boys put away their wheeled vehicles and let down by tackles from the barn loft their steel-runnered pungs and sledges which had been gathering dust and rust since spring. Heavy hauling of timber and the like now began, local sportsmen organized trotting races in their cutters (two-seater one-horse sleighs) painted gay colors. A swain who had taken his girl buggy-riding in the fall now tucked her into a smart cutter with a buffalo robe; and away they went at a fast clip over the snowy roads, to the merry jingle of sleigh bells.

The hired man on the average farm was not the pathetic type whose death Robert Frost recorded, but a stout youth. He had the right to keep a horse at his employer's expense, and every Saturday afternoon he dressed up, slicked down his hair, put on a derby hat, and drove to town in his own buggy to call on a girl, or have fun generally. For in all Northern and Western farm country there was almost always a small town within driving distance to which the farmer could haul his cash crop for shipment by rail, and where he could make his purchases. Here would be a new high school, several general stores, and (if the temperance movement had not reached it) a hotel built around a bar; two or three Protestant churches, a lawyer or two, and a doctor who also acted as dentist and veterinarian; possibly an "opera house" where strolling actors played. The barber shop was the center for sporting intelligence and smut, where waiting customers sang close-harmony in "barber-shop chords." If Germans were about there was an amateur string orchestra, brass band, or *Singverein;* possibly also a *Turnverein* for the boys to practice simple gymnastics. Smart farmers' sons went from high school or endowed academy to one of the little hilltop colleges scattered throughout the land, even to a state university to prepare for business or the professions. There were bleak and narrow aspects to this way of life, well described in Edgar Howe's grim novel of Kansas, *The Story of a Country Town* (1883), but it was active and robust. The insipidity portrayed in Sinclair Lewis's *Main Street* (1920) did not, in general, enter the life of the Northern American countryside or small town until its more enterprising people had been lured away by big industry. Many farmers' boys grew up hating this rustic routine and drudgery; Henry Ford and Frank Lloyd Wright admit in their autobiographies that revulsion against life on the farm impelled them, respectively, into automobile manufacture and architecture.

After this life had passed away forever, many became sentimental about it, and some of the best novels in American literature describe nostalgically the rural society of those days: —Mary E. Wilkins Freeman for northern New England; Willa Cather's *My Antonia* for Nebraska; Hamlin Garland for the Middle Border; O. E. Rölvaag (who wrote in Norwegian but whose *Giants in the Earth* was translated by Lincoln Colcord) for Scandinavian pioneers in the Dakotas. James Whitcomb Riley recorded Hoosier child life in verse; but nobody has better depicted this way of living in which most of our Presidents

from Lincoln to Coolidge were raised, and the impact on it
of big industry, than Sherwood Anderson in his *Poor White*
(1920).

4. Iron and Steel, Big Business and Politics

A good index of the industrial development of the Middle
West is the rise of ship tonnage passing through the "Soo"
(Saulte Ste. Marie) canal between Lakes Superior and Huron.
Roughly 100,000 tons in 1860, the burthen rose to half a
million in 1869 and 25 million in 1901. Wheat and iron ore
formed the bulk of these cargoes. The iron came from new
orefields of Michigan and Minnesota, to which the application
of the Bessemer converter process gave America cheap steel,
an essential factor of industrial development. These orefields
on Lake Superior are distant hundreds of miles from coal deposits, but cheap lake and rail transport brought them together
in the smelters of Chicago, where the first American steel rails
were rolled in 1865, and in Cleveland, Toledo, Ashtabula,
and Milwaukee. Much ore was transported to Pittsburgh, center of the northern Appalachian coalfields where native and
Irish labor, revolting against the twelve-hour shifts imposed
by the iron masters, was replaced by sturdy Hungarians and
Slavs. In the 1880's the iron and coal beds of the southern
Appalachians began to be exploited, and Birmingham, Alabama, became a Southern rival to Pittsburgh and Cleveland.
American steel production, a mere 20,000 tons in 1867, passed
the British output with 6 million tons in 1895 and reached
10 million before 1900.

In world economy the United States in 1879 was still a
country of extractive industries; by 1900 it had become one
of the greater manufacturing nations of the world. Yet the
value of farm products still greatly exceeded those of industry,
and the expanding home market precluded serious competition
with England and Germany for export markets. In 1869 there
were two million wage earners in factories and small industries, producing goods to the value of $3,385 million; in 1899
there were 4.7 million wage earners in factories alone, producing goods to the value of $11,407 million. In 1870 there
were 6.8 million workers on farms, and the value of farm
productions was $2.4 billion; in 1900 the number of farm
workers was 10.9 million, and the value of their products,
$8.5 billion. The number of horses and mules "on farms"
(apparently those in towns were not counted) rose from 7.8
million in 1867 to 25 million in 1920. Then began the long

decline, as more and more farmers relied on gasoline-powered vehicles and machinery.

In New England and the North generally, small waterpower factories declined in favor of concentrated manufacturing cities such as Fall River, Bridgeport, Paterson, Scranton, Troy, Schenectady, Youngstown, and Akron. Chicago rose triumphantly from the ashes of the great fire started by Mrs. O'Leary's cow in 1871, became the most populous American city after New York, and in 1893 staged the World's Columbian Exposition.

This development was neither steady nor orderly. Overproduction of goods and raw materials, overcapitalization of railroads, and feverish speculation in securities brought financial panics in 1873 and 1893. During the hard times that followed, labor expressed its dissatisfaction by strikes of unparalleled violence, and the farmers sought solution for their troubles in political panaceas. It was a period of cutthroat competition in which the big fish swallowed the little fish and then tried to eat one another. Competing railroads cut freight rates between important points, in the hope of obtaining the lion's share of business, until dividends ceased and the bonds became a drug in the market. The downward trend of prices from 1865 to 1900, especially marked after 1873, put a premium on labor-saving machinery, on new processes of manufacture, and on greater units for mass production. "Gentlemen's agreements" between rival producers to maintain prices and divide business, or even to pro-rate profits, were characteristic of the period after 1872. But it was found so difficult to enforce these pools that a gentlemen's agreement came to mean one that was certain to be violated. About 1880 the pool began to be superseded by the trust, a form of combination in which the affiliated companies handed over their securities and their power to a central board of trustees. John D. Rockefeller organized the first and most successful, the Standard Oil Trust, in 1879. A large measure of his success was due to improvements, economies, and original methods of marketing; but his monopoly was secured by methods condemned even by the tolerant business ethics of his day, and pronounced criminal by the courts. By playing competing railroads against each other, Standard Oil obtained rebates from their published freight rates and even forced them to pay over rebates from its competitors' freight bills to Standard Oil. If competing oil companies managed to stagger along under such handicaps, they were "frozen out" by cutting prices below cost in their selling territory, until Standard had all the business.

Thomas W. Lawson, author of *Frenzied Finance* (1905),

a plunger and speculator who acquired great wealth during this period, wrote of it cynically: "At this period Americans found they could, by the exercise of a daring and cunning of a peculiar, reckless and low order, so take advantage of the laws of the land and its economic customs as to create for themselves wealth, or the equivalent, money, to practically an unlimited extent, without the aid of time or labor or the possession of any unusual ability coming through birth or education."

The trust as a method of combination was outlawed by most of the states in the early 'eighties; but the holding company, a corporation owning the shares of other corporations, proved to be a legitimate and more efficient financial device. In popular usage, however, the term "trust" was applied to combinations of any structure, provided they had sufficient power to dictate prices. These were the trusts which became targets of popular indignation in the early twentieth century. Not until the late 1880's did the American public demand regulation of trusts, and that problem was greatly complicated by a federal form of government. The states, not the federal government, issue corporate charters (excepting transcontinental railways); and a corporation chartered by one state has the right to do business in every other. Gas, electric lighting, and water companies and street railways depended for their very existence on municipalities. Hence the corrupt alliance cemented after the Civil War between politics and business. Plain bribery was often practiced with municipal councils, which gave away for nothing franchises worth millions, while cities remained unpaved, ill-lit, and inadequately policed.

Greatest in power, and most notorious for their abuse of it, were the great railway corporations. The power of an American transcontinental railway over its exclusive territory approached the absolute; for until the automobile age people in the Far West had no alternate means of transportation. A railroad could make an industry or ruin a community merely by juggling freight rates. The funds at their disposal, often created by financial manipulation and stock-watering, were so colossal as to overshadow the budgets of state governments. Railway builders and owners, like James J. Hill, had the point of view of a feudal chieftain. Members of state legislatures were their vassals, to be coerced or bribed into voting "right" if persuasion would not serve. In their opinion, railroading was a private business, no more a fit subject for government regulation than a tailor's shop. They were unable to recognize any public interest distinct from their own. In many instances the despotism was benevolent; and if a few men became multimillionaires, their subjects also prospered. But Collis P. Huntington, Leland Stanford, and their associates who built the Central and controlled the Southern Pacific were indifferent to all save considerations of private gain. By distributing free passes to state representatives, paying their campaign expenses and giving "presents" to their wives, they evaded taxation as well as regulation. By discriminating freight charges between localities and individuals, they terrorizied merchants, farmers, and communities "until matters had reached such a pass," states a government report of 1887, "that no man dared engage in any business in which transportation largely entered without first obtaining the permission of a railroad manager." Through the press and the professions they wielded a power over public opinion comparable to that of slave-owners over the old South. Their methods were imitated by Eastern and Midwestern railroads, so far as they dared. In New Hampshire as in California, the railroad lobby, entrenched in an office near the state capitol, acted as a third chamber of initiative and revision; and few could succeed in politics unless by grace of the railroad overlord. Winston Churchill's *Coniston* (1906) and Frank Norris's *Octopus* (1901) accurately portray the social and political effects of railroad domination in these two states.

These exactions and abuses were long tolerated by Americans, so imbued were they with laissez-faire doctrine, so proud of progress, improvement, and development, and so averse from increasing the power of government. Thus it was not until 1887 that the federal government first attempted to regulate railroads and break up trusts. Congress then passed the first Interstate Commerce Act, declaring "unreasonable" rates, pooling and other unfair practices to be illegal. Enforcement was vested in the first modern American administrative board, the Interstate Commerce Commission. But administrative regulations were so foreign to the American conception of government that the federal courts insisted on their right to review orders of the Commission, and by denying its power to fix rates, emasculated the Act. So the railroads continued to charge "all the traffic would bear." Equally futile was the Sherman Anti-trust Act of 1890, which declared illegal any monopoly or combination in restraint of interstate trade. When the Supreme Court in 1895 held that purchase by the sugar trust of a controlling interest in 98 per cent of the sugar refining business of the country was not a violation of the law because not an act of interstate commerce, the Sherman Act became temporarily dead letter.

Theodore Roosevelt well summed up this last quarter of the

nineteenth century in his *Autobiography:* "A riot of individualistic materialism, under which complete freedom for the individual . . . turned out in practice to mean perfect freedom
for the strong to wrong the weak. . . . The power of the mighty
industrial overlords . . . had increased with giant strides, while
the methods of controlling them, . . . through the Government, remained archaic and therefore practically impotent."
Roosevelt also had the wit to see that merely breaking up the
trusts into smaller units was no answer; that was merely a
futile attempt to remedy by more individualism the evils that
were the result of unfettered individualism.

5. Canada Comes of Age

Canadian development lagged behind that of the United
States. Sir John Macdonald and other founders of the Dominion hoped that federation would solve everything, but the
reality fell far short of their expectations. Geography and race
offered the greatest difficulties. The Dominion, stretching from
the Strait of Belle Isle north of Newfoundland to Dawson in
the Klondike, covered 15 more degrees of longitude than the
United States; yet the depth of country north of the border
habitable by people of European stock was in no place over
400 miles wide and in many, not half that. For five months
every year the St. Lawrence was closed by ice. Under Canada's
constitution—the British North American Act of 1867—the
Dominion Parliament at Ottawa retained all reserved powers
of government. But this failed to quench provincialism in a
country whose seven provinces had very diverse interests, and
whose French population considered itself a nation apart. Enterprising, go-ahead Canadians of British stock found themselves hampered at sundry points by the French of Quebec,
whose values were still largely those of Norman peasants of
the Old Regime, and whose leaders, not content with their
provincial privileges under the Quebec Act of 1774, demanded
their extension to every other part of the Dominion. Macdonald, they claimed, had persuaded the French to federate
by promising to make all Canada bilingual.

Canada even had her own civil war five years after the one
in the United States ended. The *métis,* French-speaking half-
breeds of the Red River Colony, under the lead of Louis Riel,
seized control of that region in 1869, demanded special rights
in the Dominion, and executed some people who objected.
The *métis* were put down by British regulars, and that colony
became the Province of Manitoba in 1870. One result of this
rebellion was the formation of the Royal Canadian Mounted

Police, who proved to be more successful than the United States Army in preserving law and order in the West. But the *métis*, although given separate schools in Manitoba with French equal to English, were not satisfied. Racial minorities, as the history of the last century shows, are seldom satisfied because their leaders, to keep in power, are always stirring up fresh resentments.

Other issues, too, disturbed the Dominion. The first was the depression of 1873 which lasted a good twenty years in Canada, and slowed the growth of the country. Population increased only from 3.7 to 4.8 million between 1871 and 1891, when that of the United States rose from 38.6 to 63 million. A mild degree of protection was added to the tariff, but this seemed to do no good; and in 1874 a proposal to revive reciprocity with the United States resulted only in another snub from President Grant, and the rejection of a draft treaty by the Senate. The other big issue was the Canadian Pacific Railway. It had no sooner been chartered in 1873 than word got out, in a series of letters that rivaled James G. Blaine's for sensationalism, that the promoters had contributed $350,000 to campaign funds of the Conservative party. Sir John Macdonald's telegram, "Must have another $10,000," almost broke him, as Blaine's "Burn this letter" had lost him the presidency. And it did ruin the railway corporation. Parliament, shocked at the revelations, cut off government subsidies.

A new Liberal government under Alexander Mackenzie, a dour, self-made Scot, now tried to build the transcontinental railway piecemeal, and by 1878 had completed it as far west as Winnipeg. This was not nearly fast enough for the public, especially in British Columbia, which threatened secession if the line were not promptly pushed through. This situation, and the depression, led to a return of Macdonald and the Conservatives to power the same year. Macdonald now lent his support to a group of promoters led by George Stephen, a Montreal banker, and the Canadian Pacific Railway was rechartered on terms so liberal as to make mouths water across the border: a cash grant of $25 million, 30 million acres of land tax-exempt for 20 years, a gift of the 700 miles of railway already built, no rival road for 20 years, no rate regulation until the company was making 10 per cent on its capital! Even these were not enough; every few years the C.P.R. directors emitted cries of distress and obtained additional government loans up to $27.5 million.

George Stephen was raised to the peerage for his completion of the C.P.R., but the man who really put it through was a Yankee railroader, William C. Van Horne who, on the recommendation of James J. Hill, became general manager in 1881. The road was now vigorously pushed westward from Winnipeg, and eastward from Vancouver. Forward went the steel rails across the prairies of Manitoba and Saskatchewan, into the great plains of Alberta, spawning towns and cities like Moose Jaw, Medicine Hat, and Calgary en route; past superb Lake Louise, crossing the Selkirk range of the Rockies at Kicking Horse Pass, an elevation of over 5000 feet, while the Vancouver group worked up the valley of the Fraser river. When the last spike was driven where the two met, at Eagle Pass on 7 November 1885, less than five years had elapsed since the work had been resumed, and in that time almost half of this 2881-mile transcontinental railway had been constructed. And another 500 miles were added when the C.P.R. acquired the Intercolonial Railway from Montreal to the ice-free port of St. John, New Brunswick.

The completion of the C.P.R. coincided with the end of Louis Riel. He returned from exile to Manitoba in 1884 to head a full-fledged rebellion of *métis* and Indians. After a brief war with the Canadian army and the "Mounties," he was captured, tried for treason, and hanged, as he well deserved. This provoked an emotional explosion in Quebec, where the French population for the first time deserted the conservative guidance of their clergy, swept the provincial elections, made Sir Wilfrid Laurier leader of the Liberal party, and with the aid of discontented elements in the Maritimes and elsewhere, almost defeated the Conservatives in the general election of 1891. Sir John Macdonald won again, but the hardships of winter campaigning brought on a shock, of which this "Grand Old Man of Canada" died. A bitter controversy over sectarian schools in Ontario and Manitoba followed; the Liberals won the general election of 1896, and Laurier became premier. He rode into power on a wave of prosperity, of which the principal ingredient was a rapid development of the prairie provinces, first fruit of completing the railway. And he continued premier until defeated in 1911 on the issue of reciprocity with the United States.

Sir Wilfrid was a remarkable French Canadian gentleman, a lawyer descended from a colonel of the Carignan-Salières regiment. In his nature the energy of Theodore Roosevelt was combined with the finesse of Franklin D. Roosevelt. Loyal to the British crown and friendly to the United States, he consistently advocated Canadian nationalism. At the conference of colonial and dominion prime ministers with the British colonial secretary on the occasion of Queen Victoria's diamond jubilee, Sir Wilfrid took the lead in thwarting Joseph Chamberlain's effort to replace the loose imperial tie by a centralized system resembling the European Common Market of the 1960's.

Canada contributed 7300 volunteers to the British army in the South Africa War of 1899–1901. Her foreign relations were still conducted from London, and the Royal Canadian Navy had not yet been launched; but the Dominion entered the new century with her march toward independence almost 90 per cent achieved.

THE OLD CHISHOLM TRAIL

With my feet in the stir - rups and my hand on the horn, I'm the best damned cow - boy that ev - er was born.__ Come-a ki - yi yip-pee, come-a ki - yi - yay Come-a ki - yi - yip-pee yip-pee yay.

III

Social and Cultural Developments

1870-1900

1. *The Rise of Organized Labor*

ORGANIZED LABOR passed through phases of bewildering complexity before it won the power to meet organized capital on equal terms. There was little continuity with the antebellum period. Wage earners of the 1840's had largely become farmers, shopkeepers, and petty capitalists by the 1870's. Their places were taken by farmers' sons, discharged soldiers lured by the attractions of urban life, and a new wave of immigrants, European rather than British, who were not interested in unions and were willing to work for low wages. Annual immigration passed 300,000 in 1866 and rose to 789,000 in 1882, the highest for any year of the nineteenth century. The proportion of British and Irish immigrants fell from 45 per cent in 1861–70 to 18 per cent in 1891–1900; that of Russians, Italians, and other southern Europeans, rose in the same period from .1 to 50 per cent. In 1900, 86 per cent of the foreign-born were in states north of the Ohio and east of the Mississippi.

Ignorant of what had been tried before, American labor leaders passed through the same cycle of experiment as in the 'thirties and 'forties. There were national trade unions and local trade unions, efforts to escape from the established order through co-operation, to ameliorate it by devices like the single tax, to break it down with socialism, to organize political labor parties, and to form one big union. Yet, in spite of European dilution, the ideas of Marx, Lassalle, and Bakunin exerted far less influence than did those of Owen, Cabet, and Fourier in the 1840's.

Violent outbreaks occurred before the unions became strong. For a decade after 1867, the anthracite coal mining section of Pennsylvania, around Mauch Chunk and Pottsville, was terrorized by a secret miners' association called the Molly Maguires, composed mostly of Irish Catholics. They burned property, controlled county officials, and murdered bosses and supervisors who offended them. Finally, through legal process, the murderers were brought to trial and ten were hanged in June 1877; that broke up the Mollies. In the same year there were serious race riots in San Francisco, incited by a demagogue named Dennis Kearney, against Chinese immigrants, who had risen to 17 per cent of the population. Their competition did tend to keep wages down. This problem was solved by a series of Chinese exclusion acts, starting in 1882, which obtained support in Congress because a stupid shoe manufacturer tried to break a strike in North Adams, Massachusetts, by importing coolies.

The year 1877 was very rough. When the four eastern trunk lines (the through railroads) jauntily announced a wage cut of 10 per cent, second since the panic of 1873, the unorganized railroad employees struck and were supported by a huge army of hungry and desperate unemployed. During one week in July, traffic was suspended on the trunk lines, and every industrial center was in a turmoil. In Pittsburgh, Martinsburg, and Chicago there were pitched battles between militia and the mob; order had to be restored by federal troops. Unfortunately the reported presence of German and French socialists led the public to the easy conclusion that imported agitators were alone responsible. (Compare the South's conviction that abolitionists and other outsiders have been responsible for Negro unrest.) Few Americans realized that their country had reached a stage of industrial development which created a labor problem, or that the "Great Strike of '77" would be the first of a long series of battles between labor and capital.

Two years later, when good times and full employment were back, the labor movement developed into a contest for leadership between organizations representing labor unionism, craft unionism, and socialism. The Order of the Knights of Labor (founded 1869), native-American in leadership and largely in personnel, was an attempt to unite workers into one big union under centralized control. Its professed object was to escape from the wage system through producers' co-operation, popular education, and the union of all workers by hand or brain. Terence V. Powderly, a Pennsylvania machinist who became grand master in 1878, was an idealist who disliked the tactics of combative unionism; but the order first became powerful in 1884 by winning a railroad strike in the Southwest. Capital met labor on equal terms, for the first time in America, when the financier Jay Gould conferred with the Knights' executive board and conceded their demands. The Knights were largely responsible for a congressional act of 1885 which forbade the importation of contract labor.

Parallel with the rise of the Knights of Labor, trade unions of skilled workers grew and multiplied, while others affiliated with Marx's International or with the "Black" (anarchist) International. Knights, trade unions, socialist unions, and anarchists simultaneously struck for the eight-hour day at Chicago in 1886, when the country was prosperous and business was booming. The spectacular event of this strike was the Haymarket Square riot in Chicago on 4 May. After an English anarchist had begun inciting a mob of about 1000 strikers to violence, the police ordered them to disperse. Someone threw a dynamite bomb which, with subsequent pistol shooting, killed eight policemen and wounded sixty-seven. Eight anarchists were tried for murder and found guilty, although the bomb thrower was never identified. The verdict was sustained by the Supreme Court of the United States and four men were hanged. The horror of the crime was matched by the injustice of the punishment; and, as in the later Sacco-Vanzetti case, many Americans prominent in literature and the arts protested. In 1893, when the German-born Governor John P. Altgeld pardoned the three survivors then in jail because convinced of their innocence, he was widely denounced as an abettor of anarchy, and his political career was ruined.

As champions of the unskilled, the Knights attained a membership of about 700,000 around 1886, as compared with 250,000 in the national trade unions. Powderly, however, so mismanaged matters that the Knights lost their grip, and the van of the labor movement was usurped by an organization of skilled workers on craft lines, the American Federation of Labor.

In the late 'sixties a bullet-headed young fellow named Samuel Gompers, a British subject of mixed Hebrew and Flemish ancestry, was working in a highly unsanitary cigar-making shop in New York's lower east side, and speaking at the meetings of a local union. Cigar-making was then a sociable handicraft. The men talked or read aloud while they worked, and Gompers learned to concentrate on the economic struggle and to fight shy of intellectuals who would ride union labor to some personal utopia. He determined to divorce unionism from politics which dissipated its energy, and from radicalism which aroused public apprehension. In the hard times of the 1870's he experienced cold and hunger, the futility of charity, and the cowardice of politicians. By 1881 he and other local leaders had thought their way through to a national federation of craft unions, economic in purpose, evolutionary in method, and contending for immediate objects such as shorter hours and higher wages. Five years later the American Federation of Labor was born, and as the Knights of Labor declined it became the fighting spearhead of the American labor movement.

It is perhaps a contradiction to include the "hoboes" among the workers; but no picture of America in that era is complete without these "knights of the road" who roamed the northern part of the country, catching rides on freight trains, stealing or begging their food, and spending cold winters in local jails. The first lot were discharged soldiers of the Union army who refused to settle down. These "Weary Willies," "Tired Tims," and "Happy Hooligans" added a picturesque feature to the countryside like the Gypsies of old, and afforded cartoonists and journalists infinite material for amusement. Some were criminals, but most of them were harmless vagrants.

During this period, when England reached her nadir of unpopularity in the United States, and "twisting the British lion's tail" always won votes, the three writers who had the most influence on the American mind were English—Charles Darwin, Thomas Huxley, and Herbert Spencer. Spencer's *Social Statics* (1865) raised laissez-faire to a dogma among American business men. He had picked up a phrase of Tom Paine, "That government is best which governs least," and taught that the functions of the state should be limited to internal police and foreign protection—no public education, no limitation of hours of labor, no welfare legislation. To this he added in his *Principles of Biology* (presenting the theories of his friend Darwin) the phrase "survival of the fittest," which exactly suited the winners in the dog-eat-dog competition of that day. So deep did Spencer's theories penetrate American thought that Justice Holmes, in a dissenting opinion of 1905, felt obliged to remind his fellow jurists that *Social Statics* was not embodied in the Constitution of the United States.

Spencer's influence undoubtedly delayed factory inspection, limitation of hours, and the like. The first state labor law to be adequately enforced was the Massachusetts Ten-Hour Act of 1874 for women and children in factories. The need to provide administrative machinery for the enforcement of labor laws was generally overlooked, and even if it were, the courts were apt to declare such laws unconstitutional. The New York act of 1883 prohibiting the manufacture of cigars in tenement houses, which Gompers persuaded young Theodore Roosevelt to sponsor and Governor Cleveland to sign, was intended as an entering wedge to break up sweatshops in the cities, a rapidly growing menace. The constitutionality of this law, brought before the highest state court, was invalidated on the ground that it interfered with the profitable use of real estate, without any compensating public advantage. "It cannot be perceived how the cigar-maker is to be improved in his health or his morals by forcing him from his home and its hallowed associations and beneficent influences to ply his trade elsewhere," declared the court. Roosevelt, who had personally inspected these one-room "homes" where whole families and their lodgers ate, slept, and rolled cigars, then began to revise his conception of justice; and Gompers renewed the fight against the sweatshop.

Most state constitutions, and Amendment XIV to the Federal Constitution, forbid the government to deprive citizens of property without due process of law. As no reform can be effected without depriving someone of something that he may deem to be a property right, American courts early invented the doctrine of a superior police power, the reserved right of any state to protect the people's health, safety, and welfare. This police power had been held to justify even confiscatory reforms, such as the prohibition of lotteries, or the manufacture and sale of alcohol; but when labor and factory laws appeared on the statute books, judges began to draw the line. Corporations, securing the best lawyers, found it easy to convince courts that such laws were not a proper and reasonable exercise of the police power, and to point out conflicts with Amendment XIV or other clauses of the Federal Constitution. The Supreme Court in 1873 declined to intervene between the state of Louisiana and the New Orleans butchers, who alleged that state regulations were confiscatory. The Court explained that Amendment XIV had been adopted to protect the freed slaves, not to make the federal judiciary "a perpetual censor upon all legislation of the states . . . with authority to nullify such as it did not approve." But this was before the judges began reading Herbert Spencer.

Where a conflict with the Constitution could not be discovered, judges around 1886 began to postulate a theoretical liberty of contract, "the right of a person to sell his labor upon such terms as he deems proper."[1] A Pennsylvania statute forbidding payment of miners' wages in orders on the company store was judicially nullified by a decision declaring such a law "degrading and insulting to the laborer," and "subversive of his rights as a citizen." An Illinois court declared unconstitutional a statute limiting the hours of labor for women in sweatshops, on the ground that they had the same liberty of contract as men. In 1905 the Supreme Court of the United States took a similar view of a New York statute limiting the hours of labor in bakeries; the bakers, declared the court in effect, were sufficiently intelligent to make their own labor contracts in their own interest. Justice Holmes, whom Theodore Roosevelt had translated from the supreme judicial court of Massachusetts to the Supreme Court of the United States in 1902, dissented from 43 out of the 171 decisions in which the Supreme Court invalidated state laws in the name of due process between 1905 and 1932, when he retired. But the appointees of Presidents Taft and Wilson to the Supreme bench, with the notable exception of Justice Brandeis, continued to act as a chamber of revision on state regulatory and welfare legislation, into the first administration of Franklin D. Roosevelt.

Thus, ironically, laissez-faire as a social concept reached its logical development in American courts just as it was breaking down as a social structure before modern industrialism.

These were some of the many difficulties that labor in general encountered, the A. F. of L. in particular. Despite the loss of the great Homestead strike against the Carnegie Steel Company in 1892 (during which pacifist Andy Carnegie bawled loudly for troops), the A. F. of L. weathered the hard times of 1893–97 and turned the century with a membership of over half a million. Each national union has had to struggle for recognition, higher wages, the closed shop, and a shorter work week. The Federation carried on the struggle for a square deal from the courts, and battled socialists and other doctrinaires in its own ranks. Yet Gompers always managed to keep the A. F. of L. true to its first principles. The American unions, dealing with a body of labor divided by race and, until after World War I, constantly diluted by immigration, were slow to attain significant power. Gompers through the

---

[1] Justice Harlan, in *Adair* v. *U.S.* (1908). This theory was given the blessing of Herbert Spencer in his *Justice* (1891), a book which, together with the writings of William Graham Sumner the Yale economist, became the sacred scriptures of conservatives who wished government to keep hands off business.

A. F. of L. accomplished more than any other to raise the material standards of American labor. But neither he nor any other American trade union leader did anything to help the blacks; all were as "lily-white" in preventing the entry into unions of colored men, as the most prejudiced group in the South.

2. The State of Religion

For all the corruption and pitiful politics of the Gilded Age, it was a robust, fearless, generous era, full of gusto and joy of living, affording wide scope to individual energy and material creation. And although not one of the greatest eras in American arts and letters, it was far from barren in these, or in spiritual forces.

The Roman Catholic Church, which already had 12 million members in 1890, was faced with many problems in accommodating itself to a predominantly Protestant country wedded to the concept of separation of church and state. Apart from small upper-class groups, descendants of Lord Baltimore's friends in eastern Maryland and of French Creoles in St. Louis and Louisiana, the Catholic Church in the United States was one of recent immigrants, and therefore of the poor. Despite the Latin language of the liturgy, the different ethnic groups which composed members of that faith balked at worshipping together, and demanded priests of their own nationality who could preach and hear confession in their own old-world tongue. Italians and French Canadians in particular disliked belonging to Irish parishes; even Poles and Lithuanians demanded separate churches in the manufacturing cities of New England. This situation worked itself out in time with new native-born generations, but created so many difficulties that Peter P. Cahensly, a layman of St. Louis, started a movement to have bishops appointed on the basis of language groups instead of geography. This, with some difficulty, was prevented by James Cardinal Gibbons, Archbishop of Baltimore, and John Ireland, Archbishop of St. Paul. The Cahensly movement is understandable, because the Germans brought over the European tradition of Catholic scholarship, whilst the Irish, sons of peasants or small shopkeepers and clever in ecclesiastical as in local and state politics, obtained most of the bishoprics.

A plenary council at Baltimore in 1884, comprising over seventy bishops, monsignori, and professors of theology, did a great deal to secure uniformity in worship, to set up parochial schools and diocesan seminaries, and to found the Catholic University of America in Washington. The impulse for this came from Rome, where many members of the papal curia looked down their long noses at all things American. Rome, in general, regarded American democracy, as did the old Federalists, as a bastard brat of French Jacobinism and was concerned to protect her transatlantic faithful from Protestant influence. She had been deeply impressed by the wild guess of one prelate that a million and a half Catholics had defected to Protestantism since 1820. Consequently, Rome supported what is now called by Catholics themselves the "ghetto complex"—trying to keep Catholics living together and forbidding them to take part with Protestants even in secular American activities other than politics. Archbishop Ireland of St. Paul openly declined to go along, and in his diocese Catholics and Protestants mingled amicably. Cardinal Gibbons felt likewise; but the archbishops of Boston and New York followed the Roman line.

Liberal Catholic discontent came to a head with the publication in 1897 of a badly translated biography of Father Isaac Hecker, one of the liberals of the antebellum era. Conservative Catholics in Europe picked on this and on certain acts of American Catholics which seem insignificant enough today— the rector of the Catholic University of America accepting an honorary degree from Harvard, and priests attending a Congress of Religion at the Chicago World's Fair—as expressions of undesirable "Americanism." Their influence procured from Leo XIII in 1899 a papal letter condemning certain "American" doctrines, especially Hecker's idea that the church relax her doctrinal rigor and glorify virtue in the Roman sense rather than passive morality and monastic vows. In other words, that she favor those English Puritan values which had created the American Protestant ethic. Cardinal Gibbons and other American prelates hastened to declare that no such heresies were current in America; and in 1902 Leo XIII congratulated the American hierarchy on their people's "perfect docility of mind and alacrity of disposition."

Whether or not by "alacrity of disposition" the Holy Father meant the increasing take by Catholic charities, it is probable that the swelling stream of Peter's pence from America to the Vatican brought about a more favorable disposition in Rome. Pope Pius X in 1908 removed the American church from the jurisdiction of the Propaganda Fidei and placed it on equality with the ancient churches of France and Spain. After another half-century, it became obvious that Popes John XXIII and Paul VI were moving toward the "Americanism" condemned by Leo XIII.

The Roman Catholic Church, through emphasis on sacraments rather than sacred Scriptures, escaped the controversy

over Darwinism that rocked most of the Protestant churches
to their foundations. And it successfully rode out the storm of
German "higher criticism" of the Bible because most of the
German theologians were unintelligible. Darwin's *Origin of
Species* (1859), however, was read by almost every literate
American sooner or later. It inculcated the doctrine of evolution through natural selection and taught that man was the
end process of development from lower forms of life. Asa Gray
of Harvard begged Darwin to postulate some Grand Design,
some Beneficent Deity in all this; but Darwin could not persuade himself "that a beneficent and omnipotent God would
have designedly created the *Ichneumonidae* with the express intention of their feeding within the living bodies of caterpillars,
or . . . that the eye was expressly designed." Thomas Huxley's
Man's Place in Nature and Charles Lyell's *Geological Evi-
dences of the Antiquity of Man* (both 1863) were ready for
Americans to read after the Civil War, and pretty soon Herbert
Spencer's *Principles of Biology* (1867) and John Fiske's *Out-
lines of Cosmic Philosophy* (1874) carried the word still
further. Henry Adams could make superior fun of evolution
(which he pointed out would make U. S. Grant a better man
than George Washington), and indignant preachers might
quote Disraeli's quip, "Is man an ape or an angel? I, my Lord,
am on the side of the angels." But the more intellectual and
prominent Protestant clergy, such as Henry Ward Beecher,
James Freeman Clarke, Phillips Brooks, and James McCosh,
unable to refute Darwin's facts or challenge his conclusions,
conceded that the Book of Genesis could not be taken literally.
This was no embarrassment to the Unitarians, who already regarded the Bible as symbolical. But the evangelical churches in
general rejected the Darwinian view of the cosmos as blasphe-
mous and even persuaded several Southern states to pass laws
against the teaching of evolution in the schools. In support of
the law in Tennessee, William Jennings Bryan won the case
but lost his last battle in 1925. That law was overturned by
the Supreme Court of the United States in 1970.

The Mormons, whose sacred book had been revealed to
Joseph Smith, and the new sect of Christian Scientists, which
picked up the slack of disillusioned Christians with Mary Baker
Eddy's *Science and Health* (1875), were not greatly affected
by this controversy. But there is no doubt that it weakened the
hold of religion on the average American. He stopped reading
the Bible when it no longer could be considered divine truth;
and in so doing his character suffered. For, as Romain Rolland's Jean Christophe says, "The Bible is the marrow of lions.
Strong hearts have they who feed on it. . . . The Bible is the

backbone for people who have the will to live." Darwin may have killed Adam as an historical figure, but the old Adam in man survives; and if his intellect fails to control the fell forces he has wrested from nature, the few, if any, who survive the holocaust will tardily bear witness to the realism of the Biblical portrait of mankind.

3. Arts, Letters, and Education

Owing to a series of devastating fires in the early 1870's, the growth of urban population,[1] and the increase of wealth, the Eastern cities and Chicago were largely rebuilt between 1870 and 1900. In the process some distinguished buildings were designed by architects such as H. H. Richardson, Louis Henri Sullivan, Richard Morris Hunt, and the firm of McKim, Mead and White; but the general run of residential buildings was tiresome. Brownstone-front row houses of New York, brick rows of Philadelphia and Baltimore, and the wooden "three-deckers" of Boston were uninteresting as the outside of a shelf of books, but they met the needs of the time. Around 1890, late colonial and federal styles were revised to make satisfactory homes for the middle class. Some elaborate private residences were built for the rich—such as the Romanesque Adams and Hay houses in Washington, the French-château Vanderbilt mansions on Fifth Avenue, New York, and many Ruskin-inspired combinations of brick and stone in the Back Bay of Boston. It became the fashion in the twentieth century to sneer at America's "Victorian" architecture (and, it must be admitted, some very strange buildings were constructed); but in general the urban construction of this era was so sound that its destruction in favor of glass-and-chromium rectangles is regretted. Herbert Spencer, a well-traveled critic, was "astonished by the grandeur of New York" in 1882 in comparison with London, and in Baltimore he admired the classic front of the Peabody Institute, concealing a functional cast-iron "cathedral of books," designed by Edmund G. Lind.

Church architecture in general followed the modes of Europe, examples being St. Patrick's (Gothic) and St. Bartholomew's (Byzantine) in New York; Trinity Church, Boston

[1] New York City remained ahead, increasing from 1.36 million to 2.05 million, 1870–1900. Chicago's growth was spectacular, 443,534 to 1.7 million. Brooklyn (not yet part of New York City), Boston, Philadelphia, Baltimore, Richmond, New Orleans, Cleveland and St. Louis, combined, grew from 2.9 million to 4.86 million; San Francisco from 223,000 to 342,782. The sprawling growth of Los Angeles was yet to come.

(Provençal Romanesque), and numerous stone churches, imitating Venetian Gothic, English Perpendicular, and other medieval styles. Some excellent public buildings in the French Palais du Louvre style, such as the State-Army-Navy building in Washington, were constructed in the 1870's. But the Capitol at Washington continued to exercise an unfortunate influence on public buildings, especially state capitols, each of which had to have a dome and colonnade. The Chicago World's Fair of 1893, designed in part by Richard Morris Hunt and McKim, Mead and White, started the revival of a purer classicism.

In the meantime there arose a distinctively American urban form, which has had world-wide influence. The combination of rising land values, cheap structural steel, and the gregarious habits of American business men, produced the skyscraper. Hitherto the height of buildings had been restricted by the need for impossibly thick walls to support more than eight or ten floors, and by slow pneumatic elevators. Now, in one of the most revolutionary processes in the history of architecture, both walls and floors could be supported by a steel frame, and electric elevators could whisk one up thirty stories faster than walking up three. The first all-steel skeleton structure to be called a skyscraper was L. H. Sullivan's ten-story Auditorium Building of Chicago, finished in 1889, and the new mode reached New York in the 375-feet-high, 26-story World Building, completed in 1890. New York City's skyline, hitherto dominated by church spires and the masts of ships, by 1900 showed every variety of skyscraper; for architects were wrestling with the problem of giving the façades, with their necessarily monotonous fenestration, individuality and distinction. Today they appear to have given up the attempt. It was also in Chicago that Frank Lloyd Wright, Sullivan's favorite helper, began in 1893 to design the public and private buildings that gave him world fame.

The extension of railroads, the cheapness of iron and steel, and the public's impatience at having to shift from car to ferryboat and back for crossing rivers, led to important bridge-building. The iron bridge of the Erie Railroad over the Genesee river at Portage (1875) was one of the many triumphs of George S. Morison, then assistant to Octave Chanute, chief engineer of the Erie. Other bridges designed by Morison are the Illinois Central's over the Ohio at Cairo (1889), and, at Memphis, the first bridge to span the lower Mississippi (1892). James B. Eads of the Civil War rams and John Roebling are also great names in the history of American bridge-building. Roebling, in 1869, designed the Brooklyn Bridge completed by his son Washington in 1883. "In this structure," wrote

Lewis Mumford, "the architecture of the past, massive and protective, meets the architecture of the future, light, aerial, open to sunlight, an architecture of voids rather than solids." Louis Sullivan and his partner Dankmar Adler acknowledged the importance of the engineer's work in learning to use new raw materials: "If they are always used where they are wanted and as they are wanted," wrote Adler, "we shall have taken the first step toward the transmutation of these utterances of scientific prose into the language of poetry and art."

First steps in doing the same with nature's own gifts of trees and shrubs, land, and water, had already been taken, fortunately for the burgeoning cities, by the great landscape architect Frederick Law Olmsted. In the meantime scholarly critics like Charles Eliot Norton were quietly inculcating new artistic values that their pupils applied in the next generation. Many Americans began to feel a craving for the beautiful, but most regarded beauty as something extrinsic to be imported. Civil War profiteers, bankers, and railroad kings invaded Europe to capture "old masters," but few had the good taste of Isabella Stewart Gardner and Martin A. Ryerson. Early bequests to the public museums of fine arts that began to spring up in the 1870's were apt to prove embarrassing in the long run.

In painting, the Hudson River School and Samuel F. B. Morse were succeeded by a group of artists who sought subjects in the life of the people. In Philadelphia worked Thomas Eakins, painter of baseball games, oarsmen, pugilists, wrestlers, and surgical operations. Winslow Homer in Boston, at Prout's Neck, Maine, and in the Bahamas, painted fishermen, Civil War scenes, gay parties in sailboats, deer hunting and canoe trips, country life and children's games, recording what he saw with exceptional simplicity of vision and in a vigorous technique. Frederic Remington accomplished for the West and the cowboy what Homer had done for the East and the sea; and two great landscapists, John La Farge and William Morris Hunt, carried on the Hudson River tradition with technique acquired at Barbizon. On a lower scale of excellence, scores of minor painters have been brought to light in Maxim Karolik's collection. The Currier and Ives establishment in New York turned out lithographs of American ships, race horses, and country scenes that are now highly prized; Fanny Palmer, one of the first American women to become a painter, was the leading artist on their staff. Cheap colored reproductions of European paintings were provided in large numbers by Lewis Prang, a German-born chromolithographer working in Boston.

It was also the age of the etching, originally a diversion of the artist's studio. A display of American foreign etchings at the Centennial Exposition in 1876 started the craze; etching clubs were founded in the leading cities, and Seymour Haden and Philip G. Hamerton, the English Leonardo and Michael-angelo of this art form, lectured in the United States and brought out books on etching that were eagerly purchased. Winslow Homer, Joseph Baker, and J. Foxcroft Cole were the leading American etchers. "Everyone" collected etchings from 1880 to 1895, when they suddenly went out of fashion. "What has happened to all those grand treasures, so vast in size with their creamy margins punctuated with apt *remarques* or *vignettes?*" asks a biographer of Homer. "They all seem to have passed into a sort of limbo for unloved art objects." One finds them in golden-oak frames in dark corners of men's clubs, and in second-hand furniture shops. In time they will be eagerly collected, like the oils of the Hudson River School.

All the artists we have mentioned had a part of their artistic education in Europe, but returned to America to work. James McNeil Whistler, who "did not choose to have been born in Lowell, Mass." (but his famous subject, his Mother, had other views), remained an expatriate. John Singer Sargent, although flattered by the English society whose portraits he painted, never lost his attachment to America and returned to execute magnificent murals in the Boston Museum of Fine Arts and the Boston Public Library, and to paint luminous watercolors of American scenery.

At Concord, Massachusetts, when the centenary of the American Revolution came around, a young man of the neighborhood named Daniel Chester French designed the famous statue of the Minute Man. Later he studied in Florence under Thomas Ball, and returned to design a series of sculptured groups for the Chicago World's Fair, and several statues of Lincoln. He also helped to found the American Academy at Rome. Augustus Saint-Gaudens of New York, after studying at the Beaux-Arts and in Rome, reached fame through his statue of Hiawatha at Saratoga (1871). He worked largely at Cornish, New Hampshire, where he executed his greatest works, the memorial monument to Mrs. Henry Adams in Rock Creek Park, Washington, the Shaw Memorial in Boston, and the equestrian statue of General Sherman on Fifth Avenue, New York. Comparable in sculpture to Prang's "chromos" were the "Rogers Groups," favorites in the American home, for each told a story—Checkers up at the Farm; The Favored Scholar; Coming to the Parson; Fetching the Doctor; Weighing the Baby, and the like. John Rogers designed and executed from bronze master casts these popular plaster groups, prices of which ranged from five to twenty dollars, and sold some 100,000 of them in his lifetime.

In the fields of music and drama, America was gestating. Choral societies with fiddle and flute accompaniment, such as the Handel and Haydn and the Apollo of Boston, had been in existence since the eighteenth century; but instrumental music in its highest form, the symphony orchestra, was slow to start, and slower to attain excellence. Theodore Thomas, undaunted after the ruin of his orchestra at Philadelphia in 1876, remained the country's chief musical missionary; he became conductor of the New York Philharmonic in 1880, but had to resign after a row with Leopold Damrosch, Walter's father. He then organized his own orchestra, and became musical director of the Chicago World's Fair in 1893. The Boston Symphony Orchestra, founded by Major Henry L. Higginson in 1881, quickly attained excellence. Gustav Mahler, who came from Vienna at the turn of the century, described it in a letter to Bruno Walter as of "first rank," whilst the New York Philharmonic, of which he had become the conductor, was "a regular American orchestra, talentless and phlegmatic." Cincinnati, Chicago, and Philadelphia also had symphony orchestras before the century ended. The conductors and most of the players had to be foreigners, for want of native talent; and the few native concertos and symphonies that they felt obliged to play were second-rate.

The best American music of this era, apart from folk ballads, African spirituals, and the like, was band music to which the war had given wide currency. Patrick Sarsfield Gilmore, author of the popular war song "When Johnny Comes Marching Home Again," organized mammoth band and vocal concerts of unprecedented size and unparalleled vulgarity. At the World Peace Jubilee in Boston in 1872 he conducted an orchestra of 1000 performers, 40 soloists, and a chorus of 10,000 men and women, their not inconsiderable din being augmented by cannon roaring, church bells pealing, and fifty firemen beating out the anvil chorus of *Il Trovatore* on real anvils. Gilmore was succeeded by more restrained bandmasters such as John Philip Sousa, composer of "The Stars and Stripes Forever." And America produced some good comic operas of the Gilbert and Sullivan type, such as Reginald De Koven's *Robin Hood* (1890) and Victor Herbert's *Babes in Toyland* and *Mlle. Modiste*, which marked the turn of the century. Grand opera was an imported art form, as it still remains after the lapse of a century, but America produced some great divas of international fame, such as Lillian Nordica and Emma Eames, both from small towns in Maine.

Foundations for the American vocal artists and composers of the twentieth century were being laid by the Peabody Conservatory of Music in Baltimore, and the New England Conservatory in Boston, both dating from the late 1860's. Of American composers during this period there was no equal to Edward MacDowell. New York born, a fellow student at the Paris *Conservatoire* with Debussy and César Franck, recipient of Listz's blessing for his first piano concerto, for many years he taught music at Darmstadt. Coming to Boston in 1888 at the age of forty-seven, MacDowell played his own works with the Kneisel quartet and the Boston Symphony, and in 1896 received the new chair of music at Columbia University. This he resigned after eight years, disappointed both in the caliber of his pupils and the stuffiness of the trustees. But he was successful in the sale of his many compositions; and after his death in 1908 his widow developed their summer home at Peterborough, New Hampshire, into a colony where men and women may compose and write in peace. John Knowles Paine, who taught music at Harvard from 1862 to 1905, was happy in his pupils, including composers Foote, Mason, Converse, and Carpenter, whose works mostly belong to the next century. This Boston-Cambridge group produced able critics such as John Sullivan Dwight and William F. Apthorp, who labored, not in vain, to establish canons of musical criticism; and Alexander W. Thayer, whose monumental *Life of Beethoven* accomplished for the biography of the *maestro* what Parkman had done for colonial Canada; begun in 1866 it was not completed until after his death in 1897.

Americans were very partial to the theater, and the country produced some great actors and actresses such as Edwin Booth, Helena Modjeska (a leading actress of Warsaw who came to America seeking liberty in 1876), Nat Goodwin and Maxine Elliott, Julia Arthur, and Minnie Maddern Fiske. But a distinguished American drama lay in the future. Of the 132 plays written by Dion Boucicault, only *Rip Van Winkle* (1865) in which Joseph Jefferson starred for over thirty years, and *The Colleen Bawn*, a romantic comedy of Ireland, are remembered. As in education and music, the organizations, teachers, and promoters are more significant than the scholars and composers; actor-author-producers such as Richard Mansfield and David Belasco dominated the stage. In the absence of competition from the cinema, or the exactions of stage-hands' unions, they put on sumptuous productions of Shakespeare and adap-

tations of novels, often taking leading roles themselves. Richard
Mansfield in *Dr. Jekyll and Mr. Hyde* made your flesh creep;
his *Richard III* was so realistic that, following the royal offer
to exchange his kingdom for a horse, one of the "gallery gods"
shouted, "Youse can have mine fer ten bucks!" *Arms and the
Man,* the first of George Bernard Shaw's plays to be staged in
America, was produced by Mansfield, and he also introduced
Ibsen to America. David Belasco, born in San Francisco shortly
after the gold rush, wrote and presented *The Heart of Maryland,* in which Mrs. Leslie Carter swung on a big bell clapper
to save her soldier lover; she found the title role in *Dubarry*
more congenial. Belasco produced the stage version of *Madam
Butterfly,* which Giacomo Puccini took over, as later he did
The Girl of the Golden West, written by Belasco himself and
starring Blanche Bates. American plays of that era were regarded as "corny" in the 1960's, when the favorite Broadway
themes were chicanery, murder, rape, and incest; but they were
feasts for the eye and ear, they catered to romance, comedy,
and heroism; they gave the rising generation something to
admire and emulate.

With theater seats ranging from 25 cents to $1.50, the people
of this era had abundant opportunity to see the classic drama
as well as modern plays. All the great English and European
actors and actresses—E. H. Sothern and Julia Marlowe, Sir
Henry Irving and Ellen Terry, the Salvinis, Bernhardt, Réjane,
and Duse toured the United States. Below their level were the
vaudeville houses, especially the B. F. Keith circuit which put
on amusing skits (as yet devoid of smut), jugglers, ventrilo-
quists, trained animal acts, and the earliest, very flickering,
moving pictures. Then there were the dime museums and nick-
elodeons where one put a nickel into the slot to hear an early
gramophone play from a squeaky, cylindrical record, and the
"10-20-30-cent" theaters where for these modest prices one
could hear old melodramas like *East Lynne* and *Uncle Tom's
Cabin,* and hiss the villain.

In letters, Walt Whitman wrote some of his best work between the Civil War and his death in 1892, but it was not an
age of poetry. Minor singers such as Eugene Field, Sidney
Lanier, and James Whitcomb Riley kept a spark of verse alive,
whilst Emily Dickinson, whose poetry has outlived theirs, wrote
only for her friends and herself. Emerson, who signed off (at
the age of 65) with his "Terminus": "It is time to be old, to
take in sail," lived to a ripe old age, as did Lowell, Longfellow,
and Holmes. But the Civil War seemed to have burned out all
that was original in their genius, and they left few successors

to carry on the New England tradition in poetry. Francis Parkman, whose series on New France is distinguished by scrupulous accuracy, a superb narrative style, and a feeling for the beauty of nature and the characters of Indians and French pioneers, picked up the torch of history where Prescott dropped it, and had completed the series when death took him in 1893. Henry Adams, in the meantime, had interrupted his perennial quest for education to write his remarkable *History of the United States in the Administrations of Jefferson and Madison*. This age saw the publication of excellent American fiction and imaginative literature. Mark Twain leaped into fame with his *Jumping Frog of Calaveras County* and presently created two boys who shall neither wither nor die, *Huckleberry Finn* and *Tom Sawyer*. Henry James, at the opposite end of the literary spectrum, wrote those imperishable portraits of Americans in Europe and Europeans in America, which plumb the depths of human nature deeper than anyone except the Russian novelists dared to do. So-called "realistic" fiction (really no more realistic than *The Scarlet Letter* or *Vanity Fair*) was inaugurated by William Dean Howells's story of Silas Lapham breaking into society, James Lane Allen's *The Reign of Law* (in Kentucky), and Stephen Crane's Zola-influenced *Maggie: A Girl of the Streets*. Two other novelists whose works have survived are F. Marion Crawford, son of Thomas Crawford the sculptor, a lifelong resident of Rome who wrote a series of novels on Italian life; and Edward Bellamy, a Connecticut valley journalist who wrote the Utopian romance *Looking Backward*, well expressing the progressive optimism of the America of his day, and *The Duke of Stockbridge*, a better history of Shays's Rebellion than the formal histories.

There also flourished a school of "local colorists" who wrote stories largely in dialect (African, Down East, Irish, German, etc.) which flattered the "superior" reading classes, but today seem not worth the effort required to read them. A simple affirmative is never found in their pages; it is always, "yiss," "yea," "yup," "yah," "yessir," or "uh-huh." Most American fiction of this era, such as *When Knighthood Was in Flower* and *Little Lord Fauntleroy*, was super-romantic and trashy.

Lecturing as a method of popular education was still going strong, and the man who could get his name enrolled in Pond's Lecture Bureau was certain of a good income, plenty of travel and, not improbably, stomach ulcers. Declining Emerson lectured more and more feebly, rising Mark Twain lectured enthusiastically; visiting foreigners lectured—Oscar Wilde enjoyed a surprising success with an audience of miners at Leadville, Colorado, in 1882.

Organized education was fertilized by the peculiar temper and energy of this period. Free primary schools followed the frontier West and penetrated the South. Adult night schools and settlements, of which Jane Addams's Hull House at Chicago was the pioneer, helped to educate the immigrants in American ways and to protect them from the rougher sort of exploitation. The free public high school now reached the height of its prestige and (some will say) of its excellence, since "progressive" education had not yet been invented. Church-controlled boarding schools, reviving the Renaissance idea of training the whole boy, for which St. Paul's in Concord, New Hampshire, had pioneered in 1856, now multiplied: St. Mark's, Groton, and most of the now famous church schools, were established.

Seven women's colleges and girls' boarding schools were founded between 1861 and 1880, and the great Western state universities as well as most of the high schools became co-educational. These increasing opportunities of education for girls helped to bring about a social revolution, the admission of women to practically every occupation except stevedoring and the building trades, and to every profession except the police and the ministry; and they are now in those too. Prior to 1880 very few women were employed in American stores or offices. Salesladies then began to replace salesmen behind the counter, and the lady stenographer with her typewriter, which came into general use around 1895, replaced the Dickensian male clerk with his high stool, calf-bound ledger, steel pen, and tobacco quid; a great gain for the cleanliness and neatness of business offices. Public libraries in this era became instruments of popular adult education. They grew and multiplied, and were rendered more accessible by card catalogues and by librarians trained to serve the public rather than to conserve books.

American captains of industry, with some exceptions, were as generous in endowing higher learning as the princes of the Renaissance, and less inclined than they to interfere with the objects of the beneficence. University presidents of this era, such as Charles W. Eliot of Harvard, Andrew D. White of Cornell, Daniel Coit Gilman of Johns Hopkins, William R. Harper of Chicago, Francis Amasa Walker of M.I.T., towered over the men of wealth and tolerated no suggestion that unpopular professors be "fired." Under the guidance of these powerful presidents, simple colleges of liberal arts burst out with a congeries of professional schools, and new subjects were added to the curricula of undergraduates. Eliot, who had taught chemistry for a year in the Harvard Medical School and learned at first hand its deficiencies, announced in his first presidential report in 1870, "The whole system of medical education in this country needs thorough reformation." And he proceeded to do just that at Harvard, with the help of Dr. Oliver Wendell Holmes. A system of lectures, clinical instruction, and practical exercises was distributed through three academic years and conducted by competent professors rather than local physicians as a part-time job, and stiff examinations were given, to weed out the incompetent. American universities, wrote James Bryce in his *American Commonwealth* (1888), were making swifter progress than any other institution, and offered "the brightest promise for the future. They are supplying exactly those things which European critics have hitherto found lacking to America." Johns Hopkins University (1876), the Columbia School of Political Science (1880), and the graduate schools of other universities, now made it possible for American scholars to study for a Ph.D. in their own country instead of in Germany.

In this realm of scholarship and science, as in music and the drama, one had to wait until the next century for a harvest. Among the few Americans who gained an international reputation in science or scholarship before 1900 were J. Willard Gibbs of Yale, Basil Gildersleeve of Johns Hopkins, Charles Eliot Norton and Francis J. Child of Harvard. The American notion of a scientist still remained, as before the war, a practical inventor such as Thomas Edison; the American idea of a scholar was one who taught Latin, Greek, or mathematics in a small college. But these now forgotten teachers are not to be despised. The nation's debt to them is inestimable. Under modern circumstances, with an abundance of grants-in-aid and paid leaves of absence, they might have been productive; but they were kept so busy conveying the rudiments of a liberal education to the hordes of young barbarians who crowded their classrooms, and writing necessary textbooks, as to have no time for independent scholarship. Moreover, proper library and laboratory facilities were lacking.

4. *Games, Sports, and Joining*

Despite his racial heterogeneity the average American was becoming urban in environment and uniform in appearance, manners and thought. There were compensations: human dignity owes much to the Jewish organizers of the garment trades, whose cheap but stylish clothes wiped out class distinctions in dress both for men and women. Regional differences in cooking began to disappear before nation-wide distribution

of canned goods and other prepared foods, which provided a
more varied and (after the passage of the Pure Food and
Drugs Act) more healthful diet than earlier Americans enjoyed. Advertising had not yet reached the status of a profession; but, with psychology as handmaid, it helped to build the
great department stores of the Eastern cities and Chicago, St.
Louis and San Francisco, with such a variety of wares and
luxury in appointments that traveling Americans were no
longer dazzled by the shopping splendors of London and Paris.

As the working day shortened and the number of indoor
occupations increased, Americans began to show an interest in
outdoor sport, which the mere business of living had afforded
to their rural and frontier forebears. Games, beginning in the
colleges, spread to every age and class. Baseball as an organized sport dates from the 1850's, and was seriously taken up
by colleges and local clubs after the war. No distinction was
then made between amateurs and professionals; the Harvard
baseball team went on a "Western tour" as far as St. Louis in
the summer of 1870, winning twenty-one games including one
with the Chicago "White Stockings," and losing five, including
one with the Cincinnati "Red Stockings." Boat racing was
resumed with great enthusiasm, on Eastern lakes and rivers.
College track athletics began in 1874, as a sideshow to the intercollegiate rowing regatta at Saratoga, and the Intercollegiate
Association of Amateur Athletics was formed in 1876, Princeton winning the first meet. Shortly after, Evert J. Wendell first
ran the 100-yard dash in 10 seconds flat. And in 1896 the
American track team carried all before it in the revived Olympic games at Athens. A feature of early track meets was the
two-mile race on high-wheeled bicycles. The modern "safety"
bicycle, made possible by the invention of the pneumatic tire,
had become a national sport by 1893 and a means for city
dwellers to get out and see the country on Sundays and holi-
days; whilst the tandem bicycle "built for two" became a repu-
table vehicle for courtship. Hearst's New York *Journal* in
1895 was the first American newspaper to have a sports section; and by that time the manufacture of sporting equipment
had become big business.

Hockey, played with a six-foot curved hickory stick and a
baseball, entered the college scene on Jamaica Pond near
Boston in 1879. The Canadian game, with a flat-faced stick,
a hard rubber puck, and a "goalie" swathed in protective armor
like a knight of old, was introduced in 1895. Also from Canada
came the old North American Indian game of lacrosse. Basketball was invented in 1891 to provide a fast game in gym-
nasiums during the winter months.

Rugby football, introduced into the United States during the Civil War, became intercollegiate in 1869, when the first match was played between Princeton and Rutgers. It diverged from the English game as college strategists, notably Walter Camp of Yale, invented new formations and altered the rules to fit. Lawn tennis was introduced from Bermuda in 1874, the same year it had been patented in England; and golf was imported from Scotland in the 1880's. Both games were long considered "sissy," like smoking cigarettes. President Theodore Roosevelt never allowed a photograph of himself in tennis costume to be published, and begged his friend William H. Taft to stop injuring his presidential prospects by playing golf. In the next century both golf and tennis became so popular that towns and cities provided municipal golf courses and tennis courts.

Summer vacations, the privilege of few in 1870, had reached the clerks by 1900. Thousands of people whose parents had left homes in the country in search of more easy living, returned thither for pleasure. State, municipal, and private enterprise vied in establishing recreation parks, public bathing places, and summer resorts. The very rich built immense "cottages" at Newport, Bar Harbor, and Long Branch; the well-to-do patronized big wooden hotels in coast and mountain resorts; others boarded with farmers' families for not more than five dollars a week.

In this happy era for the capitalist, when he could get 10 per cent on his investments and paid no income tax, he indulged in various luxurious forms of expenditure, of which the most useful to the economy and the most beautiful to the eye were yachts and the breeding of race horses. Before the war there was only one American yacht club, the New York; by 1885 there were fifty in the United States and eight in Canada. Favorite type of yacht for the postwar millionaire was the big centerboard schooner, such as William Astor's 146-foot *Ambassadress*. Around 1875 the multimillionaires began building steam yachts, of which the successive queens were J. Pierpont Morgan's trio, appropriately named *Corsair*. At Bath, Maine, was built in 1879 the most gorgeous vessel that ever flew the American yacht ensign—the steel auxiliary barque *Aphrodite* (303 feet) owned by Colonel Oliver H. Payne, treasurer of the Standard Oil Company and benefactor of Cornell University.

Hundreds of yacht races were sailed every summer, but the most spectacular, viewed by thousands of spectators off Sandy Hook or Newport, were the unsuccessful attempts of British

and Canadian yachtsmen to "lift" the *America's* cup. There
were four of these in the 1870's. The contests of the 1880's
brought into prominence Edward Burgess, a Boston naturalist
who took up yacht design as a hobby. He designed the cutters
Puritan, Mayflower, and *Volunteer,* which never lost a race
to British challengers and had long subsequent careers as cruising yachts. Nathaniel G. Herreshoff of Bristol, Rhode Island,
having revolutionized yacht design with long overhangs, a
"spoon" bow, forefoot cut completely away, and a fin keel,
designed the next challenger in 1893. His *Vigilant* easily defeated Lord Dunraven's *Valkyrie II;* his *Defender* in 1895 won
three straight from *Valkyrie III,* and his *Columbia* in 1899
defeated Sir Thomas Lipton's first *Shamrock.* These handsome,
gaff-headed cutters, measuring around 90 feet on the waterline
and 125 feet over all, spread some 13,000 square feet of sail,
exclusive of spinnakers and other "kites." They were sailed
by professional skippers and crews, those of the defenders
being mostly Scandinavians.

Yachting was no millionaire's privilege. In every Eastern
harbor, in Puget Sound and San Francisco Bay, and on many
an inland lake, there were countless small boats for racing,
fishing, or just fun sailing: the Cape Cod catboat immortalized
by Winslow Homer, the "sandbagger," in which ballast had to
be shifted quickly to avoid capsizing, the plumb-stemmed
Burgess sloop, and the 21-foot knockabout.

But a sport which cost the millionaires enormous sums yet
gave pleasure to everyone, was the turf. After the Civil War,
Kentucky took the lead in breeding Thoroughbreds, and the
Kentucky Derby was first run at Churchill Downs in 1875.
Flat racing around New York City, which had got into the
hands of Tammany braves and other hoodlums before the war,
recovered prestige when Leonard W. Jerome (Sir Winston
Churchill's American grandfather), August Belmont, and
other gentleman sportsmen organized the New York Jockey
Club and established a clubhouse and race track at Jerome
Park. This was in Fordham, now a part of New York City
but then a beautiful rolling countryside, near enough for city
people to drive to in their own carriages. The stewards, by
keeping race touts and other raffish elements away, made it
possible for Jerome Park to become the American Longchamps
or Royal Ascot. At the inaugural race meeting in 1866, Kentucky, a four-year-old by Lexington out of Magnolia, for
which Jerome had paid $40,000, began a two-year winning
streak. He then joined August Belmont's nursery stud at Baby-
lon, Long Island. The Maryland Jockey Club, organized 1870,

revived Baltimore racing at Pimlico; and their annual gentle-
men-riders' steeplechase, the Grand National, was won five
times by Preakness, another son of Lexington.

Harness trotting and pacing remained the average citizen's
most popular form of horse contest. New York City had a
speedway where the driving fraternity competed informally
every pleasant day, skirting the Harlem river north of 155th
Street. The whole country waited impatiently for a horse to
make a two-minute mile in harness. In 1900, after the pneu-
matic-tired bicycle-wheel sulky had been invented, Lou Dillon
did it. Dan Patch, a pacer foaled in 1896, first broke two minutes for that gait in 1902.

There had been informal fox hunting with horses and
hounds in the South and around Philadelphia since colonial
days, but not until after the Civil War was English-style hunting introduced, with trained thoroughbreds, specially bred fox-
hounds, huntsmen and gentlemen riders in pink and ladies in
black habits on sidesaddles. This sport encountered many difficulties in America. There were never enough foxes (since the
farmers *would* shoot them), so the artificial drag had to be
introduced. It is said that when a fox pursued by the Myopia
Hunt Club ran into Lexington, descendants of the Minute Men
began taking down Revolutionary muskets from chimney
breasts, assuming that the British Redcoats were back! Hunt
clubs led to country clubs, horse shows, and hunt balls. By the
end of the century there were thirteen organized hunts in Virginia and Maryland, which afforded the best country for this
noble sport, and about fifteen more around New York, Philadelphia, and Boston. Fox hunters organized cross-country
steeplechases with amateur riders, such as the Maryland Hunt
Cup and the Rose Tree in Pennsylvania; horse races which
have escaped the foul embrace of the underworld. From England, too, was imported the four-in-hand coach, commonly
known as the "tally-ho," which furnished another luxurious
sport. In these coaches jolly parties drove to country inns, announcing their presence by traditional tunes played on long
brass coach horns, "tooled" their matched fours to race meets
and football games, and sometimes made excursions lasting a
week or more over the soft dirt roads. In New York the annual
coaching parade along Fifth Avenue was an outstanding event;
Mrs. Grover Cleveland graced the box seat of Perry Belmont's
coach in the parade of 1890.

Except for harness racing, these were the recreations of the
rich; very different was the "manly art" of pugilism, which appealed to everyone. The old-style, Queensberry rules prize-fight-
ing with bare knuckles reached its apogee in 1889 when, as

Vachel Lindsay recorded, "Nigh New Orleans, upon an emerald plain, John L. Sullivan, the strong boy of Boston, fought seventy-five red rounds with Jake Kilrain." John L. held the heavyweight title until 1892, when "Gentleman Jim" Corbett, in a match fought with boxing gloves, knocked him out in the twenty-first round; five years later Corbett yielded the belt to Bob Fitzsimmons, and that fight was the subject of the first motion picture to be exhibited nation-wide.

The American "joiner" now arose. Desire for distinction in a country of growing uniformity, and a human craving for fellowship among the urban middle classes, drew the descendants of stern anti-Masons into secret societies and fraternal orders. Freemasons and Odd Fellows, both of English origin, proved too exclusive to contain would-be joiners. The Elks, Royal Arcanum, Woodmen, Moose, and several others were founded in the twenty years after 1868. The Southern freedmen had their United Order of African Ladies and Gentlemen, and Brothers and Sisters of Pleasure and Prosperity. The Catholic church, embracing a movement it dared no longer defy, created the Knights of Columbus for its increasing membership. Based on race and ancestry were patriotic societies, the Sons and Daughters of the American Revolution, Colonial Dames, Mayflower Descendants, Daughters of the Confederacy, and the like; a drawing together of the older American stock. These, nevertheless, took the lead in civic betterment, which cannot be said of those formed by the immigrants, such as the Ancient Order of Hibernians and Sons of Italy, which were then devoted to preserving old-world traditions.

These were some of the movements and tendencies that brought a new order in American life. In 1860 the average American was a land-owning yeoman farmer; since 1900 he has been an employee. In 1860, an ambitious youth fixed his sights on a farm; since 1900 and still more since 1930, he seeks a job. In 1865 only parts of New England and the Middle States had been industrialized, American technique in general was inferior to that of Great Britain, and labor combination was making a fresh start. By 1900 industry had captured the Middle West and crossed the Mississippi; agriculture, itself transformed, had conquered the Great Plains; the United States had become the greatest iron- and steel-producing country in the world, national trade unions had given labor a new dignity and greater buying power, new combinations were dominating the business and even the political world. Feverish development and ruthless competition, conducted in a framework of pioneer individualistic mores, made this age the most lawless and picturesque that America has ever known.

IV

The Fecund Eighteen-nineties

1. *Populism and Panic*

IN 1890 AMERICAN politics lost their equilibrium and began
to pitch and toss in an effort to reach stability among wild
currents of protest that issued from the caverns of discontent.

Almost a generation had passed since the Civil War. The
older Republicans had come to revere their "Grand Old
Party" only less than the Union and the flag; to regard its
leaders as the beloved generals of a victorious army. It was
difficult for the leaders, representative men of the Middle West
who had grown up with the country, to believe that anything
was amiss. Their experience of life had been utterly different
from that of any European statesman. They had seen the
frontier of log cabin and stumpy clearings, sod house and unbroken prairie, replaced by frame houses and great barns,
well-tilled farms, and sleek cattle. The railroad, the telegraph,
the sewing machine, oil and gas lighting, and a hundred new
comforts and conveniences had come within reach of all but
the poorest during their lifetime. Towns with banks, libraries,
high schools, mansions, and theaters had sprung up where once
as barefoot boys they had hunted the squirrel and wildcat; and
the market towns of their youth had grown into manufacturing
cities. As young men they had taken part in the war for the
Union, and returned to further progress and development. If
discontented workmen and poverty-stricken farmers sometimes intruded into the picture, were not foreign agitators and

the inexorable law of supply and demand the explanation? How could there be anything wrong with a government which had wrought such miraculous changes for the better, or with a Grand Old Party which had saved the nation from disaster?

Yet the quarter-century after the war had its suffering victims who, feeling something to be radically wrong, were groping for a remedy. Kansas, in 1888, began to suffer the effects of deflation after a land boom. Virgin prairie land, and peak prices of wheat and corn in 1881, had induced excessive railway construction usually financed locally, and oversettlement of the arid western part of the state. Small towns and cities indulged in lavish expenditure, and citizens speculated wildly in building lots. The new farms were mostly bought on credit; there was one mortgage, on the average, to every other adult in the state. And in 1887 there came a summer so dry that the crops in western Kansas withered. During the next four years, one-half the people who had entered this new El Dorado trekked eastward again, with humorous mottoes on their wagon covers such as, "In God we Trusted, in Kansas we Busted." The rest made a desperate struggle to retain their farms; but with toppling prices of grain, the interest alone consumed most of the yield. Some boom towns were moved bodily out into the prairie, leaving the mortgagees to foreclose on cellar holes.

Other agricultural regions, too, were in a bad way. In one Eastern state a survey of 700 representative farms revealed an average annual yield worth $167. In the Middle West, farmers envied immigrant factory hands, who at least had their dollar a day. In the South, cotton growers struggled from year to year against a falling market, and the waste of the sharecropper system. Washington Gladden, a keen observer, wrote in 1890, "The American farmer is steadily losing ground. His burdens are heavier every year and his gains are more meagre; he is beginning to fear that he may be sinking into a servile condition. Whatever he can do by social combinations, or by united political action, to remove the disabilities under which he is suffering, he intends to do at once and with all his might."

A ready instrument of revolt was at hand in the Farmers' Alliances, originally fraternal and economic in purpose. The Northwestern Alliance organized a party of its own for the elections of 1890, and in Kansas this became a political crusade. Mary Lease, the "Kansas Pythoness," went about advising the Kansas farmers to "raise less corn and more hell"; Jerry Simpson, the "sockless Socrates" of the prairie, defeated his silk-stockinged opponent for Congress; William A. Pfeffer, champion whisker-grower of the Northwest, was elected to the

United States Senate. Two years later a convention of some
1500 delegates representing the Farmers' Alliances, the Knights
of Labor, and several minor groups, founded the People's, or
Populist, party. Their platform, drafted by Ignatius Donnelly
(Minnesota politician, discoverer of the lost Atlantis, and
champion of the Baconian theory), opened with a trenchant
indictment of the existing order, including such statements as
"The railroad corporations will either own the people or the
people must own the railroads"; and, "From the same prolific
womb of governmental injustice we breed the two great classes
of tramps and millionaires." The Populist planks included the
free and unlimited coinage of silver at the ratio of 16 to 1;
produce subtreasuries, reminiscent of the schemes of the
1780's, where farmers could deposit the yield of their farms
against treasury notes; government ownership of railroads, tele-
graphs, and telephones; a graduated income tax; the parcel post
to break the hold of the great express companies; restriction
of immigration; an eight-hour day for wage earners; popular
election of United States senators, the Australian ballot, and
the initiative and referendum. Cries of horror greeted these
"socialistic" proposals in the Eastern press; yet all but the first
three were adopted within the next generation through the
instrumentality of the older parties. General Weaver, a former
Greenbacker of Iowa, was nominated Populist candidate for
the presidency. He polled over a million votes in the presidential election of 1892 and carried four states; but Grover
Cleveland, again the Democratic candidate, carried seven
Northern states together with the solid South and obtained a
heavy majority in the electoral college. .

2. Jim Crow in the South

The winds of agrarian revolt became really torrid when they
left the prairies for the Southern savannahs and piney woods,
where they were fanned to white-heat by racial fanaticism.
Nowhere in the Union was the plight of the small farmer so
desperate as in the one-crop region of the lower South, and
nowhere else did the white farmer, the "redneck" or "cracker,"
hate so intensely. To quote Hodding Carter's *Angry Scar*,

He hated high-tariff Republicans and the nearby mill
owners who bought his cotton so cheap and sold their
bolts of cloth so dear and paid so little to the mill hands
recruited from the farm homes. He hated the unbridled
railroads which provided almost the only outlets to his
markets. If he were a tenant he hated the landlords. He

hated the local bankers and merchants for whose exclusive benefit the crop lien laws and chattel mortgages were seemingly devised, and who preyed indiscriminately on large and small landowner alike. . . . The farmer mortgaged to the merchant his future crop and stock and implements; and the merchant or banker who made the advances generally insisted that the farmer put most of his land in cotton. As the price of cotton declined, the furnish merchants became planters as well as businessmen by foreclosing upon thousands of distressed farmers. Thus did William Faulkner's tribe of Snopses so greatly replace the Sartorises and bring to its logical end whatever remained of the onetime spirit of noblesse oblige which had made more human the debilitating relationship of master and slave and landowner and tenant. But most of all the redneck hated the Negro.

When populism entered the South, it aimed at a political alliance between blacks and poor whites to break the rule of the "Bourbons." But Tom Watson, the No. 1 demagogue of this movement, turned it against the blacks. He fought the Bourbons in Georgia all through the 1880's. Elected to Congress as a Populist in 1890 by the votes of both black and white, he was defeated for a second term. He then adopted the poor-white point of view. That class simply would not vote for a biracial party. As Watson wrote, "No matter what direction progress would like to take in the South, she is held back by the never failing cry of 'nigger.'" So, after ten years of ruminating, writing bad history, and worse biography, Tom decided to hunt with the hounds. From 1906, when he became the most popular leader in the South, he outdid every other white demagogue in Negro-baiting; he lauded lynching, described Booker T. Washington as "bestial as a gorilla," and bracketed Catholics, Socialists, and Jews with Africans in his catalogue of hate.

We are getting ahead of the story. Throughout the lower South, professional rabble-rousers and "nigger-haters" arose—Tillman, Bilbo, Vardaman, Blease, and others—to challenge the Bourbon ascendancy, exploit agrarian discontent, and seize the state governments. In one state after another, between 1890 and 1908, new constitutions which by one device or another disfranchised the black, were adopted by conventions but never submitted to popular ratification. Louisiana, for instance, which had the most prosperous and cultured blacks of any Southern state, had 130,334 colored people registered as voters in 1896, but the number fell to 1342 in eight years. And

every legislature elected under these new constitutions proceeded to enact a flood of jim crow laws.

Jim Crow was a blackfaced character in a popular minstrel
show of the 1830's who did a song-and-dance routine of which
the theme was, "Jump, Jim Crow!" After the Civil War Jim's
name began to be used, like "darkey," as a slightly less insulting term than "nigger." It was now applied to the new segregation laws. Education had always been segregated in the
South, and the churches too, by the blacks' own desire; but
down to 1890 there was practically no segregation in public
transportation or elsewhere. The blacks during this period
1875-90 had been quiescent, and their leader Booker T. Washington advised them to be humble and improve themselves
by becoming better workers. His policy of gradualism, and
never claiming social equality with white people, did the colored people no good, now that rednecks were in the saddle.
And by 1900 the blacks had lost the ballot.

Jim crow cars on passenger trains came first, then jim crow
waiting rooms and lavatories, jim crow sections of streetcars
and buses, jim crow entrances to circuses, factories, and the
like. White nurses were forbidden to attend colored patients in
hospitals, and vice versa; black barbers were forbidden to cut
the hair of women or children; all colored people (except as
servants) were barred from lunch counters, bars, and restaurants run by whites; and when taxicabs came in, a colored
driver, if he managed to obtain a license, was not allowed to
carry white fares. Most of these regulations started in the
lower South and worked up; but the legal zoning of cities into
colored and white residential districts started in Baltimore in
1910 and worked down. Segregation as a principle received a
blessing from the Supreme Court in the case of *Plessy* v.
Ferguson (1896), which announced the "separate but equal"
doctrine, that segregation was legal if those segregated enjoyed equal facilities. But the blacks seldom obtained these.
They got the old, battered schools and beat-up railroad cars,
the rundown tenements and the muddy parks. Segregation
reached its height in Washington under President Wilson, when
all government offices, restaurants, and lavatories were segregated, and for the most part so remained until the Franklin
D. Roosevelt administration.

The justification often offered for jim crow laws was sanitary or sexual; blacks were said to be diseased, lousy, and lust-
ing after white girls. The hypocrisy of these claims is shown
by the fact that blacks were still in great demand as nurses
and domestic servants, even when they refused to "live in"
and spent the night in their own homes. In these domestic

relations the old friendly intimacy between the races has continued to this day; but the poor whites employed no domestic servants. The real motive of jim crow laws was to keep the black down and make him constantly sensible of his inferior status. That is why jim crow policy had so irresistible an appeal to the poor whites. Except for the "hillbillies," who lived apart and fairly respectably, these lower-class whites of the South were a very unfortunate people—poor, illiterate, and diseased; but their feeling that the poorer of them was superior to even the most cultured Negro flattered their ego and assuaged their griefs. Custom, as well as the jim crow laws, compelled every black to address the lowest dirt-eating redneck, hat in hand, as "Mr.," "Sir," or "Ma'am." But the black, no matter how respectable, had to be content with "Boy" or "Girl"; or, if elderly, "Uncle" and "Aunty"—never Mr. or Mrs. Any act of so-called insolence, such as not uncovering in the presence of whites, not stepping off a sidewalk when they approached, risked a black's being pulled out of his cabin and severely whipped. The black's daughters were free to all the lusty white lads of the neighborhood, and nothing was done about it; but if a colored man leered at a white girl of notoriously low morals, he was liable to be lynched by a mob in defense of the alleged purity of Southern womanhood.

Altogether, the thirty years from 1890 to 1920 were the darkest for the dark people of America. And, sad to relate, a perverted form of democracy was responsible; had the "Bourbons" still been governing the South, this could not have happened.[1] But the Southern gentry who abdicated the leadership they had exerted in reconstruction days, cannot escape responsibility. Some men of courage and integrity, like Harper Lee's Atticus Finch, upheld justice to the black; many more deplored the situation but failed to do anything about it; others were converted to the extremist view by hate literature such as Thomas Dixon's *Clansman*, or newspapers such as Hoke Smith's *Atlanta Journal* and Josephus Daniels's *Raleigh News and Observer*. Many pandered to the rednecks in order to be elected, or to get favors from the state legislatures for railroads, cotton mills, and the like. Several Southern writers who denounced unfairness and cruelty to blacks—notably George W. Cable and Walter Hines Page—had to move North in order to escape ostracism, or worse.

[1] In Hawaii, where there had been an immense immigration of Oriental, European, and Puerto Rican labor to work the sugar plantations, this did not happen, precisely because the ruling class, largely descendants of New England missionaries, kept a tight political control and promptly clamped down on racial enmity.

In general, the Southern black submitted to his own abasement and accepted the degraded status that his former masters forced upon him. His fellows in the North did nothing to help him. No leaders then arose to fire his sullen heart with courage and determination to resist. For that he had to wait a century after Gettysburg.

This was an era of lynchings, which reached their apex in 1892 with 226 extra-judicial mob murders, 155 of them blacks. From that date the number slowly dropped off, but no fewer than 50 blacks were lynched annually until 1913, and the total count for 1889–1918 is 2522 blacks and 702 others. Some were in Ohio, Indiana, and Illinois, a particularly bad case occurring in 1908 at Springfield, within half a mile of Abraham Lincoln's old home—property destroyed and two blacks lynched for a crime that was never committed. Of the 702 non-black lynchings, including native whites, Italians, Mexicans, Indians, and Chinese, the greater part were for horse-stealing, cattle-rustling, rape, robbery, and murder in the Far West. There, lynching was resorted to in the absence or weakness of law, whilst in the South it was used in defiance of law and the courts, often after trial and conviction, to satisfy the vicious hate of the lowest elements of the population. In New Orleans, where there had been a recent influx of Sicilians, with consequent tension, an Irish chief of police who had incurred the enmity of the Mafia, was assassinated in 1891; but of 11 Italians tried by jury, not one was found guilty. Next day a mob incited by a white lawyer invaded the jail and shot down or hanged all eleven. The Italian government demanded redress; Secretary Blaine washed his hands of the affair since it was a matter of state jurisdiction, but the United States eventually paid a small indemnity. As the Italian premier remarked, "Only savages refuse to respect the inviolability of prisoners and distrust the justice of their own courts."

The common excuse for lynching is that it was resorted to only for rape, or attempted rape, of white women. The statistics prove that sexual assaults were not even alleged in more than one case in five, and that many of those lynched for it were innocent, or the alleged assault was imaginary—as in Faulkner's *Dry September*. There is a good deal of truth in what H. L. Mencken wrote, that the typical Southern lynching was one "in which, in sheer high spirits, some convenient African is taken at random and lynched, as the newspapers say, 'on general principles.'" The most abundant alleged cause was murder or suspicion of murder, as in Lillian Smith's *Strange Fruit,* but hundreds of lynchings were for theft, alleged insult, altercations between black tenants and white landowners, or such trivial causes as killing a white man's cow or refusing to sell cotton-seed to a white man at his price. Fifty of the blacks lynched during this period were women.

Lynchings were accompanied by incidents such as cheering crowds of men, women, and children (at Waco, Texas, in 1916) witnessing the mutilation and burning alive of a black already convicted and sentenced to death for murder, and carrying away collops of his flesh as souvenirs. Horrible it is to contemplate such things; but they must be recorded, if only to prove that sadistic cruelty is no monopoly of our late enemies, or of remote eras, but part of the devil that is in all of us. Not until 1918 was anyone punished in the South for taking part in a lynching. In that year, at Winston-Salem, North Carolina, the police and home guards frustrated an attempt to lynch an innocent colored man, and fifteen white men were sentenced to serve one to six years in prison for their part in the mob.

Lynching now appears to be a closed book. The leading Southern writers of the present century have exposed it, and the decent white people of the South have revolted against it. But the blacks are no longer content with merely equal protection of the laws in cases of crime. The time has not yet arrived when the prophecy of Jeremiah xxxi.29 can be said to be fulfilled: "In those days they shall say no more, The fathers have eaten a sour grape, and the children's teeth are set on edge."

3. *President Cleveland's Second Term*

American society appeared to be in a state of dissolution, but the same old Grover Cleveland, a little stouter and more set in his ideas, was inaugurated President on 4 March 1893. A large proportion of his vote came from suffering farmers who looked to the Democrats for relief rather than to inexpert Populists. Cold comfort they obtained from the inaugural address! The situation, as the President saw it, demanded "prompt and conservative precaution" to protect a "sound and stable currency."

The administration was not three months old when a series of bank failures and industrial collapses inaugurated the panic of 1893. The treasury's gold reserve was depleted by an excess of imports and by liquidation of American securities in London after a panic there. Gold was subject to a steady drain by the monthly purchase of useless silver required by the Silver Purchase Act of 1890, and by the redemption of greenbacks which by law were promptly reissued and formed an "endless chain" for conveying gold to Europe. Cleveland summoned a special session of Congress to repeal that mischievous law. In so doing he flew in the face of his supporters, who demanded the directly opposite policy of inflating the currency with "free silver" at the ratio of 16 ounces of silver to one of gold, by which the silver dollars would have contained only 57 cents in bullion. Cleveland's discreet use of patronage provided enough Democratic votes at this special session to help the Republicans repeal their own Silver Purchase Act. Business and finance breathed more freely, but the farmers cried betrayal; and when Cleveland later broke the endless chain by a gold loan from J. P. Morgan and the Rothschilds, farmers and workingmen assumed that the President had sold out to Wall Street.

Cleveland's brusque manner of dealing with Congress did not help his party to redeem its pledge of tariff reduction. Vested interests had been built up under Republican protection, and Democratic senators from the East were no less averse from free trade than their Republican colleagues. The resulting Wilson tariff of 1894 took off a slice here and a shaving there, but remained essentially protective. Cleveland denounced the bill as smacking of "party perfidy and party dishonor"; but allowed it to become law without his signature. The best feature of the Act, a 2 per cent tax on incomes above $4000, was declared unconstitutional by a five to four decision of the Supreme Court, which fifteen years earlier had passed favorably and unanimously upon the wartime income tax. This decision (*Pollock* v. *Farmers' Loan & Trust Company*) made it necessary to adopt Amendment XVI (1913) before a federal income tax could be legally enacted.

The Wilson tariff went into effect during the worst industrial depression since the 1870's, and no worse came until 1929. Prices and wages struck rockbottom, and there seemed to be no market for anything. It was a period of soup kitchens, ragged armies of the unemployed, fervid soapbox oratory, desperate strikes. What was wrong with the United States, that it had to suffer these recurrent crises? The Democratic tariff, said the Republicans; gold, said the Populists; capitalism, said the socialists; the immutable laws of trade, said the economists; punishment for our sins, said the ministers. But Grover Cleveland, like Br'er Rabbit, "ain't sayin' nuffin'."

Chicago, where an army of floating labor attracted by the World's Fair could not be absorbed, became the plague spot of this depression. In the spring of 1894 employees in the Pullman car works struck against a wage cut that left them hardly any margin over their rents in the Pullman "model village." The American Railway Union supported the strike by refusing to handle Pullman cars. The General Managers Association, representing twenty-four railroads entering Chicago, refused to arbitrate and prepared for a trial of strength. At the suggestion of Cleveland's attorney general, the federal circuit court at Chicago served on the officers of the union a "blanket injunction" against obstructing the railroads and holding up the mails. Hooligans promptly ditched a mail train and took possession of strategic points in the switching yards. Cleveland then ordered a regiment of regulars to the city, declaring he would use every dollar in the treasury and every soldier in the army if necessary to deliver a single postcard in Chicago. Violence increased. Governor Altgeld of Illinois protested against this gratuitous interference of the federal government, and requested immediate withdrawal of the troops. Eugene V. Debs, president of the striking union, defied the injunction, was arrested, and sentenced for contempt of court. Gompers and the executive board of the A. F. of L. advised Debs's union that it was beaten, and by early August the strike was broken.

The dramatic events of this Pullman strike drove contending parties into positions far beyond their intentions. Cleveland saw the simple issue of law and order, and had no desire to help crush a strike; but he played into the hands of those who wanted federal troops as strikebreakers rather than state militia to preserve order. Governor Altgeld had no wish to help the strikers, but his protest against a doubtful assumption of federal authority placed him in the position of a rebel. Debs was trying to help the Pullman employees by boycotting the company, but the movement got out of his hands and became something like an insurrection. And the consequences went even further. The Supreme Court, to which Debs appealed against his sentence, upheld the government, declaring that even in the absence of statutory law it had a dormant power to brush away obstacles to interstate commerce—an implied power that would have made Hamilton and Marshall gasp. A new and potent weapon, the injunction, was legalized for use against strikers, Cleveland became the hero of American business, Debs received the Socialist nomination for the presidency, Altgeld was hounded from public life.

Cleveland believed that the manifest destiny of American expansion had been fulfilled. During Harrison's administration American settlers in the Hawaiian Islands had upset the royal house of Kamehameha and concluded a treaty of annexation to the United States. Cleveland, discovering that the American minister to Hawaii had taken an active part in these proceedings, withdrew the treaty from the Senate and let the new Hawaiian Republic shift for itself. Toward the Cuban insurrection that broke out in 1895 his attitude was neutral and circumspect. Nevertheless it fell to him to make a vigorous assertion of the Monroe Doctrine, and to risk war with Great Britain.

There was a long-standing boundary dispute between British Guiana and Venezuela. Lord Salisbury, the British foreign minister, refused to submit the question to international arbitration, owing to Venezuela's pretension to annex over half of a colony which, as he said, "belonged to the Throne of England before the Republic of Venezuela came into existence." In a message of 17 December 1895, President Cleveland informed Congress of Lord Salisbury's refusal, proposed to determine the disputed line himself, and declared that in his opinion any British attempt to assert jurisdiction beyond that line should be resisted by force. Panic ensued in Wall Street, dismay in England, and an outburst of jingoism in the United States. Secretary Olney's earlier note to England of 20 July, published with the President's message, included a definition of the Monroe Doctrine that alarmed Latin America, insulted Canada, and challenged England: "Today the United States is practically sovereign on this continent, and its fiat is law upon the subjects to which it confines its interposition. . . . Distance and three thousand miles of intervening ocean make any permanent political union between a European and an American state unnatural and inexpedient."

It has never been satisfactorily explained why the peaceful Cleveland and his gentlemanly corporation-lawyer secretary used such provocative language. Seven years later Olney explained himself on the ground "that in English eyes the United States was then so completely a negligible quantity that it was believed only words the equivalent of blows would be really effective." It must be admitted that they were; but still more effective were two other events—a panic in Wall Street over the possibility of war, and a telegram from William II, Emperor of Germany, congratulating President Kruger of the South African Republic for having repelled an unauthorized English colonists' raid on his territory. That event, a portent of the First World War, caused Lord Salisbury to adopt a conciliatory attitude. A treaty was signed between Britain and Venezuela submitting the controversy to arbitration, and the arbitral board reported substantially in favor of the British claim. That settled it.

The party in power is always blamed for hard times. The Populists increased their vote 50 per cent at the congressional elections of 1894, and the Republicans won back their majority in the House. So certain were they of victory in 1896 as to boast that a Republican rag doll could be elected President—a boast that Mark Hanna almost made a prophecy.

Marcus Alonzo Hanna was a great figure in the "Ohio dynasty." A big businessman satiated with wealth but avid of power, naturally intelligent though contemptuous of learning, personally upright but tolerant of corruption, Mark Hanna believed in the mission of the Republican party to promote "business" activity, whence prosperity would percolate to farmers and wage earners. Since 1890 he had been grooming for the President his amiable friend, Congressman William McKinley. Speaker Thomas B. Reed was far more able and experienced, but he had made enemies by his strong though necessary actions as speaker, as well as by a mordant wit;[1] and the "good and the great" of Maine were no match for the Ohio pols. So "Bill McKinley, author of the McKinley Bill, advance agent of prosperity," was nominated by the Republican convention. The convention pointed with pride to Republican achievement, viewed with horror the "calamitous consequences" of Democratic control, and came out somewhat equivocally for the gold standard.

Three weeks later, when the Democratic convention met at Chicago, it became evident that populism had permeated that party. Instead of converting the Democracy to caution, Cleveland had driven it into radicalism. While he strove for sound money the populist panacea of free silver had become an oriflamme to the discontented. Cornbelt economists concluded that gold was the cause of the hard times, and free silver the solution for all their ills. To argue that bimetallism was a world problem, that unlimited coinage of silver by the United States would avail nothing while the mints of Europe and India were closed to it, merely invited the retort that America must declare financial independence of London. Some wanted free coinage of silver in order to bring it back to par, others looked for cheap money to pay their mortgages; but all wanted free silver.

William Jennings Bryan, a thirty-six-year-old congressman from Nebraska, carried the Democratic convention off its feet by a speech which became famous for its peroration, "You shall not press down upon the brow of labor this crown of thorns, you shall not crucify mankind upon a cross of gold," and obtained the presidential nomination. The convention declared emphatically for free silver, and the campaign was fought on that issue. Gold Democrats bolted one way, Silver

[1] To a congressman who declared his preference to be right rather than to be President, the Speaker interjected, "The gentleman need not be disturbed, he will never be either." Of two boring congressmen he said, "They never open their mouths without subtracting from the sum of human knowledge."

Republicans the other, and the Populists supported Bryan. Apart from the silver mining interests, it was a cleancut radical-conservative contest over the first live issue in thirty years. And the new cause had an ideal leader in the "Boy Orator of the Platte":

The bard and the prophet of them all.
Prairie avenger, mountain lion,
Bryan, Bryan, Bryan, Bryan,
Gigantic troubadour, speaking like a siege gun,
Smashing Plymouth Rock with his boulders from the West.[1]

Radical only on the coinage issue, strictly orthodox in matters of morality and religion, Bryan was an honest, emotional crusader for humanity with the forensic fervor and political shrewdness that would have made him a good state leader in the age of Jackson. His object was merely to reform the government and curb privilege; but he was accused of "proposing to transfer the rewards of industry to the lap of indolence." In the hundreds of speeches that he delivered during a whirlwind tour of 13,000 miles, there was no appeal to class hatred. But his followers were full of it, and "Pitchfork Ben" Tillman of South Carolina called upon the people to throw off their bondage to a money power more insolent than the slave power. On the other side, Mark Hanna assessed metropolitan banks, insurance companies, and railroad corporations for colossal campaign contributions, which even the silver-mining interests could not match for Bryan. Employees were ordered to vote for McKinley on pain of dismissal, and their fears were aroused by the prospect of receiving wages in depreciated dollars. On Wall Street there was even talk of a secession of New York City from the Union if Bryan should win. The Democratic ticket carried the late Confederacy and most of the Far West; but the heavy electoral votes of the East and the Middle West gave McKinley an emphatic victory.

Now came high protection, plenty, and prosperity! Actually, the election of a Democratic administration could have served no useful purpose. They were not prepared, nor was the country ripe, for measures to bring financial giants under control. Free silver, if adopted, would have prolonged uncertainty and placed the United States in sullen financial isolation. Bryan's campaign was at once the last protest of the old agrarian order against industrialism, and the first attempt of the new order to

[1] Vachel Lindsay, *Collected Poems* (1925), p. 99. By permission of The Macmillan Company, New York.

clean house. Bryan was the bridge between Andrew Jackson and Theodore Roosevelt.

4. *The Spanish-American War*

William McKinley, a kindly soul in a spineless body, was inaugurated President on 4 March 1897. Mark Hanna refused a cabinet position, lest it seem payment for his efforts, but 74-year-old Senator John Sherman was persuaded to take the state department so that Mark could take his seat in the Senate. Lyman J. Gage, a Chicago banker and "gold Democrat," accepted the treasury department. Other cabinet positions went to amiable contenders for the nomination, or riggers of McKinley's; only Speaker Reed retired in a huff and would take nothing.

Business, breathing easily since the specter of Bryan running the government had been exorcised, was on the up and up. All omens for a peaceful administration were favorable. Since the one thing business wanted—except to be let alone—was more protection, the President promptly summoned a special session of Congress to raise the tariff. In a somewhat chastened spirit, the leaders of Congress proposed to set up more moderate schedules than those of 1890; but by the time every member had secured his pet interest, the Dingley tariff of 1897 was the highest protective tariff that had yet been enacted. So blatant were the monopoly-securing features of this tariff that the Republican party was badly in need of a new issue to divert popular attention.

Cuba provided the diversion. Cuba, which by geography is forced into an intimate relation with the United States, flared up in revolt, this time against Spain's inept (but hardly, by Cuban standards, over-severe) rule. Spanish efforts to suppress the insurrection were unsuccessful and revolting. American sympathy was stirred by the plight of insurgents in concentration camps, and by atrocities which were recklessly blown up by the "yellow" journals of William Randolph Hearst and Joseph Pulitzer in their race for circulation, and by Cuban exiles in the United States. Congress had repeatedly pressed the executive to "do something" about Cuba; both Cleveland and McKinley refused to do anything. In October 1897 a new Spanish premier, Sagasta, proposed to abandon the concentration policy, recalled General Weyler who had enforced it, and promised Cuba a measure of home rule. The crisis, apparently, had passed.

Unfortunately, on 15 February 1898, U.S.S. *Maine* was blown up in Havana harbor with heavy loss of life. That started a clamor for war; and when a naval court of inquiry reported

(28 March) that the cause was an external explosion by a sub-marine mine,[1] "Remember the *Maine!*" went from lip to lip. The next day McKinley sent to Madrid what turned out to be his ultimatum, demanding an immediate armistice, release of prisoners, and American mediation between Spain and Cuba. Spain's formal reply was unsatisfactory; but the Sagasta govern-ment, anxious to avoid war with the United States, moved to-ward peace with a celerity unusual at Madrid, and on 9 April the governor general of Cuba offered an armistice to the in-surgents. Next day the American minister at Madrid cabled Washington that if nothing were done to humiliate Spain he could obtain a settlement of the Cuban question on the basis of autonomy, independence, or even cession to the United States. He believed that Sagasta was ready to accord Cuba the same freedom as Britain had to Canada.

Any President with a backbone would have seized this op-portunity for an honorable solution. McKinley, a veteran of 1861, did not want war. Mark Hanna, Wall Street, big busi-ness, and a majority of the Republican senators backed him up. McKinley needed less firmness than John Adams had shown in the X Y Z affair, or Cleveland in the Venezuela crisis, to preserve peace. But Congress and the press, and "young Re-publicans" like Henry Cabot Lodge, were clamoring for war, and McKinley became obsessed with the notion that if he did not give way, the Republican party would be broken. After much prayer and hesitation, he decided to yield. A year later he confessed, "But for the inflamed state of public opinion, and the fact that Congress could no longer be held in check, a peaceful solution might have been had."

On 11 April 1898 the President sent Congress a long-winded review of the situation, making only a casual and deceptive reference to the reassuring dispatch just received from Madrid. He concluded: "I have exhausted every effort to relieve the in-tolerable condition of affairs which is at our doors. . . . I await your action." That action, of course, was a declaration of war.

"A splendid little war" is what John Hay called this war with Spain, which America entered upon as lightheartedly as if it were with a tribe of Indians, little reckoning the new and heavy responsibilities it would bring. Emphatically it was pop-ular; no war was ever more emotional or less economic in mo-

---

[1] This finding was confirmed by a careful examination of the wreck in 1911 by a board of American army and navy officers. Although it is still a mystery who set and fired the mine, it is difficult to conceive what interest any Spaniard might have had in doing it, and easy to imagine that a Cuban rebel would have planned it, in order to get the United States involved with Spain.

tive. No important business interests were looking forward to exploiting Cuba, or had even heard of the Philippines. In declaring war, Congress also declared, "The United States hereby disclaims any disposition or intention to exercise sovereignty, jurisdiction, or control over said island except for the pacification thereof, and asserts its determination, when that is accomplished, to leave the government and control of the island to its people." It did not anticipate the series of native tyrants under whom Cuba has suffered.

Europeans took sides in this war as their parents had in the Civil War. Anatole France, in *L'Anneau d'Améthyste*, depicts with matchless irony a party in a French château where the countesses beg a general of royalist views to confirm their hopes that "those American bandits" would be well thrashed. The general so predicts; America has but a tiny army, he points out, and a navy manned by stokers and mechanics, not, like the Spanish, by experienced sailors. The guests take great comfort from the rumor that the inhabitants of Boston, New York, and Philadelphia, panic-stricken over the expected appearance of a bombarding squadron, are fleeing en masse to the interior. Anatole had something there; for so apprehensive of bombardment were certain people of the Atlantic coast that the North Atlantic fleet was divided. One squadron blockaded Havana, and the other, reassuringly called the "Flying Squadron," was stationed at Hampton Roads. Senator Hale and ex-Speaker Reed of Maine so "bedevilled" the navy department, wrote assistant secretary Roosevelt, to protect Portland, that the department sent them a Civil War monitor which "quieted all that panic."

Europe came near to forming a monarchical front against the United States. Emperor William II proposed it as early as September 1897; and in Washington in April 1898, at a time when the issue of war and peace was hanging by a hair, Sir Julian Pauncefote the British ambassador sparked a joint suggestion of six European ambassadors and ministers to their respective governments that McKinley be pressured to accept the latest Spanish concessions. This move, which if carried out would have caused a fresh outburst of anglophobia in the United States, was prevented through the common sense of young Arthur James Balfour, then in charge of the British foreign office owing to the illness of Lord Salisbury. He told Sir Julian to mind his own business and stay out of any joint démarche, and the other powers did nothing, knowing that without the British navy on their side it would be impossible to influence the United States. Queen Victoria noted in her diary that the American declaration of war on Spain was "monstrous"; but almost every British political leader and journal backed the United States, realizing that England might soon need a transatlantic ally against Germany.

America rushed into this war "to free Cuba," more nearly unanimous than in any war in her history. The few who cried out against the childish jingoism, the unjust blackening of Spain's noble history, and, above all, the needlessness of the war, were dismissed as cranks or old fogies. With generous ardor young men rushed to the colors, while the bands crashed out the chords of Sousa's "Stars and Stripes Forever," and everyone sang, "There'll be a Hot Time in the Old Town To-night!" And what a comfortable feeling of unity the country obtained at last! Democrats vied in patriotism with Republicans, Bryan was colonel of a national guard regiment, the South proved equally ardent for the fight; Joe Wheeler and Fitzhugh Lee, who ended the last war as Confederate generals, were now generals of the U. S. Army. This was a closer and more personal war to Americans than either world war; it was their own little war for liberty and democracy against all that was tyrannical, treacherous, and fetid in the Old World. Each ship of the navy, from powerful *Oregon* steaming at flank speed around the Horn to be in time for the big fight, to the absurd dynamite cruiser *Vesuvius,* was known by picture and reputation to every American boy. And what heroes the war correspondents created—Hobson who sank the *Merrimack,* Lieutenant Rowan who delivered the Message to Garcia, Commodore Dewey ("You may fire when ready, Gridley"), blaspheming Bob Evans of *Iowa,* Captain Philip of *Texas* ("Don't cheer, boys, the poor fellows are dying!"), and Teddy Roosevelt with his horseless Rough Riders.

This was no war of waiting and hope deferred. On the first day of May, one week after the declaration, Dewey steamed into Manila Bay with his Pacific squadron, and without losing a single man reduced the Spanish fleet to junk. After ten weeks' fighting, the United States wrested an American empire from Spain—and it was control of the ocean that did it.

Yet Spain was a formidable power on paper, with more armored cruisers and torpedo craft than the United States had. The Spanish navy, however, was inconceivably neglected, ill-armed, and untrained; whilst the United States Navy—a creation of the last fifteen years, was smart and efficient. The Army, on the contrary, was almost completely unprepared. Russell A. Alger, an elderly politician, was at the head of the war department. There were enough Krag rifles for the regulars, but the 150,000 volunteers received Springfields and black powder. There was no khaki cloth in the country, and thousands of

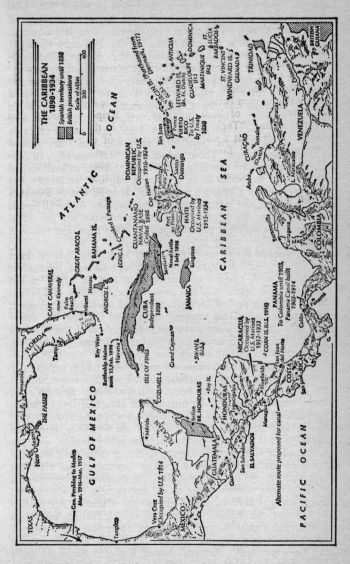

THE CARIBBEAN
1898–1934

Spanish territory until 1898
British possessions

Scale of Miles
0   200   400

TEXAS

Tampico
New Orleans
THE PASSES
Pensacola

Gen. Pershing to Mexico
Mar. 1916–Mar. 1917

GULF OF MEXICO

FLORIDA
CAPE CANAVERAL
now Kennedy
Palm Beach
Miami
Tampa
Key West
Battleship Maine
sunk 15 Feb. 1898
Havana

ATLANTIC
OCEAN

BAHAMA IS.
GREAT ABACO I.
Nassau
ANDROS I.
LONG I. Crooked I. Passage

CUBA
Independent
1898
ISLE OF PINES
Grand Cayman

Santiago
Naval battle
3 July 1898

GUANTÁNAMO
NAVAL BASE
Ceded 1898

JAMAICA
Kingston

DOMINICAN
REPUBLIC
Occupied by U.S.
1910–1924
Puerto
Plata
Cap Haïtien
Santo
Domingo
HAITI
Occupied by
U.S. Marines
1915–1934
Port
au Prince

PUERTO
RICO
to U.S.
by treaty
1898
San Juan

VIRGIN ISL. (Purchased from
Denmark, 1917)
LEEWARD IS.
(Br. Fr. Dutch)
ANTIGUA
GUADELOUPE (Fr.)
DOMINICA
MARTINIQUE
(Fr.)
ST. LUCIA
BARBADOS
ST. VINCENT
WINDWARD IS.
GRENADA

CARIBBEAN   SEA

Ven Cruz
Occupied by U.S. 1914
Tampico
MEXICO
Mérida
YUCATÁN
COZUMEL
BR. HONDURAS
Belize
Bay Is.
GUATEMALA
Guatemala
HONDURAS
Tegucigalpa
San Salvador
EL SALVADOR

NICARAGUA
Occupied by
U.S. Marines
1912–1933
Managua
Bluefields
San Juan
del Norte
CORN IS. (U.S. 1916)
COSTA RICA
San José

SWAN I.
(U.S.)

PANAMA
To Colombia until 1903.
Panama until built
1903–1914
Colón

COLOMBIA
Barranquilla
Cartagena
Magdalena R.

Aruba
(Dutch)
CURAÇAO
(Dutch)
Bonaire
L. Maracaibo
Maracaibo
Caracas
VENEZUELA
Orinoco R.

TRINIDAD
BRITISH
GUIANA

Alternate route proposed for canal

PACIFIC   OCEAN

troops fought a Cuba summer campaign in heavy blue uniforms issued for winter garrison duty. Volunteers neglected even such principles of camp sanitation as were laid down in Deuteronomy, and for every one of the 289 men killed or mortally wounded in battle, thirteen died of disease. Transporting 18,000 men to Cuba caused more confusion than conveying two million to France twenty years later. Yet the little expeditionary force was allowed to land on the beach unopposed (20–25 June), and the Captain-General of Cuba, with six weeks' warning, almost 200,000 troops on the Island and 13,000 in the city of Santiago, was able to concentrate only 1700 on the battlefields of El Caney and San Juan against 15,000 Americans. These Spaniards, well armed and entrenched, gave an excellent account of themselves and helped to promote Roosevelt from a colonelcy to the presidency. On 3 July Admiral Cervera's battle fleet steamed out of Santiago Bay to death and destruction by the guns of Admiral Sampson's Atlantic Squadron. Santiago surrendered on the 15th. Except for a military promenade in Puerto Rico, the war was over.

Spain asked for terms of peace and McKinley dictated them on 30 July:—immediate evacuation and definite relinquishment of Cuba, cession of Puerto Rico and an island in the Marianas, occupation of the city, harbor, and bay of Manila. Spain signed a preliminary peace to that effect on 12 August, sadly protesting, "This demand strips us of the very last memory of a glorious past, and expels us . . . from the Western Hemisphere, which became peopled and civilized through the proud deeds of our ancestors."

In the formal peace negotiations at Paris, which began on 1 October 1898, the only serious dispute was the disposition of the Philippines. Had they been contented under Spanish rule, there would have been no question of annexing this archipelago; but an insurrection was already on when the Spanish War broke. José Rizal, a noble leader of the Filipinos, had been executed in 1896. His successor, Emilio Aguinaldo, was encouraged by Commodore Dewey to return from exile after the battle of Manila Bay; and when the Americans had assaulted and captured the city (13 August), the *Insurrectos* organized a republic. The obvious thing to do was to turn the Philippines over to the Filipinos, like Cuba to the Cubans. But Dewey cabled that the republic represented only a faction, unable to keep order within its nominal sphere. To restore the islands to Spain would be cowardly; yet few Americans wished to "take up the white man's burden," which Rudyard Kipling begged them to do. On the other hand, Germany's obvious desire to obtain "compensation" in that quarter inclined Americans to stay.

William II of Germany, a latecomer in the European competition for colonies, hoped to purchase the Philippines from Spain and put down the insurrection himself. After the Battle of Manila Bay he sent thither a more powerful squadron than Dewey's, together with a transport lifting some 1400 troops. His naval commander, Admiral von Diederichs, established close relations with the Spanish authorities ashore and even landed troops at Mariveles on the Bataan Peninsula. A touchy situation took place when Diederichs attempted to defy Dewey's blockade of Manila, and truculently paraded his ships past the American squadron with guns trained on them. A British naval squadron under Captain Sir Edward Chichester not only co-operated with Dewey, but on 13 August 1898, when the American assault on Manila began, interposed his ships between the Americans and the Germans, who showed every evidence of trying to bluff Dewey into calling off the bombardment.

Now that China seemed to be on the point of breaking up, it began to look like a good idea to many leaders of public opinion for the United States to obtain a base in the Far East. And clearly all the Philippines must be taken, or none. McKinley hesitated long and prayerfully but finally decided, as he informed a Methodist delegation, "to take them all and to educate the Filipinos, and uplift and civilize and Christianize them." Spain was persuaded to part with the archipelago for $2 million, and on 10 December 1898 cession of the archipelago was included in the Treaty of Paris. Most Americans acquiesced, but a vigorous minority of conscientious objectors, the "anti-imperialists" led by Senator Hoar, believed it a monstrous perversion of American history to conquer and rule an Oriental country, and the necessary two-thirds majority for ratification was obtained with some difficulty. Yet time has justified the words of McKinley: "No imperial designs lurk in the American mind. They are alien to American sentiment, thought and purpose. . . . If we can benefit those remote peoples, who will object? If in the years of the future they are established in government under law and liberty, who will regret our perils and sacrifices?"

This annexation of extra-continental territory populated by an alien people created a new problem in American politics and government. The islets annexed earlier had never raised, as Puerto Rico and the Philippines did, the embarrassing question whether the Constitution followed the flag. Opinions of the Supreme Court in the Insular Cases left their status very muddled; but eventually, as in the British empire, a theory was evolved from practice. Insular possessions are dependencies of, but not part of, the United States, or included in its customs barriers unless by special act of Congress. Thus the Republican party was able to eat its cake and have it: to indulge in territorial expansion, yet maintain the tariff wall against such insular products as sugar and tobacco, as foreign. Inhabitants of the dependencies are American nationals, not citizens of the United States unless expressly granted that status by the United States. Organic acts of Congress became the constitutions of the Philippines and Puerto Rico, like the British North America Act of 1867 for Canada. Only such parts of the Federal Constitution apply as were included in these organic acts, or found applicable by the federal judiciary. President and Congress, although limited in power within the United States, were almost absolute over American dependencies. The parallel with the old British empire is suggestive; and the government at Washington, like that in Westminster, refused to admit the existence of an empire. No United States colonial office was established, no secretary for the colonies appointed. Until World War II, Puerto Rico and the Philippines were administered by the war department's bureau of insular affairs, and smaller possessions like Guam were under the navy department.

Almost half a century elapsed before McKinley's confident prediction came true. The Filipinos, most of whom had been Christians for three centuries, had no desire to be "civilized" in McKinley's sense. When Aguinaldo's troops disregarded the command of an American sentry to halt (4 February 1899), the United States Army undertook the job of making them halt, and it took about two years more and several hundred lives, to put down the Philippine insurrection. Aguinaldo—still living in 1964—finally took an oath of allegiance to the United States. General Arthur MacArthur (General Douglas MacArthur's father) acted more like an enlightened proconsul than a conqueror, announcing, "The idea of personal liberty . . . we are planting in the Orient. Wherever the American flag goes, that idea goes . . . The planting of liberty—not money—is what we seek." Military government was succeeded in 1901 by a civil Philippine Commission appointed by the President, with William H. Taft as chairman and governor general of the islands. Their population in 1900 was about seven million, of which only 4 per cent were Moslem and 5 per cent wild pagan tribes. Catholic Filipinos, the "little brown brothers" (as Governor Taft called them) who comprised the other 81 per cent, were homogeneous, intelligent, Western in ideals and civilization.

Their thirst for education was keen, and Tammany Hall could teach them little about politics. Under American rule they made a remarkable advance in education, well being, and self-government. Governor Taft, on a special mission to the Vatican, paved the way for the Philippines to purchase from the religious orders 400,000 acres of agricultural land, which were sold on easy terms to some 50,000 new landowners. The Filipinos, assured of their eventual independence, co-operated with Taft and his successors to establish a new civil code, a complete scheme of education, sanitation, good roads, a native constabulary; in 1907 a representative assembly—and baseball. Seldom has there been so successful an experiment in the now despised "colonialism" or "imperialism" as American rule in the Philippines. None of the critics' predictions that the Republic had embarked on a Roman road leading to disaster came true.

Nevertheless, acquisition of the Philippines affected America's future far more than any other settlement following the Spanish War. Cuba could be, and was, made independent, Puerto Rico was gradually advanced to commonwealth status, but responsibility for the Philippines made the United States a power in the Far East, involved her in Asiatic power politics, and made an eventual war with Japan probable. Annexing the Philippines was a major turning point in American history.

Following Japan's annexation of Formosa, and occupation of Korea, Russia, England and France began to extort from weak China permanent leases of important harbors. It became evident that unless China could be patched up, or in some way stabilized so that her vast population (six times that of Japan) would weigh in the balance of Far Eastern power, she would be sliced up by the European powers and Japan. Underlying this military menace, and the threat that each of the aggressive powers would set up barriers to American trade, there was on the part of the American people a warm feeling for China and the Chinese, fostered by medical and Christian missionaries. In the hope of arresting disintegration, Secretary of State John Hay introduced in 1899 the "open door" policy—a series of self-denying declarations by the powers that they would not interfere with vested interests and would allow a Chinese tariff commission headed by Europeans and Americans to fix and collect the customs duties. Next, in June 1900 there broke out the so-called Boxer Rebellion to cast out all "foreign devils" from China. The United States took part in a joint expeditionary force to relieve the legations at Peking; but in order to limit the objective, Hay addressed a circular note to the powers

(3 July 1900), declaring it the policy of the United States "to preserve Chinese territorial and administrative entity . . . and safeguard for the world the principle of equal and impartial trade with all parts of the Chinese Empire." The powers promptly concurred, and it is claimed by Hay's admirers that this second "open door" note prevented further partition of China. His detractors, however, contend that Europe and Japan accepted the open door policy tongue-in-cheek, merely to please the American government and public, which "mistook a phrase and a promise for an event." China was so weak, and incapable of suppressing piracy and banditry, that the Empress Dowager was forced to permit the navy of each power concerned to patrol her territorial waters, even the Yangtse river.

President Cleveland, as we have seen, had defeated every earlier attempt to annex the Hawaiian Islands. Now that American expansion was on the march, annexation was consummated by joint resolution of Congress on 7 July 1898. An organic act of 1900 conferred American citizenship on all Hawaiians and the full status of a territory of the United States, eligible for eventual statehood, which was finally accorded by Congress in 1959.

Another native kingdom in the Pacific on which the United States and other powers had designs was Samoa. Here President Grant in 1878 had obtained the naval station at Pago Pago in Tutuila by treaty with native chieftains; Germany and Great Britain followed suit. In 1899 England pulled out and sovereignty over the islands was divided between Germany and the United States. In the same year, Germany obtained some consolation for her failure to acquire the Philippines by purchasing from Spain all remnants of her Pacific empire, the Marianas group (except Guam), and the Caroline Islands. American missionaries, who hitherto had conducted all the work of civilization in these islands, wanted the United States to buy them; but the state department was not interested. During the First World War, Japan easily captured them all, as well as the Marshalls, from Germany; and in the Second World War the United States had to recover them at heavy cost.

Almost everyone in Europe expected the United States to annex Cuba. Instead, Washington promptly fulfilled the promise to make Cuba really *libre;* and the insurgents under Garcia, instead of fighting us as the Filipinos did, co-operated. For over three years the island was ruled by a United States army of occupation, fewer than 6000 troops, commanded by General Leonard Wood, a highly competent and sympathetic military governor. The outstanding features of his regime were medical. In 1900 Cuba was afflicted by a severe yellow fever epidemic. General Wood appointed a commission of four army surgeons under Dr. Walter Reed to investigate the cause. Working on a theory advanced by a Cuban physician, Dr. Carlos Finlay, they proved that the pest was transmitted by the stegomyia mosquito; and two of them, Dr. James Carroll and Dr. Jesse W. Lazear, proved it with their lives. General Wood declared war on the mosquito, and by 1901 there was not a single case of yellow fever in Havana. One of the greatest scourges of the tropics had been brought under control.

The Cuban constitutional convention that met in 1900 was induced to grant to the United States the Guantanamo naval base, and to recognize the right of the United States to intervene "for the preservation of Cuban independence," or to preserve order. Two years later the United States Army was withdrawn and Cuba turned over to her own government. The treaty provisions for intervention, known as the Platt Amendment, were incorporated in the first treaty between the United States and the Republic of Cuba; and only once invoked, in 1906. On demand of the Cuban government, the United States revoked the Platt Amendment in 1934.

Puerto Rico, handicapped by a decrepit and unsatisfactory system of law and local government, overcrowded with landless *jibaros,* enervated by hookworm and discouraged by fluctuations of the sugar market, has been an economic and social rather than a political problem. Civil government, first granted by the Foraker Act of 1900, was of the old crown-colony type: an elective assembly with a governor and executive council appointed by the President. Political parties quickly developed, the American governors were unable to keep neutral, and deadlocks occurred over the budget. Another organic Act of 1917 granted American citizenship to the Puerto Ricans and a government more responsible to the people. Since that time there has been steady progress in the economy, and in self-government. In 1971 the island, under an elected governor (Luis A. Ferre), is a commonwealth with a status similar to that of Canada in the British empire. Eventually Puerto Rico will become a state of the union unless she chooses independence.

As the presidential election of 1900 approached, the anti-imperialist movement waxed strong. It was led by statesmen such as Cleveland, Reed, and Bryan, financial magnates such as Andrew Carnegie, philosophers such as William James, college presidents such as Eliot and Jordan, writers such as Mark Twain and William Vaughan Moody. Although the rank and file of the Democrats were fully as proud as the Republicans of the victory over Spain and its fruits, the Democratic nominating convention adopted an anti-imperialist plank which, if implemented, would have caused the Philippines to be handed over immediately to the Filipinos. And the Democrats made much of scandalously inept administration by the war department in the Spanish War:—soldiers poisoned by putrid beef which smelled like embalmed corpses, and dying of typhoid in a discharge camp on Long Island. "Free silver" was trotted out again to catch Western and debtor votes. John Bull was given the usual kick in the teeth, this time for his Boer War, to catch the Irish vote. For the second, but not last time, the Democrats nominated William Jennings Bryan with former Vice President Adlai E. Stevenson for second place.

Republicans held all the trump cards—victory, world prestige, booming prosperity, and Philippine insurrection well in hand by General Arthur MacArthur. McKinley, of course, received the presidential nomination, and, in a move to isolate the irrepressible Theodore Roosevelt, the bosses saw to it that he was nominated for the vice presidency. The President conducted a "front porch campaign," receiving hand-picked delegations on the verandah of his house at Canton, Ohio, hearing their carefully censored speeches of support, and delivering in reply selected passages of patriotic platitudes. "Teddy" stumped the country in a Rough Rider hat, arousing wild enthusiasm. McKinley and Roosevelt were obviously what the people wanted. Bryan carried the solid South, together with four "silver" states of the West (Colorado, Idaho, Montana, Nevada)—but he lost his own Nebraska and won only 155 electoral votes to McKinley's 292. The President's plurality was almost 900,000 votes. Prohibitionists, Socialists, and other splinter parties polled only 4 per cent of the total. Increased Republican majorities were returned to both houses of Congress, and common stocks rose to new highs.

McKinley was inaugurated for his brief second term on 4 March 1901. Before the end of April he embarked on a rail journey around the country, accompanied by Mark Hanna and several members of the cabinet. Everywhere he was received by cheering crowds, to which he delivered familiar clichés on duty, purpose, prosperity, and the glory awaiting America. The trip ended tragically on 6 September at Buffalo, where the President was opening a Pan-American Exposition. As he always prided himself on accessibility, McKinley held a public reception, guarded by only two secret service men. An anarchist who joined the line, with a loaded revolver concealed under a handkerchief, fired two shots at the President just as he had extended a welcoming hand. One shot passed through

McKinley's stomach. An operation was performed, and the patient seemed to be improving; but infection set in, and as yet there were no wonder drugs to control it. His heart gave way, and on the 14th his kindly soul departed from his tired body.

Vice President Roosevelt, summoned while climbing Mount Marcy in the Adirondacks, hastened to Buffalo and was sworn in as President on 15 September. At the age of forty-three he was the youngest man ever to reach this high office. Senator Platt of New York, who had managed the vice presidential nomination to get rid of troublesome Teddy, told Mark Hanna at the inaugural ceremonies of 4 March that he had come especially "to see Theodore Roosevelt take the veil."

"Now look!" said Mark Hanna when he next met the Senator in October, "That damned cowboy is President of the United States!"

A HOT TIME IN THE OLD TOWN TONIGHT

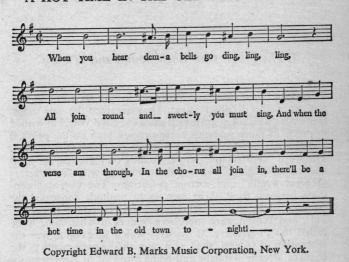

When you hear dem-a bells go ding, ling, ling,

All join round and sweet-ly you must sing, And when the

verse am through, In the cho-rus all join in, there'll be a

hot time in the old town to - night!

Copyright Edward B. Marks Music Corporation, New York.

V

Theodore Roosevelt

1901-1909

1. *The Progressive Background and "Teddy"*

THEODORE ROOSEVELT, and after him, Presidents Taft and Wilson, were liberal conservatives. They accepted the new industrial order which had grown up since the Civil War, but wished to probe its more scabrous excrescencies, both on the political and financial levels, and bring it under government regulation. The word "constructive" was constantly on their lips; socialists and reckless agitators shared their hostility with "malefactors of great wealth" and corrupt politicians. The violent dissensions between these three men as to methods concealed the essential unity of their administrations. Theodore Roosevelt, Taft, and Wilson were successive leaders of what came to be called the Progressive Movement, which in essence was the adaptation of federal, state, and municipal governments to the changes already wrought and being wrought in American society. Roosevelt called his policies the "Square Deal," Wilson his, the "New Freedom." Their philosophy was never better stated than by Elihu Root in his presidential address before the New York State Bar Association in 1912:

> The real difficulty appears to be that the new conditions
> incident to the extraordinary industrial development of the

130

last half-century are continuously and progressively demanding the readjustment of the relations between great bodies of men and the establishment of new legal rights and obligations not contemplated when existing laws were passed or existing limitations upon the powers of government were prescribed in our Constitution. In place of the old individual independence of life in which every intelligent and healthy citizen was competent to take care of himself and his family, we have come to a high degree of interdependence in which the greater part of our people have to rely for all the necessities of life upon the systematized co-operation of a vast number of other men working through complicated industrial and commercial machinery. Instead of the completeness of individual effort working out its own results in obtaining food and clothing and shelter, we have specialization and division of labor which leaves each individual unable to apply his industry and intelligence except in co-operation with a great number of others whose activity conjoined to his is necessary to produce any useful result. Instead of the give-and-take of free individual contract, the tremendous power of organization has combined great aggregations of capital in enormous industrial establishments working through vast agencies of commerce and employing great masses of men in movements of production and transportation and trade, so great in the mass that each individual concerned in them is quite helpless by himself. The relations between the employer and the employed, between the owners of aggregated capital and the units of organized labor, between the small producer, the small trader, the consumer, and the great transporting and manufacturing and distributing agencies, all present new questions for the solution of which the old reliance upon the free action of individual wills appears quite inadequate. And in many directions the intervention of that organized control which we call government seems necessary to produce the same result of justice and right conduct which obtained through the attrition of individuals before the new conditions arose.

Woodrow Wilson repeated much of this in his *The New Freedom* (1913), and added, "This is nothing short of a new social age, a new era of human relationships, a new stage-setting for the drama of life."

This seems obvious half a century later, except to the more ardent Goldwater supporters; but it was then heady stuff for most lawyers, bankers, and industrialists. These, in general, approved a clean-up of politics but saw no need to regulate business, transportation, or finance. "A tree should be allowed to grow as high as it can" expressed their laissez-faire creed, even if the tree overshadowed and sucked the life out of all bushes and plants in its radius. Several university economists, such as William Graham Sumner, pointed out that former interventions of government in business, as in colonial Canada, had been disastrous. Progressives thought otherwise, and the country supported them until World War I brought reaction. The frenzied finance of the 1920's led to the great crash and the great depression. Another Roosevelt then picked up the Progressive torch, calling it the "New Deal," and this was followed by Truman's "Fair Deal," and Kennedy's "New Frontier." All were essentially the same thing: an attempt through government action to curb the arrogance of organized wealth and the wretchedness of poverty amid plenty.

As we are now concerned with the Progressive Era, to 1917, it is pertinent to inquire why it accomplished so little that a "New Deal" was necessary; much less, for instance, than the Liberals did in Great Britain under Campbell-Bannerman and Lloyd George, who were then wrestling with similar problems. One reason was the vast scale, and the federal system, through which American Progressives had to operate. But the basic reason, as Theodore Roosevelt perceived in 1911, was the Progressives' war with themselves over basic economic policy. "Half of them are really representative of a kind of rural toryism, which wishes to attempt the impossible task of returning to the economic conditions that obtained sixty years ago" —to "bust the trusts" and break up business into old-style competing units. "The other half," continued Roosevelt, wishes "to recognize the inevitableness of combinations in business, and meet it by a corresponding increase in governmental power over big business." The progressive wing represented by William Jennings Bryan and Louis Brandeis hated bigness as such and feared the tyranny of government more than the arrogance of financiers. The other, of which Herbert Croly was the leading publicist, looked forward to a "welfare state," controlled by Congress but staffed by an intelligent and dedicated bureaucracy. Although Theodore Roosevelt, in his 1911 statement, regarded this wing as the only "proper" one for a progressive, he reacted violently against it when practised by Woodrow Wilson.

Graham Wallas, like Herbert Spencer an English publicist, deeply influenced the thinking of this generation of American liberals. His *Human Nature in Politics* (1908) was followed by lecturing at Harvard, where one of his pupils was Walter Lipp-mann, to whom his next book *The Great Society* (1914) was dedicated. In the meantime Herbert Croly in *The Promise of American Life* (1909), and Lippmann in *A Preface to Politics* (1913), had promulgated similar ideas in the United States. Brooks Adams, a publicist who had the ear of Theodore Roosevelt, pointed out in a book entitled *A Theory of Social Revolution* (1913) that revolution had always erupted under a government so rigid that no reform could be achieved through process of law. Thus, the British Parliament claimed absolute power over its colonies, and lost them; Louis XVI dis-missed Turgot and destroyed the monarchy; the cotton aristoc-racy of the South resisted restriction of slavery, and perished. Now, in 1913, a new capitalist class, having made untold sums through the application of steam to industry, had obtained con-trol of the government and would meet the same fate if it ac-quired no sense. He expressed this with the verve worthy of a grandson of J. Q. Adams.

These heralds of the welfare state were chiefly interested in the industrial worker, whose "real" wages—i.e. wages meas-ured not only by dollars but by rent and the prices of basic commodities—remained stationary or declined during this period of "Republican prosperity" and "the full dinner pail." Paul H. Douglas's basic work *Real Wages in the United States 1890–1926* shows that in eight of the years 1900–1914 "real" weekly earnings in all American industries were less than the average ($10.73) for the 1890's. The workers themselves, pain-fully aware of this, were becoming more and more skeptical of political remedies. But it would not be fair for us to denigrate the Progressives for accomplishing so little for working people, because they were the only group in the country who proposed to do anything for them, or to get away from those figments of the passing age, the "economic man" and "law of supply and demand."

One basic cause of the laborer's standstill was unrestricted immigration. In six of the ten years 1905–14 more than a million people emigrated annually to the United States. The bulk of these were no longer north Europeans, but Slavs, Jews from eastern and southern Europe, Sicilians, and Greeks. Their competition kept wages low and hampered the unions' attempts to organize; yet, low as the wages were, they were high enough to attract the poor and the ambitious from Europe. No Pro-gressives (to my knowledge) showed any interest in this prob-lem, and the nineteenth-century immigrant stocks—Irish, Germans, and Scandinavians—opposed restriction as likely to prevent their friends from coming over. An attempt by Congress to exclude illiterate immigrants, promoted by the unions, was vetoed by President Taft in 1913 for the sound reason that illiteracy, often due to lack of opportunity, was no test of character.

Common to all Progressives was belief in the perfectibility of man, and in an open society where mankind was neither chained to the past nor condemned to a deterministic future; one in which people were capable of changing their condition for better or worse. And they sincerely believed that they were the people chosen to make the word of Jefferson and Lincoln flesh indeed.

The Socialist party must also be counted in the Progressive group, for (unlike the later Communist party) having no obligation to hew to an international party line, it met American problems in an American manner. Starting on the local level, Socialists campaigned for municipal ownership of waterworks, gas and electric plants, and made very good progress. In 1911 Socialist candidates for mayor carried no fewer than eighteen American cities and almost won Cleveland and Los Angeles. Upton Sinclair in 1905 founded the Intercollegiate Socialist Society, which soon had chapters in the leading universities where lively young men and women discussed the new "gospel according to St. Marx." Eugene Debs, converted to socialism during his term in jail, edited the party's weekly, *Appeal to Reason,* and from 1900 through 1920, as candidate for the presidency, increased his vote almost tenfold. Norman Thomas, a Princeton graduate and Presbyterian minister in New York who succeeded Debs as perennial presidential candidate, was more typical of the party. It was an intellectual and middle-class party, rather than one of the workers. Debs himself regarded most of the country's labor leaders as a bunch of crooks —as indeed many of them proved to be.

By the time Theodore Roosevelt reached the presidency, an impressive amount of preliminary work had been done by Progressives in cities and states, and their efforts aroused the expectation of greater things on the federal level. The National Municipal League, organized in 1894, sponsored home-rule legislation for cities which enabled reform groups to free municipalities from the heavy hand of state control. Among these civic reformers were Charles R. Crane and Walter L. Fisher in Chicago, James D. Phelan and Rudolph Spreckels in San Francisco, Samuel M. "Golden Rule" Jones in Toledo, Seth Low of New York and Thomas L. Johnson of Cleveland. Lincoln Steffens's series on "The Shame of the Cities" in *McClure's Magazine,* starting in 1902, had an immense impact.

Theodore Roosevelt inconsistently called Steffens and his fellow writers (such as Ida Tarbell who showed up Standard Oil, Upton Sinclair of *The Jungle* fame, and Ray Stannard Baker) "the muckrakers"—a metaphor from *Pilgrim's Progress*—but they muckraked to good purpose, exposing the evils of city and state governments, unions, business, the drug trade, and whatever was curably wrong in divers segments of American life. When this new middle-class reform strain combined with the older agrarian Populists, it accomplished something. A large proportion of these pioneer Progressives were college graduates, actuated by a genuine desire for improvement, and Theodore Roosevelt was the first President to encourage them to place their talents at the service of government, reversing the process begun under Jackson of squeezing such men out of the public service into money-making.

Robert La Follette, by defeating the Republican machine of Wisconsin in 1900, started a reaction of revolt in the Middle West, helped to make his own state a progressive commonwealth (from which it has spectacularly lapsed), and went to the United States Senate where he became a power until his death in 1925. Parallel to him were Joseph W. Folk who showed up corruption in Missouri's state government and became governor in 1904; William S. U'ren who persuaded Oregon to adopt the initiative, referendum, direct primary, and popular recall of elected officials, political reforms which the Progressives expected would return state governments to the people and end corruption—and how wrong they were! Hiram Johnson in 1910 smashed the Southern Pacific Railroad domination in California and became governor of the Golden State. This reform movement, starting in the West, gradually extended eastward. In 1905 a New York attorney named Charles Evans Hughes exposed the rottenness of the great insurance companies and sent some of their moguls, such as James Hazen Hyde, into exile. In the Progressive period, many state governments recovered their vigor, experimenting with woman suffrage, the Australian ballot, the "I. and R.," the primary, factory and minimum wage legislation, and other expedients.

The federal government and the South were the last to feel the impact of Progressivism. But in 1901, with the accession of Theodore Roosevelt, the nation had a leader who caught its imagination. For Roosevelt was one of the most vital and virile figures of the century.

Roosevelt at forty-three still holds the record as the youngest President of the United States at his accession, although he was older when elected President than John F. Kennedy in 1960. None had been better equipped to administer the office. No President since John Quincy Adams had been as broadly cultivated as Roosevelt, and their careers are roughly parallel, although their backgrounds were not. Roosevelt liked to boast of his non-Anglo-Saxon blood; he was mostly old "Knicker-bocker" Dutch and his ancestors had been city merchants, bankers, and importers for generations. Born at 10 East 28th Street (now a Roosevelt shrine), Theodore suffered as a child from asthma, defective eyesight, and other physical weaknesses, but overcame them more by force of character than medical attention. Mature, he was five feet nine inches tall, weighed about 160 pounds, and had a barrel-like chest which small boys who visited the White House were invited to pommel. His education by governesses, tutors, and trips to Europe—never did he attend a school—was such as to make him a Little Lord Fauntleroy; but basic character won. After graduating from Harvard *magna cum laude,* and an early marriage, he had enough inherited wealth to build the sprawling Sagamore Hill mansion at Oyster Bay, Long Island, raise a large family and give them everything—horses, tennis courts, yachts—that the young gentry of that era enjoyed. But he was not content with being a dilettante member of the upper class. To the British ambassador in 1901 he expressed his "feeling of contempt and anger for our socially leading people" and their "lives which vary from rotten frivolity to rotten vice." Although he loved riding to hounds with the Meadowbrook set, he would ride the fourteen miles to Hempstead and back rather than suffer their "intolerable" companionship overnight. He was devoted to his parents, but ashamed that his father had not fought in the Civil War; that may explain his burning desire to get into every war during his lifetime.

Upon graduating from Harvard, Roosevelt planned to be a naturalist; then, after the death of his first wife, he became a rancher. That experience made him an enthusiast for con-serving America's natural resources. He wrote two good his-torical works, *The Naval History of the War of 1812* and *The Winning of the West.* Prior to the Spanish-American War, he had been assemblyman, police commissioner in New York City, civil service commissioner in Washington, and assistant secretary of the navy. Following his spectacular military career —storming San Juan Hill with his personally recruited Rough Riders—he was elected governor of New York, and in that office struck corruption with such vigor that in self-defense Senator Platt and the machine politicians boomed him for Vice President. Roosevelt accepted the nomination to that high but innocuous office for the political oblivion that it normally meant, and was on the point of studying law in preparation for a professional career when the anarchist's fatal shot made him President.

No American President since Lincoln was more national in his interests or so universal in his friendships. Roosevelt's reading covered the range from Herodotus to Graham Wallas, and his mind was retentive; he could discuss world history with any historian, and natural history with leading naturalists like John Muir and John Burroughs. He was the idol of the younger generation, much as John F. Kennedy later became. He had identified himself with the Far West by ranching, with New England by education, with the South because his maternal uncles had been warriors in the lost cause. Roosevelt's taste was much better than the average of his class; it was on his initiative that Augustus Saint-Gaudens designed a new gold coinage and that the bureau of engraving and printing produced the classically beautiful postage stamps of 1908. He appointed a commission of artists to advise the government on plans and positions of new public buildings in Washington, which grew visibly in beauty and distinction during his administration. People everywhere loved Roosevelt as a red-blooded, democratic American whose every action showed good sportsmanship and dynamic vitality. With the heart of a boy and the instincts of a man of action, Roosevelt had the brain of a statesman. He was the only President since the Civil War who understood, even imperfectly, what had happened to the country in the last thirty years, and he had the temperament, the brains, and the energy to grapple with problems that were crying for solution.

Roosevelt's philosophy, if his largely instinctive actions can be called that, was Hamiltonian, although his objectives were not. For Jefferson he frequently expressed contempt; the more so because his critics in finance and big business began invoking Jeffersonian democracy and state rights against governmental efforts to regulate them. Roosevelt believed, as Hamilton had, in making the federal government truly national; the "general welfare clause" of the Constitution, which had earlier been considered a limitation on the taxing power, he regarded as authority to do anything for the good of the country for which the states individually were incompetent. But he intended to direct all this activity, not toward making the rich richer, but toward giving a "square deal" to the farmer, laborer, and small businessman who was being squeezed by big business.

Roosevelt's ambition extended beyond the borders of his country. While reforming the domestic social order, he wished

America to flex her muscles and assert her strength abroad, as a world power. He seems to have had no vision of a new world order, but he did intend to make a strong, well-armed America a guarantor of world peace. Thus his place in history is that of the first four Presidents—himself, Wilson, the other Roosevelt, and Kennedy—who worked out a coherent domestic and foreign policy to meet the realities of the twentieth century. Theodore Roosevelt never looked back, only forward.

2. Consolidation and Reform

The "trust problem" was the popular name for the first object of Roosevelt's righteous zeal. The depression of the early 'nineties stimulated the railroads and the manufacturers to adopt various forms of combination, in order to eliminate competition and maintain prices. In 1897, just as prosperity was reviving, the Supreme Court found one of these organizations, the Trans-Missouri Traffic Association, invalid under the Sherman Anti-trust law, in a decision so sweeping that practically every pool or association became liable to criminal prosecution. Big business, in consequence, abandoned combination for consolidation. A group of bankers would organize a "trust" or supercorporation for the control of a single industry. With the help of the financiers who had large interests in the leading companies who made a certain product, the new trust would buy them out, issuing its own stock in exchange and assuming their bonds. An immense quantity of common stock would then be issued in anticipation of increased earnings and "unloaded" by the banker-promoters on the public, and up would go prices of the product. Never had there been so easy a method of making something out of nothing. Tobacco, agricultural machinery, tin cans, salt, sugar, dressed meat, and a score of basic products were consolidated in corporations with power to crush competition and mulct the public by increased prices of service and commodities, in order to pay dividends on a "watered" capitalization.

In many cases the merger of competing or complementary industries marked a technical advance. Trust methods, however suitable for industries such as meat-packing, were extended to others which were not, such as cotton-spinning, piano-making, and rope-making; and the economies of mass production were not often shared with laborer or consumer. The United States Steel Corporation, formed in 1901, combined the already swollen corporations of Frick, Carnegie, and others in a trust capitalized at $1,400 million, of which nearly one-seventh was issued to promoters for their services. Prices were maintained, although 10 to 12 per cent was being earned on the real capitalization, and the wages of steel workers were kept down by importing cheap labor from southern and eastern Europe. The great insurance companies of New York, instead of reducing premiums to their policy holders, paid salaries of $100,000 or more to chief executives who were often mere figureheads.

It did not always work. J. Pierpont Morgan endeavored to unite every steam and electric railway and steamship line of New England under one management, and succeeded in leaving the transportation system of that region a financial wreck, from which it has never recovered. E. H. Harriman purchased the bankrupt Union Pacific in 1893 with reserve funds of the Illinois Central system that he controlled, and made it one of the best railways in the country; but other lines that he absorbed were sucked dry and cast aside, after wiping out their stockholders' equities. The cordage trust collapsed, while the Plymouth firm which defied it, lived on. But often it did work. Standard Oil, consolidated through the ruthless ruining of competitors by John D. Rockefeller, paid an average annual dividend of 40 per cent in the 1890's. Neither the Cleveland nor the McKinley administrations had invoked the Sherman Antitrust Act against these practices.

Much the same thing was going on in England and in Europe, but not to such an extent. The American theater was so vast, and American resources so boundless, that financial or industrial consolidations found greater materials to work with. American financiers and industrialists were more sanguine and audacious than their transatlantic contemporaries; and the American government was decentralized, constantly changing in personnel, lacking organic strength and administrative traditions. The future of American democracy was imperilled by no foreign enemy, but gravely menaced by corporate greed and financial imbalance, when Roosevelt took from the bewildered Bryan Democrats the torch of reform.

Not that Roosevelt applied the torch as Bryan might have tried to do. His administration began circumspectly, as his party was the favorite of big business, and he had to deal with strong Republican majorities in House and Senate. He took over McKinley's able cabinet—John Hay in state, Elihu Root and John D. Long in war and navy—and persuaded Congress to set up a new department of commerce and labor whose first duty was to gather facts for enforcing the anti-trust laws.

Toward organized labor his attitude was ambiguous. In general he demanded a "square deal" for labor as for capital. He supported the unions in their demands for better wages and shorter hours, he enforced, for the first time in years, the eight-hour law for federal employees, and he persuaded Congress to pass progressive legislation for the District of Columbia. But he resented what he called the unions' "arrogant and domineering" attitude, and supported the open shop. In 1902 there came a test case—a strike in the anthracite coalfields of Pennsylvania, upon which the people of the Eastern states were then dependent for domestic fuel. Roosevelt summoned a conference of mine-owners and union leaders. The unions offered to arbitrate, the owners refused, and urged the President to break the strike with the army as Cleveland might have done. Roosevelt merely published the results of the conference, and public indignation then compelled the owners to submit to arbitration by a presidential commission. This episode not only strengthened his popularity, it taught him to use public opinion as a whip for recalcitrant congressmen no less than for captains of industry.

So lively, forthright, and "strenuous" (his favorite adjective) was Roosevelt in comparison with his predecessors that many wrongly assumed that he was radical and reckless. Impulsive indeed he was, but, unlike the stubborn Wilson, always willing to compromise with Congress on a half-measure in the hope of obtaining more later. In his first annual message (3 December 1901) he announced a policy with regard to trusts and corporations: enforce the existing laws, obtain full power for the federal government to inspect and regulate corporations engaged in interstate business. The first rested with him, the second with Congress.

Until he could obtain legislation strengthening the interstate commerce commission, this young President found plenty of work to do in cleansing his government of the unsavory garbage that had accumulated since the Civil War. Frauds in the post-office department were uncovered and punished. Upton Sinclair's *Jungle* drew popular as well as presidential attention to disgusting conditions in the Chicago stockyards. A government investigation substantiated his lurid charges, and Dr. H. W. Wiley, a chemist in the department of agriculture, proved by experiment the deleterious effect of preservatives and coloring matter in canned foods. The interests affected fought tooth and nail against "Socialist interference." ("It don't hurt the kids," said a candy manufacturer who diluted his coconut bars with shredded bone, "they like it!") But Congress strengthened the meat inspection service and passed the Pure Food and Drugs Act (1906), which gave consumers some protection.

Roosevelt's love of nature made conservation one of his leading policies. It was high time to put a brake on the greedy and wasteful destruction of natural resources that was encouraged by existing laws. The West, keen as ever for rapid "development," disliked this program. Taking advantage of an earlier law which his predecessors had largely ignored, Roosevelt set aside almost 150 million acres of unsold government timber land as national forest reserve, and on the suggestion of Senator La Follette withdrew from public entry some 85 million more in Alaska and the Northwest, pending a study of their mineral resources by the federal geological survey. The discovery of a gigantic system of fraud by which timber companies and ranchers were looting the public preserve enabled the President to obtain authority for transferring national forests to the department of agriculture, whose forest bureau under Gifford Pinchot administered them on scientific principles. Conservation was sweetened for the West by federal projects of irrigation. A new federal reclamation service, of which F. H. Newell was the guiding spirit, added a million and a quarter acres to the arable land of the United States by 1915. Five national parks were created in Roosevelt's administration, together with two national game preserves and fifty-one wild bird refuges.

In 1902 President Roosevelt decided to challenge another form of combination, the holding company, which was outside the scope of the decision on the Trans-Missouri case. His attorney general entered suit against the Northern Securities Company, a consolidation of Hill, Morgan, and Harriman interests that controlled four of the six transcontinental railways. By a narrow margin the Supreme Court decided for the government, thereby stopping a process of consolidation that Harriman proposed to continue until every important railway in the country came under his control.

In the realm of railway regulation, much was accomplished under Roosevelt. Rebates from published freight rates were forbidden by an Act of 1903, but more scandals and disclosures were required before government could obtain control over the rates themselves. The Hepburn Act of 1906 made regulation for the first time possible, and extended its field from interstate railways to steamship, express, and sleeping-car companies. This was further enlarged in 1910 by adding telephone and telegraph companies. The Hepburn Act authorized the interstate commerce commission, upon complaint, to determine and prescribe maximum rates. Owing to respect for the ancient principle of judicial review, appeals to federal courts had to be admitted; but the burden of proof was now on the carrier, not the commission. Railways were forced to disgorge most of the steamship lines and coal mines with which they had been wont to stifle competition. Most useful of all provisions in the Hepburn Act was the requirement placed on all common carriers to file annual accounts by a standardized system, and the power given the commission to settle disputes between railroads and shippers. Yet, as Senator La Follette contended, this law did not go far enough, since it gave the commission no power to discover the value of transportation properties or the cost of service, by which alone it could determine equitable rates.

A large part of the metropolitan press attacked Roosevelt's program as socialistic and subversive of the common weal, and himself as a reckless demagogue; the editor of the *New York Sun* even forbade the name Theodore Roosevelt to be mentioned in his journal. The President, however, was steadily growing in popularity. Merely by being himself—greeting professors and pugilists with equal warmth and discussing their hobbies with the same genuine interest, playing vigorous tennis, leading perspiring major generals on a cross-country chase, praising the good, the true, and the beautiful and denouncing the base, the false, and the ugly, preaching in hundreds of short addresses all over the country, with vigorous gesture and incisive utterance, the gospel of civic virtue and intelligent democracy—Roosevelt became an institution. Even the journals most opposed to his policies were forced to advertise them willy-nilly in their news columns. When the election of 1904 came round, the "Old Guard," as the more recalcitrant Republicans began to be called, would have preferred to nominate Mark Hanna; but "Uncle Mark" died, and Roosevelt was nominated by acclamation. The Democrats, unable to compete with Roosevelt for the progressive vote, and hoping to attract disgruntled reactionaries, put up a conservative, lackluster New York judge, Alton B. Parker. He carried nothing but the solid South. Roosevelt garnered 336 electoral votes to Parker's 140, and his popular vote, 56.4 of the total, was the largest in any presidential election between Monroe's and Harding's. The minority parties—Prohibition, Socialist, etc.—polled only 6 per cent of the total. Thus, on 4 March 1905, Roosevelt began a new term with a clear mandate for what he called "my policies."

3. *Trust and Railway Regulation to 1920*[1]

Roosevelt's attitude toward the trusts, originally one of "busting," underwent a significant change. By 1906, if not earlier, he had decided that big business was here to stay, that consolidation met a legitimate need, and that regulation rather than dissolution was the proper remedy for abuses. But he was unable to obtain congressional legislation in that direction. Bills initiated by his supporters in the House died in the Senate, which was dominated by four very able and conservative men: Nelson W. Aldrich of Rhode Island, Orville H. Platt of Connecticut, John C. Spooner of Wisconsin, and William B. Allison of Iowa. These and other like-minded men were known as the "Stand-patters," from an address of Mark Hanna in 1902 advising Ohio to "stand pat and continue Republican prosperity."

"I see no promise of any immediate and complete solution of all the problems we group together when we speak of the trust question," confessed Roosevelt at the beginning of his second administration. The authority he asked for giving the federal government plenary power to regulate all corporations engaged in interstate business was not forthcoming. Big business, however, was discredited by the panic of 1907 and by the discovery that the Sugar Trust had swindled the government out of $4 million in customs duties by false weights. Irritated by the continued attacks upon him as the destroyer of business and author of the panic, Roosevelt issued a pungent message attributing the panic "to the speculative folly and flagrant dishonesty of a few men of great wealth," describing the current malpractices, and concluding: "Our laws have failed in enforcing the performance of duty by the man of property toward the man who works for him, by the corporation toward the investor, the wage-earner and the general public."

Without fresh legislation, the President could do little more than direct prosecutions under the Sherman Act of 1890. Such prosecutions were infrequent, and in some instances successful; but they simply punished gross mischief after it had been committed, and did not always do that. Unscrambling the eggs proved to be a delicate and often impossible operation. Roosevelt was forced to conclude that the mere size and power of a combination did not render it illegal; there were "good trusts," such as the International Harvester Company, which traded fairly and passed economies on to consumers; and there

[1] Since there is no clean break in this movement prior to the Harding administration, I have carried it down to 1920, emphasizing the unity of the Progressive Era, through the Taft and Wilson administrations.

were bad trusts controlled by "malefactors of great wealth." This was about what the Supreme Court decided in the Standard Oil case of 1911: that only those acts or agreements of a monopolistic nature unduly or "unreasonably" affecting interstate commerce were to be construed as acts or agreements in restraint of trade, under the Anti-trust Act. This "rule of reason" became the guiding rule of decision, notably in the case of 1920 against the United States Steel Corporation, a consolidation from which the monopoly feature was absent. Subsequent prosecutions have been based not on mere size and power but on unfair and illegal use of power. President Wilson obtained from Congress the sort of legislation that Roosevelt demanded in vain; the Clayton Anti-trust Act proscribing certain specified trade practices, and the federal trade commission, an administrative agency clothed with police power to enforce the law.

As a result of the federal government's experience operating railways during the First World War, Congress in 1920 passed a comprehensive Transportation Act, placing the initiative and burden of rate-making on the interstate commerce commission, with a view to securing the stockholders a "fair return" on their property, and the public just freight and passenger rates. Further, the commission was given complete jurisdiction over the financing operations of the railways in order to protect the investing public and the stockholders. In 1917 even the Supreme Court went so far as to declare, "There can be nothing private or confidential in the activities and expenditures of a carrier engaged in interstate commerce." A Railway Labor Board was established to mediate disputes about wages, hours, and working conditions of railway employees, and to settle disputes. Under plenary government regulation the necessity for artificial competition had ended; and the railways, now chastened and impoverished by automobile and air competition, were encouraged to combine with a view to economical operation, as Roosevelt had recommended in his annual message of 1908.

The net result of this Progressive Era for trust and railway problems was to remove them from the political arena to administrative tribunals. Law and statesmanship cannot claim full credit for this happy consummation. With the immense growth of population and wealth since 1914, some trusts have cracked of their own weight, and unexpected competition has arisen both for them and the railroads. By 1920 the "utilities," as the electrical power companies are collectively called, were getting out of hand, and the automobile industry was about to eclipse iron and steel as the nation's biggest business.

4. The Big Stick in the Caribbean

"There is a homely adage which runs: 'Speak softly, and carry a big stick; you will go far.' " This remark, which Roosevelt used in more than one speech early in his administration, provided cartoonists with another Rooseveltian emblem to add to the toothy smile, thick glasses, and Rough Rider hat. What T.R. meant by the big stick was a strong navy; but the world feared it would be used to further political and economic "imperialism," even to conquer fresh territory in the Americas. Actually it was a very appropriate symbol for the methods that he used to get the Panama Canal started, to cure troubles in certain Caribbean republics, and to settle the Canadian-Alaskan boundary. Roosevelt accomplished much to modernize and build up the army and navy, but used them as a guarantee of peace. He evacuated Cuba, as McKinley had promised to do, intervened there once—as permitted by the Platt Amendment—to restore order, and evacuated again. He initiated self-government in the Philippines. He gave the Hague Tribunal its first case, the Pious Fund dispute with Mexico. He instructed the American delegation to the Second Hague Conference to work for restriction of naval armaments, returned to China America's share of the Boxer war indemnity, smoothed over a dangerous controversy with Japan, and refused to antagonize her by building a great military base in the Philippines, as the armed forces wanted. In advance of most Americans, he appreciated that the United States, having become one of the greater world powers, must gradually assume world responsibilities; and Woodrow Wilson's refusal to do so until pushed into it by events, aroused his undying wrath.

Roosevelt inherited from McKinley as secretary of state, John Hay, whose experience as ambassador in London made him eager to meet the new British policy of friendship halfway. And that friendship persisted, despite alarm over the "invasion" of England by American shoes, steel rails, and cotton goods, which was merely a dumping of surplus products during a glut in the home market. There is no truth in the oft-repeated story of a secret Anglo-American alliance, but there was in effect, during the entire Progressive Era, a good Anglo-American understanding. Downing Street, after a brief flirtation with Huerta in Mexico, gave Washington a free hand in the New World; and in return the state department refrained from any acts or expressions inimical to British interests, and supported British diplomacy in the Far East.

A first fruit of this understanding was a treaty clearing the way for the Panama Canal. New American responsibilities in the Caribbean and the Pacific made the speedy construction of an interoceanic canal vital. The Clayton-Bulwer Treaty stood in the way, but not the British government. The Hay-Pauncefote Treaty, signed 18 November 1901 and promptly ratified, superseded that controversial pact of 1850 and gave the United States a free hand to construct, operate, and protect an isthmian canal, subject only to the Suez Canal rules which forbade discrimination in tolls against foreign ships.

This canal had been talked about for at least four centuries, and two false starts had been made in the last century—by an American company that began one over the Nicaragua route but promptly went bankrupt; and by a French company, which did a good deal of work on the Panama route but quit in 1889 after spending $260 million and sacrificing hundreds of lives to tropical diseases. That company was now eager to recoup some of its losses by selling out to the United States. In the meantime a company financed in New York had bought a concession from Nicaragua, and by 1900 had as good as convinced Congress that Panama was an impossible "pest hole," and that the northern route was both healthy and practicable. Both companies employed expensive lobbyists in Washington. After an Isthmian Canal Commission, appointed by President McKinley and headed by Rear Admiral John G. Walker, had reported strongly in favor of the Panama route on the grounds of cost, length, and freedom from volcanic disturbances, Roosevelt became a vigorous advocate of that route. As a compromise, Congress on 28 June 1902 passed the Spooner Act. This authorized the President to acquire the French concession for $40 million if Colombia would cede a strip of land across the Isthmus of Panama "within a reasonable time," and upon reasonable terms; if not, the President was to open negotiations with Nicaragua, which Roosevelt at all costs wished to avoid. The Colombian chargé at Washington then signed a treaty granting the United States a hundred-year lease of a ten-mile-wide canal zone, for the lump sum of $10 million and an annual rental of $250,000.

The Colombian government rejected this treaty on 12 August 1903, in spite of a stiff warning from Hay that something unpleasant would happen if they did. One obstacle to ratification was the cession of sovereignty; the other was the $40 million coming to the French. That company had no right to sell its concession without the permission of Colombia, which naturally demanded a cut, especially as the company's charter was about to expire, leaving it with no assets but an incomplete ditch. Roosevelt and Hay never appreciated the reluctance of patriotic Colombians to cede sovereignty. They thought it was all a holdup.

Matters had reached an impasse by the summer of 1903, when Panama businessmen, agents of the French company, and United States Army officers, began to plan a way out—the secession of Panama from Colombia. Roosevelt and Hay officially kept clear, but the President's sympathy became notorious, and the French company's agent in Washington advised a revolutionary junta at Panama to proceed in assurance of American assistance. On 19 October three United States war vessels were ordered to the probable scene of hostilities. On 2 November their commanders were instructed to occupy the Panama railway if a revolution broke out, and to prevent Colombia from landing troops within fifty miles of the Isthmus. The secretary of state cabled the United States consul at Panama, 3 November 1903, "Uprising on Isthmus reported. Keep Department promptly and fully informed." The consul replied that afternoon, "No uprising yet. Reported will be in the night"; and, a few hours later, "Uprising occurred tonight 6; no bloodshed. Government will be organized tonight."

It was. The revolution came off according to schedule. The one Colombian gunboat on station steamed away after firing one shell which killed a sleeping Chinaman in Panama City. A landing party from U.S.S. *Nashville* confronted troops landed by the Colombian government to restore its authority; the city fire brigade formed a Panama army, a provisional government was set up, and on 4 November a declaration of Panamanian independence was read in the plaza. Two days later Secretary Hay recognized the Republic of Panama, which by cable appointed the French company's lobbyist its plenipotentiary at Washington. With him, on the 18th, Hay concluded a treaty by which Panama leased the Canal Zone "in perpetuity" to the United States and "to the entire exclusion of the exercise by Panama of any . . . sovereign rights, power or authority," for the same sum—$10 million down and $250,000 annual rent—that he had offered to Colombia.[1] Panama retained the titular sovereignty, as Colombia would have done; this was criticized in Congress but William Howard Taft, then secretary of war, said: "I agree that to the Anglo-Saxon mind a titular sovereignty is . . . a 'barren ideality,' but to the Spanish

---

[1] By a treaty of 1955 with Panama the annual rent has been raised to $1,930,000, and Presidents Eisenhower and Kennedy agreed to fly the Panama flag beside the American within the Canal Zone; but these concessions failed to satisfy Panama, whose president on 10 January 1964 demanded a revision of the treaty of 1903.

or Latin mind—poetic and sentimental, enjoying the intellectual refinements, and dwelling much on names and forms
—it is by no means unimportant." So important, in fact, that
Panamanians are now willing to risk their independence for
the right to fly their flag over the Canal Zone.

The Roosevelt administration defended its action by citing
Polk's treaty of 1846 with Colombia, by virtue of which the
United States was conceded the right to land forces on the
Isthmus to restore order and keep the Panama Railway running. Under that treaty, American forces had been landed
during several previous Panama revolutions. But to stretch
this right into an intervention to prevent Colombia from re-
covering her lawful authority, flew in the face of international
law and morality. And this has proved to be a source of infinite vexation. By exercising patience, Colombia, then recover-
ing from a devastating civil war, could have been persuaded
within a year to sign a reasonable treaty; and although only
Colombia was hit by the big stick, all Latin America trembled.
Subsequently, in the Wilson administration, the United States
paid Colombia $25 million as a balm; but the wound to her
pride rankles to this day, and the touchy little Republic of
Panama has proved to be a very difficult neighbor to the canal.
The United States is paying dear today for Roosevelt's im-
petuosity in 1903.

Roosevelt, over-eager to "make the dirt fly," made some ill-
considered appointments to the first Canal Zone commission,
who nullified the work of the engineer John F. Stevens, and
the dirt would have flown to little purpose had he not thrown
his weight in favor of a lock canal, as Stevens wanted, and
appointed Colonel George W. Goethals chief engineer and
autocrat of the Canal Zone in 1907. Open to commercial
traffic in August 1914 and formally completed six years later,
the Panama Canal was a triumph for American engineering
and organization. No less remarkable was the sanitary work
of Colonel William C. Gorgas (son of the Confederacy's chief
of ordnance), which the discoveries of Finlay and Reed in
Cuba made possible. His efforts and those of Goethals converted this area, including the cities of Panama and Colón,
earlier described by a British visitor as "a hideous dungheap of
moral and physical abomination," into a community of happy,
healthy workers, many of them imported Jamaican Negroes.

Elsewhere in the Caribbean Roosevelt wielded the big stick
energetically. A crisis arose over the question of European
intervention for the collection of the Venezuelan debt, in 1902.

Great Britain, Germany, and Italy established a blockade to force General Castro, the recalcitrant dictator, to come to terms. A showdown was avoided when Germany, discreetly pressured by Roosevelt, agreed to submit her claims to arbitration. The Hague Tribunal settled the dispute satisfactorily, scaling down the demands from some $40 million to $8 million and accepting a principle advanced by the Argentine publicist Luis Drago which outlawed the use of force for the collection of such claims. Roosevelt expressed a general satisfaction with this solution in a speech in which he said that England and Germany "kept with an honorable good faith" their disclaimer of violating the Monroe Doctrine.

Even more important was the President's announcement of the so-called "Roosevelt corollary" to the Monroe Doctrine. In his annual message of 1904 he declared, "Chronic wrongdoing, or an impotence which results in a general loosening of ties of civilized society . . . may force the United States, however reluctantly, in flagrant cases of such wrongdoing or impotence, to the exercise of an international police power." The first occasion for such "police" action arose when in 1904 the financial affairs of the Dominican Republic fell into such a desperate condition, owing to members of the government stealing the customs receipts, that she was threatened with foreclosure by European creditors. Roosevelt then announced as a "corollary" to the Monroe Doctrine that, since we could not permit European nations forcibly to collect debts in the Americas, we must ourselves assume the responsibility of seeing that "backward" states fulfilled their financial obligations. He placed an American receiver-general in charge of Dominican revenues, arranging to apply 55 per cent of customs receipts to the discharge of debts, and the rest to current expenses. This division proved to be ample for Dominican domestic needs (which the old system of stealing 90 per cent had not); but as one revolution followed another, the fiscal protectorate had to be transformed into a military occupation, and that lasted until 1924. A dangerous precedent had been established, and within a decade the United States found herself involved in domestic as well as foreign affairs of Haiti, Honduras, and Nicaragua. So burdensome did this responsibility become, so offensive to Latin America, and so utterly futile (since the evacuation by American armed forces was inevitably followed by a dictatorship or a revolution) that in 1930 the Roosevelt corollary to the Monroe Doctrine was officially repudiated by the department of state.

5. Roosevelt and World Politics

For the first time the United States had a President whom the rulers of Europe looked upon as one who understood them, and could play their game. Theodore, like his cousin Franklin, enjoyed world politics. His mediation in the Russo-Japanese War, undertaken on the suggestion of the Japanese and German emperors, is the best example. Secretary Hay being in his last illness, the President negotiated directly with premiers and crowned heads, brought the two belligerents together, and broke the deadlock from which the Treaty of Portsmouth (5 September 1905) emerged. The wisdom of that treaty is now questionable. It probably saved Japan from a beating, but her government and press persuaded the Japanese people that Roosevelt's "big stick" had done them out of vast territorial gains. And a few years later, in violation of the treaty, Japan annexed Korea. The treaty established Japan as overlord in Manchuria and enabled her to become the dominant naval power in the Pacific. Between 1941 and 1945 the United States paid heavily for the long-term results of Roosevelt's meddling, for which, ironically enough, he was awarded the Nobel peace prize.

Only thirteen months after the signing of the Treaty of Portsmouth, Japan and the United States were brought to the brink of war by segregation of the small number of Japanese children in San Francisco in a single school. These "infernal fools in California," as Roosevelt called them, aroused violent anti-American feeling in Japan; but the President, by inviting the mayor and school board to Washington and entertaining them in the White House, persuaded them to rescind their order. His part of the bargain was to conclude the "gentleman's agreement" of 1907, in which the Japanese foreign office promised to discourage further emigration to the United States. That was followed by the Root-Takahira agreement of 1908 in which both countries reaffirmed the Open Door to China and promised to maintain the status quo in the Pacific. To convince Japan that she better had, Roosevelt resorted to a typical gesture, a cruise of the United States fleet around the world in 1908–9. Sixteen post-Spanish war battleships, under the command of "Fighting Bob" Evans of Santiago fame, circled the globe, calling at four South American ports, Auckland, Sydney, and Yokohama, where the sailors had a most enthusiastic reception. This gesture convinced the world that the United States was no longer a power to be trifled with; and at the same time it showed the United States Navy, forced to fuel and provision in foreign ports, that a much better balanced fleet, with destroyer escorts and a supply train, would be required in case of war.

Roosevelt had established for his country a right that she did not yet want, to be consulted in world politics; but in the Moroccan crisis of 1905–6 he intervened to very good purpose. French extension of control over chaotic Morocco was challenged by Germany. At the suggestion of William II, the President urged France to summon a conference on the North African question, and the American representative at this Algerian Conference, Henry White, was partly responsible for a convention which kept the peace in Europe for several years. The Senate ratified this Convention reluctantly, with the qualifying amendment that it involved no departure "from the traditional American foreign policy which forbids participation by the United States in the settlement of political questions which are entirely European in their scope." President Taft, sensing the unpopularity of Roosevelt's action, refrained from participation in the second Moroccan crisis of 1911.

Roosevelt made a great mistake by announcing in 1904 that "under no circumstances" would he be a candidate for the presidency in 1908. Once having made this self-denying gesture, he lost hold over Congress during his last two years, since the members knew that they would soon have to look elsewhere for patronage and other favors. Yet his last two years of office were fruitful in reforms to which we have already alluded, such as the Hepburn Act and the Pure Food and Drug Act. And the annual presidential message of 1907 has become a classic text on the conservation of national resources.

Roosevelt himself, as more evidence accumulated of the arrogance and occasional rottenness of big business, and as a reaction against charges of subversion, socialism, treason, and insanity hurled against him by the metropolitan press, moved further to the left and even described himself as a "radical." There had been a brief panic in the stock market in 1903; and another—the worst between 1893 and 1929—occurred in 1907. Both were caused by overextension of credit, wild speculation in stocks, and inflexible currency, but Wall Street blamed it all on Roosevelt's "attacks on business." Actually, his administration stopped the 1907 landslide by pumping customs receipts into menaced New York banks, selling $150 million in bonds and notes to them on credit, and authorizing them to use these as collateral for issuing currency. This ended the drain on gold and provided money to move crops that fall. Nevertheless, the Eastern banking and business world continued to denounce Theodore in much the same terms as they later applied to his cousin Franklin. He had offended so many people that foreign observers thought he had lost his grip. But his hold on simple folk increased as time went on, and there is no doubt that he would have been triumphantly reelected in 1908 had he not tied his hands by the 1904 promise. He was still only 50 years old, and far better equipped to be President than any possible successor.

Roosevelt controlled the Republican convention of 1908 and put over the nomination on the first ballot of his favorite candidate, William H. Taft, secretary of war. The Democrats, having failed dismally with a conservative candidate in 1904, gave William J. Bryan his third presidential nomination. The effect was to stampede all disgruntled conservatives into the Taft camp; and although Bryan polled a million more votes than Parker had in 1904, he carried only the solid South and Nebraska, Colorado, Nevada, and Oklahoma.

Never did a presidential administration afford so much fun to press and public as "Teddy's." No President prior to Kennedy showed such vitality. There was hardly a day that the White House, without benefit of a publicity staff or a press conference, did not make front-page news; for Roosevelt was constantly making pronouncements on things that were not his particular concern. Embarrassing to him was the publication of his letters to "Dear Maria" (Mrs. Bellamy) Storer, wife of the American ambassador to Italy, urging her to call on the Pope and get a red hat for Archbishop Ireland. As an example of Roosevelt's quiet benevolence and good taste, Edwin Arlington Robinson, then living in a New York hall bedroom on $12 a week, was astonished one morning in 1905 to receive a letter from the White House warmly appreciating his first book of poems, and offering him a minor post in the customs house to give him security.

Young Lieutenant Douglas MacArthur, Roosevelt's aide in 1906, asked him to what he attributed his extraordinary popularity with the masses. To which he replied, "To put into words what is in their hearts and minds but not their mouths." That was it. Lincoln had the same gift.

To William H. Taft on 4 March 1909 Theodore Roosevelt handed over a government that had grown rapidly in prestige and power during the last eight years. The entire civil service had been stimulated by Roosevelt's vitality, no less than by knowledge that efficiency and intelligence would be recognized and rewarded. The whole tone and temper of government had changed for the better, an educated and public-spirited elite had again been attracted to public life, and popular interest in public affairs had never been more keen or intelligent. Yet in one respect Roosevelt failed as a leader. He inspired loyalty to himself rather than to progressive policies; he neglected, while he still possessed the power of patronage, to build up a progressive nucleus within the Republican party. The Old Guard drew a sigh of relief when Roosevelt, wishing to avoid embarrassing President Taft, embarked on a big-game hunting expedition in Africa.

VI

Taft and Wilson

1909-1917

1. *Taft Takes Over*

"BIG BILL" TAFT—he rose five feet 10½ inches and weighed 300 pounds when in the White House—was one of the most good-humored, lovable men ever elected President of the United States, and one of the unhappiest in that office. Of judicial, not political temper, he had held no elective office excepting an Ohio judgeship prior to 1909, and had set his sights on becoming a justice of the Supreme Court, which eventually he attained. An ambitious wife and Theodore Roosevelt, who trusted Taft to continue "my policies," thrust him, half appreciative and half apprehensive, into the political arena. But the results of the election were gratifying. Taft "ran ahead of his ticket" and polled a few more votes than Roosevelt had in 1904, whilst Bryan gathered fewer than on his previous two tries, carrying only the solid South and some of the old Populist states. Taft apparently had a mandate to go forward with Roosevelt progressivism.

In the measure that he failed, circumstances and personality were about equally responsible. Yet it cannot fairly be said that he did fail. His image before the American people in 1912, when he finished a bad third in a three-cornered contest,

154

was that of an amiable though stupid reactionary who had "betrayed" the Progressive cause. After fifty years have elapsed we can state with some confidence that this image was false. It would be more nearly correct to say that the Progressives, represented by Theodore Roosevelt, betrayed him. But Taft did lack the energy that a President must have to be successful; he hated the drudgery of the office, and was inept in dealing with Congress. Nevertheless, more of the Roosevelt program was enacted in the Taft administration than in the Roosevelt administration!

President Taft followed the right instinct in choosing his own cabinet instead of taking over Roosevelt's; but his choices did not include a single Progressive until 1911, when he appointed secretary of war young Henry L. Stimson, who had just been defeated for governor of New York.

His first political action was to try to unseat, as speaker of the House, "Uncle Joe" Cannon of Illinois, a vulgar blatherskite who had become just such a parliamentary "czar" as the late Speaker Reed. Under existing House rules the speaker chose the members of every committee including the rules committee which then—as in 1964—was the bottleneck through which every bill had to pass before reaching the floor. A group of liberal Republican congressmen led by George W. Norris of Nebraska proposed to defeat Cannon for the speakership when Congress convened, in the hope of changing the rules and giving new legislation a chance. Taft openly supported them while President-elect; then let them down when Senator Aldrich, Henry C. Payne (chairman of the ways and means committee), and Cannon himself called on the President five days after his inauguration and promised to support the tariff revision that he dearly wanted, if he would "call off his dogs" that were baiting Cannon. "Uncle Joe" was re-elected speaker, and Taft got the Payne-Aldrich tariff which fell far short of what he wanted. But in 1911 Progressive Republicans combined with Democrats to curb the speaker's power; and next year, after the Democratic victory in congressional elections, Champ Clark of Missouri replaced Cannon.

Roosevelt had cannily refused to burn his fingers on tariff revision, although he believed, as did almost all progressives, that the high protective schedules of the Dingley tariff of 1897 were the "nursing mothers of monopoly." Taft made tariff reduction his first objective, and promptly called a special session of Congress to do it. The usual thing happened. Lobbyists deprecated loss of protection against European "pauper labor," consumers were not represented, and the Aldrich Senate bill and Payne House bill, when brought together in a conference

committee, provided higher rates than the 1897 act which the
Republicans had promised to revise downward. At that point
the President put his foot down and obtained some concessions
which persuaded him to sign the bill. A notoriously high duty
on gloves, inserted to please a glove manufacturer who was a
friend of Cannon, was struck out; a maximum-minimum principle, to help bargaining with other countries, was inserted for
the first time in any American tariff act, and free trade with
the Philippines, which Taft as a former governor-general
ardently wanted in justice to the Filipinos, was inserted. Hides,
oil, and other raw materials were put on the free list, in addition to the "curling stones, false teeth, nux vomica, bird seed,
and silk-worm eggs" which "Mr. Dooley" declared to be now
"within th' reach iv all." Progressives in both houses, such as
Norris, Beveridge and La Follette, who had fought vigorously
against the bill, expected Taft to veto it, and thought they had
enough votes to sustain his veto; but to their dismay he not
only signed the Payne-Aldrich compromise but declared it to
be "the best tariff bill that the Republican party ever passed."
In retrospect, the Payne-Aldrich tariff, while not so good as its
supporters claimed, was not nearly so bad as its opponents
insisted. It was a slight revision, but in the right direction,
downward.

Taft next alienated the Progressives' conservationist wing
in the Ballinger-Pinchot controversy of 1909. This long and
complicated brawl overshadowed more important issues in the
public eye. The essence of it is that Gifford Pinchot, a crusader for conservation of natural resources, Roosevelt's close
friend and chief forester, accused Richard A. Ballinger, secretary of the interior, of corruptly alienating part of the national
domain to a Morgan-Guggenheim syndicate. President Taft,
instead of handling the business himself, tossed it to a special
committee of Congress, which vindicated Ballinger. But
Pinchot won in the court of public opinion, largely owing to
an effective presentation of his case by Louis D. Brandeis.
After half a century has elapsed, it seems that Pinchot went off
half-cock and that Ballinger was innocent of the charges; but
the affair was played up for far more than it was worth by the
"muckraker" periodicals, and drove a wedge between President and ex-President. Taft actually did as much or more than
Roosevelt for conservation. He was the first to reserve federal
lands where oil had been found, including Teapot Dome which
President Harding tried to give away. He asked for and obtained from Congress the authority to reserve coal lands
which Roosevelt had reserved without specific authority, and

set up a bureau of mines as guardian of the nation's mineral resources. Pinchot was replaced by the head of the Yale school of forestry, and his policy was continued by the purchase, in 1911, of great timbered tracts in the Appalachians.

The President's ineptitude and alienation of progressive elements should not blind us to his achievements. During his term the Mann-Elkins Act of 1910 strengthened the interstate commerce commission by empowering it to suspend rate increases until and unless the reasonableness thereof were ascertained, and created a new commerce court to hear appeals from the commission. The long overdue postal savings bank and parcel post wanted by the people but opposed by banks and express companies, were provided by Congress. The merit system was expanded by the addition of more postmasters to the civil service list. New Mexico and Arizona, last of the continental territories save Alaska, became the 47th and 48th states of the Union; Alaska was organized as a territory. Oklahoma, the 46th state, had been admitted under Roosevelt. Approximately twice as many prosecutions for violation of the Sherman Act were instituted during Taft's four years in office as during Roosevelt's seven. Significant of the rapidly expanding envelope of law were two amendments of the Federal Constitution, both of which were promoted by Taft. The income tax Amendment XVI, and Amendment XVII transferring the election of United States Senators from state legislatures to the people, were adopted by Congress in 1909 and 1912 respectively and ratified the following year.

Since Taft was temperamentally unable to take the strong lead that Roosevelt had in reform legislation, he got little credit for these achievements. The Republicans lost the congressional elections of 1910. The basic cause of this upset was a sharp rise in the cost of living owing (the economists tell us) to a world shortage of gold, without a corresponding rise in wages. "Real" wages, in fact, had been stationary or declining since the turn of the century. The retail cost of basic foods consumed by workingmen rose 30 per cent in 1900–1910, while real wages in industry rose but a fraction of one per cent. The Democrats, attributing a world-wide phenomenon to the Payne-Aldrich tariff, made hay in these elections, won a majority in the House for the first time since 1892, and narrowed the Republican majority in the Senate. Democratic governors were elected in several Eastern states, and in New Jersey Dr. Woodrow Wilson, president of Princeton University, took his first step toward a larger presidency.

2. Canada and the Caribbean

We left the Dominion of Canada prosperous and developing a sense of nationality under Sir Wilfrid Laurier, the liberal premier. In the decade 1893–1903, three disputes between Canada and the United States were settled by arbitration. The first was over seal fisheries in the Bering Sea; the second on the perennial question of American fishermen's rights on the coast of Newfoundland. Both arbitral decisions broadly upheld the Canadian case. But the third, over the Alaska boundary, was decided against Canada, with unfortunate results.

Just where the Alaskan "panhandle" ended and British Columbia began was disputed. The boundary had been vaguely described in the Anglo-Russian treaty of 1825. Nobody bothered much about it until 1898 when a gold strike in the Yukon made Canada insistent on a port of entry to her Yukon Territory through the Lynn Canal, on which the small American settlement of Skagway was situated. The Canadians insisted on a construction of the treaty which would have left Skagway well within their borders; the Americans demanded a line some hundred miles eastward. President Roosevelt considered the Canadian case "trumped up" and in 1903 consented to its settlement by an Anglo-American tribunal, three "impartial jurists" to each side; but he truculently informed the British government, through the curious medium of Justice Holmes, that if the board did not vote his way he would secure the boundary by armed force. The Senate only consented to the arbitration after receiving word from the White House that the three "impartial jurists" on our side would be Elihu Root, a former senator from the State of Washington, and Senator Lodge, at that time a notorious anglophobe. On the other side were two leading Canadians and Lord Alverstone, Lord Chief Justice of England.

This brandishing of the "big stick" worked. Although it has never been proved, there is strong suspicion that Alverstone was ordered by the British government to vote with the Americans, as the price of continued Anglo-American friendship in the face of rising German naval power. At any rate, that is substantially what Alverstone did. The compromise line, determined by a four-to-two vote, left Skagway inside Alaska but gave Canada the heads of the Lynn, Portland, and other inlets, and considerable territory claimed by the United States. Compromise though it was, the decision aroused violent resentment in Canada: England had let her down, and truckled to the Yankees. Like many other things in that era, reality was not so bad as appearance. Most Canadian historians now agree that their country argued a very poor case, and that the compromise did her no injury. But the controversy left a bitter taste and was partly responsible for the electorate spitting out with contempt the proffered American sugarplum of reciprocity.

President Taft in 1910 initiated a renewal of tariff reciprocity with Canada, the first since 1867, partly to ameliorate the Payne-Aldrich tariff, partly out of sheer friendliness; he owned a summer estate at Murray Bay, P.Q., and knew many leading Canadians intimately. Laurier, who had recently obtained for Canada the right to conclude her own tariff agreements, accepted the invitation, hoping thus to lower the Canadian tariff and open new markets in the United States. The Democratic majority in Congress passed a reciprocity bill which, to be valid, had to be matched by a similar bill in the Canadian parliament. For a country of 92 million population to offer practically free trade in farm, forest, and fish products to a country of 7.2 million was unprecedented, and much to the smaller country's advantage; but the "infant industries" of Canada, basking under protection, and the Canadian Pacific Railway, opposed the measure violently. Speaker Champ Clark helped whip up Canadian sentiment against it by a stupid speech in which he predicted that reciprocity would be the prelude to planting the Stars and Stripes over "every foot" of North America; and an obscure congressman proposed that Taft be instructed to open negotiations with Great Britain for the annexation of Canada. There, the "King and Country" argument was freely employed, and one of Rudyard Kipling's worst poems, "Our Lady of the Snows," was widely circulated to rebuke the impudent Yankees.

That is exactly what the Lady of the Snows did. Sir Wilfrid had to appeal to the country in a general election in September 1911. His French following, led by Henri Bourassa the eloquent Quebec nationalist, deserted the Liberal banner, and the Conservatives won 133 seats to the Liberals' 86. The *Boston Herald* thus announced the result: "Snow Lady Hits Uncle Sam in the Stomach. Grains and Foodstuffs Rise Sharply at All American Supply Centers."

Robert Laird Borden, a Nova Scotian of Scot and Loyalist ancestry and a dour, rugged personality, now succeeded suave Laurier as prime minister of the Dominion. During Sir Wilfrid's fifteen years' rule, his dream of making Canada a nation before the world had come measurably nearer fulfillment, but his hope for internal harmony had been shattered. With no statesman of his caliber to lead them, the French of Quebec became more unreasonable.

One month before "Snow Lady" handed it to Uncle Sam, President Taft submitted to the Senate two important treaties with Great Britain and France. World peace was very close to his heart, and the best method of securing it, he believed, was by judicial procedure. Hence these treaties provided for arbitration at the Hague or elsewhere of all disputes "justiciable in their nature," including those involving territory and "national honor." These treaties were received with acclamation by most of the American press as well as by Andrew Carnegie and the peace societies. But the Irish-American and German-American press, seeing their last chance of a third war with England disappearing, and encouraged by Roosevelt, led a virulent campaign against the British treaty. Both treaties were so emasculated by amendments in the Senate that the President sadly withdrew them.

The Senate was better advised in rejecting certain treaties with Caribbean countries, but the Taft administration managed to do what it wanted in that region without treaties. Philander C. Knox, secretary of state, was a corporation lawyer who cherished an odd sort of idealism to the effect that obtaining loans for the turbulent Central American republics, or pumping investment capital into them, would stabilize their governments, and cure their poverty. Knox (wrote his predecessor Root) was "antipathetic to all Spanish-American modes of thought and feeling"—a description which, unfortunately, fits many of his successors in the state department. This was illustrated by his handling of volcanic Nicaragua, where a revolution broke out against dictator Zelaya in 1909. Adolfo Díaz, who emerged triumphant (and who, miraculously, lived for 54 more years), was refused recognition until he had accepted an American bankers' loan to refund the foreign debt, and consented to American supervision of the Nicaraguan customs service. This concession occasioned, if it did not cause, an uprising against Díaz in 1912. In that civil war the intervention of about a thousand United States marines under Major Smedley D. Butler was decisive; after they had routed the rebels in a pitched battle at Coyotepe (4 October 1912), the rebellion collapsed.

Taft, in his annual message of 1912, defended this so-called "dollar diplomacy." He had gladly supported American bankers in helping "the financial rehabilitation of such countries," which needed only "a measure of stability and the means of financial regeneration to enter upon an era of peace and prosperity." Democrats and Progressives alike raised a furor against "dollar diplomacy," although it differed not from Roosevelt's with the Dominican Republic. And President Wilson continued much the same policy, even after it had been demonstrated that dollars and marines could not cure Caribbean instability.

President Taft was equally unhappy in his relations with Mexico, where the revolution against Porfirio Díaz, dictator for thirty-five years following the death of Juárez, broke out on 20 November 1910. Díaz had given his country order at the expense of every sort of liberty. The national domain of 135 million acres was cut up into latifundia, or used to augment the already swollen estates of fewer than a thousand great land owners, the *haciendados*. Díaz expropriated and allotted to his favorites the communal lands of the Indian villages, and the newcomers exacted free labor from landless peons by keeping them in perpetual debt for food and supplies. Education remained in the hands of the Catholic church. Generous concessions were given to foreign mining and other interests. The Mexican government was more autocratic than Czarist Russia, the ruling class more concentrated and powerful, the condition of the people worse. Taft, and Republicans generally, regarded Díaz as a great statesman, not only because he preserved order, but "for the reason" (wrote the President to Mrs. Taft) "that we have two billions American capital in Mexico that will be greatly endangered if Díaz were to die."

This revolution which, after many vicissitudes, regenerated Mexico, obtained slight sympathy in Washington, and no support. Francisco I. Madero, a gentle, dreamy liberal who succeeded Díaz, was unable to keep order or satisfy the land-hungry peons. In February 1913 a counter-revolution by half the army and most of the *haciendados* cornered Madero in Mexico City. At that juncture, a super-gangster, General Victoriano Huerta, won the support of Henry Lane Wilson the professional diplomat whom Taft had appointed ambassador to Mexico, and who with singular lack of judgment called Madero "a man of disordered intellect . . . comparable to a Nero." Wilson helped Huerta engineer a coup d'état against Madero and presented him to the diplomatic corps as the next president of Mexico. Huerta's henchmen promptly murdered both Madero and the vice president. It remained for Woodrow Wilson to try to undo what Henry Lane Wilson had done.

3. Insurgents and the Election of 1912

Theodore Roosevelt, after enjoying good hunting in Africa and a triumphal progress through Europe, returned to New York in June 1910. Greeted with hysterical enthusiasm, he

settled down at Sagamore Hill to pursue his many nonpolitical
interests. The weekly *Outlook,* of which he became associate
editor, afforded him an organ; but the role of sage was uncon-
genial to "Teddy," and the public would not be denied seeing
and hearing him. Before the summer was over, he was making
public addresses in the West, indicating unmistakably that
shooting lions and dining with crowned heads had not dulled
his fighting edge for reform. His ideas, clarified and systematized as the "New Nationalism," included not merely his former policies of honesty in government, regulation of big business and conservation of natural resources, but the relatively
new conception of social justice—the reconstruction of society
by political action. This principle involved vigorous criticism
of recent decisions of the Supreme Court as largely reconsti-
tuted by Taft (only Justices Holmes and Day remained of
Roosevelt's appointees), which had nullified social legislation
in the states. In his Osawatomie speech of 31 August 1910
Roosevelt announced, "I stand for the square deal . . . I mean
not merely that I stand for fair play under the present rules of
the game, but . . . for having those rules changed so as to
work for a more substantial equality of opportunity and of
reward for equally good service. . . . We must drive special
interests out of politics."

Conservative Republicans shuddered and President Taft
worried. "I have had a hard time," he wrote to T.R. in May
1910. "I have been conscientiously trying to carry out your
policies." But the two old friends were being pulled apart. Insurgents and displaced progressives like Pinchot were continually flattering Roosevelt and entreating him to save the country
in 1912, on the assumption that Taft had surrendered to the
Old Guard.

After the Democratic victories of 1910 and the Republicans'
loss of the House, it was clear that Taft could not succeed
himself. Early in 1911 Senator La Follette, spokesman for the
"insurgents," organized a National Progressive Republican
League to liberalize the Republican party. Upon obtaining
what he thought to be Roosevelt's promise not to run again,
La Follette became a candidate for the Republican nomination.
But he was unable to build up much strength outside the
Mississippi valley, and when addressing a convention of nation-wide newspaper men early in 1912 he collapsed and
babbled incoherently. This incident lost La Follette an influ-
ential part of his following. Insurgents who preferred Roosevelt anyway now flocked to their old leader, who on 21 February announced, "My hat is in the ring." Bored by inactivity,

Roosevelt was easily persuaded that he was indispensable to carry on progressive policies. His public utterances became increasingly radical. He urged that democracy be given an economic as well as a political connotation, declared that the rich man "holds his wealth subject to the general right of the community to regulate its business use as the public welfare requires," and that the police power of the state should be broadened to embrace all necessary forms of regulation. On the political side he advocated not only the initiative and the referendum, but the recall of judicial decisions; since, as his friend Brooks Adams pointed out, the Supreme Court had arrogated the powers of a third legislative chamber to quash reform legislation. Roosevelt's radicalism alienated thousands of Republican voters and cost him the support of friends such as Lodge, Knox, Root, and Stimson.

La Follette stayed in the fight, and the three-cornered contest for the Republican nomination became unseemly and bitter. Taft denounced Roosevelt for stirring up class hatred; Roosevelt accused Taft of biting the hand that fed him; La Follette described the ex-President as a conceited playboy; and many other things were said that would better have been left unsaid. Roosevelt knew that he could not win against the regular party organization, but wherever the law permitted he entered presidential preference primaries in the hope that a display of popularity might frighten the Old Guard. Thirteen states chose delegates through popular primaries, and in these Roosevelt obtained 278 delegates, Taft 46, and La Follette 36. Roosevelt had an overwhelming support by the rank and file, but the bosses were for Taft, and the Republican "rotten boroughs" in the South returned a solid block of Taft delegates who represented little more than federal office-holders. Credentials of some 200 delegates were in dispute. The conservatives, by electing Elihu Root temporary chairman, obtained control of the convention machinery and awarded almost every contested seat to a Taft man. On the ground that he had been robbed, Roosevelt instructed his friends to walk out, and Taft was easily renominated. Old-timers thought of the split Democratic convention of 1860, and shuddered.

Roosevelt and his followers at once took steps to found a new party. On 5 August 1912 the first Progressive party convention met at Chicago amid scenes of febrile enthusiasm. "We stand at Armageddon, and we battle for the Lord!" announced Roosevelt to enraptured followers, who paraded around the convention hall singing "Onward, Christian Soldiers" and other stirring melodies. Another remark of the

beloved leader, "I am feeling like a bull moose," gave the new
party an appropriate symbol, beside the Republican elephant
and the Democratic donkey.

Denial of the nomination to Roosevelt, and the subsequent
formation of the Bull Moose party, brief though that party's
life proved to be, were crucial in political history. They
squeezed liberal and progressive elements out of the "Grand
Old Party" and gave the Democrats their first real opportunity
since the Civil War.

The Progressive party hoped to break the solid South; but
Roosevelt had entertained Booker Washington at dinner at
the White House, and the South had a candidate of her own.
This was Woodrow Wilson, born in Staunton, Virginia, in
1856, a year earlier than Taft, two years earlier than Roosevelt. Son and grandson of Presbyterian ministers, Wilson followed a quiet academic career until 1902, when he became
president of Princeton University. While Roosevelt fought
political privilege in the nation, Wilson contended with social
privilege at Princeton. His attempts to break up the club system and the graduate school ran afoul of wealthy alumni and
foundered. Wilson then stepped off the academic vessel.

Politics in that era was considered closed to professors,
even to those with a national reputation for political literature
such as Wilson. But it so happened that in 1910 the Democrats of New Jersey wished to achieve respectability with a
new sort of candidate. At the suggestion of George Harvey of
Harper's Weekly, the bosses nominated Wilson and the people
elected him governor. Chosen for the job of window dressing,
Wilson proceeded to clean up the shop. New Jersey gasped,
Harvey dropped him as an ingrate, but a silent gentleman
from Texas named Edward M. House took him up, and
Wilson became a leading candidate for the presidential nomination in 1912.

The Democratic party had changed singularly little since
the Civil War. It was composed of a progressive Western wing
represented by Bryan; Irish-Americans of the big Eastern cities
and Chicago and recently naturalized immigrants who followed the Irish bosses; the solid South, including the Snopses,
the rednecks, and almost every white man in the late Confederacy; and multimillionaire William Randolph Hearst with
his nation-wide string of yellow journals. Only tradition and
the hope of victory held these curiously incongruous elements
together, but the issues of liquor and religion that split the
party in 1924 had not arisen, and Southerners sympathized
with rebels against Wall Street. In only one election since the

Civil War (1904) had the party polled less than 43 per cent of the total vote cast for president; but it wanted leadership. Bryan had thrice failed, and the majority leaders in Congress were elderly and timid. When the Democratic national convention met in June 1912, the majority were pledged for Champ Clark of Missouri, candidate of Tammany Hall and of Hearst. Congressman Oscar W. Underwood of Alabama was candidate of the "Bourbons," as the Democratic Old Guard was called; Governor Wilson represented the progressive wing. William Jennings Bryan, still a power in his party, required all his art and eloquence to "drive the money-changers from the temple" and obtain the nomination of Woodrow Wilson on the forty-sixth ballot.

The presidential election then became a three-cornered contest between Taft, Roosevelt, and Wilson; but really between the two last as rival bidders for the popular feeling against privilege. It was a year of social unrest. A new syndicalist movement, the Industrial Workers of the World, which had organized the migratory harvest hands of the West, was now contesting the skilled-worker field with the American Federation of Labor. The I.W.W. took charge of a great strike in the polyglot textile city of Lawrence, Massachusetts, and displayed to the shocked middle class red banners with godless mottoes. Incidentally, the Lawrence strike brought out the fact that the woolen industry, which enjoyed the highest protection under the Payne-Aldrich tariff, was paying starvation wages; male operatives earned a maximum of $10 for a 54-hour week. Thus the campaign was fought with revolution looming as an alternative to reform; and in that year the Socialist party under Eugene V. Debs polled 6 per cent of the total vote, highest in their history.

Taft and the Republicans accepted the ultra-conservative role now thrust upon them, preaching checks and balances and protection of minorities as the essence of freedom. There was little to choose between the Democratic and Progressive platforms. The latter, as Roosevelt said, "represented the first effort on a large scale to translate abstract formulas of economic and social justice into concrete American nationalism." With the Roosevelt doctrine of regulation the Democrats substantially agreed; Wilson's "New Freedom" was composed of the same ingredients as Roosevelt's "New Nationalism." Their method of campaigning, however, had no more in common than their personalities. Roosevelt, with biblical imagery and a voice like a shrilling fife, stirred men to wrath, to combat, and to antique virtue; Wilson, serene and confident, lifted men

out of themselves by phrases that sang in their hearts, to a
vision of a better world. It was the Old Testament against the
New.

The writer, who cast his first presidential ballot that year,
asked a middle-aged gentleman at the polls how to vote: "Vote
for Roosevelt, pray for Taft, but bet on Wilson!" was the reply.
Wilson received only 42 per cent of the popular vote but won
an overwhelming majority in the electoral college. Roosevelt
carried California, Michigan, South Dakota, Washington,
Minnesota, and Pennsylvania. Taft, with 23 per cent of the
vote, carried only Utah and Vermont. Roosevelt's percentage
of the vote was 27, and if that could have been added to the
President's, Taft would have won.

A popular cartoon the morning after depicted a cocked-
hatted Federalist, a log-cabin Whig, assorted Anti-Masons,
Greenbackers, and the like, welcoming a limping elephant to
"The Home for Old Parties." Ardent Progressives thought
back to 1856 and ahead to 1916; Wilson would be just another
bland Buchanan. But Roosevelt told a friend, "We are beaten.
You can't hold a party like the Progressives together. . . .
There are no loaves and fishes." And how right he was! The
Old Guard neither died nor surrendered. The Republicans
obtained 127 members in the House as against 18 Progressives; and nothing was left but deflated enthusiasm and a
defeated candidate to keep the Bull Moose alive. Many good
men, such as Senator Albert J. Beveridge of Indiana, were lost
to politics; but in his case at least the country benefited, because Beveridge concentrated on his classic biography of Chief
Justice Marshall. President Taft became professor of constitutional law at Yale, and later attained his heart's desire, chief
justiceship of the Supreme Court.

Woodrow Wilson, instead of playing the role of Buchanan,
welded his party into a fit instrument of his purpose "to square
every process of our national life again with the standards we
so proudly set up at the beginning and have always carried
at our hearts." Thus, the election of 1912 began an era in
American political history that long endured, one in which the
Democratic party replaced the Republican as the party of new
ideas and positive leadership. After stand-patters had ousted
progressives from the Republican party's organization, Wilson
took them over and "stole the Bull Moose's thunder." Theodore Roosevelt's twin principles of social justice at home and
vigorous leadership abroad have been forwarded by every
Democratic president; whilst Republican presidents and defeated Republican presidential candidates have tended to check
reform at home and retire to isolation in foreign policy.

4. The First Wilson Administration

Many Americans like myself who were born in the late nineteenth century and brought up in the early twentieth, look upon the years prior to 1914 as a golden age of the Republic. In part, this feeling was due to our youth; in part to the fact that the great middle class could command goods and services that are now beyond their reach. But there was also a euphoria in the air, peace among the nations, and a feeling that justice and prosperity for all was attainable through good will and progressive legislation. Even pessimistic Henry Adams wrote in his *Education* that, owing to Roosevelt's successful efforts to end the Russo-Japanese War, "for the first time in 1500 years a true Roman *Pax* was in sight."

Yet few people expected more than a respectable presidency. Wilson lacked the common touch, and loved humanity in the abstract rather than people in particular. He was fully as "red-blooded" as Roosevelt; had played football at Princeton and helped coach the team when a professor. But he could not mingle with crowds to advantage or talk naturally with horse wranglers and prizefighters. Through eight years of office he was always aloof and often alone. "Wilson is clean, strong, high-minded and cold-blooded," wrote warm-hearted Franklin K. Lane who became his secretary of the interior. Wilson's warm affections embraced only family and a few friends; his puckish humor, often at his own expense, was shown only to intimates. He was very stubborn and prone to take refuge from facts in generalities. Loving the quiet places of life and preferring the slow ways of persuasion to the quick ones of force, his misfortune was to be President in an era of fierce international strife and internal discord.

Colonel House, who had earned his honorary military title by unofficially advising a governor of Texas, now became the President's closest friend and adviser. The Colonel was no "Texas type" but a well traveled and cosmopolitan gentleman of independent means who was interested in getting things done in a progressive direction. He had published anonymously a utopian novel, *Philip Dru, Administrator,* in which one may find much of the New Freedom, and the New Deal too. House helped the President to select his cabinet. Bryan as secretary of state, which insured the support of his immense following, appeared to be a master-stroke until there was work for Bryan to do. William G. McAdoo, the President's campaign manager and future son-in-law, became secretary of the treasury. Lindley M. Garrison, a New Jersey judge whom Wilson appointed secretary of war, was dropped

when war became imminent. Lane, Canadian by birth and
Californian by residence, proved a good secretary of the interior to reconcile the Far West with conservation. The others
were nonentities. The cabinet was not a strong group. The
majority were Southerners, as by the rule of seniority were
most of the chairmen of House and Senate committees. New
England, for the first time since Jackson's administration, was
not represented, although Massachusetts, for the first time
since Jefferson, had voted with Virginia.

Wilson's inaugural address was a stirring plea for action on
the tariff, conservation, banking, and regulation of "the larger
economic interests of the nation," in the interest of "humanity." It concluded: "Men's hearts wait upon us; men's lives
hang in the balance. . . . I summon all honest men, all patriotic, all forward-looking men, to my side. God helping me, I
will not fail them, if they will counsel and sustain me."

When Congress met on 7 April 1913, President Wilson revived a practice abandoned by Jefferson, of addressing both
houses in person. A slight thing in itself, this act caught popular approval. It restored the President's initiative in law-mak-
ing and established good relations between "the two ends of
Pennsylvania Avenue." For Wilson's power over men left him
when he stepped off the rostrum; unlike Roosevelt, he could
not persuade or browbeat a recalcitrant congressman in private
conversation. But 114 out of 290 Democratic members of the
House were there for the first time, and readily followed him.

Congress had been summoned to a special session to revise
the tariff. The resulting Underwood tariff of 3 October 1913
was the lowest since the Civil War. Duties were reduced on
958 items and more than a hundred were placed on the free
list. Appended to the Underwood tariff bill was a graduated
federal tax on incomes above $3000, constitutional since
Amendment XVI (1913) overrode the earlier Supreme Court
decision that an income tax was unconstitutional. Despite the
jeremiads of business, the new tariff worked admirably during
the few years of peace in which it could be tested, and the
income tax brought not only abundant revenue but a mass of
statistical information about the distribution of the national
wealth that was of immense value to lawmakers of the future.
And his victory in the matter of the tariff clinched the President's control of Congress.

The greatest measure of Wilson's first year was the Federal
Reserve Act of 23 December 1913, which reconstructed the
national banking and currency system. The existing system,
inelastic and obsolete, had contributed largely to the panic of
1907. A great central bank would have been the ideal substi-

tute; but the tradition of Jackson's contest with the B.U.S. was still strong in the Democratic party, and federal investigation had uncovered the existence of a so-called "money trust" controlled by a handful of New York and Boston financiers. By the Federal Reserve Act, drafted by Carter Glass of Virginia, the country was divided into twelve districts, each with a federal reserve bank which was a private corporation empowered to issue banknotes against commercial paper and other liquid assets. The Federal Reserve Board, appointed by the President and connected with the treasury department, controls the rate of discount and superintends the twelve federal reserve banks, which in turn are articulated with such local banks as wish to become members of the system. That the Democratic party, with its rural constituencies, could have passed the most important piece of financial legislation since Hamilton's day was no less remarkable than the persistency with which President Wilson kept Congress to its task, even refusing a Christmas recess until this bill was ready for his signature. Wilson serenely ignored the torrent of abuse heaped on him by the big bankers; and the Federal Reserve Act is clearly the crowning achievement of his domestic legislation.

A law establishing the Federal Trade Commission and the Clayton Antitrust Act of 1914, enacted repeated recommendations by President Roosevelt—who refused to admit the connection. The Clayton Act included what Samuel Gompers called "labor's charter of freedom": a section declaring that unions could never be considered unlawful combinations *per se;* that strikes, boycotting, and picketing were not, as such, violations of federal law; and that the injunction could no longer be used by federal courts in labor disputes.

This list does not exhaust the reform and social legislation initiated by Wilson and enacted by Congress. A rural credits law, a workmen's compensation act for the federal civil service, and a law excluding from interstate commerce the products of child labor, were passed in 1916.[1] The La Follette Seamen's Act of 1915, culmination of twenty years' agitation by Andrew Furuseth of the seamen's union, did much for sailors' well-being but did not, as its advocates predicted, restore American supremacy at sea. Nor, for that matter, did the United States Shipping Board, created in 1916. All in all, the Democratic party exhibited the most harmonious co-operation between Capitol and White House since Grant's administra-

---

[1] The last was declared unconstitutional by the Supreme Court, as was a second law passed in 1918, laying special taxes on factories employing children under 14. Congress in 1924 initiated a child-labor amendment to override these decisions, but it failed of ratification.

tion. It proved that statesmanship was no monopoly of the Republicans, and it took over the Progressives' weapons, lock, stock, and barrel.

5. Woodrow Wilson and Mexico

In a speech of 17 October 1913 President Wilson announced to the doubting ears of Latin America that the United States would never add a foot to her territory by conquest, nor did she; but Wilson continued in the Caribbean the "dollar diplomacy" of Taft and Knox which he had denounced. Nicaragua was persuaded to sign a treaty similar to Roosevelt's with Panama, but with no cession of sovereignty, giving the United States the exclusive right to build a Nicaragua canal, and granting a 99-year lease of two small islands and a site for a naval base, which was never used. Haiti, in a state of appalling anarchy and degradation, was occupied in 1915 by United States Marines, and nineteen years elapsed before they could complete their work of pacification and road building, and withdraw. The Dominican Republic, at the same time, was advanced from the status of a financial receivership to that of a Marine Corps occupation, which lasted until 1924. Sumner Welles of the state department then set up a democratic government which was promptly overthrown by the dictator Trujillo, who lasted until 1961. And Haiti, after being evacuated by the Marines, began slipping back into her old ways, and fell under another cruel and ruthless dictator. In Asia, however, Wilson renounced American participation in the three-power bankers' loan to China, which Knox had arranged.

From Taft and Knox, Wilson and Bryan inherited a serious problem about Mexico. Bully Huerta, having been installed president as the result of a coup which the American minister helped to pull off, aimed to set up a regime similar to that of Porfirio Díaz, including the protection of foreign investments. England recognized him; Wilson recalled the mischievous American minister and refused recognition. At the same time there was a controversy with Britain over shipping tolls in the Panama Canal. We were obliged by treaty to treat all nations' ships equally, but Congress defiantly passed a law in 1912 exempting American-flag ships from tolls. By a secret agreement between Colonel House and Sir William Tyrrell, secretary to the British foreign minister, Wilson promised to press Congress to repeal the tolls exemption—and Congress did; whilst Tyrrell agreed that the foreign office would withdraw recognition of Huerta and follow our lead in Mexico, which it did.

Apart from this sensible agreement, Wilson's Mexican policy floundered. Huerta created an "incident" by arresting a paymaster and party from U.S.S. *Dolphin* at Tampico. Although they were promptly released, the Admiral demanded an apology and a salute to the flag; Huerta declined, and on 21 April 1914 Admiral Frank F. Fletcher, under orders from Washington, landed a force at Vera Cruz (selected for this demonstration in order to choke off Huerta's consignments of munitions from Germany), and captured the city against armed resistance, mostly sniping from buildings.

It looked as if a second Mexican War were beginning, with Wilson playing the role of Polk. Instead, Wilson adopted "watchful waiting," as he called it, and by occupying Vera Cruz and its customs house, Huerta's only source of cash was closed. This starved him out of office, he fled the country in July 1914, and American forces evacuated Vera Cruz. A victory for Wilson, apparently; but Huerta's departure made matters worse, because all Mexican political elements splintered into factions under rival leaders, each printing money, raising soldiers, killing, looting, and destroying property. The principal rivals were Emiliano Zapata, an illiterate Indian whose chief concern was to give the peons land in his state of Morelos, which he reduced to anarchy in the process; Pancho Villa, a jolly, swashbuckling bandit who controlled most of the north; and General Venustiano Carranza, a well-educated liberal with a claim to be the constitutionally elected president.

William Jennings Bryan was the strangest secretary of state in the history of the Republic. His sincere desire to preserve peace was expressed in the promotion of compulsory arbitration treaties with all and sundry nations. He had so little sense of dignity as to go on the Chautauqua circuit, along with Tyrolean yodelers and vaudeville acts. He did not even pretend to understand Mexico; after hearing a cogent report on the situation by the President's special agent Bryan remarked, "I just can't understand why those people are fighting their brothers!" And he went so far on one occasion as to allude to Pancho Villa, in whose presence no virtuous woman was safe, as a "Sir Galahad." So Wilson let Bryan play with arbitration treaties, and handled Mexican policy himself. He and Secretary Lansing, who succeeded Bryan in mid-1915, tried again and again, alone or with the help of the "A.B.C. Powers"—Argentine, Brazil, and Chile—to bring all Mexican revolutionists to a "get-together," make peace, and hold a fair election. Carranza thwarted all such efforts because he considered himself to be the constitutionally elected president, and saw no more reason to make tenders to Villa and Zapata than Lincoln did to Davis. Owing to this intransigence, Wilson acquired an intense dislike for Carranza, a man of his own age and similar character: honest, dogmatic, stubborn. Wilson stuck out his long chin, pursed his prim lips, and stared angrily through his pince-nez at Carranza, while Carranza, his beard bristling, glared back at Wilson through steel-rimmed glasses and refused to budge an inch.

The Mexican won. On 19 October 1915 the United States and the A.B.C. Powers, augmented by Guatemala and Uruguay, recognized Carranza as the legitimate president. But for two or three years he was unable to bring about even a truce in the civil war. Now came to the fore Pancho Villa, whom righteous Wilson and simple Bryan had favored. Since he had nothing to lose and everything to gain by embroiling his country with the United States, Villa in January 1916 murdered in cold blood seventeen American mining engineers. Two months later he raided the town of Columbus, New Mexico, set fire to it, and killed some sixteen citizens. Wilson ordered a large part of the regular army and the national guard to the border, and a column over 6000 strong under General John J. ("Black Jack") Pershing pursued Villa some 300 miles into Mexico (April 1916). There the fox went to earth, and Carranza threw every obstacle in the way of the hounds, demanding their withdrawal in a bitter, insulting note. Wilson replied calmly, but required the release of twenty-three American soldiers captured by Carranza forces—or else. The Mexican yielded on that point, but won his main objective. Wilson, now that war with Germany had become probable, followed his military advisers in pulling all American troops out of Mexico by early February 1917, without taking Villa. The cost of this intervention was well worth the practice it afforded the army, but the results were nil, and Wilson had to resume "watchful waiting" as the alternative to war.

Carranza now had a respite in which he promulgated the Constitution of 1917, on which the government of Mexico rests today; but its nationalization of church and oil lands lit a fresh dispute with the United States which smoldered during the First World War, and blazed up in the 1920's. By that time Carranza, Zapata, and Villa had all been assassinated, and General Álvaro Obregón was President of Mexico. Carranza, for standing stiffly on the principle of nonintervention, for letting his country work out her own destiny, has become one of the heroes of modern Mexico. That he reached that stature was due in no small measure to the patience and forbearance of the man he detested, Woodrow Wilson.

Wilson's achievements during his first term were remarkable

The Princeton professor had become leader of a party refractory to leadership and converted it from state-rights tradition to enlightened nationalism. But complaints were being voiced both from the left and the right. The Bryan wing of the party in 1913–14 demanded legislation to destroy the financial oligarchy of New York and Boston, regulate the stock exchanges, place a heavy tax on corporations, and more stringent anti-trust laws. They got none of these things, and organized labor did not obtain the restriction on unlimited immigration that it wanted. The blacks, whose leaders had supported Wilson in 1912, got less than nothing. Racial segregation was extended to almost every federal department, and there took place a wholesale firing of black postmasters and other minor federal officials in the South; since (as Wilson's collector of internal revenue in Georgia announced), "A Negro's place is in the cornfield." In the congressional elections of 1914 the Democratic majorities in both houses were much reduced, mostly owing to disillusioned Progressives deserting Wilson after he had placated the bankers by putting "safe" men in charge of the federal reserve system. Judged by the test case of Mexico, Wilson had shown little capacity for leadership in world affairs; that would come under the greater test of the war in Europe. Nevertheless, according to Brooks Adams's definition of administration as "the capacity of co-ordinating . . . conflicting social energies in a single organism, so adroitly that they shall operate as a unity," Wilson had proved himself a great administrator.

VII

The First World War:
The Neutrality Period

1914-1917

1. America's Reaction to the War

BETWEEN THE FIRING on Fort Sumter and the attack on Pearl Harbor there was no shock to American public opinion comparable to that of the outbreak of the European war in August 1914. Almost every shade of American opinion had assumed that a general European war was unthinkable, because nobody cared to think about it. International arbitration was making notable progress, and the two Hague Conventions as well as the London Naval Conference of 1909 were devoted to making war unlikely to occur, or less horrible if it did. Norman Angell's *The Great Illusion* (1910) proved that modern war was unprofitable for both victors and vanquished. So who would dare to start one? There might be little wars—we were on the brink of one with Mexico—but surely no more big ones after the Russo-Japanese War? Balkan wars in 1912–13 caused some misgivings; but these, it was assumed, were just squabbles of petty princes. Surely the so-called Concert of Europe, which meant the foreign offices of the leading powers in consultation, would prevent any really big conflict from breaking out?

That Concert fell into cacophony when Austria-Hungary declared war on Serbia (28 July 1914) for presumably harboring the terrorist organization which assassinated Archduke Franz Ferdinand. Germany backed her ally Austria to the limit, Russia mobilized in the hope of protecting her small ally, and Germany declared war on Russia and on France, Russia's ally (1–3 August). German armies crashed through neutral Belgium to crush France; and Britain, honoring her pledge to defend Belgian neutrality, declared war on Germany.

The initial American reaction was horror, disgust, and determination to keep out of it. President Wilson proclaimed American neutrality on 4 August, and in a message to the Senate on the 19th declared, "The United States must be neutral in fact as well as in name. . . . We must be impartial in thought as well as in action, must put a curb upon our sentiments." Walter Hines Page, American ambassador at London, later an ardent advocate of supporting the Allies, wrote to Colonel House in August that America presented a "magnificent spectacle. . . . We escape murder, we escape brutalization." Even Theodore Roosevelt, later a strident advocate of intervention, was unmoved by the invasion of Belgium. In *The Outlook* of 22 August he wrote, "I am not now taking sides"; in September he praised the Germans as a "stern, virile and masterful people," and declared that it would be "folly to jump into the war."

America could not be "impartial in thought" in the face of such a universal catastrophe, and the public in general became divided emotionally into pro-Ally, pro-German, or pro-neutral before the war was a month old. Leaders in pro-Ally sentiment were college-educated and well-to-do people on the East and West coasts and in the South. These, mostly English in race and culture, cherished the traditional American love of France; and those who had visited Europe in the last years of peace needed no propaganda to perceive that Germany was the aggressor and that England and France had done everything honorably possible to avoid war. Canada, moreover, went to war when England did, and gave freely of her men and money. There was an immediate rush of young American college graduates to obtain commissions in the British army or the French foreign legion; to form the Lafayette Escadrille of the French air force, and to organize an American ambulance service to help the Allies. Pro-Ally bazaars and relief organizations sprang up in almost every American city; and in these circles neutral or pro-German sentiment became taboo. The educated white people of the South, who alone in America remembered the devastation of war, warmheartedly supported the Allied cause from the beginning, although somewhat shaken when England declared cotton to be contraband.

The great heart of the country, on the contrary, and working people in general, were both neutral and pacifist. Even recent immigrants embraced American isolationism with fervor; the European war represented part of what they had come over to get away from. The Mid-Westerner could think no ill of Germans because so many of them were his good neighbors. Progressives who had launched a long-range program to fulfill Herbert Croly's *Promise of American Life* loathed war not only for its waste and suffering but because it would interrupt progress toward social justice. Many simple people dismissed the war as a natural result of monarchical rivalries—Edward VII was nasty to his nephew William II, Nicholas II was jealous of the emperors of Germany and Austria. Others found the socialist, economic-determinism explanation convincing; the war was caused by rivalry for foreign markets and colonies, munitions-makers' zeal to sell their wares, and the bankers' lust to glut themselves on war profits. It followed that both sides in the European war were guilty, both were horrible; and to preserve America's integrity and perhaps regenerate an Old World exhausted from fighting, she must neither rearm nor fight. So reasoned Westerners who had won their land by fighting Indians, and Eastern progressives who accepted the Marxian argument. Henry Ford, jeered by the Eastern press but supported by warm Western hearts, even chartered a steamship, filled it with preachers, pacifists, and assorted cranks, and took it to Europe to persuade the warring governments to "get the boys out of the trenches by Christmas." And some otherwise sensible people argued that if the United States went to war, she would be torn apart by the foreign-language groups. The Hearst newspapers, the Chicago *Tribune*, Irish-Americans who cherished an implacable hostility toward Britain, and German-Americans, by and large, were determined to keep America neutral.

There was a general opinion that the war would be short. After fighting a month or two, the belligerents would be exhausted, financially and otherwise. Many American army officers believed that nothing could stop Germany, that she would crush France in a matter of weeks, then turn on Russia and invade England. The Allied victory of the Marne in September proved that France was far from decadent; and England's valiant efforts to build a new army out of the remnants of the "old contemptibles" compelled admiration. Allied propaganda directed at America was well handled; German propaganda was singularly truculent and ineffective. It left no doubt that

Germany was autocratic and militaristic, and that her victory would impose the mailed fist on the Western world. A German patriot's "Hymn of Hate" against England was widely read and deprecated, and Kipling's reply, "The Hun is at the gate!" was appreciated; for there was no answer to his rhetorical questions, "What stands if Freedom fall? Who dies if England live?"

There now developed a controversy over neutral rights which, in other hands than Wilson's, might have drawn in the United States against the Allies.

2. Neutrality Problems

Keeping the sea lanes open was vital to England's very existence then, as in the Napoleonic Wars, and as to us in World War II and today; but it took a long time and a fresh look to convince the United States that her interest was identical with England's. Since the Allies had preponderant naval power, they used it by a blockade of Germany, which meant stopping and taking into port all neutral ships bound for Europe, and condemning those which were carrying cargoes to Germany, even if initially consigned to neutral European countries like Scandinavia. These procedures were contrary to traditional principles of freedom of the seas and neutral rights, which Americans had defended in the early days of the Republic and fought for in 1812; but (as the British made haste to point out) they were a very slight extension of the methods of blockade which the Union navy had applied to the Confederacy in 1862–65. The British government was in a dilemma— a tight blockade of Germany was essential if they were to win, but American ill will would make defeat certain. Wilson and Bryan, falling back on principles of neutral rights which had survived the age of sail, embarked on a policy of protest by diplomatic notes that recalled the equally futile note-writing by James Madison in 1807–12. Protests became fainter as the American stake in Allied victory became greater, and not only through sentiment. The Allies kept the sea lanes open and placed enormous orders for food and munitions in the United States, which relieved a serious economic recession in 1914. These purchases, moreover, were largely financed by the floating of British, French, and Russian bond issues in the United States, and by direct loans from American bankers. Not that this influenced (as the Nye Senate report of 1935 claimed it did) American desire for war. The business and financial interests who followed their pocketbooks, and Wall Street generally, remained strong for neutrality until early 1917, because that status offered them all the profits of war without the corresponding sacrifices. And the financial stake in Allied victory had no influence whatsoever on President Wilson.

Germany in 1914 as in 1939 (and like Napoleon in 1812) expected to defeat the sea powers by overrunning the continent. Generals Hindenburg and Ludendorff beat the Russians so badly at the Tannenberg and Masurian Lakes (26 August–15 September 1914) that Russia ceased to be an asset to the Allies. Joffre saved Paris and the Channel ports in his victory over the German army of invasion at the Marne (5–12 September). The Germans fell back to the Aisne, whence a series of bloody assaults by the Allies failed to dislodge them. By the end of 1914 the war on the western front had become a war of positions, of trenches: a ghastly, blown-up version of the Union and Confederate lines before Petersburg in 1865. In this kind of war the defense had the advantage, and every attempt of the Allies for three years to break or turn the German positions failed after grievous loss of lives.

On the oceans, England as the dominant naval power was able to contain the German high-seas fleet in port, except for hit-and-run bombardments and an occasional commerce-destroying sortie. She was able to establish and enforce an effective blockade of the Central Powers, adding greatly to the list of items to be considered contraband and so liable by international law to be taken from a neutral ship. This was reasonable, since the manufacture of modern explosives and weapons now required a vast array of new materials—copper and cotton, for instance. Germany retaliated against the blockade by commerce destroying, as the Confederacy had done in 1862. But Germany could wage war in the air and under the ocean. The U-boats, as the Germans called their submarines, confined their efforts to warships until 1915. But on 4 February 1915 the Emperor announced that all waters around the British Isles constituted a war zone in which any merchant ship attempting to trade with the Allies would be destroyed. This was what forced America into war.

The distinction between British and German violations of neutral rights was clear. No citizen of a neutral state lost his life as a result of the British blockade, and all neutral cargoes seized were paid for at war prices. But the U-boat warfare took a toll of some 200 American lives on the high seas when America was still neutral, and other neutrals suffered far more. President Wilson, foreseeing what would happen, informed the German government on 10 February 1915 that the United States would hold it "to a strict accountability" for "property endangered or lives lost." Thereby he took a stand that inevitably led to war, unless either his or the German government backed down.

Soon came tests of "strict accountability." On 1 May 1915 the American tanker *Gulflight* was torpedoed and sunk without warning. Germany offered to make reparation for this "unfortunate accident," but refused to abandon submarine warfare. Six days later a U-boat torpedoed and sank Cunard liner *Lusitania* off the coast of Ireland, with the loss of over 1100 civilians, including 128 American citizens, some of them women. The sinking of the *Lusitania* was criminally stupid; it was no excuse to point out that the German embassy had warned passengers not to sail on the ill-fated ship, and that she carried munitions for the Allied armies. By existing laws of neutrality an enemy merchant ship captured on the high seas should have been brought into port; or if that were impractical, the passengers and crew should be taken off before scuttling. But the U-boat sank her without warning and made no effort to rescue the hapless passengers. A thrill of horror ran through America; but President Wilson, in an address on 10 May, pronounced a smug phrase that he lived to regret: "There is such a thing as a man being too proud to fight." Leaders like Theodore Roosevelt clamored for war, and the press took up the cry. That, as it turned out, might have been the best moment for the United States to have entered the war. Had she been able to bring her strength to bear in 1916, the war would probably have been over within a year; the disastrous loss of life and breakdown of civilized standards would have ended two years earlier than it did, and the Russian revolution would not have taken place, at least not then.

America was not yet emotionally prepared for war, and Wilson in 1915, like Jefferson in 1807, refused to be stampeded into it. On 13 May he demanded that the German government disavow the sinking of the *Lusitania,* make reparation, and "prevent the recurrence of anything so obviously subversive of the principles of warfare." The German reply procrastinated, and on 9 June Wilson sent a more peremptory note: "The lives of noncombatants cannot lawfully or rightfully be put in jeopardy by the capture or destruction of an unresisting merchantman." He denied altogether the legality of a "war zone," unheard of in earlier wars. Secretary Bryan, regarding this protest as dangerously close to an ultimatum, resigned rather than sign it. His own solution was to renounce responsibility for the lives of Americans who chose passage on belligerent ships. "Germany," he said, "has a right to prevent contraband from going to the Allies, and a ship carrying contraband should not rely upon passengers to protect her from

an attack—it would be like putting women and children in
front of an army."

3. *Preparedness and the Election of 1916*

Closely interwoven with the problem of defending neutral
rights was the issue of military "preparedness," as it was called,
for war; although usually advanced as the only way to keep
America out of war. Preparedness was first advocated by those
who, after the *Lusitania* sinking, believed that America must
eventually intervene on the side of England and France. It
was opposed by pacifists, and by all pro-German or anti-
British elements, who realized that there was no chance of
America's intervening on the German side.

The preparedness people, who in general were the same as
the pro-Allied interventionists, invited British veterans like Ian
Hay to address meetings. But the most effective propagandists
were Americans who risked or gave their lives in the Allied
cause—Edouard Genet (a descendant of the "Citoyen") and
others who formed the Lafayette Escadrille, Steve Galatti and
his American Field Service; members of the Foreign Legion
like Alan Seeger who wrote "I Have a Rendezvous with
Death." The Navy League and other societies begged Congress
to prepare, arguing that only strong armed forces could preserve neutrality. Long did the President remain deaf to their
appeals. On the initiative of Grenville Clark, Theodore Roosevelt, Jr. and other New York business and professional men,
General Leonard Wood and the war department organized
in the summer of 1915 the first Plattsburg training camp, in
which some 1200 civilian volunteers received instruction in
modern warfare under regular army officers, paying for their
own food, uniforms, and travel expenses. The idea spread, and
in the following summer some 16,000 men were enrolled in a
number of "Plattsburgs," thus creating a cadre of trained
officers for the new army. But the Plattsburg idea received no
blessing from Wilson prior to a speech of 4 November 1915 in
which he set forth a program of preparedness, justifying his
conversion by quoting Ezekiel xxxiii.6: "But if the watchman
see the sword come, and blow not the trumpet, and the people
be not warned . . . his blood will I require at the watchman's
hand."

Bryan and La Follette now attempted to persuade the public
that preparedness was merely a scheme of warmongers and
profiteers, of whom Wilson was the dupe. Many labor and
farm organizations fell in line; and their efforts were reflected
in the Gore-McLemore resolutions of Congress, ordering the

government to forbid American citizens to travel on armed merchant ships of belligerents. Wilson moved promptly to defeat these resolutions and succeeded, helped by press disclosures that the German-American Alliance was trying to intimidate congressmen into voting for them. In January 1916 the President toured the country to promote military preparedness and to propagate the view that the only way to "keep out of war" was to make America so strong that nobody would dare attack her. Monster preparedness parades were held in several cities, and Wilson marched in the one at Washington. On 7 March 1916 the President appointed Newton D. Baker secretary of war. As mayor of Cleveland, Baker had opposed preparedness, but he now became its vigorous and effective advocate.

During the summer of 1916 Congress, urged by Baker, Daniels, and Wilson, provided a significant strengthening of the armed forces. Most important was the "Big Navy Act" of 29 August embodying a ten-year plan of construction, which anticipated making the United States Navy equal to any two others in the world. The handicap that American trade was under, depending on foreign merchantmen to carry exports, converted the Democratic party to building up the merchant marine, and the United States Shipping Board Act of 7 September 1916 appropriated $50 million for the purchase or construction of merchant ships.

The Allies, finding the lack of defensive armament on their merchant ships to be no protection against their being sunk at sight, began arming them; the German government countered by threatening to sink all such ships without warning. Unarmed, however, was French channel steamer *Sussex*, torpedoed by a U-boat next month (24 March 1916) with a loss of 80 civilian lives, some of them American. Secretary Lansing on 18 April notified Germany that her methods of submarine warfare were "utterly incompatible with the principles of humanity" as well as with international law; that unless they were abandoned, diplomatic relations would be severed. This warning placed the German government in a dilemma. Was American neutrality worth the concession demanded? Was not the U-boat Germany's God-given weapon for victory? For the time being the Kaiser temporized. On 4 May he promised that U-boats would no longer attack merchantmen without sufficient warning to give their complement a chance for life—a temporary victory for Wilson.

In the wake of the *Sussex* incident came the Irish Sinn-Fein rebellion of Easter Monday, 24 April, which the British suppressed, executing several of the leaders. This produced an explosion of American anglophobia, and not only in Irish circles. Publication by the British of a blacklist of 87 American and 350 Latin-American firms which were dealing directly or indirectly with Germany, caused Wilson's attitude to harden against the Allies.

Early in that year, he had sent Colonel House on a secret mission to England, France, and Germany in the hope of persuading their governments to let him mediate and end the war. He had little encouragement in London or Paris, as the British and French army heads were confident of breaking the German lines in a spring drive; and none in Berlin, because Germany now held all the cards for victory. The Chancellor told the Colonel that he would entertain no peace offer that did not include big war indemnities and a permanent German control of Poland and Belgium.

So the slaughter continued. In February began the great Battle for Verdun. "They shall not pass!" declared General Pétain, nor did they; but the defense of Verdun cost France some 350,000 men. On 31 May–1 June occurred the Battle of Jutland, greatest sea action of the war, in which the Royal Navy drove the Imperial high seas fleet back to its mine-protected harbors, losing six capital ships in the process. On 1 July 1916 opened the Battle of the Somme, in which the tank made its debut on the field of Mars. The French paid with 200,000 lives, and the British almost double, to recover a few square miles of territory. Even heavier was the cost of a Russian offensive in Galicia, eventually stopped by the Germans and Austrians at the cost of almost a million men, and demoralization of the Russian army. By mid-November, when every contending nation had been bled white, a ghastly quiet again descended on the western front.

The presidential election had already been decided. Wilson and the Democrats planned the political campaign with unusual subtlety. They understood that the outcome would largely depend on whether the party could hold the progressives and Irish-Americans, now alienated by preparedness and fear of involvement in war, on England's side. Well timed was the President's nomination of Louis D. Brandeis, foremost pro-labor and social-justice lawyer of the country, to the Supreme Court. He was confirmed by the Senate on 1 June after a bitter struggle with Republicans and big business interests. The Rural Credits Act of 17 July, creating twelve federal farm loan banks with an initial capital of $60 million, to provide cheap mortgages to farmers, came next. On 19 August, a Workmen's Compensation Act for federal employees was passed. A nation-wide railroad strike, threatened by the four railroad unions, to which management refused any concession, was prevented by the President's pushing through Congress the Adamson Act of 3 September, adopting the eight-hour day and other benefits for the railroad brotherhoods. The Jones Act of 29 August 1916 granted autonomy to the Philippines.

By this time the Democrats had appropriated almost every plank in the Bull Moose platform of 1912. And Mid-Western support of Wilson was enhanced by an incident of the Democratic nominating convention in June. Governor Martin H. Glynn of New York in a keynote speech cited one instance after another when presidential diplomacy had averted war. After each item the convention roared, "We didn't go to war!" and this, translated into the slogan "He kept us out of war!" became the oriflamme of the presidential election. But Wilson was careful to make no promise to continue neutrality under any and every condition.

Though pro-Ally in leadership, the Republican party dared not alienate Mid-Western pacifists or the "hyphenated Americans," as Theodore Roosevelt contemptuously called those whose old-world loyalties and hatreds outweighed their new-world citizenship. It nominated Charles Evans Hughes, associate justice of the Supreme Court, on a vague platform accusing Wilson of following a vacillating and timid domestic and foreign policy, truckling to the railroad brotherhoods and to Mexican bandits. For this was the summer of armed mobilization on the Mexican border and Pershing's unsuccessful pursuit of Villa. The Bull Moose party held a convention, only to expire "not with a bang but with a whimper," when Theodore Roosevelt advised his followers to return as penitents to the Republican fold.

The election itself was highly exciting. Both candidates stumped the country, but Wilson had the advantage in capitalizing on neutrality and his party's legislative achievements. Hughes was a poor speaker; his full beard, suitable for a Supreme Court justice, looked comical to the younger generation of smooth-shaven voters, and his arguments in the face of Democratic legislative achievements misfired. Nevertheless, Hughes almost won; it was the closest contest since 1876. When the early returns on 7 November showed that the Republicans had made a clean sweep of the Eastern states with a heavy electoral vote, even the Democratic New York *World* conceded defeat. But California had not yet been heard from. Hughes had made several "boners" when speaking in that state, especially by not calling on Governor Hiram Johnson, the Bull Moose vice-presidential candidate in 1912, and he lost the Golden State by fewer than 4000 votes. California's electoral vote put Wilson across. The President polled 49.3 per cent of the vote, and won 277 in the electoral college; Hughes polled 46 per cent and 254 electoral votes. About half the Socialist party voted for Wilson, as did about two-thirds of the Progressives. The German-American vote divided. Hughes's surprising strength in the Eastern cities is ascribed to Irish-Americans deserting Wilson for not protesting against the execution of Irish rebels or doing anything about anti-clericalism in Mexico.

Now Wilson was free, untrammeled by political considerations, to make a final attempt to mediate in the European war; or, if that failed, to enter it on the Allied side.

4. *From Wilson's Re-election to War*

It is odd that Wilson, a student of history and author of an excellent book covering the Civil War, should not have seen that the European situation in 1917 was similar to that of America in 1864. Too much had been sacrificed, too much hate had been aroused, for a compromise peace. Even had European statesmen been of the caliber of Castlereagh and Talleyrand, they would not have dared disappoint the hopes of their people by "letting the enemy off easy," as the man in the street put it.

Wilson's peace effort must be set straight, because it has been distorted to mean that he thwarted a sincere attempt of Germany to end the war on fair terms. The outstanding facts are these:—On 12 December 1916, before the President was ready to start his final peace drive, Chancellor Bethmann-Hollweg anticipated him by announcing that the Imperial government was ready to negotiate with the Allies. The Kaiser, Marshal Hindenburg, General Falkenhayn, and Admiral Tirpitz allowed the chancellor to try this peace move because German victories of 1916, which included knocking Romania out of the war, put them in a strong bargaining position; yet they were frustrated (as Napoleon had been, and as Hitler would be in 1940) by "perfidious Albion's" firm control of the ocean. The only bar to a complete victory, they thought, was the Wilson-imposed shackles on the submarines. Bethmann-Hollweg, a wise and moderate man, saw clearly that if America entered the war, Germany's doom was sealed; before that happened, he must negotiate peace. But he had to promise the warlords that if this attempt did not succeed, unrestricted submarine warfare would be adopted as the last chance of breaking down England and winning the war. Suppose America did come in, argued the warlords, she could never bring her potential strength to bear before England would be brought to her knees by starvation.

Bethmann-Hollweg's announcement created a sensation and raised the question of what terms Germany would demand. Wilson now issued a note (18 December 1916) calling on all belligerents to state "the precise objects which would . . . satisfy them and their people that the war had been fought out." Lloyd George replied that Britain's terms would be "complete restitution, full reparation, and effectual guarantees" for the future. The German chancellor evaded Wilson's query because he knew that if he stated the minimum that his government had decided to accept—annexation of Luxemburg, a slice of eastern France and of Russia's Baltic provinces, protectorate over Belgium and Poland, and a vast war indemnity—neutral opinion would be alienated. His game was to use Wilson to get the Allies into a peace conference, while the Central Powers still occupied Belgium and large sections of Italy, France, and Russia. The Allied governments saw the trap and indignantly refused.

Having failed in this effort, President Wilson on 22 January 1917 delivered before the Senate his "Peace Without Victory" address. Holding forth the hope of a better world, organized in a league of peace after the war, he declared that such a peace must be a compromise, not a victorious one; a peace which would not leave the vanquished nations impoverished, bitter, and filled with feelings of revenge. He declared that he spoke "for the silent mass of mankind everywhere who have as yet had no . . . opportunity to speak their real hearts out concerning the death and ruin." Wilson's words lifted the hearts of plain people everywhere, and he became a sort of apostle. But "the silent mass of mankind" in Europe also wanted victory. They had not endured heavy sacrifices since 1914 only to be cheated out of it by noble sentiments. That, fundamentally, not machinations of "wicked" statesmen, is why the fundamental contradiction of Wilson's policy was never resolved. It was just as in 1863, when the Vice President of the Confederacy wrote that most Americans were tired of civil war and craved peace, "but as we do not want peace without independence, so they do not want peace without union."

On the last day of January 1917 the German government, through its ambassador in Washington, communicated a watered-down version of its minimum peace terms, which were bad enough; but far more deadly was the simultaneous announcement that unrestricted submarine warfare would start next day. This meant that the U-boats would be instructed to sink at sight any American or other neutral ship, armed or un-armed, that ventured into the German-declared war zone around the British Isles, or the Mediterranean. On 3 February Wilson replied by breaking diplomatic relations with Germany.

The next three weeks were a period of watchful waiting on the President's part, hoping in vain that the Germans might not dare carry out their threats. He even discouraged further military preparedness, fearing lest too much build-up would suggest to Germany that we really were preparing for war. The army bill passed by Congress on 22 February appro-priated only a normal $250 million for that fiscal year. Gen-eral Hugh L. Scott, the army's chief of staff, wrote (15 February), "We are not allowed to ask for any money or to get ready in a serious way, until the soft pedal is taken off." The greatest personal obstacle to adequate preparedness was Josephus Daniels, secretary of the navy. He obstructed efforts of the navy to put itself on a war footing, on the ground that defensive measures might be construed by Germany as "overt acts." Even after the breach of diplomatic relations he refused to sign contracts for building new destroyers authorized by Congress, lest this "provoke" Germany. His assistant secretary, a young man named Franklin D. Roosevelt, had to persuade a New York shipping magnate to stop urging Wilson to get rid of Daniels, before the secretary would sign the contracts.

Wilson at this juncture seemed weak and vacillating, even pusillanimous, to many good citizens, but most of the country supported his every effort to evade or avoid war. We who re-member those days are charitable to Woodrow Wilson, for many of us experienced the same emotional throes that he did. The years 1915–17, like 1775–76 and 1860–61, were times that tried men's souls. Should America "turn the other cheek" to Germany, to keep herself strong and free, "the hope of the world"? Or must a strong and virile nation help save her friends from being conquered by the "mailed fist"? The war on the western front had become a stalemate, a magnified Spot-sylvania or Petersburg; but this affected different people differ-ent ways. It convinced the faint-hearted, as well as the igno-rant, that America should virtually stay aloof and let poor Europe destroy herself; but it strengthened stout hearts in their belief that America should play a noble part, pile in to ensure an Allied victory and, if possible, conclude the sort of peace which would prevent its happening again. Wilson him-self was appalled at the prospect of war, but the story that he told Frank Cobb, the veteran news correspondent and editor of the New York *World*, "Once lead this people into war, and they'll forget there ever was such a thing as tolerance," has been proved by Professor Auerbach to be apocryphal.

So Wilson waited, hoping for something to turn up. What did turn up was a diplomatic bombshell—the "Zimmermann Note." This was a dispatch from the German minister of foreign affairs through diplomatic channels to President Carranza, proposing a German-Mexican alliance against the United States: Mexico to get New Mexico, Arizona and Texas as her share of the loot. Carranza was further invited to detach Japan from the Allies and persuade her to attack the United States, presumably to have Hawaii as her reward. The British intercepted and decoded this dispatch and sent it to Wilson. Zimmermann's note brought to a head the entire subject of German espionage in the United States. The Austrian ambassador, two attachés of the German embassy at Washington, and others, had earlier been expelled for promoting strikes of longshoremen and explosions in munitions works. The leading German secret agent made a practice of planting time-bombs on docked ships about to carry cargoes to the Allies. American secret service unearthed documents indicating that before the end of 1915 Germany had spent $27 million in the United States for propaganda and espionage, almost half of it on General Huerta and his exiled friends to promote a counter-revolution in Mexico.

On 26 February the President addressed Congress in joint session to ask for authority to arm American merchant ships in their defense and to "employ any other instrumentalities or methods to protect them on their lawful occasions." What he had in mind was an armed neutrality or quasi-war, like the one with France in 1798; but Congress would not allow him even that. A group of die-hard pacifists, led by Senators La Follette and Norris, talked the bill to death, and the 64th Congress ended on 5 March without doing anything. "A little group of willful men," said Wilson, "have rendered the great government of the United States helpless and contemptible." The President went ahead and started arming merchant ships anyway, and summoned the 65th Congress, elected in November, to a special session on 2 April.

In the meantime, the U-boats were being hideously successful. On 18 March three unarmed American merchantmen were sunk without warning, and with heavy loss of life. This overt act, coupled with the disclosure of the Zimmermann note, started a landslide of public meetings, petitions, and manifestos for a declaration of war. News of the first Russian revolution, and the abdication of the Czar, on 15 March, not only fanned the flame but removed the last taint of autocracy from the Allied cause.

On the evening of 2 April, first day's session of the new Congress, the President reviewed his efforts to restore peace, declaring: "Neutrality is no longer feasible or desirable when the peace of the world is involved and the freedom of its peoples, and the menace to that peace and freedom lies in the existence of autocratic governments backed by organized force which is controlled wholly by their will. We have no quarrel with the German people," he added. "We have no feeling towards them but one of sympathy and friendship. . . . *The world must be made safe for democracy.*"

With a profound sense of the solemn and even tragical character of the step I am taking and of the grave responsibilities which it involves, but in unhesitating obedience to what I deem my constitutional duty, I advise that Congress declare the recent course of the Imperial German government to be, in fact, nothing less than war against the government and people of the United States; that it formally accept the status of belligerent which has thus been thrust upon it; and that it take immediate steps not only to put the country in a more thorough state of defence, but also to exert all its power and employ all its resources to bring the government of the German Empire to terms and end the war.

He concluded with a noble peroration:

It is a fearful thing to lead this great peaceful people into war, into the most terrible and disastrous of all wars, civilization itself seeming to be in the balance. But the right is more precious than peace, and we shall fight for the things which we have always carried nearest our hearts,—for democracy, for the right of those who submit to authority to have a voice in their own government, for the rights and liberties of small nations, for a universal dominion of right by such a concert of free peoples as shall bring peace and safety to all nations and make the world itself at last free. To such a task we can dedicate our lives and our fortunes, everything that we are and everything that we have, with the pride of those who know that the day has come when America is privileged to spend her blood and her might for the principles that gave her birth and happiness and the peace which she has treasured. God helping her she can do no other.

Ironically, this was Holy Week. The Senate passed a declaration of war on the German Empire, 82 to 6, on 4 April; the House concurred, 373 to 50, in the small hours of Good Friday, the 6th. That afternoon the President signed the declaration, not with joy but in deep sorrow.

I DIDN'T RAISE MY BOY TO BE A SOLDIER

Not only the American declaration of war but Wilson's words heartened the people of the Allied countries, especially the young men who were fighting; for he raised their hopes anew, persuading them (alas for their disillusion!) that this new ally not only assured victory to their side but a just and lasting peace.

After the war, one frequently heard both in America and Britain that America's entry into the war was a tragic mistake; that otherwise there would have been a "peace without victory" in 1917. Now that we know more about what went on behind the scenes, we can see that this was mere wishful thinking. The only basis on which the German chancellor had been authorized by his military to conclude peace was the annexationist terms we have already mentioned; and, as the military situation continued to favor Germany through 1917, there was no reason for her to modify these terms. Had America not come in, and the Allies been so desperate as to make peace in 1917, that peace would have registered an overwhelming German victory in the west, as the Treaty of Brest-Litovsk with Russia, giving Germany the Ukraine, the Baltic provinces and Poland, actually did in the east. Germany would have kept Belgium, Luxemburg, Alsace-Lorraine, and part of France. No peace of that sort could have lasted—it would have been a mere interval between wars.

VIII

The United States in the First World War

1917-1920

1. Naval Operations

THE UNITED STATES declared war on Germany on 6 April
1917, and the first two American republics to follow her
example were Panama and Cuba. Congress at the President's
recommendation declared war on the crumbling Austrian empire on 7 December 1917. It never did declare war on the
other two central powers, Turkey and Bulgaria.

The old tradition of avoiding "foreign entanglements" was
still so strong that the United States never formally allied with
the Allies. President Wilson made it clear that we were merely
"associates" in the same war. England and France, in their
hours of greatest need, had concluded secret treaties with
Russia, Italy, and Japan, promising them certain enemy territories after victory. Whether or not Wilson knew about these
is uncertain; but, even had he not, he believed that the Allied
governments contemplated a traditional peace settlement, annexing large chunks of enemy territory as Germany had done
in 1871, and we in 1848. This he was determined to prevent;
so he kept America's hands free of territorial commitment,

bided his time, and on 8 January 1918 announced the "Fourteen Points" as a basis of peace.[1]

"President Wilson and his Fourteen Points bore me," said Clemenceau, the "tiger" of France. "Even God Almighty has only ten!"

This appearance of aloofness did not preclude full and frank interchange of views and information with the foreign offices and military and naval staffs of the Allies. But months elapsed before America contributed anything substantial in naval or military power to the war against Germany.

It happened thus, largely because "preparedness," starting late, had proceeded by halts and jerks. The fleet was far from being ready "from stem to stern" as Secretary Daniels claimed. Daniels's main interest in the navy was to make it a "floating university" for the bluejackets, and to improve their morals by banning alcoholic beverages from ships and shore stations. But he had a very efficient assistant secretary, Franklin D. Roosevelt; and the commander in chief of the Atlantic Fleet, Admiral Henry T. Mayo, was one of the best fleet commanders in our history. Both navy and marine corps, eager to begin fighting, were restrained by the Chief of Naval Operations, Admiral William S. Benson. A confirmed anglophobe, Benson opposed American entrance into the war (so far as his position permitted) and now proposed that the United States Navy fight a defensive war on the western side of the Atlantic. His first orders to the battle fleet were to concentrate in the Caribbean, presumably to protect the Panama Canal, and a cruiser squadron was ordered to remain in the Pacific to "watch" Japan, one of the Allies. Fortunately, the President had been prevailed upon by Ambassador Page to send to London the president of the Naval War College, Rear Admiral William S. Sims, a few days before the declaration of war. Sims was under oral orders to "keep the department posted," and Admiral Benson dispatched him with the discouraging remark, "We would as soon fight the British as the Germans."

The general situation of the Allies could hardly have been worse than in the spring of 1917. General Nivelle's offensive against the Chemin-des-Dames section of the western front was

---

[1] Wilson's Fourteen Points may thus be summarized:—(1) "Open covenants openly arrived at"; (2) Freedom of the seas; (3) No economic barriers; (4) Disarmament; (5) Adjustment of colonial claims; (6, 7, 8) Evacuation of Russia, Belgium, and France, including Alsace-Lorraine; (9) Readjustment of the Italian frontiers; (10) Autonomy of parts of the Austrian Empire; (11) Evacuation of the Balkans; (12) Emancipation of Turkey's subject peoples; (13) An independent Poland, with access to the sea; (14) A League of Nations. It should be noted that "self-determination" as a general principle was not one of the points.

a hideous failure, provoking mutinies in several French divisions. The Canadian army was bled white taking Vimy Ridge, and the British Arras offensive, of which that was a part, also ended in mud and blood. Sims reported the Allied naval situation to be equally bad. Admiral Jellicoe, First Lord of the Admiralty, informed him that sinkings of Allied and neutral merchant and fishing vessels averaged almost 570,000 tons per month in February and March, and bade fair to reach 900,000 tons in April. They actually fell little short of that appalling figure, which the more powerful U-boats of World War II never attained. England had only three weeks' supply of food, and if something were not done promptly to stop losses and repair the lifeline, the Allies would have to throw in the sponge before the end of the year.

Before leaving Washington, Sims had been told that President Wilson was "decidedly of the opinion that ships should be convoyed." Upon arrival in England he found, to his surprise, that the Admiralty had not yet done so. Sims helped Lloyd George to put convoys across. The predicted frictions and collisions proved to be few and unimportant, and the convoy system more than any other single factor (and this is equally true of the Second World War) enabled American troops and supplies to cross the Atlantic safely.

Secretary Daniels, replying to an urgent appeal from Admiral Sims and the Royal Navy, decided in April to send destroyers to Queenstown (now Cobh), Ireland, to be used as escort-of-convoy and antisubmarine patrol under British command. The first six, under Commander J. K. Taussig, arrived on 4 May and went right to work; by 5 July there were thirty-four of them, together with six converted yachts and several ancient 400-ton torpedo boats of the Asiatic Fleet, which Lieutenant Commander Harold R. Stark had brought halfway around the world. This was the first time that American warships had operated under foreign command. The senior British naval officer at Queenstown, Vice Admiral Sir Lewis Bayly, was a crusty old sea dog; but the American destroyer officers were devoted to "Uncle Lewis"; and he, after a year had elapsed, issued an order which ended, "To command you is an honor, to work with you is a pleasure." A destroyer flotilla was sent to Brest, under Rear Admiral Henry B. Wilson, with the particular task of escorting troop-laden transports. These destroyers were equipped with underwater listening gear to detect submarines, and with depth charges which could destroy a submerged U-boat if properly placed. Both were primitive in comparison with the sonar and depth weapons of World War II, but effective against the small submarines of this war. On 17 November an American destroyer made its first kill of a U-boat. In the meantime convoys and aggressive patrolling had reduced Allied and neutral monthly shipping losses from 875,000 tons in April to 293,000 tons in November; and although they later rose to over 300,000 tons monthly, these figures were more than offset by new construction. Submarine operations now became very hazardous, and the United States could send troops and supplies abroad with confidence that they would arrive. Not one loaded transport was lost.

Admiral Mayo, with his staff officer Commander Ernest J. King, took part in a naval conference in which all the Allies including Russia and Japan were represented, at London in early September 1917. He then crossed to France and participated in a naval bombardment mission against Ostend. As a result of his experience and observations, Admiral Mayo persuaded the navy department to send more destroyers to Queenstown and Brest, to establish naval air stations in France, Ireland, and Britain to help the antisubmarine war, to take major responsibility for setting up a 250-mile mine barrage across the North Sea, and to send a battleship division to augment the British grand fleet at Scapa Flow. Rear Admiral Hugh L. Rodman commanded this contingent in U.S.S. *New York*. These battlewagons never saw action, as the German high seas fleet prudently stayed in port. A fleet of 120 subchasers of the same 110-foot model that proved serviceable twenty-five years later, was sent to European waters, beginning in June 1917. The SCs, commanded by naval ensigns or young reserve officers, carried depth-charges aft and proved their value both as patrols and escort vessels. They had one memorable battle with the Austrian navy in the Adriatic. Small-craft and destroyer service proved to be the best sort of training for future high command.

Pioneers in naval aviation, who became noted admirals by World War II, were Lieutenant Richard E. Byrd the explorer, who commanded the first United States–Canadian naval air station at Halifax; Lieutenant "Pat" Bellinger, who made an altitude record of 10,000 feet in 1915, and Lieutenant J. H. Towers, third naval officer to win his wings, whose endurance record of 6 hours 10½ minutes airborne in 1912 stood for years. Lieutenant Artemus L. Gates, who made a remarkable rescue under shore fire of a splashed R.A.F. flyer off Dunkerque, became the first assistant secretary of the navy for air.

Naval aviation units sent to France were long dependent on foreign-built planes. One outfit was given a "flying coffin" seaplane which the French navy had rejected. Another had to go to Italy for Capronis, the flying of which to northern air bases was more hazardous than air combat, owing to the bad design and poor workmanship of their motors. Gradually these aviation units were supplied with Curtiss float planes, of which over 500 were in use by the end of the war, at 27 different European bases. These aircraft helped to protect convoys by spying lurking U-boats; some were converted to bombers and joined the army air force in its rather ineffective air raids on German military installations.

At the same time a tremendous effort was made to build up the American merchant marine, for which the shipping board, created in 1916, had done little but set up an organization. On 16 April 1917 Congress created an emergency fleet corporation with unlimited power and generous funds to requisition, purchase, construct, and operate ships without limitation. This, in co-operation with the inter-Allied shipping council, proceeded to build a "bridge to France." By seizing interned German ships, buying neutral ships, taking over all private shipping, constructing enormous new shipyards at Hog Island in the Delaware river and elsewhere, building steel ships, reviving defunct New England and West Coast yards to build wooden ships, even producing concrete ships, the emergency fleet corporation succeeded in increasing available tonnage from one to ten million tons, laying down two ships for every one sunk by the U-boats.

At the outbreak of the war, the United States Navy owned only three transports; merchantmen and freighters had to be chartered to get the initial troop contingent across the Atlantic in June. The 109 interned German ships which were commandeered were in bad shape, as their crews had done everything possible to destroy the engines; but a remarkable repair job was done by American mechanics, and these ex-German liners, starting with 54,000-ton *Vaterland* (renamed *Leviathan*), carried 558,000 troops overseas. Even so, almost half the transport tonnage used by the U.S. Army was British. About half the American troops sent to Europe were landed at British ports, mostly Liverpool, proceeding to France in a cross-channel fleet of small converted transports. The other half were landed at French outports, mostly Brest.

Naturally, the German admiralty did not take this lying down. In 1918 it sent six long-range U-boats to the American coast, in the hope of interrupting the transatlantic movement. They made a good bag of coastal schooners, fishing vessels, and small neutral freighters, cut cables and planted mines off Long Island, but never came to grips with the escorted troop convoys. All the damage inflicted on the transport fleet was done in European waters. *Tuscania* and *Moldana* were sunk, with a total loss of 222 lives; six transports homeward bound were torpedoed, and four of them sunk. Only three escort vessels of the United States Navy were lost in the course of the war. Germany, on the other hand, lost 203 U-boats; 137 of them to the British navy, three to the French, and four to the United States Navy. Thirteen of the enemy submarines were sunk by gunfire of the mystery or Q-ships, armed merchantmen with masked batteries, of which the British employed no fewer than 180 during the war. In addition, 176 U-boats surrendered to the Allies at the war's end. Submarines in World War I had a much shorter firing range than in World War II, and could not get off a torpedo without sighting the victim through a periscope; hence the most effective method of defeating them was the convoy, whose escorting destroyers and other warships drove off or kept down prowling submarines even when unable to sink them.

2. The American Expeditionary Force

Naval operations were geared to those of the army because their purpose was to control the Atlantic so that men and supplies for the Allied and associated armies could get across. The United States Army, numbering but 200,000 officers and men (133,000 regulars and 67,000 National Guard) on 1 April 1917, was probably even less prepared for war than the navy. Pershing's "punitive expedition" of 1916 had taught it something, but chasing Pancho Villa around northern Mexico was not much preparation for trench warfare on the western front.

One great obstacle to quick and abundant American reinforcement of the Allies was the need for intensive training in the sort of warfare the troops would have to wage. The 1st Infantry Division, a regular army outfit, arrived in France in time to parade down the Champs Elysées on 4 July 1917, but it was broken up into small units and distributed for training into different parts of the front. About 180,000 American troops had arrived in France by the end of the year, eight months after the declaration of war, but as yet they had done practically no fighting. The second division to start was the 42nd Infantry (Rainbow) of which Colonel Douglas MacArthur was chief of staff. This was an amalgamation of national guard units from twenty-six different states, to supply the necessary components for a division of 27,000 officers and men. Parts of this division and of the 26th (Yankee) saw action in February 1918 under French command. By that time the Allied military situation had become so desperate that a "race to France" of American forces began. One more infantry division—the 2nd of the regular army—arrived in March. By the end of the war, the United States had created an army of 4 million men, transported more than half of them to France, and placed about 1,300,000 on the firing line. This was a tribute to the organizing genius of Newton D. Baker, secretary of war; but it took time.

General Hugh L. Scott, the army's chief of staff, persuaded President Wilson, Secretary Baker, and Congress, to adopt conscription. The Selective Service Act of 18 May 1917 required all men between the ages of 21 and 30 inclusive to register for service. Certain congressmen, recalling the draft riots of 1863, prophesied that conscription would be attended by rioting and that no draftee would ever reach the firing line; but these predictions proved mistaken. When the registration offices closed at sundown 5 June, 9.6 million men had been registered. Although this number was enlarged to 24.2 million in the registrations of 1918, which extended the age limits to 18 and 45, only 2.2 million men were actually inducted into the army by the draft. And of the twenty-nine divisions (of approximately 1000 officers and 27,000 men each) who saw action in France, only eleven were draftee divisions; the rest were seven regular and eleven national guard divisions, all volunteers.

Training these men, which took an average of eight months before action, the building of cantonments at about thirty training camps, providing them with modern weapons and equipment, and finally getting them "over there," were mighty problems not altogether solved. American field artillery largely depended on French 75s, and aviation units (as we have seen) on foreign aircraft, partly because the American equivalents were slow to get into production, partly because available shipping was crammed with beans, bullets, and soldiers. Colonel Roosevelt, as the ex-President now styled himself, created confusion by demanding that he be made commanding general of a division of "horse riflemen," as he called them, to be recruited from his friends and admirers and leap into action after six weeks' training. Clemenceau wanted it as a fillip to French morale, and President Wilson was willing to indulge Roosevelt's last grasp for glory; but General Scott and all top army generals set their faces sternly against the Colonel's scheme; he was too old for a field command, and knew nothing about modern warfare. This rejection convinced Roosevelt that Woodrow Wilson was a crafty villain, and he continued to attack him by voice and pen.

The American Expeditionary Force of 1917–18 was a jolly, singing army compared with the grim, tight-lipped American

Army of 1942–45. Music and banners were not wanting; New York's tin-pan alley ground out some excellent marching songs such as Irving Berlin's "Oh, How I Hate To Get Up in the Morning!" Official propaganda aimed to make the A.E.F. feel like knights errant rescuing damsel France from the wicked Hun; "Mademoiselle from Armentières" and her sisters worked hard to make it worth their while. "We cried more over the Americans leaving for the front than over our own men," said a French peasant woman at a village near the front lines— "They were so young and looked so innocent, and were so far from home." The "doughboy" learned tactics of trench warfare surprisingly quickly; his élan, fighting spirit, and contempt for death made a deep impression on allies as well as enemies. He was far better taken care of than in earlier wars: better medicine, sanitation, field and base hospitals (but, as yet, no wonder drugs to check infection from wounds); Y.M.C.A., Red Cross, and Salvation Army; long leaves in Paris, with guided tours. And he was the better fighter because he wanted desperately to get it "over, over there" and go home.

The A.E.F. was fortunate to arrive on the western front at a time when a war of maneuver was beginning to replace the boring and deadly trench warfare. The excessive slaughter in this war was caused by an enhancement of what we have observed in the Civil War—the increased lethal power of explosives. Trenches, dugouts, barbed-wire tangles, and concrete emplacements were efforts to protect the human body, whose defenses were no better than at the dawn of history, from the effects of these explosives. But for a hundred or a thousand infantrymen, with no other armor than a steel helmet, to go "over the top" and try to take an enemy trench system by assault was suicidal, even when preceded by days of preparatory cannon fire. If Ludendorff had chosen to keep the German army sitting tight in its fixed positions across northern France, it is difficult to see how the Allies could have reached a decision, even with millions of Americans to throw in. But the war of maneuver gave American forces a chance to count. Doughboys who expected to attack the enemy in one surging, shouting line, as at Fredericksburg, watched with fascination the methodical way in which the French took out a newly established German position. Little knots of three or four men, each group with a machine-gun, would approach the enemy from different angles, and while one engaged his attention the others would make a leap forward. The Americans soon learned these tactics, and their losses were not great. Out of 1,390,000 American troops and sailors who saw active combat service, 49,000 were killed in action or died of wounds; 230,000 more

THE AMERICAN EXPEDITIONARY FORCE

were wounded. Yet, as in previous wars, deaths from disease, 57,000 in number, exceeded those from fighting. To a great extent these were caused by an influenza-pneumonia pandemic that swept through the camps in America and France in the fall of 1918.[1]

The army as well as the navy had an air arm in this war. The 1st Aero (later 1st Bombardment) Squadron was organized in 1913 with nine "pusher" biplanes, mostly Curtiss J-2s. It served with General Pershing in Mexico, making what was then a record non-stop flight of 4 hours 22 minutes. The officers and men of this unit sailed for France in 1917, where they were amalgamated with the Lafayette Escadrille and began combat duty with French Nieuports in March 1918. By the time of the Argonne offensive, this aero squadron had expanded to three, which proved very useful for observation and reconnaissance, and even tried a little bombing behind enemy lines. Lieutenant Eddie Rickenbacker, the American "ace" of this war, shot down 26 enemy planes; but the French and German aces made much higher scores. Colonel William Mitchell acquired his basic idea, that the next war could be won by air bombing alone, and Major Carl ("Tooey") Spaatz acquired the experience that led to his eminence in World War II. Major Fiorello LaGuardia, later a famous mayor of New York, commanded the A.A.F. base in northern Italy.

The army had only 55 planes and 4500 aviators when the war began. When it closed, there were 3227 U.S.A.A.F. De Haviland 4s—a British design—of which 1885 had been shipped to France, and 13,574 Liberty engines—12-cylinder, 450 horsepower of American design—of which 5460 had been shipped abroad, over 1000 of them for the Allies. All these planes were of wood construction, and a special organization had to be set up to persuade the radical workers of the I.W.W., the "Wobblies" of the Far West, to turn out airplane fir and spruce.

At the top of the military hierarchy was President Wilson. He had only vague childhood memories of the Civil War, knew nothing of military or naval affairs, and so followed his military advisers and left them initiative and a wide discretion. Wilson's directive to Pershing simply stated that the general was "vested with all necessary authority to carry on the war vigorously," and when Foch and Haig opposed "Black Jack"

---

[1] L. V. Ayres, *Statistical Summary*, p. 127; but battle losses in the A.E.F. were twice those of disease. Figures for killed and died of wounds of the other combatants, as given in W. L. Langer, *Encyclopaedia of World History*, p. 960, are: Italy, 460,000; Great Britain, 947,000 (adding the Canadian and other empire losses brings it close to 1 million); Austria, 1.2 million; France, 1.4 million; Russia, 1.7 million; Germany, 1.8 million.

and tried to appeal over him to the President, they got nowhere. But when Foch, in the crisis of 1918, was made supreme allied commander, Wilson made it clear that Pershing
was subordinate to him.

The President had complete confidence in war secretary
Baker, and was adamant in rejecting requests for favors from
congressmen and others. But he did not have the same confidence in Secretary Daniels. After the war was over, Admiral
Sims accused Daniels and Admiral Benson of delaying victory
at sea by a year through their policy of feeding out mere dribs
and drabs of naval power to the theater where alone it could
count.

In this war, America with no plan of her own, fitted herself
into the naval and western front strategy already existing.
Hence Wilson was not faced as Lincoln had been, and F. D.
Roosevelt would be, with the necessity of making important
strategic decisions. His role was largely that of a top-level co-
ordinator of military activity, and super-cheerleader of the
nation.

3. *The Big Push of 1918*

At the time the United States entered the war, European
military authorities thought that an American reinforcement of
half a million men would be ample to ensure victory. Events
in the second half of 1917 upset that calculation. In October
the Italian lines against Austria, which had been almost stationary for two years, were broken at Caporetto by an Austro-
German drive. The Italian retreat became the rout so vividly
described in Ernest Hemingway's *Farewell to Arms*. The
French army was unable to start a fresh offensive after Nivelle's
failure, but the British tried again. Haig's western front offensive of 31 July to 10 November, a rain-drenched tragedy
known as the Third Battle of Ypres or Passchendaele, cost
400,000 more casualties, made no appreciable gain, and
brought the British and Canadian armies to the verge of ex-
haustion.

Even worse for the Allied cause was the second Russian
revolution, the most important non-military event of World
War I. Russia not only left her allies cold but became the first
communist state in the world, dedicated to the destruction of
religion, property, and most of the values that had been built
up in the Western world since ancient Greece.

Whilst this is no place to detail the causes of the Russian
overturn—all being outside any possible American influence—
the main events must be given in outline, since they led in-

AMERICAN PARTICIPATION
IN THE ALLIED OFFENSIVE
OF 1918

Scale of Miles
0   25   50

NORTH SEA

ENGLAND

STR. OF DOVER

Ostend
Nieuport
Ghent
Schelde R.

BRUSSELS

BELGIUM

GERMANY

Ypres
Armentieres
Lille
YPRES-LYS
AUG. 19-NOV. 11
Divisions engaged:
27-30-37-91

Bethune
Lens
Mons

LINE OF NOV. 11

Arras
LINE OF JULY 18
Cambrai

Meuse R.

Amiens
SOMME
AUG. 8-NOV. 11
Divisions engaged: 27-30-part of 33

Sedan

LUXEM-
BOURG

Cantigny
Montdidier
Noyon
Oise
Laon
OISE-AISNE
AUG. 18-NOV. 11
Divisions engaged:
28-32-77

Compiegne
Soissons
Aisne R.
Rheims

FRANCE

AISNE-MARNE
JULY 18-AUG. 6
Divisions engaged:
1-2-3-4-26-28-32-42

Chateau Thierry

MEUSE-ARGONNE
SEPT. 20-NOV. 11
Divisions engaged:
1-2-3-4-5-26-28-29-32-33-35-37-42-77
78-79-80-82-89-90-91 (6 in reserve)

Verdun

Metz

ST. MIHIEL SEPT. 12-16
Divisions engaged:
1-2-4-5-26-42-82-89-90
(In reserve: 3-33-35-78-80-91)

Marne R.
Seine R.
Somme R.

PARIS

exorably to the "cold war" of 1945. The inept imperial Russian government was overthrown by mutinous troops, and Emperor Nicholas II abdicated on 15 March 1917. The provisional government which succeeded, announced far-reaching reforms and pledged a vigorous prosecution of the war. That did not suit the Soviet (Workers' and Soldiers' Council) of Petrograd (now Leningrad), which demanded immediate peace negotiations. This Soviet, representing but a fraction of one per cent of the Russian people, probably would not have gone far but for a clever coup of the German government. Collecting the principal Bolshevik leaders then in exile, headed by Vladimir Lenin, it sent them to Petrograd by special train in order to undermine the Russian government. After the July offensive of the Russian army against Austria had failed, Alexander Kerensky took over the provisional government. Unable to keep order yet unwilling to make peace, he was overthrown on 6 November 1917 by the Petrograd Soviet, led by Lenin and Trotsky. These two, with Josef Stalin as one of their ministers, organized a Communist All-Russian government, cynically dissolved the constituent assembly which met on the 25th because it contained an anti-communist majority, and demanded that the Allies promptly conclude a peace on the principle of "no annexations, no indemnities."

The Allies naturally rejected this principle, when victory (with the help of America) seemed within their grasp; and when they refused, the Communists turned to the German government which, tongue in cheek, accepted and negotiated a truce on 1 December, which led to the treaty of Brest-Litovsk. Thus Russia was out of the war by December, and had been practically so since July. This meant that the Central Powers, leaving only token forces on the eastern and not much on the Italian front, could concentrate on a massive drive toward the Channel ports and Paris, to break the deadlock, as the submarine war had not done, and reach a decision before American troops arrived in strength. When her westward offensive started, Germany had 207 divisions on that front against the Allies' 173, of which only nine were American.[1]

Field Marshal Ludendorff opened this German offensive on 21 March 1918 with an assault on the British lines from Arras to La Fère. Within a week the Germans had advanced 25 to 40 miles. On 9 April came the second offensive; once again the British were hurled back on a broad front from Ypres to Armentières, and General Haig issued an appeal, "With our backs to the wall and believing in the justice of our cause, each one of us must fight on to the end." In late May the third offensive, against the French armies between Noyon and Rheims, was equally successful; the Germans were now back on the Marne, whence Joffre had expelled them in 1914, and within cannon shot of Paris; on Good Friday a shell from a "Big Bertha" 56 miles away exploded in the Paris church of St. Eustache, killing hundreds of worshippers. On 14 April the Allies placed General Ferdinand Foch in supreme command of all their forces, and on 5 June Pershing and the British commander in chief joined Foch in requesting that more American troops be sent over immediately, even if untrained. One week later this plea was supported by the premiers of Great Britain, France, and Italy, who warned Wilson, "There is great danger of the war being lost unless the numerical inferiority of the Allies can be remedied as rapidly as possible by the advent of American troops." Another 313,000 troops were shipped across in July. Wilson, Baker, and Pershing were determined that these should eventually form a separate Ameri-

---

[1] B. H. Liddell Hart, *The Real War*, p. 366. Actually there were only 4½ U.S. divisions, but as they were almost double the strength of European divisions, his count is 9.

can army, but under stress of the emergency Pershing placed all his forces at the disposal of Foch, who dispersed them among the Allied armies where they were most needed.

On 28 May the 1st Division helped to repulse the German drive on Montdidier, and captured the heights of Cantigny. A marine brigade of the 2nd Division and elements of the 3rd and 28th helped the French to stem the third German onslaught at Château-Thierry. On 6 June the marines, under Pershing's chief of staff General Harbord, with elements of two infantry divisions, took the offensive at Belleau Wood, a square mile held as a crucial strongpoint by seasoned German troops. It took them about a week to capture that bit of forest, and their losses (55 per cent) were heavy; but this action, the toughest that the Marine Corps encountered before Tarawa, astounded the Germans, and ensured the Marine Corps—then associated in the public mind with hunting Haitian bandits—a warm place in the hearts of the American people.

Ludendorff now rested his armies for three weeks, a valuable interval for the French and British to recuperate, and for the Americans to increase their strength. On 15 July opened the last phase of the German 1918 offensive, known as the Second Battle of the Marne. The Germans attacked simultaneously on both sides of Rheims. In the words of their General Walther Reinhardt, "We well-nigh reached the objectives prescribed for our shock divisions for July 15th and 16th . . . with the exception of the one division on our right wing. This encountered American units." In three days the German assault played itself out, and on 18 July Foch called upon the 1st and 2nd American Divisions, the 1st French Colonial and the Gordon Highlanders, to spearhead a counterattack at Soissons. (It was in this offensive that the poet Joyce Kilmer was killed, and buried by a tree stump—no complete tree could be found.) The counterattack, brilliantly executed, "turned the tide of war," wrote General Pershing. The German Chancellor, who on 15 July was expecting any day to receive peace overtures from the Allies, wrote, "On the 18th even the most optimistic among us knew that all was lost. The history of the world was played out in three days."

With the passing of this crisis on the Marne, Pershing on 10 August obtained Allied consent to his cherished plan for an independent American army. Colonel George C. Marshall became his operations officer. In the meantime, the British, Canadians, Australians, and Americans had delivered a successful counterattack south of the Somme which, at comparatively slight cost, made a deep penetration of the German lines. Ludendorff now told the Kaiser that he had better open peace negotiations because all chance of German victory had vanished.

While the French and British gave Ludendorff the one-two in the north, Foch assigned to Pershing the task of pinching out the Saint-Mihiel salient, south of Verdun. This place was strategically important as a rail junction and entrance to the Briey iron basin. Pershing planned the capture of Saint-Mihiel as the opening gun of an operation which would go through to Metz and eventually take over the front thence to Switzerland. But Foch, in a stormy interview with Pershing on 30 August, insisted that after taking Saint-Mihiel the new American army must come to the Allies' assistance to break the German lines to the north. Since Foch was the generalissimo, Pershing had no choice but to obey. Douglas MacArthur believed that this "was one of the great mistakes of the war," a bad example of inflexibility.

The Germans, recognizing that Saint-Mihiel was untenable in the face of a determined assault, were preparing to withdraw when, early in the morning of 12 September, blanketed by heavy fog, the American-led army, ten American and three French divisions, attacked. In two days this force wiped out the Saint-Mihiel salient, captured 15,000 prisoners and 443 guns at a cost of fewer than 8000 casualties.

General Foch's plan involved American co-operation in a gigantic Allied offensive from Ypres to Verdun. The time was propitious. The last Austrian offensive against Italy had failed, and the revived Italian army was about to resume the offensive (Battle of Vittorio-Veneto). Bulgaria cracked up in September, and Turkey would follow in October. The American First Army was assigned the sector between the Meuse and the Argonne forest, with Sedan as the ultimate objective. The Meuse-Argonne battle, launched on 26 September, was the greatest in which American troops had ever fought, and it was not until 1944 that the numbers involved—1,031,000, of which 135,000 were French, 896,000 American—were surpassed.

The entire forward movement was a complete success. The Hindenburg line, Germany's last line of defense, was broken by the British in the northern sector. The American advance was suspended 14 October owing to logistic difficulties; but it no longer mattered, as the Central Powers were falling apart. In the hope of conciliating Wilson, Germany hastily established a parliamentary system, and Prince Max of Baden, who formed a liberal government, on 3 October addressed peace overtures to the President on the basis of his Fourteen Points. On 30 October, Austria asked Italy for an armistice. After a month of diplomatic fencing, in which the Germans were necessarily worsted, Marshal Foch was instructed by the Allied governments to negotiate an armistice. Mutiny in the German navy and revolution in Munich, the Rhine cities, and Berlin rendered the Germans impotent to offer further resistance; but in the vain hope that a complete change in the form of government might win milder terms of peace, the Kaiser was forced to abdicate. Two days later the armistice was signed in Foch's dining car on a siding in the forest of Compiègne, and at 1100 on 11 November the greatest and most costly war that the world had yet known came to an end. It happened so suddenly and spectacularly that both sides were left gasping; and a German corporal named Adolf Hitler, then hospitalized and temporarily blinded by a gas attack, sobbed bitterly and decided to become an agitator and avenge Germany.

What caused this amazingly sudden collapse of the most arrogant and powerful military nation since imperial Rome? The fortitude of the British, French, and Italians through years of uncertainty and disappointment was essential. The fresh, powerful American Expeditionary Force, which could have put over a million men into action in 1919, gave the final push. Control of the ocean by the Allies defeated the U-boats, made the transatlantic flow of men and supplies possible, and all but strangled Germany. Her people already on short rations, with every prospect of their becoming shorter, were not inclined to gamble on continuing the war, even though over two million men were still under arms and full of fight.

4. The War at Home

To these exploits of American soldiers and sailors on the "field of honor," the war of opinion at home stands in painful contrast. In order to convert Americans from their traditional isolationism, the President condoned a terrific propaganda drive to make people love the war and hate the enemy.

George Creel, who headed the committee on public information established by Congress, undertook to mobilize American emotions as Bernard Baruch was mobilizing industry, and Secretary Baker the manpower. Artists, advertisers, poets, historians, photographers, educators, actors were enlisted in the campaign, the country was inundated by a flood of printed material (as yet there were very few private radio sets), while some 75,000 "four-minute men" let loose a barrage of oratory at movie houses and public gatherings. Motion pictures displayed to horrified audiences the barbarities of the "Hun";

pamphlets written by supposed experts "proved" that Germans had always been depraved, and thousands of canned editorials told the average man what to think. This whipping-up of hatred helped to defeat the President's main objective of a just and lasting peace; anyone overheard observing that there were good Germans as well as bad became suspect; speakers trying to explain that the establishment of a League of Nations after victory was the President's main object in going to war, were accused of trying to make the world soft for an unspeakable enemy.

On the excuse, or the belief, that the country was honeycombed with secret agents of the Kaiser, Congress passed the Espionage Act of 15 June 1917 and the Sedition Act of 16 May 1918, as extreme as any similar legislation in Europe. The first fixed a fine of $10,000 and 20 years' imprisonment upon anyone who interfered with the draft or encouraged disloyalty; the Sedition Act extended these penalties to anyone obstructing the sale of United States bonds, discouraging recruiting, uttering "disloyal or abusive language" about the government, the Constitution, the flag, or even the uniform. Under these laws the government arrested over 1500 persons for disloyalty, and among those convicted and sentenced to long prison terms were Eugene V. Debs the Socialist presidential candidate, for threatening that Socialists would not support the war, and Victor L. Berger, the first Socialist to be elected to Congress. Berger was re-elected to Congress in 1918 but expelled by the House—like Jack Wilkes from Parliament in the reign of George III. Even worse than the official crusade against sedition was the unofficial spy-hunting that engaged the energy of frustrated old women of both sexes. It was a wonderful opportunity to bring patriotism to the aid of neighborhood feuds and personal grudges. German-Americans, who did as much to support the war as any group, suffered the most. Stay-at-home patriots indulged in an orgy of hate, which even extended to passing state laws forbidding the teaching of German in schools or colleges, throwing German books out of public libraries, forbidding German or Austrian musicians to play in public or their music to be performed.

The bright side of the war on the home front is the control of food production and distribution under Herbert C. Hoover, a mining engineer who happened to be in England when the war broke, and who promptly organized a commission for Belgian relief. Hoover's task was to increase the production and decrease the consumption of food in America so that armies and civilians overseas might be adequately fed. He was empowered to fix the prices of staples, license food distributors, co-ordinate purchases, supervise exports, prohibit hoarding or profiteering, and stimulate production. He fixed the price of wheat at $2.20 a bushel, establishing a grain corporation to buy and sell it, organized the supply and purchase of meat, corralled the supply of sugar. But his major achievements were done by persuasion, not force, as befitted one of Quaker background. He induced people to cut down waste and reduce consumption by voluntary wheatless Mondays, meatless Tuesdays, and the like, which became an accepted part of the war effort; to save wheat, Americans returned to the "rye 'n Injun" bread of colonial days and experimented with unattractive if nutritious substitutes such as dogfish, sugarless candy, vegetable lamb, whale meat, and horse steak. As a result of "Hooverizing," the United States was able to export in 1918 approximately thrice her normal amounts of breadstuffs, meats, and sugar.

A fuel administration, under the direction of Harry A. Garfield, introduced daylight saving and gasless days which motorists generally respected, and closed non-essential manufacturing plants in an effort to conserve coal. A war trade board licensed foreign trade and blacklisted firms suspected of trading with the enemy. A war industries board, of which Bernard M. Baruch was the leading figure, co-ordinated purchases for the government and the Allies. A labor administration regulated relations between capital and labor, arbitrated industrial disputes, fixed hours and wages in certain industries, and banned strikes as contrary to public interest. A war finance corporation was authorized to supervise the floating of security issues, and underwriting of loans to industries engaged in the production of war materials.

To keep the Allies financially viable, as well as pay for our own part in the war—which was costing about $44 million a day at the end—income and all other taxes were increased and new ones applied, and about one-third of war costs were met by taxation; the rest by loans. There was no difficulty in raising $18.5 billion in liberty and victory bonds at the low interest rates of 3.5 to 4.25 per cent. Yet the country did not go off the gold standard, and inflation was kept at a minimum, compared with World War II.

5. The Peace Conference and the League

Thus, by 11 November 1918 the war was won, so far as arms could do it. Now came the great test of what kind of peace the Allies would impose and the Central Powers accept. For a "peace without victory" had long since been ruled out, even by President Wilson.

So many mistakes were made around the beginning of peace negotiations as to support the Swedish chancellor Oxenstiern's lament *Quantula sapientia mundus regitur,* "By how little wisdom is the world governed!" First of all, the Allies, victims of their own propaganda which made the Kaiser the No. 1 villain, refused to negotiate with him; William II had to abdicate, and the moderately democratic government that followed never established itself in the hearts of the people. Germans needed someone to look up to, and in the absence of royalty they erected twin idols: Hindenburg and Hitler. Second, Wilson's unwise appeal to return only Democrats to Congress in the fall elections, which the voters disregarded, was interpreted as a repudiation of the President and all he stood for; so that when the President decided to attend the Paris Peace Conference in person, he went with diminished prestige. Republican leaders and their friends in Paris—notably Frank Simonds the war correspondent and Judson C. Welliver of the New York *Sun*—urged the French public almost daily to pay no attention to Wilson and his dreams of a League of Nations— he had been repudiated. Yet even under these discouraging circumstances Wilson's character, and the hold he had on the plain people of England, France and Italy, enabled him to obtain a peace which, if not what he had wanted, was much better than what the Allied leaders would have achieved without him.

When the fighting reached its climax in the fall of 1918 a movement for "unconditional surrender" started; super-patriots began to sport buttons with Grant's old slogan. General Pershing even protested against an armistice, wished to march right on to Berlin. But Wilson and the Allies had given Marshal Foch authority to negotiate an armistice, and that great soldier declared, "War is only a means to results. If the Germans now sign an armistice under our conditions, those results are in our possession. This being achieved, no man has the right to cause another drop of blood to be shed." This sounds very noble; but, as we can see now, signing an armistice on the basis of the Fourteen Points gave the Germans a complaint that they had been betrayed, when the ensuing treaty so little resembled said points. And simply letting the German army go home and demobilize instead of occupying the country gave Hitler the further talking point that Germany had not been beaten in 1918, only "betrayed."

The Armistice was supposed to be in force for only sixty

days, which it was thought would be sufficient to conclude a treaty of peace. Actually, the Peace Conference did not even open for ten weeks, and peace-making required six months more, even though no German or Austrian delegation was allowed to debate the terms. During this time the Armistice was formally renewed monthly. And one of its severest terms, continuing the blockade until Germany signed a peace treaty, was relentlessly enforced, since the Allies wished to prevent a renewal of the war by Germany in case her government did not like the terms. This continued blockade caused more suffering in Germany than even the war, created a dangerous bitterness, and fed that desire for revenge which Hitler later exploited.

The two powerful leaders with whom Wilson had to contend at Paris were Clemenceau and Lloyd George. The "tiger of France," old and cynical—he had seen our Civil War and been through the war of 1870–71—was willing to accept a League of Nations provided France obtained security for the future. But his one idea of security was the traditional one of leaving Germany so weak, by massive reparations and territorial cessions, that she could be no further threat to France. Lloyd George, the clever, shallow premier of Great Britain, wanted reparations for his country and continued power for himself; he had successfully waged an electoral campaign in December 1918 on the slogans "Hang the Kaiser!" and "Make Germany Pay!" Orlando, for Italy, wanted vast cessions of territory from the defunct Austrian empire; and Mussolini later rode to power on the claim that he never got them. Wilson knew little of the seething nationalism in Europe, but he had a corps of experts (recruited by Colonel House) on every conceivable economic and territorial problem, and conscientiously tried to minimize war indemnities and obtain boundaries that would satisfy the populations. Whilst it is not true that the feature of the treaty closest to his heart, the League of Nations, prolonged the Peace Conference, it is now clear that the Allies could and should, before the new year dawned, have lifted the blockade, fed the hungry, and drafted a preliminary treaty leaving the working out of a definitive treaty and league to professional diplomats at a plenary conference with those of the defeated powers.

President Wilson cherished the hope that a League of Nations, in itself, would prevent future wars; and, with no other force but international law and public opinion, enforce peace. A story circulated in Paris tells of a conversation he had with Clemenceau. It went approximately as follows:

Wilson: My one object in promoting the League of Nations is to prevent future wars.

Clemenceau: You can never prevent war by no matter what scheme or organization unless we can all agree on three fundamental principles.

Wilson: What are they?

Clemenceau: First, to declare and enforce racial equality. Japan already has a resolution to that effect before the Conference. She demands that it be incorporated in the Treaty. Do you accept?

Wilson: No, I'm afraid not. The race question is very touchy in the United States, and the Southern and West Coast senators would defeat any treaty containing such a clause.

Clemenceau: The second thing we must do is to establish freedom of immigration; no country to close her borders to foreigners wishing to come to live there. Do you agree?

Wilson: No; my country is determined to exclude Orientals absolutely, and Congress is already considering restrictions to European immigration.

Clemenceau: The third condition of an enduring peace is free trade throughout the world. How would you like that?

Wilson: I personally would like to see it, and my party has lowered the American tariff; but I could never get Congress to agree to a customs union with Europe, Asia, and Africa.

Clemenceau: Very well, then; the only way to maintain peace is to remain strong ourselves and keep our past and potential enemies weak. No conceivable League of Nations can do that.

Although Wilson had plenty of experts to tell him what was right, he made an unfortunate choice of peace commissioners. Secretary Lansing took a narrow legal point of view and disliked the League. General Tasker H. Bliss, army chief of staff, was competent for military questions only; Henry White, one of our best career diplomats, was approaching senility. The best of the commissioners, Colonel House (who for the first time had official standing), was an expert negotiator but, before the end of the Conference, he lost Wilson's confidence. A prudent President would have appointed a senator or a prominent Republican of international repute such as Taft, Elihu Root, or Hughes, who had already gone on record for a League of Nations. Mrs. Wilson apparently was jealous of

House's influence on her husband and probably was the wedge that split them apart. This was unfortunate, because House's realism complemented Wilson's idealism; and when they parted, the stature of each was diminished.

Russia was the red ghost at the Peace Conference. She was represented in Paris only by committees of emigrés, ranging from socialists to monarchists; but her shadow hovered over the deliberations. The Bolsheviks (as the Russian Communists were then called) were in power, dedicated to establishing a "dictatorship of the proletariat" (meaning themselves) in Russia, and eventually throughout the world. During the Peace Conference they set up a communist regime in Hungary under Bela Kun, which was quickly snuffed out; but who could tell whether that might not happen elsewhere? Communist groups in every continental country looked to Moscow for guidance.

Wilson and Lloyd George sent a secret mission to sound out Lenin in March 1919. He was willing to negotiate, but nothing came of it, nor could any negotiation have quenched the implacable hatred the Communist party felt for the "bourgeois imperialists." The French government refused to treat in any way with the Bolsheviks because their regime, cruel and amoral beyond any in the memory of man, they believed to be certain to go. And, to make sure that it would go, the British and the French secretly supported counterrevolutionary Russian armies, which pressed into that unhappy country from three sides. President Wilson went along to the extent of sending a small American force to Archangel, ostensibly to prevent a cache of military supplies reaching Germany, and participating in a Japanese-directed invasion of Siberia, to see that Japan did not go too far. But the Russian army, reorganized by the redoubtable Trotsky, defeated all invasions and counterrevolutions; and by mid-June 1919 the Communist party was supreme in Russia.

The effect of all this on the Peace Conference, and on Wilson, was to dispose him to compromise the Fourteen Points and accept things in the treaty, such as an indefinite war indemnity, that he knew were wrong. When he felt like pulling out and telling the Allies to make peace their own way, he reflected that if he did, all Europe east of the Rhine might go Red. And, if he had quit, he would have called down on his head, his party and his country, the charge of loving "the Huns" more than the Allies. For there were other ghosts than Russia's hovering over the peace table—the spirits of millions of men killed; who, in the words of one of them, the poet John McCrae, cried

> If ye break faith with us who die
> We shall not sleep, though poppies grow
> In Flanders fields.

To blame Woodrow Wilson, in that atmosphere, for failing to do what was hard enough to do after a second world war, is palpably unfair.

Wilson successfully resisted some of the more extreme demands of the Allies. He denied Fiume to Italy—an action which caused Orlando to withdraw from the Conference in a huff, and enabled Republicans at home to mobilize Italian-Americans against the treaty. He protested against the cession of Shantung to Japan but wrung from her a promise, which Japan honored, to evacuate that Chinese province. He refused to permit the Allies to charge Germany with the whole cost of the war—a sum which Lloyd George estimated at approximately $120 billion. He resisted Clemenceau's desire to detach the entire Rhineland from Germany and set up an Alsace-Lorraine in reverse. He resisted the Polish demand for East Prussia, because it was inhabited mainly by Germans.

The Treaty of Versailles, which the Germans signed on 28 June 1919, was not so drastic as France and Italy wanted, or harsh enough to keep Germany down. It required her to admit war guilt, stripped her of all colonies and Alsace-Lorraine, imposed military and naval disarmament, saddled her with an immediate indemnity of $15 billion and a future reparations bill of indeterminate amount, and placed her economic system under temporary Allied control. Other treaties drawn up simultaneously or shortly after, set up, out of the debris of the Austro-Hungarian empire, the new republic of Czechoslovakia, restored the independence of Poland, and gave her a corridor to the Baltic. By adding the Slavic sections of the old Dual Monarchy to Serbia, that kingdom became Yugoslavia, and Rumania's territory was almost doubled at the expense of Hungary. In general the revised boundaries of Europe were carefully worked out on the basis of language and race, but it was economically impractical to make every new boundary follow an ethnic line, and, in case of doubt, the Germans and Austrians naturally were the ones to suffer. Nor should it be forgotten that the fate of four debatable territories—the Saar, Schleswig, lower East Prussia, and Upper Silesia—were settled by plebiscites, three of which were won by Germany. German cries over territorial losses—enhanced to screams under Hitler—convinced many people of good will in America and Europe that grave injustice had been done; but from the viewpoint of 1964 the squawks and howls over that "horrible" Treaty of

Versailles seem faintly ridiculous. Its only really bad features, which few outside Germany criticized at the time,[1] were the flexible indemnity which promoted financial instability in Germany, and the disarmament clauses which rendered the German Republic powerless to defend itself. But the treaty also set up a reparations committee which eventually let Germany off easily on the financial side, so that by 1929 such parts of the treaty as were keeping Germany poor and insolvent had been removed by mutual consent.

Wilson and most of the European statesmen agreed that through a permanent international organization for settling disputes and correcting injustices, all crooked things in the treaty could be put straight. "The settlements," said Wilson, "may be temporary, but the processes must be permanent." It was he who insisted that the League be an integral part of the treaty. On 25 January 1919 the Peace Conference sustained him and assigned to a special committee, of which he was chairman, the task of drawing up the League Covenant. The final draft was adopted by the Conference on 14 February 1919, and published immediately.

The function of the League of Nations, as set forth in the preamble, was "to promote international co-operation and to achieve international peace and security." Membership was open to all nations and self-governing dominions. An assembly, in which every member nation had a vote; a council, of which the five great powers were permanent members and four others were to be elected; a permanent secretariat at Geneva and a court of international justice at the Hague, completed the machinery for world organization. Members of the League pledged themselves to "respect and preserve as against external aggression the territorial integrity and existing political independence" of one another (Art. X); to submit to inquiry and arbitration every dispute threatening peace; to refrain from war with any nation that complied with an arbitral award by the League; and to employ military, financial, and economic sanctions against nations resorting to war in disregard of the League. In order to counter the charge of territorial aggrandizement, the League would administer the colonies of former enemies by the mandate system, a new and excellent feature

---

[1] A notable exception was John M. Keynes's *The Economic Consequences of the Peace,* which came out in January 1920 and had an immense impact on public opinion on both sides of the Atlantic. Keynes, owing to his later heading a school of economic thought, has become a classic; but Allyn A. Young in *The New Republic,* 25 Feb. 1920, punctured several of his sophistries. It was Keynes who invented the cliché of Wilson, the simple Presbyterian elder, being "bamboozled" by those slick operators Lloyd George and Clemenceau.

of the Versailles Treaty for which Wilson and House were largely responsible. This meant that the former German colonies in Africa, China, and the Pacific, instead of being divided up as booty in the time-honored fashion, were placed under the trusteeship of England, France, Australia, New Zealand, or Japan, which were accountable to the League for promoting the welfare of the natives.

6. The Eclipse of Liberalism

In June 1919 when Wilson finally left Paris for home, House counseled him to meet the Senate in the same conciliatory spirit that he had used with Lloyd George and Clemenceau. At that suggestion the President stuck out his jaw and said he was going to fight for the treaty. That he did, to his death.

The fight had already started, and the Senate was in an ugly mood. The League was no exclusive brain-child of Wilson, nor was it "sprung" on the people unawares. In 1915 a number of leading Americans, including former President Taft, Elihu Root, and President Lowell of Harvard, had organized a "League To Enforce Peace" society and promoted it by voice and pen. Senator Lodge delivered a commencement address on the subject in 1915 and told the League To Enforce Peace on 27 May 1916 that George Washington's warning against entangling alliances was never meant to exclude America from joining other nations in "a method . . . to diminish war and encourage peace." Even Theodore Roosevelt gave tentative support, and the Democratic platform of 1916 contained a League of Nations plank. In May 1918 there was held at Philadelphia a "win the war for Permanent Peace" convention, addressed by Taft, Lowell, Rabbi Stephen S. Wise, Charles E. Hughes, Senator John Sharp Williams, and several industrial leaders. Not only intellectuals but labor unions and financial organizations, and most of the press of the United States, had definitely endorsed the League of Nations idea well before the armistice. But during the long-drawn-out peace negotiations, hostility both to the idea of an international league, and to the actual Covenant that Wilson brought home, gathered momentum.

Many of the arguments against it were rational. Theodore Roosevelt, for instance, pointed out that the League was unlikely to preserve peace without armed forces under its exclusive control; and before condemning him, let us ask ourselves whether the United Nations could have prevented the cold war from getting hot, without NATO and American atomic power? Or whether there is now any likelihood of preserving peace without an enforceable world law? Most of the opposition, however, was irrational and emotional, compounded of personal hostility to Wilson and senatorial pique, German-American excitement over the alleged betrayal of Germany, Italian-American anger over Italy's not getting Fiume; Irish-American frenzy over Sinn Fein; conservative dislike of "leniency" toward Germany, liberal disapproval of "severity" toward Germany, and a general feeling that America, having expended her all, only to be tricked by European diplomats, should avoid future entanglements.

At one extreme in the Senate were Borah, Johnson, Knox, Moses, McCormick, La Follette and other Republicans, who were unwilling to let Wilson get away with another triumph and persuaded themselves that any departure from the traditional policy of isolation would be suicidal. At the other extreme were Democrats loyal to Wilson who felt honor bound not to let him and the Allies down, and who believed that the League was the only possible method of preventing another war. In between were members of both parties who believed in the wisdom of a few reservations, such as a declaration that Article X would not obligate the United States to go to war to preserve every new boundary set up under the Treaty of Versailles. More than three-fourths of the senators were ready to vote for the League in some form or other. If Wilson had been willing to accept a few reservations such as the one recognizing "the validity of . . . regional understandings like the Monroe Doctrine," which he himself had inserted in the Covenant, he could have obtained ratification that summer. But his basic stubbornness came to the fore, and he would yield nothing more than a few innocuous interpretations.

What a futile controversy! The Covenant proved to be far too weak to restrain a major power, and no reservations proposed in the Senate could have made it materially weaker. But it was at least worth a try.

Wilson's prideful belief that God and the people were with him—the *hubris* which in Greek tragedies always destroyed the proud—led him to make a direct appeal to the electorate. On 4 September 1919 he set out on a speaking tour through the Middle and Far West. He spoke with superb eloquence, passionate conviction, and the tongue of prophecy: "I can predict with absolute certainty that within another generation there will be another world war if the nations of the world do not concert the method by which to prevent it"; and, "What the Germans used were toys compared to what would be used in the next war." But much of the effect of his speeches was spoiled by arguments of irreconcilables who stalked him re-

lentlessly from city to city. On 25 September he spoke at
Pueblo, Colorado; that night he suffered a physical collapse.
And with that vanished all hope of the United States subscrib-
ing to a new world order.

When safely back in the White House, it became clear that
the President was incapacitated by arteriosclerosis and a throm-
bosis that paralyzed his left arm and leg. For at least two
months he hovered between life and death, and his physique
never fully recovered. Nobody was permitted so see him except his secretary Joseph Tumulty, his daughters, Mrs. Wilson,
Dr. Grayson, his personal physician, and, occasionally, Bernard
Baruch. Mrs. Wilson and Grayson acted as an informal council
of regency. Colonel House's letters were not answered; some of
them not opened. Even Sir Edward (now Viscount) Grey, a
pioneer for the League, a liberal whom Wilson trusted and admired, sent by the British government to try to persuade him
to accept reservations, was not admitted to the presence. For
two months the President could do no more than scrawl a
shaky signature to documents that his wife or physician thrust
at him. After that, his mind became clear enough to follow
what was going on, and he could dictate letters, talk for a few
minutes at a time with cabinet members, and receive an occasional distinguished visitor.

This was definitely the situation envisaged by the Constitution: "In the case of" the President's "inability to discharge the
powers and duties of the said office, the same shall devolve on
the Vice President." But, when this was propounded by Secretary Lansing, Mrs. Wilson and Joe Tumulty opposed it so
vigorously that he went no further. And who was to declare
presidential disability? The Constitution and the laws said
nothing about that. Moreover, Vice President Thomas R.
Marshall was a colorless character whose one utterance recorded for fame is, "What this country needs is a good five-
cent cigar!" One shuddered to think of him as President, and
he was terrified at the prospect himself; but the bitter irony is
that if he had become President at this juncture he would have
made the necessary concessions and the Treaty would have
been ratified. In any case, the President's disability was temporary. From about 1 November he had full control of his mental
faculties.

Senator Henry Cabot Lodge, with malignant ingenuity, maneuvered the Senate to doom the Treaty and the League, while
pretending to favor both with reservations. On 6 November
1919 Senator Gilbert M. Hitchcock of Nebraska, who had
managed the pro-League campaign, was admitted to the President's sick chamber to convey the bad news that the Democrats

could not raise even a bare majority for ratification without reservations. "Is it possible?" said Wilson, groaning. "It might be wise to compromise," the Senator ventured to say. "Let Lodge compromise!" said Wilson. Even Mrs. Wilson begged him to accept the Lodge reservations. "Better a thousand times to go down fighting than to dip your colors to dishonorable compromise," he replied.

And so, fighting, the ship went down. On 19 November the Senate took a vote on ratifying the Treaty of Versailles, and the noes won. Brought up for reconsideration next session, it once more failed of two-thirds majority and on 19 March 1920 the Senate returned it to the President with formal notice of inability to ratify.

In the meantime there were sad doings on the domestic front. President Wilson's third attorney general, A. Mitchell Palmer, was a Pennsylvania politician with a presidential bee in his bonnet. Appointed alien property custodian in 1917, he sequestered some $600 million worth of German and Austrian property in the United States, and saw to it that his friends got some of the bargains when this property was sold. As attorney general, Palmer decided (like Joseph McCarthy more than thirty years later) that the way to fame and power was to crack down on the "Reds." Pro-Germans were no longer dangerous, but the success of the Bolsheviks in Russia, their provocative and threatening language, and their growing control over all socialist elements everywhere, now made them the chief target of American fears. Wilson, at the first cabinet meeting since his breakdown, in April 1920, said, "Palmer, do not let this country see red!" But Palmer had been doing just that for five months. He instigated a series of lawless raids on homes and labor headquarters, on a single night of January 1920, arresting more than 4000 alleged communists in 33 different cities. In New England, hundreds of people were arrested who had no connection with radicalism of any kind. In Detroit, 300 men were arrested on false charges, held for a week in jail and denied food for 24 hours, only to be found innocent of any involvement in revolutionary movements. The raids yielded almost nothing in the way of arms or revolutionaries, but Palmer emerged from the episode a national hero. And what made his action the more abominable is that he was a practicing Quaker, even using the traditional "thee" instead of "you." In New York, the anti-radical campaign reached its climax when the state legislature expelled five Socialist members of the assembly, although the Socialist party was legally recognized and the members were innocent of any offense. This went too far, even for conservatives; the Chicago *Tribune*,

Senator Harding, and Charles Evans Hughes denounced their action. In Massachusetts the Sacco and Vanzetti case, though having nothing directly to do with the raids, was an offshoot of the same whipped-up anti-red hysteria.

Early in 1920 a movement against Palmer by the labor department, led by Secretary William B. Wilson and his assistant Louis Post, turned deportation proceedings to a saner direction. Post insisted on giving aliens proper counsel and fair hearings. He canceled action against dozens of them, and by spring released nearly half those arrested in Palmer's January raids. Palmer demanded that Post be fired for his "tender solicitude for social revolution," but when Post was haled before a congressional committee, he made such a convincing presentation that his critics were forced to back down. In the end, although 5000 arrest warrants had been sworn out, only a few more than 600 aliens were actually deported.

Palmer now let his attempts to capitalize on the "Red Menace" get out of hand. He issued a series of warnings of a revolutionary plot which would be launched on 1 May 1920, to overthrow the United States government. The National Guard was called out, and in New York City the entire police force was put on 24-hour duty. May Day passed without a single shot being fired or bomb exploded. As a result, the country concluded that Palmer had cried wolf once too often.

There was a lot more of this sort of thing going around; more hate literature, more nasty, sour, and angry groups promoting "hundred per cent Americanism" than at any earlier period of our history, or any later one prior to the 1950's. Anti-Semitism appeared openly for the first time in America, and was nourished by Henry Ford, of all people. The Dearborn newspaper that he controlled reprinted that hoary fake, "The Protocols of the Elders of Zion," supposedly proving a Jewish conspiracy to destroy civilization; and Ford either wrote or had compiled for him a book *The International Jew* (1920), which blamed the war and everything else on that race. There were also anti-Catholic pamphlets accusing the Knights of Columbus of indulging in obscene rites. The Ku Klux Klan was revived and did well, especially in the North and West; the Klan elected governors in Oklahoma and Oregon, and in 1924 practically took over Indiana. Favorite targets of the Klansmen were alcohol and adultery; but when David Stephenson, "Grand Dragon" of Indiana, who had made millions out of membership fees and selling nightshirts, was convicted of raping a young woman and causing her death, the Klan began to decline.

Another source of trouble, which the peddlers of hate

whipped up, was the northward move of many Southern blacks to work in war industries and better their condition. This, as usual, was resented by white workers, especially recent immigrants, and led to bloody riots. In one at East St. Louis, Illinois, in 1917 forty-seven people, mostly blacks, were killed and hundreds wounded. In July of 1919, the month that President Wilson returned from Paris and submitted the Treaty to the Senate, there occurred in the capital city the most serious race riots in its history between whites and blacks, not quelled until thousands of troops had been brought in to help the police, and six people killed. In the same month there was a three-day race riot in Chicago in which thirty-six people were killed. There were also major racial disorders that year in New York and Omaha, at least seven in the South, mostly occasioned by black veterans of the war having the "impudence" to demand their rights as citizens.

But for his disability, Woodrow Wilson could have been nominated for a third presidential term by the Democratic national convention. Palmer for a time thought he would get it; but he and McAdoo, the President's son-in-law, killed each other off, and Governor James A. Cox of Ohio obtained the nomination. Cox was little known nationally, like Franklin Pierce, and as unimportant. Reversing the usual procedure, his vice-presidential nominee, Franklin D. Roosevelt, was the man with a future.

Much the same happened in the Republican camp. The tycoons of the party wanted General Leonard Wood, who was exploiting a grievance of having been kept out of glory in the war, like his old friend Colonel Roosevelt. But the General and Governor Frank Lowden of Illinois could not get the necessary majority; and the bosses, after deciding on Senator Warren G. Harding of Ohio in a "smoke-filled room," put him across. They were about to impose another "pol" of the same kidney for second place, when the delegates got their backs up, and nominated Calvin Coolidge. Fame had recently thrust herself upon Governor Coolidge when, in the course of a Boston police strike, he declared that there was "no right to strike against the public safety by anybody, anywhere, anytime." This caught the imagination of a public jittery about the Red Menace.

The voters gave Harding 16,152,200 votes, with 404 in the electoral college, and Cox 9,147,353 with 127 electoral votes. The winner's plurality, 61 per cent of the total, came nearest to a political landslide in our history, prior to 1964. Harding, or whoever wrote his campaign speeches, gauged the public temper correctly when he announced, "America's present need is not heroics but healing; not nostrums but normalcy; not revolution but restoration . . . not surgery but serenity." At least half the 920,000 votes polled by Socialist candidate Debs, who was still in jail for opposing the war, registered protest by people disillusioned with Wilson but unwilling to go Republican.

So emphatic an overturn needs explanation. It was not merely dislike of the League of Nations. A group of prominent Leaguers, including Taft, Hoover, Hughes, and college presidents Nicholas Murray Butler of Columbia and Lowell of Harvard, urged people to vote for Harding as the only way to support the League—an odd piece of bad judgment that they later regretted. Walter Lippmann, who lived through those years of turmoil, in 1964 diagnosed the reaction as "the backwash of the excitement and the sacrifice, when the people were war-weary and angry at the disappointing peace which followed the war." Others have said that the people were tired of being "pushed around" by rationing, restrictions, drafts, and the like. Possibly so; but Herbert Hoover, as the most conspicuous pusher-arounder of the war, was elected President in 1928. Disillusion over the peace, especially by the three principal groups of "hyphenated Americans" who felt that Germany, Ireland, and Italy had been "betrayed," and the feeling that all America's sacrifices had been in vain, doubtless had much to do with the people's revulsion from the Democrats. But, in my opinion, the principal architect of Democratic defeat was George Creel and the propaganda corps. His campaign of hate during the war got the people all hopped up for fighting Germany to an unconditional surrender, marching on Berlin, hanging the Kaiser, and all that; so when the war ended abruptly before even half the armed forces had seen action, the public, suddenly let down, turned its emotions against something else. The Red Menace siphoned off a part of the hate, but most of it boomeranged on the administration which had led us into a "futile and useless war."

Whatever may have been the reason or reasons for the 1920 vote, it is certain that World War I was the most popular war in our history while it lasted, and the most hated after it was over. American books, plays, and movies on the war, such as Dos Passos's *Three Soldiers,* Hemingway's *Farewell to Arms,* and Laurence Stallings and Maxwell Anderson's *What Price Glory?* presented the war as unrelieved boredom, horror, and filth. And no general officer in the war ever received an important political office.

President Wilson, a shadow of his former self but still stern and dignified, just managed to be driven to the Capitol in an open car with President-elect Harding on 4 March 1921. He then passed into the shadows.

Woodrow Wilson, even after half a century has elapsed, is a difficult President to evaluate; especially for one who joyfully followed his leadership both in peace and war, saw him in action in Paris, suffered disillusion at the outcome, yet with the lapse of time has become tolerant of the President's mistakes. Wilson was a great leader because he sensed the aspirations of plain people and expressed them in phrases that rang like a great bronze bell. He showed flexibility, one of the attributes of statesmanship, in his shift from a pacifist to a belligerent policy, and in his negotiations at Paris; he was stubborn only at the end, when his efforts had worn him out. He was a prophet, foretelling that if America fell back into isolation she would surely be involved in another and more terrible war; that the only way to prevent that was to stop it from starting. His faults, which may forever deny him that veneration which the American people give to the memory of Lincoln, of Washington and even of Franklin D. Roosevelt, were a stubborn pride and a distaste for personal contacts. These were but the infirmities of a noble mind. Many turned against him for the

OH! HOW I HATE TO GET UP IN THE MORNING

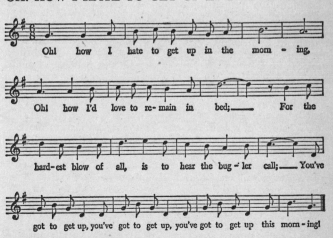

Oh! how I hate to get up in the morn - ing,
Oh! how I'd love to re- main in bed;___ For the
hard-est blow of all, is to hear the bug - ler call;___ You've
got to get up, you've got to get up, you've got to get up this morn-ing!

same reason that a certain citizen of ancient Athens turned against Aristides because he was sick and tired of hearing that statesman called "the Just." Wilson's attitude about everything that he did was irritatingly virtuous.

Yet every hard thought about Wilson may vanish if we shift our attention from him to ourselves. He threw America's strength into the war, to accomplish something of transcendent benefit to his country and to mankind—an organization to ensure a peaceful solution for international conflicts. Maybe the goal was too high. Maybe he should not have made the attempt. But in that desperate gamble there is something far more admirable than what the United States Senate did, contrary to his advice and exhortation. Their action, which in some measure was forced by the people, and which the people approved in the next election, resulted in degrading America's war of 1917–18 to a mere hit-and-run operation.

IX

The Great Change

1902-1939

1. *The Auto and the Ad Men*

THROUGHOUT THESE crowded years of progressive legislation, violent politics, war waging and peace making, the American people were undergoing profound changes in their environment, their racial composition, their mental processes, and their moral climate. Rural America was moving to the city, horsey America was becoming motor-conscious, the American "melting pot" stopped bubbling; female America broke out of her former "only place, the home," and morally Puritan America, having put over the puritanical Amendment XVIII, became a country of wild drinking and loose morals. All these things interacted; but the invention of the internal combustion engine[1] and its multifarious applications to transport and power, was the material key to the Great Change.

The "horseless carriage," as the automobile was first called in America, was just that; a strongly built buggy with solid rubber tires and a one-cylinder gasoline engine geared to the rear axle by a bicycle chain. Just as the early steamships looked

---

[1] The gas or gasoline engine was invented by N. A. Otto in 1876, the oil or diesel engine in 1892 by Rudolf Diesel, both Germans; but, as with other basic inventions, many years elapsed before their practical application to power and transportation was consummated.

like sailing vessels, so motor vehicle designs changed slowly from those of carriages. First you had the "runabout" steered by a tiller; then you added a "tonneau" with a rear-opening door to make a "touring car." Better springs and pneumatic tires made the riding less rough; a canvas top and side-curtains protected passengers from rain; and by the end of World War I the average speed of cars had so increased that the public demanded a hardtop "limousine," "sedan," or "cabriolet," hitherto the privilege of the rich.

As these terms indicate, and also "chassis," "garage," "chauffeur," and even "automobile," France was the original home of the motor car. At the time of the Paris Exposition of 1900, cars were almost driving horses off the Champs-Elysées. But in America for eight or ten years more the automobile was an imported toy, a plaything of the rich, disliked because it was smelly, noisy, and frightened horses. Automobiling was one of those things like tennis- and golf-playing, smoking cigarettes and wearing wrist watches, which politicians did not dare to be seen doing. Theodore Roosevelt wrote in 1905 that he had taken but two "auto rides" during his presidency and would take no more, because on the last one his chauffeur had been held up for speeding, which created undesirable publicity. Woodrow Wilson, president of Princeton in 1907, cautioned the students against indulging in the "snobbery" of motoring. "Nothing," he said, "has spread socialistic feelings in this country more" than this "picture of the arrogance of wealth."

The greatest obstacle to making the automobile popular was neither price nor prejudice but bad roads. Outside the cities these at best were macadamized, but more often just plain dirt. Maintained locally, they were full of ruts and potholes because farmers driving slow-moving wagons and buggies did not care to be taxed to keep them in good shape. Such roads were uncomfortable for the new vehicles at best, and impossible during snow or long wet spells. In 1902 there appeared a book by Arthur J. Eddy entitled *Two Thousand Miles on an Automobile*. Eddy drove a two-seat, one-cylinder car that could make up to 30 miles per hour but seldom went more than 20 on the roads that he encountered, and suffered a puncture and tire-change about every 100 miles. But the principal hazard was a skittish horse with timid driver. In some villages, speed limits were as low as 10 miles per hour, and the pioneer motorist was apt to be brought up short by a gate bearing the sign "No Horseless Carriages Allowed," guarded by a bearded deputy sheriff with a shotgun. The first Glidden Tour, of 34 autos in October 1903, took eight days to reach Pittsburgh from New York City.

Although there were cheap American cars before Ford's, there was no rugged, all-purpose car selling for less than $1500 until Henry Ford brought out his Model T in 1908. Six years later he invented the assembly-line method of mass production; and a few months after that, to the astonishment of the world and the indignation of other employers, Ford announced a minimum wage of $5 a day for his workers. The Model T "tin lizzie" or "flivver," as it was nicknamed, sold over half a million in 1916, two million in 1923, and by 1927 when its production ceased (Ford having unwillingly substituted the slightly more sophisticated Model A), the staggering total of 15 million cars had been sold. The price, which started at $825 for the two-seat runabout in 1908, when down to $260 in 1925. And after Ford had established an assembly plant in England, American cars began to invade the European market. A significant fact in American economic history is that in 1929 the value of automotive exports surpassed that of cotton exports, which had held first place since the Civil War.

Model T was the car that revolutionized American life. The farmer now had a vehicle that he could use for pleasure, with a pickup truck attachment to carry crops to market; or, with rear wheel jacked up and a homemade attachment, saw wood, fill the silo, do everything (it was said) but wash the dishes. The skilled worker in town or city could live miles from his job and drive his family into the country after supper or on Sundays. Even the Southern black's lot was bettered by the Ford car, which the most benighted Ku-Kluxers did not deny to him, provided it was bought locally. The car not only afforded him recreation, but at a pinch his family could pile in and drive north to seek a job. The automobile, in connection with gasoline-driven agricultural machinery, emancipated the Western wheat farmer from his land. Without animals to feed, he could shut up house as soon as the crop was harvested and roll to California or Florida for the winter. Filling stations and service garages sprang up along main roads, enterprising farm wives established country restaurants to cater to "joy-riders," and small-time entrepreneurs set up dance halls for playboys and their "pick-ups." "Ye olde gifte shoppes" burgeoned to compete for the motorist's dollar, and country inns whose only patrons had been traveling salesmen, now redecorated and hung out "Old Colonial" signs. Others established tourist camps with individual cabins ("fireplace and flush toilet"), which after World War II were largely superseded by motels.

But none of these things were possible without good roads. Prior to World War I, at least nine out of ten car owners in the Northern states "put up" their cars in winter and went back to horse or steam transportation. Country doctors had to maintain a horse, buggy, and sleigh to get about when roads were impassable because of mud or snow. And at best, on dirt roads, the motorist had to wear linen duster, goggles, and veil for protection from the clouds of dust that every car raised. As late as 1920 an official of Jackson County, Missouri, named Harry Truman, when making his rounds, had to ballast the rear of his Dodge with concrete blocks to avoid being capsized in potholes. But by 1925, when more than half the families, in the North at least, either owned a car or were about to buy one on the installment plan, appropriations for hard-top roads began to pour freely out of state legislatures. The "balloon tire" made riding less rattly; and the gasoline-run bulldozer began its victorious onslaught on American scenery.

Congress in 1916 passed an act matching state appropriations for through roads, dollar for dollar. This did not satisfy the road-hungry public, and in 1954 the federal government began paying 90 per cent of the cost of roads approved by the secretary of the interior. A new and fruitful source of corruption was opened by the vast road-building programs since World War II, in the extravagant widenings, straightenings, over- and under-passes, loops and cross-country expressways, construction of which was stimulated far more by profits than by any pressing need of the traveling public. Politicians love to appropriate money for new roads; they can tip off their friends to profit by land-taking, curry favor with contractors by voting extra funds for non-contractual alterations, and with labor for overtime. The urge to get in and out of the city is ruining the city; gaping holes are torn through it to make place for urban expressways. No home is safe, no distinguished architecture of the past is spared, no amenities such as century-old trees by a quiet riverside are respected.

All earlier types of transportation suffered. The rural trolley car was the first to go; it could not compete with the faster, gasoline- or diesel-driven bus that whipped people from place to place in half the time. Livery stables, of which every small town boasted at least one, carriage and wagon factories, harness makers, grain stores and other industries that fed horse transport, went bankrupt; hayfields where the horse's provender had been grown, reverted to brush and forest like the tobacco "old fields" of Virginia. Last horse-driven industry to be motorized was the funeral; until the 1930's it was thought indecorous for a corpse to be hustled to the grave in a motor hearse. Coastal steamboats and freighters died a lingering death, not so much owing to the change of propulsion—gasoline being too dear for freighters and the diesel engine too expensive initially—but from road-truck competition. World War I brought a last spurt in the building of wooden sailing vessels, but most of them were permanently beached in the postwar slump. Coastal steamships hung on to 1937, when the famous Fall River Line expired in its ninety-first year. The railroads, America's pride in the early part of the century, are now emitting ominous death-rattles, despite the adoption of electric-driven diesel engines and accelerated schedules.

Although Ford sold more "flivvers" than all other American cars combined, he had plenty of competition near his price range, notably the Dodge and the Maxwell. The motor-car industry in America began "all over the place" in the North and Middle West. Around 1910 thousands of mechanically minded youngsters were building their own "jalopies" in a tool-shed and dreaming of becoming another Ford; most of the tycoons of Willys-Overland, Buick, Oldsmobile, Cadillac, Packard, and Chrysler started that way. George M. Pierce of the elegant, prestigious but now defunct Pierce-Arrow, started by making bird cages, then went to bicycle manufacture, and as early as 1901 brought out his first motor car, powered by a one-cylinder French engine. Over 2000 different "makes" of autos have existed in the United States. Prior to World War I, more autos were being built in New England than in Michigan; but Ford's success attracted others to the Detroit complex, and one by one the little plants—Metz, Moon and Stanley Steamer of Boston, Winton of Cleveland, and hundreds more—went broke or were absorbed. Cadillac survived as a name, though absorbed by General Motors, thanks to pioneering in 1912 the self-starter, which did even more than windshields and front doors to attract women drivers.

Consolidation was not confined to the motor car factories. During this era the existence of every local store became precarious. "Great Atlantic & Pacific" bought out over 15,000 little groceries by 1932; Woolworth, pioneer in the five-and-dime field, purchased on such an immense scale that he could undersell everybody; the success of "Piggly-Wiggly—All Over the World" sparked tens of thousands of "Stop and Shop" supermarkets to which the housewife drove in her car and served herself. Efficient, perhaps; profitable, certainly; but thousands of friendly neighborhood stores were ruined. This situation, in the 1950's, produced a series of state "fair trade" laws pegging retail prices so that small stores could survive the competition of the chains.

Ford's Model T largely sold itself, but the fierce competition among his rivals fed a relatively new business—"high-powered" salesmanship and advertising. The motor car industry did even more than drugs, cosmetics, and appliances to exalt advertising to the dignity of a profession. Prior to 1910, advertisements were relatively few and simple. In newspapers and magazines, apart from positions- and help-wanted notices, and for the department stores, advertisements were mostly of cures for physical ills—Lydia E. Pinkham's comfortable nostrum for the weaker sex, Dr. Sloan's Liniment for Man or Beast, Fletcher's Castoria ("Children Cry for It"); or bald claims for superior excellence of competing articles in daily use. But the Motor Age changed advertising to a series of prestigious urges to spend and buy:—a bigger car than your neighbor's; a luxury cruise, an all-electric kitchen, mink coat and diamonds for Mother. Emerson, over a century ago, complained that the stockjobber had supplanted the robber baron; in our time the writers of advertising copy, more highly paid than archbishops or college presidents, seem to have convinced the American public that to make money and spend it is the good life. They have become the priesthood to what William James aptly called "the bitch-goddess, Success." Bruce Barton, chairman of the board of Batten, Barton, Durstine & Osborne, in a book called *The Man Nobody Knows* (1925), presented Jesus Christ to the nation as a back-slapping good guy, a go-getter and regular Rotarian.

Whilst advertising needed constant regulation to prevent defacing the countryside with billboards and claiming cure-all virtues for innocuous or harmful pills, it did contribute something positive to the economy besides employing thousands of models, photographers, and copy-writers. Advertising revenue enabled magazines and newspapers, which otherwise would have succumbed to radio competition, to survive; and some big advertisers acquired a social conscience. Texaco, for instance, has supported the broadcasting of grand opera. Advertising also promoted the revolution of rising expectations. Factory operatives by 1916 were no longer content to walk to work, wear secondhand clothes, live in cold-water "walk-ups," and have few if any recreations. Mom wanted nice new clothes for the children, and, later a radio to while away the tedium of household chores, a weekly hair-do, a vacuum cleaner, and a washing machine; Dad wanted above all things a car. Employers had to pay high enough wages for the workers to buy, and provide the leisure hours for them to enjoy, these gadgets which the advertisers had taught them it was "un-American" to be without. Nor were they denied; and by the time the big crash came, American workingmen had acquired such middle-class values that even the Great Depression did not thrust them back to the status of a helpless proletariat, as the communists hoped and predicted. Thus, advertising, more than any factor, has made the luxuries of yesterday the necessities of today; and if any profession is to be crowned or cursed for bringing about the present state of society it is that of the "ad men."

The increasing application of internal-combustion engines to power led to geographical dislocation in the economy. Certain coal-mining regions became depressed areas; oil-producing regions attracted population and wealth, and lucky land owners who happened to "strike oil" became multimillionaires of the vulgar type portrayed in Edna Ferber's *Cimarron* (1930). California, the leading oil-producing state in 1925, and Texas, which began pulling ahead of her, owe no small measure of their phenomenal increase in population to the enhanced demand for their underground riches in petroleum.

2. Aviation, 1903–1960

The successful application of the internal-combustion engine to aviation took much longer than it did to road or rail transport. Substituting engine for horse to propel a wheeled vehicle, or converting a steamboat to diesel power, was simple in comparison. But man had to learn to fly before he could apply power to aircraft, and he faced far more difficult problems of engine and structural design than ever did the builders of ships and cars.

For centuries Europeans had dreamed of flying; Leonardo da Vinci designed a helicopter, Tennyson foretold "airy navies grappling in the central blue," and for decades American schoolboys had pestered their teachers with paper darts shaped like the latest delta-winged plane of 1964. Balloons had been used to some extent since the late eighteenth century. But the balloon without power was at the mercy of the wind and, with power, it led to a dead-end development—the Zeppelin and the blimp.

Active experimenting in and scientific study of aerodynamics began only in the second half of the nineteenth century. Three lines of endeavor pulled together to bring about the first powered heavier-than-air flights, in 1903. First there was the work of mathematicians and physicists such as Samuel P. Langley of the Smithsonian (whose *Experiments in Aerodynamics of* 1891 is basic), aided by experiments in kite-flying by the meteorologist A. Lawrence Rotch, and Alexander Graham Bell, inventor of the telephone. But Langley never constructed a successful "flying machine" because he relied exclusively on science, not experience. Second were the gliders, notably Otto Lilienthal of Germany who crashed fatally in 1896 after making over 2000 successful glides, and Octave Chanute whose employee Augustus M. Herring began gliding from sand dunes on Lake Michigan that year, and who lived to advise the Wrights. Third were the amateurs—writers, students, and promoters of man-made flight. These were a band of brothers, unmoved by gain, unterrified by popular skepticism and the belief that "God never meant man to fly." God made the birds, however, and all pioneers of aviation studied meticulously the flying methods of birds, especially the seagull, the stork, the albatross, and the condor; even the humble sparrow contributed by suggesting to Chanute the "tail down" landing.

Of American amateurs, the most important was James Means, a retired shoe manufacturer who founded the Boston Aëronautical Society in 1895 and the same year began the publication of the *Aëronautical Annual*. Therein professionals like Langley shared knowledge and aspirations with each other and the amateurs. Orville Wright wrote to Means early in 1908, "The old *Annuals* were largely responsible for the active interest which led us to begin experiments in aeronautics."

Orville and Wilbur Wright were the men who pulled all three lines together to produce the first powered flights. Sons of a Protestant bishop, in 1896 they were just two young men in their twenties who owned a bicycle business in Dayton, Ohio. After reading everything on the subject by Langley, Chanute, and others, they decided that the three essential problems to be solved before powered and guided flight would be possible were wing design, balance and control aloft, and the application of power. In 1900 they began gliding a plane of their own design and construction at Kitty Hawk on the outer coast of North Carolina, not far from Roanoke Island where the first Virginia colony was founded. They tried wing-warping for lateral control, and a front elevator for longitudinal control; they experimented with miniature models in a home-made wind tunnel, and in 1902 flew almost 1000 successful glides. Building their own four-cylinder, 200-pound, 12-horsepower gasoline engine—since none in the market was light enough— they fitted it to their third glider, and on the morning of 17 December 1903 made their first four powered flights—of 120 to 582 feet over the ground, lasting from twelve seconds to a minute, against a strong wind. The deed was done, and the Wrights won because they learned to fly before applying power.

But it took them five years to prove that they had won, for they were shy of the press which had sneered at their efforts,

and declined financial aid. Quietly they continued experimenting, and in 1905 designed an improved airplane in which Wilbur flew over 24 miles in 38 minutes. In the meantime other
aviation pioneers, mainly foreign, were receiving all the publicity, and working on the problem of stability, which the
Wrights had not solved. Santos-Dumont of Brazil got into the
running in 1906; and Glenn Curtiss, a former motorcycle
racer, constructed a rival plane to the Wrights', which flew a
mile on 4 July 1908. That fall, poker-faced Wilbur Wright
took the brothers' latest airplane (35-horsepower with a payload of one passenger plus 100 pounds) to France, and "Vil-
bure Vritch," as the French pronounced his name, made a
sensation, especially by his perfect control of the plane in all
kinds of wind. He also established new world records for distance—62 miles in six minutes short of two hours, and altitude
—361 feet! In the meantime, Brother Orville was demonstrat-
ing a two-seater model over Fort Myer, Virginia, which the
Army had already ordered.

Few things in our history are more admirable than the skill,
the pluck, the quiet self-confidence, the alertness to reject fixed
ideas and to work out new ones, and the absence of pose and
publicity, with which these Wright brothers made the dream of
ages—man's conquest of the air—come true.

Aviation history now accelerated. Louis Blériot flew his
French monoplane across the English Channel in July 1909,
and next month the first international aviation meet, with Curtiss and Wright planes entered, was held at Rheims. Henry
Farman won the endurance prize by a flight of 112 miles, and
Curtiss took the speed prize at 43 miles an hour. "Flying circuses" of "barnstorming" aviators now became features of
country fairs.

Glenn Curtiss pioneered seaplanes for water take-offs and
landings; the navy ordered two in 1911 after Eugene Ely had
flown one off the deck of cruiser *Birmingham*, and landed another, assisted by the first arresting hook and chain, on battleship *Pennsylvania*. In 1914 the navy established at Pensacola
the first training school for aviators. Although air power was
not a decisive factor in World War I, it took that war to pull
aircraft construction out of the "sailcloth, sticks and string"
complex into using light, tough, steel alloys, and to provide a
nucleus of trained pilots.

The interest of American universities in airplane dynamics
may be said to have begun in 1914 when Jerome C. Hunsaker
brought back from England reports on what had been accomplished at the Teddington laboratory, and Edwin B. Wilson,

first to put airplane stability into mathematical form, began to lecture on it at M.I.T. Wilson and Hunsaker's report on dynamic stability was the first to be issued by the National Advisory Committee for Aeronautics, in 1915. After the war, universities began establishing schools of flight engineering, and great progress was made in every scientific aspect of aviation. Inventors, notably Elmer A. Sperry, devised new instruments such as the automatic pilot and altimeter, to help man emulate the birds. Celestial navigation made greater strides than it had for 1000 years, owing to the air navigator's imperative need for a quick fix of his position. Lieutenant Commander Albert C. Read USN made the first transatlantic flight in 1919 in flying boat NC-4, Newfoundland to Portugal, with one stop in the Azores. A few weeks later, John Alcock and Arthur W. Brown of the R.A.F. made the first non-stop transatlantic flight, Newfoundland to Ireland, in 16 hours 12 minutes. The United States Navy established a Bureau of Aeronautics in 1921 and converted a collier to its first carrier, U.S.S. *Langley.* Two army lieutenants in a Fokker monoplane, in 1923, made the first non-stop flight across the United States, from Long Island to San Diego; it took them 26 hours 50 minutes. Three years later, Congress passed the Air Commerce Act, creating in the commerce department a bureau of aeronautics that was authorized to license planes and pilots, set up and enforce rules for air traffic, investigate accidents, and test new aircraft for safety. On 9 May 1926 Lieutenant Commander Richard E. Byrd made the first flight over the North Pole, in a plane powered by a 220-horsepower Wright Whirlwind engine. The same model engine, in the Ryan monoplane "Spirit of St. Louis" enabled twenty-five-year-old Charles A. Lindbergh to make a non-stop flight of 3735 miles from Roosevelt Field, Long Island, to Le Bourget airdrome, Paris, in 33 hours 39 minutes, on 20–21 May 1927.

Now, at last, man could emulate Walt Whitman's "Man-of-War Bird"—

Thou born to match the gale, (thou art all wings,)
To cope with heaven and earth and sea and hurricane . . .
At dusk thou look'st on Senegal, at morn America.

Cross-Channel passenger air lines began both in England and France in 1919, but commercial aviation was slow to get under way in the United States; the first regularly scheduled passenger service, between Boston and New York, started in 1927. The principal aircraft designers and builders who survived those lean years were Glenn Curtiss at Garden City, Glenn Martin at Cleveland, William Boeing at Seattle, Claude Ryan at San Diego, Donald Douglas at Santa Monica, and William Stout at Detroit. Pan American Airways got its first mail contract, Key West to Cuba, in July 1927, and within three years had thrown an air loop around South America. United, American, and Trans-World Airlines were organized in 1929.

The age of the modern airliner began in 1932, when Douglas sold to T.W.A. two dozen two-engined DC-2's capable of carrying a payload of 12 passengers at 150 m.p.h., and the Boeing-247, with retractable landing gear and cowled, air-cooled engines, began to operate. These were the first two compact, all-metal planes, resembling giant birds. Douglas's DC-3 (two 900-horsepower Wright cyclone engines, payload of 21 passengers) of 1936, has been called "the Model T of aircraft." Almost 11,000 of these fast, durable planes, costing about $100,000 each, were produced in the next decade. Then came a famous trio: the Douglas DC-4 Skymaster, the Lockheed Constellation, and the Boeing-207 Stratoliner, first plane with a pressurized cabin, carrying 40 passengers at 175 miles per hour. The Skymaster, designated C-54, became the Army's workhorse in World War II.

American women were now getting into aviation. Ellen Church, the pioneer hostess, got her first job with Boeing in 1930. Amelia Earhart, pioneer aviatrix to make a non-stop transaltantic flight (1928), lost her life trying to circumnavigate the globe in 1937.

Aviation now grew at a fantastic pace. Pan American opened trans-Pacific service, San Francisco to Manila via Hawaii, Midway, Wake, and Guam, with Martin M-130 flying boats, and transatlantic service New York to Lisbon via Horta, in 1939. In the year of Pearl Harbor, American Airlines carried over 3 million passengers, and 24,000 private planes—mostly one-engine Piper Cubs and the like—were owned in the United States.

Again a great war made such demands on airplane designers, manufacturers, and pilots that civilian aviation eventually profited. The air became a normal medium for transportation. Seaplanes used for transoceanic flights during the war were now replaced by faster, jet-propelled land planes. Between 1941 and 1957 the number of airports in the United States tripled, the number of certified pilots increased sixfold, the number of passengers carried rose from 3.5 to 48.5 million, the ton-miles of air cargo from 5.3 to 266.5 million.

While the airplane was helping the automobile to ruin the railroads (passenger traffic dropped from 1270 million in 1920 to 413 million in 1957), the number of automobile registrations, 30 million in 1937, rose to 67 million (one-sixth of them trucks) in 1957. Privately owned aircraft, both because of their initial cost and upkeep, and the stiff requirements for pilot licenses, had not even begun to compete with privately owned autos. There were only 84,089 of them (including 823 rotocraft and 413 gliders) in the country by 1962. Air enthusiasts look forward to the day when every American family will have a little airplane or helicopter on its roof or in its backyard. Others doubt whether there is any future for civil aviation other than the present pattern of big, fast jets, flying frequent inter-city passenger and cargo shuttles, and crossing the oceans in as many hours as a ship takes days.

3. *Immigration*

Two postwar policies that helped to create a revolution in American life were immigration restriction and the prohibition of alcoholic beverages.

Unlimited and unrestricted immigration, except for Orientals, paupers, imbeciles, and prostitutes, had been national policy down to World War I. The fear of labor leaders that they could never hold wage gains made during the war if it continued, was the primary pressure for reversing this policy. Labor was helped by a group of intellectuals who feared that the overwhelming number of immigrants from southern and eastern Europe, with different folkways and traditions from those of northern Europe, were a menace to American society. Kenneth Roberts the Maine novelist, in a series of articles in the *Saturday Evening Post,* argued that further unrestricted immigration would flood the country with "human parasites" and produce "a hybrid race of good-for-nothing mongrels." Such arguments appealed to "hundred per centers" after the war and determined the quota basis for the new immigration laws. The first of these, the Johnson Act of 1921, signed by President Harding after a similar law had been vetoed by President Wilson, limited the number of aliens admitted annually to 3 per cent of the number of foreign-born of that nationality already in the United States, according to the census of 1910. The total allowed was 358,000 of which 200,000 were allotted to northern European countries and 155,000 to those of southern and eastern Europe. This was cried out upon as unjust and undemocratic; but Sicilians were suspect, owing to their having imported the Mafia (now called Cosa Nostra) organization for crime, and eastern European immigration was suspect because largely Jewish and possibly "Red." So Congress in 1924 passed a new Johnson Act applying the same system more drastically. Admitted annually were 2 per cent of each foreign-born group resident in the United States in 1890, prior to the great wave of southern and eastern European immigration. After exhaustive calculations had been made of national origins of all Americans in 1890, a third act, in 1929, fixed the total annual quota at 150,000, of which 132,000 were allotted to northern Europe and only 20,000 to southern and eastern Europe and Asia. The count was made of white inhabitants only, in order to keep Africa from having any quotas. With certain exceptions, such as favoring "displaced persons" from Europe and allotting minimum quotas to Asiatic and African countries, this system was still in force in 1964.

Another restriction was the visa system adopted in the act of 1924. This meant that every prospective immigrant had to establish his right to come in under his country's quota, his eligibility respecting character, lack of communist or anarchist affiliation, and the unlikelihood of his becoming a public charge. The process required many documents, much time, and so much red tape as to discourage all but the most persistent.

This legislation did not apply to immigrants from countries in the New World, and those from Canada, Mexico, and the West Indies greatly increased. "Net" immigration from Europe and Asia (that is, total number of immigrants less departures), after hovering around 200,000 to 1930, dropped during the Great Depression to a minus quantity, and only rose again to between 21,000 and 56,000 annually in the years from 1936 to World War II, when fascism produced a new crop of refugees. The total number arriving from Europe in 1933—23,068—was the smallest since 1831.

The social effects of this restrictive policy were tremendous. The foreign-language press declined in numbers and influence. The so-called "ghettos" in the cities where recent immigrants congregated in search of friends and jobs, gradually faded out; but new ones have been created by the migration of Southern Negroes and Puerto Ricans to Northern cities. Absence of cheap immigrant labor permitted average "real" weekly wages in the United States, which we left at $10.73 per week in 1914, to rise to $13.14 in 1926, despite an immense increase in the cost of living; and in the same period, real wages in the largely unionized building trades rose from $18.22 to $23.94, miners' wages from $11.56 to $15.03, printers' from $19.67 to $21.63, and others in like proportion. Labor "never had it so good" as in the years between the postwar recession of 1920–21 and the crash of 1929. So good, in fact, that the unions lost a large proportion of their dues-paying members.[1]

Middle- and upper-class Americans outside the South had always been dependent on recent immigrants for domestic service; now that source was largely cut off. The number of "private household workers"—cooks, butlers, laundresses, housekeepers, and miscellaneous maids—declined between 1900 and 1950, although the total population in that period had increased 140 per cent.[2] There were probably fewer than half a million domestic workers in the United States in 1964, although wages had risen spectacularly—from about $10 for a long week around 1900 to $65–$85 for a 5½ day week; all this without benefit of a union but with free board and lodging. The main reasons for this decline have been the reduction of immigration, and the increasing demand for women in war and other industries. This shortage of domestic "help" has been a social revolution in itself. It has increased the number of restaurants, since men and women who dislike working in a household seem to prefer the far greater drudgery in a public eatery. The rarity of domestic servants has stimulated the production of home labor-saving devices and of packaged, precooked, and frozen foods to save the housewife time and trouble. Private hospitality has progressively declined; it is now evident that the "gracious living" of past generations was made possible only by a household of skilled domestic servants. Cocktail parties have become the only practicable form of home entertainment for all but the very rich. The people upon whom the weight of this domestic revolution has fallen are the women brought up with plenty of servants who now, in middle age, must perform every household chore for which they were not trained, and which they never expected to do. The brave and successful response to this challenge by America's "thoroughbreds" is a tribute to their character, and one to which no male social scientist has yet alluded.

One prediction about the effects of immigration restriction—that the total population of the United States would level off around 1950 to about 145 million—was not realized. The total reached 179.3 million in 1960, and was estimated at 191 million

---

[1] See above, Chapter XLIX. "Real" wages means wages in terms of purchasing power for rent and essential food. Actual money wages were far higher than these figures, because prices had risen too.

[2] *Historical Statistics of U.S.*, p. 77. The figures do not include children's nurses, or their successors the baby-sitters; but do include "accommodators" and other servants who live out.

for 1965. That this has happened is due primarily to the decline in the death rate, but in part to the increase of early marriages.

4. *Bootlegging and Other Sports*

The ratification of Amendment XIX to the Constitution in 1920, making women's suffrage national, shortly followed that of the Prohibition Amendment XVIII outlawing alcoholic beverages; and the two were closely connected. The women's rights movement, starting in the 1840's and marching to victory under Carrie Chapman Catt and Susan B. Anthony, joined forces with the Prohibition movement toward the end of the century. The Women's Christian Temperance Union founded by Frances Willard, and the Anti-Saloon League whose militant leader was Wayne B. Wheeler, determined to make the nation "dry." Evangelical churches lent vigorous support. Statewide prohibition of the manufacture, sale, and consumption of alcoholic beverages had made great strides since Neal Dow's Maine Law of 1851. Twenty-seven states were dry by 1917, and in many of the others "local option" prevailed; a county or municipality could vote itself dry even when the state at large stayed wet. The total per capita consumption of alcoholic beverages, reduced to "absolute alcohol," among the people of the United States fifteen years of age up, was 1.96 gallons in 1916–19, the lowest since the 1870's.

This orderly progress in temperance was rudely interrupted by the Volstead Act of 28 October 1919, which defined prohibited intoxicating liquors as any containing over one-half of one per cent alcohol; and by Amendment XVIII, which, after an intense and successful campaign by pressure groups, went into effect in January 1920. The reasons for so precipitate an enlargement of the federal government's power over the citizenry were many. The dry states complained that they could not enforce Prohibition when adjacent states were wet; the war induced a "spirit of sacrifice," and the German-American Alliance, by combining defense of *Bierstube* with "Hoch der Kaiser!" made drinking seem faintly treasonable. Wives of workingmen wanted their husbands to bring home their pay instead of spending half of it with "the boys" in a saloon; the liquor industry had been proved a major factor in political corruption and was tied in with prostitution, gambling, and other vices. Many businessmen and manufacturers favored Prohibition, hoping it would eliminate "blue Monday" absenteeism. The Anti-Saloon League printed some 100 million flyers, posters, and pamphlets, mostly to further the idea that alcohol was mainly responsible for poverty, disease, crime, insanity, and degeneracy, and that national Prohibition would empty the jails, the asylums, and the poorhouses. William Jennings Bryan, as one might expect, was always bone-dry; Theodore Roosevelt, after much hemming and hawing, went along; Taft opposed Amendment XVIII but as chief justice did his best to enforce it, as did Hughes who became chief justice in 1930. Woodrow Wilson straddled, fearing lest a stand either way defeat the League of Nations. Labor unions, in general, did not support Prohibition because it threw out of work many thousand brewers, distillers, waiters, and bartenders.

No sooner had national prohibition become law than the country seemed to regret it, and a new occupation, bootlegging, sprang up to quench the public thirst. The federal government in ten years made over half a million arrests for breaking the Volstead Act, and secured over 300,000 convictions; but smuggling increased. The Canadian and Mexican borders were full of "leaks." Small craft easily ran cargoes from Cuba into Florida and the Gulf states; mountain moonshiners multiplied; obliging vineyards in California and New York provided kegs of grape juice in which, with a little time and a yeast cake, one could emulate the miracle of Cana; carloads of grapes went to Italian- and Greek-Americans to be trodden out in a traditional winepress and allowed to ferment. Off every seaport from Maine to Miami, outside the three-mile limit, rode a fleet of ocean-going ships loaded with every variety of wine and liquor. Motor launches, too fast for coast guard or enforcement agents to catch, ran these cargoes ashore, where they were transferred to trucks and cars owned by bootleggers; but the truckloads often got "hijacked" by other criminals, and in any case the strong liquor was "cut" with water before being sold. Millions of gallons of industrial alcohol, manufacture of which was permitted, were converted into bootleg whisky or gin, and bottled under counterfeit labels; poisonous wood alcohol, inexpertly "converted," caused numerous deaths. Liquor and wine, imported under license for "medicinal purposes," easily found its way to the stomachs of healthy citizens. Every city became studded with "speakeasies" to replace the saloon, almost every urban family patronized a local bootlegger, and in defiant states like Rhode Island, which refused either to ratify Amendment XVIII or help enforce it, one could buy a bottle of British gin right off the shelves of a grocery store for ten dollars. Those who did not care to patronize bootleggers and so contribute to crime and political corruption, made their own "bathtub" gin at home or got along with home-brewed beer and cider. Bravado induced numerous young people to drink who otherwise would not have done so; restaurants which refused to break the law themselves provided "set-ups" of ice, soda water, and ginger ale to be energized by whatever the patrons brought.

There were many social effects of Prohibition, apart from the encouragement of lawbreaking and the building up of a criminal class that turned to gambling and drugs when Amendment XVIII was repealed in 1933. The high point in the Chicago gang war that was fed by bootlegging was the "St. Valentine's Day Massacre" of 1929. Al Capone ran one gang; George ("Bugs") Moran, the other. In four years there had been 215 unsolved murders in the Windy City. The Capone hoods, disguised as policemen, machine-gunned six of the Moran gang in a garage where they were waiting to buy a truckload of liquor from hijackers. Nobody was punished for this multiple murder; it took the federal government to get the planner, Capone, for evasion of income taxes. And the Chicago alliance between police and organized crime has never been broken.

Since beer and wine did not pay bootleggers like strong liquor, the country's drinking habits were changed from the one to the other. College students who before Prohibition would have in a keg of beer and sit around singing the "Dartmouth Stein Song," and "Under the Anheuser Busch," now got drunk quickly on bathtub gin and could manage no lyric more complicated than "How Dry I Am!" Woman, emancipated by Amendment XIX, enthusiastically connived at breaking Amendment XVIII and now helped her husband to spend on liquor the savings that formerly went to the saloon. Hip-flask drinking certainly helped the revolution in sexual standards that we shall discuss shortly. And it encouraged hypocrisy in politics.

Both major parties successfully blinked the issue for a decade. The Republicans, strongest in the rural communities and the middle classes, in general stood behind what President Hoover called "an experiment noble in motive and far-reaching in purpose." The Democrats were torn between Southern constituencies which were immovably dry because Prohibition was supposed to help "keep the Negroes in order," and Northern cities, full of Irish-, German-, and Italian-Americans who were incurably wet. This division almost split the party in 1924 when the drys supported McAdoo and the wets Alfred E. Smith. The wets, having gained the upper hand by 1928, then nominated Al Smith, who proposed to abandon national prohibition and return the alcohol problem to the States. This stand was partly responsible for his spectacular success in the urban centers of the North, as well as for his defeat in the solid South and West.

President Hoover, who really tried to enforce the Volstead Act, appointed a commission to investigate the question of law enforcement. This Wickersham Commission submitted, in January 1931, a confused report to the effect that federal prohibition was unenforceable but should be enforced, that it was a failure but should be retained! By 1932 the "noble experiment" was so palpable a failure that the Republican party favored a "revision" of Amendment XVIII: the Democrats demanded outright repeal. Following Franklin D. Roosevelt's overwhelming victory, Congress in February 1933 recommended Amendment XXI repealing federal prohibition, which was promptly ratified, in December. The problem of liquor control was thus thrown back where it had been before 1917. A few states continued to be dry; but many others played around with laws forbidding drinking without a meal, or allowing fortified wine to be sold in drinking places, or keeping a state monopoly of the sale of alcoholic beverages in original packages.

Yet national prohibition did have a favorable effect on the drinking habits of the nation. The per capita consumption by those fifteen years of age and up, reduced to "absolute alcohol," was less than one gallon in 1934, the first full year after the repeal of Amendment XVIII. It rose for the first time to over two gallons ten years later, and has hovered around that figure ever since, but never approached those of 1901–15. The figure for 1962, 2.11 gallons per capita, was less than one-third that of France (which, despite the myth that the French drink only wine, is the leading consumer of alcohol among the nations), and less than that of Italy, Switzerland, the Antipodes, West Germany, and Belgium. Canada's consumption per capita is a little less than that of the United States, Britain's about 77 per cent of America's. But this is not the whole story, as only the legally sold, heavily taxed alcohol is included; there is no knowing how much "moonshine," "white mule," and other homemade and smuggled liquors have passed down the national or international gullet. Evin M. Jellinek, who has applied himself to this problem, figures that roughly 4,470,000 Americans, about 4 per cent of the population twenty years old and up, were alcoholics in 1960; no pleasant thing to contemplate.

The growth of leisure led to a vast increase in sports, especially in spectator sports like professional baseball, football, basketball, and hockey. College football, too, became professional when it spread from the older Eastern colleges to Notre Dame (whose Knute Rockne was the first of the high-pressure coaches), the Western Conference, and the South, for which Huey Long built the Sugar Bowl. Football squads lived in special quarters, practiced the year round, were supported by "athletic scholarships," and graduated in physical education. "Yes, we had to go out and buy a football team," said the president of a Texas university to the writer, around 1940. "Otherwise, we could get no money for scholastic purposes out of the rich oil men."

Pugilism continued its popular appeal, especially after fights could be followed on television. Jack Johnson, in 1908, the first black to become heavyweight champion, kept the belt longer than any predecessor except John L. Sullivan, knocking out one "white hope" after another until Jess Willard gave him the K.O. in 1915. Jack Dempsey held the championship for seven years, 1919–26, when he lost on points to Gene Tunney, one of the lightest men ever to win the belt, a really scientific fighter; Gene married a New York heiress and retired from the ring. After five more championships won by white men, including the giant Italian Primo Carnera, there came an almost unbroken series of black winners, starting with Joe Louis and concluding with Cassius Marcellus Clay in 1964.*

In professional baseball, "Ty" Cobb, the hero of the early part of the century, gave way to George Herman ("Babe") Ruth, who began belting out home runs in 1915 and so continued for 22 years, chalking up a total of 714 four-baggers— 60 in the single season of 1927—for the New York Yankees. There never was another baseball player like "The Babe." A natural ham actor, his stream of Homeric insults to his opponents was alone worth the price of admission, and he could even dramatize striking out.

The horse, superseded for transport, was now bred entirely for hunting, hacking, and racing. Horse-racing became a favorite spectator sport and vehicle for gambling. States like Massachusetts, which had outlawed horse-racing because of its drain on the savings of those least able to afford to gamble, mindful of the revenue to be derived from pari-mutuel machines, not only legalized horse-racing in the 1930's but dog-racing too; and the once puritanical state of New Hampshire capped this by establishing an official sweepstakes in 1964. With increasing specialization, all records were broken. Citation, a bay thoroughbred, had won more than a million dollars for his owners, and many millions for the bookmakers, when he retired in 1951 at the age of six, having set up a new record of 1:33⅗ for a mile run, and won the "triple crown"—the Kentucky Derby, Preakness, and Belmont Stakes. The greatest sire in American turf history was Man o' War, by Fair Play out of Mahubah, both of the old Diomed-Lexington stock. He won $83,000 as a

* Continuing through Joe Frazier in 1971.

two-year-old in 1919, retired in 1921, and for the next 26 years at stud near Lexington, Kentucky, sired the famous steeple-chaser Battleship and hundreds of other racers and hunters.

Golf and tennis, which were regarded by the American public as effete games of the idle rich around the turn of the century, now became popular. Francis Ouimet, a former caddy, by winning the open golf championship at The Country Club, Brookline, in 1913, proved that you did not have to be a Scot or a gentleman to be good at golf, and golf courses were laid out by hundreds of clubs and municipalities in every state. Golf never became wholly professionalized; contenders in tournaments still have to pay their own expenses. But tennis became semi-professionalized when the proliferating tennis clubs began paying all expenses of stars in order to attract a big "gate." The 1920's were the era of William T. ("Big Bill") Tilden, men's singles champion for seven years, and Helen Wills the women's singles champion. The international Davis Cup was won by American teams from 1922 through 1926, but for the next ten years the United States contestants had to be satisfied with second place to France or Great Britain. Skiing, hardly known in the United States before World War I, rapidly caught on after the invention of the ski-lift to save the time and effort of zig-zagging uphill. It has created new winter resorts in the West, and made the fortunes of northern New England villages which formerly hibernated. But the most popular "participation" sports, as always, were fishing and shooting. Every man of wealth on the Eastern seaboard had to have his local duck-blind, join a Southern club for shooting quail and wild turkey, and a New Brunswick fishing club for taking salmon. The small-town and country lads continued to whip local streams and ponds for trout and bass, or to roam the woods with a shotgun in search of ruffed grouse and pheasant, or with a rifle for deer. New fishing developments were casting a line from beaches beyond the surf for "stripers," and catching enormous game fishes like the marlin from motor boats.

Thus the most significant developments of sport since 1902 have been the spread of gentlemanly sports to working people, the devising of new games, the growth of professionalism, and increasing public interest both as spectators and participants. At the turn of the century an ordinary citizen who wanted exercise other than shooting and fishing had a narrow choice:—"sand lot" baseball, sailing a small boat in summer, skating, snow-shoeing, or gymnasium in winter. Today he has better shooting and fishing than ever, together with a choice of golf, tennis, bowling, skiing, and other sports, all with womenfolk participating; or he may stay home and gaze at a variety of games on television.

5. *The Sexual Upheaval*

The mores or sexual relations in European countries have fluctuated through the ages, and are a difficult subject upon which to generalize, owing to public reticence and lack of records. It is, however, fair to say that the so-called Protestant ethic—which is really the Christian ethic—in sexual morals prevailed in the United States from at least the early nineteenth century to around 1910; and that, whilst laws and principles have changed little in fifty years, practices have undergone a radical revolution.

The Protestant ethic allowed the sexual instinct to be gratified only within marriage. It disapproved of premarital intercourse as well as adultery, and regarded the Catholic countries of Europe as hopelessly immoral, although Irish Catholics and the French bourgeoisie were, if anything, more austere in sex matters than descendants of early Puritans. Virginity before and chastity after marriage, absolute requirements for girls and women, were also enjoined on men; but for them, especially for young men whose marriages had to be postponed until they could support a wife, public opinion condoned prostitution as an outlet. Nobody can tell how far these ethics were actually respected around 1910, but they were the norm for middle-class Protestant Anglo-Saxons, Irish Catholics, and most of the immigrants from northern Europe. Dr. Kinsey in his famous *Reports* on sexual behavior (1948–53) seems to have been surprised because sexual practices varied from class to class. Any observant boy who grew up around the turn of the century could have told him that. While middle-class intellectuals observed fairly well the principles of the Protestant ethic, the daughters of certain immigrant peoples were notoriously "easy." These were known as "chippies," in contrast to professional "tarts." And, in towns and cities, the daily visit of the iceman, who prior to mechanical refrigeration, replenished ice-chests with big blocks of pond ice, was the traditional consoler of frustrated wives and lonely widows.

The women's organizations which promoted Prohibition and female emancipation, complained of the "double standard" which required a girl to be a virgin at marriage, but not a man; they and the clergy, with some success, promoted the Christian principle that there should be a single standard of chastity for both. H. L. Mencken *In Defense of Women* (1918) snorted at this "hysterical denunciation" of the double standard. "What these virtuous beldames actually desire," he asserted, "is not that the male be reduced to chemical purity, but that the franchise of dalliance be extended to themselves." That is about what has happened. The revolution in sexual relations is one aspect of the emancipation of American women—of their escape from the Protestant purdah into business, the professions, and the arts; and from the country to the city. In that process they willingly shed the angel's wings clamped on them by sentimentalists and romantic poets.

Around 1910 there was a great to-do about prostitution and venereal disease. Houses of ill-fame to meet every taste and purse existed in the major cities (in New Orleans a guide book to them was printed annually), and there was at least one in every town. Some cities, notably San Francisco, had "red light districts," where one-dollar whores displayed their dubious charms behind windows for the benefit of sailors, lumberjacks, and cowboys whose vocations required prolonged absence from women. Many inmates were there because they preferred "woman's oldest profession" to hard work, but others were recruited by deception from the hinterland, Europe, and Mexico. Reginald Wright Kauffman's novel *The House of Bondage* (1910) created a sensation by describing the seduction of an innocent country girl into prostitution, leaving her a hopeless syphilitic. The United States Immigration Commission conducted an investigation of this "white slave" traffic, proving that girls were being imported from Europe, voluntarily or otherwise, at prices ranging from $200 to $2000; this report led Congress to pass the Mann or White Slave Traffic Act, making it a felony to bring women for immoral purposes into the United States, or across state lines. In the next four or five years, forty-five states passed laws against third persons—procurers and madams—profiting from prostitution, and some thirty cities closed their red light districts.

These halfhearted and indifferently enforced efforts at reform were moved less by moral fervor than by the ravages of venereal disease. "Elaborate surveys," wrote one contemporary authority, "show the frequency of gonorrhea and syphilis at this period to have been one per cent among men, and almost a half of one per cent among women in the United States." Now that the religious sanction to sexual continence declined, and young people no longer feared future torment for sins observed by the All-Seeing Eye, it was hoped that fear of infection would prove a deterrent. The American Social Hygiene Association, formed in 1914, worked on sex education and the regulation of the social evil, and the League of Nations set up a committee on the white slave traffic which at least brought it into the open.

Parallel with efforts to enforce the Protestant ethic by force or fear, it was crumbling from within. The loose morals of the 1920's are generally ascribed to the First World War; but a general laxity was observable for at least seven years before America entered that war. Increased knowledge of sexual hygiene counteracted the terror of infection. The automobile offered an easy spot for courtship away from the family parlor or porch. Moving pictures were becoming more attractive and lascivious; the sight of Theda Bara very lightly clad, in close and luscious embrace with a lover, could not help but be suggestive. Dancing, formerly confined to supervised homes and ballrooms, could now be practiced in all manner of night clubs and country dance halls; and instead of the sedate waltz and two-step, one now had the hesitation waltz, the Argentine tango (both banned by the Federation of Women's Clubs in 1914), the bunny-hug, the fox trot, and the turkey trot.

Women's costumes, too, were undergoing a revolution; the knee-length skirt did not arrive until after the war, but the stiff, carapace-like corset, which for generations had helped protect weak women from enterprising males, went out; girls whose parents did not allow them to follow the fashion had to discard their corsets surreptitiously in cars and dressing rooms, or risk being called "Old Ironsides" by the boys. The drinking of hard liquor by women and young girls started about the same time; dancing made them thirsty, and the more they drank the more wildly they danced. And jazz, which the Reverend Henry Van Dyke called "a sensual teasing of the strings of sensual passion," was now the principle dance music.

Thus a revolution in sexual morals was well under way before the war started, but the war quickened it. American troops who went overseas indulged in experiences denied to them by law and custom at home, and paternal government gave them prophylaxis to prevent venereal disease. Nurses, Red Cross and Y.W.C.A. workers had their eyes opened. All returned to a country where there was more of everything—money, leisure, cars, sexy movies, dance halls, jazz; not more liquor for a time, but Prohibition made drinking more exciting, and the sort of liquor one got removed inhibitions.

Coincident with the weakening of religious sanction, a pseudo-scientific version of psychology began to supplant it. Doctors Sigmund Freud of Vienna, Carl Jung of Switzerland, and Havelock Ellis of England were the prophets. Ellis's great work, *Studies in the Psychology of Sex,* a sober and scientific case book, began circulating in America around 1910. Both

Freud and Jung had lectured in the United States before the war, and by 1916 there were 500 practicing psychoanalysts in New York City alone. But it was not until after the war that their doctrines, through translations and popular simplifications and distortions, began to infiltrate. One of the saddest things in history is the way the doctrines of scientific innovators become distorted before they reach the mass of the people. Sir Isaac Newton was a deeply religious man, but got the reputation of postulating a purely mechanical universe; Darwin's doctrine of evolution was distorted to mean that man was descended from a monkey; Karl Marx would never have recognized the societies in which he has been substituted for God; and Dr. Freud, an austere man of impeccable morals who mainly wished to take off the wraps which prevented medical research in sex phenomena, became, in the writings of his unprofessional disciples, the prophet of promiscuity. In 1919–20 one began to hear college students comparing their dreams and prattling knowingly (as they thought) about complexes, inhibitions, infantile sexuality, introverts and extroverts, and the libido. Probably Ellis, Freud, and Jung did much good by throwing light on the dark places of the subsconscious, and opening discussion. But on the young of the "lost generation" (as those of the 1920's liked to call themselves) the effect was catastrophic. By presenting inhibition or repression of natural impulses as an unmixed evil which would warp one's character and even ruin one's life, it followed that the Protestant ethic was wrong; that instead of resisting temptation and channeling the sex impulse into marriage, it should be indulged from the age of puberty. A girl who objected to being kissed and handled by her swain of the evening was apt to be silenced by a quotation alleged to be from Jung; a young man indifferent to girls would now be accused of being permanently in love with his mother; virginity became something to get rid of, chastity a medieval relic. Katherine Anthony the feminist, who had promoted the emancipation of women, was astounded in 1921 at "the wild conduct of the young, who are certainly out of bounds since the war." And the same year an ironical Irish journalist, after seeing for himself American postwar mores remarked, "Unbalanced by prolonged contemplation of the tedious virtues of New England, a generation has arisen whose great illusion is that the transvaluation of all values may be effected by promiscuity."

Chaperonage of middle- and upper-class unmarried girls was never as strict in North America as in Latin countries; but what there was now disappeared when the girls most needed protection. Emily Post's first edition of her famous book on etiquette, in 1922, devoted a chapter to "Chaperons and other Conventions." For the edition of 1937 this chapter became "The Vanished Chaperon and Other Lost Conventions." Training, said Madam Post, was replacing protection. The girls were now supposed to be sufficiently intelligent to take care of their own morals, and doubtless most of them were. Moreover, the "wages of sin" were no longer "death." Unmarried mothers were no longer driven from their homes or regarded as moral lepers. Hawthorne's Hester Prynne, or Sarah Orne Jewett's Joanna in *The Country of the Pointed Firs,* who spent her life in lonely exile to expiate one sexual slip, would have been unthinkable by 1936.

Other signs of the times were that in 1929 *The Ladies' Home Journal* first admitted advertisements of lipstick and cigarette manufacturers first dared to show pictures of women smoking. The rate of divorces to marriages doubled between 1910 and 1928, and has continued to rise.

This revolution in the sexual mores of teen-agers and the young married soon received literary expression. Francis Scott Key Fitzgerald of Minnesota, who left Princeton to serve as an infantry officer in the war, created a sensation in 1920 when he described what was going on, in his first two books: *This Side of Paradise,* and *Flappers and Philosophers.* At the same time John Held, Jr., originally from Utah, became the artist of the flappers, as the free-and-easy girls were called. James T. Farrell in 1932 began describing the life of Chicago's no longer priest-ridden Irish-Americans in the *Studs Lonigan* trilogy, using four-letter words seldom before seen in print; and William Faulkner of Mississippi, after serving in the Royal Canadian Air Force, stripped the romance off the South with stark tales like *Sanctuary* (1931). These are among the best of the American novelists who informed the older generation what was going on, and the rising generation what to expect. Priests and parsons, college presidents, the Christian Endeavor Society, the Y.W.C.A., and other organizations thundered against immorality; state legislatures added new regulations to the existing sumptuary laws such as prohibiting bobbed hair or knee-length skirts. Judge Ben Lindsay of the juvenile court of Denver tried to meet the problem in 1927 by proposing to legalize birth control, and trial or "companionate" marriages; but he was howled down by believers in the older moral code. Nothing worked; the "lost generation" proceeded to go to hell or salvation in its own way.

The revolution we have been describing occurred, sooner

or later, throughout the Western world. It came earlier in Sweden, Germany, and Australia than in America, about the same time in France and southern Europe; somewhat later in Britain and Latin America. European lecturers in the United States, with knowing leers, regarded developments on this side as long overdue. There was no need for sex to break out in Moslem, Hindu, or Buddhist countries, or in Japan or black Africa, where sensuousness had the sanction of religion. And nowhere in the Christian world was the revolution complete. The old mores remained, embalmed in law and preached from pulpits; and millions of people, probably a majority of the population in the United States, resisted tempting offers to rebuild their lives around a core of sex.

By the time World War II broke out, most people expected that the sexual revolution had about run its course; on the contrary, the war speeded up the movement. And during the postwar years other influences came in to relax old principles still further. The fears and tensions of the cold war tempted people to be merry, since tomorrow they might die. Stream-of-consciousness literature and movies pioneered by James Joyce's *Ulysses* increased in volume and in crudeness; the wraps were removed from frankly pornographic literature which formerly had to be smuggled; and by following "permissiveness" to its logical conclusion, crime was condoned and sexual deviation tolerated. A peculiarly nasty product of the new freedom are the teen-age monsters of both sexes who take drugs, riot, rob, and kill "just for kicks."

Another and less reprehensible development has been the prevalent very early marriage. This, in part, is owing to a desire of young men to escape the draft; in part, the supposed need of young students and working people to combine two incomes in one; in part, a praiseworthy escape into security from the social compulsion toward promiscuity.

Advocates of the new morals claim that the lifting of nineteenth-century repressions, inhibitions, etc., "freed" the rising generation, made them more natural, wholesome, and the like. Probably some oversexed persons were injured by their efforts to be faithful to the Christian ethic. But, how many of the "pure in heart" have been ruined by the present stimuli striking at them every day and from every direction, urging them to surrender to the cruder demands of the flesh? A recent glorifier of the Viennese doctor claims that Freud "demolished the ideals of the hypocritical Victorian age and turned a glaring light on the underworld by revealing the 'filth' that had been repressed into the unconscious."

Possibly that would have been the best place to have left it.

6. Letters, Arts, and Sciences

The "one hundred per cent Americans" of 1919–20 were not content to fight Reds, Parlor Pinks, Democrats, supporters of the League of Nations, and friends of England and France. Intellectuals, especially professors, attracted a good part of their hostility. The colleges and universities were accused of being hotbeds of sedition by Vice President Coolidge in a series of articles in *The Delineator* (1921); but next year Upton Sinclair in *The Goose Step* presented the same institutions as centers of reaction, literary annexes to Wall Street!

Widespread distrust of intellectuals is not surprising, for in this era the peculiarly American form of what Julien Benda called *la trahison des clercs*, was to attack American traditions. Charles A. Beard in his *Economic Origins of the Constitution* (1913) paved the way for a host of writers who maintained that the Federal Constitution was the work of wealthy tricksters to keep democracy down; and in 1927 he produced his *Rise of American Civilization* to prove that there were no heroes or even leaders in American history, only economic trends. Debunking (the word was coined by William E. Woodward in his novel *Bunk*, 1923) became a literary mode; every American hero from Columbus to Coolidge was successively "debunked" —Woodward himself did it to Washington, Grant, and Lafayette. After the war, almost every American writer who had the price fled to Europe; one could find scores of them in certain Parisian cafés declaring to anyone who would listen, that America was "finished"—an "impossible" place for a "cultivated man" to live; or, in the words of T. S. Eliot (a poet whom they admired but who would have no truck with them), a "waste land." From Paris, Harold E. Stearns in 1921 edited a remarkable symposium entitled *Civilization in the United States,* one long moan by thirty solemn young men on American mediocrity, sterility, conformity, and smug prosperity. Frank M. Colby, for instance, wrote a chapter on American Humor merely to say that there was none. What, one wonders, was the matter with Finley Peter Dunne, the creator of Mr. Dooley, or Will Rogers the "Cowboy Philosopher," or Bob Benchley, or that incomparable pair of radio comedians "Amos 'n Andy".

But the greatest debunker of all—one who debunked even the other debunkers—was H. L. Mencken "the bad boy of Baltimore" whose chosen medium was *The American Mercury*. Mencken wrote in a pungent style with an original vocabulary that demanded and got attention, and he was no gentle satirist like Mr. Dooley. He lashed out at almost every group in American society—the "booboisie," the "anthropoids" of the Alleghenies; the *Gelehrten* ("as pathetic an ass as a university professor of history"), the politicians ("crooks and charlatans"), evangelists ("gaudy zanies"), orators ("the seemly bosh of the late Woodrow"), parsons and priests ("mountebanks"), and guardians of public morals ("wowsers"). Mencken was no social reformer but a saucy iconoclast who had something amusing to say about every region, class, and profession in America. He despised democracy and freely predicted that it would dissolve into despotism; he discerned very little good in American life. "Almost the only thing I believe in with a childlike and unquestioning faith," he wrote, "is free speech"; yet he refused to "sympathize with the pedagogues who . . . are heaved out of some fresh-water college for trying to exercise it," because "nothing a pedagogue says, as a pedagogue, is worth hearing." Mencken in his inimitable style emitted a good deal of sound common sense against the folderols of Dewey-inspired education in his day. His merry extravagance and cynicism might have broken down American smugness if that had been his objective; but he had no objective, so his writings had less influence than those of Beard and the ponderous debunkers.

Conrad Aiken, almost alone of Harold Stearns's contributors, found something healthy in American life, praising the "energy, vitality and confidence" of the rising generation of American poets such as Eliot, Frost, Fletcher, Sandburg, Ezra Pound, Cummings, Wheelock, Amy Lowell, Edna St. Vincent Millay, and Elinor Wylie. These and many others did their best work between the two world wars. New York, especially Greenwich Village, was a center of the English-speaking literary world disputed only by London; and Chicago, where the "New Poetry" was launched in 1912, was not far behind with the novels of Robert Herrick, Floyd Dell, and Theodore Dreiser.

Novels that successfully exploited the flatness of small-town life were Sinclair Lewis's *Main Street* (1920) and *Babbitt* (1922), which added two types to our gallery; Sherwood Anderson's *Winesburg, Ohio* (1919), *Poor White* (1920), and *Triumph of the Egg* (1922). Lewis satirized the average American but never achieved anything resembling a literary style, whilst Anderson, in singularly moving and felicitous language, described those who lived "lives of quiet desperation." The Pulitzer prizes for fiction, which began in 1918, were generally awarded, prior to World War II, to conventional novelists such as Edith Wharton (Sinclair Lewis was so angry at not getting it for *Main Street* that he refused one for *Arrowsmith*); but other Pulitzer prizes were intelligently bestowed. Most of the above-mentioned poets received one; and the prize for American biography was given to three really great books, *The Education of Henry Adams*, Beveridge's *Marshall*, and Freeman's *Lee*. The prize for the best American play was thrice awarded to the greatest dramatist of that era, Eugene O'Neill, whose *Anna Christie, Beyond the Horizon, Strange Interlude,* and *Mourning Becomes Electra*, came as close to the humor, the irony, the tragedy, and the human understanding of the ancient Greek dramatists as any playwright is likely to attain for another century.

American literature had many categories besides the above. Books like Edwin D. Slosson's *Creative Chemistry* (1919) became enormously popular, as were the works of English scientists and philosophers. There was an immense curiosity among educated Americans to learn history, philosophy, and science painlessly. H. G. Wells's *Outline of History* (1920) and Will Durant's *Story of Philosophy* (1926) were superficial and popular works which catered to this appetite.

Whilst a febrile despair, a Byronic disillusion, a belief that life had no meaning, that Western civilization was declining into chaos, characterized many of the poets and prose writers of the economically lush 1920's, the following decade of depression, which included the rise of Hitler and Stalin, persuaded most American authors that their country had something worth preserving. Sinclair Lewis in *It Can't Happen Here* (1935) painted a terrifying picture of how America could go fascist; Archibald MacLeish, who had been writing lyric poetry, came out with *The Irresponsibles* (1940), a stirring appeal to artists and men of letters to stop horsing around with strange gods and goddesses, and rally to the defense of American traditions. The same year Ernest Hemingway, after observing the death throes of the Spanish Republic, published *For Whom the Bell Tolls* as a warning to his country, and Dos Passos, after portraying in his *U.S.A.* trilogy of 1930–36 a rootless and disintegrating society, came to a halt in *The Ground We Stand On*. Edna St. Vincent Millay, having burned her "candle at both ends," turned to spiritual values in *Huntsman, What Quarry?* (1939); and Stephen Vincent Benét, who had never lost faith in America, delivered a solemn warning in "Litany for Dictatorships" (1936). John Steinbeck, after writing the Rabelaisian *Tortilla Flat* about Mexicans in California, produced *The Grapes of Wrath* in 1939. This story of a ruined family's journey from their Oklahoma dust bowl to the promised land of California was the one great novel to portray the tragedy of the Great Depression for the rural proletariat.

Painting in America remained in a healthy condition

throughout this era. The Armory Show of 1913 introduced New York to the avant-garde of Europe—Gauguin, Picasso, and Duchamp's "Nude Descending a Staircase." But American artists struck out on lines of their own. Some, like Thomas Hart Benton, continued the Hudson River tradition of glorifying American scenery, but the majority depicted American life —in brisk movement, as with Waldo Pierce's "Trotting Race at a Country Fair"; with satire, as in Grant Wood's "American Gothic"; with pathos, as in George Biddle's "Sacco and Vanzetti." Biddle himself observed that in an exhibition of 1936 there were no nudes, portraits, or still-lifes among the American paintings; the majority dealt with the current scene or reflected a social criticism of American life. It was not a great age in American sculpture, largely for lack of demand; pallid busts no longer adorned the drawing-rooms of the rich, the public wanted no more statues of heroes, and architecture was becoming stark; but we had a few very distinguished works like Paul Manship's "Prometheus" at Rockefeller Center; George G. Barnard's two statues of Nature in the Metropolitan Museum, Anna Hyatt Huntington's "Joan of Arc" in New York, and Joseph Coletti's high-relief sculptures in the Baltimore Cathedral. Daniel Chester French in 1922 crowned his long career with the heroic statue in the Lincoln Memorial, which his friend Henry Bacon had designed.

In American music it was not a great age for original compositions. John Alden Carpenter of Chicago, composer in the classical tradition, came to terms with the modern age in his "Skyscrapers" ballet, produced both in New York and Munich in 1926–28. The most distinctive contributions to American music were made by blacks. Their syncopated "rag-time" melodies developed into jazz. The black soldiers' bands brought jazz to Europe during the war; and before long, inspired by expert practitioners such as Duke Ellington and Bessie Smith, saxophones were wailing, trumpets shrieking, and "blues" singers moaning jazz music around the world.

The most successful American composers between-wars were New York City boys like Aaron Copland and George Gershwin, and Roy E. Harris of Utah, who applied symphonic methods to jazz and translated this folk art into music. Gershwin's *Of Thee I Sing* (1932) was a side-splitting musical satire on American politics in the Gilbert and Sullivan manner, and his *Porgy and Bess* (1935), based on the compassionately humorous play *Porgy* by DuBose Heyward about African life in Charleston, has become a veritable American opera. So, too, is Rogers and Hammerstein's *Oklahoma!* Harris's Folk Song

Symphonies and Walter Piston's "Third Symphony" of 1947 were in the same tradition.

Besides the works of these *maestros* there was a general dissemination of good music among the people by skilled teachers:—Archibald T. Davison and his assistant G. Wallace Woodworth, whose coaching of the Harvard Glee Club stimulated every college vocal society, and Thomas W. Surette, whose *Concord Series* of musical reprints went nationwide, and whose Concord Summer School of Music trained hundreds of teachers in the philosophy of "nothing but the best" music to be sung in schools and colleges.

Broadcasting music by radio began in 1920; forty years later there were 200 million radio and television sets in America. Discriminating listeners skipped the commercials, the "soap opera," and other trash to enjoy chamber music, symphonies, and operas. Supplementing radio were millions of phonographs playing everything from blues to Beethoven. Eighty-four new symphony orchestras were established in the depression decade, but the nation supported very few opera companies. Music conservatories flourished; great foundations like the Guggenheim patronized budding genius. And totalitarian terror brought to America some distinguished European composers and musicians such as Stravinsky, Hindemith, Bartók, and Schönberg.

American scholarship and science now came of age. The great change came after 1910 when men of wealth (notably Rockefeller, Carnegie, Guggenheim) and the foundations that they set up, endowed libraries and laboratories where scholars and scientists could labor without going to Europe, and established scholarship and research funds which enabled them to do creative work without the physical drag of teaching elements to undergraduates. Americans received no Nobel awards for physics or medicine prior to 1923, and only Theodore W. Richards got one in chemistry. Thereafter, about one in three of the Nobel prizes in physics, one in five of those in chemistry, one in four of those in medicine, have gone to Americans.

The most striking advances were in the fields of astronomy, physics, and medicine. Working with the giant telescope of Mt. Wilson Observatory, which enabled them to plot thousands of new galaxies, astronomers like Harlow Shapley discovered an indefinitely expanding universe. Physicists invented the cyclotron to break down atoms, and founded the new science of nuclear physics. Einstein and Fermi were two great European physicists who found refuge in America from Hitler and Mussolini.

Of all these subjects, medical science, which closely affected the lives of the people, underwent a revolution in this period. The rural general practitioner of 1910 made endless house calls, driving long distances day and night in his buggy, as well as seeing patients in his office, which was generally at his home. Only rarely would a doctor send a patient to a hospital, of which there were few outside the great cities. Childbirth in a hospital was virtually unknown; surgeons even performed caesareans and other major operations in the patient's home, usually on the kitchen table. Specialists, mostly graduates of European universities, were available only in certain cities. The first effect of the automobile on medicine was to extend the doctor's range. Maurice H. Richardson of Boston, the country's leading specialist in appendectomy, kept two big limousines and day-and-night chauffeurs; after an urgent telephone call he would pick up a nurse, an assistant, and his instruments and be driven over abominable roads 100 miles or more into the country to perform an operation—often for nothing if the patient was poor. He once remarked to this writer, "Ten appendectomies this week; total take, $200 and a barrel of apples."

The men who did most to inaugurate an era when any patient, almost anywhere, could have the entire corpus of medical knowledge at his disposal, were a quartet of young medical geniuses who came to Johns Hopkins University during the 1890's and remained active well into the twentieth century. These were William H. Welch, pathologist; Howard A. Kelly, gynecologist; William S. Halsted, surgeon; and William Osler, beloved physician and medical scholar. All were great teachers as well as men of science; they and their pupils implemented and continued the revolution in medicine and surgery that began with Eliot's reforms at Harvard in 1870.[1]

The founding in 1903 of the Rockefeller Institute for Medical Research—one of the many institutions through which the Rockefeller family have put their ill-gotten wealth to the service of mankind—is a second landmark. For there could be little progress in medicine without research, and that required training and adequate support. The Institute was a first step leading to the vast and continuing expansion of facilities for medical research. Seven years later appeared the Flexner report on Medical Education, result of a two-year investigation

[1] Osler, a Canadian graduate of McGill, became Regius Professor of Medicine at Oxford in 1909, was created a baronet by King George V, and died in 1919. The others remained active up to their deaths: "Popsy" Welch in 1934, Halsted in 1922, and Kelly in 1943. For Eliot's reforms, see Chapter XLVII above.

supported by the American Medical Association and financed by one of the Carnegie foundations. Dr. Abraham Flexner exposed numerous "degree mills" which even granted M.D.'s by correspondence; he found the average medical school inadequately staffed by busy general practitioners who had neither time nor inclination for research; indeed, the only first-class medical school, he said, was the Johns Hopkins. This report stimulated the good medical schools to improve, encouraged wealthy foundations and individuals to provide funds, and promoted the development of medical specialties. As an example, Boston has become the world's center for children's diseases, owing to pediatricians such as Kenneth D. Blackfan and James L. Gamble, and the Children's Hospital that they served; and also for the study of tropical diseases, owing to the research and field trips of Drs. Richard P. Strong and George C. Shattuck. Another significant development was the clinic where a number of specialists gathered to minister to human ills; the Mayo Clinic at Rochester, Minnesota, is the most famous.

Diseases which had hitherto baffled the medical profession were now attacked by doctors, chemists, bacteriologists, and physicists, working in the laboratories of universities, governments, and the foundations. Results were spectacular. In the first third of the century, infant mortality in the United States declined by two-thirds, and life expectancy increased from 49 to 59 years. The death rate for tuberculosis dropped from 180 to 49 per 100,000, for typhoid from 36 to 2, for diphtheria from 43 to 2, for measles from 12 to 1, for pneumonia from 158 to 50. Sulfa drugs and penicillin made pneumonia no longer something to be dreaded. Yellow fever and smallpox were practically wiped out, and the war on malaria, pellagra, hookworm, and similar diseases was brilliantly successful. Sir Frederick Banting in Canada discovered insulin to treat diabetes just in time to save the life of Dr. George Minot of the Harvard Medical School; Minot and his colleague William P. Murphy then proceeded to find the liver-extract treatment for pernicious anemia. Intensive research promoted new and better anesthesia, and additional researches made possible the brain surgery of Harvey Cushing, the cardiac treatments of Paul Dudley White (which probably saved President Eisenhower's life), and the heart surgery of Alfred Blalock and Robert Gross. Rickets and tooth decay yielded to vitamin treatment, and that discovery led to general dietary reform as well as to a great deal of quackery in "wonder drugs" sold by pharmaceutical companies at staggering profits. Adrenalin proved helpful in cardiac disorders and gave relief to sufferers from asthma. New methods of ameliorating apparently fatal burns saved thousands of lives of soldiers and sailors in World War II. The fight against coccus infections was sensational. English and American doctors experimented with sulfanilamide (whose therapeutic qualities were discovered by Gerhard Domagk in 1935 when working for the German dye industry) and its numerous derivatives, and found that it could be successfully used against a host of coccal infections including meningitis, gonorrhea, undulant fever, and pneumonia.

Yet it was typical of America that, side by side with the great medical schools and research laboratories, there flourished throughout the country a considerable number of medical heresies, notably the chiropractors. "This preposterous quackery," wrote H. L. Mencken in 1927, which claimed to cure all human ills by "thrusts, lunges, yanks, hooks, and bounces, is now all the rage in the back reaches of the Republic, and even begins to conquer the less civilized of the big cities"— notably Los Angeles, haven of strange sects. The osteopaths, well established by 1910, though still unorthodox, have become more respectable with the lapse of years and no longer pretend to work miracles by manipulation of the spinal column.

Polar exploration was one of the most important scientific exploits of this era, and, just as all the major maritime discoveries had been made under sail, so the discovery of the two poles was made by foot and by dog.

Admiral Robert E. Peary thus attained the North Pole in 1909 as a result of exploring and studying the Arctic regions and cultivating the Eskimo for over twenty years. He decided that the best way to attain the coveted pole was to thrust as far into the Arctic ice as possible in a ship, and dash northward by dog train, establishing caches of provisions en route for the return journey. After two such attempts, which came within three degrees of the pole, he left his ship about 435 miles from the objective in March 1909, and took off with 33 men, 19 sleds, and 133 huskies. Every five days a cache was established and a section of the expedition returned. At the last of these, at lat. 87° 48′ N, Peary with his black assistant Matthew A. Henson, four Eskimos, five sleds, and 40 dogs, made his final dash, and on 6 April reached the top of the world. Three weeks later, he was back on board his ship.

The conquest of the South Pole took more time, because there is no human life in the Antarctic, and the land is only supportable by humans with large stockpiles of food and fuel. The Norwegian Roald Amundsen did it after a decade of experience in polar regions. In his 70-foot sloop *Gjoa,* in 1903–5, he made the Northwest passage, Atlantic to Pacific, which Cabot, Frobisher, and countless others had vainly sought. In 1910 he commanded a modest expedition in the ship *Fram* to the Antarctic, taking Eskimo dogs and sleds. With them he crossed the great Ross Barrier, and on 14 December 1911 raised his country's flag over the South Pole, and returned safely. The English explorer Robert F. Scott, using the same methods, arrived there a month later; but Scott with his four companions died of exposure on the return trip.

A new chapter in Antarctic exploration was opened when Richard E. Byrd, a United States naval officer, applied the internal combustion engine and the airplane. After making the first flight over the North Pole on 9 May 1926, and a transatlantic flight too, he obtained private funds for air exploration of the Antarctic. This, he rightly estimated, was of far more potential value than the Arctic, because it is a solid continent, not an ice-covered ocean. From New Zealand he jumped off in barque *Bear* to Ross Ice Shelf, where the open ocean most nearly approaches the pole and there at lat. 78° 30′ S established the base that he named Little America, in October 1928. Thence, after a month of careful preparation, he departed with a crew of three in the tri-motored plane *Floyd Bennett,* flew over the South Pole on 28 November, and returned to base in less than 19 hours. Byrd, as able a writer as explorer and leader, records this exploit in his *Little America* (1930).

OF THEE I SING

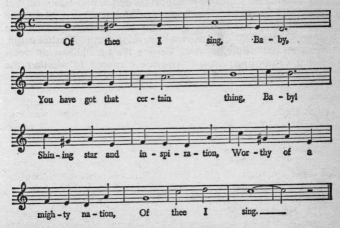

Of thee I sing, Ba-by,

You have got that cer-tain thing, Ba-by!

Shin-ing star and in-spi-ra-tion, Wor-thy of a

migh-ty na-tion, Of thee I sing.——

For Byrd, this was just a beginning. Promoted rear admiral by act of Congress, he lectured and worked for funds for several years, and in 1934 established an advanced base on lat. 80° S and spent five months there alone in the Antarctic waste to make meteorological and other observations. In addition he explored and charted a large part of Antarctica. His book *Discovery* (1935) relates his experiences. It aroused universal interest in the Antarctic for strategic and economic possibilities. President Roosevelt appointed Admiral Byrd commander of the U.S. Antarctic Service, in 1939, and for two years he made further explorations of the Southern continent by airplane and motorized sled or tractor. Then World War II interrupted his work.

The stock market crash of 1929 and the depression that followed punctuated the era that we have been describing. No quarter-century of American history had wrought so many changes in society, or so few in politics. After a crusade to "make the world safe for democracy," America turned away from Europe. After a century and a half of asking the world to "give me your tired, your poor, your huddled masses yearning to breathe free," her door was shut. After a century of increasing temperance, prohibition had been adopted, then repealed. After three centuries in which Christian morals had been maintained by law, religion, and custom, "permissiveness" had conquered St. Augustine and John Milton, becoming a dominant principle in education and sexual relations. Yet there had been gain as well as loss: the rise of real wages, the siphoning of private fortunes into research institutions, the improved quality of American literature, music, scholarship, science, and medicine. And, despite the breakdown of traditional values and virtues, America managed to weather the Great Depression and the Second World War.

X

Republican Ascendancy

1921-1933

1. *Harding and the "Ohio Gang"*

EIGHT YEARS OF Democratic rule were followed by twelve of Republican ascendancy under three inept Presidents—Warren G. Harding, Calvin Coolidge, and Herbert Hoover. Yet Hoover and Coolidge were good men and the former had elements of greatness. Their failure to cope with difficult problems must be shared by their party, which until 1931 controlled both houses of Congress; the G.O.P., like the aristocrats who returned to power in France after the fall of Napoleon, had "forgotten nothing and learned nothing." Progressive Republicans, having been piped away by Theodore Roosevelt into the Bull Moose wilderness, had to straggle back on their knees, if at all; for the party was now in the hands of conservatives and reactionaries. They, in general, regarded the Democratic interlude of 1913–21 as abnormal, the war which Wilson had led them into as a failure, and his New Freedom an unnecessary obstruction to free enterprise. Hoover's favorite cliché, "The American system of rugged individualism," Vice President Coolidge's epigram, "The business of America is business," and Harding's election slogan, a return to "normalcy," expressed their views. McKinley's administration, to which Harding liked to compare his, was normal; Theodore

259

Roosevelt's and all since were abnormal. The Harding-Coolidge plurality of 61 per cent seemed a clear mandate for isolation in foreign policy, favoring big business in domestic policy, and government keeping hands off individuals, no matter how rugged.

Warren Gamaliel Harding was what everyone called a "nice" man—handsome, genial, well dressed, outwardly dignified; his big plurality was probably due to many more women voting for him than for colorless, flat-faced Governor Cox. He was a "typical American," son of an Ohio physician, lawyer and journalist in a small Ohio town, director of the local bank and telephone company, pillar of the Baptist church, favorite orator, state senator, and always a "regular" Republican. Mrs. Harding, an angular and ambitious widow five years his senior, groomed Warren into respectability and made his newspaper pay. Politically he had grown up as a "spieler" (orator in the slang of that day) for Senator Joseph B. Foraker, whose intimates were known as the "Ohio gang." Foraker, after years of feuding with Theodore Roosevelt, had been driven from public life by the disclosure that he had been on the Standard Oil payroll while serving as senator. At that juncture Harry M. Daugherty, Foraker's hatchet man, took up Harding and managed his campaign for the Senate in 1914. Harding's senatorial career proved so satisfactory to party stalwarts and big business that Daugherty began an astute and successful campaign to make him President of the United States. And with him the "Ohio gang" moved into Washington.

President Harding's top cabinet appointments—Charles Evans Hughes as secretary of state, Andrew W. Mellon the Pittsburgh aluminum millionaire secretary of the treasury, Herbert Hoover secretary of commerce—were excellent. But most of the other cabinet posts and several leading administrative positions went to the gang. Harry M. Daugherty, a lobbyist by profession, became attorney general; a senatorial friend, Albert B. Fall, who looked like a ballyhoo-man at a country fair but served the oil interests well, secretary of the interior; Will H. Hays, Harding's campaign manager, postmaster general. Of the local cronies, a former county sheriff was appointed director of the mint, a Marion lawyer whose financial experience was limited to a few months' presidency of the local bank became governor of the federal reserve banking system; "Colonel" Charles R. Forbes, a chance acquaintance who, it subsequently appeared, had deserted from the army, became head of the Veterans' Bureau. A local doctor named Sawyer, who had helped Mrs. Harding (a hypochondriac and believer in soothsayers and clairvoyants), was suddenly jumped from civilian life to an army "generalcy," as the President called it, to be White House physician. A loutish fellow named Jess Smith, valet-secretary to Daugherty, was given an office in the department of justice and became the primary "fixer" of the administration. Gaston B. Means, another hanger-on, was the gang's bootlegger while holding office in the department of justice. After serving a term in the penitentiary (subsequent to Harding's death) for selling permits for "medicinal" whisky, Means disclosed that he had collected the cool sum of $7 million in bribes from bootleggers, and turned over the money to Jess Smith. But by that time Smith had committed suicide and could not deny it.

Other friends of the President were equally shady characters; there was never so raffish a "court" as that of Warren G. Harding. And what a change in the White House! In contrast to the jolly country-house atmosphere of the Theodore Roosevelt administration, the sick-room smell of the latter part of Wilson's, and the good taste and republican elegance of the future Kennedy administration, that of Harding's was of the bar-room. T.R.'s daughter Mrs. Nicholas Longworth, inadvertently straying into an upstairs room during a state reception, found a recently vacated poker table littered with cigar stubs, glasses, and partly empty whisky bottles; and if she had explored below stairs she might have found a young mistress of the President, brought in through a back door, waiting for him in a cloakroom. To escape such respectability as Mrs. Harding imposed on the White House, the President, of an evening, would steal away to the home of Jess Smith or some other crony, to play more poker and drink heavily.

These were indeed the "hollow men" as T. S. Eliot characterized the postwar politicians of the Western world. There was nothing in them but wind, greed, and a certain low cunning.

Congress, too, was full of hollow men; William E. Borah, perpetual senator from Idaho, was the most pretentious and the emptiest, although he looked more like a statesman than any senator since Daniel Webster. Borah would support any liberal bill with great rumbling oratory, yet in the end vote with the regular Republicans. Senator Norris said of him, "He fights until he sees the whites of their eyes." Or, for a hollow man from New England, take George Holden Tinkham, bachelor congressman from one of the Boston districts, a big-game hunter with an impressive though greasy beard. Tinkham was immovable because he did favors at Washington for most of his constituents—getting pensions for those who were not entitled to them, sending a wreath to everyone's funeral, a present for every bride, and a graduation gift to every young person in his district. No Democrat in Democratic Boston dared oppose him, and one campaign for re-election was conducted in absentia by his efficient lady secretary. Every summer Tinkham went globe-trotting, and on his return gave out pronouncements on world developments that invariably were wrong. But he could get anything he wanted from the federal government because he had taken the precaution, when Prohibition was looming, to buy a small hotel in the District and equip it with a good ten years' supply of alcoholic beverages, with which he was very generous; this being his private stock, enforcement agents did not dare touch it.

Harding was the best of the lot—a vulgar good fellow who wished to make everyone happy and saw nothing incongruous in promoting a small-town banker to the most powerful and responsible financial position in the government. That was the older American way, the Andrew Jackson way; anybody was qualified for any office, provided his politics were right. But Harding was completely out of his depth in the presidency. Typical was his outburst to a secretary after hearing his advisers discuss a financial matter: "John, I can't make a damn thing out of this tax problem. I listen to one side and they seem right, and then—God!—I talk to the other side, and they seem just as right. I know somewhere there is a book that will give me the truth, but hell, I couldn't read the book. I know somewhere there is an economist who knows the truth, but I don't know where to find him and haven't the sense to know and trust him when I find him. God! what a job!" Uncomfortable with Hughes, Mellon, and Hoover, the statesmen in his cabinet, Harding became increasingly dependent for advice on the "good fellows"—Daugherty, Hays, and Fall.

But Harding had a heart, and he wished to do something for peace. One of his first kind acts (one which Wilson had refused to do) was to pardon several victims of prosecution under the wartime Sedition Act, notably Eugene Debs who had served two years of a ten-year sentence for saying no more than the Federalist leaders had said in 1812, or the Whigs in 1846. The pardon was to have been given in 1922, but Harding upped it to the previous December "so Debs could spend Christmas with his family."

2. The Republicans and Foreign Affairs

Harding's biggest bid for peace was the Naval Disarmament Conference of 1921–22, first of several futile efforts toward disarmament. The "Big Navy" Act of 1916, if fully implemented by Congress, would have made the United States Navy "incomparably the most adequate navy in the world," as President Wilson put it. Lloyd George, instead of welcoming this development, which would partly have relieved the Royal Navy of world-wide responsibilities, chose to regard it as a challenge; and Britain, impoverished by her hard-won victory, could never match the American program. So the British premier proposed an international meeting for naval disarmament. Harding and Hughes, eager to accomplish something for peace, gladly accepted, and the conference opened at Washington on 12 November 1921, with delegates from three major (United States, Britain, Japan), two medium (France and Italy), and four minor (Belgium, Holland, Portugal, China) naval powers.

Secretary Hughes astounded the conference and electrified the world by announcing in his opening speech that the United States was prepared to scrap new naval construction on which $300 million had already been spent, if Britain and Japan would do likewise. After long bargaining, it was agreed to scrap a great deal of naval tonnage built or building, and to limit future building. The Washington treaties, signed 6 February 1922, set up a 5:5:3 ratio in battleship and aircraft carrier tonnage between Britain, America, and Japan. A ten-year "holiday" was declared on building capital ships, and the tonnage of battleships was restricted to 35,000. Although this ratio allowed Japan to become the strongest naval power in the western Pacific (since America had two, and Britain three, oceans to defend), Japanese consent had to be purchased by a supplementary agreement on military bases. The United States renounced strengthening, in a military sense, any of her bases such as Guam and Manila that lay west of Pearl Harbor; and England similarly denied the same to herself east of Singapore or north of Australia. This provision actually reversed the 5:5:3 ratio to favor Japan, as the United States and Great Britain learned to their sorrow twenty years later.

Naval limitation was undoubtedly popular. Congress never authorized naval construction up to treaty strength until the eve of World War II, and the Kellogg-Briand Peace Pact which President Coolidge added to the Republican preserve-the-peace armory was ratified by the United States Senate (15 January 1929) by a vote of 81 to 1. Initiated by the French premier Aristide Briand, supported by the British prime minister Ramsay Macdonald, this pact was negotiated for the United States by Secretary of State Frank B. Kellogg. It provided that the contracting powers "renounce war as an instrument of national policy," and promised to solve "all disputes or conflicts of whatever nature or of whatever origin" by "pacific means." No fewer than 62 nations, including Italy, Japan, and Germany, adhered to the Kellogg-Briand Pact, which may fairly be called an attempt to keep the peace by incantation. It was taken seriously by the democratic nations, and the breach of it by the Axis powers became the basis of war criminals' trials after World War II.

These methods of preserving the peace—by naval limitation, by incantation, and (in the Roosevelt administration) by negation—would have been effective among nations that wanted peace. They were worse than useless in a world in which three nations—Germany, Italy, and Japan—wanted war; for they merely served to lull the democracies into a false feeling of security, while giving the militarists elsewhere a chance to plot, plan, and prepare for a war that would enable them to divide the world.

Uncle Sam's isolationist bark was much worse than his bite. After World War I was over, many efforts were made both by the government and private charity to relieve suffering in Europe and the Middle East. In July 1921 the Soviet government persuaded the well-known Russian writer Maxim Gorky to appeal for relief from starvation in Russia. Allegedly this was the result of drought and crop failures, but primarily it was due to the Soviet government's abolition of private property and forced collection of food from the peasants. Although Lenin had made it clear that the communists were bent on upsetting every capitalist government, and that the United States was their principal target, America responded generously to Gorky's appeals to her "bourgeois" sentiment of humanity. The American Relief Association, headed by Secretary Hoover, with funds contributed partly by private charity but mainly by the United States government, moved into Russia promptly and vigorously. By August 1922 two hundred Americans were there, directing 18,000 stations at which more than 4 million children and 6 million adults were fed. Medical assistance, too, was provided on a massive scale. A conservative estimate of the number of Russian lives saved through the efforts of the A.R.A. is 11 million. But this great effort is now written down by Soviet historians as an effort of American capitalists to overthrow the Communist regime; the most that they can admit is that A.R.A. "gave a certain help to the starving."

Near East Relief, another massive charitable effort, was financed wholly from private sources. The Rev. James L. Barton, a former missionary in Turkey, and Cleveland H. Dodge, financier and philanthropist, ran it with the help of a

Milking Time

Delineations of Country Life by Winslow Homer

Shoveling Out

Rogers Group, *Coming to the Parson*, 1889

POST CIVIL WAR ARCHITECTURE AND SCULPTURE

The Syracuse, New York, Savings Bank, 1875

Finish of the 1870 race off Staten Island. *Cambria, Dauntless, America, Idler, Magic*

America's CUP RACE

Volunteer, the 1887 defender

Kentucky

TWO GREAT AMERICAN THOROUGHBREDS

Man O'War

WILLIAM McKINLEY AND THEODORE ROOSEVELT
Taken at McKinley's home, after the election of 1900

PRESIDENT WILSON AND GENERAL PERSHING
On the President's visit to the army in January 1919

A Curtiss Triad A-1 of 1912

EARLY AVIATION

NC-4 Arriving Lisbon, May 1919, after her first ocean crossing

THE "GREAT FOUR" OF JOHNS HOPKINS, by John Singer Sargent
William H. Welch, William S. Halsted, William Osler,
Howard A. Kelly

TVA's HIWASSEE DAM in North Carolina

SENATOR AND MRS. GEORGE W. NORRIS

WILLIAM LYON
MACKENZIE KING

REAR ADMIRAL RICHARD E. BYRD, USN

PRESIDENT FRANKLIN DELANO ROOSEVELT

President Harry S. Truman

President Dwight D. Eisenhower

PRESIDENT JOHN F. KENNEDY

board of trustees that included Taft, Root, Hughes, and F. D. Roosevelt. The condition of the people around the Aegean was particularly deplorable, because, after the world war ended, hostilities continued between Greece and Turkey. These culminated in 1922 with the Greeks taking a bad beating and being forced to evacuate every person of their race and religion from Turkish territory. Almost a million and a half refugees from Asia crossed the Aegean; in revenge, all Moslems had to leave Greece. Near East Relief undertook not only to feed and clothe these "displaced persons," earliest of that unfortunate class in modern times, but to build them houses, set up schools for their children, and industries to employ them. Between 1919 and 1930 it disbursed some $91 million in money and $25 million worth of food in Greece, Turkey, Armenia, Macedonia, Persia, and Mesopotamia. About one-quarter of all this was sent to alleviate famine and disease in the Russian Caucasus, where conditions following the civil war were unspeakably bad; all this in addition to what the A.R.A. was doing in other parts of Russia.

Nor did America turn her back on Europe in the matter of war debts and German reparations. During the war, in addition to private loans, the Allies received over $7 billion from the United States government, to which $3.2 billion more were added after the armistice. These debts were to bear interest at 5 per cent. From Great Britain alone $4 billion was due; but Britain had made similar loans to other Allies amounting to $10.5 billion. Arthur Balfour proposed in 1922 that all inter-allied war debts be canceled, and to many Americans this seemed a just solution, considering how late we had entered the war and that most of the loans had been spent in the United States. But such generosity was politically explosive, and the Fordney-McCumber tariff act, an upward revision all along the line, prevented Europe from repaying her debts by the export of goods.

In 1923 Congress consented to a radical reduction of war debts, ranging from 30 per cent of both capital and interest for Britain to 80 per cent for Italy, together with extension of the time of repayment to 62 years. During the Great Depression the European governments were unable to continue these payments. President Hoover advised, and Congress consented, to a moratorium on war debts for a year. After that there was a general default, Finland and Cuba alone meeting their financial obligations in full. Americans felt that they had been very generous, but Europeans asserted that "U.S." stood for "Uncle Shylock" and mutual recriminations helped to prolong American neutrality in World War II.

German reparations, fixed at $33 billion in 1921, were in-separable from the inter-allied war debts because the Allies expected to use them to repay each other and the United States. The government of the German Republic became in-volved in runaway inflation, until a postage stamp cost a mil-lion marks, and suspended reparation payments in December 1922. France countered by invading the Ruhr, the German miners struck, and this attempt to collect debts by force was a dismal failure. Roland W. Boyden, a Boston lawyer of great acumen who had been unofficial "observer" for Presidents Wilson and Harding on the Reparations Commission, publicly criticized French policy and advocated that both debts and reparations be settled on the principle of "ability to pay," which finally was done. Secretary Hughes appointed a com-mittee headed by the Chicago financier Charles G. Dawes (later Vice President under Coolidge), which arranged for an American loan to enable Germany to pay something, per-suaded France to evacuate the Ruhr, and to help the German Republic establish a new and sound currency. Germany had to be bailed out again in 1929; this time it was the Wall Street financier Owen D. Young, appointed by President Hoover, who did the trick and persuaded Germany's creditors to scale down reparations to $27 billion, to be paid within 60 years. Germany met this reduced payment only by floating bonds in the United States. By 1931, when Germany finally defaulted in the depth of her depression, she had paid $4.5 billion in reparations, of which $2.5 billion had been borrowed from hopeful American investors. In the same period the Allies had paid $2.6 billion to the United States, which thus footed over half the German reparations which were actually paid, as well as allowing three-quarters of the Allied debts to go by default.

The three Republican Presidents and their secretaries of state, Hughes, Kellogg, and Henry L. Stimson, managed to maintain an uneasy peace in the Far East where the breakup of China into spheres controlled by war lords offered tempt-ing opportunities for aggression, especially by Japan. That country, under a liberal government since the war, honored her trust commitments under the League of Nations, canceled the "Twenty-one Demands" which would have made China her satellite, withdrew her armies from Siberia, Manchuria, and the Shantung peninsula as she had promised to do, and joined in the nine-power treaty of 1922. In this treaty the powers which had Far Eastern interests promised to "safe-guard the rights and interests of China," mutually agreeing to respect her sovereignty, independence, and administrative integrity, and to refrain from creating "spheres of influence" or seeking special privileges or concessions.

But the Japanese liberals, the only hope of preserving peace in the Orient, lost out to the militarists, who played up Japan's short end of the 5:5:3 ratio in the naval limitation treaties as insulting and unconstitutional, and resented the exclusion of Japanese from the United States by the Act of 1924. These things, together with too frequent instances of American intolerance toward Japanese-Americans, offended Nipponese pride and offset the gratitude for generous American help after the Tokyo earthquake of 1923. That earthquake did, however, postpone a crisis because the havoc that it created and the superstitious dread it aroused caused the military secret societies to postpone the coup d'état they had planned. The Japanese militarists, who bore a strong resemblance in methods and objectives to Hitler's Nazis, were planning to seize the government and throw the detested white man out of East Asia. World War II in the Far East really began on 18 September 1931 when General Hayashi moved his army from Korea into Manchuria. The Japanese government, ignorant of this "Manchuria Incident" until it was accomplished, was forced to acquiesce under threat of assassination, and declared Manchuria to be the independent kingdom of Manchukuo, under a puppet monarch.

All this violated treaties, the Kellogg Pact, and the League Covenant, by which Japan was bound. Without waiting for League action Secretary Stimson informed Japan that the United States would not recognize the legality of any development which impaired American treaty rights or violated the open-door policy. He would have gone further but for President Hoover's Quakerish qualms. A commission of the League of Nations condemned the Japanese aggression in September 1932; Japan countered by withdrawing from the League. The militarists consolidated their power by assassinating the Japanese premier and other important ministers of state, and entered on a vigorous program of economic and military preparation for invading China proper.

In Mexico and Central America, the Republican administrations liquidated a very sticky situation with Mexico but became deeply involved in Nicaragua.

Álvaro Obregón was elected constitutional president of Mexico in 1920 after the assassination of Wilson's old antagonist Carranza, and Plutarco Calles succeeded him in 1924. Both kept order fairly well; but both were resolved to carry out the basic principles of the Mexican Revolution—to nationalize all foreign oil, mining, and other properties, and destroy the power of the Roman Catholic church. Calles aroused resentment in the United States by conducting a heavy flirtation with the Soviets; in his era it was more profitable for Mexican politicians to make pilgrimages to Lenin's tomb in Moscow than to Our Lady of Guadalupe. American oil interests, especially those of Doheny and Sinclair which had been smirched by the Teapot Dome affair, wanted war; and Secretary Kellogg, who had negotiated the pact outlawing war, was almost converted to armed intervention. President Coolidge appeared to take the same point of view by declaring that Americans and their property abroad were part of the public domain. Thus, by the close of 1926 it looked as if another war with Mexico were about to begin. But a remarkable uprise of public sentiment, expressed by the liberal press, labor unions, Protestant church groups, and others, even converted the United States Senate, which on 25 January 1927 resolved unanimously that our differences with Mexico be settled by arbitration. "Cool Cal," sensitive to public opinion, then recalled his interventionist ambassador and appointed Dwight W. Morrow, a partner of the House of Morgan, ambassador to Mexico. Morrow succeeded in repairing most of the damage done by his predecessors there and his superiors in Washington. He really liked the Mexicans, he despised dollar diplomacy, he negotiated informally, and took Will Rogers on an inspection tour, knowing that the "cowboy philosopher's" reports would improve the average American's picture of the Mexicans. Charles Lindbergh, invited to visit Mexico City, was received with wild enthusiasm; Morrow built a house at Cuernavaca and employed Diego Rivera to decorate the town hall with murals.

The Mexican Congress now modified some of its oil and mineral legislation in line with American objections, and Morrow obtained an adjustment of land questions, claims, and the Catholic question. For several years the new understanding inaugurated by Morrow remained undisturbed, while in the United States admiration for Mexican culture and a growing appreciation of the social ideals of the Mexican revolution made a good base for the future.

Obregón, re-elected President of Mexico in 1928, was assassinated before he could take office. After three temporary presidents whom Calles promoted and sustained, Lázaro Cardenas was elected president in 1934.

Despite the reluctance of Republican administrations to get involved in Latin America, circumstances forced President Coolidge into a hot little row in Nicaragua. The previous intervention in that volcanic country, begun under President Taft, had barely been liquidated and the marines' legation guard withdrawn from Managua (August 1925) when civil war erupted. So, honoring a request from the then government of Nicaragua to help preserve order along the Corinto-Managua railroad, back came the marines—some 2000 of them by February 1927, and many more before the troubles were over. President Coolidge sent Henry L. Stimson, who had just returned from a trouble-shooting trip to the Philippines, to Managua to "straighten the matter out," which that remarkable man effected within five weeks. He brought the leaders of both sides together, obtained the "agreement of Tipitata" to stop fighting, allowed the presidential incumbent to stay in for a year and then to hold a free election supervised by the marines, who in the meantime would train a native national guard to maintain order. Stimson returned home to find that Coolidge had appointed him governor general of the Philippines.

So far, so good; but one of the twelve opposition generals, Augusto Sandino, refused to co-operate and continued the fight from his mountain redoubt in northern Nicaragua. Sandino was of different metal from the bandit chiefs with whom the marines had dealt in Hispaniola. A troublemaker from school days, he had escaped justice for murder and lived for several years in Mexico, where he made useful contacts with communists and other left-wing elements. Like the guerrillas in Viet-Nam, when hard-pressed he was always able to retire to a safe asylum over the border, recruit, and return to fight again. The Communist party played him up as a hero of liberation and not only collected arms and money for him but fooled gullible liberals in the United States and Europe into supporting Sandino as the savior of his country from the "imperialists." The New York *Nation,* edited by pacifist Oswald Garrison Villard, gave Sandino full support while he was spreading terror and torture through Nicaraguan villages. Henry Barbusse, author of *Le feu,* called Sandino "Le George Washington de l'Amérique Centrale"; and the Chinese communists named a division after him.

Sandino was a precursor of Fidel Castro; had he won, Nicaragua could have become another Red satellite. "General don Augusto Cesar Sandino," as he styled himself, called his forces, "El Ejército Autonomista de Centro America," indicating that he intended to take over neighboring republics as well; and his middle name, added by himself, suggested that he proposed to play the role of Octavian in uniting Central America against "el grotesco imperialismo Yanki."

Owing largely to the marines, he did not win. Sandino never had many troops, but his friends saw that they were well sup-

plied with weapons and munitions. The marines had a tactical
air squadron which helped turn the tide. In November 1928,
the presidential election brought about the first peaceful change
of government in Nicaraguan history. But Sandino, after spending over a year recruiting in Mexico, struck again in 1930,
financed by world-wide contributions from left-wingers. Again
repulsed, again he returned; this time he was hurled back into
Honduras by the new national guard led by Captain Lewis B.
("Chesty") Puller USMC. Once more returning, he was arrested
by the national guard and executed by a firing squad led by
Colonel Anastacio Somoza, the guard's *jefe*. Somoza now assumed the presidency and became a dictator. But Nicaragua
was at peace; and under the "good neighbor" policy of Franklin D. Roosevelt there were no more forcible interventions in
Latin America.

Although the Philippines were not yet "foreign," it will be
convenient at this point to follow thither Governor General
Stimson. The lax and extravagant proconsulship of President
Wilson's appointee, F. Burton Harrison, was succeeded in
1921 by the severe one of General Leonard Wood, who made
the mistake of attempting to apply army discipline to an easygoing people. Stimson quickly established friendly relations
with the Filipino leaders Osmeña, Roxas, and Quezón, and
accomplished a great deal for the economy and education in
the islands. What is more, he broke down racial segregation
and treated the Filipinos as social equals. One good aspect of
President Coolidge's penchant for inactivity was to refrain
from giving his appointees abroad the usual stream of orders
and advice. Stimson was allowed to do what he thought best
during his year as governor general, and he laid a basis for
future friendly relations between America and the Philippine
Republic.

3. *Postwar Canada*

The Dominion of Canada, having entered the war with
England and taken part in the bloody offensive on the Western
front, suffered heavier casualties proportionally than the
United States, and acquired a huge national debt—$2.2 billion.
As her population in 1921 was only 8.8 million, about the
same as that of Pennsylvania, this was more burdensome than
the $24 billion which the United States national debt reached
in the same year. Canada entered, somewhat later, the American wave of postwar prosperity, and from 1921 on the United
States was her best customer.

Differences between the two countries were as significant as the resemblances. Canada's frontier of settlement had not ended in 1890, like that of the United States. Following the war, prairie settlement placed many thousand more acres under wheat cultivation in Saskatchewan, Alberta, and the Peace River district. And, when the United States began to restrict immigration, Canada encouraged it, setting up emigration offices not only in Britain, but in Paris, Warsaw, Danzig and other eastern European cities, and in many cases paying immigrants' passages. In 1926, for instance, 136,000 people emigrated to Canada, almost half as many as the United States allowed under the quota system. But more than 100,000 Canadians, on an average, emigrated to the United States annually between 1920 and 1927.

A movement similar to the earlier Populist-Progressive one in the United States, arose in Canada's prairie provinces, based upon the same agrarian discontent. A 50 per cent wartime increase of farm acreage was followed by a drop in the price of wheat from $2.19 per bushel in 1919 to 60 cents next year. This brought forth an agrarian party, called the National Progressives, which entered federal politics in 1920, captured several provincial governments, and seriously impinged on the traditional two-party system, winning 65 seats out of 235 in the Dominion House of Commons in 1921. The government proceeded to take over two great railway systems, the Canadian Northern and the Grand Trunk, which became the Canadian National. Sir Henry Thornton, a native of Indiana, who had served for twenty years in the engineering department of the Pennsylvania Railroad, became an important figure in army transportation in England during World War I. Appointed president of the Canadian National in 1922, he made it pay its running expenses. And, as another indication of close Canadian-American relations, William Howard Taft served, while professor of law at Yale, on a commission of three to appraise the value of the Grand Trunk system when it was nationalized. He dissented from the decision of the two Canadian members to give no compensation to the holders of common stock.

State socialism and welfare legislation in Canada went much further than in the United States. The street railways of Toronto were taken over by the municipality, and the Ontario Hydro-Electric Corporation, later imitated by the Tennessee Valley Authority, pioneered successfully in government ownership of electric power.

Sir Wilfrid Laurier, the Grand Old Man of Canada and leader of the Liberal party, died in 1919. William Lyon Mackenzie King, namesake and grandson of the rebellion leader of 1837, became his political heir. After graduating in law from Toronto, King took a Ph.D. in economics at Harvard, continued his studies in London, returned to Canada, and as minister of labour in the Laurier government, became responsible for an important Industrial Investigation Act. This was much admired in the United States and, after his defeat in the election of 1911, led to King's becoming a highly placed member of the Rockefeller Foundation for investigating and adjusting industrial disputes. In the United States, King was instrumental in settling major conflicts, such as a strike between coal miners and the Rockefellers' Colorado Fuel and Iron Company in which the bloody "Ludlow Massacre" occurred. Returning again to Canada in 1919, Mackenzie King was chosen leader of the Liberals by a party convention. He was then forty-five years old, the same age as Arthur Meighen, a distinguished lawyer and member of the House of Commons who succeeded Sir Robert Borden as leader of the Unionist party in 1920. Meighen's majority in the House of Commons, eaten away by the Progressives' winning by-elections, became so tenuous that a general election was held in December 1921. The Progressives won 65 seats, the Conservatives 50, and the Liberals 117. The governor general then summoned Mackenzie King to construct a new government; but with a very slim majority he was unable to do much in the domestic area.

The Liberal party traditionally favored close and friendly relations with the United States, whilst the Unionists (generally called the Conservatives) tended toward the traditional British association. Both parties continued the earlier Canadian policy of gently but firmly pulling their country loose from imperial influence. Sir Robert Borden, prime minister at the time of the Paris Peace Conference, insisted that Canada sign and ratify the Treaty of Versailles separately from Britain, and on her receiving a seat in the League Assembly and becoming eligible to a place on the Council. The folly of the American anti-Leaguers' contention that Canada's place in the League meant a double vote for "perfidious Albion," was proved in 1922 when Lloyd George contemplated war with Turkey. The British prime minister announced that he expected Canada in the League of Nations to vote for sanctions against Turkey, but Mackenzie King refused to commit the Dominion. A year later the Canadian government, remembering how England had let her down in the Alaska boundary controversy, herself negotiated a treaty with the United States for control of the halibut fishery in the Pacific. This quasi-independence was legalized by the Imperial Conferences between Britain and her

Dominions in 1923 and 1926, which agreed that any part of the British Empire might negotiate and sign treaties affecting only itself. Canada now organized her own foreign service. Early in 1927 Vincent Massey was sent to Washington as Canadian minister; and William Phillips, former undersecretary of state and ambassador to Belgium, went to Ottawa as the first United States minister to Canada. Both posts were later raised to embassies.

Mackenzie King, hampered by his slight majority, appealed to the country in 1925. The surprising results were an increase of Conservative members and disintegration of the Progressives. Canada was prosperous and wheat prices going up, the farmers having organized a system of big co-operatives and wheat pools for price support. King, with an even more slender majority than before, nevertheless decided to "muddle through"—as John Diefenbaker later did. But he was gravely embarrassed by a series of scandals paralleling those of the late President Harding.

These scandals were the indirect result of Amendment XVIII being added to the United States Constitution while Canada left the liquor question to the provinces. Several of these tried prohibition, but by the end of 1926 Ontario, Quebec, the Maritimes, and all but three prairie provinces had rejected America's "noble experiment." And the manufacture and export of alcoholic beverages had then reached stupendous proportions, owing to demands from across the border. A parliamentary committee in 1926 revealed that a rum-runner gang in Montreal had bribed excise officers and customs officials to release liquor for export without paying taxes, and in return had smuggled in American textiles, tobacco, and other articles without paying duty. Canada was rocked by the revelation of this "unholy partnership between the government and a gang of bootleggers," as the opposition described it; and although the scandals did not smirch King personally, political considerations forced him to resign. Parliament was dissolved, and a very exciting campaign ensued. There were more serious issues, but King's Harvard degree and lack of war service were brought up against him; the Liberals retorted by pointing out that Meighen had named a son after Theodore Roosevelt! (This paralleled the efforts of "Big Bill" Thompson, mayor of Chicago, and other demagogues, to drive former Rhodes scholars or anyone with British relations out of American political life.) Despite the alleged "welter of wickedness," the Liberals won; King returned to power, constructed a strong cabinet including seven French Canadians, and "cleaned house" in the customs service.

Thus Mackenzie King was premier when Canada celebrated her diamond jubilee on 1 July 1927, sixtieth anniversary of Confederation. On this occasion, in contrast to what happened in 1867, President Coolidge sent warm greetings (for him), and the United States was represented not only by Minister Phillips but by Charles Lindbergh. Immediately after the celebration at Ottawa, a new Peace Bridge between Buffalo and Fort Erie, scene of such bitter fighting in the War of 1812, was dedicated. Vice President Dawes, Secretary Kellogg, and Governor Al Smith represented the United States, and Stanley Baldwin and the Prince of Wales, Great Britain.

Although Canada was now a nation in her relations with the outside world, internally the Dominion government had lost power to the provinces; this in spite of the Canadian constitution having been expressly drafted to exorcise the specter of state rights. Owing to the profound economic and racial differences between the Canadian provinces, and the vast distances between some of them, they had acquired by 1920 prerogatives and powers far greater than the reserved rights of the American states. Certain appeals by the provinces to the supreme court of the British empire (the judicial committee of the privy council)—notably the Toronto Electric case of 1925 —resulted in several federal laws of a welfare nature being found unconstitutional. Consequently, the Dominion government had to act with circumspection and leave social experimentation largely to the provinces. Mackenzie King dominated Canadian politics for twenty years because he appreciated this situation and acted accordingly. A bachelor premier, he lacked the personal charm of Laurier or the human warmth of Macdonald, inspired slight affection, and created no personal following like that of the Roosevelts. Yet he managed to hold the volatile French Canadians in the Liberal party without alienating the Protestants; he placated the farm groups and the rising manufacturers, and accepted half-measures when it would have been unwise to demand the whole loaf. King had the blandness of Buchanan, the shrewdness of Coolidge, and a peculiar talent for easing the strains and stresses of religion, language, and sectionalism to which the Dominion was subject.

American heedlessness of the interests and aspirations of her nearest neighbor and best customer is almost incredible. One incident will suffice. Early in 1929, toward the close of the Coolidge administration, the House of Representatives began to hold hearings preliminary to jacking up tariff schedules, for which there was no excuse in that booming era. Proposed prohibitory rates on imports from Canada raised such a furor of anti-American feeling in the Canadian press, and so many threats of retaliation, that the American minister at Ottawa, William Phillips, visited Washington at the request of Mackenzie King, to see if he could do anything to moderate the greed of the tariff-mongers. Phillips called on President-elect Hoover who, as former secretary of commerce, he assumed would be interested, and pointed out that if the threatened high tariff schedules against Canadian products became law, the Conservatives would ride to power on a wave of anti-American resentment. Hoover, completely indifferent, referred the diplomat to the congressional ways and means committee, which consented to hear him. Phillips, gathering from the committee's questions that their ideas of Canadian geography were completely vague, obtained an atlas from the Library of Congress to point out where each province was located and to illustrate his exposition of their interests and powers of retaliation. He was politely dismissed with the astonishing remark that the committee was not interested in exports from the United States, only in keeping out imports.

Over a year passed and the depression struck in before the Hawley-Smoot tariff, highest in American history, was enacted, in disregard of Canadian feelings, and of many American export interests too. Objections from the American Bankers Association and a protest signed by over 1000 economists had no effect on Congress, and President Hoover signed the bill on 17 June 1930. Canada, of course, retaliated; and as one result, no fewer than 87 branch factories for American automobiles, textiles, agricultural machinery, cordage, and other manufactures were set up in Canada within a year. A catastrophic drop of United States exports to Canada, following Canadian retaliation, deepened the depression. It took Roosevelt and the New Deal to lower the barrier.

Mackenzie King initiated negotiations with the United States for building the deep-draft St. Lawrence Seaway, but did not remain in power long enough to conclude the treaty in 1932. That treaty was rejected by the United States Senate, largely because American railroads and the Eastern cities feared that the St. Lawrence, improved so that ocean freighters could steam into the Great Lakes, would siphon away their trade.[1] Canada returned the Senate's compliment by refusing to go along with the Quoddy Project, a scheme on which President Roosevelt had set his heart, to make electric power from the tides of Passamaquoddy Bay.

In the meantime, the imperial relationship of Canada, as well as that of other British Dominions, or Commonwealths

[1] The St. Lawrence Seaway was completed in 1959.

as they now began to be called, had been defined by the Statute of Westminster, passed by the Parliament of Great Britain
on 11 December 1931. By virtue of this fundamental law,
which embodied even more concessions than American radicals
had demanded in 1775, Parliament renounced its ancient right
to legislate for Canada, unless at Canada's request, as well
as the royal prerogative of disallowing acts of the Canadian
parliament. But the judicial committee of the Privy Council
continued to act as an imperial supreme court, hearing cases
appealed from the Dominion supreme court. The governor
general of Canada now became a personal representative of
the British crown, not the proconsul of a British government;
and since the death of the much-beloved Lord Tweedsmuir
(John Buchan) in 1940, most of the governors general have
been Canadians. The right of Canada to conduct her own
foreign relations and to decide on war or peace was implicitly
if not explicitly recognized; and Canadians, while proudly
clinging to their right to be British subjects, have their own
Canadian citizenship.

Thus, so far as the United States and other nations were
concerned, Canada had become an independent nation.

4. The Harding Scandals and the Coolidge Administration

Jess Smith's suicide was the first indication that the Ohio
gang had overreached itself. Shortly after, it was brought to
the President's attention that his pal "Colonel" Forbes, director
of the Veterans' Bureau, had been taking a cut on the building
of hospitals and profiting from the sale of excess war materials.
Forbes had to resign, and in March 1923 his principal legal
adviser committed suicide. All this so worried President Harding that he decided to take a trip across the country and up
to Alaska. Uneasy and depressed, he fell ill of ptomaine poi-
soning, then of pneumonia, and died of an embolism at San
Francisco on 2 August 1923.

Now the oil scandals burst forth. A Washington correspondent of the St. Louis *Post-Dispatch* obtained the evidence, and
Senators Thomas J. Walsh and Gerald Nye made it public.
Albert B. Fall, secretary of the interior, with the passive connivance of Edwin M. Denby (a complete nonentity whom
Harding had made navy secretary) entered into a corrupt alliance with the Doheny and Sinclair oil interests to turn over to
them valuable petroleum deposits, which President Wilson had
reserved for the navy. The Elk Hill oil reserve in California

was leased to Doheny and the Teapot Dome oil reserve in Wyoming to Sinclair. In return for these favors they built some oil storage tanks for the navy in Pearl Harbor; but Fall got at least $100,000 from Doheny and $300,000 from Sinclair. The Senate investigation forced both secretaries to resign, the oil leases were canceled, and the government recovered $6 million. Criminal proscutions sent Fall and Sinclair to prison for short terms, but the rest got off.

Other revelations besmirched the Harding administration. His appointee as custodian of alien property, who had sold valuable German chemical patents for a song, was dismissed from office and convicted of a criminal conspiracy to defraud the government. Harry Daugherty, who regarded the office of attorney general as an opportunity to reward friends and, it is said, to protect Harding from *his* friends, was dismissed for misconduct involving the illegal sale of liquor permits and pardons. A Senate committee found him guilty of these and other malpractices, but the jury that tried him could not agree. As Will Rogers remarked, it was hard to convince a jury of criminal corruption in those lush times, because most of the jurors secretly admired people who got away with it.

When these scandals and others even less savory about Harding's personal conduct were ventilated, Calvin Coolidge was President of the United States, at the age of fifty-one. The first President from New England since Franklin Pierce, born in a small farming community in the Vermont hills, he had graduated from Amherst College, become a lawyer in Northampton, Massachusetts, and ascended from the lower to the higher brackets of state politics. Good luck, and a firm stand in the Boston police strike of 1919, made him Vice President. A mean, thin-lipped little man, a respectable mediocrity, he lived parsimoniously but admired men of wealth, and his political principles were those current in 1901. People thought Coolidge brighter than he was because he seldom said anything; but, as he admitted, he was "usually able to make enough noise" to get what he wanted. Mrs. Coolidge was a handsome and gracious lady, without whom the formal parties at the White House would have been unbearably grim. She helped this dour, abstemious, and unimaginative figure to become one of the most popular American Presidents. "Silent Cal" by his frugality, unpretentiousness, and taciturnity seems to have afforded vicarious satisfaction to a generation that was extravagant, pretentious, and voluble. Actually, Coolidge was democratic by habit rather than by conviction, and his taciturnity was calculated—"I have never been hurt by what I have not said," is one of his aphorisms. He regarded the progressive movement since Theodore Roosevelt's day with cynical distrust. Consequently, although he had a moral integrity wanting in his predecessor, there was no change in political or economic policy between the Harding and the Coolidge administrations. Policies of high tariff, tax reduction, and government support to industry were pushed to extremes, and a high plateau of prosperity was attained.

Since the President exalted inactivity to a fine art, there is not much to say about his administration except in foreign affairs, which we have already mentioned, and the prelude to the Great Depression, which is to come. He gave no lead to Congress or the country, took it easy in the White House with a long nap every afternoon, and maintained a somewhat feeble health by riding a mechanical horse. He had no intimate adviser like Wilson's House or Roosevelt's Hopkins; the nearest was his personal secretary C. Bascom Slemp, a former Republican congressman from Virginia who was an expert "fixer" and saved his boss a lot of trouble by placating petitioners for favors and jobs. Coolidge and the men whom he and Harding appointed to the great federal commissions did nothing to stop or even discourage the wild speculation that was going on. His one positive achievement was to use the presidential veto. Congress overrode him and passed a veterans' bonus, but his vetoes of the McNary-Haugen Farm relief bills in 1927–28 killed that particular measure for subsidizing the farmers, and rendered them far more vulnerable than they need have been to the Great Depression. Income and inheritance taxes were reduced during his second term, but he signed the Jones-White Act of 1928 for doubling the subsidy to builders of merchant ships, and needled Congress into building some much-needed cruisers.

In the nineteenth century, revelations such as those of Harding's administration—the worst since Grant's—would have brought a political reaction; but Coolidge's personality restored the people's confidence in the Republicans; and Coolidge, like all Vice Presidents, eager to be "President in his own right," won the Republican nomination unanimously in 1924. The Democrats hanged themselves because their nominating convention in New York was deadlocked for 102 ballots between William McAdoo the "Dry" candidate, and Al Smith the darling of the "wets"; and the sordid story, including a Tammany claque in the galleries, went to the public over the radio. Finally the convention settled on a corporation lawyer, John W. Davis, with William Jennings Bryan's innocuous brother Charles as running mate in the hope of taking off the Wall Street curse. Progressivism rose from its grave in the shape of a new party called the Conference for Political Action. This was formed by farmer groups, disgusted liberals, and radicals from both parties, allied with the Socialists; it nominated Robert La Follette for the presidency, and polled 4.8 million votes—more than Roosevelt did in 1912—but carried only Wisconsin. "Republican prosperity" had returned, the economy was booming, and with wheat back at $2.20 the farmers were no longer after politicians' scalps. Coolidge won 54 per cent of the popular vote, and 382 in the electoral college; Davis received little more than half Coolidge's vote, and 136 in the electoral college. The Communists, who now called themselves the Workers' party, under William Z. Foster, polled only 33,000 votes.

XI

———————————

The Hoover Administration

1929-1933

1. *The Election of 1928*

WHEN THE ELECTION of 1928 approached, President Coolidge secretly aspired to a third term. But his sphinx-like announcement, "I do not choose to run," was taken as a refusal, and with ill-concealed disgust he saw his secretary of commerce, Herbert C. Hoover, run away with the Republican nomination.

Hoover, a mining engineer by profession, a graduate of Stanford University, had well earned his reputation as a humanitarian by his administration of food distribution in the war, and of Belgium and Russian relief. In the commerce department he had won the confidence of business. Although never before elected to public office, he seemed to be a new type of political leader, a socially-minded efficiency expert. People did not resent his being a millionaire, since he had been born on an Iowa farm and had worked up to success.

The Democratic nominee, Alfred E. Smith, represented a very different type of democracy. A product of "The Sidewalks of New York" (his favorite theme song) and of Tammany, he was the first man without a farm background and the first Irish Catholic to receive the presidential nomination of a major party. It was high time; the urban workers and recent immigrants had been an indispensable prop to the Democratic party since Jefferson's day. Al Smith rose superior to ward politics, and, without losing the common touch, served as governor of New York for four terms, 1919–28. Smith here showed an unexpected gift for administration; under his leadership the state government introduced an executive budget, reorganized departments and agencies, and created a cabinet system responsible to the governor. On questions of power regulation, labor, and social reform Smith was progressive; on the prohibition issue, an out-and-out "wet." In the convention his name was placed in nomination by Franklin D. Roosevelt who, paraphrasing a poem of Wordsworth, described Al as "the Happy Warrior of the political battlefield."

An exciting campaign followed. The Happy Warrior happily addressed immense, enthusiastic crowds in the cities of the North and East, but when he invaded the rural regions of the South and West he received a chill reception. Both parties raised big campaign funds, the Republicans the bigger; but it was not money that defeated Al. He carried all the great urban centers; yet Hoover, with Charles Curtis—an Osage Indian—as Vice President, received 58 per cent of the popular vote and an overwhelming electoral college majority of 357, carrying every state but eight and smashing the solid South. Explanations of this overwhelming victory are not hard to find. The average workingman was contented, the average businessman prosperous, and neither had any desire for change. "You can't lick this Prosperity thing," said Will Rogers; "even the fellow that hasn't got any is all excited over the idea." Smith, as a Catholic, a Tammany brave, a New Yorker, and a wet, grated on the average rural American. His "Brooklyn accent," manners, and background did not seem proper to a President.

2. Herbert Hoover and the Boom

The stock market crash of October 1929 was a natural consequence of the greatest orgy of speculation and over-optimism since the South Sea Bubble of 1720. After a postwar recession (or minor depression) of 1920, security prices recovered, business readjusted, and a major advance began after Harding's death in 1923. Increased investment was largely responsible for the rise until 1925, when speculation raised it to a giddy height. A general euphoria drew more and more "suckers" into the speculative market; brokerage houses opened branches in small towns and near college campuses; widows, factory workers, bootblacks, and waiters risked their savings to make a "fast buck" in stocks, and even those who did not, eagerly followed *the* market, meaning the daily New York

Stock Exchange quotations, which made more headlines than crime or international affairs. Probably not more than 600,000 stockbrokers' accounts, out of an estimated 1.5 million, were trading on margin—but that was enough to breed a tremendous wave of speculation.

American prosperity, Germany's remarkable recovery after 1924, and the growth of world trade justified a rise in security values, but they rose much further than was justified. And when speculation began to get out of hand, neither the federal nor the state governments did anything effective to check it. They, of course, could not check human greed and folly; but the Federal Reserve Board and Trade Commission might have applied certain brakes. The main reason they did not is that, since 1921, these bodies had been diluted by political hacks or Republican financiers who did not believe in the regulative functions which they were supposed to perform. Thus, the Federal Reserve Board was unable to make up its mind what to do, or to do anything, at critical junctures. Secretary Hoover worried about "this fever of speculation," as he called it in a press release of 1 January 1926, warned against overextension of installment buying, and even criticized the easy credit policies of the Federal Reserve system; but when he failed to win President Coolidge or Secretary Mellon to his views, he smothered his concern and took pains to say nothing that might weaken the prevalent optimism. Coolidge, who saved money from his presidential salary, and who never gambled a nickel in a slot machine, much less a dollar in stocks, regarded the speculative orgy with detached complacency; his philosophy forbade interference with "the law of supply and demand." And no wonder people were overconfident, since even some old progressives and socialists went overboard. Walter Lippmann in 1928 praised the "unplanned activities of big businessmen," and early next year Lincoln Steffens, who had hailed the Russian revolution as the socialist heaven, wrote, "Big business in America is producing what the Socialists held up as their goal: food, shelter and clothing for all. . . . It is a great country this; as great as Rome."

There was a great deal wrong, besides overspeculation, with the national economy and the laws regulating it. Corporations, which as early as 1919 employed 86.5 per cent of all wage earners in industry, were proliferating under practically no control. Certain states such as Delaware and New Jersey allowed anyone paying a registration fee to incorporate a company, leaving its directors free to issue new stock, and with no obligation to make an annual report or accounting. The number of Delaware incorporations, with authorized capital stock of $20 million or more, rose from 55 in 1925 to 619 in 1929. One characteristic device was to form a holding company comprising a large number of electric light and other power corporations, the "utilities" as these were called. Holding companies were often so rigged that an outsider who bought stock knew nothing of what was going on, and the insiders profited, just as railway construction groups did in the days of President Grant. Stockholders of three of the biggest—Electric Bond & Share, Standard Gas & Electric, and Cities Service (235,000 shareholders in 1925)—were not vouchsafed any information about the subsidiaries' earnings, on which theirs depended.

Stock pools burgeoned and blossomed. A group of men would get together, buy a sizeable block of stock of no matter what, then trade shares back and forth, hiking the price and pulling in outsiders who hoped to get in on the profits. When the stock reached an agreed point, members of the pool dumped it on the market, took their profits and retired, leaving the suckers to take the rap. The reverse was a "bear raid" on a stock already doing well. Rumors would be circulated that the company was being badly managed or overcapitalized, by operators who sold short, drove down the stock, and bought it back at a very attractive price. Joseph P. Kennedy, father of the late President, thwarted just such a raid on the Yellow Cab Company, then owned by John D. Hertz who became the Rent-a-Car tycoon. Hertz's friend Walter Howey, editor of the *Boston American,* enlisted Kennedy's aid to save Yellow Cab from ruin. The Bostonian installed special telephones and a ticker tape in a hotel suite, and with a borrowed $5 million placed both buy and sell orders from points all around the country, utterly confusing the raiders and stabilizing the stock at 51. This successful maneuver had the effect of attracting the favorable attention of William Randolph Hearst to Joseph P. Kennedy, with political results that we shall observe shortly.

A more typical case involving a future secretary of defense is that of a holding company called United States and Foreign Securities Corporation, chartered under the laws of Maryland by the New York investment house of Dillon, Read & Company. It had practically unlimited powers to "purchase, hold and deal with investment securities," and "engage in commercial, manufacturing and industrial enterprises." Upon its organization Dillon, Read absorbed 500,000 shares of the common stock at 20 cents a share; and of these, their partner James V. Forrestal took 37,000 shares which, after buying more later at a slightly higher price, cost him $28,539.50. Forrestal transferred about 20,000 of his shares to Beekman Company, Ltd. of Canada, a sort of ghost corporation set up by Dillon, Read and run by their employees for the particular purpose of juggling United States & Foreign Securities and other stock. Beekman Ltd. was wholly owned by the Beekman Corporation of Delaware, whose entire stock was owned by Mr. and Mrs. Forrestal. Beekman Ltd. sold 16,788 shares of Forrestal's U.S. & Foreign Securities stock to the public at 53. This stock rose to 72 before the great crash of October 1929, then went down to 1⅜ in 1932. There was also much trading and borrowing back and forth between the two Beekman corporations and Mr. Forrestal, who realized a profit of $864,000. The reason for this curious set-up, then legal, was to enable him to evade paying income tax or capital gains from the sale of this stock, which had cost him less than $29,000. Forrestal, recognizing a moral obligation, paid a large sum in back taxes after the Pecora Committee had reported the facts; but the little fellows who had bought this worthless stock, lost their shirts.

Most of the subsidiaries of the utilities' holding companies kept going more or less profitably during the depression, and the communities they served did not suffer; but there were many cases of a local industry upon which a community depended being scuttled by high finance. Organizers of a super-hardware holding company, for instance, would discover a small corporation making locks and bolts, which under conservative management made steady profits and owned a cash reserve of a million dollars. The holding company would bid up the stock, tempting local holders to sell out at a profit; then, as soon as the holding company had 51 per cent of the shares, whoosh! The cash reserve was siphoned off into its own treasury, and the locks and bolts shop closed as "uneconomical," leaving the community to support the people thus thrown out of work. This sort of thing is still going on in the 1960's, but it was much more prevalent forty years earlier.

The boom was world-wide, and the two promoters who were most successful in fleecing the American lambs were foreigners: Samuel E. Insull, originally from London, and Ivar Kreuger the Swedish match king; both were featured on covers of *Time* magazine as financial geniuses. Insull, who emigrated young to Chicago, became chairman of 65 company directorates which operated in the utilities field in 23 different states. He was no common crook, but a public-spirited magnate who saved the city of Chicago from bankruptcy, built it a palatial opera house, and started a natural-gas pipeline from the Texas panhandle to Lake Michigan. Regarding the depression as temporary, he continued to overextend in 1930, and his elaborate edifice crashed in April 1932 with a loss to American investors of $700 million. Insull found a pleasant asylum in Greece; extradited, he was acquitted of breaking the law. Not so nice was the career of Ivar Kreuger, who even counterfeited Italian government bonds to deceive auditors. "Uncle Ivar" looked so virtuous and claimed to be on such intimate terms with European statesmen that he was able to buy American companies like Diamond Match "on a shoestring," and to employ the old Boston firm of Lee, Higginson & Company as his American outlet. Investors as well as speculators, attracted by this respectable backing, bought about $250 million of his worthless securities; even Harvard University had a substantial slice of Kreuger & Toll in its treasury when the match king, at last found out, committed suicide in 1932.

Loans to brokers for purchasing or carrying securities had reached $8.5 billion by October 1929, and banks everywhere had made unwise loans for speculation. New issues of common stock to the unprecedented amount of $5.1 billion were floated in the United States during the twelve months before the crash.

Warnings of the coming debacle were not wanting. William Z. Ripley, Harvard economist, published two articles in *The Atlantic* in 1926 which exposed what he called the "honeyfugling, hornswoggling and skulduggery" of corporate practices; but not enough people listened. Roger W. Babson on 5 September 1929 predicted, "There is a crash coming, and it may be a terrific one," involving even "a decline of from 60 to 80 points in the Dow-Jones barometer." But *Barron's Weekly* devoted a large part of its next issue to sneering at Babson as "the Sage of Wellesley,"[1] a "scaremonger," pointing out that he had advised investors to get out of the market in 1926. Alexander D. Noyes, veteran financial editor of the *New York Times,* did his utmost to prick the bubble of perpetually rising stocks and eternally increasing prosperity, only to be denounced as "trying to discredit or stop American prosperity." Herbert Hoover during the campaign of 1928 made only negligible references to speculation and predicted, "We shall soon with the help of God be in sight of the day when poverty will be banished from this nation." President Coolidge's last message, of 4 December 1928, declared that the nation might "regard the present with satisfaction and anticipate the future with optimism"; no United States Congress "has met with a more pleasing prospect than that which appears at the present

[1] On 28 October 1929, after Babson's prophecy had been fulfilled by a decline of 80 points in one day, *Barron's Weekly* began taking the line that the panic was the fault of Babson and others who warned of it.

time." On 16 October 1929, Professor Irving Fisher of Yale touched the acme of prophetic folly, announcing, "Stock prices have reached what looks like a permanently high plateau."

3. *The 1929 Crash and the Great Depression*

The stock market had already begun to act queerly. On 23 October there was a spectacular drop during the last hour of trading, and the 24th, when almost 13 million shares changed hands, became known as "Black Thursday." Spokesmen for bankers and brokers insisted that the worst was over, but 28 and 29 October were even more terrible days, from which there was no recovery. Stocks reached new lows on 13 November, rose slightly during the early months of 1930, but in April began a downward slide that continued with only brief interruptions to rock-bottom in mid-1932.

At this point a table of the highest and lowest prices of twelve representative common stocks, and of five selected products of the soil, tell the story better than any description.

PRICES OF COMMON STOCKS[1]

	1929		1932	
	HIGHEST	LOWEST	HIGHEST	LOWEST
American Telephone & Telegraph	310¼	193¼	137⅜	69¾
Cities Service	68½	20	6⅞	1¼
Electric Bond & Share	189	50	48	5
General Electric	403	168⅛	26⅛[2]	8½
General Motors	91¾	33½	24⅝	7⅝
Kreuger & Toll	46⅜	21⅛	(dead)	—
National Cash Register	148¾	59	18¾	6¼
Radio Corporation of America	114¾	26	13½	2½
Remington Rand	57¾	20⅜	7½	1
Sears, Roebuck	181	80	37⅜	9⅞
United States Smelting, Refining & Mining	72⅞	29⅞	22¾	10
United States Steel	261¾	150	52⅝	21¼

WHOLESALE PRICES OF SELECTED COMMODITIES
ANNUAL AVERAGES TO NEAREST HALF-CENT[3]

	1925	1929	1930	1931	1932	1933	1935	1936
Wheat, bushel	$1.435	$1.035	$0.67	$0.40	$0.38	$0.75	$0.83	$1.025
Corn, bushel	0.70	0.80	0.60	0.32	0.315	0.52	0.655	1.05
Raw cotton, pound	0.235	0.19	0.135	0.085	0.065	0.085	0.12	0.12
Wool, pound	1.40	0.985	0.765	0.62	0.46	0.665	0.725	0.88
Tobacco, pound	0.17	0.185	0.13	0.08	0.105	0.13	0.185	0.235

[1] *Commercial and Financial Chronicle*, Vols. CXXX (1930) and CXXXVII (1933).

[2] After issuing five new shares to each share outstanding; multiply by 5 for comparison with 1929.

[3] *Historical Statistics of the U.S.*, pp. 123, 29–7, 302. The corn, wheat, and tobacco prices are "season average received by farmers."

Whilst the boom of 1926–29 made the stock market crash inevitable, there was nothing inevitable about the Great Depression that followed. This reached its nadir in 1932–33. Although alleviated by the bold expedients of the New Deal, it did not really end until 1939–40 when America began to rearm. As yet there is no consensus among economists as to why a prolonged depression followed the crash. Not all agree to this writer's generalization that the national economy was honeycombed with weakness, giving "Coolidge prosperity" a fine appearance over a rotten foundation. Optimism, justified in the early 1920's, had been carried to extremes owing to lack of insight and want of courage to say "Stop!" on the part of leaders in business, finance, politics, and the universities. These, imbued with laissez-faire doctrine and overrating the importance of maintaining public confidence, refrained from making candid statements or taking steps to curb or cure the abuses, a small fraction of which we have described. At the same time, efforts were made to prevent declines of farm products and raw materials, which were the result of increasing abundance. This created world-wide overproduction of basic commodities such as wheat, rubber, coffee, cotton, sugar, copper, silver, and zinc, intensified by bumper crops in Europe in 1929.

Economic analysis, a science then in its infancy, failed to discern the serious faults in American and European economics and their increasing vulnerability to shock. Among the weak points were the tremendous volume of stock-market, mortgage, and installment-buying debts; the chaotic American banking system, precarious European currencies, and the war reparations question, supposedly but not really settled. President Hoover, in his message of 2 December 1930, rightly pointed out that soft spots in European economy infected America. But even he did not see that the American boom helped to make Europe vulnerable by checking the outflow of American capital and sucking a counter-current of European investment and call-money into New York. This depleted European gold reserves, undermined currencies, and created industrial instability.

Thus, the stock-market crash of 1929 started a downward spiral in prices, production, employment, and foreign trade, which the Hawley-Smoot tariff of 1930 and intensified protection in European countries—everyone for himself—made even worse. Collapse in commodity prices reduced buying power everywhere and increased unemployment in all industrialized countries. In 1931, when President Hoover thought he had the depression by the tail, the collapse of the *Kreditanstalt* of

CHART OF STOCK MARKET AND
OTHER FLUCTUATIONS

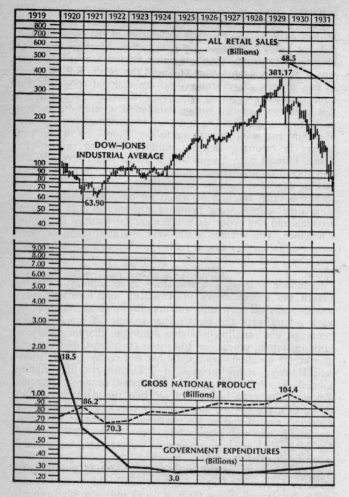

Vienna, and Britain's abandonment of her sacred gold standard, intensified world-wide conditions. The business world

From Forbes Investographs; courtesy Forbes, Inc., New York

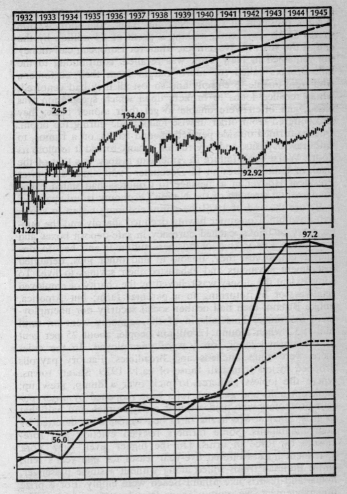

seemed to be crumbling everywhere; communists were full of
glee over the imminent collapse of representative government
and the capitalist system.

Efforts to arrest the avalanche were not strong enough to be
effective. Many financiers appeared to be more interested in

profiting from the bear market than in stopping it; Albert H. Wiggin, president of Chase National Bank, sold short 42,506 shares of his own bank, making a profit of $4 million by the end of the year. By November, whatever European call-money still remained in New York was recalled, contributing to the fall. Brokers called for more margin from their customers, who were unable to comply and so lost all they had ventured; banks recalled loans to brokers upon which speculation was based, and often were unable to get their money back; they also suffered from other unwise loans made during the boom. Queues formed outside perfectly sound banks, on a rumor, to withdraw deposits, and any run on a bank forced it to close its doors. Worst bank failure in American history was that of the Bank of United States on 11 December 1930—nine days after President Hoover in a message to Congress had stated, "The fundamental strength of the Nation's economy is unimpaired."

Before the end of 1929 the entire economy began to snowball downhill. Consumer buying declined sharply and the public, leery of banks, cached currency in safe-deposit boxes and mattresses. Every kind of business suffered, and had to discharge employees; they, unable to find other jobs, defaulted installment payments and exhausted their savings to live. To some extent the misery was relieved by the charity of employed relatives, or by returning to a parental farm; but America, unlike Britain, then had neither social security nor unemployment insurance. This tailspin of the economy went on until mid-1932 when around 12 million people, about 25 per cent of the normal labor force, were unemployed. In the cities there were soup kitchens and breadlines. Factory payrolls dropped to less than half those of early 1929. Shanty towns, where the jobless gathered to pick over a dump, grew up; bankrupt mills and garment lofts were reopened by unscrupulous promoters who paid a dollar a day to men and half that to girls. Small towns in the farm belt were almost deserted by their inhabitants. Some farmers resisted eviction and foreclosure by force of arms. On the higher level, New York apartment houses offered five-year leases for one year's rent, entire Pullman trains rolled along without a single passenger, hotels and resorts like Miami Beach were empty. For a prize understatement we nominate ex-President Coolidge's "The country is not in good condition," in his syndicated press column on 20 January 1931.

Looking backward, there is reason to believe that the Great Depression created less misery than that of 1893–96, when nothing but private charity stood between the unemployed and starvation. The researches of Joseph S. Davis bring out some alleviating factors, such as low prices stimulating the sale of household gadgetry; a higher percentage of farms acquired radio, electricity, and running water during the 1930's than in the previous decade.[1] Life expectancy continued to lengthen and the death rate to decline, especially among the African population, and lack of jobs induced more young people to complete high school. Popular psychology made the Great Depression seem worse than it really was because the public had so frequently been fooled by "permanent plateau of prosperity" talk that it seemed abnormal, unnatural, and abominable. In the 1890's, on the other hand, alternate booming and hard times were taken for granted.

No nation ever faced a business decline more optimistically than America did this one. Nobody highly placed in government or finance admitted the existence of a depression for six months or more after the crash. Everyone wanted to stop the decline, but nobody knew how. Incantation was the favorite method for the first six months. Brookmire Economic Service, heading the procession, quoted an opinion of a British industrialist after an American inspection tour of 26 October 1929: "I look on the events of the last week as an incident . . . prices reached at the peak will look cheap . . . it is quite impossible to be anything but optimistic about America." The National Association of Manufacturers began covering tattered billboards with a cartoon designed by Howard Chandler Christy representing an attractive Miss Columbia saying "Business is Good. Keep it Good. Nothing can stop US." Old John D. Rockefeller issued a fatuous statement to the affect that "fundamental conditions of the country are sound," and that "he and his son are accumulating shares."

President Hoover became the leading exorciser with public statements such as, "Any lack of confidence in . . . the basic strength of business . . . is foolish" (November 1929). "Business and industry have turned the corner" (21 January 1930). "We have now passed the worst" (1 May 1930). On 28 June 1930, when wheat had dropped to 68 cents a bushel—and would go to 38 cents—and cotton had dropped to 13 cents a pound—and would go to 6.5 cents—James J. Davis, secretary of labor, dropped this gem: "Courage and resource are already swinging us back on the road to recovery. And we are fortunate in having a President who sets us a shining example of that courage and initiative."

More than talk was needed to swell the shrunken gourd and plump the shriveled shell. President Hoover did his best ac-

[1] See Chapter XII, section 3, for some of the causes of this.

cording to his lights, and he had a warm heart which responded to the suffering. But he was restrained from taking any bold, imaginative steps by wrong estimates of the situation, and by his laissez-faire philosophy, which taught him that nature would cure all, whilst government intervention might ruin all. At his elbow was Andrew Mellon, secretary of the treasury, whose one idea was to keep hands off and let the slump liquidate itself; his formula, Hoover admitted, was "liquidate labor, liquidate stocks, liquidate the farmer, liquidate real estate." Mellon wanted it to go right to the bottom; thought that would be a good thing. "People will work harder, live a more moral life. Values will be adjusted, and enterprising people will pick up the wrecks from less competent people." There were plenty of tycoons who had enough income from rents and bonds to weather a prolonged depression themselves, but found consolation in the hope that it would destroy the labor unions and bring back old times when "a dollar a day is a white man's pay."

That was not what Hoover wanted. He aimed to end the depression promptly and to relieve present suffering. He asked for a big charity drive in the winter of 1929–30 and it yielded only a miserable $15 million. But he was unwilling to recommend, or the Congress to vote, direct relief; poor relief was traditionally the prerogative of state and local governments, churches, and private charity. Senators Costigan of Colorado, Bronson Cutting of New Mexico, and the younger La Follette of Wisconsin pled for a big federal program of public works, presenting statistics proving the breakdown of private and local charity; but every proposal was met by stubborn presidential opposition. When the House threatened to pass a bill appropriating $2 billion for public works, Hoover intervened with the warning, "This is not unemployment relief. It is the most gigantic pork-barrel ever perpetrated by the American Congress."

Not until 1932, when the Democrats controlled the House, and a coalition of Democrats and Republican progressives ran the Senate, were vital measures taken to cope with the depression. By that time an estimated one to two million men were roaming the country looking for jobs or handouts, and more than 100 cities had no relief money left. In January President Hoover signed a bill creating the Reconstruction Finance Corporation for lending money to railroads, banks, agricultural agencies, industry, and commerce. During the rest of the Hoover administration, the RFC stopped many bankruptcies by feeding in money at the top, but this did little to restore the economy. In the next three years, under Roosevelt, with vastly greater appropriations, the RFC came to the aid of 7000 banks and trust companies to the tune of $3.5 billion. Loans to mortgage-loan companies and to insurance companies and railroads took up $1 billion more. Loans to industry and to agriculture in one form or another came to over $2.6 billion.

RFC assistance to banks, mortgage and insurance companies, railroads and industries undoubtedly prevented more serious losses, and to that extent checked the downward spiral. But many loans merely put off the day of reckoning for banks that were beyond saving. And the RFC gave little relief to the people who most urgently needed it. For the theory behind it, as Will Rogers said, was "The money was all appropriated for the top in the hopes it would trickle down to the needy." Mounting figures of unemployment from 4.3 million in 1930 to 12 million in 1932,[1] figures which Hoover simply refused to believe, proved that the depression was getting worse rather than better.

President Hoover meant very well, labored hard to find solutions, and sought advice; but nothing seemed to work because, being the prisoner of fixed ideas, and surrounded by likeminded men, he refused to try anything new or bold. The year 1933, when he left office, marks the grave of the laissez-faire nineteenth-century state, so far as America was concerned. It had already been buried in every European country, and in Japan.

We owe admiration as well as pity to the simple folk of America who suffered so grievously under the depression. Many by mid-1932 were angry and desperate, but they still had faith in their country and its institutions; surprisingly few listened to strange voices which told them that fascism Mussolini-style, or communism Moscow-style, was the only answer. They were only waiting for a leader to show them the way out.[2]

[1] These are annual averages, from *Historical Statistics of the U.S.*, p. 73; the A. F. of L. figures, as given in Lionel Robbins, *The Great Depression* (1935), p. 213, are 3 million in 1930, 10.5 million in 1932. It is significant that Germany, the only country with a larger proportion of unemployed in those years, underwent the Hitler revolution in 1933.
[2] Two persistent depression myths may be mentioned here: (1) That hundreds of brokers and bankers hurled themselves out of skyscraper windows, or otherwise committed suicide after the big crash. Actually the number of suicides remained normal. (2) That the jobless were only taken care of by selling apples. What happened was that an apple growers' association in the Northwest arranged to market their surplus production by hiring unemployed men to sell apples on the streets of leading cities. This gimmick worked so well that, according to Mr. Hoover, many left good jobs to hawk apples.

4. The Accession of Franklin D. Roosevelt

The eruption of Franklin D. Roosevelt into the political arena in 1928 was a surprise. "F.D.R.," born to a patrician Hudson river family in 1882, graduated from Groton and Harvard (where he was regarded as a playboy) and the Columbia Law School. For a few years he engaged in law and business in New York City with very moderate success; but he made a successful marriage in 1905 with Eleanor Roosevelt, niece of his remote cousin Theodore, whom he greatly admired. The Dutchess County Roosevelts to whom Franklin belonged had been Democrats since Andrew Jackson days; so, as a Democrat, "Frank," as his friends called him, was elected to the New York Senate. Support of Woodrow Wilson in the campaign of 1912 earned him the assistant secretaryship of the navy, which enabled him to counteract some of the folly of Josephus Daniels; and that, in turn, led to his vice-presidential nomination on the losing Cox ticket in 1920. Next year a sudden and severe attack of polio at his summer home in Campobello, New Brunswick, left him apparently a hopeless invalid; but during the next seven years he fought his way back to health, used his leisure for thought, study, and correspondence, and emerged from forced retirement a changed man. Still charming and jaunty in manner, he was deeply ambitious to do something for his country and lend fresh luster to the Roosevelt name.

His political comeback was signaled by nominating Al Smith in the Democratic convention of 1924 with the "happy warrior" speech; and Al later persuaded him to take the Democratic candidacy for governor of New York in 1928. To those who objected that Roosevelt was still a cripple, the Happy Warrior replied, "The Governor of New York State does not have to be an acrobat!" Although Al lost his native state in the presidential election, the magic of the Roosevelt name elected F.D.R. governor; and at Albany he did so well, with the assistance of an able staff of economists and social workers, that in 1930 he was re-elected by a majority of 700,000. That made him a leading contender for his party's presidential nomination.

Herbert Hoover was renominated by the Republicans as the only alternative to admitting failure. For the Democratic nomination, assumed to mean election, there was a free-for-all. Al Smith wanted it again, but the politicians recalled his poor showing in 1928 and divided their efforts between F.D.R. and "Cactus Jack" Garner of Texas, then speaker of the house. Other aspirants were William McAdoo, President Wilson's son-in-law; Newton D. Baker, Wilson's able secretary of war; Owen D. Young, who had helped put the German Republic on its financial feet; Governor Harry F. Byrd of Virginia; even Governor "Alfalfa Bill" Murray of Oklahoma. Joseph P. Kennedy, father of a future President, then a free-lance financier who had got out of the stock market in time, decided that Roosevelt was the man. Kennedy raised money for his campaign and attended the nominating convention. When it looked like a deadlock between Roosevelt and Garner, he talked on the telephone to William Randolph Hearst, who was under obligation to him for stopping the raid on Yellow Cab during the big boom. As the only California Democrat willing to spend money, Hearst controlled the California delegation. They were pledged to Garner, but Kennedy, with the help of Jim Farley, convinced the multimillionaire publisher that if he did not switch California's vote to Roosevelt, either Baker or Smith, both of whom he hated, would be nominated. Hearst switched; Garner, anxious to avoid a deadlock, released his pledged delegates, and California's 44 votes helped to nominate Roosevelt. Garner accepted the vice-presidential nomination, which was more to his liking since it gave him plenty of time for hunting and shooting in Texas.

Roosevelt, who before his nomination had seemed to many people merely "a nice man who very much wanted to be President," electrified the country by a bold, aggressive campaign. Although he now had a wide radio network at his disposal, the candidate, to prove his physical vigor and exert his personal magnetism, embarked upon an old-fashioned stumping tour which took him into almost every state of the Union. He set forth a comprehensive scheme of reform and recovery, embracing the repeal of Prohibition, unemployment relief, lower tariffs, and legislation to save agriculture, rehabilitate the railroads, protect consumers and investors, and slash government expenses; all of it contained in the party platform. The keynote was a "New Deal" to the "forgotten man." For some odd reason this last phrase aroused the fury of conservatives; even Al Smith, when he first heard Roosevelt plead for "the forgotten man at the bottom of the economic pyramid," burst out with "This is no time for demagogues!"

President Hoover, laboring under the dead weight of the deepening depression, recited his efforts to cope with it, mumbled prophecies to the effect that a Democratic victory would mean that "The grass will grow in the streets of a hundred cities," and reaffirmed his faith in rugged individualism and the American system. "Any change of policies will bring disaster to every fireside in America."

Most of the voters, fearing that the "American system" needed desperate measures to be saved, were ready to take a chance on the New Deal. On election day Roosevelt received almost 22.8 million votes with 57.3 per cent of all cast, and won 472 electors; Hoover polled 15.8 million votes—39.6 cent, with only 59 votes in the electoral college. It is a tribute to the average American's faith in his country and her institutions that the Socialist and Communist parties, both insisting that capitalism had collapsed, polled fewer than a million votes. And the Democrats elected emphatic majorities to both houses of Congress. There was never a stronger popular mandate in American history for a new program or policy, or a clearer repudiation of laissez-faire. As Will Rogers put it, "The little fellow felt that he never had a chance and he didn't till November the Eighth. And did he grab it!"

Unfortunately the so-called "lame duck" Amendment XX to the Constitution, altering the beginning of a new presidential administration from 4 March to 20 January, and the opening of a new Congress to 3 January, was not ratified by the requisite number of states until 6 February 1933. Consequently there was an embarrassing gap between the November election and 4 March, when F.D.R. could take over. Hoover at that time made a sincere but fruitless effort to persuade the President-elect to agree to participate in an international conference to stabilize currency and exchange, and to make a public declaration against inflation, expensive government projects, and unbalancing the budget. In other words, the President-elect should (as Hoover wrote to Senator David A. Reed on 20 February) agree to "the abandonment of 90 per cent of the so-called new deal." Roosevelt refused to commit himself in advance to break his platform. It was like the situation in February 1861 when John Tyler demanded that the Republicans abandon the principles on which they were elected, as the price of union. Hoover later declared that "fear" of New Deal radicalism was what caused the governors of twenty-two states to close all banks prior to 4 March. But the banks had been failing right through the depression—almost 5000 of them since 1929; and the threatened failure of many more early in 1933 was simply the built-up result of the economic tailspin.

Before we dismiss Herbert Hoover from his unhappy four years in Washington to his happy thirty-one years of semi-retirement, we should remember that some degree of F.D.R.'s success in dealing with the depression is owed to Hoover's proving that conventional methods had failed. If Al Smith, whose economic presuppositions were the same as Hoover's, had been elected President in 1928, he probably would have repeated the same mistakes.

When Franklin D. Roosevelt took the oath of office on 4 March 1933, the stock market had already started that upswing from its all-time low which continued to 1938. But the general situation was catastrophic, and the new President made no effort to minimize it. The first paragraph of his inaugural address sounded like a trumpet call:

First of all, let me assert my firm belief that the only thing we have to fear is fear itself—nameless, unreasoning, unjustified terror which paralyzes needed efforts to convert retreat into advance. In every dark hour of our national life a leadership of frankness and vigor has met with that understanding and support of the people themselves which is essential to victory. I am convinced that you will again give that support to leadership in these critical days.

Then came the adagio:

Values have shrunk to fantastic levels; taxes have risen; our ability to pay has fallen; government of all kinds is faced by serious curtailment of income; the means of exchange are frozen in the currents of trade; the withered leaves of industrial enterprise lie on every side; farmers find no markets for their produce; the savings of many years in thousands of families are gone. More important, a host of unemployed citizens face the grim problem of existence and an equally great number toil with little return. Only a foolish optimist can deny the dark realities of the moment.

There followed an excoriation of the "money changers" who "have fled from their high seats in the temple of our civilization"; and of the "false leadership" which had attempted to solve problems through exhortation. "They have no vision, and when there is no vision the people perish." But Roosevelt had no intention of emulating his predecessor in relying upon exhortation. "This nation," he said, "asks for action, and action now!" Setting forth a general program which he promised shortly to elaborate in detail, he warned Congress and the country that the emergency called for emergency measures; and that if "the normal balance of executive and legislative authority" prove inadequate "to meet the unprecedented task before us," he would ask Congress for "broad executive power to wage a war against the emergency as great as the power that would be given to me if we were in fact invaded by a foreign foe." He concluded:

The people of the United States . . . in their need . . . have registered a mandate that they want direct, vigorous leadership. They have asked for discipline and direction under leadership. They have made me the present instrument of their wishes. In the spirit of the gift I take it. . . . May God guide me in the days to come.

"America hasn't been as happy in three years as they are today," wrote Will Rogers in his column on 5 March. "No money, no banks, no work, no nothing, but they know they got a man in there who is wise to Congress, wise to our so-called big men. The whole country is with him."[1]

That very day I asked a New Hampshire countrywoman, in a town which always voted heavily Republican, what they thought of the new President. Here is her answer, which millions all over the land would have endorsed:

"We feel that our country has been given back to us."

[1] Will Rogers, *How We Elect Our Presidents*, p. 141.

XII

The New Deal

1. *Roosevelt Himself*

There are seasons, in human affairs, of inward and outward revolutions, when new depths seem to be broken up in the soul, when new wants are unfolded in multitudes, and a new and undefined good is thirsted for. There are periods when the principles of experience need to be modified, when hope and trust and instinct claim a share with prudence in the guidance of affairs, when, in truth, *to dare* is the highest wisdom.[1]

THUS WROTE William Ellery Channing in 1829. One of those seasons had arrived, and the man who dared to dare was President of the United States. Franklin D. Roosevelt, who occupied the chief magistracy for twelve years and thirty-nine days, was one of the most remarkable characters who ever occupied that high office; and he held it during two major crises, the Great Depression and World War II. A patrician by birth and education, endowed with an independent fortune, he was a democrat not only by conviction; he really loved people as no other President has except Lincoln, and as no other American statesman had since Franklin. Appreciation he prized; opposition often angered but never soured him. Widely traveled in youth and young manhood, Roosevelt knew Europe well. A great reader, especially of American history and political science, he found time to collect postage stamps and books

---

[1] William Ellery Channing, *Complete Works* (1884), p. 459.

on the United States Navy. No American President has been a success without prior political experience; and Roosevelt had had plenty of that, in the New York assembly, the governor's chair, and as assistant secretary of the navy. In addition, he had political acumen, a sense of the "art of the possible," and knew how to work through established political machinery. Not claiming omniscience—"there is no indispensable man," he said in a campaign speech—he summoned all manner of experts to Washington to furnish ideas and formulate legislation to get the country out of its desperate plight. He combined audacity with caution; stubborn as to ultimate ends, he was an opportunist as to means, and knew when to compromise. A natural dramatist, he was able to project his personal charm both in public appearances and in those radio "fireside chats" in which he seemed to be taking the whole country into his confidence. Thus he won loyalty to his ideals as well as to his person.

Indispensable to Roosevelt's well being and success was Mrs. Roosevelt, whom the whole country before long was calling by her first name. Franklin found traveling difficult, but Eleanor went everywhere, by car, train, and airplane, even to Pacific Ocean bases during World War II. She visited and talked to all sorts and conditions of people, giving them a feeling that the government really cared about them. She took a particular interest in the disoriented and confused young people then graduating from schools and colleges, and was instrumental in preventing thousands of them from going Red. Among the colored people she became a legendary benefactress; and, in so doing, alienated the white South. She maintained the atmosphere of a gentleman's country home in the White House, amid all the hurly-burly of the New Deal. But she never intruded upon or tried to influence the President's policy; in fact, she disapproved much of it, notably his neutrality policy toward the civil war in Spain. Eleanor Roosevelt survived her husband for eighteen years, but cheerfully continued her good works almost to the day of her death.

Roosevelt's first cabinet included two men over sixty: Cordell Hull, secretary of state who had been congressman and senator from Tennessee for thirty years, and William H. Woodin, secretary of the treasury, who came of a family of Pennsylvania ironmasters. Others were James A. Farley, who had expertly managed the campaign and thus received the postmaster-generalship, chief source of patronage; Henry A. Wallace, second-generation editor of a farm journal and the world's greatest authority on hybrid corn, secretary of agriculture; Harold L. Ickes, elderly, peppery, persnickety Bull-Mooser and

conservationist from Chicago, secretary of the interior; and
Frances Perkins, social worker from New York, secretary of
labor. There was something odd about every one of these
except Hull, a Southern statesman of the old school, and
Farley, a typical Irish Democrat. Woodin played the guitar
and composed songs; Wallace was a religious mystic; Ickes
had a persecution complex; and although "Madam" Perkins, as
she was called, had a man's brain, it was odd to have a woman
in the cabinet, especially in the labor office. Several members
were former Republicans. Wallace's father, Henry C. Wallace,
had been secretary of agriculture in the Harding administration, and the most frustrated member of that cabinet.

Roosevelt had the same facility as Lincoln in profiting from
the expertise of his advisers while overlooking their quirks; he
could use the slow, ruminating mind of a Hull as well as the
brittle cleverness of a Bill Bullitt. Raymond Moley of Ohio,
professor of public law at Columbia, and Rexford G. Tugwell,
professor of economics in the same university, became respectively assistant secretaries of state and agriculture; several
others with a similar professorial background were highly
placed.

Many of the unofficial cabinet, the "brain-trusters" whom
Roosevelt brought to Washington, were more important than
the real cabinet. Harry Hopkins, son of a Mid-Western harness
maker, was the most brainy, whether in social welfare matters
in which he had been trained, or in later war issues which were
completely new to him. Winston Churchill once called Hopkins
"Mr. Root of the Matter," because he had an astonishing
ability to get to the bottom of a problem in the shortest time.
Thomas C. "Tommy the Cork" Corcoran, with his quick mind
and Irish wit, and Benjamin Cohen, quiet, scholarly, and
thorough, were an important part of the setup. Collectively
the "New Dealers," within and without the cabinet, were well
educated, at home in the world of ideas, talkers and discussers,
eager to put their intelligence to the service of the government.

"I pledge you, I pledge myself, to a New Deal for the
American people," said Roosevelt in his speech accepting the
Democratic nomination. That theme, which he returned to
frequently during the campaign, gave a collective name to his
policies—the New Deal. The series of measures that he inaugurated was a natural development from his cousin's Square
Deal and Wilson's New Freedom. The only really new thing
about it was a conscious effort, through legislation, to enhance
the welfare and eventual security of simple folk throughout
the country. These, at his accession, felt completely helpless,
humiliated by the business and financial barons who had de-

ceived them, and neglected by the previous administrations.

The transfer of wealth from the rich to the poor by government action had been suggested by Theodore Roosevelt in his Bull Moose campaign; and the income and inheritance taxes now made it possible. This policy, which Roosevelt and the Democrats pursued relentlessly, led to what was named, in scorn, the Welfare State. It did not prevent rewards to the skill and organizing ability of able individuals, as the increase of great fortunes since World War II has proved; but it vastly increased the power of organized labor and gave the ordinary citizen a feeling of financial security against old age, sickness, and unemployment which he had never enjoyed, and a participation in government such as he had never felt since Lincoln's era. At the same time a large part of the middle class, especially those who had retired on pensions or annuities, felt squeezed between the upper and nether millstones.

Thus the New Deal was just what the term implied—a new deal of old cards, no longer stacked against the common man. Opponents called it near-fascism or near-communism, but it was American as a bale of hay—an opportunist, rule-of-thumb method of curing deep-seated ills. Probably it saved the capitalist system in the United States; there is no knowing what might have happened under another administration like Hoover's. The German Republic fell before Hitler largely because it kept telling the people, "The government can do nothing for you." And, as proof that the Roosevelt administration was trying to avoid excessive governmental power rather than promote socialism, in his very first measure, the Banking Act, the President refused to consider nationalization. He insisted on leaving the banks free and independent, subject only to the regulation of the Glass-Steagall Banking Act. The New Deal seemed newer than it really was, partly because progressive principles had largely been forgotten for thirteen years, but mostly because the cards were dealt with such bewildering rapidity.

2. The Hundred Days and After

During the first "Hundred Days" of the Roosevelt administration, the President made ten speeches, sent Congress fifteen messages, eased many laws to enactment, talked to the press twice a week, conferred personally or by telephone with foreign statesmen, and made many important decisions. Yet he remained serene, confident, and smiling. Here are the legislative and executive landmarks of those hundred days in 1933:—

9 March	Emergency Banking Act
20 March	Economy Act
31 March	Civilian Conservation Corps
19 April	Gold standard abandoned (ratified 5 June)
12 May	Federal Emergency Relief Act
"	Agricultural Adjustment Act
"	Emergency Farm Mortgage Act
18 May	Tennessee Valley Authority Act
27 May	Truth-in-Securities Act
13 June	Home Owner's Loan Act
16 June	National Industrial Recovery Act
"	Glass-Steagall Banking Act
"	Farm Credit Act

The Emergency Banking bill, which the President and Secretary Woodin had worked on with the help of directors of the Federal Reserve Board, was submitted to Congress on the very day it convened, 9 March, and passed in the record time of eight hours. It provided for reopening the banks, then closed throughout the country, under a system of licenses and conservators, and gave the treasury power to prevent hoarding gold and to issue more currency. On Sunday, 12 March, the President delivered the first of his fireside chats, in which, as Will Rogers said, he took up the complicated subject of banking "and made everybody understand it, even the bankers." The banks reopened on Monday, the stock market rose on Wednesday, and a federal bond issue was oversubscribed the first day of issue.

The Economy Act was initiated by F.D.R. and Lewis Douglas, director of the budget, to redeem a platform pledge to reduce the cost of government. All federal appointees took at least a 15 per cent salary cut, and other savings were effected. This, as it turned out, was a false start; what the country wanted and the economy needed was more federal spending. The salary cuts were restored before the end of the year.

The Civilian Conservation Corps was a device to give unemployed young men useful work, preventing them from drifting into subversive organizations, and to help conserve natural resources. By mid-June, 1300 CCC camps had been set up under army control and recruited by the department of labor; by August, over 300,000 young men were at work; and before the camps were wound up in wartime, some 2½ million men had passed through them, 17 million acres of new forests had been planted, numerous dams built to stop soil erosion, and an immense amount of other useful outdoor work performed in

federal and state parks. The CCC might also have been a valuable backlog for the future army, but for pacifist pressure
which deprived the army of an opportunity to give the young
men even close-order drill. Even so, the camps vastly improved
the health and well-being of the men who would have to fight
another war before long.

On 19 April the President, against the advice of most of his
economic advisers, but with the unexpected support of the
House of Morgan, announced that the United States was going
off the gold standard, as England had done two years earlier.
Congress backed him up on 5 June. This was the most revolutionary act of the New Deal, since it broke the implicit contract between government and public to the effect that all
government bonds, and bills from $20 up, were to be paid in
"gold coin." But it helped foreign trade, stopped the drain of
gold to Europe, and the domestic economy reacted buoyantly;
prices and stocks rose. Winston Churchill congratulated Roosevelt on the "noble and heroic sanity" of this step.

The off-gold order was followed by the London World
Monetary and Economic Conference on currency and exchange of June–July 1933, attended by representatives of over
fifty nations. President Hoover, who believed that the Great
Depression was essentially a world affair and that currency
stabilization was the answer, had promised American participation. The professed object of this conference was to obtain an
agreement of the principal countries to peg the wildly fluctu-
ating international exchange, and agree on gold or some other
standard for currency. Roosevelt's only positive contribution
was a proposal made to Georges Bonnet, the French finance
minister, before the conference opened: a stabilization fund to
keep the dollar, the pound sterling, and the franc in a fixed
relation. But the French government turned that down.

Every shade of opinion was represented in the large delegation that Roosevelt sent to London: senators, congressmen,
bankers, economists, Democrats, and Republicans. They argued
scandalously among themselves; on one occasion, Senator Key
Pittman, the Nevada free silver advocate, was seen pursuing
a "gold bug" down the hall with a drawn bowie knife! And, as
if there were not already enough confusion, over 100 members
of Congress signed a petition to Roosevelt to send the radio
priest Father Coughlin to London as an "adviser"! As the
President insisted on taking a summer sailing cruise along the
New England coast while this conference was going on, his
influence on it was intermittent and haphazard. Briefly, the conference became a tussle between gold-standard countries such

as France, Holland, and Belgium, and those which had gone off gold, mainly Britain, Canada, Scandinavia, and the United States. The former wished to protect their foreign trade by getting everyone else back on gold; the latter were determined to stay off, and to promote inflation to raise domestic prices and increase foreign trade. In the so-called Thomas amendment to the Agricultural Adjustment Act, Congress had given the President power at his discretion to devalue the dollar as much as 50 per cent, to issue fiat money, and to establish bimetallism. He was determined not to surrender those advantages by international agreement. In mid-June, after security prices had again broken in New York, F.D.R. sent Moley to London, and that economist succeeded in obtaining a rather innocuous resolution by the Conference in favor of exchange stabilization and eventual return to the gold standard. Moley urged the President to accept this; Secretary Woodin wanted it; but F.D.R., with only his yachting mates Henry Morgenthau Jr. and Louis M. Howe having the presidential ear, refused to be bound, and in a strong message from Campobello on 3 July "torpedoed" the Conference agreement. Thus lightly the President accepted a policy of managed currency and exchange, which still obtained in 1964.

Many conservative financiers at home and abroad were horrified; but Bernard Baruch and Russell Leffingwell of the House of Morgan approved, as did Winston Churchill and John M. Keynes who said, "President Roosevelt is magnificently right." After the lapse of thirty years, there can be no doubt that Roosevelt was right in protecting his administration's fiscal freedom but the manner in which he acted offended many people, and Moley had to be sacrificed to appease Cordell Hull.

The Federal Emergency Relief Act of 12 May appropriated $500 million (later increased to $5 billion) for direct relief to states, cities, towns, and counties. Harry Hopkins, who headed this, and the Civil Works Administration which grew out of it, correctly estimated that the unemployed wanted work rather than a mere dole, and organized on that basis. By January 1934 CWA had over 4 million people on its rolls, and at its peak, 400,000 separate projects were under way: roads, schoolhouses, airports (500 new ones and as many improved), parks, sewers, everything that Hopkins could think up that would be of public benefit. Work relief, as it was called, proved to be one of the best morale builders of the New Deal; it gave the recipients self-respect to feel that they were doing something useful. Governor Landon of Kansas, who contested the presidency with Roosevelt in 1936, wrote to him two years earlier, "This civil works program is one of the soundest, most constructive policies of your administration, and I cannot urge too strongly its continuance."

Next in importance came the National Industrial Recovery Act of 16 June, the (for a time) famous NRA. Title I of this law prescribed the drafting and application of "codes" to every sort of industry, with multiple objectives—recovery and reform, encouraging collective bargaining, setting up maximum hours (and sometimes prices) and minimum wages, and forbidding child labor. NRA was administered by General Hugh S. Johnson, a West Pointer who had had charge of the draft in World War I and had occupied a high place in army logistics. By hard work and persuasion, with the symbol of a blue eagle clutching a cogwheel allotted to every firm and store that adopted the system, he codified some 700 industries. Businessmen in general did not like NRA; they wished to be free to raise prices and cut wages as soon as they were out of the woods; and Title I was declared unconstitutional by the Supreme Court in 1935. Before that occurred, some 4 million unemployed had been reabsorbed into industry, and about 23 million workers were under codes.

The Works Projects Administration, the second part of NRA, the Supreme Court allowed to stand. Administered by Harry Hopkins, WPA spent billions on reforestation, flood control, rural electrification, water works, sewage plants, school buildings, slum clearance, and students' scholarships. A feature of the WPA which caught the public eye and became nicknamed "boondoggling," was the setting up of projects to employ artists, musicians, writers, and other "white collar" workers. Post offices and other public buildings were decorated with murals; regional and state guides were written; libraries in municipal and state buildings were catalogued by out-of-work librarians, and indigent graduate students were employed to inventory archives and copy old shipping lists, to the subsequent profit of American historians. The federal theater at its peak employed over 15,000 actors and other workers, at an average wage of $20 a week. Under the direction of John Houseman, Orson Welles, and others, new plays were written and produced, and the classics revived; some had long runs on Broadway and toured the "provinces." On the fine arts projects, artist George Biddle observes that they were "as humane, democratic and intelligent, as any art program the world over. . . . They had developed through trial and error. They were no brain-trust fantasy, but were suited to our needs, our tradition and our temperament."

The AAA, the Agricultural Adjustment Act of 12 May,

administered by Secretary Wallace, attempted to placate the perennial grievances of our tillers of the soil. Starting with the principles of the McNary-Haugen Farm Relief bill which President Coolidge vetoed, it went even further to meet the glut of farm products and the abysmally low prices. Wheat and corn then commanded a smaller price per bushel than they had in the colonies three centuries earlier. AAA authorized the agriculture department, through a system of county agents, to reduce planting of staple commodities such as grain, cotton, tobacco, peanuts, and sugar; to plow under 10 million acres of the cotton acreage already planted (for which the owners were paid $200 million), and to reduce the breeding of pigs and meat cattle. Opponents of the New Deal made much of the slaughter of 6 million piglets that fall; but the Federal Surplus Relief Corporation froze the pork and distributed over 100 million pounds of it to families on relief. Tobacco growers who had received $43 million for their 1933 crop, got $120 million in 1934, and comparable results were attained in other farm products. The national farm income increased from $5.6 billion in 1932 to $8.7 billion in 1935. Destruction of food, and paying farmers not to produce, went against the grain; but, in the long run, no other way has been found in thirty years to meet the recurrent problem of giving the farmers an adequate return for their pains. "Agriculture cannot survive in a capitalistic society as a philanthropic enterprise," said Secretary Wallace. Sentimentalists who weep over controlled production by farmers "do not suggest that clothing factories should go on producing *ad infinitum,* regardless of effective demand for their merchandise."

On the same day, 12 May, that the AAA became law, Congress passed the Emergency Farm Mortgage Act which halted foreclosures and provided federal refunding of mortgages. One month later, Congress set up a Home Owner's Loan Corporation to refinance small mortgages on private dwellings; within a year it had approved over 300,000 loans amounting to almost $1 billion. This was the most popular enactment of the New Deal as it prevented so many citizens from losing their homes.

Legislation to reform and regulate the stock exchange and the banks began with the Truth-in-Securities Act of 27 May 1933. This bill was drafted by two law professors, Felix Frankfurter and James M. Landis, who had studied existing legislation in Great Britain. It provided that new securities be registered before a public commission, and that every offering contain full information to enable the prospective purchaser to judge the value of the issue and the condition of the corporation. Directors were made criminally liable for omitting significant information or for willful misstatement of fact.

After an interval of several months, during which the New York Stock Exchange had opportunity to curb malpractices but remained recalcitrant, two of the leading "brain-trusters," Ben Cohen and Thomas C. Corcoran, drafted a bill which Speaker Sam Rayburn guided to enactment on 6 June 1934, creating the Securities and Exchange Commission. This body had power to license stock exchanges and to register all securities in which they dealt. It prohibited pools and such devices for manipulating the market, and empowered the Federal Reserve Board to determine the extension of credit for marginal and speculative loans. Subsequent legislation enlarged the authority of the Securities and Exchange Commission over the public utilities. President Roosevelt, to the consternation of many, appointed as chairman of the Securities Commission Joseph P. Kennedy, one of the leading plungers before the crash. But as one who knew all the "angles" of the market, and was convinced of the need of reform, Kennedy was the man to do it. Supported by some of the more liberal and penitent moguls of finance such as James V. Forrestal, Robert Lovett, and W. Averell Harriman, the SEC formulated rules to prevent future skulduggery, stepped up the required margin for stock trading from 10 to 45 per cent, and also worked hard to obtain new financing. For about a year the corporations were defiant, alleging that Kennedy and "That Man in the White House" had ruined business; then Swift & Company broke the deadlock with a $43 million bond issue that was promptly subscribed, and by the fall of 1935 some $800 million of new financing had been effected. Kennedy now removed himself and his large family to the London embassy, and saturnine James M. Landis succeeded him as head of the SEC.

When the "Fighting First" Division, United States Army, crashed through a little Sicilian town named Nicosia in July 1943, they were not aware that it was the birthplace of a fighting American judge, Ferdinand Pecora. In New York City, after graduating from law school, Pecora made a name for himself as assistant district attorney, and as a judge. Appointed counsel to the Senate committee on banking and currency in January 1933, he conducted a sensational investigation of what had been going on in the field of investment banking. Typically Sicilian in appearance, angry and sarcastic at times but always in command of himself and the situation, Pecora interrogated such titans of finance as Morgan, Dillon, Aldrich, Forrestal, Otto Kahn, and Wiggin, uncovering the story of chicanery in high places from which we culled a few facts for an earlier chapter. The investigation had a major influence on the Truth-in-Securities Act already mentioned, and on the Glass-Steagall Banking Act of June 1933. This law required banks to get out of the investment business, and placed severe restrictions on the use of banking funds for speculation. And it gave a federal guarantee for individual bank deposits. This revolutionary device, which even Roosevelt thought dangerous, was pushed through by a group of congressmen led by Arthur H. Vandenberg of Michigan, against the opposition of the American Bankers' Association. Insurance of bank deposits turned out to be one of the most brilliant achievements of the Hundred Days.

Many of the laws that we have briefly described were regarded by their authors and by the President as temporary relief measures; but this banking law, as well as the two acts regulating the securities markets, were intended as permanent reforms and, though amended by later enactments, are still in force. Of the same nature were the Social Security Act of 1935 which initiated a comprehensive federal system of unemployment and old age insurance, and the Public Utilities Holding Company Act of the same year, passed in spite of a high-pressure lobby organized by Wendell Willkie. So, too, were the several conservation measures which we shall take up shortly.

Winston Churchill, out of office and not yet acquainted with F.D.R., remarked on the efforts of his future partner, "The courage, the power and the scale of his effort must enlist the ardent sympathy of every country, and his success could not fail to lift the whole world forward with the sunlight of an easier and more genial age. . . . Roosevelt is an explorer who has embarked on a voyage as uncertain as that of Columbus, and upon a quest which might conceivably be as important as the discovery of the New World."

Long, exhausting, and tortuous has been that voyage in quest of peace and security, and it may well be that none now living may sight that promised land. But Roosevelt had at least got them through the Red Sea, with no other miracle than the fortuitous union of courage, faith, and sagacity.

3. Conservation and the TVA

On 18 May 1933, President Roosevelt signed the Tennessee Valley Authority Act, the famous TVA, a great and permanent achievement of the New Deal. It deserves special mention as a revolutionary attempt to do something constructive for the poor, whom "ye have always with you." Most of the New Deal measures were based on the theory that the only thing government could do to relieve poverty was relief—mostly by taxing the "haves" for benefit of the "have-nots." TVA was based on a constructive concept, to raise the collective well-being of millions of people by controlling a mighty river in such wise as to produce electric power, rebuild the fertility of eroded farms, and enhance the living conditions of those inhabiting the valley.

This idea was sold to F.D.R. by Senator George Norris of Nebraska, one of the most remarkable statesmen in our modern history. Unimpressive, simple in his tastes—he never acquired a dinner coat during thirty years in Washington—no great orator, with arched eyebrows that gave his countenance a look of perpetual surprise, but always a little sad over the greed and folly that he encountered daily, Norris was a liberal progressive who linked the 1890's with the 1930's. Always contending on the liberal side and often beaten, he never gave up, reminding one of the warriors for Irish freedom described by Shaemas O'Sheel:

> They went forth to battle, but they always fell;
> Something they saw above the sullen shields.

What Norris saw was "the one great central problem, the use of the earth for the good of man." Born in Ohio in 1861, teacher, lawyer, and judge in a small Nebraska town, Norris had served his state in Congress as representative and senator for thirty years, always a Republican. And although he found more support for his idea among the Democrats, he never abandoned the dream of his youth to make the Republican party an instrument of human progress and justice, an example of "pure and enlightened government." His first blistering experience was that of the hard times in Nebraska in the 1890's. "Only those who have lived in the heart of the nation's food-producing regions," he wrote, "know fully the agony of these cycles of crop failures, heavy indebtedness upon the land, and ruinous farm commodity prices." He followed Theodore Roosevelt into the Progressive party, and was chosen to the Senate in 1912. There he became interested in flood control and other aspects of conservation. For thirty years he fought the Pacific Gas & Electric Company's grab of the Hetch Hetchy reservoir and power system in California, and lost. He fought American entry into World War I, and lost. During the discouraging Harding administration he found a cause that he finally led to victory—the TVA.

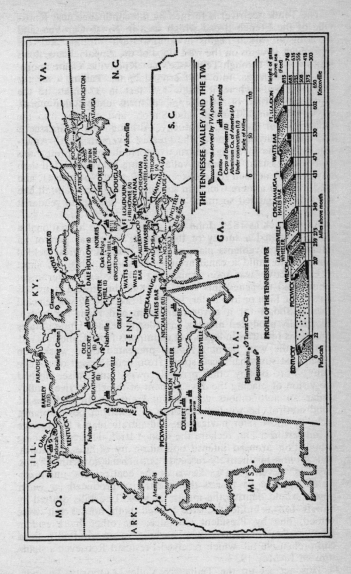

THE TENNESSEE VALLEY AND THE TVA

Dams:
Corps of Engineers (E)
Aluminum Co. of America (A)
Under construction (U)

▨ Area served by TVA power.
▲ Steam plants

Scale of Miles
0   50   100

PROFILE OF THE TENNESSEE RIVER

Height of gates above sea (feet)

745
635
556
508
418
300

815 685 595
530
471 431 349 225 259 209 22
Miles above mouth

Paducah 6 0

KENTUCKY PICKWICK WILSON WHEELER GUNTERSVILLE HALES BAR CHICKAMAUGA WATTS BAR FT. LOUDOUN

602 650
Knoxville

The Tennessee river is formed by the confluence near Knox-ville of the French Broad which rises in North Carolina, and the Holston which begins in southwestern Virginia and, fed by smaller streams on the west slope of the Appalachians, flows southwesterly through Tennessee, past Knoxville, Chattanooga, and Chickamauga, into northern Alabama. Passing over the Muscle Shoals where it drops 137 feet in 37 miles, to the northeast corner of Mississippi, it turns almost due north, passes Pittsburgh Landing and Shiloh, and empties into the Ohio river at Paducah, Kentucky. Although the Tennessee is 652 miles long and one of the greatest rivers in North Amer-ica, it became a raging, destructive torrent in the spring rains (the southeastern Tennessee valley having heavier rainfall than any other American region except the Pacific Northwest), and died away to a mere trickle in summer. Moreover, rainfall had eroded and gullied so much of the valley land as to render it sterile.

As far back as 1825, John C. Calhoun, still in his nationalist mood, initiated a survey of the Muscle Shoals as part of an internal improvements plan, and as a result Congress helped Alabama to build a canal around the shoals. This, too short to be effective, was soon abandoned. The federal government rebuilt and reopened this canal in 1890, but found it useless at extreme high or low water. In 1917 President Wilson selected Muscle Shoals for a government dam and plant for hydro-electrically produced nitrates, in order to render United States munitions factories independent of imports from Chile.

After the war, Senator Norris prevented these works, on which vast sums had been spent, from being leased or sold to Henry Ford or any other privately owned enterprise. He had the vision of placing the development of the entire river valley under an autonomous governmental agency. In addition to flood control, he wanted authority to construct power plants, locks to allow river navigation, and nitrate plants to produce cheap fertilizer and reclaim the eroded land. This far-reaching proposition aroused intense opposition by utilities, railroads, and all who instinctively resisted "putting the government into business." Even John L. Lewis of the coal miners' union ob-jected because he feared that electricity produced by water power would deprive the miners of jobs! Two bills drafted by Norris for a limited scheme passed both houses but were vetoed, one by President Coolidge, the other by President Hoover. Senator Norris, who never gave up, drafted a third comprehensive bill which received President Roosevelt's signa-ture on 18 May 1933.

This act set up the Tennessee Valley Authority, an independent public body based on the Panama Canal Commission precedent, for the development of an area three-fourths the size of England. It is directed by a board of three men appointed by the President of the United States. The first board comprised Arthur E. Morgan, a flood-control expert, Harcourt A. Morgan, an agricultural scientist, and David E. Lilienthal, then thirty-four years old, lately a member of the Wisconsin public service commission. The basic Act transferred to TVA all government-owned property at Muscle Shoals, made the Board responsible for flood control and developing navigation, and gave it authority to build and operate dams and reservoirs, to generate and sell electric power, and to manufacture and distribute fertilizer. And it made possible any number of other programs to raise the "economic and social well being of the people living in said river basin."

The Authority already owned the Wilson dam at Muscle Shoals. It started work on the first new one, appropriately named Norris, on 1 October 1933 and completed it in May 1936. This was the first of six completed before World War II. All were multi-purpose dams, including locks for navigation and a hydro-electric plant; some contributed to flood control by creating storage reservoirs on tributaries of the Tennessee.

The men who ran the Authority had the sense to see that the well being of this great valley must be promoted in a variety of ways. First, by flood control. Floods, still a hazard on the Ohio, the Connecticut, and many other American rivers, are now a thing of the past on the Tennessee. Second, by commercial navigation. By means of massive locks the haulage increased from 33 million ton-miles in 1932—mostly short runs of gravel barges—to 2.2 billion ton-miles in 1963—mostly diesel-power barges carrying every sort of commodity on long haul. Third, by development of cheap electric power for homes and factories. Generated at the dams on the main river and some of its tributaries, it is distributed to the ultimate consumer through 158 locally owned co-operatives, municipalities, or private companies. These deliver the current to individuals at less than one cent per kilowatt hour, compared with the average nation-wide rate of 2.4 cents charged by private utilities. By 1950 when the low-cost hydro-electric potential of the river was nearing full realization, TVA began building steam power plants operated by coal brought downstream by barge or by rail from the mines of Kentucky, Tennessee, and Illinois. Finally, by improvement of farming. A group of TVA chemists set to work to lower the cost of fertilizer by producing concentrated phosphate; and in late 1936 TVA was operating its first electric phosphorus furnace. In order to persuade farmers to use this to advantage, demonstration farms were developed with the co-operation of agricultural colleges, local bodies, and farm owners; 54,000 farms, covering more than 6.6 million acres, have participated. TVA also provided free seedlings for reforestation. With the help of state nurseries it has reforested over a million acres of valley land since 1933.

The TVA has few compulsory powers. It enjoys the right of eminent domain, and can remove obstructions to navigation, but in general operates through partnership with local authorities, and the voluntary co-operation of individuals. Although dependent on Congress for appropriations for non-revenue-producing activities, it remains independent of the Washington bureaucracy. More than 200 private companies now manufacture and market products developed by TVA. Thus it is not a super-government; both in theory and practice TVA is worlds apart from the Soviet system of forcing collectivized farming on the peasants and regulating what they sow and reap. Farmers' co-operatives were organized in all but ten of the 125 valley counties. And, since World War II, it has been the model for man's similar schemes in other parts of the world.

Senator Norris could not rest after the original act received President Roosevelt's signature. He became the leader of a long and weary battle for congressional appropriations, to defend TVA from politicians who wanted to control it, and the utilities which accused it of "creeping socialism." It seemed monstrous to elderly senators such as Kenneth D. McKellar of Tennessee that this autonomous authority should operate in their bailiwick, dictate where dams and power plants should be built, and handle its personnel by the merit system. The utilities' major quarrel with TVA was probably based on its policy of providing electricity to the public at lowest possible cost, both to stimulate consumption and act as a "yardstick" for public bodies regulating the rates charged by private companies. Since the private utilities' policy was based on charging high rates for limited consumption, they considered TVA's low rate-high use policy ruinous. But in thirty years' time most of them came to accept it.

In World War II the Oak Ridge center for atomic fission was located within the Tennessee valley to use TVA power. This and other applications of its power to national defense, made new friends for TVA. Senator Norris noted with satisfaction that big utilities men on the National Defense Advisory Committee pressed Congress to provide funds for building Cherokee dam on the Holston river to provide power for aluminum production. This important dam, first of a number of wartime additions to TVA's power capacity, was built in the record time of sixteen months in 1940–41. Incidentally, the Authority created some fourscore public parks for boating and bathing.

This great enterprise has been one of the country's major contributions in the twentieth century. It proved that a democratic state could be progressive; that by invention, farsighted planning, and popular co-operation it could benefit the entire society within its orbit; that a great river, instead of being a destroyer, could become a boon to the dwellers on its watershed. President Kennedy, addressing an assembly at the Muscle Shoals on the thirtieth anniversary of TVA in 1963, well said: "The tremendous economic growth of this region, its private industry and its private income, make it clear to all that TVA is a fitting answer to socialism—and it certainly has not been creeping."

The Soil Conservation Act of 1936, replacing the emergency AAA, provided for the reforestation of immense areas of marginal land throughout the country. Next year Senator Norris proposed the creation of six more regional authorities like TVA, starting with the Missouri valley which needed it most. Owing in part to the failure of the states concerned to agree, in part to the utilities' lobby, none of these proposals reached law. But the Roosevelt administration is remembered for several great multi-purpose dams in the West. It completed Boulder dam on the Colorado river, begun under President Coolidge. This is a godsend to Los Angeles and Southern California as a source of electric power. The 550-foot-high Grand Coulee dam on the Columbia river in eastern Washington, completed in 1941, created a lake 150 miles long, and provided almost 2 million kilowatts' power, as well as irrigation, for a barren section of the old Oregon country known as the "Scablands." Twenty years later, the value of crops grown on this former desert was $42 million. On the lower Columbia, about 35 miles upstream from Portland, army engineers in 1938 completed Bonneville dam to tame the five-mile Cascade Rapids. These, like the Muscle Shoals, had closed a vital part of the river to shipping. And, through a series of other dams and locks, the Columbia is now navigable for boats of nine-foot draught up to Pasco, 324 miles from the bar which the ship *Columbia* was the first to cross. Several other dams and hydro-electric plants have been built on this great river by privately financed utilities. And in October 1964 a treaty with Canada, providing for joint exploitation of the upper Columbia, was ratified.

The problem of how to distribute and dispose of this newly generated electric power aroused, as we have seen in the case of TVA, a bitter controversy between the administration and the utilities. These, wedded to the "high rate–low use" concept, refused, as unprofitable, to extend light and power lines into thinly inhabited rural areas. So, in contrast to poor countries like Norway where, owing to government control of water power, almost every farmhouse had enjoyed electric light since the early years of the century, only one out of ten American farms had it in 1933; and as for electrical milking and other machines, it was clear that if the farmers were to continue dependent on privately financed utilities, they might wait forever—except in the Tennessee valley.

The Rural Electrification Administration, originally set up as a relief project, became an independent agency in 1936. REA owes as much to Morris Llewellyn Cooke as TVA does to Senator Norris; and Norris helped REA too. Cooke, a Lehigh University graduate in engineering, a main-line Philadelphian sixty-three years old, had made a power survey of Pennsylvania which convinced him that only government support would get electricity into the back-country, and sold the idea to F.D.R. and Harold Ickes. Cooke first tried to persuade the utilities to accept low-interest loans from the government for extending their lines into the country, but met with a flat refusal. He then decided to promote non-profit co-operatives among the farmers. After much opposition by the utilities' lobby, REA got the money from Congress and, by the end of 1941, had lent $434 million to rural co-operative power plants. And in five years the number of farms having electric light and power increased from about 750,000 to 2,250,000. By 1950, 90 per cent of all farms in the United States were electrified.

Conservationists got through Congress during the Hoover administration a very important law, the Shipstead-Nolan Act of 1930, "to promote better protection and highest public use of the lands of the United States." And the country now had a President and secretary of the interior who were aggressive conservationists. The Roosevelt administration promoted or completed several national parks, including the Olympic, Isle Royale, Shenandoah, and Great Smoky Mountains. Since 1927 a voluntary organization called the Quetico-Superior Council had been trying to make an international park out of the Superior National Forest in Minnesota and the Quetico Park in Ontario, to protect the lake country on both sides of the old Indian fur-trade portage between Lake Superior and Lake of the Woods. The guiding spirit of this Council was a Harvard graduate named Ernest C. Oberholtzer, who loved the wilderness and wished to preserve this last big unspoiled tract in the

Middle West for posterity. Only by putting it under the National Forest Service could its natural beauty, the maze of lakes and streams, the primeval forest, the fish and game, be protected from spoliation. The Shipstead-Nolan act gave the authority, but the Quetico-Superior project, requiring concurrent action between Minnesota, the United States, Ontario, and the Dominion of Canada, was exceedingly difficult to implement. Opposition developed from Minnesota paper and pulpwood interests which wished to strip the region of its timber and ruin the lake shores by building dams so that logs could be run out at a minimum of expense. Ickes approved the Oberholtzer program, and the President instructed Secretary Hull to negotiate a treaty with Canada to carry it out; but before that could be done, World War II broke out. The state of Minnesota raised objections, but the project was completed by the Humphrey Act of June 1956, and included in the Wilderness Act of 1964.

George W. Norris, whose career is a standing reproach to those "tired liberals" who give up after a few defeats, died in 1944; a concentration of money on an obscure local candidate had defeated him for re-election to the Senate. His own simple conclusion to his efforts was this: "If in the peaceful years ahead new vigor comes to old and wooded hills, not only in the basin of the Tennessee but throughout America, and in other regions of the world, and laughter replaces the silence of impoverished peoples, that is well."

4. *The New Deal and Foreign Affairs*

We have already seen how the President "torpedoed" the London Economic Conference in the summer of 1933, in order to retain America's freedom to manipulate currency and exchange to her own advantage. The rise of Hitler, however, caused a change of heart, and Henry Morgenthau Jr., Woodin's successor in the treasury, negotiated a tripartite pact with Great Britain and France in 1936, for stabilizing the dollar-pound-franc exchange.

A constructive measure for lowering trade barriers was the Reciprocal Trade Agreements Act passed by Congress in 1934 at the earnest insistence of Secretary Hull. This allowed the President to lower customs duties against a nation as much as 50 per cent in return for similar favors. Since these agreements did not have to be ratified by the Senate, the traditional log-rolling and pressure politics were bypassed. By the end of 1938, American exports to the sixteen nations with which Hull had concluded these agreements had increased 40 per cent over the figures of 1930.

Since 1919, official American relations with Russia had been with the Kerensky government in exile. Recognition of Soviet Russia was brought about partly in the hope of trade, and also because it became clear that the communist regime was there to stay. Russia in 1933 appeared to be moving toward the "bourgeois prejudices" which earlier she had despised; hence many Americans thought, quite erroneously, that the Russian was now going the way of the French Revolution. But Stalin and his colleagues knew exactly what they were doing. They modified the rigid communist system to make it work, but were still inseparable from the Comintern, organ of the Third International, and continued to promote world-wide revolution so far as they could, including the United States.

Recognition was accorded in November 1933 after Maxim Litvinov, the foreign minister, had visited Washington and promised not only to end communist propaganda in the United States and guarantee religious freedom in Russia, but negotiate a settlement of claims and debts. Stalin broke faith on all three counts, and the expected trade failed to materialize.

The main trend of New Deal foreign policy until 1940 was to continue to avoid European commitments, but to cultivate New World solidarity, and to attempt to persuade Japan through diplomacy to respect the integrity of China. The Latin-American aspect really worked. Secretary Hull's reciprocity agreements helped every American republic to get out of the depression, and at Montevideo in December he signed a treaty to the effect that "no state has the right to intervene in the internal or external affairs of another." This made binding Hoover's disavowal of the Roosevelt corollary to the Monroe Doctrine. In accordance with this "Good Neighbor" policy, the United States in 1934 formally renounced her right to intervene in Cuba under the Platt Amendment, withdrew the last of the marines from Haiti, and increased Panama's annuity for the Canal Zone. Roosevelt himself attended an Inter-American Conference for Peace at Buenos Aires in 1936, promising to consult with Latin-American nations "for mutual safety."

Another troublesome situation with Mexico arose in 1938, under President Cardenas, who identified himself with the interests of the peons and union labor. Partly as a result of their complaints against British and American oil companies in Mexico, Cardenas expropriated all foreign oil properties in 1938. After four years of negotiations, a commission valued the confiscated properties at $24 million—about one-tenth of what the oil companies claimed; and the companies obeyed the state department's advice to accept.

These acts implemented the Good Neighbor policy and resulted in Pan-American solidarity in World War II.

5. *The Opposition and the Supreme Court*

On 1 March 1934 Justice Stone of the Supreme Court wrote to Herbert Hoover, "It seems clear that the honeymoon is over, and that we may witness the beginning of real political discussion." Or, as another put it, business, having emerged from its storm cellar with the help of the administration, forgot that there had ever been a storm. With the gross national product rising by 20 per cent in 1934, and the Dow-Jones index of common stock prices going from 41.2 in mid-1932 to 100 in mid-1933, the old adage came true again:

> The devil was sick, the devil a monk would be;
> The devil was well, the devil a monk was he!

Business and finance had many emotional and some legitimate grievances against the New Deal. The popular image of financiers and businessmen as generous promoters of the common weal had been destroyed; that of a beneficent federal government had taken its place. Industrial tycoons found it irritating to be forced to confer with "young whipper-snappers" of the "brain trust" about codes, labor relations, and the like. Railroads and trusts were used to regulation, but manufacturers, investment houses, and stock exchanges were not. Washington brain-trusters were not always tactful, and the spectacle of their drafting bills which the 74th Congress "rubber-stamped" infuriated people both in and out of Congress. Many conservatives persuaded themselves that the New Deal was destroying the historic American pattern of individual responsibility and local initiative by placing the nation's future in the hands of starry-eyed professors and power-mad bureaucrats. Soon it began to be whispered, then written, then shouted, that the Roosevelt administration was becoming totalitarian, assimilating American policy to that of Hitler or Stalin. Many a business leader began to look upon himself as Horatius at the Bridge, "facing fearful odds, for the ashes of his fathers, and the temple of his gods." The American Liberty League, founded in 1934 by a group of conservative Democrats led by Al Smith, John W. Davis, and the Du Ponts, played variations on that theme. Senator Connally of Texas expressed the popular reaction: "If the government had not got into business, there would be no business today. As soon as the business man sees a slight improvement he starts shouting, 'The government must get out of business.'"

Roosevelt made a conciliatory fireside chat on 30 September 1934 in which he declared his faith in "the driving power of individual initiative and the incentive of fair private profit," with the qualification that "obligations to the public interest" must be accepted. He had given up the hope of partnership with business, because most of the business leaders with whom he conferred simply wanted repeal of New Deal legislation and to let laissez-faire resume its fateful course. "One of my principal tasks," wrote the President in November, was "to prevent bankers and business men from committing suicide." Wisely he elected to remain "above the battle" in the congressional elections of 1934, and forbade cabinet members—except irrepressible Jim Farley—to make campaign speeches. The election proved Roosevelt's strength. The Democrats added nine members to their majority in the House, and several new Democratic senators, including the hitherto unknown Harry Truman, were sent to the Senate.

Congress now (14 August 1935) passed one of the most far-reaching laws of the New Deal, the Social Security Act. This provided for unemployment compensation by a one per cent tax (since increased to 10.4 per cent) on payrolls, half withheld from the employee's salary, half paid by the employer; a federal bonus to state old-age assistance of half what the state paid, in addition to a straight old-age pension; grants to the states for children's health and welfare, to the blind, and to extend state public health services.

A host of cases challenging the constitutionality of these measures reached the Supreme Court. Charles Evans Hughes was still chief justice; and, of the associate justices, only Brandeis, Stone, and Cardozo could be expected to find constitutional the vast extensions of federal power assumed by President and Congress in 1933–34. In May 1935 the Supreme Court, in the Schechter poultry case, destroyed the National Industrial Recovery Act in a unanimous and sweeping decision. Congress, said the Court, cannot delegate unfettered power to the President to issue whatever edicts he thinks advisable for the good of trade or industry. The NRA constituted an improper exercise of the commerce power, for if the commerce clause were so construed, "the federal authority would embrace practically all the activities of the people and the authority of the state over its domestic concerns would exist only by sufferance." Thus ended a law which the President had described as "the most important and far-reaching ever enacted by the American Congress." Actually, NRA had run its course and done its work; the blue eagle was not greatly missed.

On 6 January 1936, the Supreme Court invalidated the AAA (Agricultural Adjustment Act) as an improper exercise of the taxing power and an invasion of the reserved rights of the states. "This is coercion by economic pressure," said Justice Roberts, who conjured up the terrifying consequences that would flow from the taxation of one part of the community for the benefit of another. But Justice Stone, dissenting, warned his colleagues against a "tortured construction of the Constitution," and observed, with some asperity, "Courts are not the only agency of government that must be assumed to have capacity to govern."

Although the Supreme Court passed favorably on TVA and other leading measures of the New Deal such as the Wagner Labor Act, it invalidated several other measures of importance to the administration. Justices of the Supreme Court are long-lived and were not then subject to a retirement age, and there had been no vacancy during President Roosevelt's first term. F.D.R., feeling that the country could not afford to wait for the six septuagenarians on the Court to make their last decisions, in February 1937 made the startling suggestion to Congress that it authorize him to appoint one new Justice for every one over seventy years of age who had not retired. This was his first big mistake. The public may have been irritated by the obstructionism of the Supreme Court, but it did not wish that revered institution to be tampered with. From almost every quarter the proposal was denounced as an attempt to "pack" the Court, and Congress refused to pass the desired law: But, if Roosevelt lost his battle, he won the campaign. The Court itself, while the debate was under way, managed to find reasons for passing favorably on new laws differing little from those formerly under the ban:—a farm-mortgage act, the National Labor Relations Act, and Social Security. The old justices began to die or retire, and in the next four years, Roosevelt was able to appoint a virtually new court:—Senators James F. Byrnes of South Carolina and Hugo Black of Alabama, Stanley Reed of Kentucky, Professor Felix Frankfurter who had raised up a new generation of lawyers and jurists, Professor William O. Douglas, who had served on the SEC; and Governor Frank Murphy of Michigan. In 1941, when Chief Justice Hughes retired, Harlan F. Stone, a wise and tolerant associate justice, became his successor.

This new court completed the retreat from the constitutional position taken by its predecessor and renewed the tradition of

Marshall and Story. It returned to that broad interpretation of the commerce, taxing, and general welfare clauses of the Constitution and of Amendment XIV which made possible the application of the Constitution to an industrial nation. The principles of those famous dissenters, Justices Holmes and Brandeis, became cornerstones for the new majority.

6. Demagogues and Deviationists

While the strongest opposition to Roosevelt came from the right, the noisiest came from the left. The depression not only spawned demagogues and cranks, each with his own panacea, but had a devastating effect on many young college graduates and other jobless intellectuals. It seemed to prove that representative government and capitalism were finished. Whither, then, to turn? Polarity being a weakness of intellectuals, many decided to save America by embracing one of the two competing ideologies in Europe—fascism and communism. Seward Collins, a graduate of Hill School and Princeton, founded *The American Review*, which became the organ of an American fascist party. Lawrence Dennis of Exeter and Harvard, a repentant Wall Street banker, turned toward Hitler as a new god; his *The Coming of American Fascism* came out in 1936. William D. Pelley of North Carolina organized the Silver Shirts, "the flower of our Protestant Christian manhood" he called these middle-class hoodlums, who imitated Hitler's storm troopers by terrorizing Jews, communists, and liberals, but with minimum success. Pelley counted on becoming the American *Führer* when Hitler took over, and his lieutenants picked out expensive mansions from Newport to Palm Beach for future headquarters as *Gauleiter*. Other fascist groups were formed, claiming that they alone could save America from the Jews and communists toward which Franklin D. Roosevelt (Rosenveltd according to them)[1] was driving it. Those movements even enjoyed a half-hearted approval by the Hearst press in 1934–35, Hearst himself having been deeply impressed by Hitler in Berlin. Many a college student, visiting Germany during the depression, observed the *Hitler Jugend* marching, singing, and doing something, returned home to find apathy and unemployment, and became a Nazi convert. This American fascist movement never became serious, but it made some

[1] One of the yarns in which many people believed during the New Deal was that F.D.R. was the descendant of a German Jew named Rosenveltd whom Peter Stuyvesant had exiled to Hyde Park because he engaged in seditious activities in New Amsterdam.

notable converts who turned traitor to the United States during the next war—the poet Ezra Pound who broadcast for Mussolini, and Fred Kaltenbach, one of Hearst's favorite European correspondents, who performed the same service for Hitler.

At the other pole was the American Communist party, which always obeyed orders from Moscow. Hitherto the Soviets followed the "hard line"—founding communist trade unions, agitating incessantly and denouncing the socialists as well as the bourgeoisie. The Communist party, following this line, organized the unions in two big textile strikes in the 1920's, at Passaic and New Bedford, and lost both. In 1934, however, Stalin, alarmed at the growing power of Hitler, adopted the "soft line" of infiltrating regular unions and co-operating with liberals and socialists to set up "Popular Front" governments in Europe. Earl Browder, head of the American Communist party, obeying his master's voice, ordered members to liquidate "every old idea that stands as an obstacle between us and the masses." The New York *Daily Worker* stopped insulting socialists but continued to attack President Roosevelt as a covert fascist, and the New Deal as "the death rattle of capitalism." Communists infiltrated the Minnesota Farmer-Labor party, and in some instances local units of the regular parties, by attending caucuses and electing themselves as delegates. Chuckle-headed union leaders—notably those of the Chicago meat packers—thought they "could use the Commies" and let them into the organization, only to find that they were the ones used. One such take-over threatened the entire structure of national defense; this was the National Maritime Union, which held up shipments to France in 1940, but became super-patriotic when Hitler attacked Russia.

Besides infiltrating labor unions, the communists joined with pacifists and other liberals in organizing "front" organizations, notably the American League Against War and Fascism, which capitalized on sentiments common to most Americans. This League held an annual congress from 1933 on, to orate and pass resolutions, on the model of the International Congress Against War at Amsterdam, organized by Barbusse and Romain Rolland. Controlled from the start by communists, this League claimed to have two million members and very likely did, as propaganda against American participation in the European war fell in with the national mood. The Reds also took over the National Negro Congress organized by anti-communist leaders such as Ralph Bunche; the American Student Union, which claimed 20,000 members, and the American Youth Congress, founded by vague "young" (mostly aged 40 and up) liberals, but soon captured by really young and determined communists.

Communism, presented as an ideal form of society and a gospel of all-embracing love for mankind, appealed to muddled young intellectuals, many of whom were persuaded that this, not fascism as Anne Morrow Lindbergh predicted, was "the wave of the future." They were horrified by the excesses of the Nazis but conveniently overlooked those of the Soviets— the purges and executions, the five and a half million *kulaks* (land-owning peasants) liquidated or transported to Siberia between 1928 and 1934; the five million starved in the famine of 1932–33—because these were either concealed and denied, or were presented as a necessary prelude to an ideal society. Communism also attracted young scientists whose political education had been neglected, because it was presented as a completely logical, scientific reorganization of government and society. Encouraged by the party, several talented young men like Whittaker Chambers and Alger Hiss sought and obtained positions—mostly unimportant ones—in the federal government. They formed a communist cell in Washington and met frequently to laugh their heads off over the futile efforts of "that cripple Roosevelt" to cure a tottering capitalist system. They attempted to ingratiate themselves with Russia by stealing government documents—mostly innocuous reports by foreign service representatives in Europe—and copying them for transmittal to Moscow. Hiss's odd typewriter became the means of his later conviction. These men confidently expected to be named top commissars of the Soviet United States, just as Hitler's supporters looked to the Fuehrer to bestow similar favors after beating America to her knees.

In the relatively temperate regions between the two political poles were bred a number of native American movements, each under a leader with a particular nostrum for ending the depression. One of the most formidable was the Reverend Charles E. Coughlin "the radio priest," Irish-Canadian rector of the parish of Royal Oak near Detroit. In 1926 he began operating the "Shrine of the Little Flower Radio Station" and preaching what he called a Christian solution of the nation's economic difficulties, namely, juggling the currency. A consummate radio orator, his Irish humor attracted attention to his theories; and as a free-silver and paper-money man he appealed to the old populist faith that gold was the root of all evil and New York bankers the devils. By 1934 ten million people were listening to Coughlin's radio broadcasts, and voluntary contributions of half a million dollars a year were rolling in to the Shrine of the Little Flower. Up to that time, Coughlin supported Roosevelt and the New Deal, which he even called "Christ's deal." But in 1934 he decided that the President had gone over to the bankers and began to attack the "Jew deal," anti-Semitism being one of Coughlin's favorite stocks in trade.

Dr. Francis E. Townsend, a sixty-six-year-old physician of Long Beach, California, was impelled into the crackpot political arena by the distressing spectacle of helpless and hopeless old folk who had lost their jobs and spent their savings and knew not where to turn. In 1933 he announced the "Townsend Plan" to cure the depression—to give everyone over sixty years of age a federal pension of $150 a month, provided he spent it. The idea went over big in California, haven of the elderly and retired; and with the aid of a real estate promoter named Robert E. Clement, Townsend Clubs spread countrywide. A Democrat named John S. McGroarty, the "poet laureate of California," introduced a bill in Congress which would give every oldster $200 a month for life. After it had been pointed out that this would channel about one-half the national income into the pockets of one-eleventh of the population, the bill was dropped.

Upton Sinclair, the most prolific author in American literary history, a Socialist for thirty years, joined the Democratic party in California to campaign for the governorship on a platform of End Poverty in California, EPIC for short. His ideas were ancient—reorganizing society in co-operative phalanstaries like Brook Farm and New Harmony, which had failed a century earlier. With the aid of a popular utopian novel that he wrote for the occasion, *I, Governor of California and How I Ended Poverty,* Sinclair captured the Democratic nomination for governor in 1934. Since he was a Democrat, the administration had to support him, as did Father Coughlin and a number of Eastern intellectuals such as Theodore Dreiser. Roosevelt rather liked Sinclair, and regarded his proposed experiments as interesting and innocuous. Not so, however, the fat cats of California. In the first of our all-out, heavily financed campaigns directed by a public relations firm of advertising men, the immense corpus of Sinclair's published literature was combed for odd or offensive statements, and documents were forged to prove him a communist and a traitor. The Republican candidate for governor stole some of his thunder by endorsing the New Deal and the Townsend Plan, and Sinclair was snowed under. That was the end of EPIC, but this state campaign was significant for proving the influence of the public relations profession. No major presidential campaign since 1948 has been waged without their fabulously expensive aid to one or both sides.

There were several other "small, sour and angry" schemes, as Emerson described their prototypes a century earlier; but the really formidable one, which had the administration trembling for a time, was "Every Man a King," led by Huey P. "Kingfish" Long of Louisiana. Huey was the most amusing and terrifying of all demagogues thrown up by the Great Depression; and, unlike the others, he had a firm state base to work from. Born into a "hillbilly" family in the piney-woods of northern Louisiana, Huey worked his way to a law degree by the age of twenty-one. When he entered state politics, the regular Democratic machine had been in power for fifty years without doing anything for the people. By appealing to the "Cajuns" (descendants of the displaced Acadians), the "sapsuckers" of the piney-woods, and the hillbillies, using a slogan he got from Bryan, "Every Man a King," Long got himself elected governor in 1928. Within a few years, having persuaded the voters to elect a "rubber-stamp" legislature, and by using bribery, violence, and blackmail, he had the entire state and local government, down to the policemen and firemen, under his control. Louisiana became a government like that of Mexico under Calles or the Argentine Republic under Perón. Huey did accomplish a lot of good. He built schools and enlarged the university, extended hard-top roads into the up-country, abolished the poll tax so that blacks could vote; they and the poor whites adored him. But he was also a clown, a vindictive bully, and a coward who evaded the wartime draft and went about surrounded by an armed bodyguard. Aiming at national power, he got himself elected to the United States Senate in 1930 as a first step. Fellow senators, shocked by his improprieties, regarded him with his pudgy face, pug nose, pop eyes, red hair, and ungrammatical speech, as an ignorant buffoon. But they underestimated Huey, and he regarded most of them as stuffed shirts.

Long supported Roosevelt in 1932, but broke with him next year; the President, one of the first to regard him as dangerous, retaliated by denying him federal patronage. Huey retorted with what he called the Share-the-Wealth program, which outdid even Dr. Townsend, or the Social Credit people in Canada. By a capital levy on fortunes and inheritance, he would present every American family with a $5000 house, $2000 annual income, and sundry other benefits. Poor folk and crackpots all over the country poured in their praise of Share-the-Wealth, and Long announced his candidature for the presidency early in 1935. He was then only forty-two years old.

Congress adjourned at the end of August 1935, and the

Kingfish returned to his kingdom. On the evening of 8 September as he was crossing the rotunda of the state capitol, he was assassinated by a man whose family he had ruined. There was a sigh of relief in Washington; but the simple folk of Louisiana sing ballads about Huey Long to this day, and his successors are still in control of the state.

The Kingfish's crown now passed to Congressman William Lemke of North Dakota. After the defeat in May 1935 of Lemke's bill to refinance farm mortgages by the issue of $8 billion worth of greenbacks, this congressman announced himself as candidate for the presidency of the Union party, or National Union for Social Justice, an inflationist organization founded (over the air) by Father Coughlin to support his views. Lemke, a Republican and a graduate of Yale Law School, aped the dress and speech of the impoverished Dakota farmers whom he championed. He characterized Roosevelt as "the bewildered Kerensky of a provisional government." Father Coughlin and Dr. Townsend supported him, and the Reverend Gerald L. K. Smith, who had been Huey Long's principal assistant in his Share-the-Wealth movement, promised to deliver the alleged six million followers of the Kingfish to the Union party. H. L. Mencken, who was present at the Union party convention in Cleveland in 1936, described Smith's speech as "a magnificent amalgam of each and every American species of rabble-rousing. . . . It ran the keyboard from the softest sobs and gurgles to the most earsplitting whoops and howls, and when it was over the 9000 delegates simply lay back in their pews and yelled." Father Coughlin was not at his best before a live audience, but when he referred to "Franklin Double-Crossing Roosevelt," the crowd went wild again. Dr. Townsend was there too, somewhat abashed because his realtor executive had skipped with $90,000 from the till. It looked as if this combination of Western agrarianism, the old folks, Huey's "Share-the-Wealth," and Coughlin's Irish brogue would make this party a mighty force. It nominated Lemke for the presidency, and for vice president Thomas C. O'Brien, a Harvard graduate who had been general counsel for the railroad brotherhoods and was counted on to get their vote.

7. The Election of 1936

As the presidential election approached, the clamor against President Roosevelt so increased both in pitch and volume that many political seers believed that the New Deal was doomed. H. L. Mencken declared in March that "this dreadful burlesque of civilized government" was at the end of its turn, that the "brain trust" had better pack up and go home, and the Republicans "begin to grasp the fact" that they can beat F.D.R. "with a Chinaman, or even a Republican!"

Governor Alfred M. Landon of Kansas, selected to do the job, was thrifty, cagey, and folksy, and no fool. An old Bull Mooser, if elected he would have continued the New Deal under another name. Hoover "wowed" the Republican convention by predicting that a continuance of Democratic rule would result in "violence and outrage," "class hatred . . . preached from the White House," "despotism," "universal bankruptcy," and other horrors. Yet the platform promised to do everything that Democrats had done, without destroying "free enterprise, private competition, and equality of opportunity."

The Democratic convention met in a jubilant mood, renominated President Roosevelt by acclamation, endorsed the entire New Deal, and promised to extend and expand it.

This campaign of 1936 was very heated. The Republicans' best argument was that the New Deal had not materially increased employment—there had been 12.8 million unemployed in 1933, and were still 9 million in 1936. The Democrats answered that the numbers of jobless would have been far worse without the New Deal, and that, anyway, the upturn had come and everyone except the bankrupt bankers and speculators was feeling better. Most of the newspapers, and very many business people, supported Landon. "Save the American Way of Life" was the slogan. A poll conducted by the *Literary Digest* predicted Landon's election. Then, in one of the greatest landslides in political history, Roosevelt received 60.7 per cent of the popular vote, and won 523 presidential electors out of 531. Lemke's Union party polled 892,000 votes, about the same that Norman Thomas the Socialist candidate had received in 1932. Earl Browder the Communist leader, who vainly tried to make a "popular front" with Thomas, obtained only 80,000 votes.

It was an old saying, "As Maine goes, so goes the nation." Jim Farley now changed this to "As Maine goes, so goes Vermont." These were the only two states that Landon carried, but his popular vote was 36 per cent of the total. The Republican minority in Congress dwindled, but still constituted strong opposition, a good thing for the country.

This unmistakable mandate for his policies encouraged Roosevelt to deal with the Supreme Court (as we have already noted) and to enlarge his methods to provide economic recovery.

XIII

The Second Roosevelt Administration

1937-1941

1. *The New Deal and Labor*

THE OVERWHELMING ENDORSEMENT of Roosevelt in 1936, followed by an almost equally strong one in 1940, did not mean that everybody loved F.D.R. Among those who did not, hatred was more bitter, vituperation more shrill, nasty rumors more prevalent, than against any President in our history—except possibly Lincoln. In most business and some professional circles it was the fashion never to mention his name—he was "That Man" or even "That Madman" in the White House. Nice old gentlemen wished he might drop dead or regretted that age and conscience prevented them from assassinating him. What reason was there for this virulence? The philosopher Alfred North Whitehead, who regarded Roosevelt as the greatest ruler since the Emperor Augustus, observed that similar things had been said in his youth about Gladstone, and for the same reason—that he was "a traitor to his class." If somebody like Bryan had been at the head of the New Deal it would have been understandable; but for a Hudson river patrician, a graduate of Groton and Harvard, to act that way, was abominable.

Big business and finance had deservedly lost status and popular respect since 1929, but blamed it on Roosevelt. And, worst of all, he had done his best to peg wages at trade-union levels. Almost every man of wealth had enough resources to tide him over any conceivable depression, but he wanted the downward spiral to hit rock bottom, smash the labor unions, and re-establish the free labor market of the previous century. Roosevelt's successful effort to prevent that was his unpardonable crime; but in the eyes of the country at large, his greatest achievement. A section of the National Industrial Recovery Act, the NRA of 1933, declared that employees had the right to collective bargaining through their own representatives, that there should be no interference, restraint, or coercion by employers in their organizing, that the "yellow dog contract" which required a worker as a condition of employment to join a company union or refrain from joining some other union, was no longer legal.

Under the impetus of the NRA, organized labor more than recovered its losses of the preceding decade, and by 1936 the A. F. of L. boasted a membership of 3.4 million. When employers who questioned the constitutionality of the NRA refused to be bound by its provisions or to accept the rulings of the Board, an epidemic of strikes and lockouts swept the country. Labor, certain of government support, presumed upon its new position and antagonized public opinion; industry, determined to recoup depression losses and unterrified by the New Deal, employed traditional weapons of strikebreakers, injunctions, and company unions. During 1934 recovery was delayed by a strike in the automobile industry, a nation-wide textile strike, and a general strike in San Francisco. All were unsuccessful, and the last two were smashed by the militia and by self-constituted vigilantes.

After the NRA had been declared unconstitutional by the Supreme Court, many of its labor provisions were re-enacted in the Wagner-Connery Act of 5 July 1935. This set up a federally appointed National Labor Relations Board, authorized to investigate complaints and issue "cease and desist" orders against "unfair practices" in labor relations. The Supreme Court sustained the constitutionality both of the Wagner-Connery Act and the NLRB. Chief Justice Hughes insisted that the connection between manufacturing and commerce was obvious and that the protection of the "right of employees to self-organization and freedom in the choice of representatives for collective bargaining" had an intimate relation with interstate commerce.

As one might have expected, the NLRB was bitterly hated and severely attacked by the great corporations and employers of labor, because it meant almost continuous government interposition between employer and employee. But the Board made an excellent record. In the five years ending January 1941, it handled some 33,000 cases involving over 7 million workers, and amicably disposed of more than 90 per cent of them. Of 3166 strikes certified to the Board, 2383 were settled peaceably. In case after case its findings were sustained by the Supreme Court. The NLRB now beat back all attempts to repeal its authority and curtail its powers, and, by the beginning of the third Roosevelt administration, the opposition was silenced if not converted.

An important development within the ranks of labor was the emergence in 1935 of the Congress of Industrial Organizations, the C.I.O., a secession from the A. F. of L. by workers impatient with Sam Gompers's cautious policy. Under the dynamic leadership of John L. Lewis of the United Mine Workers, the C.I.O. set out to unionize industries which had heretofore resisted, such as steel, automobile, textile, and public utilities. Union after union seceded from the A. F. of L. to the new organization; hundreds of thousands of unskilled and semi-skilled laborers signed up with the only union which appeared to have any interest in them; journalists and other "white collar" workers organized professional affiliates. By midsummer 1937 the C.I.O. had an estimated membership of four million. Heady with success, John L. Lewis called a series of strikes directed not toward improvement in hours and wages, but to secure the closed shop, and establish the C.I.O.'s exclusive right to represent workers in collective bargaining. He defended the new technique of the "sit-down" strike, taking possession of the premises and refusing to get out until demands had been granted. To this weapon many employers surrendered; United States Steel met the demands of the C.I.O. in March 1937. Others, notably General Motors and Republic Steel, challenged the legality of the sit-down and called upon the courts to rescue their property. The courts responded with injunctions, and when workers resisted the court orders, things erupted. The intervention of Governor Murphy of Michigan prevented widespread violence in the automobile industries of that state, but in May 1937 there was bitter strife in South Chicago, where police, defending the property of Goodyear Tire, killed ten people. Public opinion turned against the C.I.O. and the sit-down, and by midsummer 1937 it appeared that the new organization might forfeit many of its early gains.

In June 1938 Congress passed a bill drawn by Senator Black of Alabama, designed to put "a ceiling over hours and a floor under wages." This Fair Labor Standards Act had as an objective the "elimination of labor conditions detrimental to the maintenance of the minimum standards of living necessary for health, efficiency and well being of workers." It provided for an eventual maximum working week of forty hours, and minimum wage of forty cents an hour. The wage increase affected 700,000 workers, and the hours provision ultimately reached some 13 million people. President Roosevelt characterized the Fair Labor Standards Act as "the most far-reaching, far-sighted program for the benefit of workers ever adopted in this or any other country." Its constitutionality was challenged, but sustained in a unanimous opinion of the Supreme Court.

2. Canada in the Depression

Although the stock-market crash of October 1929 affected fewer people, proportionally, in Canada than in the United States, the Great Depression dug as deep or deeper in the Dominion as in the United States. As the Canadian historian A. R. M. Lower has put it, "revelry on the warm sand beaches of the 1920's was followed by the freezing rain of the 1930's, with its ghastly tale of unemployment. Only a continent as fat as North America could have stood such heating and such chilling."

Since the depression was world-wide, Canada, dependent on foreign trade, felt its effects very severely. Over one-third of her gross national product was derived from sale of products, mostly raw materials, abroad. Prices for newsprint, metals, and lumber tumbled to new lows; wheat fell from $1.60 a bushel in 1929 to 38 cents in late 1932, and the production from 567 million bushels in 1928 to 182 million in 1934. Industrial centers in Ontario, protected by the tariff, suffered from lack of consumer demand, and hundreds of thousands of workers were laid off. The Canadian National incurred deficits of over $60 million a year, and the bloated C.P.R. even passed dividends. The Maritimes suffered least because they were poor anyway; their mixed farming and fishing at least afforded them plenty to eat even when exports fell off. British Columbia, whose fishing and lumber interests depended on foreign demand, was badly beaten down. But the prairie wheat-growing provinces suffered most, since they lost not only their markets but their crops in two years of drought. Under the weight of cumulative disaster, the promising co-operative wheat pools established in 1923-24 simply died. And the traditional Canadian resource in hard times of emigrating to the United States was no longer available because there were no jobs across the border. Over 200,000 Canadians entered the United States in 1924; only 6000 in 1933.

The Conservatives won the general election of 1930, partly as a reaction against the high United States tariff, partly because Mackenzie King refused to take radical steps to remedy unemployment or support the tumbling price of wheat. The new Conservative leader Richard B. Bennett, who spent money lavishly in the campaign, now became prime minister. Bennett, descended from a colonial Connecticut family which moved to Nova Scotia before the American Revolution, was a robust, dynamic man who, after making a personal fortune from railroads and a paper mill, had served as minister of finance under Meighen. A natural conservative like Herbert Hoover, Bennett was forced by the Great Depression to favor measures as radical as Roosevelt's.

Owing to that steady increase of provincial powers of government at the expense of the Dominion, which we have already noted, the provinces, with comparatively weak resources, now had commitments for social welfare which they could no longer bear. Bennett's first attempt to redeem Conservative campaign promises to end the depression took the form of raising customs duties, in the hope of giving Canada bargaining power to break down the high tariffs of the United States, France, Italy, and—beginning in 1931—Great Britain. He did wrest concessions from the mother country after an imperial economic conference in 1932. The Dominion parliament also voted large sums for unemployment relief to be distributed by the provincial governments; and over a period of seven years it lent over $100 million to the prairie provinces.

Radical parties arose in the Canadian west, as in the United States, dedicated to ending the depression in one swoop. The Co-operative Commonwealth Federation (C.C.F.), led by the Reverend J. S. Woodsworth, resembled old Kansas Populism with a veneer of British Labour party philosophy. The other, the Social Credit party, was founded in Alberta by a school principal and head of a fundamentalist Bible institute named William Aberhardt. Believing that the basic trouble with Canadian society was inadequate distribution of purchasing power, this "funny money party," as opponents called it, advocated the federal government's paying every citizen a "social dividend" of $25 a month. Simple farmers who hadn't seen that much money for years were naturally impressed. Social Credit swept Alberta in 1935 but accomplished nothing because the Dominion government disallowed all provincial laws in the field of banking and currency.

Comparable to the United States Senate's Pecora investigation of banking and investment houses, was a Canadian royal commission on price spreads. Harry H. Stevens, Bennett's minister of trade and commerce, who earlier had uncovered the customs corruption of the 1920's, presided. This commission revealed startling cases of price manipulation and stock watering, wholesale evasion of wages and hours, shops charging $2.50 each for garments made in sweatshops at $1.50 a dozen, and similar abuses. They reported "that the corporate form of business not only gives freedom from legal liability but also facilitates the evasion of moral responsibility for inequitable and uneconomic practices." Bennett tried to suppress the report, but Stevens gave it out, and made speeches emphasizing some of the more reprehensible cases of exploitation. He was forced to resign, and started a small businessmen's party of his own.

Now, to the astonishment of all Canada, and the dismay of Republicans across the border who had been pointing with pride to the Bennett approach as the proper one to end the depression, the Premier suddenly came out with measures out-Rooseveling Roosevelt! Apparently he had been "sold" on the New Deal by his brother-in-law William D. Herridge, whom he had appointed Canadian ambassador at Washington. Herridge was an Ottawa lawyer of great charm, and an idealist who became a sort of honorary member of the Roosevelt "brain trust." With a general election already scheduled for 1935, Bennett rocked the country with a series of radio addresses declaring that the capitalist system must be reformed by measures "more comprehensive, more far-reaching than any scheme of reform which this country has ever known." Parliament then proceeded to enact "Bennett's New Deal"—minimum wages, 48-hour week in industry and a weekly day of rest, unemployment and social insurance; and set up commissions to regulate industry, enforce business standards, and market Canadian products.

It was too late for Bennett to be the F.D.R. of Canada. Personally he was overbearing and arrogant; his sudden conversion to radicalism alienated thousands of his own party, and failed to impress the others as sincere. Mackenzie King and the Liberals swept every province except British Columbia, which the Conservatives took, and Alberta, which Social Credit won. "Funny money" and the C.C.F. obtained 24 seats in the new Parliament of 1935, and the Conservatives only 40; but the Liberals won 179, biggest majority since Confederation. Bennett retired to England where possibly the conferring of a peerage by George V consoled him for most of his New Deal measures being declared unconstitutional by the judicial committee of the Privy Council.

Mackenzie King in April 1935 again became premier of Canada and remained in office for thirteen years, through two more general elections and the Second World War. This short, thick-set man, a confirmed bachelor with a mild and diffident air, no great orator, endowed with few attributes of leadership, was nevertheless a remarkably astute statesman. He had the "feel" of Canada's ambivalent position toward the United States and Great Britain, the peculiar relation between Ottawa and the provinces, and between French Canada and English Canada. Through a French deputy premier, Ernest Lapointe, he kept the habitants of Quebec in line; by various measures he placated the embattled farmers of the west. And the most important of Bennett's New Deal measures, the Unemployment and Social Insurance Act, was re-enacted in 1940 after a parliamentary amendment to the British North America Act of 1867 had overridden the Privy Council decision.

Mackenzie King and Franklin D. Roosevelt, who had known each other during King's United States career, now became warm personal friends, although King (says his biographer) "was too studious, spinsterish and precious for the lusty inner White House circle." President Roosevelt, now that Canada had abandoned high protection, reciprocated, and in an agreement concluded at Washington in November 1935, United States duties on some 200 Canadian products were lowered. Secretary Hull, a glutton for reciprocal trade agreements, built on this good start with a Britain-Canada-United States conference at Washington in 1937. Out of that came a tripartite trade agreement of 17 November 1938. This was a bold stroke at the tariffs that had enhanced the depression by placing national economics in watertight compartments. And at Kingston, Ontario, in August 1938, President Roosevelt promised "that the people of the United States will not stand idly by if domination of Canadian soil is threatened by any other Empire," a promise which King reciprocated shortly after. From the outbreak of war in Europe Roosevelt passed to King by letter or telephone everything he learned that might be of interest to Canada; and that close partnership was cemented during the war.

3. *New Deal for Indians and Negroes*

We left the American Indian of the West in the midst of his prolonged depression which followed the passage of the well-meaning Dawes Act of 1887.[1] That situation continued to within the third decade of the twentieth century. The general assumption behind the federal government's policy was an anticipated disappearance of the Indians as a separate and distinct race. Hence it was a good thing to help the process—not, of course, by the earlier crude methods of starvation, disease, and extermination, but by promoting the breakup of reservations into individually owned allotments. Land ownership, it was believed, would make the redskins responsible citizens and assimilate them to the American Way of life. The interior department speeded up this process through shortening by several years the time that an Indian had to occupy his allotment before receiving fee-simple title, and sell it. In one year 60 per cent of all Indians receiving titles to their allotments sold out, and most of them squandered the proceeds.

This does not, however, apply to the Five Civilized Tribes of Oklahoma. They managed to retain much of their own culture, while adapting themselves to that of the Anglo-Saxon American; and many became eminent. Will Rogers, Senator R. L. Owen, and Admiral Joseph J. ("Jocko") Clarke, a great carrier group commander in World War II, were Cherokee; Charles Curtis, Vice President under Hoover, was an Osage, and the list might be extended indefinitely by including artists, professional singers, and ballerinas.

The appointment of Albert B. Fall as secretary of the interior by President Harding boded ill for the poor Indian, now a victim marked for slaughter in that general assault on the public domain in the name of "development." Fall did not try to steal the Navajo oil lands, because by the time their leases came up for auction, he had been frightened by the Teapot Dome disclosures; but he sponsored a barefaced attempt to rob the Pueblo Indians of Arizona and New Mexico of a large proportion of their irrigated land. Since 1877 some 3000 white families had moved in on the Pueblo domain, either as squatters or by illegal purchase from individual Indians. In 1913 the Supreme Court of the United States invalidated these purchases. The white claimants then appealed for relief to Congress, which with Fall's approval drafted the so-called Bursum bill, throwing on the Indians the burden of proving ownership of their ancestral lands; failure to do so would vest title in the white squatter. This attempt at a wholesale steal caused the Pueblo Indians to act in concert for the first time since their great revolt of 1680. Forming an All Pueblo Council, they appealed to Congress and the public, and under the leadership

[1] See above, Chapter II.

of John Collier, a social-work director of California, not only defeated the Bursum bill but persuaded Congress to set up a fair procedure for determining ownership of the disputed property.

In an act of 1924 Congress conferred United States citizenship on all Indians born within the United States who did not already have it. This boon was received with considerable skepticism, especially as many states refused to let Indians vote—New Mexico and Arizona did not do so until 1948. What most Indians wanted was to be let alone on their diminished reservations, to live their own way. Reservation Indians, not taxed and not subject to the draft, in a sense were privileged, even if poor in goods. Most of them preferred to continue that way rather than be individual landowners with the duties that landowning imposed.

A New Deal for the Indians really began under President Coolidge when his secretary of the interior, Hubert Work, employed a private organization financed by John D. Rockefeller, Jr. to conduct a thorough investigation of the economic and social condition of reservation Indians. Their report, issued in 1928 and known by the name of the head investigator Lewis Meriam, declared, "An overwhelming majority of the Indians are poor, even extremely poor, and they are not adjusted to the . . . system of the dominant white civilization." It showed up the abuses of the allotment system, and recommended that it be abolished. It exposed the failure of the government's educational policy of placing Indian children in boarding schools where only English was spoken, and where they were supposed to learn the "three R's" and a trade. The boarding schools turned out to be regular Dotheboys Halls, where the children were overworked, undernourished (an average of 11 cents per day per capita being allowed for food), and taught very little of any use to them. Meriam urged replacement of these by day schools located within communities where their parents lived and, wherever possible, integrated with public school systems. It further declared that the Indian service should become "an efficient educational agency, devoting its main energies to the social and economic advancement of the Indians," so that they may either "be absorbed into the prevailing civilization" or "be fitted to live in the presence of that civilization" with "a minimum standard of health and decency."

The Meriam report made a deep impression. Before the Hoover administration ended, many of the boarding schools had been abolished in favor of day schools, and responsibility for health on the reservations had been transferred to the National Health Service. But Hoover's secretary of the interior was premature in predicting in 1931 that the Indian Service had "turned the corner" and would "work itself out of a job in 25 years."

For a radical change of policy, the redskins had to wait for the Roosevelt administration. Harold Ickes, the new secretary of the interior, appointed as commissioner of Indian affairs John Collier, the crusader who had helped the Pueblos. Under his aggressive leadership the administration embarked on a program of helping the Indians to stay Indian—strengthening tribal governments, fostering arts and crafts, and in general following the advice of ethnologists who believed that the Indians not only had a culture worth preserving but the right to preserve it. Congress, at the request of Ickes, passed the Indian Reorganization Act of 18 June 1934, embodying this concept and definitely repealing the allotment plan of 1887, which had reduced tribal holdings from 138 million to 48 million acres. It even provided for acquiring new land for the use of the Indian reservations which needed it. President Roosevelt accepted the thesis that the Indians were not headed for extinction; they must be helped to achieve a respected though distinctive status under the American flag. This was a return to Chief Justice Marshall's decisions in which he tried in vain to protect the Eastern Indians from the rapacity of frontiersmen and the roguery of politicians. Now the Democratic party, hostile to Indians and Negroes for a century, became the champion of both.

The American black probably suffered even more than whites from the Great Depression, but he benefited by the New Deal and made notable advances toward his goal of integration—the direct opposite to what most Indians wanted. Disaffection of Africans to the party of Abraham Lincoln started in 1928 when the Republicans began to build a "lily-white" organization in the South. President Roosevelt, on the contrary, gained a large following among the colored. Segregation in federal offices in Washington, which the three Republican Presidents had allowed to stand, was abolished. Roosevelt made a beginning of integrating racially the armed forces, and insisted that in every industry, defense or otherwise, set up under the New Deal, blacks should receive an equal chance of employment. He appointed many to office; and in almost every new commission and bureau there were one or more black advisers on race relations. Mrs. Roosevelt was close to Mrs. Mary Bethune, head of the National Council of Negro Women. Secretary Ickes, who had been president of the Chicago branch of the National Association for the Advancement of Colored People (NAACP), was particularly assiduous in finding posts for qualified blacks; in 1946 there were four times the number of black federal employees as in 1933. Blacks benefited equally from New Deal projects like the AAA, the TVA, and the CCC, and the housing and other welfare programs. Even a few of the labor unions which formerly had rigidly excluded blacks from membership, now opened their doors.

Throughout this period the Communist party was playing for the blacks, with the attractive bait of setting up an all-black state in the South. James W. Ford, a Negro, received second place on their presidential ticket. But the vast majority of colored citizens of the United States merely shifted their allegiance from the Republican to the Democratic Party.

Whilst the Roosevelt administration favored integration of blacks in federal activities, it did not attempt the colossal task of forcing it on Southern states and committees, or of putting blacks on their electoral rolls. Even in so comparatively liberal a Southern city as Richmond, blacks were not allowed to use the public libraries until 1947. Undoubtedly the black made great progress toward political and economic equality between 1933 and 1945; but at the latter date he was still very far from his—or his leaders'—goal.

4. Conclusion to the New Deal

With the farm and labor legislation of 1938, the domestic program of the New Deal was rounded out. Not all the cards had been dealt, but the nature of the game was fairly well established. So, what was really accomplished?

First, the relief of distress and the rise of employment. There was a recession in 1937 and unemployment again rose above 10 million the next year; but from that time on, with the help of war orders after 1939, it dropped almost to nothing. Wages and prices remained steady.

Second, more had been done for the physical rehabilitation of the country, and to stop the waste of natural resources, than in any similar period. The TVA, the big new dams, reforestation to halt the spread of the dust bowl, and the new national parks, reversed that earlier trend of despoiling natural resources.

Third, the thesis that the federal government is ultimately responsible for the people's welfare, employment, and security, became generally accepted. This principle, implicit in Wilson's New Freedom, received wide and general application only in the New Deal. It began with relief to the unemployed, entered the domains of agriculture and labor, and established elaborate programs of rural rehabilitation. As proof of the welfare principle's general acceptance, the Republicans adopted it from

1940 on, their quarrel being no longer with the welfare state as such but with the haphazard and wasteful way in which it was administered by the Democrats. That charge in a great measure is true; but, considering the pressing emergency and the proliferation of new boards, commissions, and administrative agencies, waste and misspent efforts were inevitable.

Fourth, Roosevelt reasserted the presidential leadership which had been forfeited by his three predecessors and promoted the growth of federal power which had halted since the First World War. Yet, despite all the hullabaloo attributing to him dictatorship, fascism, communism, and the like, he consistently acted within the framework of the Constitution. When the Supreme Court declared a measure like NRA unconstitutional, the President obeyed and the blue eagle died. This was very different from President Jackson's "Marshall has made his decision, now let him execute it!" And Roosevelt's unsuccessful attempt to "pack" the Supreme Court was far less radical than Jefferson's plan to destroy it by impeachment.

Fifth, economic and social planning by the federal government became an established fact. American corporations such as General Motors and United States Steel had long planned operations for years ahead, but Americans were congenitally suspicious of governmental planning, and Roosevelt's National Resources Planning Board aroused more frenzied opposition from senators such as Taft, Tydings, and Byrd, than anything else in the New Deal. They appear to have suspected Roosevelt of attempting to put over a Russian-style "five-year plan." In the course of the 1940's, under the stress of a war that required intelligent foresight if it were to be won, planning ceased to be a dirty word and became a necessity in modern administration.

Of basic importance in the political field was a growing appreciation of the nature and function of the state. Laissez-faire, not without gallant rear-guard actions, gave way to a realization that the state was a natural medium for man's self-expression, like organized religion, fraternal orders, and social clubs. It became clear—though far from indisputably so—that there was no inherent conflict between *imperium* and *libertas,* authority and freedom. The flexibility of the Federal Constitution was spectacularly vindicated. James Madison in *The Federalist* had predicted that only a federal government over a large area could reconcile conflicting economic interests and subordinate private to public welfare. In spite of the vastly increasing size and complexity of the United States, it now appeared that Madison was right.

Besides temporary expedients such as the employment of

youth in CCC camps, the organizing of "white collar" projects and public works relief, the New Deal achieved many things of permanent benefit. Such were the conservation program, including TVA; the regulation of the stock market, the rural electrification program, and the enhanced status of union labor. This expansion of governmental functions and regulation inevitably affected the economic life of the nation. But the movement left so much scope to private enterprise that, in the end, the entire economy was strengthened. The New Deal did more to shore up and buttress a capitalist system tottering under the blows of depression, than it did to weaken or destroy it. The American system came dangerously near collapse in 1932–33, with over 12 million unemployed. Could it have stood 20 million, 30 million unemployed? Huey Long, for one, thought not; he truculently told the Senate that he might be heading a mob to storm the capitol and hang his fellow senators! Such things have happened in many countries; and there was no assurance that it could not happen here, if the people lost faith in their government.

Franklin D. Roosevelt's administration saved twentieth-century American capitalism by purging it of gross abuses and forcing an accommodation to the larger public interest. This historian, for one, believes him to have been the most effective American conservative since Alexander Hamilton, as well as the most successful democrat since Lincoln. As Roosevelt remarked in a fireside chat of 1938, democracy had disappeared in certain European nations because their governments said, "We can do nothing for you." But "We in America know that our democratic institutions can be preserved and made to work." And to this task of providing security without impairing fundamental liberties, Roosevelt devoted his major peacetime energies.

"The only sure bulwark of continuing liberty," Roosevelt further observed, "is a government strong enough to protect the interests of the people, and a people strong enough and well enough informed to maintain its sovereign control over its government." In 1940, when it became doubtful whether liberty or democracy could survive overt attempts by totalitarian states to conquer the world, it was of utmost importance to mankind that the American democracy weathered the Great Depression and emerged strong and courageous; that the American people were refreshed in their democratic faith, determined to defend it at home and to fight for it abroad. Once more the United States, in Turgot's phrase, was "the hope of the human race."

5. War in Europe and Asia

Had any pollster been looking for one idea on which the vast majority of the American people agreed, when under the New Deal experiment they agreed on nothing else, it would have been that if Europe were so wicked or stupid as to start another war, America would resolutely stay out. On this point even communists agreed with the Liberty League. Roosevelt reflected this feeling by failing even to mention foreign relations in his second inaugural address, delivered on 20 January 1937. Yet the collective security which the League of Nations supposedly had established was already giving way to uninhibited aggression by dictators or oligarchies. Hitler in 1935 denounced the German disarmament clauses in the Treaty of Versailles, one year later he occupied the Rhineland, and nobody did anything about it. Toward Italy, already at war with Ethiopia, the League of Nations applied partial economic sanctions, but by May 1936 the indestructible Emperor Haile Selassie was in exile and his country annexed to Italy. That summer, General Franco began a civil war in Spain; in the fall Hitler and Mussolini established the "Rome-Berlin Axis." And before Roosevelt's second inauguration, Japan was deeply engaged in undeclared war with China. Thus there were plenty of warnings of the next international debacle, had Roosevelt cared to allude to them. He doubtless refrained from doing so because anything he might have said would have created violent dissension among American groups and parties on whom he depended to continue his domestic program.

Of all these evil portents, the most sinister was the rise of Adolf Hitler. The hold of that uneducated paranoiac over the German people, with their long tradition of culture and decency (to which they have since returned), is a phenomenon which even the Germans themselves find hard to explain. In part, no doubt, it was due to the poverty and disorganization of Germany after her defeat in World War I; but other nations, notably Austria and Poland, had suffered even more than Germany, and made little trouble. Hitler rose on a tide of resentment over the Treaty of Versailles; but the victors had redressed most of the severities imposed by that treaty, and (with the aid of American loans) had relieved Germany from the burden of war reparations before Hitler reached power. There was much talk of *Lebensraum,* room for expansion; but the Netherlands and Scandinavia suffered similar pressure without trying to wreck the European world. Probably the conclusion that Franklin D. Roosevelt reached is the right one. Hitler, a frustrated fanatic, based his Nazi party on the residuary hatred, barbarism, and cruelty inherent in modern society. He hated the Jews, hated democracy, hated the Christian religion in which he was reared, hated all foreigners, and in general everything that was good, true, or beautiful. For brutality, sadistic cruelty, and villainy he may be compared only with Genghis Khan in ancient days, or to Stalin in ours. As Winston Churchill wrote, Hitler "called from the depths of defeat the dark and savage furies latent in the most numerous, most serviceable, ruthless, contradictory, and ill-starred race in Europe."

Never since Jefferson's time had America, and never in recorded history had England, been in so pacifist a mood as in 1933–39; Hitler was canny enough to play upon this. He pronounced President Roosevelt's speech of 16 May 1933, expressing American hopes for peace and disarmament, a "ray of comfort." Hitler and the warlords of Japan secretly worked for war but publicly advocated peace, and although this fooled the democracies, no hypocrisy was intended. For their concept of peace was as different from ours as Soviet "democracy" is from real democracy. For Hitler, peace meant getting all he wanted for Germany; in Japan, it meant a "feudal peace" of all eastern Asia under Japanese hegemony.

The Spanish civil war, exceedingly cruel and bloody, was won by General Franco early in 1939, and a fascist-type dictatorship set up. It had somewhat the same relation to World War II as "bleeding Kansas" to the American Civil War. Ernest Hemingway, who volunteered to fight for the republican cause, recalled in his novel *For Whom the Bell Tolls* the solemn words of John Donne. The bell in Spain tolled not only for that unhappy country; *"It tolls for thee."*

We may now conclude what Winston Churchill called "the long, dismal, drawling tides of drift and surrender, of wrong measurements and feeble impulses." Unknown to anyone but the participants, Hitler at a meeting with his foreign minister and his top generals, announced his plans for conquest on 5 November 1937. His object, he said, was to acquire new territory for Germany in Europe's heartland. This could only be done by force. It was the Fuehrer's unalterable resolve to apply force by 1943 if the opportunity did not occur sooner, as he expected it would. The generals and the foreign minister who objected were dismissed.

The bell tolled for Austria in March 1938, when Hitler invaded that hapless remnant of the Hapsburg empire and annexed it to Germany; nobody stopped him. The next victim was Czechoslovakia. That secession state from the old Austro-Hungarian Empire had prospered since 1920 under the rule of able statesmen such as Masaryk and Beneš. But in its western part, the Sudeten Germans, once the ruling class under Austrian domination, regarded the Slavic Czechs and Slovaks with hatred and contempt, and hailed Hitler as the German savior who would put them in the saddle again. Czechoslovakia had a strong, well-trained army and valuable munitions works which would have been a danger to Hitler when he attacked France and Russia, as he intended to do. In May 1938 he decided to move on this country and divide or annex it. Neville Chamberlain, the British prime minister, thrice visited Hitler in September 1938, and was completely deceived by the Fuehrer's promise that he wanted only a fringe of the German-speaking part. In the final meeting at Munich on 28–29 September, Chamberlain, Mussolini, and French premier Daladier agreed to Hitler's terms; and Chamberlain returned to England, announcing cheerily "peace in our time."

In the one year 1938 Hitler had annexed and brought under his absolute rule 6.7 million Austrians and 3.5 million Sudeten Germans. And these were not annexations in the traditional sense, giving full rights to the annexed people, and at least a year's time for objectors to sell out and leave. The Czechs or Austrians who did not relish joining the German Reich had to flee, or be liquidated; the Jews were liquidated anyway.

Hitler was not yet appeased. In March 1939, again breaking solemn promises, he moved his army into Prague, divided the rest of Czechoslovakia into two German satellite states, and again cynically announced that he now had all he wanted. Mussolini followed suit by invading and seizing Albania.

These sorry episodes made Chamberlain and his inevitable umbrella figures of contempt, and "appeasement" a dirty word in the political vocabulary.

On the other side of the world the Japanese militarists, resurrecting from their dim and distant past the slogan *Hakko ichiu* —"bringing the eight corners of the world under one roof" —were riding high. Their movement had many points of resemblance to Hitler's Nazism. It entertained the same enticing ambition of wide dominion; in this instance, an empire of East Asia. Dissolving China offered a good start toward eventually bringing all Asiatic colonies or dependencies of Europe and America—India, Burma, Indonesia, Indochina, the Philippines—under Japanese hegemony. Emperor Hirohito deplored these tendencies, but was helpless before a movement that invoked his name and used his moral authority.

After the "China incident" of 7 July 1937 inaugurated un-

declared war between Japan and China, the American government concentrated on diplomatic efforts to "bring Japan to her
senses" and restore peace in the Far East. This was completely
ineffectual, and the Japanese militarists made a concerted
effort to drive American and European missionary, educational,
medical, and cultural activities out of China, as the Chinese
communists have since done. American churches, hospitals,
schools, and colleges were bombed despite flag markings on
their roofs; American missionaries and their families were
killed; there were so many "accidents" of this sort that a cynic
reported the most dangerous spot in an air raid to be an American mission. A small river gunboat of the navy's Yangtze
river patrol, U.S.S. *Panay*, was "accidentally" bombed and
sunk by Japanese planes on 12 December 1937. When the
Japanese government apologized and offered to pay indemnity
to the victims, a sigh of relief passed over the length and
breadth of America. In a Gallup poll conducted during the
second week of January 1938, 70 per cent of the American
voters who were interviewed and had an opinion on the subject, favored complete withdrawal from China—Asiatic Fleet,
marines, missionaries, medical missions, and all.

Well, why not? the reader may ask, since that is what Mao
Tse-tung's government has forced us to do in the end. Would
not a China under Japanese rule have been better for the world
than a Red China? Possibly; for the end is not yet in sight. But
no responsible American statesman would contemplate going
back on our plighted word to China, and treating her as the
European powers had treated Czechoslovakia. And they knew
from many historical examples, recent and remote, that mili-
tarist cliques are never satisfied, and that nothing short of the
control of all Asia and the Pacific Ocean would satisfy the
Japanese. We had to risk a war in the 1940's rather than take
on an infinitely stronger enemy later.

In 1939 the Japanese captured Shanghai and proceeded to
make life intolerable for Americans and Europeans in the international settlement. President Roosevelt now contemplated
the imposition of economic sanctions on Japan to make her
leaders stop, look, and listen. His first step, on 26 July 1939, was
to denounce the existing treaty of commerce with Japan. This
received almost unanimous approval, even from isolationists.
There matters stood in the Far East when war broke out in
Europe in September 1939.

That bell also tolled for the United States, but its somber
notes fell dim and muffled on American ears. To threats of the
war lords the average American was indifferent. He thought
of Europe as decadent, given to secret diplomacy, class con-

flict, and evasion of debts. He was sorry for "John Chinaman" and detested the "Japs," but he felt that if 450 million Chinese could not defend themselves against 73 million Japanese there was nothing he should or could do about it. Isolationism was not so much a reasoned principle as an instinctive belief in our safety behind ocean barriers. The world was indeed out of joint, but what obligation had we to set it right?

Perversely the American people and their Congress read awry the lessons of the First World War. First, it had been a mistake for us to enter the war, which might otherwise have ended in a draw. Second, the war was caused by competitive armaments; hence the Washington treaty of 1922 and later agreements on naval limitation. Third, the war was caused by fear, so let everyone agree, "no more war"; hence the Kellogg-Briand pact to outlaw war. Fourth, according to Senator Nye's investigation, it was caused by bankers and munitions manufacturers who made money out of war; so if we took all the profit out of war, peace could be maintained. Fifth, it was caused by the United States insisting on neutral rights; so if we renounced neutral rights we could keep out of any future war. All methods were tried—peace by isolation, peace by arms limitation, peace by incantation; and, in the Roosevelt administration, peace by negation, which was expected to dispose of the last two causes. The neutrality acts passed by Congress between 1935 and 1939, only half approved by the President but signed by him, forbade the sale or transport of arms and munitions to a belligerent, private loans to a belligerent, or the entry of American ships into war zones. Everyone ignored Woodrow Wilson's warning that the only way to prevent American involvement in another world war was to prevent it from starting. Typical of our military preparedness is the story of the B-17, the heavy bomber of the forthcoming war: the Army Air Force was allowed to develop it under the subterfuge that it was needed for coast defense against hostile fleets; and only 13 were completed when war began in Europe.

As the poet Edna St. Vincent Millay wrote, "Longing to wed with Peace, what did we do?—Sketched her a fortress on a paper pad."

Law could have gone no further than the neutrality acts did to "keep us out of war"; but as President Roosevelt later observed, "Our arms embargo played right into the hands of the aggressor nations." Germany, Japan, and to a less degree Italy, were feverishly preparing for land, sea, and air warfare; England, France, and Russia were barely beginning to do so; and American neutrality legislation assured the Axis that when they got ready to strike, their victims would be shut off from obtaining implements of war from America.

Roosevelt was watching with growing concern the menaces to peace in Europe and Asia. Speaking in Chicago shortly after the beginning of the "China incident" in 1937, he called for a quarantine against aggressor nations. If lawlessness and violence rage unrestrained, he warned, "Let no one imagine that America will escape, that America may expect mercy, that this Western Hemisphere will not be attacked." These prophetic words awakened no popular response, and in many quarters the President was denounced as a warmonger. In January 1938 he proposed to the British government a conference of leading powers in Washington to discuss the underlying causes of turmoil in Europe. Chamberlain brushed him off; he preferred the appeasement approach to Hitler, and felt that Japan's doings in China did not concern Britain. In September the President reminded all signatory nations of their "outlawry of war" under the Kellogg-Briand pact, and appealed for arbitration of the Sudeten question. Nobody replied. On 14 April 1939 he sent a personal message to Hitler and Mussolini asking them to promise not to attack about twenty small countries in Europe during the next ten years. Hitler made an insulting reply, and then bullied some of the countries (which he was about to gobble up) into assuring Roosevelt that they had no cause to fear good neighbor Germany. Mussolini at first refused to read the message, then sneered at it before his underlings as "a result of infantile paralysis."

Hitler, far from sated with Czechoslovakia, in 1939 turned his hungry glare on Poland, with which he had recently signed a non-aggression pact. The "Polish corridor" to the Baltic was the grievance. Poland allowed German trains and cars free transit across the corridor; but to Hitler this was a degrading situation. In North American terms it was as if the United States felt insulted because trains from Buffalo to Detroit crossed the Ontario peninsula, and demanded that Canada cede her territory up to and including Toronto.

The British and French governments, now cured of their delusions about Hitler, reversed their policy and (31 March) made too late the rash move of guaranteeing against aggression Poland and Rumania, which they were incapable of helping. The guarantee would have made sense if English and French diplomacy had made a partner of Russia, as Stalin was ready to do; but Chamberlain's government fiddled, Poland quibbled, and Stalin made a right-about-face. On 24 August 1939, the Western world was stupefied by the news that Stalin and Hitler, who had been violently abusing each other for five years, had shaken hands in a non-aggression pact. The world did not yet know the secret clauses, in which they also agreed to partition Poland.

After his usual preparatory propaganda of fake frontier incidents, Hitler launched his attack on Poland on 1 September 1939. Two days later, Great Britain and France declared war on Germany. The British dominions followed suit shortly. World War II was on.

′ For two dreadful weeks the German mechanized army smashed through Poland in a "Blitzkrieg" without parallel in earlier warfare, while bombing planes reduced Polish towns and villages to rubble. The Russians moved in from the east, taking over what they held to be Russian Poland. Attacked from both sides by overwhelming force, with no military aid from anyone, Poland was conquered before the end of September. Germany and Russia divided the country between them. At comparatively slight cost Hitler had acquired 21 million more subjects, together with vast agricultural and industrial resources.

In the west, Germany stood securely behind the newly completed Siegfried line, while Britain and France, the one unable and the other unwilling to take the offensive, relied upon an imperfect blockade to bring her to terms. Hitler refrained from a western offensive because he hoped to buy peace with the sacrifice of Poland. There ensued a period of inaction which Senator Borah called the "phony war," and which Churchill named "the winter of illusion." It was like the "all quiet along the Potomac" period in the American Civil War. Any illusions about Russia were dispelled when Stalin picked a quarrel with his democratic neighbor Finland, and in March 1940 forced her to yield large slices of territory. Shortly after, Stalin annexed the three other Baltic states (Estonia, Latvia, Lithuania) and recovered Bessarabia and the Bukovina from Romania; thus completing, as he thought, a barrier defense against a possible change of policy by Hitler.

Early in April 1940, the phony war came to a dramatic end. Without warning Germany moved into Denmark, a nation with which Hitler had recently concluded a non-aggression pact, and then into Norway. This attack was well planned, and the co-operation of the Norse traitor Quisling almost resulted in that government's being taken over. The king escaped to England, and the British tried to help; but their efforts were "too little and too late"; within less than two months they had been driven out, and Hitler controlled Norway.

One month after the invasion of Scandinavia came the blow in the West. Here the French army, already weakened by communist and fascist propaganda, trusted to a series of modern forts, called the Maginot line after its designer. But the Maginot line ended at the frontier of Belgium, whose king was so scrupulously neutral and so eager to keep out of war that he neglected even rudimentary defense. On 10 May the German army invaded Belgium and neutral Holland, while the *Luftwaffe*, the German air force, rained death on those countries and on northeastern France. In five days the Netherlands were conquered, Rotterdam laid in ruins by air assault. Already the German Panzer (armored) divisions, slipping around the end of the Maginot line, had crashed through the Ardennes Forest, enveloped a French army, and smashed ahead toward the channel ports. On 21 May the Germans reached the English Channel, cutting off the British expeditionary force which had been rushed to the aid of Belgium and France. A week later Belgium surrendered, and the British were left to their fate. Their evacuation has well been called "the miracle of Dunkerque." Every available warship, yacht, power boat, fisherman, barge, and tug, was pressed into service; and with a suicide division holding the front and the Royal Air Force screening, 338,000 men were transported to England. But they did not take their weapons, and evacuations do not win wars.

The German army now swung south, and in two weeks cut the French army to pieces. On 10 June 1940 Mussolini, with his jackal instinct to be in at the kill, declared war on France. Five days later Paris fell, and Premier Reynaud, in desperation, appealed to Roosevelt for "clouds of planes." But Roosevelt could give only sympathy, and a hastily formed French government under the aged Marshal Pétain sued for peace. Hitler exacted a savage price. He occupied half of France, leaving the southern part to be ruled, from Vichy, by Pétain and Laval, who were forced to collaborate with the victors, even to recruit workers for German war industry and to deliver French Jews to torture and death. In one month Hitler's mechanized armies had done what the Kaiser's forces had been unable to accomplish in four years.

Now England stood alone. "We have just one more battle to win," said Hitler's propaganda minister Goebbels to cheering thousands; but Hitler was unprepared with landing craft and equipment to launch a massive amphibious operation. While these instruments were being built and assembled in northern France, the Luftwaffe under Marshal Goering tried to soften up England by bombing. In September 1940 this air assault rose to a furious crescendo. Cities like London, Coventry, and Birmingham suffered massive destruction; civilian casualties ran into the tens of thousands. England was saved by her scientists, such as Watson-Watt and Tizard, who developed radar and persuaded the government to set up a chain of radar warning posts about southern and eastern England; and by the gallantry of her Spitfire and Hurricane fighter pilots, who exacted an insupportable toll of the invaders. By October the German air force had to acknowledge that it had failed.

In this hour of mortal peril England found her soul, under the inspiration of a great leader. The reins of government, on 11 May 1940, had passed from the faltering hands of Chamberlain into the iron grip of Winston Churchill, who announced, when he took office, that he had nought to offer his country but "blood, toil, tears, and sweat." Undismayed by disaster, he confronted life with antique courage, and infused that courage into freedom-loving peoples everywhere. At the threat of invasion, he thus hurled defiance at Germany:

> We shall not flag or fail, we shall go on to the end, we shall fight in France, we shall fight on the seas and oceans . . . we shall fight on the landing grounds, we shall fight in the fields and in the streets, we shall fight in the hills; we shall never surrender. And even if . . . this island . . . were subjugated and starving, then our Empire beyond the seas, armed and guarded by the British Fleet, would carry on the struggle, until, in God's good time, the new world, with all its power and might, steps forth to the rescue and liberation of the old.

Would America respond? President Roosevelt was among the first to do so. In a speech to the graduating class of the University of Virginia, on 10 June 1940, he announced, "We will extend to the opponents of force the material resources of this nation; and, at the same time . . . speed up the use of these resources in order that we . . . in the Americas may have equipment and training equal to the task of any emergency."

6. *"Short of War"* to Pearl Harbor

Americans were not neutral in thought to this war, as Wilson had asked them to be in the earlier one. An overwhelming majority desired the defeat of Hitler and his satellites, but also wanted to keep out of the war. One concession, however, was wrung from a reluctant Congress—a modification of neutrality legislation which permitted belligerents to obtain war materials from this country on a "cash and carry" basis. Britain and France promptly took advantage of the new law by placing large orders with American manufacturers, but it would be months or years before tanks began to roll off assembly lines and planes out of hangars in sufficient quantity to match Germany.

The fall of France raised the distinct possibility of the fall of England too, bringing Hitler's forces within striking distance of America. Another shock was the Tripartite Pact of 27 September 1940, in which Japan formally joined the European Axis. This pact stipulated that if any one of the three got into war with the United States the other two would pitch in. For the United States Navy this posed the problem of fighting a two-ocean war with a smaller than one-ocean fleet.

President Roosevelt had a political calculating machine in his head, an intricate instrument in which Gallup polls, the strength of armed forces, and the probability of England's survival; the personalities of governors, senators, and congressmen, and of Mussolini, Hitler, Churchill, Chiang, and General Tojo the Japanese premier; the Irish, German, Italian, and Jewish votes in the approaching presidential election; the "Help the Allies" people and the "America Firsters," were combined with fine points of political maneuvering. The fall of France, fed into the F.D.R. calculating machine, caused wheels to whir and gears to click with dynamic intensity. Out came a solution: the "short of war" policy (1) to help keep England fighting in Europe (2) to gain time for American rearmament; and (3) to restrain Japan by diplomacy and naval "deterrence." Whether Roosevelt really believed that this policy would "keep us out of war" is debatable. But he had to assume that it would, until after the presidential election of 1940 in which he flouted tradition by running for a third term, and until events abroad convinced the American people that war was their only alternative to a shameful and ultimately disastrous appeasement.

In any case, an essential and most beneficial part of the "short of war" policy was to build up the navy. On 14 June 1940, the day that Hitler took Paris, President Roosevelt signed a naval expansion bill that had been under discussion for months. Three days later Admiral Stark, Chief of Naval Operations, asked Congress for $4 billion more to begin building a "two-ocean navy," and got it. The navy then had about 1.2 million tons of combatant shipping; this bill authorized a more than double increase. But, as Admiral Stark said, "Dollars cannot buy yesterday." For two years at least the Americas would be very vulnerable in the event of a German victory.

On 15 June 1940, the day after approving the first of these new navy bills, President Roosevelt appointed a group of eminent civilian scientists members of a new National Defense Research Committee. Vannevar Bush, president of the Carnegie

Institution of Washington, was the chairman. From this N.D.R.C. stemmed most of the scientific research done for the armed forces during the war.

The President was ready for bolder steps, and announced them frankly. The stories built up by anti-Roosevelt fanatics like Clare Boothe Luce ("He *lied* us into war") have no foundation in fact. His radio fireside chat of 26 May 1940, his Charlottesville speech of 10 June which we have already quoted, gave fair notice that he was no longer neutral, merely non-belligerent. At the same time (June 1940), in order to make his administration bipartisan, he replaced the colorless war and navy secretaries in his cabinet with two prominent Republicans—seventy-two-year-old Henry L. Stimson, who had been secretary of war under Taft and of state under Hoover, and Frank Knox, vice-presidential candidate in 1936. By the end of 1940 there were also new and stronger Democrats in the cabinet: Frank Walker replaced Jim Farley as postmaster general; Robert H. Jackson came in as attorney general, Jesse Jones as secretary of commerce.

In pursuance of the new presidential policy came a series of bold moves. The Act of Havana, passed at a Pan American meeting in July 1940, promised protection to all America, and gave notice that any transfer of Europe's American colonies to Hitler would be resisted. In August Roosevelt conferred with Mackenzie King and concluded a United States-Canada defense pact which gave each country free use of the other's naval facilities. In mid-September Congress passed the first peacetime conscription in our history—the Burke-Wadsworth Act, providing for registration of all men between the ages of 21 and 35, and the induction into the armed services of 800,000 draftees. That month the President announced an arrangement whereby the United States transferred to Britain fifty destroyers which had been "in mothballs" for twenty years, and received in return 99-year leases on naval and air bases in the British West Indies, Argentia (Newfoundland), and Bermuda. This, said the President, was "an epochal and far-reaching act of preparation for continental defense in the face of grave danger."

It was charged, both in this country and by the Axis powers, that these measures were unneutral, which indeed they were; openly so. Attorney General Jackson advised the President that Hitler could no longer invoke the protection of international law, after successively violating the neutrality of Denmark, Norway, Belgium, and Holland. But this did not lessen our respect for the neutrality of other nations.

Although the destroyer-bases deal met with general approval, Roosevelt's foreign policy sharply divided American opinion.

Critics charged that it was dragging the United States inexorably into an "imperialistic" war with which we had no legitimate concern; supporters insisted that only by helping Britain and France to defeat Hitler could we save democracy from destruction and ourselves from ultimate attack. The issue was fought out in the halls of Congress, in the press, over the radio, on public platforms, in bars, offices, and homes. Party lines were shattered, labor organizations split, business relations strained, old friendships broken. William Allen White's Committee to Defend America by Aiding the Allies organized branches in a thousand towns, sent out hundreds of speakers and millions of letters and pamphlets to arouse the nation to its danger. The opposition organization, the America First Committee, top-billing Charles Lindbergh, paraded, picketed, protested, and preached an amalgam of isolationism and pacifism, with overtones of anti-Semitism; and it came out after the war that the "America Firsters" had accepted financial support from Germany. Newspapers like the New York *Times* and *Herald-Tribune* ranged themselves behind the presidential policy, while the Chicago *Tribune* found itself in a congenial alliance with Hearst ringing an alarm-bell against "being dragged into war to save England."

In the midst of this debate came the presidential election. The Republican party, having clung to the unheroic position of isolationism, stood pat. Its three leading contenders for the presidential nomination, Senators Robert Taft of Ohio and Arthur Vandenberg of Michigan and District Attorney Thomas Dewey of New York, were isolationists in varying degree. In the meantime, a group of amateur politicians had been building up a political maverick, Wendell Willkie, a Wall Street lawyer and counsel for the big utilities. Willkie was critical of the New Deal, not of its basic principles but of its inefficiency, and a frank proponent of aid to the Allies. His sincerity and personal charm appealed to an electorate sick of political clap-trap, and inspired a devotion such as no other Republican enjoyed between "Teddy" and "Ike." When the Republican convention met at Philadelphia in June, seasoned politicians found that they could not hold the rising tide of Willkie sentiment. On the sixth ballot he was nominated.

The Democrats were in a quandary. The President had never been more popular, or his leadership more essential than in this crisis. Democratic state conventions called for his renomination. But would he accept the nomination for a third term, and would the American people acquiesce in this challenge to the sacrosanct two-term tradition? Roosevelt himself maintained an inscrutable silence. The Democratic convention, without guidance, renominated him on the first ballot. Roosevelt replied by radio that "in the face of the danger which confronts our time" he had no right to refuse. But there is no doubt that F.D.R. loved power and gladly accepted this responsibility.

Two leading Democrats were very sore about this. Jim Farley, who had even fewer qualifications for the high office than Cal Coolidge, thought he should have been nominated. Vice President Garner was persuaded to decline a third term as Vice President in the expectation he would be promoted, but the convention passed him over for both places and gave Henry Wallace the lesser one.

The campaign that followed lacked real issues, since Willkie supported the President's "short of war" measures, and most of the New Deal. It was not clear that Willkie could do better what Roosevelt was doing well, and he labored under the handicap of the support of odd-balls such as the Reverends Gerald Smith and Charles Coughlin. Although many Southern politicians disliked the New Deal because it was doing so much for the blacks, the South in general, with its gallant tradition, applauded the President's determination to help the Allies; and, ahead of any other part of the country, prepared mentally for the war that the nation had to fight.

In the November election Roosevelt received 449 electoral votes, Willkie only 82. Apart from Maine and Vermont, the Republicans carried only the isolationist heartland of the midwest, but Willkie received 45 per cent of the popular vote. The Socialist, Communist, and other splinter parties only received one-half of one per cent. The two-term tradition had been shattered; it required Amendment XXII to the Constitution, the Republicans' posthumous revenge on F.D.R., to put it together again.

The President naturally interpreted re-election as an endorsement of his foreign as well as his domestic policies. When Congress met early in January 1941 he appealed for support of nations who were fighting in defense of what he called the Four Freedoms—freedom of speech, freedom of religion, freedom from want, freedom from fear. Four days later he submitted a program designed to circumvent existing limitations of the neutrality legislation and make American war materials immediately available to the Allies. This was the Lend-Lease Act, which authorized the President to "sell, transfer, exchange, lease, lend" any defense articles "to the government of any country whose defense the President deems vital to the defense of the United States," and made available to such nations the facilities of American shipyards. This touched off a prolonged and bitter debate which reached its nadir in Senator Burton K. Wheeler's statement that Lend-Lease "will plow under every fourth American boy." After the isolationists had had their say, administration supporters passed the bill by substantial majorities and it became law 11 March 1941. Lend-Lease made the United States the "arsenal of democracy," as F.D.R. said. Under its provisions America not only provided the enemies of the Axis with $50 billion in arms, foodstuffs, and services, but geared her own production to war needs and officially abandoned any pretense at neutrality. And Lend-Lease had the advantage of preventing another postwar controversy over debts.

Events now moved rapidly. A few weeks after the passage of Lend-Lease the United States seized all Axis shipping in American ports. In April 1941 it took Greenland under protection and announced that the navy would patrol the sea lanes in defense zones. In May came the transfer of 50 oil tankers to Britain, and, after the sinking of an American freighter by a U-boat, the proclamation of an "unlimited national emergency." In June the United States froze all Axis assets and closed the consulates. On 24 June the President announced that Lend-Lease would be extended to a new ally—Russia. For on 22 June Hitler, in one of the astounding about-faces common to dictators, broke his 1939 pact and set out to conquer that vast country. It was one of those colossal mistakes in strategy which undid all earlier faults by England and France. Now they had an ally capable of pinning down the bulk of the German army on an eastern front.

An administration bill to extend conscription for the duration of the emergency, and keep under the colors the national guard regiments then receiving training, passed the House only by a majority of one vote. Many Congressmen who voted to "send the boys home" were really for having them stay but feared the wrath of their constituents. Republicans in the House voted 133 to 21 against this selective service bill, 143 to 21 against repeal of the arms embargo, and 135 to 24 against Lend-Lease. But public opinion was hardening. And when, after a battle on 4 September between *U-642* and U.S.S. *Greer,* the President ordered the navy to "shoot on sight" any German submarine encountered, most of the nation applauded. From that date, the United States was engaged in a *de facto* naval war with Germany. U.S.S. *Kearny,* torpedoed on 17 October, survived, but destroyer *Reuben James* was sunk by a U-boat 600 miles west of Iceland on the 31st. Seven American merchantmen were sunk by German warships before war was declared.

In the meantime President Roosevelt, like Wilson a generation earlier, had moved to obtain a statement of war aims from the Allies. On 10 August 1941 he and Winston Churchill met in Argentia Bay, Newfoundland, and there drew up the Atlantic Charter containing certain "common principles" on which they based "their hopes for a better future for the world." These included the already proclaimed Four Freedoms, a renunciation of territorial aggrandizement, a promise of the restoration of self-government to those deprived of it, and to all equal access to trade and raw materials.

For over a year, tension had been mounting in the Far East. The Japanese warlords, meeting unexpected resistance in China, now planned to swing south and gobble up the Philippines, Malaya, and Indonesia. In order to realize this "Greater East Asia Co-Prosperity Sphere," as they called it, Japan had to risk fighting Great Britain, France, the Netherlands, and the United States, which between them controlled the coveted territories. In the summer of 1940 Japan wrested permission to build airfields in Indochina from the helpless Vichy government of France. The United States struck back with a small loan to China and a partial embargo on exports to Japan. Congress, in July 1940, gave the President power to restrict export of war materials needed for American defense, or to license their export to friendly nations. In the same month, Congress passed the Two-Ocean Navy Act. Very cautiously, Roosevelt began imposing embargoes on various strategic materials, including scrap iron; and a Gallup poll indicated 96 per cent popular approval.

In July 1941 events began moving toward a crisis. On the 25th, Japan announced that she had assumed a protectorate of the whole of French Indochina. Next day, President Roosevelt took three momentous steps. He received the armed forces of the Philippine Commonwealth into the United States Army, appointed General Douglas MacArthur to command all army forces in the Far East, and issued an executive order freezing Japanese financial assets in the United States. Great Britain and the Netherlands followed suit, cutting off Japan's source of credit and imports of rubber, scrap iron, and fuel oil. The Japanese warlords decided to make war on these three countries within three or four months, unless the flow of oil and other strategic supplies was restored. For Japan was "eating her own tail" in the matter of oil; her armies must have fuel or evacuate the mainland, a loss of face that the military would not contemplate. This embargo on oil and credit brought Japan to the point of war.

The final negotiations were a mere sparring for time by two governments that considered war all but inevitable. The Japanese wanted time to organize their military and naval push to the south; the United States wanted time to prepare the defense of the Philippines and strengthen the navy. Through the summer and fall of 1941 Secretary Hull made it clear that Japan could have all the goods and credit she wanted, if she would begin a military evacuation of China and Indochina. Prince Konoye, the Japanese premier, on 14 October asked General Tojo, the war minister, to begin at least a token withdrawal. Tojo refused, confident that Japan could beat America, Britain, and any other country that stood in her way; and a few days later Tojo became prime minister. On 20 November he presented Japan's ultimatum. He promised to occupy no more Asiatic territory if the United States would stop reinforcing the Philippines; he would evacuate southern Indochina only if the United States would cut off aid to Chiang Kai-shek and "unfreeze" Japanese assets in the United States, leaving Japan free to complete her subjugation of China. Tojo did not expect that the United States would accept such terms, which were appropriate only for a defeated nation, and his plans for further aggression were already hardened. On 26 November 1941 the Japanese striking force of six big carriers carrying 423 planes, two battleships, two heavy cruisers, and eleven destroyers, sortied from it rendezvous in the Kurile Islands for the fatal destination of Pearl Harbor.

No inkling of even the existence of that force leaked out. A few days earlier, however, Japanese troop-laden transports and warships were reported steaming south off Formosa. Hence on 27 November, Washington sent a "war warning" message to Pearl Harbor and Manila, indicating an attack against the Philippines, Thailand, or the Malay Peninsula, but not mentioning Pearl Harbor as a possibility. Nobody in Washington thought that Japan was capable of striking a one-two blow, nor that, if she were, she would be so foolish as to drive divided America into war, united and angry. The Japanese warlords thought it necessary to destroy the Pacific Fleet, without the warning of a declaration of war, to prevent its interfering with their plans of conquest.

On 7 December at 6 a.m. the six Japanese carriers, with their escorting warships, reached their planned launching point 275 miles north of Pearl Harbor. The carriers commenced launching bombers and fighters immediately. The first attack group sighted Oahu at 7:40. "Pearl Harbor was asleep in the morning mist," wrote Commander Itaya who led the first formation. "Calm and serene inside the harbor . . . important ships of the Pacific Fleet, strung out and anchored two ships side by side."

Perfect targets. At 7:55 the bombs began to fall and aerial torpedoes aimed at the battleships to drop in the harbor. It seemed almost unbelievable to the sailors, as they rushed to man their anti-aircraft guns; confusion was almost complete, but courage was not wanting. Not until 7:58 did Rear Admiral Bellinger, the naval air commander, broadcast the message that shook the United States as nothing had since the firing on Fort Sumter:

AIR RAID, PEARL HARBOR—THIS IS NO DRILL.

XIV

On the Defensive

1941-1942

1. *World-wide Disaster*

AT THE END OF THIS sad and bloody day, 7 December 1941, the "day that shall live in infamy" as President Roosevelt said of it, 2403 American sailors, soldiers, marines, and civilians had been killed, and 1178 more wounded; 149 planes had been destroyed on the ground or in the water, U.S.S. *Arizona* was destroyed beyond possible repair, *Oklahoma* shattered and capsized, four other battleships were resting on the bottom or run aground to prevent sinking, two naval auxiliaries destroyed, three destroyers and a few other vessels badly damaged. All at a cost of twenty-nine planes and pilots to the Japanese striking force, which returned undetected to its home waters.

Nor was this all. Although General MacArthur's Far Eastern command was notified of the attack on Pearl Harbor at 3:00 a.m., 8 December (corresponding to 8:00 a.m., 7 December at Oahu), a Japanese bomber attack from Formosa caught the B-17s grounded on fields near Manila at noon, and destroyed most of them. Before dawn Japanese troops landed on the Malay Peninsula, and at 8:30 a.m. Guam was bombed from nearby Saipan.

To millions of Americans, whether at breakfast in Hawaii,

or reading the Sunday paper in the West, or sitting down to dinner in the East, this news of disaster after disaster seemed fantastic, incredible. As the awful details poured in, hour after hour, incredulity turned to anger and an implacable determination to avenge these unprovoked and dastardly attacks. On 8 December, Congress with but one dissenting vote declared a state of war with Japan; on 11 December, Germany and Italy, faithful to the tripartite pact, declared war on the United States. President Roosevelt, in his war message following that declaration, declared, "Never before has there been a greater challenge to life, liberty and civilization."

Yet, in attacking Pearl Harbor, Japan conferred a moral benefit on the nation which was the chief object of her rage and hatred. Senator Arthur Vandenberg of Michigan, who had been one of the leading isolationists before that event, remarked five years later that Pearl Harbor "drove most of us to the irresistible conclusion that world peace is indivisible. We learned that the oceans are no longer moats around our ramparts. We learned that mass destruction is a progressive science which defies both time and space and reduces human flesh and blood to cruel impotence."

The situation in Hawaii was not so bad as first it seemed; providentially, three fleet aircraft carriers *Lexington, Enterprise,* and *Saratoga* were at sea. These and their air groups constituted a striking force far more valuable than the lost battleships, all but two of which were salvaged and repaired in time to fight again.

In the Far East, on the other hand, the situation was calamitous. Thailand surrendered to the Japanese, who promptly landed troops at various points on the Malay Peninsula and began a relentless march on the British base at Singapore. On 10 December the Rising Sun flag was hoisted on Guam, which had been bravely but pitifully defended by a few hundred Americans and Chamorros. The same day, England met her Pearl Harbor when the Japanese air force sank H.M.S. *Prince of Wales* and *Repulse* off the Malay Peninsula. Other Japanese task forces occupied the Gilbert Islands, captured Hong Kong, and jumped the Borneo oilfields. On Wake Island, lonely outpost in the Central Pacific, Commander W. S. Cunningham and a small marine defense force beat off a Japanese attack on 11 December, only to be overwhelmed by another on the 23rd, before the navy managed to come to their rescue. In the Philippines, on 10 December, Japanese bombers destroyed Cavite navy yard. During the seventeen days before Christmas the enemy made nine amphibious landings in the Philippines. General MacArthur evacuated Manila on 27 December, withdrew his army to the Bataan Peninsula, and set up head-quarters on the island fortress of Corregidor.

The defense of Bataan and the Rock of Corregidor, although valiant and inspiring, proved to be a melancholy confirmation of Mahan's theory of sea power. The Japanese, controlling all sea and air approaches, enveloped both Peninsula and Rock in a tight blockade, landing fresh troops behind the American lines at will. After three months, over half the fighting men were disabled by wounds or by disease, and all were at the point of starvation. On 8 April the "battling bastards of Bataan," about 12,500 Americans and over 60,000 Filipinos, surrendered unconditionally. Only a couple of thousand escaped to Corregidor before the ranks of the prisoners were thinned by the infamous "death march" from Bataan to Japanese prison camps.

In the hope of restoring confidence to the Australians, President Roosevelt ordered General MacArthur to leave the Philippines and set up headquarters in the sub-continent. He left by motor torpedo boat on 11 March, promising to return, as indeed he did. On 6 May 1942, after the Japanese had captured the main defenses of Corregidor, General Jonathan M. Wainwright was forced to surrender the Rock together with its 11,000 defenders, and a Philippine army of over 50,000. There had been no such capitulation in American history since Appomattox.

In the meantime the Japanese had won their every objective in Southeast Asia. The Malay barrier (Sumatra, Java, Bali, Timor, and smaller islands), which barred the enemy from the Indian Ocean and Australia, was desperately defended by soldiers, sailors, and aviators of the United States, Great Britain, the Netherlands, and Australia under a combined command; a hopeless task. The Japanese would seize a strategic point in Borneo or Celebes, operate or build an airfield there, soften up the next objective by air bombing, occupy it with an amphibious force, and go on to the next. Admiral Hart's Asiatic Fleet, with British and Dutch allies, fought a series of valiant engagements in January and February 1942—Balikpapan, Bali, Bandung Strait, Java Sea—always greatly outnumbered, always defeated. Singapore, on which England had lavished millions of pounds, fell on 15 February. Java surrendered on 9 May; Rangoon, capital and chief seaport of Burma, had been occupied the day before. The Japanese were now in control of East Asia. India and Australia were tremblingly aware that their turn might come next.

Never in modern history has there been so quick or valuable a series of conquests; even Hitler's were inferior. The prestige of the white races fell so low that even victory over Japan could not win it back; and all countries that the Japanese conquered, though no longer Japanese, are no longer colonies.

The Atlantic sea lanes had to be kept open for supplies, and for building up a United States army in England for eventual invasion of the continent. American destroyers now helped to escort convoys all the way across, and used the sharp training facilities of the British bases in Northern Ireland. Sinkings in the North Atlantic fell off promptly; soon we knew why. Admiral Doenitz was moving wolf-packs over to the American east coast, where he rightly anticipated rich pickings from non-convoyed tankers and merchantmen. The navy, pressed to build more big ships, had neglected small vessels suitable for coastal convoy, hoping to improvise them if the need arose; but the Germans were not so accommodating as to wait.

The U-boat offensive opened on 12 January 1942 off Cape Cod, and a severe one it was. Most United States destroyers were tied to North Atlantic escort duty; only five subchasers were in commission; there were fewer than 100 planes to patrol coastal waters between Newfoundland and New Orleans; no merchantmen had yet been armed. Under these conditions, frightful destruction was wrought in shipping lanes between the Canadian border and Jacksonville. During January-April 1942, almost 200 ships were sunk in North American, Gulf, and Caribbean waters, or around Bermuda. Doenitz then shifted his wolf-packs to the Straits of Florida, the Gulf of Mexico, and the Caribbean; and in those waters 182 ships totaling over 751,000 tons were sunk in May and June 1942. Vessels were torpedoed 30 miles off New York City, within sight of Virginia Beach, off the Passes to the Mississippi, off the Panama Canal entrance. Since tourist resorts from Atlantic City to Miami Beach were not even required to turn off neon signs and water-front lights until 18 April 1942, or to black out completely for another month, hapless freighters and tankers passing them were silhouetted for the benefit of the U-boats. Over half the victims in southern waters were tankers, the sinking of which not only fried the water-borne survivors in burning oil, but threatened the success of military operations in Europe and the Pacific. Puerto Rico suffered from inability to move crops or import necessary food; sugar and coffee had to be rationed in the United States; "good neighbors" in Latin America began to doubt big neighbor's ability to win. The north-south sea lane, along the east coast through the Caribbean to Rio de Janeiro and the River Plate, had to be maintained equally with the west-east line to Great Britain, and the Pacific sea lines.

But the U-boats were knocking down the ships like tenpins. New construction of merchantmen in Allied and neutral countries amounted to less than 600,000 tons in June 1942 when the total loss almost touched 800,000 tons; and in half a year the British and American navies had sunk less than one month's production of new U-boats. Obviously, if this ratio continued, a "torpedo curtain" would soon be dropped between the United States and Europe.

Fortunately Admiral Ernest J. King, who had directed the "short of war" phase, became "Cominch," commander in chief of the United States fleet, on 20 December 1941. He took energetic measures to combat the submarine menace. The first need was for small escort vessels. The slogan "sixty vessels in sixty days" was nailed to the mast in April 1942; and 67 vessels actually came through by 4 May, when a second 60-60 program was already under way. Scientists were mobilized to find more efficient means of tracking and sinking U-boats. Inshore and offshore patrols were organized with converted yachts—the "Hooligan Navy" as it was nicknamed. As more escorts became available, an interlocking convoy system was worked out; the trunk line New York to Key West was fed freight by numerous branch lines which extended north to Canada and south to Brazil. In the second half of 1942 coastal convoys lost only 0.5 per cent of their ships; the transatlantic convoys lost only 1.4 per cent in a whole year. By April 1943 there was every day at sea in the American half of the North Atlantic, an average of 31 convoys with 145 escorts and 673 merchant ships, as well as 120 ships traveling alone and unescorted, and the heavily escorted troop convoys. There was nothing like a well-escorted convoy to bait the U-boats, or a well-equipped destroyer to kill them with depth charges or the forward-throwing hedgehog; but you had to have enough destroyers so that some of them could peel off and hunt. A big, fast, four-engined plane like the Liberator, equipped with guns, microwave radar, and depth bombs, was an effective instrument to sink a submarine, especially when it could be located by radio transmission.

It took time for these new methods and weapons to be adopted or produced in sufficient quantities to be effective. Throughout 1942 the U-boats enjoyed a succession of field days at our expense. And, in the meantime, this battle had extended into the Arctic Ocean and the South Atlantic. The first, the most dangerous and disagreeable of all convoy routes, had to be used to get lend-lease goods to Russia through Murmansk or Archangel. Although the British navy did most of the escorting over this route—losing in that service eleven warships—about half the merchantmen concerned were American, and their losses were severe. Another extension of the Atlantic battle lay southward. Most of the Latin American nations broke relations with or declared war on the Axis and Japan, and Brazil gave the Allies substantial aid. She declared war on the Axis in August 1942, after Doenitz had sunk five Brazilian ships within sight of shore. In conjunction with the Brazilian navy, with the British naval command in West Africa, and using an airfield built by United States Army engineers on lonely Ascension Island, an effective air-sea patrol of the Atlantic Narrows was then established.

2. *The Strategy and Direction of the War*

Although America, as we have seen, learned wrong all the lessons of World War I as to how to maintain peace, the leaders of the armed forces, especially General Marshall and Admiral King, learned right how to conduct a coalition war. The first lesson was to have a plan ready if and when war came. So, before World War II engulfed America, the United States Joint Chiefs of Staff (as heads of army, navy, and army air force shortly became) held a secret conference with their British opposite numbers. The resulting "ABC-1" staff agreement of 27 March 1941 set forth that, if and when America entered the war, her primary military effort would be exerted in the European theater. This concept of "Beat the Axis First" was arrived at because Germany and Italy, by knocking out France, had control of the entire western coast of Europe, and Germany's U-boats threatened to cut sea communication between the Old World and the New. Germany, too, had a greater war potential than Japan, and it was feared she might uncork some devastating secret weapon if given the time—as she did, but too late to win.

The informal alliance thus formed continued throughout the war, through the American Joint Chiefs of Staff and the British Chiefs of Staff. Meeting together as the Combined Chiefs of Staff, they, under President Roosevelt and Prime Minister Churchill, initiated strategy, drafted plans, allocated forces, and directed the war. Russia was represented by Marshall Stalin, and China by Chiang Kai-shek at two plenary C.C.S. conferences. Each of these two allies fought his own war with ample aid from England and America, but with slight regard for their strategy or wishes.

America was fortunate in having a very able war direction. Vital members of the Joint Chiefs of Staff throughout the war were General H. H. ("Hap") Arnold, head of the army air force; chief of staff General George C. Marshall, a V.M.I. graduate who combined the patient wisdom of Washington with the strategic savvy of Lee; Admiral Ernest J. King, chief of naval operations and commander in chief of the fleet, a tough, experienced naval officer who took a world-wide view of strategy and seldom, if ever, made a mistake. These three in concert with President Roosevelt formed a winning team. There had been nothing like that since the Lincoln-Grant-Farragut team of 1864–65.

At the cabinet level, America was equally strong. Cordell Hull, secretary of state, was becoming slightly infirm, but he had an energetic under-secretary, Sumner Welles; Henry L. Stimson, secretary of war, was full of brains and energy. Frank Knox, secretary of the navy, also had an able under-secretary, James Forrestal, who handled all matters of procurement for the navy, as assistant secretary Robert Patterson did for the army. Forrestal succeeded Knox after the latter's death in 1944, and later became the first secretary of defense. Over these staffs and heads of departments, and also over innumerable boards and committees which dealt with various phases of the war, were Churchill and Roosevelt. The "P.M." was Britain's greatest war leader since the elder Pitt. His energy and pluck saved England in her darkest hour, which he, in his remarkable history of the war, calls "Her Finest Hour." He called leading scientists into consultation at the top levels of government. He visited every British front to give the soldiers and sailors the inspiration of his presence, always smoking a long cigar and making the "V for Victory" sign with two upraised fingers.

Roosevelt, too, was a great war President, in a class with Lincoln; and, like Lincoln's, his greatness came from a capacity to lead and inspire, rather than from skill in administration. He was an opportunist, with a flair for the attainable, rather than, as in the case of Wilson, for the ideal; but, no less than Wilson, he looked ahead to a world of peace and justice. He kept a boyish zest for life, and his courage and energy triumphed over the crippling disease of his young manhood and enabled him for twelve years to carry the greatest burden that any modern statesman has been called upon to bear. His understanding of other nations enabled him to deal successfully with Latin America, neutrals, and representatives of the overrun democracies; and his death, when victory was in sight, was almost universally mourned. He respected his military advisers, and in the few instances in which he overrode them, his judgment was sound. He sometimes worked in devious ways, through his wise but much detested confidential assistant,

Harry Hopkins, and he needed the wisdom of the serpent to deal with clashing personalities and opposing interests.

Although much had been accomplished in military perparedness when Pearl Harbor broke—far more, relatively, than in 1812 or 1917—much more remained to be done. Congress promptly repealed its prohibition against sending draftees outside the Western Hemisphere, and extended their period of service to six months after the war's end—no "three months men" in this war. All men between 18 and 45 were made liable to military service. Standards of physical fitness and intelligence were exacting, and many failed to qualify. Including voluntary enlistments, over 15 million people served in the armed forces during the war; 10 million in the army, 4 million in the navy and coast guard, 600,000 in the marine corps. About 275,000 women served as nurses, in the "Waves," "Wacs," "Spars," or as lady marines.

The training problem was prodigious. Morale was easier to achieve for the navy and marine corps, whose recruits were volunteers; it never seemed to occur to them that America could be defeated. But the average "G.I." (General Issue), the nickname for infantrymen in this war, was a more or less unwilling draftee, who had been brought up in a pacifist atmosphere. He could be trained *to* fight, but it was well said of General Patton that he alone could make them *want* to fight. And far more was required of the G.I. than of the "doughboy" of World War I, or the "boys in blue," or gray, of 1861. There was any number of special forces, such as the army rangers for raiding, and the navy's UDT's or "frogmen," who swam up to enemy-held beaches, made soundings, and blew obstacles. Air forces had already become highly specialized. There were fighter planes, high-level bombers, torpedo-and dive-bombers, operating both from ships and shore, and several other types, for which pilots and crewmen had to be trained. And we required an enormous amount of research to replace plane types which proved unequal to their tasks, by newer, faster, and bigger ones. To fight a global war it was necessary to build dozens of naval bases and hundreds of airfields all over the world. Specially packaged units called Lions, Cubs, Oaks, and Acorns were organized with men and matérial all ready to rush in and build a base or airfield as soon as a site was secured.

The work of the service forces was very important. In this war the average soldier required at least double the World War I equipment. An infantry division of 8000 fighting men required 600 more to keep it fed, supplied, paid, doctored, amused, transported, and its equipment repaired. By the end of the war, so many artillery and other elements were added that a "reinforced" infantry division totaled 20,000 or more men. Remarkable progress was made by the medical corps. Infection and disease, always the bane of armies, in every war prior to 1917 had accounted for more deaths than the fighting. Thanks to abundant food, clothing, hospitals, and skillful physicians, the health of the armed forces in World War II compared favorably with that of the civilian population. The development of sulfa drugs and penicillin, the use of plasma for transfusions, control of mosquitoes and other insects, new techniques for the treatment of the terrible burns incident to bursting shells and Japanese kamikaze tactics, and prompt evacuation of wounded, reduced the death rate from wounds to less than half that of World War I, and enabled about two-thirds of all wounded to return to duty. The increasing role of artillery and the bomb in warfare is shown by the fact that, whilst 94 per cent of wounds in the Civil War were caused by rifle bullets, 72 per cent of those in the two world wars and the Korean War were inflicted by shell fragments.

The United States Navy entered the war well prepared except for antiaircraft and antisubmarine work, which happened to be among its most pressing needs. Fortunately, in conjunction with the marines, it had undertaken training for amphibious warfare, anticipating that to deliver troops to a fighting area would be no simple matter of sea transport and landing them on a wharf, but landing under fire on enemy-held beaches. Consequently the navy began building a new line of "lettered" vessels specially designed for amphibious warfare: the 460-foot LSD (Landing Ship, Dock), which spawned loaded landing craft from a miniature lake in its bowels; the 330-foot LST (Landing Ship, Tank), a two-decker floating garage, which became the workhorse of the fleet; the 180-foot LCI (Landing Craft, Infantry) for bringing soldiers directly to a beach; and a variety of small landing craft that could be lowered by the davits of a big transport. After 1940, with money available for high wages and overtime in the shipyards, it became possible to build a destroyer in five months instead of a year, and a big carrier in fifteen months instead of thirty-five.

The Maritime Commission, created by Congress in 1936 and headed by Rear Admiral Emory S. Land, received new powers in July 1941, and drew up blueprints for an emergency freighter that could be built quickly and inexpensively. The first of these Liberty ships—appropriately named *Patrick*

Henry—was launched in September, and 139 more came out that year. The bigger and faster Victory ship followed. In November 1941, when Congress repealed the Neutrality Act forbidding merchantmen to arm in self-defense, the navy began installing naval guns with bluejacket crews on freighters.

In the realm of production the United States enjoyed advantages over every other country that enabled it to become an "arsenal of democracy" while fighting the war. Lend-Lease and the big defense appropriations of 1940–41 had already added 6 million workers to the payrolls, wiping out unemployment. Yet there were ominous lags and shortages. The steel industry did not expand its capacity quickly enough, and the automobile industry was reluctant to shift from pleasure cars to war vehicles when restored prosperity released a flood of new car orders. Pearl Harbor galvanized American industry into a confusion of high-speed planning and production, which had to be straightened out by the War Production Board before anything useful could be accomplished. In 1942 the curve of production rose sharply; American industry produced not only enough matériel and weapons for the United States, but supplied the Allies. But our deficiencies were many.

Stockpiles of bauxite, aluminum, and chrome, which would have to reach America through submarine-infested waters, were lacking in 1941. Japan's quick conquests cut off the western world's principal sources of rubber, quinine, and manila fiber, and one of the chief sources of oil. As iron and horses had been essential to earlier wars, so steel, oil, and rubber were to this; armies no longer "marched on their stomachs," as Napoleon remarked, or wriggled ahead on their bellies, as in World War I, but rolled in motor vehicles on rubber tires; naval vessels were no longer fired by coal, but by black or diesel oil; high-test avgas was required for aircraft. Oil production had to be vastly increased in the United States and in Venezuela. New synthetic rubber plants, reworked tires, and wild caoutchouc imports from the Amazon lifted rubber production to over a million tons in 1944.

Mighty as America's effort was, it did not add up to total war, as the term was understood in the British Commonwealth, Germany, or Japan. There was no firm control over manpower, no conscription of women, little direction of talent to useful activities. A few edibles were rationed, but most Americans ate more heartily than before. Gasoline and tires were rationed, but hundreds of thousands of cars managed to stay on the road for purposes remotely connected with the war. Personal and corporation taxes were increased, but there was no limit on profits, or to what workers could earn, if they chose to work overtime; and as prices of most essentials were kept down, the standard of living rose. The country was never invaded, except by U-boats penetrating the three-mile limit, and a large measure of the "blood, sweat and tears" that Churchill promised his countrymen, were spared to his country's ally.

Only about 40 per cent of the cost of the war was met by taxation, the rest by borrowing; about $97 billion was subscribed in government bonds. The United States Treasury went into the red by over $40 billion annually, and borrowed freely from banks at 1 to 1.5 per cent interest—rates which would have astounded Salmon P. Chase. The national debt rose to $250 billion. Total cost of the war, exclusive of postwar pensions, interest payments, Marshall Plan, etc., came to about $350 billion, ten times that of World War I.

It was a grim, austere war for the American fighting forces, compared with World War I. No brass bands or bugles, no "Over There" or marching songs, no flaunting colors; no public farewells to boys going overseas, not even a ship's bell to mark the watches. It was typical that when the Japanese surrendered on board *Missouri* on 2 September 1945, "The Star-Spangled Banner" had to be played from a disk over the intercom system, and Admiral Halsey had only coffee to offer his guests.

3. *Turn of the Tide*

On Christmas Eve 1941 Admiral King warned, "The way to victory is long; the going will be hard." Hard indeed it was. Admiral Chester W. Nimitz, who at the same time received the command of the Pacific Fleet, was forced to bide his time until new naval construction and more trained troops gave him adequate reinforcements.

Since no British fleet remained in the Pacific, the Combined Chiefs of Staff entrusted the conduct of the Pacific war to the American Joint Chiefs of Staff, and they perforce adopted a strategy of active defense. Distances were immense, and the only hope of eventually defeating Japan was to hold fast to what we had, and prepare for future offensives. Islands still in American possession such as the Hawaiian and Samoan groups must be defended; the sea-air lanes to New Zealand and to Australia must be protected; and that meant tying up a large part of the fleet to escort transports and supply ships. Nothing much could be done for five months except to make hit-and-run raids with carrier planes. Of these the most spectacular was the air assault on Tokyo 18 April 1942. That was delivered by Colonel James H. Doolittle's B-25's from Admiral Halsey's carrier *Hornet,* a base that President Roosevelt humorously called

"Shangri-La," after the idyllic land in James Hilton's *Lost Horizon*. The planes did little damage, and most of their crews had to bail out over China; but the news that Tokyo had actually been bombed lifted American morale, and encouraged the Japanese high command to retrieve face by an imprudent offensive. America learned more from adversity than Japan did from victory.

Instead of organizing their new conquests, the Japanese succumbed to what one of their admirals after the war ruefully called "victory disease." They decided to wrest more Pacific territory—Papua, Fijis, New Caledonia, Solomons, western Aleutians, Midway Island—from the Allies and set up an impregnable "ribbon defense." These islands, in connection with those that Japan already held, were near enough to one another for patrol planes to protect, and to be bases for disrupting the lifeline between the United States and the British antipodes.

Admiral Yamamoto, greatest Japanese sea lord since Togo, wished to provoke a major battle with our Pacific Fleet. A good prophet, he pointed out that the United States Navy must be annihilated, if ever, in 1942, before American productive capacity replaced the Pearl Harbor losses. He hoped that after another defeat, the "soft" American people would force their government to quit and leave Japan in possession of her most valuable conquests. Then she could proceed at her leisure to conquer the rest of China and so become the most powerful empire in the world, capable of defying even Germany, if Hitler conquered all Europe.

The Japanese navy in 1942 was, by any standards, a great navy. Japan had the two largest and most powerful battleships in the world, displacing 68,000 tons, with 18-inch guns; the American *Iowa* class, none of which were completed before 1943, were of 45,000 tons with 16-inch guns. She had a fleet of fast and powerful 8-inch gunned cruisers built in defiance of former treaty restrictions, comparable to the later American *Baltimore* class. She had the fastest and most modern destroyers, twice as many big carriers as the United States Navy, and her carrier planes were superior in the fighter and torpedo-bomber types. Japanese torpedoes were faster, more powerful, and more sure-firing than those made in the United States, and employment of them was at once more lavish and more intelligent. Japanese naval gunnery was excellent; Japanese warships were intensely trained for night fighting, as the Americans were not. They lacked only radar, which American ships began to install in 1942. Flushed with triumph after triumph in the Southwest Pacific, the Japanese army and navy were confident of victory.

Why, then, did Japan fail? Because, owing to a combination of stupid strategy on her part and good strategy and good luck on ours, the numerically inferior Pacific Fleet defeated her in the battles of the Coral Sea, Midway, and Guadalcanal. And after 1942 it was too late, as Yamamoto predicted. The United States Navy had learned many salutary lessons, acquired unprecedented strength, and become an irresistible force in the air, on the surface, and under water.

The Battle of the Coral Sea (7–8 May 1942) frustrated the first forward lunge in the new Japanese offensive, to capture Port Moresby, a strategic base in Papua, New Guinea. This was the first naval battle in which no ship of either side sighted one of the other; the fighting was done by carrier plane against carrier plane, or carrier plane against ship. Admiral Nimitz sent carriers *Lexington* and *Yorktown* and a support group of cruisers into the Coral Sea, under the command of Rear Admiral Frank Jack Fletcher. The resulting engagement was a comedy of errors. Each side in this new sort of naval warfare made mistakes, but the Japanese made more; and although their losses were inferior to ours, they dared not press on to occupy Port Moresby. For Australia, Coral Sea was the decisive battle, saving her from possible invasion.

In the next and more vital Japanese offensive, Yamamoto went all-out. Personally assuming command, he brought with him almost every capital ship of the Japanese navy except the carriers damaged in the Coral Sea. His first objective was to capture Midway, a tiny atoll at the tip end of the Hawaiian chain, 1134 miles northwest of Pearl Harbor, where the United States had an advanced naval and air base. Yamamoto wanted Midway as a staging point for air raids to render Pearl Harbor untenable by the American Pacific Fleet. Minor objectives were Attu and Kiska, two barren islands in the western Aleutians which he wanted as the northern anchor of the new ribbon defense. Yamamoto's dearest object, however, was to force Nimitz to give battle with his numerically inferior Pacific Fleet. He had his wish, but this time the battle did not go to the strong.

Nimitz guessed what Yamamoto was up to, but had only a small fleet to stop him. First, he reinforced Midway with planes to the saturation point. Next, he sent out Rear Admiral Raymond A. Spruance to command carriers *Enterprise* and *Hornet* with their attendant cruisers and destroyers; Rear Admiral Fletcher in carrier *Yorktown* (damaged in the Coral Sea but promptly repaired) hastened to join. On 4 June 1942, the Japanese four-carrier force, advancing undetected under a

foul-weather front, was near enough Midway to batter the air
base. A brave group of twenty-six obsolete marine fighter
planes, together with antiaircraft guns on the island, disposed
of about one-third of the enemy attackers. The rest bombed
Midway severely but not lethally.

Admiral Nagumo, the Japanese carrier-force commander,

had a painful surprise on the morning of 4 June, when he learned from a reconnaissance plane that American flattops were approaching. Nagumo then made the fatal decision of the battle. He ordered his reserve attack group, then arming for a second strike on Midway, to be rearmed with the different sort of bombs used against ships, and turned his prows northeast-

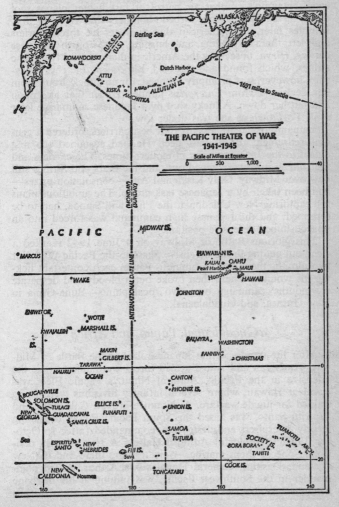

THE PACIFIC THEATER OF WAR
1941-1945
Scale of Miles at Equator
0   500   1,000

ward to close with the American carriers. Spruance and Fletcher already had several flights of torpedo- and dive-bombers flying toward the Japanese; and, owing to Nagumo's mistake, they had the good fortune to catch three of his four carriers in the vulnerable situation of rearming and refueling planes. But the carrier-plane battle opened ill for the Americans. Nagumo's combat air patrol of fast fighter planes shot down 35 of the 41 slow torpedo-bombers that came in first. Minutes later, the American dive-bombers hit three carriers and left them exploding and burning. The fourth Japanese carrier, *Hiryu,* unseen by the American fliers, got off two plane strikes, which found and disabled *Yorktown.* Fletcher's flag-ship, however, was promptly avenged, for an attack group from her deck and from *Enterprise* jumped *Hiryu* that afternoon and put her down. A lucky shot by a Japanese submarine later sank *Yorktown* as she was under tow.

Yamamoto, having lost his four best carriers, ordered a general retirement of his vast fleet. He had sustained the first defeat to the Japanese navy in modern times. The carriers and their air groups were wiped out, and the Stars and Stripes still flew over Midway. Only Kiska and Attu—consolation prizes—had been taken by a Japanese task group. The ambitious plans for capturing New Caledonia, the Fijis, and Samoa, had to be scrapped; and the Japanese high command was forced into an unaccustomed defensive position.

This glorious Battle of Midway on 4 June 1942 marked a clean-cut ending to the defensive phase in the Pacific War. For two months there was an ominous pause, each contestant licking his wounds. There then broke out a bloody and desperate six months' campaign over two focal points—Buna-Gona in New Guinea, and Guadalcanal.

4. *Guadalcanal, Papua, and Africa*

After the repulse of the Japanese fleet in the Battle of Midway, American and Allied armed forces were able to take the offensive in the Pacific. Admiral Nimitz's Pacific Fleet was based at Hawaii, where several infantry divisions were being trained for jungle warfare. At Nouméa in New Caledonia, and Espiritu Santo, was based the South Pacific Force, consisting largely of cruisers and destroyers, commanded (after 16 October 1942) by colorful Admiral Halsey. A few infantry divisions—one of them marine—were training there and in New Zealand. Dashing General Douglas MacArthur, Allied commander in the Southwest Pacific, was fuming at his Brisbane headquarters for lack of forces to resume the offensive. His troops were mostly Australian; and the small fleet under him was partly Australian, partly American.

Although the Japanese had been beaten back from the Coral Sea, they still held Tulagi in the Solomons, and Rabaul on New Britain. These were anchors to a formidable barrier, which for short we call the Bismarcks barrier, to an Allied advance toward Japan. The islands here are so close to one another that all approaches and surrounding waters could be controlled by land-based planes. Hence this barrier had to be breached if ever we were to approach Japan. And the campaign to do it was sparked off by the news that Japanese had taken Buna and Gona on the north coast of Papua (the tail of the New Guinea bird), and were building an airfield on Guadalcanal, whence they would be able to bomb our advanced base at Espiritu Santo. Admiral King in Washington decided that this must not be; the South Pacific Force was hurriedly assembled, and presently nineteen transports, escorted by cruisers and destroyers, with three carriers loosely attached, were converging on the mountainous, jungle-clad Solomon Islands. On 7 August 1942, the 1st Marine Division under General Alexander A. Vandegrift landed at Tulagi and Guadalcanal, surprised the enemy, and seized the harbor of the one island and the airfield on the other.

There then began the prolonged and bloody struggle for Guadalcanal; an island hardly more valuable than the battlefield of Gettysburg, yet even more violently contested. The Japanese could not afford to let us establish a base there, and we could not afford to let it go. Ships, planes, and troops were committed by both sides. Seven major naval battles were fought until Ironbottom Sound, as our sailors named the waters between Guadalcanal and Florida Islands, was strewn with the hulls of ships and the bodies of seamen. The first of these battles, named after Savo Island which guards the western entrance to Ironbottom Sound, was the worst defeat ever suffered by the United States Navy. Admiral Mikawa, with a force no stronger than ours, pulled off a complete surprise on the night of 9 August, sinking one Australian and three American heavy cruisers, with no loss to himself. That was Japan's great opportunity to pile in and overwhelm the marines ashore; but overconfidence led her to reinforce Guadalcanal only by dribs and drabs. One reinforcement group was defeated by Rear Admiral Norman Scott off Cape Esperance on the night of 11–12 October. And the great Naval Battle of Guadalcanal raged for two long nights between 12 and 15 November 1942, with furious daylight air-ship battles between. Rear Admirals Scott and D. J. Callaghan were killed; but Rear Admiral Willis

A. Lee won the second night engagement, in U.S.S. *Washington*, by sinking a Japanese battleship. There were also two carrier actions outside the Solomons, and another surface action in Ironbottom Sound in which we lost cruiser *Northampton* to the smartest of the Japanese rear admirals, Raizo Tanaka. Every few nights a "Tokyo Express" of fast destroyer transports, crowded with troops, raced down "the Slot"—the central channel between the Solomons—dropped the troops overboard to swim ashore, and was out of American air range by morning. Every few days we did the same thing from Espiritu Santo—except that our reinforcements went ashore dry-shod. On shore, the marines, reinforced by two army divisions, fought desperately and successfully. The Airsols command, comprising army, navy, and marine corps planes of the United States, Australia, and New Zealand, gradually won control of the air. And on 9 February 1943, six months after the landings, the Japanese evacuated Guadalcanal.

In this campaign, American soldiers took the measure of the supposedly invincible Japanese jungle fighters who had overrun half Eastern Asia, and found that they could be beaten. And the navy learned, the hard way, how to fight night battles and shoot down enemy planes. After Guadalcanal had been secured, the navy lost no more battles.

In the meantime, the western prong of this Japanese offensive had been stopped on the north coast of Papua, New Guinea by American and Australian troops under Generals Eichelberger and Sir Edmund Herring. The fighting, in malaria-infested mangrove swamps against a trapped and never-surrendering enemy, was the most horrible of the entire war. With the aid of air power, the combined armies won through, and by the end of January 1943 Papua up to Huon Gulf was in Allied hands.

The counteroffensive against Japan had made a good start.

President Roosevelt and Winston Churchill, meeting in the White House in June 1942, could not agree on time or place of the first Allied offensive against the Axis, nor could their military advisers. The Americans wanted priority for a cross-channel operation against the Germans in France, a beachhead to be secured in 1942, and a strike at the heart of the Reich in 1943. They discounted the value of peripheral operations—such as the raids on Dieppe and Norway—which the British favored continuing for a couple of years before mounting any massive invasion; for the British wished at all hazards to prevent trench warfare developing. But something had to be done to help Russia, which alone of the Allies was now bearing the brunt of the war. Stalin sent Molotov to Washington to beg for a "second front, now" and all left-wing elements in England and America took up the cry. Churchill and Roosevelt could not stand the obloquy of fighting another "phony war." On 25 July 1942 they decided to occupy French North Africa—Operation "Torch." The object was to secure a strategic springboard for invading Italy. That had to do for a "second front."

Oran and Algiers on the Mediterranean, and Casablanca on the Atlantic coast of Morocco, were selected as the three harbors to be seized by amphibious forces. General Dwight D. Eisenhower was appointed commander in chief, with Admiral Sir Andrew Cunningham RN as over-all commander of naval forces. In less than four months the United States and Great Britain had to train thousands of troops for amphibious warfare, divert hundreds of ships to new duties and, as Eisenhower wrote, occupy "the rim of a continent where no major military campaign had been conducted for centuries."

On 23 October General Sir Bernard Montgomery launched the second battle of El Alamein against the German Afrika Korps under Rommel. On the same day Rear Admiral H. Kent Hewitt, commanding the Western Naval Task Force, sailed from Hampton Roads. America had invaded Africa in Jefferson's day, and Africa had been brought to America in the persons of her sons and daughters; but never before had an amphibious operation been projected across an ocean. The complex operation went like clockwork. By midnight 7–8 November all three task forces (those for Oran and Algiers under British command) had reached their destinations, unscathed and unreported. French, Spaniards, Germans, and Italians were completely surprised. Admiral Hewitt had to fight a naval battle with the French fleet off Casablanca and sink most of it, in order to get General Patton's troops ashore safely; but there was little resistance from the French army. Admiral Darlan—second to Marshal Pétain in the Vichy government—who happened to be in Algiers, was so impressed by the strength of the Anglo-American landings that Eisenhower was able to persuade him, and Marshal Pétain secretly ordered him, to issue a cease-fire order to all French forces in North Africa on 11 November.

This "Darlan deal," as it was called, aroused vicious attacks on the sincerity of Eisenhower, Roosevelt, and Churchill from left-wing elements. They were accused of compromise with fascism, yielding to the enemy, etc. But through that deal the United States and Great Britain saved thousands of their soldiers' lives and gained new bases, and support of the French in North Africa, and eventually a new ally.

Although caught flatfooted by the invasion, the Germans reacted promptly, flying 20,000 men across the Sicilian straits within a few days and establishing fighter and bomber bases on Tunisian airfields. General Eisenhower moved, too, but the difficulties he faced from mountain and desert, narrow twisting roads, the rainy season which grounded his aircraft and, not least, from his own half-trained troops, prevented his reaching Bizerte and Tunis in 1942.

Early in January 1943 Roosevelt and Churchill and the Combined Chiefs of Staff met at Casablanca to plan future operations. For the first time Allied prospects seemed favorable; this, as Churchill said, was "the end of the beginning." The Russians had turned the tide at the decisive battle of Stalingrad, Auchinleck and Montgomery had saved Egypt, air and naval forces were fast being built up in Morocco and Algeria, Mussolini could no longer call the Mediterranean *mare nostrum*. And General de Gaulle, though furious at not being given the Allied command in Africa, consented to appear and shake hands all around.

Allied chiefs at Casablanca decided to invade Sicily as soon as Tunisia was secured, and promised "to draw as much weight as possible off the Russian armies by engaging the enemy as heavily as possible at the best selected point." And they made the momentous announcement that the war would end only with "unconditional surrender" of all enemies, European and Asiatic. That formula, borrowed from General Grant's declaration before Fort Donelson, was the second major strategic decision of the war. Not well thought out as to the consequences, it may have been a mistake. The reasons prompting it were the failure of the armistice of 11 November 1918 to eliminate the German menace; the Darlan deal, creating suspicion that Roosevelt contemplated a similar deal with Mussolini and Hitler; and a desire to reassure Russia that we would not let her down. On Mussolini the formula had no effect, since he was almost ready to quit, but it may have helped Hitler to persuade his people to fight to the bitter end.

While Roosevelt and Churchill were discussing grand strategy, the Germans seized the initiative. Swift counterattacks and the arrival of Rommel's Afrika Korps gave them ground superiority, which Rommel exploited in brilliant fashion. On 14 February 1943 he hurled his armor through the Kasserine Pass, turned northward toward Tebessa, and threatened to cut the Allied armies in two. The untried American forces were badly beaten for a time. But General Patton, with two new

armored divisions and powerful new tanks, and clearing skies
that permitted the Allied air force to deliver punishing blows,
turned the tide.

This was Rommel's last offensive. Montgomery had caught
up with him, and the two antagonists squared off for a last
round. Hammered front and rear, pounded by the most devastating aerial attack of the North African campaign, Rommel
acknowledged defeat and retreated northward into Tunisia. The
Allied armies, now half a million strong, closed in for the kill.
Then, as Montgomery broke the German lines in the south
and raced for Tunis, Omar Bradley, commanding II Corps,
United States Army, smashed into Bizerte. Both cities fell on
7 May 1943. Cornered on Cape Bon, the German army, still
275,000 strong, surrendered on 13 May. It was the greatest
victory that British and American arms had yet won.

Now that North Africa was cleared of the enemy, the Mediterranean became open to Allied merchant ships throughout its
entire length, though still subject to air attack from Italy and
southern France, which the Germans occupied as soon as they
heard of the Darlan deal. The now spliced lifeline of the
British Empire to India through Suez made it possible to reinforce Russia via the Persian Gulf. And the way was open
at last for a blow at what Churchill mistakenly called "the soft
underbelly" of Europe.

5. *The U-Boat Mastered, Italy Invaded*

At the Casablanca conference in January 1943 the Combined Chiefs of Staff gave antisubmarine warfare number one
priority. In terms of construction, this meant that American
shipyards had to slow up on producing beaching and landing
craft for amphibious operations, and concentrate on escort vessels, especially the new DE (destroyer-escort) and the CVE
(escort or "jeep" carrier), which could carry bombing planes
into submarine-infested waters.

The Battle of the Atlantic came to a head in 1943. At the
turn of the year Hitler appointed to command the German
navy his submarine expert Admiral Doenitz, and concentrated
on producing more and better U-boats and new types which
could submerge for long periods. The number operating in the
Atlantic more than doubled, and their effectiveness was increased by sending big supply subs—"milch cows"—into waters
around the neutral Azores, enabling U-boats to replenish without returning to France. But the number of Allied ships and
planes capable of dealing with them more than quadrupled.
A fresh German blitz on the North Atlantic and other routes,

in March 1943, accounted for 108 merchant ships aggregating over 625,000 tons. Echelons of wolf-packs, preceded by U-boats whose sole duty was to shadow convoys, attacked by day as well as night. These sinkings, occurring at the worst season in the North Atlantic when the temperature of the water hovers around 30° F, were accompanied by heavy loss of life. The big question in mid-1943 was whether existing U-boat types could be mastered in time to enable America to get enough men and weapons across to beat Germany before the new U-boats got into production. By April 1943 the Allies were definitely ahead. At a conference with Hitler on the 11th, Doenitz admitted the loss of 40 U-boats and 6 Italian submarines since New Year's.

An increased number of convoys and escorts, many new antisubmarine devices, better training, and the work of scientists and technicians were getting results. The British put on a great drive in the Bay of Biscay against U-boats that were approaching or departing from their French bases. This, in conjunction with successes elsewhere, brought the total bag up to 41 in May. At the same time the United States began using her new escort carriers in convoys between Norfolk and the Mediterranean. These, screened by the new DE's, went out after every submarine detected within 300 miles of the convoy route and sank a considerable number, even some of the big "milch cows." The latter were already driven from their pastures when Portugal permitted the Allies to use air bases in the Azores. That closed the last stretch in the North Atlantic which long-range bomber planes had been unable to reach. And new merchant ship construction was now well ahead of losses.

Germany built 198 U-boats between 1 May 1943 and the end of the year, and lost 186. Transatlantic convoys were now so well defended that tonnage losses during these eight months were less than in the single months of June and November 1942. Admiral Doenitz, feeling that he must make a tonnage score, no matter where, now began sending his best long-legged U-boats into the Indian Ocean, where as yet there were no convoys. But he kept enough in home waters, occasionally to send wolf-packs full cry after transatlantic traffic; the Battle of the Atlantic did not end until Germany surrendered.

Operation "Torch" flickered so long that "Overlord," the invasion of Normandy, had to be postponed to 1944. Something had to be done against the Axis during the rest of 1943, or the people would howl for action; and that something obviously had to start from the newly won Allied base in North Africa.

The plan selected was to overrun Sicily, cross the Strait of Messina to Calabria, and work up the Italian peninsula. This offered a chance of complete control of the Mediterranean as well as an objective dear to Churchill's heart, knocking Italy out of the war. D-day for the attack on Sicily was set for 10 July, and General Eisenhower commanded. This was the biggest amphibious assault of the war. About 250,000 British and American troops landed simultaneously, eight divisions abreast, in deep darkness. The more numerous Italian and German defenders of Sicily were completely surprised. General Patton's American Seventh Army was put ashore by Admiral Hewitt's Eighth Fleet on the southwestern shore of Sicily; General Montgomery's British Eighth Army, which included a Canadian division, landed to the right and almost up to Syracuse. The new LST and other beaching craft, here employed in large numbers for the first time, assisted in getting troops, tanks, and field artillery ashore so promptly that within a few hours the invaders controlled 150 miles of coastline, and substantial beachheads. The smoothness with which these landings were carried off, the celerity with which enemy opposition was overwhelmed, deeply impressed the German and Italian high commands. The Germans concluded that only a delaying operation was possible; the Italians decided it was time to quit.

After a sharp battle at the Gela beachhead with a German armored division, the Seventh Army swept across Sicily, marching at a rate that matched Stonewall Jackson's "foot cavalry" in the Civil War. On 22 July General Patton made a triumphal entry into Palermo and set up headquarters in the ancient palace of the Norman kings, whence, like another Tancred or Roger, he directed the campaign along the north coast of Sicily. That big island was in the Allied bag by 17 August 1943.

Italy was heartily sick of the war into which Mussolini had forced her. On 25 July, six days after Allied air forces had delivered a 560-plane bombing raid on Rome, the little king summoned up enough courage to force *il Duce* to resign. Marshal Badoglio, who told the king that the war was absolutely and completely lost, took over the government and began to probe for peace. Owing to the Italian love of bargaining and the "unconditional surrender" slogan which made bargaining difficult, negotiations dragged along until 3 September. This gave the Germans time to rush reinforcements into Italy and to seize key points such as Genoa, Leghorn, and Rome.

General Eisenhower had already been ordered by the Combined Chiefs of Staff to invade Italy at the earliest possible date. Salerno, south of the Sorrento peninsula, was chosen for

the main landing. In early September 1943 the Allied Fifth
Army, commanded by General Mark W. Clark, with two
British and two American infantry divisions in the assault,
took off from a dozen ports between Oran and Alexandria.
En route the familiar voice of General "Ike" was heard broadcasting news of the Italian surrender, so all hands expected a
walkover. They had a bitter surprise. Some very tough and
unco-operative Germans were at the beachhead, and D-day at
Salerno, 9 September, was very costly. The German air force
was active and enterprising, and tried a new weapon, the radio-
guided bomb which put several ships out of business. A series
of vicious tank attacks, to divide the American from the British
divisions, was thwarted by the invaders, ably assisted by naval
gunfire; and on 16 September the Germans started an orderly
retirement northward. Fifth Army on 1 October entered
Naples, which the Germans had done their best to destroy.

Here, with the great harbor secured and the Foggia airdrome on the other side of Italy in Allied hands, the Italian
campaign should have been halted. But Churchill and General
Sir Alan Brooke justified continuing up the Italian "boot," on
the ground that the battle of Italy pinned down and used up
German divisions which might resist the Normandy landing
in 1944. Actually the Italian campaign failed to draw German
reserves from France, and by June 1944 the Allies were
employing in Italy double the number of the Germans in that
area. It developed, as General Sir Henry Wilson said, into a
"slow, painful advance through difficult terrain against a determined and resourceful enemy, skilled in the exploitation of
natural obstacles by mines and demolition." Marshal Kesselring, fighting a series of delaying operations along prepared
mountain entrenchments, exploited these natural advantages
to the full; and none of the Allied generals except Guillaume,
who commanded a French army corps, showed much ability
to cope with German tactics. From Naples to Rome is but
100 miles; yet the Allies, with numerical superiority on land
and in the air, and with control of adjacent waters, took eight
months to cover that ground. Fighting in the Apennines was
vividly described by the war correspondent Ernie Pyle, as consisting of "almost inconceivable misery," in mud and frost.
G.I.'s "lived like men of prehistoric times, and a club would
have become them more than a machine gun."

Rome was the objective of the winter campaign of 1943–44,
but some of the most mountainous terrain in Europe barred the
way. Churchill persuaded the C.C.S. to try and break the stalemate by an amphibious landing in the rear of the Germans at
Anzio, 37 miles south of Rome. Although the Anzio landing

(22 January 1944) by one British and one United States division was a complete surprise, Marshal Kesselring reacted swiftly. His air force sank a number of transports and warships, and the troops had to dig into an open plain, where they were subjected to constant air and infantry counterattack. Anzio beachhead, which should have been a spearhead, became instead a beleaguered fort.

To the south, the Eighth Army launched a series of savage attacks against the ancient monastery of Monte Cassino, anchor of another German line. For three months the Allies wore themselves out in futile attempts to take the place by storm. Finally, the Eighth Army, which by this time included American, British, Polish, Indian, and French divisions, enveloped and captured Monte Cassino (19 May); a Canadian force advanced up the Adriatic coast; Mark Clark's Fifth Army burst through the iron ring around Anzio on 25 May, and advanced north against stubborn rear-guard resistance.

By the morning of 4 June 1944, as Kesselring's forces were retiring toward a new defense line, columns of Allied troops were rushing along all roads that led to Rome. By midnight the Fifth Army was there.

For one brief day the liberation of Rome held the attention of the Allied nations. Then, on 6 June, came the news that the Allies had landed on the coast of Normandy.

6. Leap-Frogging in the Pacific

During the five months that followed the securing of Guadalcanal, the only active area in the Pacific war was the Aleutians. Here Rear Admiral Charles H. McMorris won a daylight surface action, the Battle of the Komandorski Islands, on 24 March 1943, against a Japanese fleet of twice his strength. The Japanese were then cleaned out of Attu, and the western Aleutians developed as air bases. These, usually "socked in" by foul weather, were of little use; the Aleutians had better have been left to the Aleuts.

During this lull in the Pacific war—owing to our efforts in Europe and the loss of four aircraft carriers—army and navy strategists were discussing ways and means of getting at Japan. Thousands of atolls and islands—the Gilberts, Marshalls, Carolines, Marianas, and Bonins—plastered with airfields and bristling with defenses, sprawled across the ocean like a maze of gigantic spider webs, blocking every route north of the equator; and, south of the line, Japan still held the Bismarck Archipelago, all the Solomons except Guadalcanal and nearby islands, and New Guinea excepting its Papuan tail. General

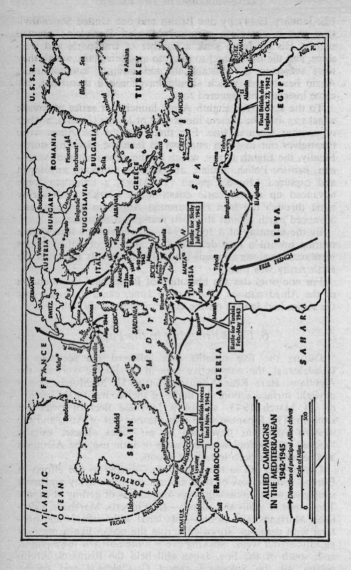

Map labels (within image):

USSR

SUEZ CANAL
Nile R.
Cairo
Alexandria
El Alamein

Final British drive begins Oct. 23, 1942

EGYPT

TURKEY
Ankara
Black Sea
CYPRUS
Istanbul
RHODES
CRETE
Khania

ROMANIA
Bucharest
Ploesti
Danube R.
Sofia
BULGARIA
Belgrade
YUGOSLAVIA
Zagreb
GREECE
Athens
ALBANIA

LIBYA
Tobruk
Derna
Bardia
Benghazi
El Agheila

FREE FRENCH

Budapest
HUNGARY
Vienna
AUSTRIA
GERMANY
SWITZ.
Trieste
Venice
Po R.
Genoa
Turin
ITALY
Rome
Anzio Jan. 22, 1944
MT. CASSINO
Salerno Sept. 9, 1944
Naples
Foggia
CORSICA
SARDINIA

Battle for Sicily July–Aug. 1943
SICILY
Palermo
Catania
MALTA

TUNISIA
Bizerte
Tunis
Bône
Sfax
Mareth
Gabès

Battle for Tunisia Feb.–May 1943

Tripoli

MEDITERRANEAN SEA

FRANCE
Vichy
Lyon
Bordeaux
Aug. 1944
Rhône R.
Marseille
Toulon
(Lib. 28 Aug. '44)
BALEARIC IS.

SPAIN
Madrid

PORTUGAL
Lisbon
ATLANTIC OCEAN

Gibraltar
Tangier
SP. MOROCCO
FR. MOROCCO
Port Lyautey
Mehdia
Fedhala
Casablanca
Safi

ALGERIA
Oran
Algiers

SAHARA

U.S. and British forces land Nov. 8, 1942

FROM U.S.
FROM ENGLAND

ALLIED CAMPAIGNS IN THE MEDITERRANEAN 1942–1945
➤ Direction of principal Allied drives
Scale of Miles
0   500

384

MacArthur wished to advance by what he called the New Guinea-Mindanao axis; but Rabaul, planted like a baleful spider at the center of a web across that axis, would have to be eliminated first. And as long as Japan held the central island complexes, she could feed in air and naval forces at will against his communications. So it was decided that Admiral Nimitz must take a broom to the Gilberts, the Marshalls, and the Carolines, while MacArthur and Halsey cleaned out the Bismarcks. All could then join forces for a final push into the Philippines and on to the coast of China, or even Japan.

Accordingly the plans for mid-1943 to mid-1944 began with preliminary operations to sweep up enemy spiders' webs. The central Solomons were the first objective. After three sharp naval actions up the Solomons' slot in July (battles of Kula Gulf, Kolombangara, and Vella Gulf) and a number of PT actions (in one of which future President Kennedy lost his boat but distinguished himself), the navy won control of surrounding waters, and Munda field with adjacent positions was captured by the army after a tough jungle campaign. In New Guinea and on Cape Gloucester, New Britain, a series of shore-to-shore amphibious operations secured the main passage from the Coral Sea through the Bismarcks barrier into the western Pacific.

Japan could now be approached in a series of bold leaps instead of a multitude of short hops. Independently, General MacArthur and Rear Admiral Theodore S. Wilkinson thought up "leap-frogging," or, as Wilkinson called it in baseball phraseology, "hitting 'em where they ain't." The essence of this strategy was to by-pass the principal Japanese strongpoints like Truk and Rabaul, sealing them off with sea and air power, leaving their garrisons to "wither on the vine," while we constructed a new air and naval base in some less strongly defended spot several hundred miles nearer Japan. After the war was over General Tojo told General MacArthur that leap-frogging, the success of United States submarines against the Japanese merchant marine, and the projection of fire power by aircraft carriers deep into enemy territory were the three main factors that defeated his country.

Now began a campaign to neutralize Rabaul. On 1 November Admiral Wilkinson's III Amphibious Force leap-frogged onto a slice of undefended coast in Bougainville and established a defensive perimeter for the Seabees to build fighter and bomber strips. A Japanese fleet based on Rabaul sortied to challenge but was decisively beaten (Battle of Empress Augusta Bay, 2 November 1943) by Rear Admiral A. S. Merrill's cruiser and destroyer force. On the 5th and 11th, planes from stately old *Saratoga* and the new carriers *Essex, Bunker Hill, Independence,* and *Princeton* pounded Rabaul, and bombers based on Bougainville continued the good work daily. Enemy air forces, even after stripping planes off carriers to defend Rabaul, were gradually worn away. On 25 November, in the Battle of Cape St. George, Captain Arleigh ("31-knot") Burke, commanding a destroyer squadron, defeated a Japanese attempt to reinforce Bougainville, and sank three of their five destroyers. Thus, by 25 March 1944, when Wilkinson's III 'Phib had taken Green Island and General MacArthur's VII 'Phib had occupied Manus in the Admiralty Islands, the Bismarcks barrier was broken, Rabaul rendered impotent, and almost 100,000 Japanese troops were neutralized.

The Gilberts and Marshalls campaigns were the first big amphibious operations in the Pacific. Some 200 sail of ships, Fifth Fleet carrying 108,000 soldiers, sailors, marines, and aviators under the command of Rear Admirals Raymond Spruance and Kelly Turner, and Major General H. M. ("Howling Mad") Smith, converged on two coral atolls of the Gilbert group. Makin, where the enemy had no great strength, was taken early by one regiment; but Tarawa, a small, strongly defended position behind a long coral-reef apron, was a very tough nut. The lives of almost 1000 marines and sailors were required to dispose of 4000 no-surrender Japanese on an islet not three miles long. But Tarawa taught invaluable lessons for future landings, and provided another airfield.

The new Gilberts bases helped aircraft to neutralize the many Japanese airdromes in the Marshalls. Fast carrier forces under Rear Admiral Marc Mitscher roamed about the group, ships pounding and aircraft bombing. Consequently, not one Japanese plane was available in the Marshalls on D-day, 31 January 1944. Massive amphibious forces under Rear Admirals Harry Hill and Turner, with close air and gunfire support, covered landings at both ends of the great atoll of Kwajalein. On 17 February another force moved into Eniwetok, westernmost of the Marshalls. The Japanese troops, as usual, resisted to the last man; but the Marshalls not only cost many fewer casualties than tiny Tarawa, but were conquered without the loss of a single ship. The Japanese navy dared not challenge because its air arm had been sliced off to defend Rabaul; and on 20 February its capital ships and aircraft were chased out of the important naval base of Truk, with heavy loss, by a round-the-clock carrier raid.

Mobile surface forces and air power needed mobile logistics, and got them. Outstanding in the pattern for Pacific victory was the supply base—Service Squadron 10, a logistic counterpart to the fast carrier forces. While the flattops carried the naval air arm to within striking distance of the enemy, "Servron 10," composed of tankers, ammunition ships, refrigerator ships, repair ships, fleet tugs, escort carriers with replacement planes, and several other types of auxiliaries, acted as a traveling annex to Pearl Harbor to provide the fleet with food, fuel, bullets, spare parts, and spare planes. The Pacific Fleet actually recovered its independence of land bases, which had been lost when sail gave way to steam.

While Spruance and Turner were crashing through the Gilberts and Marshalls, "MacArthur's navy," the Seventh Fleet under Admirals Kinkaid and Barbey, was leap-frogging along the New Guinea coast. Hollandia and Aitape airfields were secured by the end of April. Biak Island, posed like a fly over the neck of the New Guinea bird, fell on 17 May 1944. Admiral Toyoda, commander in chief of the Japanese fleet (Yamamoto having been shot down over Bougainville), planned to stop the Americans right there with his two superbattleships; but before he got around to it a more dangerous American movement engaged his attention, and VII 'Phib was able to take the western end of New Guinea by 15 September 1944. MacArthur's air forces were now within bombing distance of the Philippines.

The movement that diverted Admiral Toyoda's attention was directed against the Marianas. Of this group, a bastion on Japan's inner line of defense, the principal islands are Saipan, Tinian, and Guam. So, when Admiral Nimitz's victorious team moved into Saipan on 15 June, Japan had to do something better than the last-ditch local resistance she had offered in the Marshalls. And by now her navy had trained new air groups.

Vice Admiral Ozawa's fleet, deploying into the Philippine Sea, comprised nine carriers, five battleships, and seven heavy cruisers. Admiral Spruance's Fifth Fleet (seven *Essex*-class and eight light carriers, seven battleships, three heavy and six light cruisers), moved out to meet him, preceded by a screen of submarines. Spruance played his usual cool game, taking risks boldly when they seemed commensurate with the damage he might inflict, yet never forgetting that his main duty was to protect the amphibious forces at Saipan. The Battle of the Philippine Sea broke at 10 a.m., 19 June 1944, when hundreds of Japanese planes were detected flying toward the American carriers, then about 100 miles northwest of Guam. Sixty miles out, Hellcat fighters intercepted the Japanese planes, and only forty broke through. The antiaircraft fire of Spruance's ships was so accurate and deadly that these planes scored only two hits, on battleships that suffered little damage. As a result of the day's fighting, the Japanese lost over 345 planes at the cost of only 17 American aircraft. Ozawa lost three carriers (two to United States submarines), his air groups were wiped out, and he had no time to train new ones before the next great battle, in October.

Now the conquest of the Marianas could proceed without enemy interference. By 1 August 1944 the three major islands, Saipan, Tinian, and Guam, were in American possession. Airfield and harbor development went on briskly. Admiral Nimitz moved his headquarters to the hills above Agaña in Guam, and by fall, Marianas-based B-29's were bombing southern Japan.

The more sagacious Japanese now knew they were beaten; but they dared not admit it, and nerved their people to another year of bitter resistance in the vain hope that America might tire of the war when victory was within her grasp.

XV

Victory

1944-1945

1. The Invasion of Europe

GENERAL CARL ("TOOEY") SPAATZ of the United States Army
Air Force, America's foremost aviator, believed with Air Chief
Marshal "Bomber" Harris of the Royal Air Force that Germany could be defeated by air bombing; no invasion would be
necessary. In July and August 1943 the R.A.F. and VIII
A.A.F. together inflicted the most destructive air bombing of
the European war:—repeated attacks on Hamburg which
wiped out over half the city, killed 42,600, and injured 37,000
people. "Those who sowed the wind are reaping the whirlwind," remarked Winston Churchill. Worse was to come; but
this air offensive never became a substitute for land invasion.
Bombing German cities, almost nightly by the R.A.F. and
every clear day by the A.A.F., did not seriously diminish Germany's well dispersed war production, and failed to break her
civilian morale. It was also frightfully expensive. In six days of
October 1943, culminating in a raid on the ball-bearing plants
at Schweinfurt, the VIII A.A.F. lost 148 bombers and their
crews.

One reason for these heavy casualties was the lack of fighter
planes long-legged enough to escort the bombers from their

bases in England or Italy. But by the spring of 1944 we had the P-38 Lightning, P-47 Thunderbolt, and P-51 Mustang, which could fly to Berlin and back, fighting a good part of the way. Air power, besides obstructing the movement of enemy armies, was now applied with increasing precision and violence to the key centers of German war production.

In the week of 19–25 February 1944, 3800 heavy bombers of the VIII and XV A.A.F., escorted by fighters, attacked twelve targets vital to the German aircraft industry, as far south as Ratisbon and Augsburg. Our losses were 226 bombers, 28 fighters, and about 2600 men; but some 600 German planes were shot down. German aircraft production did recuperate, but these February bombing missions denied many hundred aircraft to the enemy when he needed them most. By 14 April, when this long-sustained bomber offensive ended, and control of the U.S. Strategic Air Forces in Europe passed to General Eisenhower, the Allied air forces had established a thirty-to-one superiority over the Luftwaffe. On Normandy D-day General Eisenhower told his troops, "If you see fighting aircraft over you, they will be ours," and so they were.

This air war in Europe cost the lives of some 158,000 British, Canadian, and American aviators, but it was indispensable to the success of the coming invasion.

Planning for the continental invasion began at London early in 1943, by an Anglo-American staff under the direction of General Sir Frederick Morgan. The Combined Chiefs of Staffs set the date for May or June 1944. General Eisenhower, who in the conduct of North African and Mediterranean operations had revealed superior talents, was appointed to command all invasion forces of both nations. In January 1944 "Ike" flew to London where he received his directive: "You will enter the continent of Europe and, in conjunction with the other United Nations, undertake operations aimed at the heart of Germany and the destruction of her armed forces."

Never since 1688 had an invading army crossed the English Channel, and there was no "Protestant wind" behind this one. The coastal defenses of Hitler's *Festung Europa* were formidable: underwater obstacles and mines, artillery emplacements, pill boxes, wire entanglements, tank traps, land mines, and other hazards to stop invaders on the beaches. Behind these defenses were stationed 58 German divisions, only 14 of them, fortunately, in Normandy and Brittany. Yet the Allies had reason for confidence. They could select their point of attack. For six weeks Allied air forces had been smashing roads and bridges in northern France, reducing the enemy transportation

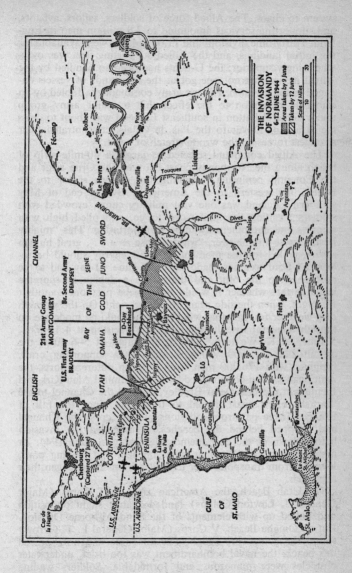

THE INVASION OF NORMANDY
6-12 JUNE 1944

Areas taken by 9 June
Taken by 12 June

Scale of Miles
0   10   20

ENGLISH   CHANNEL

Rouen
Seine R.
Bolbec
Pont Audemer
Fécamp
Le Havre
Touques
Deauville
Trouville
Lisieux
Dives
Falaise
Argentan

21st Army Group
MONTGOMERY

Br. Second Army
DEMPSEY

U.S. First Army
BRADLEY

D-Day Beachhead

BAY   OF   THE   SEINE

UTAH   OMAHA   GOLD   JUNO   SWORD

BR. AIRBORNE

Pointe du Hoc
Vierville
Isigny
Bayeux
Caumont
St. Lô
Vire
Flers
Orne
Caen

U.S. AIRBORNE

COTENTIN   PENINSULA

Ste. Mère Eglise
Carentan
La Haye du Puits
Coutances
Avranches
Granville

Cherbourg
(Captured 27 June)
Cap de
la Hague

GULF
OF
ST. MALO

St. Michel
St. Malo

system to chaos. The Allied force of soldiers, sailors, aviators, and supporting services amounted to 2.8 million men in England. Thirty-nine divisions and 11,000 planes were available for the initial landings, and the Allied supporting fleet was overwhelmingly superior; the U-boats had been so handled by the Allied navies that not one got at the thousands of vessels engaged in the invasion. Hitler's army commanders, fooled by an elaborate deception to the effect that a major army group under General Patton in southeast England was about to cross the Straits of Dover to the Pas de Calais, concentrated their strongest forces on the wrong stretch of coast.

The Allied command selected as target a 40-mile strip of beach along the Normandy coast between the Orne river and the Cotentin peninsula, assigning the eastern sector to the British, the western to the Americans. By the end of May southern England was one vast military camp, crowded with soldiers awaiting the final word to go, and piled high with supplies and equipment awaiting transportation. This "mighty host," wrote Eisenhower, "was as tense as a . . . great human spring, coiled for the moment when its energy should be released." Foul weather made up on 4 June, D-day had to be postponed to the 6th, and there was a debate at supreme headquarters whether it would have to be postponed another fortnight, when the tide again would be right. On the strength of a weather forecast that wind and sea would be moderate on the 6th, General Eisenhower made the decision at 4:15 a.m., 5 June, "O.K. We'll go." During the night of 5–6 June, the assault fleet of 600 warships and 4000 supporting craft, freighted with 176,000 men from a dozen different ports, the American section commanded by Rear Admiral Alan Kirk and Lieutenant General Omar Bradley, crossed the Channel to the "far shore," a coast denied to the Allies since the fall of France. Three paratroop divisions, flown across the Channel and dropped behind the beaches, spearheaded the invasion before dawn of the ever-memorable D-day, 6 June 1944. At first light the naval bombardment opened, and landing craft, lowered from transports over ten miles from shore, began their approach.

On Utah Beach, the American right, VII Corps (Major General J. Lawton Collins) landed against slight opposition and linked up with elements of the 82nd Airborne Division. But on Omaha Beach, V Corps (Major General L. T. Gerow) found the going very rough. The air force had not bombed this beach, the naval bombardment was too brief, underwater obstacles were numerous and formidable. Soldiers wading ashore fell when wounded into a maze of mined obstacles, and were drowned by the rising tide; those who reached dry land had to cross a 50-yard-wide beach exposed to cunningly contrived crossfire from concrete pill boxes that naval gunfire could not reach. Men huddled for protection under a low sea wall until company officers rallied them to root the defenders out of their prepared positions. Sheer guts and sound training saved the day at Omaha, not forgetting the naval gunfire support that rained shells on the Germans as soon as shore fire control parties were able to indicate targets.

The even bigger British assault force under Admiral Vian and General Dempsey had an easier landing on the eastern beaches, but bore the brunt of the next week's fighting. Caen, behind the British beaches, was the hinge of the Allied beachhead, where the Germans directed their main counterattacks. In both sectors the D-day assault was brilliantly successful; but the landings were only the beginning of a long and costly campaign.

In the first week the Allies landed 326,000 men, 50,000 vehicles, and over 100,000 tons of supplies, to build up an invading army faster than the Germans could reinforce theirs. They now controlled a beachhead some 7 miles in length and from five to fifteen miles in depth. Two artificial harbors called "mulberrys," built out of sunken ships with connecting pontoon units, facilitated this rapid build-up on the landing beaches, but a northwest gale which blew up on 19 June so badly damaged them that the capture of Cherbourg became highly urgent. Cherbourg surrendered on 26 June after the Germans had wrecked the harbor.

The Battle of Normandy lasted until 24 July. By that time the British had captured Caen; the Americans had taken Saint-Lô, gateway to the South. The enemy, unable to bring up reinforcements, his communications wrecked and planes grounded, was bewildered. Rommel thought the situation hopeless and was preparing to try to negotiate with Eisenhower for a separate peace when Hitler had him arrested and killed. Other high-ranking officers attempted to assassinate Hitler on 20 July, as the only way to end the war; but the Fuehrer survived, the conspirators were tortured to death, and the war went on. Hitler now trusted to secret weapons to win. His new V-1 "buzz bombs," launched from positions in Belgium and northern France, were spreading death and destruction on London, and the V-2 guided missiles were ready.

The Battle for France began on 25 July when General Patton's Third Army hit the German lines west of Saint-Lô. Within two days VII Corps had reached Coutances, hemming in remnants of the German army along the coast. By the end

of July, Avranches had fallen, and the Americans stood at the
threshold of Brittany. In the face of this fast and furious attack
the German withdrawal turned into something like a rout.
Nothing could stop Patton except running out of gas. One
wing of his army turned west and within a week overran Brittany, leaving only Brest, Lorient, and Saint-Nazaire for leisurely
reduction. Another wing turned east, and within two weeks
reached the Loire and Le Mans. In a desperate gamble Hitler
ordered the German Seventh Army to break through the
American army at Avranches. Most of it was destroyed in the
ensuing Battle of the Falaise Gap; only remnants of armor
fought their way through and sped east to prepare for the
defense of Germany.

On 15 August the Allies launched their long-awaited invasion of southern France. General Eisenhower insisted on this
operation, against strong opposition from Churchill, in order
to capture the major port of Marseilles for logistic supply, and
deploy the American Seventh Army (Lieutenant General Alexander C. Patch) and the First French Army (General de
Lattre de Tassigny) on his southern flank for the invasion of
Germany. The coast of Provence was so lightly defended that
the amphibious assault commanded by Admiral H. Kent
Hewitt USN was a pushover. Toulon and Marseilles were soon
liberated, Seventh Army rolled up the Rhone valley, captured
Lyon, and by mid-September linked with Patton's Third Army.

"Liberate Paris by Christmas and none of us can ask for
more," said Churchill to Eisenhower. First Army (Lieutenant
General Courtney H. Hodges) rolled to the Seine; Patton's
Third boiled out into the open country north of the Loire and
swept eastward through Orleans to Troyes. Paris rose against
the German garrison, and with the aid of General Leclerc's
2nd Armored Division was liberated on 25 August, four
months ahead of Churchill's request. General Charles de
Gaulle now entered the city in triumph and assumed the presidency of a French provisional government.

Patton's spearheads reached the Marne on 28 August and
overran Rheims and Verdun. To the north, Montgomery's
British and Canadians pushed along the coast into Belgium,
captured Brussels, and entered Antwerp 4 September. By the
11th, the American First Army had liberated Luxemburg and
near Aachen crossed the border into Germany. Within six
weeks all France had been cleared of the enemy, and from
Belgium to Switzerland Allied armies stood poised for the invasion of Germany. Hitler had lost almost half a million men,
but his amazing hold over the Germans had not relaxed, and
they were ready for a last counterblow that cost the Allies dear.

On other fronts, Russia had recovered most of her invaded territory, and in the spring of 1944 the Soviet armies reached the Dnieper river in the north and the Carpathians in the south. Stalin, having promised to start a new offensive when the Allies entered Normandy, on 23 June advanced along an 800-mile front from Leningrad to the Carpathians. In the space of five weeks Russians swept across the Ukraine and Poland and up to the gates of Warsaw where they paused, despicably, instead of helping Polish patriots to liberate the capital. Rumania threw in the sponge when another Red army crossed her borders, and so deprived the Germans of their last source of crude oil. In Italy the Germans were being driven back on their last line of defense, guarding the Po valley.

Although in mid-September 1944 the Allies held the initiative on the western front, they were unable to exploit it owing to a serious problem of logistics. Not only were the supply lines very, very long; the sea approach to Antwerp was still denied by a stubborn German defense of the lower Scheldt. This situation presented Eisenhower with one of his most difficult strategic problems. Field Marshal Montgomery wanted to push ahead through Holland into the heart of Germany and plunge through to Berlin. General Patton was no less confident of his ability to smash into Germany from the south. Logistical supply permitted a modest advance on a broad front, or a deep stab on a single front, but not both. Because Eisenhower deemed it essential to clear the way to Antwerp, capture Calais and Dunkerque, and overrun the V-1 and V-2 bomb emplacements which were raining guided missiles on London, priority in the scarce gasoline supply was given to Montgomery, who wasted it; and his favored operation, taking Arnhem by paratroop drop, was badly defeated, stopping the ground offensive cold. The sad prospect of another winter's campaign in Europe now loomed.

2. *The Battle for Leyte Gulf*

By 1 August 1944, when the Marianas and New Guinea were in American or Australian possession, the question of where to move next had virtually been decided at a conference in Honolulu between General MacArthur, Admiral Nimitz, and President Roosevelt. The President, pointing to Saipan on the map, said, "Douglas, where do we go from here?" "Leyte, Mr. President; and then Luzon!" And that is how it was done.

The Joint Chiefs of Staff set the date for the invasion of Leyte as 20 December 1944, but at the suggestion of aggressive Admiral Halsey, with General MacArthur's glad approval,

the timetable was stepped up two months. Central Pacific forces
under Admirals Nimitz and Halsey, and Southwest Pacific
forces under General MacArthur and Admiral Kinkaid, combined in one massive thrust into Leyte. That island was chosen
as the nearest practicable base from which to begin the liberation of the Philippines, and also because land-based planes on
previously captured islands could cover the invasion. Early in
the morning of 20 October 1944, 73 transports and 50 LST's
entered Leyte Gulf, exactly where Magellan's ships had sailed,
423 years before. The landings on Leyte by Sixth Army (Lieutenant General Walter Krueger) went off according to schedule, and that afternoon General MacArthur and President
Osmeña of the Philippines splashed ashore from a landing craft.
Before a microphone, MacArthur delivered an impressive
liberation speech beginning, "People of the Philippines, I have
returned."

He certainly had; but how long could he stay? The Japanese
were not taking this lying down. At Tokyo the war lords decided to commit the entire Japanese fleet, smash American
forces afloat, and so isolate MacArthur that he would be virtually back at Bataan. From that decision there resulted, on
25 October, the Battle for Leyte Gulf, greatest sea fight of this
or of any other war.

Admiral Toyoda put into execution a plan based on ruse
and surprise, factors dear to Japanese strategists; but his plan
required a division of the Japanese fleet into three parts, which
proved to be fatal. Admiral Nishimura's Southern Force of
battleships and cruisers was to come through Surigao Strait,
break into Leyte Gulf at daybreak 25 October, and there
rendezvous with Kurita's more powerful Center Force, which
was to thread San Bernardino Strait and come around Samar
from the north. Either separately was strong enough to make
mincemeat of Admiral Kinkaid's amphibious forces in Leyte
Gulf and cut off General Krueger's troops from their sea-
borne lifeline. Way was to be cleared for Kurita by Admiral
Ozawa's Northern Force built around four carriers, whose mission was to entice Halsey's Task Force 38, the American carrier
force, up north.

That part of the plan worked only too well, but the rest of
it worked not at all. Admiral Kinkaid deployed almost every
battleship, cruiser, and destroyer that had supported the Leyte
landings, and placed them under the command of Rear Admiral Jesse Oldendorf, to catch Nishimura as he came through
Surigao Strait in the early hours of 25 October. Two destroyer
torpedo attacks nicked Nishimura of one battleship and three
destroyers, and what was left of his "T" was crossed by

Oldendorf's battleships and cruisers. Their high-caliber fire sank the other enemy battleship, and what was left of the Southern Force fled, most of it to be harried and sunk after dawn by carrier planes. This smashing night victory—the Battle of Surigao Strait—was the battlewagons' revenge for Pearl Harbor; five of those engaged had been sunk or grounded on 7 December 1941.

Scarcely had Surigao Strait been cleared when the most critical of the three actions began. Kurita's massive Center Force, built around his biggest battleships and heavy cruisers, had been damaged and delayed the previous day, first by American submarines, then by the Halsey-Mitscher carrier planes. Halsey overestimated the damage that his bombers had done; and, after his search planes had found Admiral Ozawa's Northern Force coming down from Japan (with the express mission of luring him north), the Admiral could think of nothing but to sink those carriers. So, without leaving even a destroyer to watch San Bernardino Strait, Halsey roared up north to dispose of the enemy flattops.

Thus, Kurita, to his great astonishment, was able to thread the strait unopposed, and approach the northern entrance to Leyte Gulf undetected. At one of the critical moments of the war, off the island of Samar, at 6:45 a.m., 25 October, Kurita ran smack into a force of six escort carriers under Rear Admiral Clifton Sprague. One of three groups of "baby flattops" that were providing air cover for the amphibious forces in Leyte Gulf, the last thing they expected was a fight with battleships, heavy cruisers, and destroyers. The ensuing Battle off Samar was the most gallant naval action in our history, and the most bloody—1130 killed, 913 wounded. Kurita, who still had the 18-inch-gunned *Yamato* and three more battleships, eight cruisers, and ten destroyers, should have been able to destroy Sprague's feebly armed escort carriers; but as soon as the Japanese big guns opened at a range of 14 miles, Sprague turned into the wind to launch planes, called for help from two other escort carrier groups, and sent his destroyers and DE's to make desperate gunfire and torpedo attacks. After a running fight of an hour and a half, two American escort carriers and two destroyer types were lost; but the American bombs and torpedoes had sunk three Japanese heavy cruisers and, by repeated relentless air attacks, so badly mauled and scattered the other enemy ships that Admiral Kurita broke off action and retired. Thus, because the enemy commander lacked gumption, and Sprague had plenty; and also because the Japanese had no air support, a fleet more than ten times as powerful as the Americans in gunfire was defeated.

Up north, Admiral Marc Mitscher's carriers were slicing off bombers and fighter planes against Ozawa's carriers which had decoyed Halsey. In this battle off Cape Engaño, all four Japanese carriers were sunk.

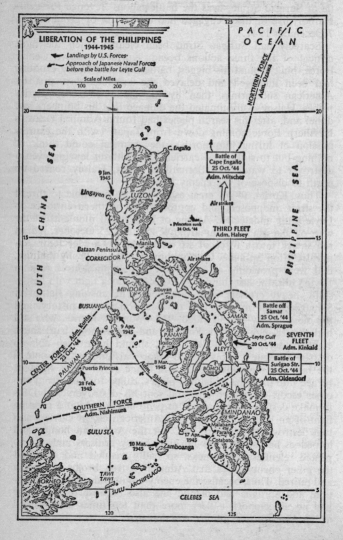

LIBERATION OF THE PHILIPPINES
1944-1945

→ Landings by U.S. Forces
⇢ Approach of Japanese Naval Forces
before the battle for Leyte Gulf

Scale of Miles
0   100   200   300

PACIFIC OCEAN

NORTHERN FORCE
Adm. Ozawa

C. Engaño

Battle of
Cape Engaño
25 Oct. '44
Adm. Mitscher

9 Jan. 1945

Lingayen Gulf

LUZON

Air strikes

Princeton sunk
24 Oct. '44

THIRD FLEET
Adm. Halsey

Manila

Bataan Peninsula
CORREGIDOR I.

Air strikes

SOUTH CHINA SEA

PHILIPPINE SEA

MINDORO

Sibuyan Sea

BUSUANGA

SAMAR

Battle off
Samar
25 Oct. '44
Adm. Sprague

9 Apr. 1945

PANAY

Iloilo

CEBU

LEYTE

Leyte Gulf
20 Oct. '44

SEVENTH FLEET
Adm. Kinkaid

CENTER FORCE
Adm. Kurita
23 Oct. '44

PALAWAN

Puerto Princesa

8 Mar. 1945

Adm. Shima

BOHOL

Battle of
Surigao Str.
25 Oct. '44
Adm. Oldendorf

28 Feb. 1945

SOUTHERN FORCE
Adm. Nishimura

24 Oct. '44

MINDANAO

SULU SEA

Malabang
Parang
Cotabato

17 Apr. 1945

10 Mar. 1945
Zamboanga

TAWI TAWI

SULU ARCHIPELAGO

N. BORNEO

CELEBES SEA

This three-part battle for Leyte Gulf on 25 October 1944 left the United States Navy in complete command of Philippine waters; never again could the Japanese navy offer a real threat. But two months' fighting ashore were required against the hard-fighting, no-surrender Japanese infantry, before Leyte and Samar were in MacArthur's hands.

3. Political Interlude

As the Allied armed forces lunged on to victory, another presidential election came up, first in wartime since 1864. Eighty years earlier, the Democratic party had nominated a disgruntled general, attacked the conduct of the war, and called for a compromise peace. Now, in 1944, a hard core of isolationists, supported by the Chicago *Tribune* and the Hearst press, wished to reverse the "beat Germany first" decision and promote General MacArthur, supposedly a "martyr" to Roosevelt's "jealousy," for the Republican presidential nomination. But the General, although he felt slighted and hoped to become President some day, insisted first on fulfilling his promise to liberate the Philippines. A Gallup poll in the Midwest farming country in September 1943 gave General MacArthur a decided preference over Roosevelt for next President. Many voters in the old liberal-progressive farm bloc, especially German-Americans, never believed in any necessity to fight Hitler, and the Pearl Harbor attack turned all their belligerent feelings westward.

For the present, however, almost every Republican supported the war and endorsed a postwar international organization. In the 1942 congressional elections the Republicans increased their strength in the House 30 per cent, giving them high hopes of winning the presidency in 1944.

Wendell Willkie by now was a world figure, owing to several visits to Allied countries, and inspiring speeches in support of the war. But he made the tactical error of entering the presidential primary in Wisconsin, where the voters wanted no advocate of "One World," but an isolationist who would promise to "bring the boys home" from Europe. There he met a stunning defeat, and withdrew. Thomas E. Dewey, who had proved himself a competent administrator as governor of New York, was nominated by the Republican convention on the first ballot. Republican strategy was to concentrate on the argument that no party could be safely entrusted with office for more than twelve years without a hardening of political arteries, and that the country needed new and younger men for the tasks of peace and reconstruction. Respecting President Roosevelt's health the charge was only too true; but his physicians reported him still to be fit as a fiddle. The Democratic national convention renominated him on the first ballot for a fourth term, but there was a change in the second place on the ticket. Roosevelt, tired of Wallace's left-wing vagaries, gave the nod to Senator Harry Truman of Missouri—another instance of his good judgment.

The issue was never in doubt. Roosevelt carried 36 states with 432 electoral votes; Dewey, 12 states with 99 electoral votes, and Roosevelt's popular plurality was about 3.5 million. The Democrats won 242 seats in the House, as against 190 Republicans. That marked the end of isolationism as a positive political factor. But, in a sense, it "went underground," to emerge nastily as McCarthyism.

4. Victory in Europe

After the failure of the Arnhem air drop, the war lost its momentum and settled down to what General Eisenhower called "the dirtiest kind of infantry slugging." The Germans now held their strongest defensive positions since the beginning of the invasion. Rundstedt and Kesselring, their ablest generals, were now commanders in the west and in Italy. Floods, intense cold, rain and snow in the winter of 1944-45 combined to help the defense.

In the confused fighting that stretched from October to mid-December 1944 we can distinguish a series of battles, each as bitter and as costly as any since the Civil War. The first, taking them in geographical order, was the battle for the Scheldt estuary. The task of clearing the enemy out of the islands, whose possession by the Germans prevented Allied use of Antwerp, was assigned to the Canadian First Army. The reduction of Walcheren cost the Allies more casualties than the conquest of Sicily, and not until the end of November could Allied ships unload at Antwerp, and so shorten the logistics line.

The second major battle was for Aachen, near the junction of Belgium, Holland, and Germany. General Hodges's First Army launched the attack on 2 October, fighting through five miles of German fortifications. By the middle of the month the city was surrounded; then came a week of street fighting before the ancient capital of Charlemagne capitulated—first German city to fall to the Allies.

General Omar Bradley now brought Ninth Army north to co-operate with the First in a campaign to capture the Roer river dams—third of the major battles. An assault by seventeen divisions through the Hürtgen Forest to Düren failed to do it.

The country was not unlike that Wilderness in which Grant and Lee had tangled eighty years earlier. Three divisions alone, the 4th, 9th, and 28th, suffered almost 13,000 casualties. The Americans reached the Roer river on 3 December, and there they were stalled until early February.

In the south, General Patton's Third Army jumped off in early November to capture Metz, northern Lorraine, and the industrial Saar basin. Only once before in modern times—in 1871—had the fortress city of Metz fallen to an invader. Patton proved that if need be, he could be methodical, instead of dashing. First he enveloped Metz, reducing one by one the forts that encircled it. Then came a week of street fighting. The city fell on 22 November and Third Army, fighting its way through the heaviest fortifications of the Siegfried line, plunged into the Saar. This campaign cost the Americans 29,000 battle casualties, but netted them 37,000 prisoners.

In conjunction with Patton's advance, Lieutenant General Jacob L. Devers's Sixth Army Group, which incorporated Patch's and De Lattre de Tassigny's armies, entered Alsace, and Strasbourg fell on 23 November. The French then turned north along the Rhine, the Americans south. These operations, obscured by the more dramatic fighting to the north, cost the Allies 33,000 more casualties.

By mid-December the Allied armies were poised along the border from Holland to Switzerland, ready to plunge deep into Germany. Then came a dramatic change of fortune: a German counteroffensive, recalling Jubal Early's raid on Washington in 1864, but on a vast scale. Rundstedt's name was given to this desperate thrust through the Ardennes Forest, but the idea was Hitler's. His objective was to split the Allied army groups, drive through to the coast, and recapture Antwerp. Eisenhower had taken the calculated risk of spreading thin his forces in the rugged Ardennes, through which Rundstedt had crashed with his main force in May 1940. Now the Germans prepared to repeat that successful campaign. Because the bad weather prevented Allied air reconnaissance, they achieved surprise and initial success along a fifty-mile front, on 16 December. After the first shock, Allied resistance stiffened. The Germans concentrated on the center of the Allied line. They almost reached the Meuse on 26 December, but were checked at Bastogne, headquarters of General Troy Middleton's VIII Corps, focal point of a network of roads essential to the Germans. Middleton decided to hold it at all costs, without adequate forces. Late in the night of 17 December the 101st Airborne Division, then in a rest center 100 miles behind the lines, was ordered to Bastogne; the men piled into trucks and

jeeps and pulled into Bastogne on the 18th, just before the
German tide flooded around the town. This reinforcement
beefed up the strength of the defenders to some 18,000 men.

There followed one of the fiercest land battles of the war.
The Americans seized outlying villages, and set up a perimeter
defense. For six days the enemy hurled armor and planes at
them, persistently probing for a weak spot, and found not one.
Foul weather prevented aerial reinforcement of the defenders.
On 22 December the American situation appeared hopeless and
the Germans presented a formal demand for surrender, to
which General "Tony" McAuliffe of the 101st Airborne gave
the simple answer "Nuts!" Next day the weather cleared, and
planes began dropping supplies; by Christmas Eve, with bomber
and fighter support, the situation looked more hopeful. In the
meantime, Patton's Third Army had made a great left wheel
and started pell-mell north to the rescue of the besieged garrison. On 26 December his 4th Armored Division broke
through the German encirclement and Bastogne was saved.
The Battle of the Bulge, as we named it, was not over, but by
15 January 1945 the original lines of mid-December had been
restored. Rundstedt had held up the Allied advance by a full
month, but at a cost of 120,000 men, 1600 planes, and a good
part of his armor. Never thereafter were the Germans able to
put up an effective defense.

At the end of January, Eisenhower regrouped his armies and
resumed advance toward the Rhine. In the meantime the
Russians had sprung their winter offensive, which surpassed
the campaign in the west in numbers involved and territory
recaptured. The Russian army jumped off on a 1000-mile front
early in January, crossed the Vistula, and swept toward Germany. While one group of armies in the center took Warsaw
and raced across Poland to the Oder river, others stabbed into
Germany from the north and south, moved into Hungary and
Czechoslovakia, and threatened Vienna.

In the final Allied campaign in the west we can distinguish
three stages: the advance to the Rhine, from late January to
21 March; the crossing of the Rhine and the Battle of the Ruhr,
21 March to 14 April; and the annihilation of all enemy opposition, 14 April to the surrender on 7 May 1945. Omitting
details, the 7th of March was one of the dramatic days of the
war. On that day a detachment of the 9th Armored Division
captured a bridge over the Rhine at Remagen, just as the
Germans were about to blow it. A fleet of navy landing craft
were brought up in trucks to help General Hodges's First
Army get across; it then fanned out, securing the highway

running south to Munich. And on 22 March Patton, beating "Monty" to the river, began crossing the Rhine at Oppenheim.

The next move after vaulting the Rhine barrier was to encircle the Ruhr. Moving at breakneck speed, First Army swung north, Lieutenant General William H. Simpson's Ninth turned south, and a giant pincer closed on the Ruhr. Encircled, pounded on all sides, hammered day and night by swarms of bombers, the German armies caught in the pocket disintegrated. By 18 April the bag of prisoners reached the total of 325,000, and organized resistance ceased. It was, said General Marshall, the largest envelopment operation in the history of American warfare; and it should be noted that this was Marshall's idea, violently opposed by Sir Alan Brooke and Montgomery, who wished to concentrate all Allied ground forces in one knifelike thrust across northern Europe. That concept, if carried out, would have created an impossible congestion and left the Ruhr in enemy hands.

Now Montgomery drove toward Bremen and Hamburg, Patton raced for Kassel, and Patch sped through Bavaria toward Czechoslovakia.

As the Allied armies penetrated Germany, Austria, and Poland, they came upon one torture camp after another— Buchenwald, Dachau, Belsen, Auschwitz, Linz, Lublin—and what they saw sickened them. These atrocious camps had been started in 1937 for Jews, gypsies, and anti-Nazi Germans and Austrians; during the war Hitler used them for prisoners of all nationalities, civilians and soldiers, men, women, and children, and for Jews rounded up in Italy, France, Holland, and Hungary. All Jews were killed in the hope of exterminating the entire race, hordes of prisoners were scientifically murdered; multitudes died of disease, starvation, and maltreatment. Much of this wholesale murder was done in the name of "science," and with the criminal collusion of German physicians, who appear to have absorbed the Nazi contempt for humanity. Nothing in their experience had prepared Americans for these revelations of human depravity; many are still incredulous. But the evidence is conclusive that the total number of civilians done to death by Hitler's orders exceeded 6 million. And the pathetic story of one of the least of these, the diary of the little Dutch girl Anne Frank, has probably done more to convince the world of the hatred inherent in the Nazi doctrine than the solemn postwar trials.

As German resistance crumbled and victory appeared certain, the Allied world was plunged into mourning by the news that a great leader had died. President Roosevelt, returning in

February a sick man from the Yalta conference of the Combined Chiefs of Staff, went to his winter home in Warm Springs, Georgia, to prepare for the inauguration of the United Nations at San Francisco. On 12 April, as he was drafting a Jefferson Day address, he suffered a cerebral hemorrhage which brought instant death. The last words he wrote were an epitome of his career: "The only limit to our realization of tomorrow will be our doubts of today. Let us move forward with strong and active faith."

Now the end of Hitler's Germany approached. The Western Allies rolled unopposed to the Elbe; the Russians thrust at Berlin. Advance detachments of the two armies met at Torgau on 25 April, severing Germany. On the last day of April, Hitler died a coward's death, killing first his mistress and then himself in a bombproof bunker under Berlin. German resistance was also collapsing in northern Italy. On 4 May General Mark Clark's Fifth Army, which had fought all the way up the boot of Italy, met, at the Brenner Pass, General Patch's Seventh, coming down through Austria, and next day German resistance in Italy ceased. Italian partisans had already captured and killed Mussolini, on 28 April. Thus ended, in ruin, horror, and despair the Axis that pretended to rule the world, and the Reich which Hitler had boasted would last a thousand years.

Admiral Doenitz, Hitler's designated heir and second Fuehrer, tried desperately to arrange a surrender to the Western Allies, instead of to Russia. Loyalty to our Eastern ally—a loyalty not reciprocated—caused General Eisenhower sternly to decline these advances. On 7 May General Jodl signed an unconditional surrender at Allied headquarters in Rheims, and the war came to an end in the West.

5. Victory in the Pacific

Well before the landings on Leyte on 20 October 1944, the Joint Chiefs of Staff decided that as soon as the aircraft carrier fleet could be relieved from supporting MacArthur in the Philippines, it should help secure island bases for a final assault on Japan. Tokyo, Saipan, and Formosa make an isosceles triangle with legs 1500 miles long. The eastern leg, Saipan-Tokyo, was already being used by the B-29 Superforts to bomb the Japanese homeland, but a halfway house was wanted through which fighter support could stage, or where damaged Superforts could call. Iwo Jima fitted the bill. Kelly Turner's seasoned Fifth Fleet team, with Major General Harry Schmidt commanding the marines, landed on 19 February 1945. Mount Suribachi, scene of the famous flag-raising, was captured on

23 February; after that it was a steady, bloody advance of the marines against the holed-up enemy, with constant naval fire support. Even before organized resistance ceased on 14 March, the B-29's began using the Iwo airfields; and it is estimated that by this means thousands of American lives were saved. But Iwo Jima cost the navy and marine corps 6855 deaths and 21,000 other casualties.

In the meantime another angle of the triangle, whose apex was Tokyo, had been shifted to Okinawa in the Ryukyus, several hundred miles nearer Japan than is Formosa, and less stoutly defended. Sixty-mile-long Okinawa, where Commodore Perry had called in 1853, was an integral part of Japan. It was expected that when we attacked the Japanese would "throw the book at us," and they did. They had few warships left and American command of the sea prevented reinforcement of the island garrison; but they had plenty of planes and self-sacrificing pilots to employ the deadly kamikaze tactics. The Kamikaze ("Divine Wind") Corps was organized as a desperate expedient after the use of proximity-fuzed antiaircraft shells by the United States Navy had made it almost impossible for a conventional bomber to hit a ship. The kamikaze pilots were trained to crash a ship, which meant certain death for a large part of its crew, and probable loss of the vessel. These tactics had already been tried in the Philippines campaign, with devastating success, and no defense against them had yet been found, except to station radar picket destroyers around the fleet, to take the rap and pass the word.

The Spruance-Turner team was in charge of the amphibious assault on Okinawa, with Lieutenant General Simon Bolivar Buckner (who lost his life there) commanding Tenth Army. American amphibious technique was now so perfected that when the four divisions went ashore on Okinawa on Easter Sunday, 1 April, the Japanese abandoned beaches and airfields and retired to prepared positions on the southern end of the island. Here they put up a desperate resistance, exacting a heavy toll of American lives, before the island was conquered late in June. In the meantime the navy, which had to cover the operation and furnish fire support, took a terrible beating from the kamikaze planes. Thirty-two ships were sunk, and sixty-one others were so badly damaged as to be out of the war; casualties were heavy even on the ships that survived. The carrier task force, besides supporting this operation, made carrier-plane raids on Tokyo and on Japanese airfields, and when the superbattleship *Yamato* sortied in early April, she was promptly sunk by air attack. Seven carriers were badly damaged by kamikazes—*Franklin, Wasp,* and *Bunker Hill* between them lost 2211 men killed and 798 wounded—but not one was sunk. The invasion of Okinawa cost us more than 12,500 sailors, soldiers, and aviators; but the island was indispensable as a base, not only in the closing weeks of World War II but in the cold war that followed.

Germany was now defeated and the Allies could give their undivided attention to knocking out Japan. A new British offensive, by land and sea, captured Mandalay and Rangoon in the spring of 1945 and pushed the Japanese out of Burma. While in great secrecy scientists were preparing the atomic bombs at Los Alamos, the navy and the army air force redoubled the fury of their attacks on the Japanese home islands. There were bombings by carrier planes, naval bombardments, and B-29 bombing raids. Large parts of Tokyo and other industrial cities were destroyed by incendiary bombs.

During these assaults on the outlying Japanese islands, General Eichelberger's Eighth Army and Admiral Kinkaid's Seventh Fleet—both under General MacArthur—were completing the liberation of the Philippines. They captured the ruins of Manila, where the Japanese made a house-to-house defense, on 4 March 1945. There the Philippine Commonwealth, soon to become the Philippine Republic, was already re-established by MacArthur. The General did not feel that he had redeemed his promise until the rest of the archipelago was liberated; and before Japan surrendered, Palawan, Panay, Negros, Cebu, Bohol, Mindanao, and Sulu had been taken by a series of assaults spearheaded by Rear Admiral Dan Barbey's VII 'Phib.

Nor must one forget the Pacific Fleet submarines whose destruction of merchant shipping was one of the three main factors that brought victory over Japan. Some 50 American submarines operating daily in the Pacific, in 1944 under Admiral Lockwood, were almost twice as effective as over 100 German U-boats operating daily in the Atlantic in 1942–43. Japan had 6 million tons of merchant shipping at the start of the war and added another 4 million tons by conquest and new construction; but at the end she had left only 1.8 million tons, mostly small wooden vessels in the Inland Sea, and was completely cut off from her island conquests. United States forces alone sank 2117 Japanese merchant vessels of almost 8 million tons during the war, and 60 per cent of this was done by submarines, of which 50 were lost in action. Japanese submarines sank several valuable warships but inflicted slight damage on the American merchant marine; and 128 of the Japanese submarines were lost, U.S.S. *England* sinking six in thirteen days of May 1944.

The Combined Chiefs of Staff, meeting at Quebec in September 1944, figured that it would take eighteen months after the surrender of Germany to defeat Japan. Actually, the war in the Pacific ended with a terrific bang only three months after V-E Day. President Truman and Winston Churchill, meeting with the C.C.S. at Potsdam, presented Japan with an ultimatum on 26 July 1945. The surrender must be complete, and include Allied occupation of Japan, and the return of all Japanese conquests since 1895 to their former owners. But the Japanese people were assured that the occupation would end as soon as "a peacefully inclined and responsible government" was established, and that they would neither "be enslaved as a race or destroyed as a nation." The alternative was "prompt and utter destruction." If Suzuki, the Japanese premier, had made up his mind promptly to accept the Potsdam declaration as a basis for peace, there would have been no atomic bomb explosion over Japan. But Suzuki was more afraid of the Japanese militarists than he was of American power.

The fearful consequences were the result of prolonged experiment and development in atomic fission. In 1939 Albert Einstein, Enrico Fermi, Leo Szilard, and other physicists who had sought refuge in the United States from tyranny in their native countries, warned President Roosevelt of the danger of Germany's obtaining a lead in uranium fission. The President entrusted a project of that nature to the Office of Scientific Research and Development, set up in May 1941. On 2 December 1942 Fermi and others achieved the first self-sustaining nuclear chain reaction, halfway mark to the atomic bomb. Army engineers under General W. S. Groves then took over and built a small city at Oak Ridge, Tennessee, for producing the atomic bomb. By 1944 research had so progressed that a special physics laboratory was erected at Los Alamos, New Mexico, for which J. R. Oppenheimer was responsible; and on 16 July 1945 the first atomic bomb was exploded there.

President Truman conveyed the news at Potsdam to Winston Churchill, who remarked, "This is the Second Coming, in wrath." That indeed it was for Japan.

We had it, but whether or not to use it was another question. President Truman's committee of high officials and top atomic scientists recommended that atomic bombs be exploded over Japan at once, and without warning. On 25 July the President issued the necessary order to the XX Army Air Force at Saipan, whither the first two bombs had been sent, to prepare to drop them at the first favorable moment after 3 August, if Japan had not by then accepted surrender. He and Secretary of State Byrnes waited in vain for word from Japan. All they got was a silly statement from Suzuki that the Potsdam Declaration was unworthy of notice. So the fateful order stood. "Enola Gay," as the chosen B-29 was called, was commanded by Colonel Paul W. Tibbets. At 9:15 a.m., 6 August, the bomb was toggled out at an altitude of 31,600 feet over Hiroshima. This city had been given the tragic target assignment as the second most important military center in Japan. The bomb wiped out the Second Japanese Army to a man, razed four square miles of the city, and killed 60,175 people, including the soldiers. Around noon 9 August, a few hours after Russia had declared war on Japan, the second atomic bomb exploded over Nagasaki, killing 36,000 more.[1]

Although many Americans have expressed contrition over exploding the first atomic bombs, it is difficult to see how the Pacific war could otherwise have been concluded, except by a long and bitter invasion of Japan; or what difference it would have made after the war if the secret had temporarily been withheld. The explosion over Hiroshima caused fewer civilian casualties than the repeated B-29 bombings of Tokyo, and those big bombers would have had to wipe out one city after another if the war had not ended in August. Japan had enough military capability—more than 5000 planes with kamikaze-trained pilots and at least 2 million ground troops—to have made our planned invasion of the Japanese home islands in the fall of 1945 an exceedingly bloody affair for both sides. And that would have been followed by a series of bitterly protracted battles on Japanese soil, the effects of which even time could hardly have healed. Moreover, as Russia would have been a full partner in these campaigns, the end result would have been partition of Japan, as happened to Germany.

Even after the two atomic bombs had been dropped, and the Potsdam declaration had been clarified to assure Japan that she could keep her emperor, the surrender was a very near thing. Hirohito had to override his two chief military advisers and take the responsibility of accepting the Potsdam terms. That he did on 14 August, but even after that a military coup d'état to sequester the emperor, kill his cabinet, and continue the war was narrowly averted. Hirohito showed great moral courage; and the promise to retain him in power despite the wishes of Russia (which wanted the war prolonged and Japan given over to anarchy) was a very wise decision.

After preliminary arrangements had been made at Manila

---

[1] Official Japanese statement of 31 July 1959 for Hiroshima. Samuél Glasstone, *Effects of Nuclear Weapons* (Atomic Energy Commission, 1957), p. 455, for Nagasaki.

with General MacArthur's and Admiral Nimitz's staffs, an advance party was flown into Atsugi airfield near Tokyo on 28 August. Scores of ships of the United States Pacific Fleet, and of the British Far Eastern Fleet, then entered Tokyo Bay. On 2 September 1945 General MacArthur, General Umezu, the Japanese foreign minister, and representatives of Great Britain, China, Russia, Australia, Canada, New Zealand, the Netherlands, and France, signed the surrender documents on the deck of battleship *Missouri*, a few miles from the spot where Commodore Perry's treaty had been signed ninety-two years before.

At 9:25 a.m., as the formalities closed, a flight of hundreds of aircraft swept over *Missouri* and her sister ships. General MacArthur then addressed a broadcast to the people of the United States:

> Today the guns are silent. A great tragedy has ended. A great victory has been won. . . .
>
> A new era is upon us. . . . Victory itself brings with it profound concern, both for our future security, and the survival of civilization.
>
> Men since the beginning of time have sought peace. . . . Military alliances, balances of power, leagues of nations, all in turn failed, leaving the only path to be by the way of the crucible of war. . . .
>
> The utter destructiveness of war now blots out this alternative. We have had our last chance. If we do not devise some greater and more equitable system, Armageddon will be at our door. The problem basically is theological and involves a spiritual recrudescence. . . .

XVI

The Truman Administrations

1945-1953

1. *The Iron Curtain*

BEFORE BEWILDERED Harry Truman takes the helm on 12 April 1945, one month before the end of the war in Europe and four months before victory in the Pacific, we must speak of relations with Russia in the latter part of the Roosevelt regime.

Almost every American admired Russia's war effort and wished to remain friendly with her government and people. But this did not suit Stalin. Churchill and Roosevelt made several basic errors in their relations with the Soviets. First, they believed that if they were "nice to Russia" and helped her to the extent of their ability, Russia would co-operate to support a free world—in the Western sense—after the war. Nothing could have been more mistaken. Stalin could, when he chose, be very pleasant and reasonable as in the conferences at Tehran and Yalta; even at Potsdam after the death of Roosevelt, who liked referring to him as "Uncle Joe." The flapdoodle written about Stalin by such people as Eric Johnston, president of the American Chamber of Commerce, and Ambassador Joseph Davies, is astounding. Davies, who lived at Moscow in an atmosphere of caviar and champagne, even declared that to question Stalin's good faith was "bad Chris-

tianity, bad sportsmanship, bad sense." Wendell Willkie glorified the Russian regime in his book *One World*. Roosevelt had
the conceit to suppose that his personal charm could win over
Stalin; but it bounced off that human steel like echo-ranging
sonar off the hull of a U-boat. Even Truman returned from
Potsdam saying, "I like Uncle Joe," and telling how they had
discussed (through an interpreter) the raising of corn and
pigs. Actually, Stalin never abandoned the Communist party's
objective of revolutionizing the world. He naturally accepted
all the help he could get from the Western powers in his war
with Hitler, but he intended to control every country bordering Russia on the west, and to revolutionize the rest of Europe
with the aid of communists in Italy and France; the more
useful to him and dangerous to their own countries by virtue
of their guerrilla experience resisting Hitler and Mussolini.
Ambassador Averell Harriman and George Kennan warned
Washington what would happen after the war, but nobody of
importance listened, and the policy of "be nice to Russia"
continued.

The second reason why the Western Allies went all out to
please Stalin was the indispensability of Russia's war effort.
Hitler put forth Germany's greatest strength on the eastern
front, where Russia, nearly to the end of the war, engaged
between 125 and 200 German divisions. It was essential for
victory in the West that this vast host continue on the eastern
front. Here the Western Allies paid the penalty for not having
managed to beat Germany a year earlier, when they would have
had far less need of Russian support.

Russia had been neutral to the war in the Pacific, but the
Western Allies mistakenly assumed that Japan could not be
defeated without Russian aid. Otherwise, it was feared, the
Allies would have to fight a long and bloody campaign against
a Japanese army in Manchuria after conquering Japan. The
Combined Chiefs of Staff badly wanted Russia to declare war
on Japan; even General MacArthur prior to Yalta said it was
necessary. Actually, Allied military intelligence was so defective that without its knowledge the strongest elements of the
Japanese army in Manchuria had been removed to defend the
Marianas, Okinawa, and the home islands; by mid-1945 that
army was a mere "paper tiger," to use a favorite Chinese
phrase.

The final mistake was the assumption that a joint regime,
communist and non-communist, would work in defeated or
liberated countries, like the "popular front" governments before the war. Churchill visited Moscow in October 1944 and
negotiated with Stalin a division of spheres of future influence

in the Balkins. The British were to have Greece, the Russians Rumania, and they would split Yugoslavia and Hungary fifty-fifty. Roosevelt and the state department did not like this, as savoring of secret treaties in World War I, but did nothing about it. The event proved that no popular front with communists could have any other result but a Communist party take-over. It was not generally known that within a month of the death of Hitler, Moscow had ordered all communists every-where to restore the "hard line."

All these false assumptions prevailed when Churchill and Roosevelt met Stalin at Yalta in the Crimea in February 1945. The Battle of the Bulge was then barely over, the Philippines had not yet been liberated or Okinawa even invaded. Five months earlier, future lines of demarcation between the Rus-sian and Allied armies in Germany had been agreed upon; and at the moment, when the Western Allies had not even crossed the Rhine, the Russians were fast approaching the Oder river. Moreover, the atomic bomb had not yet been tried out; the army told Roosevelt that he could not depend on it. Had it been tried and a proved success, the anxiety about Russian sup-port either in the West or in the East would not have existed.

This is the background to the agreements at Yalta. In return for Stalin's promise to fight Japan two or three months at most after Germany surrendered, Russia was promised the southern half of Sakhalin Island, which Japan had won in her war of 1904, and the recognition of her "pre-eminent interests" in Manchuria; and the Allies promised to make Chiang recognize these interests. The touchy subject of money reparations from Germany was postponed. Poland, on which Russia had in-flicted two of the dirtiest deals of the war—the Katyn massacre of captured Polish officers, and the halt of Russian armies ten miles from Warsaw to enable the Nazis to massacre Polish patriots—was "sold down the river." Stalin refused to recog-nize the non-communist Polish government-in-exile which had been functioning in London for six years. His own puppet Polish government was already set up, and his only concession was to promise to add a few democratic leaders to that govern-ment. He also agreed to establish interim governments, "broadly representative of all democratic elements," in the rest of liberated Europe—Austria, Hungary, Czechoslovakia, Bul-garia, and Rumania—to be followed by free elections. These agreements were merely oral, not defined in a treaty; for in the "spirit of Yalta" Roosevelt and Churchill trusted that Stalin would keep faith, which he never had any intention of doing.

The Yalta agreements, even the one about Poland, might have worked if they had been respected by Stalin; but none of them were except the promise to fight Japan, which delivered Manchuria to Russia in return for a five days' war.

Wherever Russian armies penetrated—excepting Austria and Czechoslovakia—they set up communist governments, and the local Communist party saw to it that the elections, if held at all, would be a farce. By mid-March 1945 Winston Churchill was writing to Roosevelt that everything in Europe supposedly settled at Yalta had broken down, and F.D.R. showed signs of admitting error before his death on 12 April. In the meantime, General Eisenhower, in accordance with the Yalta agreements, had pulled Patton's army back from Prague, since Czechoslovakia was in the Soviet sphere of influence, and allowed Russian troops to take Berlin. Even if these positions had later been abandoned, they would have been good bargaining points.

Thus the cold war began as soon as the hot war was over. Earl Browder, head of the Communist party in the United States, was the first victim of the "hard line." For his continuing to preach friendly collaboration between the United States and Russia, which he had been ordered to do in 1941, he was contemptuously deposed in May 1945 by orders from Moscow. This caused all his lieutenants to weep and grovel for having "deserted the workers." Browder was replaced by William Z. Foster, willing to follow the "party line" wheresoever it might lead. The Russian government confidently expected capitalist society to collapse as a result of the war—for had not Karl Marx so prophesied?—and that the Western Allies would be unable to prevent communism from taking over one country after another. The United Nations had already been formed, but Stalin counted on neutralizing it if he could not control it.

Harry Truman, acceding to the presidency on 12 April 1945, knew little of what had been going on. He naturally tried to continue the policy of collaboration with Russia in the hope that Stalin would prove reasonable. Averell Harriman, American ambassador at Moscow, warned him that Russia was violating most of the Yalta agreements; but he thought, and Truman agreed, that Russian need for American financial aid in reconstruction would keep Stalin in line. And it was largely to obtain reassurance from Russia that Truman attended the last of the big wartime conferences, at Potsdam, on 17 July 1945. He and Clement Attlee, the new Labour premier of Great Britain (Winston Churchill having been defeated in a general election), agreed to what they supposed to be temporary arrangements, pending a general peace treaty. For occupation purposes Germany was divided down the middle, and as a result the Russians proceeded to strip East Germany of most of its machinery and set up a communist government there. West

Germany was divided into three zones of occupation between Britain, the United States, and France. And, as a minor reflection of this partition, both Berlin and Vienna were divided into occupation zones. The Western powers also acquiesced in Russian annexation of eastern Poland, and in the Polish Reds' occupying East Prussia and Germany up to the Neisse river.

The Potsdam agreements, concluded after the need for Russian armed help had ceased, but while Russian armies occupied most of eastern Europe, were less excusable than those of Yalta, but still defensible as one more effort to win Russia to a stable peace settlement. So it is not surprising that both agreements came to be regarded by average citizens of the United States and Great Britain—not to speak of those of Poland, Austria, and the other countries who suffered from them—as a gross betrayal of the principles for which the Western Allies had been fighting. "Yalta" became a pejorative word, a signal for booes and hisses at Republican and other rallies. These agreements and the settlements that stemmed from them were based on the fallacy that the golden rule would work on the Russian government, which regarded Christian ethics as outmoded, and agreements or treaties to be respected only so long as they aided the supposed interests of "the revolution." The enormous backlog of good will that Russia had built up in Britain and the United States, and on which she could have drawn for relief and reconstruction, was dissipated by this mad grasp for power. But it took a long time to dissipate. A strong section of the British Labour party, and hundreds of French and Italian intellectuals, continued to defend Stalin's every move and to attack the United States as a "warmongering, imperialist" power.

In America many liberal elements—notably *The Nation*, now edited by Freda Kirchwey—similarly played dupes. Charles A. Beard in his last book warned readers that Truman was trying to pick a quarrel with Russia; and in 1948 a splinter party was formed on this assumption under the aegis of former Vice President Wallace, who insisted that only continual concessions to Russia would ensure world peace. As late as 1958 Bertrand Russell, the most vocal British spokesman of this point of view, wrote that if "no alternative remains except communist domination or the extinction of the human race, the former alternative is the lesser of two evils." Translated into the slogan "Better Red than Dead," and promoted by "Ban the Bomb" parades in England and America, this apparently inescapable dilemma made a wide appeal.

Winston Churchill, speaking before President Truman in March 1946 at Westminster College in Fulton, Missouri, said,

"From Stettin in the Baltic to Trieste in the Adriatic an iron curtain has descended across the Continent." It certainly had; and presently another iron curtain would shut out most of the Asiatic continent. But years had to elapse before people recognized a basic principle: the children of a big revolution, such as Napoleon, Hitler, Mussolini, Stalin, and Mao, can never stop. To satisfy their followers they have to postulate dangers from within and without, and drive on and on until they win all, or lose all. They may make truces, but never peace. Dean Acheson, who pointed this out in 1946, and President Truman, after he had considered all possible alternatives, came to the conclusion that the only possible way to deal with Russia in such wise as to prevent another and more terrible world war, was to convince her that she could not profit by war. Congressional revival of the army draft in 1948 was one sign. Truman's decision in January 1950, to continue and intensify research and production of thermonuclear weapons, definitely marks the adoption of this policy by the United States government. From the vantage point of 1971, it appears to have succeeded.

2. Harry's First Term

Harry S Truman, almost sixty-one years old at his accession, was an inconspicuous-looking President, but one of the most conspicuously successful. He could easily have got lost in a crowd, so typically Middle-Western were his face and figure; but he had in abundance the courage and integrity which were most needed during the postwar years, and good judgment as well. By experience Truman was as well prepared for the presidency as any of his immediate predecessors—a farm and small-town childhood, service in World War I, ward politics in Kansas City, country grass-root politics, and ten years in the United States Senate. Eastern Republicans said, "Who's Truman?" just as the Whigs in 1844 said, "Who is Polk?" They soon found out.

Harry was brought up on a prosperous 440-acre farm in Jackson County, Missouri. There were all kinds of animals which the boy learned to handle, corn to shuck, wheat to thresh, and hay to pitch; and this background lasted in his speech and earthy wit. At the age of six his parents removed to Independence, the old jumping-off place of the Oregon Trail, then a typical country town. The Trumans had been Confederates in the Civil War—the President's mother said she would rather sleep on the floor of the White House than in Lincoln's bed!—and Democrats ever since. Bible readers, they indoctrinated Harry with a love of good literature, espe-

cially history; as a lad he read avidly Plutarch's *Lives*, Jacob
Abbott's popular works, and the history of the Civil War,
about which his family and neighbors were rich in stories and
legends. Few statesmen have profited as much from history as
Truman did; from the antics of the Republican Radicals in
1862–65 he learned how to avoid pitfalls when he became
chairman of a senate committee on World War II; from
Andrew Johnson's conduct he learned mistakes to be avoided
when succeeding a great President; from General McClellan's
case he learned how to deal with an insubordinate general; and
from Jefferson's example in the Alien and Sedition hysteria of
1798 he learned to keep calm in the presence of Joe McCarthy.

As a youth Harry worked in a bank in Kansas City, joined
the National Guard and, as a captain of field artillery, fought
in the St. Mihiel and Meuse-Argonne campaigns of 1918.
Returning to Independence, he married his early love, Bess
Wallace, opened a haberdashery in Kansas City which failed
in the postwar recession, and entered local politics. Under the
aegis of the Pendergasts, Tammany-type bosses of Kansas City,
he was elected a county official. In this office he was proud of
having good modern roads constructed to help the farmers get
about. Jim Pendergast, who wanted a friend in the United
States Senate, helped Harry to get elected in 1934, much as
Daugherty had promoted Harding; but in the Senate Truman
proved to be of a different breed from the hapless good fellow
of Marion. As chairman of a special committee to investigate
the national defense program he attracted the attention of
President and public by issuing a series of devastating though
constructive reports, exposing the haphazard and wasteful
manner in which war contracts had been awarded on the cost-
plus basis, extortion by labor unions, and the shoving aside of
small business. These led to his being on the winning ticket
in 1944. Now he was President of the United States. On his
first day of office Truman remarked to a newspaperman, "Did
you ever have a bull or a load of hay fall on you? If you ever
did, you know how I felt last night."

President Truman's native intelligence enabled him to grasp
quickly the situation into which he was so suddenly thrown,
and on which he had not been briefed by Roosevelt. He had
to have a few boon companions from Missouri around the
White House for relaxation, but he won the friendship and
respect of gentlemen in politics such as Dean Acheson, soldiers
such as General Marshall, and foreign statesmen such as
Clement Attlee. He made good cabinet, judicial, and ambas-
sadorial appointments; he kept a firm hand on the new department of defense and the foreign service; and with more fateful

decisions than almost any President in our time, he made the fewest mistakes. Truman was always folksy, always the politician, but nobody can reasonably deny that he attained the stature of a statesman. He was magnanimous to critics and opponents—unless they did something he considered personally insulting such as criticizing his daughter Margaret's singing. But he did not object to criticism of his own piano playing.

We may now mention some domestic problems of Truman's first administration, although the situation was such that no issue could be completely isolated as domestic. Demobilization, for instance. No sooner was the war over than a popular clamor arose to "send the boys home." The army planned to discharge 5.5 million men by 1 July 1946, but this was too slow to suit the voters, and congressional pressure forced the army to speed it up. By the spring of 1950 it was down to 600,000 men and there were only ten divisions even partially ready for action—fewer than in Belgium and Holland. "It was no demobilization, it was a rout," said General Marshall. America was deprived of deterrent ground forces, and communist hopes were raised that America as a great power was slipping, by the will of the people.

To offset this impression of weakness, America confounded all the Marxist prophets by remaining prosperous. There was an enormous unsatisfied demand for consumer goods, which did not want purchasers, as almost every class in the community had money to spend. The new cars were attractive, although double the prices of 1941 models. Television, now nation-wide, dishwashing machines, and electric stoves absorbed millions of dollars. Prices went up, too, especially after Congress in 1946 removed most of the restrictions, but incomes went up even more. Even the farmers continued to benefit from high war prices for their cattle, grains, and cotton because of the demand in Europe, and the federal government's willingness to extend credit so that Europeans could buy them.

Veterans were easily absorbed into industry, and even more readily into schools. An act of Congress known as "the G.I. Bill of Rights" in 1944 offered full scholarships in colleges or universities or trade schools with subsistence, for a maximum of four years, to every able and honorably discharged member of the armed forces who applied. Some 12 million men and women availed themselves of the privilege. There was, of course, a great deal of waste in the scheme—chiropractor academies and sundry degree mills were hurriedly organized to get G.I. dollars—but on the whole it was a brilliant success, rendering several million young Americans better prepared to cope with life in an atomic age. In addition, Senator J. W.

Fulbright of Arkansas fathered a bill to provide for exchange of teachers and students between American and foreign universities.

President Truman did his best to prevent a postwar reaction such as that of the 1920's. In his address of 5 September 1945 to Congress he outlined a 21-point program of progressive legislation, in accordance with a "Fair Deal," as he renamed the no longer New Deal. But Congress and the country were in no mood for more social experiments. He was also troubled by the attitude of labor. During the war the unions had been riding high, and their members made big money out of war-pressured overtime. Once the war was over and industry converted to peacetime production, management did not attempt to reduce wages but cut out overtime, and many workers were furious at having their "take-home pay" thus reduced by as much as 50 per cent. At the same time the cost of living was rising sharply because Congress refused to continue price controls as Truman requested. On the plea of the cattlemen and packers that if controls were taken off beef everyone could have beefsteak, the legal limit was removed in July 1946, and beefsteak jumped from around 50 cents to over a dollar a pound, where it has been ever since. Eight basic commodities jumped 25 per cent, and "real wages" declined 12 per cent in one year.

These were the main reasons for strikes for higher wages in coal, motor cars, steel, electric appliances, and railroads. The coal strike threatened American industry and European recovery, and John L. Lewis, the leader responsible, defied both President and courts and got away with it. The strike of the railway brotherhoods, hitherto the most conservative and responsible unions, threatened to tie up the entire transportation system; Truman ended that by promising to use the army to operate the trains. The arrogance and irresponsibility of union labor leaders, a poor return for their favors from the New Deal, produced a strong anti-union feeling in the public which was reflected in the congressional elections of 1946. A Republican majority in both houses was returned for the first time in fifteen years. And the new 80th Congress passed the Taft-Hartley Act which outlawed the closed shop, made unions liable for damages caused by breach of contract, required a 60-day "cooling-off period" before a strike, forbade unions to make political contributions or exact excessive dues, and required elected union officials to take an oath that they were not communists. It was passed over the President's veto and despite outraged cries from labor leaders that the bill meant "slavery" and "fascism" for the workers. That was nonsense, as the later prosperity of union labor proves; but this act, a tribute to the political courage and integrity of Senator Robert Taft, produced a salutary purging of communists who had infiltrated the unions (not, unfortunately, of the criminal element as well) and forced the union leaders, with some notable exceptions, to be more circumspect and less greedy.

President Truman continued Harold Ickes, watchdog of the national domain, as secretary of the interior; but Ickes resigned with loud snorts in 1946 because Truman nominated as undersecretary of the navy Edwin W. Pauley, a Texas oil magnate who had his eye on the tideland oil reserves. Pauley's nomination was withdrawn and Truman defended these oil reserves, but during the Eisenhower administration Congress presented them, up to the three-mile limit, to the Gulf states and California.

Although Truman came from a former slave state, he was sympathetic with the demands of blacks for a civil rights act to secure them their long-denied right to vote in the lower South, and at least diminish their other disabilities. Congress not only refused to pass a civil rights bill but, when the Democratic party at the presidential nominating convention of 1948 adopted a strong civil rights plank and renominated Truman, many Southern Democrats seceded from the convention, waving the Confederate battle flag, and formed a splinter party, the so-called Dixiecrats. They held a convention at Montgomery, the old Confederate capital, and nominated Governor Strom Thurmond of South Carolina for the presidency. At the other end of the political spectrum a new progressive party was formed, with former Vice President Henry Wallace as leader, on the issue that Truman was risking war with Russia. At the same time, things were going badly for the United States in China, and McCarthyism—of which more anon—was raising its ugly head. So, when the Republicans again nominated Governor Dewey, almost everyone but Harry thought that they would win.

Truman waged an aggressive campaign, denouncing the 80th Congress as only he could, and everywhere addressing enthusiastic crowds who cried, "Pour it on, Harry!" "Give it to 'em!" He won about 50 per cent of the vote and 303 electoral votes. Dewey, a poor campaigner, with an unimpressive personality, polled 46 per cent of the popular vote, but only 189 in the electoral college. Thurmond carried several states of the lower South, with 39 electoral votes; Wallace, with a popular vote of over a million, carried not one state. And the Democrats recaptured control of Congress.

Harry Truman could now look forward to four years as

"President in his own right"—and a troubled term indeed it was.

3. *The United Nations and the Cold War*

The United Nations was established shortly after Truman became President, and he entertained high hopes of its ability to quench the angry passions of postwar and prevent a new war. Secretary Hull had initiated the movement under President Roosevelt who, profiting by Woodrow Wilson's mistakes, took care to have prominent Republicans included in every committee appointed to plan this new international organization. Senator Arthur H. Vandenberg of Michigan, once a forthright isolationist, undertook the task of bringing his colleagues around to international co-operation. A meeting of representatives of Great Britain, the United States, Russia, and China at Washington in the autumn of 1944 drafted a preliminary outline, basis of the charter which issued from a plenary conference of fifty different nations at San Francisco in April 1945.

The charter of the United Nations established an international body measurably stronger than the old League of Nations. But it had the same basic defect of giving each of the "big five" on the top Security Council—the United States, Britain, Russia, China, and France—a veto on every decision. This veto was not proposed by Russia, although she exercised it *ad nauseam;* it was insisted upon by Britain and America because their respective governments knew that the people would never consent to ratification without such protection to their sovereignty. Russia also wanted a veto on discussions in the Security Council, but did not get that. Each member nation had one vote in the General Assembly, and complete freedom of discussion there. The point in which the United Nations went beyond the old League was a provision for the use of force against aggression. The Security Council could recommend the General Assembly to sever diplomatic relations, or apply economic sanctions, or go to war against an aggressor. It could even set up a permanent international military force; but owing to Russian opposition, this never came about. It had the right to appoint a commission (UNESCO) to help backward or impoverished nations, and to draw up an international Bill of Rights. Both were done, and UNESCO did a great deal of good, considering its limited budget; but the Bill of Rights has remained a dead letter to most of the members of the new league.

The Senate ratified the United Nations charter by a vote of 89 to 2 on 28 July 1945; and on 10 January 1946 the first session of the Assembly of 51 nations met in London. Next year the Sperry plant at Lake Success, Long Island, became the temporary home of the United Nations, which decided to have its permanent headquarters in the United States. After investigating various sites on the Eastern seaboard, the UN settled on New York City as its capital, and built the high building at the foot of East 43rd Street, where it has been since 1950.

Until the United Nations began functioning, the situation in Europe had to be dealt with in another manner. At Potsdam a Council of Foreign Ministers of the big powers was set up to oversee the Allied Control Council, which in turn oversaw the military administration of occupied Germany and Austria.

Efforts of the Allied Control Council to revive German industry and give the defeated people something to live for, were thwarted by Russian insistence on gutting German factories under the excuse of reparations; the real motive being to reduce that country to such a state that it would turn in despair to communism. James F. Byrnes, new secretary of state, declared in September 1946 that his country would no longer accept responsibility for "the needless aggravation of economic distress" caused by the Allied Control Council's failing to agree on anything, owing to Russia's repeated *niet*.

In the meantime, the trial of German war criminals at Nuremberg, whose records revealed an unimaginable depth of depravity, were being held, and twelve high Nazis, including Goering, Jodl, and Ribbentrop, were sentenced to death. The occupying authorities were also concerned with the "denazification" of Germany and the encouragement of the supposedly purified electorate to set up a new republican government, which was done in 1949.

An enormous relief program, abbreviated as UNRRA, was set up by the Allies before the end of the war and adopted by the United Nations. Under the successive leads of Governor Herbert H. Lehman and Mayor Fiorello H. La Guardia, UNRRA spent about a billion dollars a year—the United States contributing 68 per cent—for relief in continental Europe. UNRRA had responsibility for feeding and, if possible, resettling displaced persons, of whom there were almost ten million in Europe—Germans driven out of Poland and Czechoslovakia, Slavs who fled before advancing Russian armies, and others. It spent a large part of its effort and money transporting Jews, who saw no future for themselves in Europe, to the British-mandated territory of Palestine, thus creating a new problem for the United Nations.

In 1943 the treasury department, consulting with corresponding departments in several other countries, began laying plans to stabilize currencies and provide credit for postwar international trade and investment. An international conference which met in the summer of 1944 at Bretton Woods, New Hampshire, drafted, and Congress ratified, two new agencies: the International Monetary Fund and the International Bank for Reconstruction and Development. The Fund, designed to stabilize exchange rates and discourage restrictions on international payments, was provided initially with a capital of $8.8 billion, to which the United States contributed about one-third. The International or World Bank had authority to lend and borrow money and to underwrite private loans for eligible projects.

What was to be done about atomic energy and the bomb? Experiments at Bikini Atoll in the Marshall Islands in 1946 confirmed what the wartime explosions at Hiroshima and Nagasaki had indicated, that mankind had acquired a force which, if uncontrolled, could destroy civilization. At its first session the United Nations general assembly appointed an atomic energy commission on which twelve countries were represented. Bernard Baruch, the American member, presented a plan for creating an international authority to control every phase of the production of atomic energy, using it only for peaceful purposes, and forbidding the further manufacture of atomic weapons. Had this plan been adopted, America would have destroyed her stock of atomic bombs and made no more. Considering that the United States then had a monopoly of atomic weapons, this was a magnanimous proposal, and all countries on the atomic energy commission accepted it except Russia and Poland. They refused, pretending to regard as espionage the inspection necessary to enforce the plan, but really because they hoped and expected, through the work of their own scientists and the use of atomic secrets stolen from the United States, to match or surpass the American atomic arsenal. Russia made the counter-proposal that the United States destroy all her atomic weapons immediately, and every country promise to manufacture no more. As no such promise, without the sanction of inspection, was worth the paper it was written on, the Russian proposal got nowhere. But, considering the vast amount of breast-beating that there has been in the United States about the atomic bomb, we should remember that the Baruch plan offered to renounce American superiority in the race for more destructive weapons, if every country would devote atomic research to peaceful objects and permit inspection.

In Great Britain even the imposition of controls on trading by the Labour government did not prevent a financial crisis in

1947. The United States government extended a loan of $3.75 billion, but that did not recoup the loss of Britain's former export markets. At the same time, the economy of France, Italy, and other countries was teetering on the verge of collapse, with prospects of communist take-over to follow. To check this, General George C. Marshall, now secretary of state, announced at Harvard Commencement in 1947 what became known as the Marshall Plan. President Truman was behind it, and George Kennan on the policy planning staff of the state department had a good deal to do with working it out. The key idea was this: European countries which needed help should make their own reconstruction plans, not so much for immediate relief as "to permit the emergence of political and social conditions in which free institutions can exist"; the United States would provide the cash to get started. The essence, as Marshall made clear, was that the European nations must plan themselves.

Marshall's idea was taken up with enthusiasm by every European country not under communist control. Sixteen nations sent representatives to a conference in Paris, which drew up a comprehensive plan for European recovery:—new factories, new hydro-electric projects, monetary stability, lowering of trade barriers, and a thousand different things. Russia, offered the same benefits, rejected them as a cloak for American capitalist exploitation, and prevented her satellites from joining. (The real reason for Russian opposition was fear that the plan would destroy Stalin's hope for a general capitalist collapse.) Truman presented the Marshall Plan to Congress in December 1947, recommending that the United States contribute $17 billion out of the total four-year estimate of $22 billion. The leading champion of the bill in the Senate was Senator Vandenberg; the leading opponent, Senator Taft. While Congress was still arguing pro and con in February 1948, the communists pulled off a coup d'état in democratic Czechoslovakia, and took over a country with which Americans had many strong racial and sentimental ties. America's old friend Jan Masaryk was liquidated by the classic Prague method of defenestration, and the iron curtain clanged down outside that unfortunate country.

This made votes for the Foreign Assistance Act, passed by heavy majorities on 3 April 1948. Congress voted $5.3 billion immediately for the Marshall Plan, and an additional $275 million for Greece and Turkey. This was only a beginning of foreign aid by the United States, which came to $80 billion by 1 July 1961.

In retrospect, the Marshall Plan was the best thing the

United States could have done for Europe; and the factor that made it work was Europe's enthusiasm and positive contribution, in brains, money, and know-how, to saving herself. Communists did their best to sabotage it by propaganda, by persuading stevedores to refuse to handle American shipments, and by other tricks of the Marxian trade; but in spite of their efforts, and of the initial skepticism of old-fashioned European industrialists, the economy of the once war-ravaged countries built up so rapidly that in a little more than a decade the balance of trade with the United States had turned in Europe's favor.

Strokes and counterstrokes in the cold war went on through 1947 and 1948. The first showdown occurred in the Mediterranean, where the West won three rounds. Russia, in an effort to expand her dependent empire of communist satellites, was putting intolerable pressure on the government of Iran (Persia), threatening Turkey, and supporting a civil war against the government of Greece; a particularly cruel war, since the communist guerrillas, invading from Albania, Yugoslavia, and Bulgaria, carried off thousands of Greek children for forced labor. Great Britain, which had been giving extensive financial and military aid to the Greek government but was now in the midst of her financial crisis, gave notice that she would have to abandon Greece and Turkey. President Truman made a quick decision to pick up both. On 12 March 1947 he sent a message to Congress embodying not only a request for appropriations for Greece and Turkey, but what came to be known as the Truman Doctrine. One of the primary objectives of the foreign policy of the United States, he said, "is the creation of conditions in which we and other nations will be able to work out a way of life free from coercion. . . . I believe that it must be the policy of the United States to support freed peoples who are resisting attempted subjugation by armed minorities or by outside pressures."

Truman felt so strongly about this that he even went in person to the House ways and means committee to lobby for aid to Greece—an unprecedented step for a President. He told me in 1960 how reporters flocked around the doors which shut them from the secret hearing; how Senator Taft, who had opposed every European commitment, got up and left the room in the middle of it, and Truman thought, "My God! he's going to give them a hostile statement and wreck the whole thing!" But Taft told them nothing and supported the appropriation for aid to Greece. All left-wing elements in the United States deplored this. They insisted that the Greek monarchy was out of date, corrupt, inept; the virile Communist party should be allowed to take over. They were disappointed. King Paul of Greece exhibited such skill and energy as to win the civil war; and Tito, the communist dictator of Yugoslavia, having broken temporarily with Stalin, refused any longer to harbor guerrillas. Turkey so strengthened her defenses as to become almost impregnable; and Stalin, deciding that this *Drang nach Osten* did not pay, stopped harassing Iran.

Another crucial spot where England abdicated was Palestine. She had held the mandate here since 1919, and in accordance with Balfour's promise of 1917, facilitated Jewish immigration to their motherland. This aroused the implacable hostility of the Arab population, which insisted on limiting the Jewish quota to a mere trickle. That was impossible to enforce after World War II, when thousands of displaced Jews from central and eastern Europe, who were wanted nowhere else, were eager to go to Palestine; and many did, illegally. President Truman took an active interest in their plight, but the British government announced that it could no longer keep the peace and must give up its Palestine mandate. The United Nations now rendered a judgment of Solomon, dividing Palestine between a separate Arab state and the new Republic of Israel. The United States recognized Israel in May 1948. Military experts and thousands of others predicted that the Arabs would soon drive the Jews into the Mediterranean. But Israel successfully defended herself against five Arab states and has become a virile modern republic despite a constant state of war with her Arab neighbors, implacably hostile to her very existence.

There were strokes and counterstrokes in Europe too. After the Western Allies had helped West Germany to set up a representative government (Russia having refused to co-operate), Stalin on 24 June 1948 ordered a blockade of the noncommunist zones of Berlin, hoping to squeeze out the Allies and annex their zones to East Germany. General Lucius D. Clay, the stalwart and intelligent commander of American occupation forces in Europe, warned the President that to lose Berlin would be to lose the entire Western position in Europe; and Harry saw the point. The American and British air forces promptly organized an airlift by transport planes that fed, clothed, and heated West Berlin for 321 days; 2.5 million tons of supplies were flown in, and the city's products flown out. The Berlin airlift was a striking demonstration of what air power could accomplish, and of the value of firmness and strength when confronting communists. Stalin ended the blockade on 12 May 1949, but minor hampering of trains, motor convoys, and aircraft which have to cross East Germany to reach Berlin, has continued ever since.

This menace, in return, brought about another initiative by President Truman, resulting in the North Atlantic Treaty of 4 April 1949 between the United States, Canada, and ten nations of Western Europe. Each pledged itself to resist any armed attack against any one member. Under this treaty NATO, the North Atlantic Treaty Organization, was set up. Never before had the United States gone so far in a peacetime promise to fight under certain conditions, or to recognize a frontier extending far overseas. The Senate ratified it by a vote of 82 to 13; one of the negative votes being that of Senator Taft, who declared that NATO might seem to threaten Russia and provoke her to attack. The President's military assistance program for the NATO nations was accepted by the House, and the first shipments of arms reached Europe that month. General Eisenhower resigned the presidency of Columbia University to become supreme commander of NATO forces; Britain, France, and Italy began rearming, and in 1954 West Germany was admitted. Russia looked upon the creation of NATO as a declaration of hostility; pacifists and left-wingers everywhere deplored its existence as "shaking the mailed fist," and all that; but there can no longer be any doubt that the NATO armed forces were a major deterrent to Russia's trying any more communist putsches in Europe.

Truman's policy, "containment" as it was called, worked. Russia made no conquests in Western Europe or the Near East after her military occupations in the confused period immediately following the war. But containment was not applied early enough in the Far East.

4. *China and the Occupation of Japan*

The basic cause of the Pacific war of 1941–45 was the attempt of the United States to protect the integrity of China against Japan. Yet, a few years after the war was over, China became an implacable enemy of America, and within twenty years, so great a threat to world peace as to alarm even Russia. How could this have happened? The answer, in a word, is the weakness of Generalissimo Chiang Kai-shek's *kuomintang* or nationalist government, and the cleverness of the Chinese communists in exploiting that weakness.

Throughout the war, Roosevelt treated Chiang's China as a full-fledged ally, and led the way in renouncing (January 1943) the extraterritorial privileges which had been extorted from the last Manchu emperors. Churchill growled, considering Chiang a weak reed, but acquiesced. But throughout the war Mao Tse-tung maintained a communist government in

North China, abstained from fighting Japan, and pinned down a large part of Chiang's army. Chiang was isolated from his allies, not only by the Reds but by Japanese blockade and conquest of Burma, Thailand, and Indochina. Just as the Western Allies made great sacrifices to send aid to Russia through the Arctic Ocean, so they flew supplies to Chiang, and to General Chennault's XIV Army Air Force, over the Himalayas "hump."

Early in the war Roosevelt sent General Joseph Stilwell to help Chiang because he was the only general officer of the army who knew the Chinese and could speak their language. Stilwell—aptly nicknamed "Vinegar Joe"—did a wonderful job training the few Chinese troops entrusted to him, but so antagonized the Generalissimo by indiscreet remarks about him and his ineffective administration that in September 1944, when F.D.R. urged Chiang to make Stilwell commander in chief of the Chinese army, Chiang demanded and obtained his recall.

When Japan surrendered in August 1945, Chiang was about at the end of his resources. He nominally controlled over half China, but runaway inflation had alienated the professional classes, and his high officials, chosen mainly from among Madame Chiang's relatives, were inept and corrupt. At this juncture General Albert C. Wedemeyer, who had relieved Stilwell as United States commander in the Chinese theater of war, proved to be the seer. In dispatches of mid-August 1945 to the Joint Chiefs of Staff he demanded priority for occupation of Manchuria and the Chinese seaports, in order to prevent the Chinese Reds from taking over. Japan, a country under orderly government, he thought could wait; but Asia was then "an enormous pot, seething and boiling, the fumes of which may readily snuff out the advancements gained by Allied sacrifices the past several years."

That is exactly what happened, but neither Admiral Nimitz nor General MacArthur agreed. The latter insisted that the prompt occupation of Japan was paramount and should be given highest priority in the allotment of forces and logistics. Had Wedemeyer's advice been listened to, strong Allied forces, not really needed for the occupation of Japan, could have been landed in China to help Chiang protect himself from the Chinese Reds. Seventh Fleet did help the "G'mo" to transport troops by sea to strategic points for receiving the surrender of Japanese mainland armies, but naturally could not influence events in the interior.

Trouble with Russia began immediately. A Russian army pressed through Manchuria into Jehol province, even after the

Japanese cease-fire of 16 August (exactly one week after Russia declared war), and forced the Japanese forces there to surrender to them instead of to Chiang, as Stalin had agreed. For quick promise-breaking there has been nothing to equal that of a Russo-Chinese treaty of 14 August in which Stalin formed an alliance with Chiang. A few days later he decided that the Reds were going to win, and began aiding them to overthrow the Nationalist Chinese government.

Many people high in the United States government were also in favor of shifting partners. Chiang seemed hopeless, and several journalists who had been with Mao pictured his government as not really communist but bent only on distributing land to the Chinese peasants. Truman and the state department rejected the idea of dumping Chiang, but they and the Joint Chiefs of Staff were determined not to become involved in a Chinese civil war, especially since we would soon lack the military capability to intervene. Owing to popular insistence on "sending the boys home," over 3 million of them were returned from Pacific Ocean areas to the United States between September 1945 and March 1946. As General Wedemeyer put it, "America fought the war like a football game, after which the winner leaves the field and celebrates."

President Truman in December 1945 sent out General Marshall in the vain hope of mediating peace between the two Chinas and setting up a popular front government. He did obtain a cease-fire, as the Reds were now building up their strength with Russian aid. When they were ready, fighting broke out all along the line where the two forces confronted each other. Money, arms, and munitions to the tune of $2 billion were poured in by us to help Chiang, but that was not enough. He over-extended himself, many of his generals surrendered or sold out to Mao, turning their American arms against Chiang, and by the end of 1949 the Nationalist government was forced to evacuate the mainland and establish itself in Formosa (Taiwan), where it still remains in 1971. Mao promptly consolidated his position by liquidating the Chinese who would not go along, by the tens of millions; he expelled all American or European missionaries, teachers, and businessmen and taught, or forced, the Chinese to hate the nations who had helped them against Japan.

Such was the sad issue of World War II in China; a result profoundly shocking and distressing to the American people. All their century-long efforts to help China with medical and other missionaries, with "Open Door" and the Nine-Power treaty, and, finally, by fighting Japan, went for nought. Traditional Sino-American friendship was changed into hate, and a peaceful policy distorted into "imperialism," "war-mongering," and all the tiresome slogans that communists hurl against those who oppose their power. But the charge that traitors or fools in the American government "lost" China is fantastic. It was Chiang who lost China; not "all the king's horses and all the king's men" could protect that amiable, loyal, but inept leader against the determined drive of Mao, supported by Russia. An army of a million Americans might have done it, but that was out of the question.

Fortunately we have something pleasant to relate in the post-war Asiatic world: the military occupation of Japan. This began with the formal surrender on board U.S.S. *Missouri* (2 September 1945) and lasted until 1952. It was a brilliant success mainly for two reasons. The Western Allies had the wisdom to profit by the mistake of "hang the Kaiser" policy in 1918; and, despite outraged shrieks of communist and left-wingers, kept Emperor Hirohito, a man of peace, in power. His government, intact, faithfully carried out the occupying authority's orders, and the Japanese people, chastened by defeat but with their godlike symbol still on his throne, accepted the situation stoically, went about their business without agitation, and respected the forces of occupation.

The second wise and fortunate circumstance was the appointment of General Douglas MacArthur as SCAP (Supreme Commander Allied Powers) by President Truman, and the set-up which gave him complete authority over Japan. Russia was kept out of it by giving her a representative on an international Pacific Commission in Washington, with the proviso that if the members disagreed—as they usually did—General MacArthur could decide. Thus the dissension and frustration of the four-nation commission on occupied Germany was avoided.

His conduct of the occupation of Japan constitutes General MacArthur's greatest claim to fame; and probably he thought so, too, since he wrote, after it was over, "If the historian of the future should deem my service worthy of some slight reference, it would be my hope that he mention me not as a commander engaged in campaigns and battles, even though victorious to American arms, but rather as that one whose sacred duty it became, once the guns were silenced, to carry to the land of our vanquished foe the solace and hope and faith of Christian morals."

His task was colossal, for he had to demilitarize a military empire and give a poor and defeated people the skills and confidence to create a viable state, all within the framework of the Golden Rule. "I decided that this was to be, for the first time in history perhaps, a *Christian* occupation," said the General to me in 1950; and that it was.

Almost anyone but MacArthur would have been daunted by the problem of directing the administration of a nation of 83 million people in an area equal to California but only one-sixth arable, with a maximum of 2200 American civilians and 60,000 troops, reduced to fewer than 5000 during the Korean War. Sixty per cent of the houses in Tokyo had been destroyed. Some 4 million Japanese soldiers and sailors had to be demobilized, a cool million of them in various Pacific bases which had been bypassed in accordance with the "leap-frog" strategy. All enemy commanders in the Pacific obeyed their Emperor's orders to surrender, and their troops were returned to Japan by the United States and Australian navies, and by such Japanese transports and merchant ships as were still afloat. But about 375,000 of the Manchurian army, who had been forced to surrender to the Russians, were kept for years in Siberia doing forced labor; only in 1950 did Russia begin returning those who had been indoctrinated as communists, in the hope of disrupting the occupation policy and throwing Japan into turmoil. They did produce a number of riots and strikes but, thanks to the pervasive loyalty to the emperor, and to MacArthur's having encouraged the workers to form trade unions and giving them social security, the returning Reds fell far short of their goal.

General MacArthur, living in the American embassy in Tokyo and using the downtown Dai-Ichi building as an office, superintended every aspect of the occupation. He got rid of the secret police, purged the civil service of unrepentant militarists, abolished the secret societies which had helped bring on the war, broke up the *zaibatsu* system of cartels which had strangled Japanese industry, and even brought about a comprehensive land reform. This confirmed tenant farmers' plots to them in full ownership and compensated the landlords, but insisted, against landlord opposition, that the deeds be registered. Over 4.5 million acres were distributed to the peasants, and a strong co-operative movement encouraged among them. All this was accomplished without undue inflation, thanks to the Diet's adopting a plan by Joseph M. Dodge of Detroit. On the political side, the General gave his blessing to a new constitution drafted by liberal Japanese elements, which set up a democratic and representative government. The Emperor, with obvious relief, renounced his divine attributes but became more popular than ever because MacArthur encouraged him to travel about the country and let the people see him. Women were given the vote, and in the first general election in 1946 they won 39 seats in the Diet. Religious discrimination was abolished, and the state religion disestablished.

During this transition, the United States poured food, clothing, medicaments, and other supplies into Japan—$517 million in one year, 1949. The General, summoning a corps of American economists as consultants, undertook to rebuild Japanese business and find new markets for handicrafts and heavy industry. Even the arts were not neglected; a fine arts commission under SCAP saw to it that relief funds were allocated to prevent the ancient temples of Nikko, Kyoto, and other places from decaying, and the leading museums were reopened. Especially praiseworthy was the work of SCAP's public health and welfare section, headed by General C. F. Sams, a chief surgeon of the United States Army. The entire population was vaccinated twice. A control program over tuberculosis resulted in a 40 per cent reduction of deaths from the "white plague." Diphtheria, dysentery, and typhoid cases were reduced 80 to 90 per cent under the occupation; cholera ceased to be. A beginning was made to encourage cattle-raising to correct the protein deficiency in the Japanese diet.

The United States Navy under Vice Admiral C. Turner Joy, an integral part of SCAP, co-operated in many ways to further the General's policy. Rear Admiral B. W. Decker, commanding the Yokosuka naval base, found jobs building furniture, boats, and yachts to occupy workers thrown out of employment by the liquidation of the Japanese navy. He even set them to growing mushrooms in the vast underground complex that the Japanese had built as a command post to resist the invasion that never came off. Ascertaining that former gangster elements had muscled into relief distribution, Decker, to the astonishment of the natives, organized the women to take over.

MacArthur became immensely popular although he kept himself rigorously aloof; crowds gathered at the exit to the Dai-Ichi building just to see him. And this, in spite of the war crimes trials for which no fewer than 720 officers and civilians were executed and 3480 given prison terms. The war crimes tribunal consisted of eleven judges, each representing an allied country or commonwealth, presided over by Sir William Webb of the Supreme Court of Queensland, Australia. Most of the convictions and executions were for torturing and beheading prisoners. General Tojo, another former premier, and five former cabinet ministers were also sentenced to death for having conspired to bring on the war. This tribunal was completely independent of SCAP. General MacArthur approved the execution of officers who had tortured prisoners, but deplored the imprisonment of civilians, particularly of foreign minister Mamoru Shigemitsu, who signed the surrender, and of the emperor's confidential adviser Koichi Kido, who had been instrumental in bringing it about. I have reason to believe that the tribunal did this to please the Russian member, in return for his voting to acquit others; and that Stalin hoped to liquidate the old governing class, as he was doing in Poland, to let in communism. Fortunately, Russian and Anglo-American leftist pressure to try the emperor as a war criminal was defeated.

On 8 September 1951 John Foster Dulles concluded for the state department a treaty with Japan that ended the state of war, and the occupation. No reparations were extorted, but the United States obtained the right to military bases and airfields at specific places in Japan and on Okinawa. And Japanese good will built up under SCAP has lasted.

"Could I have but a line a century hence," wrote General MacArthur, "crediting a contribution to the advance of peace, I would yield every honor which has been accorded by war."

Here's your line, General; this historian salutes you. Your efforts for peace and good will entitle you to a place among the immortals. No proconsul, no conqueror in ancient or modern times succeeded to the degree that you did in winning the hearts of a proud and warlike people who had suffered defeat. Your victory was a dual one—military, and in the highest sense, spiritual.

5. The Korean War

A peaceful Sunday in Japan, 25 June 1950, was interrupted by very bad, surprising news. An army from North Korea had suddenly burst into South Korea and apparently was carrying everything before it.

Korea had been divided across the middle, along lat. 38° N, before the end of World War II; the northern part to be occupied by Russia and the southern by the United States. This happened before the Russians had demonstrated that by temporary occupation they meant permanent communization. They set up a Red North Korea, while the Western Allies brought back from exile the aged patriot Syngman Rhee and supported a representative government under him. Lieutenant General John R. Hodge, one of the best leaders in the Pacific war, was unable to cope with the situation, having no long-established government or well-disciplined people to deal with, as MacArthur had in Japan. The Koreans, notorious individualists, organized no fewer than eighty political parties, and President Rhee, an exile since 1912, unknown to most of his compatriots,

THE KOREAN WAR 433

had no flair for government. He did not even have the human materials to set up a viable administration, as the Japanese had monopolized all top and middle-layer positions. At Potsdam, Stalin had promised to promote union of Korea under one government, but every effort of the United Nations to do so was foiled by the Russian veto. An assembly, boycotted by the Russians, met in 1948 and promulgated the Republic of Korea with Rhee as president, but the authority of this "R.O.K." ended at the 38th parallel. North of it was the "People's Republic of Korea" headed by a vigorous young Moscow-trained communist named Kim Il Sung. After Russian troops evacuated North Korea, the United States pulled her garrison out of the southern half, leaving only a small military mission to help Rhee create his own army.

This evacuation of the Republic of Korea was ordered by the Joint Chiefs of Staff with the approval of President Truman, General MacArthur, and the state department. The main reason for creating this sensitive power vacuum was the radical reduction in American armed forces. Moreover, the Joint Chiefs of Staff and all intelligence agencies believed that Europe was the danger point; that if war came it would be started there by Russia and be an atomic duel. Consequently, to strengthen American retaliatory power, to "get a bigger bang for a buck" as the phrase ran, the defense department built up a long-range "strategic" air force, with a stockpile of atomic bombs, but neglected both navy and ground forces. When Secretary Acheson announced in a speech of 12 January 1950 that the American defense perimeter in the Pacific included Japan, Okinawa, Formosa, and the Philippines, implying that South Korea belonged to "other areas" which would have to defend themselves initially, nobody objected.[1]

Although General MacArthur's command was braced to resist Russian aggression early in 1950, they expected it to take the form of a sudden invasion of Hokkaido; for Stalin had demanded, and Truman denied, a military occupation of this northern Japanese island. SCAP's military intelligence was so inadequate that 70,000 North Korean troops, complete with tanks and armor, were able to assemble behind the 38th parallel without its knowledge. Mao of course was behind this push,

[1] This speech was held up against Acheson in the Presidential election of 1952 as an "invitation" to the communists to overrun South Korea. He was able to prove that his perimeter was exactly the same as one previously defined by General MacArthur. Moreover, he repeatedly asked Congress to provide military aid for South Korea, even after the House on 19 January defeated the aid bill which the state department had requested.

which Kim would not have dared to undertake unsupported;
but Stalin probably did not know what was cooking, or the
Russian seat on the UN Security Council would not then have
been vacant.

The communist powers counted on no interference by the
United States, much less by the United Nations. But South
Korea had to be defended, to protect the Korean people and
because of its strategic position across the Strait of Tsushima
from Japan. President Truman acted promptly and decisively.
Before the end of the first day of the Red invasion—24 June
in Washington—he had sent orders to General MacArthur to

THE KOREAN WAR
- - - Principal railways
Scale of Miles
0   50   100

do his best to help stem the tide, and brought the situation before the Security Council of the United Nations. The Council, after ordering North Korea to desist from her aggression, made this a United Nations war on the 27th by calling on all members to provide assistance to South Korea. Ten eventually did.

General MacArthur, first as SCAP and United States Commander in Chief Far East, and from 8 July Commander in Chief United Nations forces, conducted this "police action," as it was officially called. On 9 July he informed the Joint Chiefs of Staff that it was going to be a major operation, and asked that the 1st Marine Division and four army infantry divisions be sent to him at once. That took time, the Reds really got the jump, and the first phase of this war went very ill for the United Nations. Before substantial forces could reach Korea, the Reds had overrun most of the peninsula, leaving the Allies only the southeastern port of Pusan and a small perimeter. This happened because of the surprise, because the South Korean ground troops were ill trained, as were the first American soldiers who arrived by airlift from Japan. Young draftees with no battle experience, they were soft from occupation duty.

A combined task force built around U.S.S. *Juneau* and H.M.S. *Jamaica* knocked out the North Korean navy and several troop-laden transports on 2 July, and from that time UN control of the sea was uncontested; but the Reds generally managed to move beyond the range of naval gunfire. The most useful contributions by the navy, other than bombardments, were helicopters and light bombers of the marine corps air wing, operating from escort carriers to give close support to ground troops, and to evacuate the wounded. The helicopter really came into its own during this war. By mid-August the United States, by drawing units from Hawaii, Puerto Rico, and the Mediterranean, had 65,000 troops, and the British Commonwealth one division, in the Pusan perimeter.

Counteroffensive began in mid-September 1950. The concept, MacArthur's own, was to bypass and cut off the Red troops south of lat. 38° by making an amphibious landing at Inchon, outport to Seoul, and then to drive up through North Korea to the Yalu. This bold gamble was suggested, said the General, by reading Parkman's account of Wolfe's assault on Quebec in 1759. His own staff didn't like it; the navy didn't like it, owing to the 30-foot range of tide at Inchon; the Joint Chiefs of Staff didn't like it; but he insisted. The navy put its best brains into the plan, and the Inchon landing, commanded by Rear Admiral Struble and effected by the 1st Marine Division on 15 September 1950, was a brilliant success. Unfortunately, it made MacArthur infallible, in his own opinion.

Inchon landing led to the capture of Seoul (25 September), cutting the Reds' communications with South Korea and forcing thousands to surrender. On 7 October the UN General Assembly approved MacArthur's crossing the 38th parallel and attempting to reunite all Korea. He had already opened his northward offensive. Eighth Army (Lieutenant General Walton H. Walker) advanced along the west coast, captured Pyongyang the North Korean capital on 19 October, and pressed on to the Yalu. But MacArthur now made a grave strategic error by dividing his army and ordering X Corps to be re-embarked at Inchon and landed at Wonsan on the east coast, there to make a second northward march parallel to that of Eighth Army. The navy opposed it. Vice Admiral C. Turner Joy, the U.S. Navy's commander in the Far East, observed that X Corps could have marched the 150 miles overland to Wonsan with less effort and time than was consumed, with the limited shipping at his disposal, to lift it 800 miles around the peninsula. And the South Korean Army (the ROK) was already marching on Wonsan and took it on 10 October. But MacArthur insisted. X Corps (Major General Edward M. Almond) was landed by the navy at Wonsan on 26 October, advanced rapidly, spearheaded by the 1st Marine Division, and by 1 November was near the Chosin reservoir in northern Korea. If the two columns could meet on the Yalu, Korea would be enveloped.

This daring strategy was adopted by General MacArthur, either on the assumption that China would not intervene—at Wake Island on 14 October he assured President Truman that there was "very little chance" of it—or on the assumption that a vigorous lunge to the Yalu would convince Mao he had better not intervene. Unfortunately, Mao had decided to pile in. By mid-November some 200,000 Chinese troops had crossed the Yalu and taken up mountainous positions between Walker's Eighth Army and Almond's X Corps. The Red offensive began on 25 November, the Chinese attacking first Walker's right flank and, a week later, Almond's left.

To meet this "entirely new war" as MacArthur well called this phase of the Korean struggle, he proposed to bomb bridges over the Yalu, bomb the Chinese assembly area north of it, facilitate the invasion of China by Chiang's army on Formosa, and blockade the entire Chinese coast. It is possible, even probable, that this would have worked; for when communists are faced with resolute, determined and superior force, they usually retreat. But would Russia have come to China's aid? That is the big question which can never be answered until communist archives yield their secrets.

The fact that this was a United Nations, not a United States, war, was the main reason MacArthur's strategy could not be adopted. Several members of the UN, especially Britain, insisted on keeping it a limited war and dared not risk another world conflict. Russia had exploded an atomic bomb the previous fall, and nobody knew how many she had; supposing China were invaded and Stalin decided to help his ally Mao, the first Russian counterattack would probably be a lethal rain of atomic bombs on Britain. Hence MacArthur's directive of 27 September 1950 ordered him under no circumstances to send planes or troops across the border into China or Russian Siberia, which touches the northeast corner of Korea. Even Winston Churchill, leader of the British opposition, pointed out that to get the United States and the United Nations "entangled inextricably in a war with China" would play Stalin's game.

Nor could Korea be considered apart from other Asiatic areas in turmoil. France had half her army, some 150,000 men, trying to put down the Viet-Minh revolt in Indochina; the British were fighting communist guerrillas in Malaya; President Quirino of the independent Philippines was still fighting the "Huks," and in India fastidious, superior Nehru was doing his best to appease Mao after Red China's annexation of Tibet.

Truman, having placed this operation under UN control, had no choice but to respect our allies' wishes. Moreover, there was little military support for MacArthur's invade-China plan outside his own staff. General Eisenhower, leaving for Europe as supreme commander of NATO, opposed it; General Omar Bradley, expressing the views of the Joint Chiefs of Staff, later told Congress that MacArthur proposed "the wrong war, at the wrong place and at the wrong time, and with the wrong enemy."

The Chinese offensive that began on 25 November was not only a surprise; it took advantage of MacArthur's mistake of dividing the UN army into two columns separated by a mountainous wilderness. The Chinese who lunged into this strategic vacuum attacked each strung-out column on its exposed flank, announcing their presence in the initial engagements by eerie bugle calls, weird whistles, chirps, and howls. There then began what our troops called "the big bug-out"—a fighting retreat against attacks of vastly superior strength, through mountain passes and valleys, in bitter cold and deep snow. The story of Oliver Smith's 1st Marine Division retiring from the Chosin reservoir, beating off attacks by three Chinese armies, is one of the most glorious in the annals of that gallant corps, recalling Xenophon's retreat of the immortal ten thousand to the sea. The marines reached Hungnam on the east coast and, together with the rest of X Corps (a total of 105,000), were transferred by the navy on 11–21 December to Pusan. Eighth Army's fighting retreat, covering 300 miles in three weeks, was assisted by a combined fleet under a British admiral which evacuated several units from west coast seaports. The Reds now had ample air power, with Russian planes and pilots, to contest the UN air forces, but fortunately for us they had no naval power, and only frequent bombardments by the combined navies prevented them from exploiting their success to the point of annihilation.

December 15, when Eighth Army was back again below the 38th parallel, marks the nadir of the Korean War. The Republicans, led by Senator Taft and encouraged by gains in the fall elections, demanded the dismissal of Dean Acheson as an "appeaser" of the Reds, and cheerfully expressed their willingness to abandon the defense of Europe in order to help MacArthur in Asia.[1] Former President Hoover, proposing that American policy revert to the last century, demanded that all United States forces be withdrawn from Europe, Asia, and Africa to "Fortress America," in order to preserve this "Gibraltar of Western Civilization." His sentiment was cheered by Americans who hated communism, hated England and Europe, hated new deals and new frontiers, and saw no need to bother with anything outside our own borders. But Truman and the Joint Chiefs of Staff stood firm. On 29 December General MacArthur received a new directive from the J. C. S. to defend all Korea, with a fresh warning that this was a limited war and there would be no blockade of China or "unleashing" Chiang from Formosa. MacArthur made a scorching reply, reiterating his plan for bombing Manchuria; Truman repeated the former directive. MacArthur replied (30 December) that this would mean the annihilation of the UN army.

A poor prophecy, indeed. The tide of battle had already turned. General Walker, killed on 23 December, was replaced as Commanding General Eighth Army by Major General Matthew B. Ridgway, who had commanded an airborne division in the 1943 invasion of Sicily. He found the morale of the now 15-nation UN army appallingly low, and bent his major efforts to improving it. By January 1951, when Ridgway had

---

[1] But several leading Republicans, such as Henry Cabot Lodge, Jr., John Foster Dulles, Thomas E. Dewey, and Harold Stassen, supported the President.

some 365,000 troops under his command, he had prepared positions ready to meet a fresh assault by Mao's half-million Chinese "volunteers" and North Koreans. Under his expert and inspiring leadership, with the Allied navies battering Chinese troop concentrations and communication lines along both coasts, the UN army advanced, recaptured Seoul on 14 March 1951, and recovered South Korea up to and a little beyond the 38th parallel. It was Ridgway who pulled victory out of defeat.

On 24 March 1951 MacArthur released to the press what he called a military appraisal containing a fresh plan to end the war. Arguing that the enemy had no industrial capability to wage modern war and that any forward move by us across the Yalu "would doom Red China to the risk of immediate military collapse," there should be no difficulty, he observed, in negotiating peace at once; and he stood ready to confer with the Chinese commander in chief to that effect. Not only was the plan foolish in itself, the release flouted an earlier presidential directive to the General to make no public statement on policy without his permission. Truman now decided that MacArthur must be relieved. The final straw was a letter from the General to Joseph Martin, Republican leader of the House, which Martin released to the press on 6 April. It said that Korea was the crucial spot where the war for global supremacy must be decided, "that here we fight Europe's war with arms while the diplomats there still fight it with words"; and ended with his favorite slogan, "There is no substitute for victory."

Truman consulted Generals Bradley and Marshall, Acheson and Harriman; all agreed that MacArthur must go. The actual orders were unnecessarily abrupt, because hurriedly drafted and dated at half past midnight 11 April in order to forestall a morning-paper scoop by the Chicago *Tribune*.

Then, what a blow-up! It reminded Winston Churchill of the dismissal of his ancestor the Duke of Marlborough by Queen Anne in 1711. Super patriots half-masted American flags, Senator Nixon demanded the General's immediate reinstatement. Senator Jenner threatened to impeach the President, to "cut out this whole cancerous conspiracy out of our government." Senator McCarthy denounced Truman as "a s.o.b. who decided to remove MacArthur when drunk." A Gallup poll reported that the public favored the General against the President 69 to 29. MacArthur received wildly enthusiastic greetings on his return to the United States, culminating in an address to both houses of Congress which drew tears even from the television audience when he quoted the army ballad "Old Soldiers Never Die, They Just Fade Away."

MacArthur's egotism forced him to regard any operation that he commanded as crucial. Thus, during World War II, he objected to the war against Germany being given priority, inveighed against Admiral Nimitz being given independent authority in the Pacific, and wished the entire strength of the United States and the British Commonwealth to be directed against Japan, under his command. So, naturally, he regarded the Korean War as the center of the world-wide struggle against communism. During World War II he had largely confined his extreme views to conversations, but now he felt strong enough to appeal over the President's head to the Republican party and public opinion. He never crossed the Rubicon, to be sure, but his horse's front hoofs were in the water.

One may debate endlessly whether MacArthur's plan to crush China would or would not have brought in Russia and started a third world war. But there can be no doubt that Truman was right in relieving a general whose attitude to his civilian commander in chief had become insufferable. The only valid criticism of the President is that he did not sack the General months earlier, at the end of August 1950, when he gave a statement to the press castigating "those who invariably in the past have propagandized a policy of defeatism and appeasement in the Pacific." Everyone knew that "those" meant Truman and Acheson. The General himself told me that a theater commander should be allowed to act independently, with no orders from President, United Nations, or anyone; and he repeated the statement so that there could be no doubt of his meaning. Any such supreme military power is incompatible with representative and responsible government.

Unable to admit a mistake, MacArthur later attributed his army's retreat in 1950 to traitors in the British embassy at Washington passing his plans to the Reds—as if the communists hadn't plenty of spies in Korea. The retreat was the result of his own bad strategy in the face of a Chinese concentration which either his intelligence service failed to report or which he and his staff disregarded.

Moreover, there is a substitute for total victory: peace, the only proper objective of war; and if Korea brought back into the international arena the concept of limited war for specific objectives, so much the better. The "unconditional surrender" kind of war was evolving into a war of mutual annihilation, as MacArthur himself told many people, including myself, before the Korean War broke. Limited war is also in the American tradition. We did not go on fighting in 1814 to conquer Canada, we did not try to take over all Mexico in 1848, we did not attempt to annex the troublesome Caribbean republics. It is regrettable that MacArthur's overweening ego prevented him, fundamentally a man of peace, from seeing this.

General Ridgway, succeeding MacArthur as SCAP, won peace in Korea. Armistice negotiations began on 10 July 1951 and continued until 5 March 1953 at Panmunjom, wearing out Admiral Joy and other negotiators. There were intermittent hostilities during that period. Cease-fire and the restoration of the 38° boundary were easy to obtain; what strung out the talks was the repatriation of prisoners, of which the UN had upward of 70,000. The Reds demanded that every one be returned to them, but the vast majority, unwilling draftees, preferred to stay out of communist territory. As a result of UN insistence that every man choose for himself, they were finally permitted to do so, and three out of four elected to stay south. On the other side, 21 American prisoners were "brainwashed" in captivity and threw in their lot with Red China. During these truce talks, the Reds pulled off a wonderful propaganda stunt, the germ warfare hoax. They accused Americans of dropping insects infected with cholera within their lines from aircraft, and supported this preposterous charge with confessions signed under torture by imprisoned aviators. This monstrous accusation was firmly believed by communists everywhere, and by thousands of fellow travelers and humanitarians. Investigation by the United Nations completely exploded it.

No formal peace treaty has yet (1971) been concluded; the situation in Korea is still an armed truce along the 38th parallel. But the Korean War was a clean-cut victory for the United States and the United Nations. It stopped a major communist lunge southward, and may well have saved Japan from being engulfed in the Red tide. It proved that the UN was no "paper tiger"—that it would and could fight if necessary. After the lapse of more than 20 years, it is clear that the Korean War was worth its cost in lives and money; but a major political party in the United States, and a part of the Labour party in Great Britain, took up the cry that it was a miserable failure.[1]

---

[1] The following statistics are from David Rees, *Korea the Limited War* (1964), Appendix A:—The United States furnished seven divisions and most of her Pacific Fleet. The British furnished their Far Eastern Fleet and the Commonwealth Division, composed of units from Britain, Australia, Canada, and New Zealand. Belgium, Colombia, Ethiopia, France, Greece, Netherlands, Philippines, and Thailand each sent one infantry battalion. Turkey sent one infantry brigade—superlative fighters—and there were smaller units from Luxemburg and the Union of South Africa. The war cost the United States 33,529 killed in action, died of wounds, or in captivity. The other United Nations lost 3194

6. The Election of 1952

Eleven years after his retirement, President Truman's achievements for world peace, national security, and European reconstruction shine out from the somber postwar atmosphere, but a large section of the American public in 1950–52 could see nothing but failure. He and General Marshall had "lost" China; he and Dean Acheson then "lost" the Korean War; hero MacArthur when (by his own statement) only ten days' fighting were needed to achieve complete victory, had been brutally cashiered; the Soviets may have been "contained" in Europe, but were getting ready to leap at our throats. Public opinion, unable to understand failure following the superb victory of 1945, readily picked on Truman and the Democrats as instruments of defeat. It was helped into this frame of mind by the charges and innuendoes of the House Committee on Un-American Activities ("the most un-American thing in America in its day," wrote Truman in his *Memoirs*), and by the spectacular demagoguery of Senator Joseph McCarthy of Wisconsin.

Against this background of malaise, suspicion, and frustration, an inglorious witch hunt was sparked off by several incidents. Alger Hiss was suspected, if not proved, to have been a communist when employed by the state department; Klaus Fuchs in England was convicted of feeding atomic secrets to Russia, and Russian defector Igor Gouzenko revealed the existence of a gigantic communist spy ring in Canada. It was so sinister that Mackenzie King said he "could not believe" that Stalin "countenanced" it—an attitude which shortened but did not end King's long premiership.[1] Ten top American communists were convicted under the Smith Act of 1939 of conspiracy to overthrow the government. All this fed a neat theory to explain recent events. During "twenty years of treason," as Senator McCarthy put it, the Democrats, led by Roosevelt and Truman, had "conspired" to deliver America to the Reds.

---

dead, 2769 missing or prisoners. Included in the UN figures are 1263 killed, 1188 missing or prisoners, in the Commonwealth Division. Of these 1263, 686 were British, 294 Canadian. I have been unable to find any reliable figures on R.O.K. forces or casualties; these were at least equal to those of the UN.

[1] King retired 20 April 1948 after 7619 days in office, and was succeeded as premier by his foreign secretary Louis St. Laurent. The significance of the spy disclosures is explained by the fact that Britain, Canada, and the U.S., the only three countries known to have developed atomic fission, had agreed in 1946 mutually to protect their scientists' atomic secrets. The biggest leak discovered in the United States was the Rosenbergs', for which they were convicted in 1951 and executed.

F.D.R. got into World War II mainly to help Russia, gave away everything to Stalin at Yalta; Harry presented China to the Reds and recalled General MacArthur because he was about to beat them; Alger Hisses were concealed in every government office, college, and corporation, ready to take over when Stalin pushed the button. This utterly preposterous theory almost tore the country apart then; it even played a role in later presidential campaigns. These efforts to "root out" subversives from government, colleges, and even business, ruined the careers and reputations of thousands of patriotic Americans whose only offense was to have lent their names to some "front" organization during World War II.

The conspiracy theory would never have been so widely received but for the histrionics and diabolical cunning of Senator Joseph R. McCarthy of Wisconsin. Estimates of him and his objectives vary, from pure white to deepest black. He was probably simply a plain rogue who wanted power to make Presidents and cabinet officials jump when he cracked the whip; but in the opinion of many he, like Huey Long, aimed at the presidency. McCarthy had none of the redeeming qualities of Huey Long. Cruel and greedy, he did nothing for the people of his native state. He was also one of the most colossal liars in our history. During a part of the war he had been air combat intelligence officer in the marines' 4th air wing; in his political campaigns, however, he claimed to have been a tail gunner on countless combat missions, responsible for killing thousands of the enemy. In competition with the younger La Follette he was elected to the Senate from Wisconsin in 1946 as a Republican. There, in search for a popular cause, he first took up that of German "martyrs" in the war criminal trials,[1] but that got him nowhere; on the advice of a prominent Catholic prelate he turned to the Red Menace. McCarthy's favorite method in speaking was to wave a document, announcing "I have in my hand" a list furnished confidentially by some patriot in the government "whose name I shall never reveal," containing the names of ten, fifty, or two hundred "card-carrying Communists" in the department of state. The document might have been a form letter or a laundry list; audiences never got a look at it.

In July 1950 a Senate committee under Millard Tydings of Maryland investigated McCarthy's charges and reported that

[1] McCarthy was three-quarters Irish blood, one-quarter German. The German-American farmers and small business men of Wisconsin, who bitterly resented being drawn into two wars against their mother country and refused to believe ill of Hitler, regarded McCarthy as their champion against the Anglo-Saxons.

they were "a fraud and a hoax perpetrated on the Senate of the United States and on the American people. They represent perhaps the most nefarious campaign of half-truth and untruth in the history of the Republic." McCarthy then charged the Tydings committee with being "soft" on communism, and with the aid of a big public relations firm, paid for by rightist organizations, brought so many false charges against Senator Tydings that he was defeated for re-election.

McCarthy now moved to bigger game—Dean Acheson and General Marshall, the alleged executioners of Chiang's government. He obtained valuable support from the so-called "China lobby," financed by a New York importer who anticipated a whopping trade with China if Chiang were restored. He even charged General Marshall with treason, and Dean Acheson made a perfect target for his hatred and malice. Educated at Groton, Yale, and Harvard Law School, Acheson was too handsome, well-groomed, self-assured, and ironical for the average congressman to stomach. "I look at that fellow," said Senator Hugh Butler of Nebraska, "I watch his smart-aleck manner and his British clothes and that . . . everlasting New Dealism in everything he says and does, and I want to shout, 'Get out! Get out! You stand for everything that has been wrong with the United States for years!' "

Nobody who did not live through that period will ever believe what a sound and fury made up. McCarthy had a country-wide following. He was the idol of the Boston Irish, despite his vile attacks on men whom they had elected. Cardinal Spellman extended his blessing; rising young politicians such as John F. Kennedy hedged. Actually, not one of the hundreds of "subversives" accused by McCarthy as being in the state department was found guilty after full investigation or trial. Many leading Republicans deplored all this, but the general run of politicians were delighted to have a new, hot issue; and the Republican platform of 1952 played up the "betrayal" of Chiang, the "loss" of the Korean War, and the "negative" nature of Truman's containment policy in Europe.

The Republicans' political strategy for 1952 was based on the inescapable fact that they had been a minority party for twenty years and were declining. Most of the rising generation regarded the G.O.P. as hopeless old fuddy-duddies; many racial and occupational groups such as blacks, Jews, and organized labor had abandoned them. Thus, to win, the Republicans must have a new issue or a glamour boy like the late Wendell Willkie, or both. McCarthy supplied the issue, but who would lead the procession? General MacArthur might have ridden the elephant. Willing enough, he was invited to give the keynote address to the Republican nominating convention at Chicago in July. It was received with slight enthusiasm, since the politicians knew that the General had no grass-roots support; he had failed as an avowed candidate in 1948—eleven votes on the first ballot, none on the third—and veterans did not like him. Thus the most logical conservative candidate was Senator Taft —"Mr. Republican" as he was often called. None more deserved to be President, for Taft had integrity, a deep knowledge of the governmental structure, and political courage. As in the case of Henry Clay, courage lost Taft the nomination; he had made too many enemies, notably the labor union leaders, owing to the Taft-Hartley Act. Tom Dewey, twice defeated, did not care to try again, but he marshaled delegates to win the nomination for a really glamorous candidate—General Eisenhower. "Ike" had no more political experience than MacArthur, but he was well liked by the G.I.'s; and his achievements in Europe, which included running two international coalitions, suggested that he had a flair for politics. He received 845 votes for the nomination, Taft had 280, Stassen 77, and MacArthur received 4. Senator Richard Nixon of California received second place on the ticket as a reward for having uncovered the former communist connections of Alger Hiss, when a member of the Un-American Activities Committee. He had no other qualifications; it was a case similar to Coolidge's winning the vice-presidential nomination for a few strong words about the Boston police strike.

Another factor that worked against the Democrats in this election was the "Truman scandals," exposed in part by congressional investigations, in part by an article "The Scandalous Years" in *Look* magazine. These were the pardoning of convicted criminals who had important Democratic friends, such as Mayor Curley of Boston, and favors extended to and bribes received by officeholders. A group of lobbyists known as "influence peddlers" had sprung up in Washington. They offered, in return for a modest 5 per cent, to connect businessmen who wanted contracts with the "right" person in the administration, or to "fix" cases by persuading the department of justice to lay off income tax evaders and other offenders. A congressional investigation of this shady business, led by Senator Fulbright of Arkansas, discovered that General Harry Vaughan, an old National Guard buddy whom Truman had appointed his military aide, had befriended perfume smugglers and accepted gifts from a grateful influence peddler, and that the wife of an examiner of loans for the Reconstruction Finance Corporation had received a $10,000 mink coat after he had approved a loan to a Florida motel. The R.F.C. had been a useful means of "pump priming" under the New Deal; but now, having out-lived its usefulness, it was extending loans to tottering corpora-tions or dubious projects such as snake farms and gambling casinos, and the arranging of such loans was a chief source of income to the 5 per centers.

Other investigations uncovered "fixing" in the bureau of internal revenue and the department of justice. An assistant attorney general and the President's appointments secretary were convicted and jailed on conspiracy charges, as was a former commissioner of internal revenue for tax evasion. The picture has a strong family resemblance to that of the "good guys" under Harding. Truman's easygoing old pals were re-sponsible for most of the high-level corruption, but not for scandals in the tax department. Here the basic trouble, which had been going on since 1933, was infiltration of federal tax collecting offices in the big cities from Boston to San Francisco by dishonest members of local Democratic machines.

President Truman was too complacent about these goings-on. Not covetous himself, he found it hard to believe that his friends were greedy and corrupt as the records proved. Even-tually he administered mild purges to the department of justice and the bureau of internal revenue, and reorganized the R.F.C. But the mink coat plagued him in the next campaign, like the bloody shirt of yore.

Harry could have tried for a third term despite Amendment XXII to the Constitution because it was not ratified in time to prevent him from having it. But, seeing how the wind blew, he definitely declined to be a candidate in March 1952. Senator Estes Kefauver of Tennessee, one of the leading contestants for the Democratic nomination, stumped the country in a coon-skin cap to emulate Davy Crockett, but he had two strikes against him. Advocacy of civil rights cost him the support of the dominant white South, and by showing up the alliance between ward politics and organized crime his name had be-come anathema to Democratic bosses in the cities. Ambassador Averell Harriman of New York was thought to be too closely identified with the foreign service to win the election. On the third ballot, Governor Adlai E. Stevenson of Illinois, grandson of the likenamed Vice President under Grover Cleveland, re-ceived the nomination.

Stevenson was an intelligent gentleman, skilled in adminis-tration, full of constructive ideas on domestic and foreign policy. He attracted the support of professors and other intel-lectuals (whom Eisenhower dubbed "eggheads") who thought they had found another F.D.R. Probably no Democrat could have beaten Eisenhower that year; but Stevenson's speeches were too epigrammatic and intellectual to interest the public, and the burden of the Truman scandals and malaise over the Korean War and China were too much for him to surmount or cure. General Eisenhower wrote prose which, even when corrected by the members of his political staff, was repetitive and obscure; but his pleasing personality and wide grin, said to have been worth several divisions during the war, attracted votes. "I Like Ike" stickers went up on cars, buildings, and trees all over the country. It was more important to know what Ike liked, but he carefully left that vague.

In the presidential election of 1952, the Eisenhower-Nixon ticket won 55.2 per cent of the popular vote, greatest plurality since 1936, and 442 electoral votes. Stevenson polled 44.5 per cent and 89 electoral votes, mostly in the South. The remaining three-tenths of one per cent was divided among six splinter parties, including a new Constitution party which nominated General MacArthur. His financial admirers, undismayed by his polling only 17,000 votes out of over 61 million, financed a ridiculous campaign to persuade the presidential electors to ditch General "Ike" and elect General "Doug."

After seeing General Eisenhower inaugurated, Truman retired to his home in Independence, Missouri. As was said in a famous Western epitaph which Harry liked to quote, "He did his damndest." Economic reconstruction of Europe, airlift to Berlin, containment of Soviet power by NATO, help to Greece and Turkey, bold acceptance of the Korean challenge, placing that war under the United Nations, maintaining the supremacy of civil over military government; all make a shining record for the little man from Missouri.

XVII

The Eisenhower Administrations

1953-1961

1. *The President and His Domestic Policy*

GENERAL OF THE ARMY Dwight D. Eisenhower became President of the United States on 20 January 1953, at the age of sixty-two. No President since George Washington entered office with a greater bank of good will on which to draw, at home and from abroad. Everyone "liked Ike" even if he did not vote for him; the British and European soldiers and statesmen, who had met him during the war or as head of NATO, felt that he understood their problems; even the Soviets seemed to thaw a little when the Beria-Bulganin team succeeded Stalin. Most Americans now felt that "everything would be all right"— Korean War concluded, budget balanced, no more starry-eyed visionaries in the top ranks of government, or crypto-communists in the lower echelons, no dubious characters from city wards slinking in and out of the White House to "fix" things. And, above all, a President tested by battle, intellectual enough to be head of a great university, strong enough to bang the heads of the service chiefs together and work out a defense policy that the country could afford. Eisenhower's "historic role," wrote Walter Lippmann, was to be "restorer of peace and order after an age of violence and faction."

Eisenhower was one of the best men ever elected President of the United States, and the people endorsed his first term by re-electing him with even greater majorities in 1956. His genial character and transparent honesty inspired loyalty to himself and confidence in his administration. Yet he failed in the historic role cast for him by producer Lippmann. Peace and order were not restored abroad; violence and faction were not quenched at home. What went wrong? To put it simply, Dulles on the international scene, and the President's want of political experience on the domestic scene. Eisenhower who, like Hoover, had never occupied an elective office, disliked politics and politicians and attempted to leave sordid questions of patronage to others. And fundamentally, Eisenhower had a conception of the presidency which precluded positive leadership while leaving plenty of time for golf. Consciously or unconsciously he became a constitutional monarch, a symbolic chief of state, rather than a dynamic initiator of policy; he mediated, smoothed over difficulties, but left leadership to the Republicans in Congress. He hoped to inaugurate another Era of Good Feelings, as Monroe had done in 1820. He hoped to end the cold war and restore normal international relations. Unfortunately conditions at home and abroad were such that no dayspring of peace and tranquility could have dawned in 1953, no matter how much good will emerged from the White House, and that good will became an ill wind in the hands of his secretary of state, John Foster Dulles.

The President organized his administration somewhat like a military staff. Men below him were supposed to work out in detail what needed to be done; the President had to make the ultimate decision, but he disliked doing any preliminary thinking about it himself. Contradictory recommendations would come to him on defense and other matters from two or three different departments, each already watered down while passing up from lower echelons. The President, who studied no problem deeply himself, would return the differing recommendations and order an all-round agreement on which to base his decisions; thus almost every decision was a compromise, and often a wishy-washy one. His health was always precarious, and in 1955 he suffered a serious heart attack which for weeks made it difficult for him to transact public business; and at all times, to maintain his strength, he spent an unusual amount of time for a president, relaxing at Camp David or his Gettysburg farm, or playing golf.

Eisenhower's cabinet appointments met with general approval, for they seemed to accord with Harding's epigram that the country needed "more business in government and less government in business." The appointment of John Foster Dulles, two years senior to Eisenhower, as secretary of state, seemed an ideal choice; on his record Dulles seemed the best equipped man in all our history to head the foreign service. Grandson of one secretary of state (John W. Foster, under the second President Harrison); nephew of another (Robert Lansing, under Wilson); Princeton graduate, member of a leading law firm of New York, Dulles had been intermittently in public life since 1907 when he played secretary to his grandfather at the Hague Convention. He had had a part in drafting the United Nations constitution, and served under Truman as consultant in the state department while still an avowed Republican. As such he negotiated the excellent treaty of peace with Japan and persuaded the Philippine Republic, which wanted a Versailles sort of treaty, to accept it. With his hunched shoulders and woeful countenance occasionally lit by a wry smile, always hard-working, always ready to fly to the ends of the earth (559,988 miles by careful count as secretary) when he thought it would do good, Dulles was a conscientious student of foreign affairs. His speech was slow and he often managed to bore rather than impress the foreign statesmen with whom he talked. His failure to attain his and Eisenhower's avowed objectives of world peace and containment of communism was due in great part to conditions beyond his control; but in good part to his pedagogical methods of handling strange and explosive situations.

For other cabinet appointments, Eisenhower sought out leaders of big business. The new department of defense, established by Congress under Truman in the hope of co-ordinating the three armed forces, was given to Charles E. Wilson of Detroit, president since 1941 of General Motors, one of the country's biggest and most successful corporations. That sounded fine; but the President did not know that sixty-three-year-old Wilson, a mere figurehead in Detroit, had lost any capacity he might have had for businesslike administration.[1] In the second Eisenhower administration Wilson was replaced by Neil H. McElroy, a Harvard graduate with a glamorous

[1] An assistant secretary of the army has given me an account of a typical "day with Wilson." When he arrived, by appointment with an important defense matter, Wilson, instead of listening to him, insisted on discussing whether or not to fold up some petty air force facility in Georgia. In succession Admiral Radford and General Twining of the J. C. S., and Secretary Quarles of the air force, came in by appointment, each with an important subject for decision. Wilson drew them into the air force discussion, which continued during lunch, after which all four were dismissed without the important questions being brought up.

personality, president of the Procter & Gamble soap firm of Cincinnati. After this ineffective minister had served for two years he was relieved by Thomas S. Gates, Jr., a Philadelphia investment banker and former secretary of the navy, who made a really hard-working, competent defense secretary, putting in a twelve-hour day at the Pentagon. Until he came in, and to some extent even later, the method of allotting funds to the several armed services and of making up the total defense budget, was incredibly bad. A rigid fixed percentage of the total was allotted to each arm—23 per cent to the army, 28 per cent to the navy and marines, and 46 per cent to the air force. This "vertical" budgeting resulted in each force developing its wants independent of the other two, so that the defense picture was never viewed in the aggregate. No wonder that General Maxwell D. Taylor, who relieved General Ridgway as chief of staff in 1955, found inspiration from 1 Corinthians xiv:8 for the title of his book, *The Uncertain Trumpet*.

In view of Republican promises to economize, reduce the national debt, check inflation, and promote prosperity, an appointment equal in importance to state and defense was the secretary of the treasury. George M. Humphrey of Cleveland, chairman of the board of several important steel and coal companies, was Eisenhower's choice. He was not a good team worker, consistently trying to pare down expenditures on defense during the cold war, even publicly attacking the President's budget in 1957 by announcing that the necessary taxes would produce "a depression that will curl your hair." Joseph M. Dodge, the new director of the budget, should have been given the treasury, as he had shown financial genius under Truman by stabilizing the currencies of Japan, Austria, and Germany. Both his hands and Humphrey's were tied, because the administration insisted on an independent Federal Reserve Board. This stemmed from the outmoded "free market" concept, the heart of Republican ideology. There was a severe recession in 1957–58 which might have developed into a major depression but for the controls established during the Roosevelt administrations.

Eisenhower's first secretary of the interior, Governor Douglas MacKay of Oregon, and Postmaster General Arthur E. Summerfield were automobile distributors by profession. Adlai Stevenson remarked, "The New Dealers have all left Washington to make way for the car dealers." MacKay was a notorious foe to conservation and public power developments. Ezra Taft Benson of Utah, a graduate of Brigham Young University and one of the Twelve Apostles of the Mormon church, who strongly disapproved the welfare state, became secretary of agriculture. Despite the hostility of Western farmers who resented his efforts to reduce price supports, Benson held office through both Eisenhower terms. Sinclair Weeks, a Harvard graduate and former senator from Massachusetts, director of several New England corporations and of the National Association of Manufacturers, appropriately became secretary of commerce. He signaled the return of the *caveat emptor* concept to the federal government by firing Allen Astin, chief of the bureau of standards, who had offended several drug manufacturers and others by down-grading their products. This caused a nation-wide protest from consumers, and Astin got his job back. For cabinet lady, Eisenhower appointed to the newly established department of health, education and welfare, Mrs. Oveta Culp Hobby, wife of a wealthy Texas publisher. Nelson Rockefeller became her deputy. For attorney general, Eisenhower chose a legal aid to Governor Dewey, Herbert Brownell. To round out the picture and have one Democrat in it, the department of labor was given to Martin Durkin, president of the Journeymen Plumbers' and Steamfitters' Union. As one liberal paper quipped, "Ike's cabinet consists of eight millionaires and a plumber." But Durkin was so unhappy in this company that he resigned before the year was out.

More important than the cabinet, as the turnstile through which most visitors and all business had to pass to reach the President, was Sherman Adams, Dartmouth graduate, former congressman, and state governor. He had taken an active part in the Eisenhower campaign, and the President chose him as special assistant. He had cabinet rank and occupied a position similar to that of Harry Hopkins in Roosevelt's and of Harry Vaughan's in Truman's; but enjoyed far more power than either. After he had become almost indispensable to the valetudinarian President, Adams unfortunately intervened with the Federal Trade Commission and the S.E.C. on behalf of a shady manipulator and income tax evader named Bernard Goldfine, from whom he had received expensive gifts and hospitality. When this came out, the President had to accept Adams's resignation, and the "gray eminence" of the administration returned to New Hampshire to raise chickens.

Every administration, one may say, has its own pattern of corruption. "Fixing," that of Truman's, did not now altogether disappear, as the Adams-Goldfine episode reveals; but the typical thing under Eisenhower was conflict of interest. Business men who accepted cabinet appointments were supposed to "divest" themselves of pecuniary interests in companies to which government contracts might be awarded, and most of them did. But it later came out that Harold E. Talbott, president of the Dayton-Wright airplane company, who became secretary of the air force, retained half-interest in a management-engineering firm for which he solicited business while in government service; and that Robert T. Ross in the defense department awarded millions of dollars' worth to a firm of which his wife was president. Both men were forced by the defense secretary to resign, and both considered themselves "martyrs" —they had sacrificed so much money to serve the nation, why shouldn't they make a little on the side? This seems to have been a prevalent ethical attitude, well illustrated in a popular novel of the era, Sloan Wilson's *The Man in the Gray Flannel Suit*.

A somewhat different affair, which rocked the country with laughter but caused Secretary Benson great embarrassment, was the great cheese scandal. On 1 April 1954 Elder Benson dropped the price-support level for all dairy products from 90 to 75 per cent parity. Prior to that date, the big cheese distributors of Wisconsin and bordering states had contracted to sell 90 million pounds of their local "cheddar" to the government at the high support price of 37 cents per pound. Immediately after, they bought back almost the same amount from the government at 34¼ cents, making a profit of nearly $2.5 million on cheese that never left their warehouses. Neither Benson nor his subordinates profited, and they prevented its happening again.

Walter Lippmann predicted that responsibility would cure the Republicans of trying to prove that the Democrats had sold out to Moscow. So far as foreign policy was concerned, this worked; when John Foster Dulles, as Republican as Bob Taft, scrapped campaign boasts and in most essentials followed Truman's policy, the congressional Republicans fumed and growled but kept quiet. Far different was it with McCarthyism. Eisenhower extended security checks to all government agencies and purged the service of over 6900 "security risks" in seventeen months. None of these were really serious cases—mostly clerks who drank or talked too much or who had expensive girl friends. But Secretary Dulles gravely damaged the morale of his department just when America's world position required the recruitment of good men, by a pusillanimous catering to McCarthy, forcing the resignation of professional foreign service officers as punishment for giving the "wrong" advice— from the Republican point of view—about China. This display of zeal failed to appease McCarthy, who shifted his attacks to the Eisenhower administration. And no one who witnessed his appearances on TV can doubt that the Senator hoped to convict the President of being "soft on communism"; even to succeed him.

So long as McCarthy confined his smears to professors, scholars, and the foreign service, the general run of Americans, who disliked intellectuals and the "white spat boys," seemed to be with him. And the President kept silent except for attacking "book burners" in an address at Dartmouth College, which was about as effective as a speech against witch-hangers in Salem might have been.[1] But when McCarthy swung on the Protestant clergy and the United States Army in March 1954, the administration began to take notice. Army secretary Robert Ten Broeck Stevens (one of the President's best appointments), with his attorney Joseph N. Welch, fought back vigorously; and when McCarthy demanded that he be allowed to fish in F.B.I. files for the names of new victims, Eisenhower denounced him as one who tried "to set himself above the laws of our land" and "to override orders of the President." The Senate then censured him by an emphatic vote. McCarthy himself collapsed, but the poisonous suspicion that he injected into the body politic will take many years to leach out. As Eisenhower states in his memoirs, "McCarthyism took its toll on many individuals and on the nation. No one was safe from charges recklessly made from inside the walls of congressional immunity. Teachers, government employees, and even ministers became vulnerable. . . . The cost was often tragic." For success in dividing a country by sowing suspicion of treason in high places, there has been no one to equal Joe McCarthy since Marat in the French Revolution.

"Dynamic conservatism," a favorite phrase of the President's, was carried out in a number of ways, along the welfare line recently condemned during the election. Eisenhower canceled the few remaining price and rent controls, and wound up the discredited RFC; but with his approval Congress enlarged social security to embrace some 10 million more people—domestic servants who needed it least, farm hands who needed it most, and government employees who had it anyway. Unemployment compensation, too, was extended to an additional 4 million people. The nation-wide minimum wage was raised to a dollar an hour, laws were enacted to curb corruption and

[1] The allusion was to the activities of two henchmen of McCarthy in Europe, visiting U.S. Information Bureau libraries and designating the books of authors (such as Dos Passos, Hemingway, and Thoreau) who were on a list of "subversives" compiled by some excited old lady, to be eliminated. This sort of activity so resembled those of Hitler's brown shirts that many Europeans seriously feared that America was going fascist.

racketeering in the unions, and a moderate public housing program was passed by Congress in 1955. Next year a $40 billion highway program was launched. Eisenhower promoted a bill for federal aid to the states for building new schoolhouses, to the tune of $50 million a year; but the bill failed after being amended so that racially segregated schools were excluded.

Most amusing of unconscious tributes by Republicans to the New Deal was their adoption of Henry Wallace's "soil bank." This meant paying farmers to take marginal arable land out of cultivation and plant it with trees or put it to other uses. Soil banks, together with price supports that Elder Benson could never get rid of, shot up federal grants to farmers to $5 billion in 1959. In addition, the government lost over $1.2 billion in the years 1953–55 through purchasing and storing farm products to get rid of surpluses. The difference between Eisenhower "dynamic conservatism" and the no less dynamic liberalism of Truman, seems to have been that the Republicans passed such measures reluctantly, with sighs and groans over the political necessity, and many a backward glance to the good old days before the war.

According to Lewis L. Strauss, onetime Chairman of the Atomic Energy Commission, the TVA was the "sacred cow" of the New Deal, but the Republicans regarded it as a maverick steer to be jabbed and sniped at on sight. Hence the so-called Dixon-Yates deal. The gist of this complicated affair is about as follows. In 1953 TVA proposed to build a new steam generating plant at Fulton, Tennessee, primarily to meet the growing power requirements of Memphis. President Eisenhower disapproved, Congress refused to provide funds, and as a substitute the administration backed a complex arrangement. The Atomic Energy Commission, TVA's largest single power customer, would contract with a combination of two private companies, known as "Dixon-Yates" from the names of their presidents, to provide energy which AEC would then turn over to TVA for ultimate delivery to Memphis; the basic idea being to give a private company a slice of the Authority's territory and a guaranteed profit. Although engineers demonstrated that this bizarre arrangement would cost the public $5.5 million more annually than would the proposed Fulton plant, President Eisenhower gave the deal his blessing. He also refused to reappoint Gordon Clapp, the TVA chairman who had fought for the new plant, and later replaced him by one who considered Dixon-Yates a "good deal." After AEC had signed the contract with Dixon-Yates, it came out that a consultant of the Bureau of the Budget who had helped arrange the deal was an official of the banking firm selected to finance it. The deal collapsed in 1955 when the city of Memphis declared it would build its own municipal plant rather than be dependent on Dixon-Yates. Later the department of justice found the agreement so contrary to public policy as to be "null and void." The same year, a commission headed by Herbert Hoover to recommend "streamlining" the federal government, proposed that TVA be required to sell all its steam plants to private firms. But no such law went through Congress, and the passage of an act in 1959, allowing the Authority to issue bonds to provide for expansion, guaranteed the "sacred cow" ample fodder for the future.

So many deals of the Dixon-Yates type were attempted, and enough of them succeeded, to justify the Democrats' coining the phrase "The Give-away Program" for the Eisenhower administration's power and conservation policy. Hell's Canyon on the Snake river, for instance, was abandoned to a private utility; a bankrupt mining company was allowed to recoup its fortunes by stripping part of the Rouge River National Forest of its timber; in two years 566 leases for drilling oil wells were granted in wild life refuges. Democrats supported, Republicans defeated, a bill to set up a federal atomic power plant, and the administration farmed out Oak Ridge to Union Carbide, and the Hanford atomic energy plant to General Electric. The President, however, vetoed the biggest attempted "steal," the Natural Gas Bill which would have relieved that booming industry of price regulation. On the whole, the net picture of the Eisenhower administration of conservation is one of carelessness, not corruption, want of understanding about flood control and the preservation of mineral, oil, and forest reserves; and a disposition to let private capital exploit resources that rightfully belong to the public.

When we turn to civil rights, the picture is much brighter. President Eisenhower made some excellent appointments to the Supreme Court bench, including that of Earl Warren of California as Chief Justice, and under him the Supreme Court made several decisions safeguarding the rights of individuals in the security and loyalty cases that had been sparked off by McCarthy. All these paled in comparison with the epoch-making decision in the school segregation case.

Under Chief Justice Fuller, the Supreme Court in *Plessy* v. *Ferguson* (1896) gave legal sanction to the jim crow laws, holding that Amendment XIV to the Constitution did not forbid segregation of Negroes in schools, etc., provided that public facilities reserved for the colored were equal to those whence they were excluded. Justice Harlan of Kentucky dissented. In 1954 the principle behind his dissent became the unanimous opinion of the court, delivered by Chief Justice Warren in the case of *Brown* v. *Board of Education of Topeka:* "We conclude that in the field of public education the doctrine of 'separate but equal' has no place. Separate educational facilities are inherently unequal."

Although the Court conceded that states might move gradually toward desegregating schools, several of the former slave states resorted to every possible legal device, as well as pressure and intimidation, to block even a beginning of integration. One method, practiced in Virginia and eventually declared illegal by the Supreme Court, was to abandon the public school system and set up a series of so-called private schools for white children, the state paying the fees. In the lower South, the Supreme Court's decision was to all intents and purposes nullified and has remained so through 1971. John C. Calhoun would have been delighted! For, powerful as the federal government has become, the American system still is federal, which means that "interposition" by a state government—a word now revived from the Kentucky and Virginia Resolutions of 1798—can thwart federal law when the great majority of the people, in this instance the Southern whites, is in violent disagreement.

Some progress was made in large cities in the upper South and the border area, such as Washington, Baltimore, Louisville, and St. Louis. There schools reopened quietly on an integrated basis. But 2300 districts, including all in the deep South and Virginia, remained segregated. In the high school of Little Rock, Arkansas, which a couple of qualified colored children tried to enter in the fall of 1957, intervention by a rabble-rousing governor and threats of mob action led President Eisenhower to send federal troops to maintain order. Protests and disorders reached their height that year and the next. The Little Rock school board appealed to the Supreme Court, which in September 1958 (case of *Cooper* v. *Aaron*) declared, "The constitutional rights [of the children] are not to be sacrificed or yielded to the violence and disorder which have followed the actions of the Governor and Legislature. . . . Law and order are not to be preserved by depriving the Negro children of their constitutional rights." President Eisenhower, after Senator Richard Russell of Georgia had insolently compared him to Hitler for sending troops to Little Rock, replied: "When a State refuses to utilize its police powers to protect persons who are peaceably exercising their rights under the Constitution as defined in such [Federal] court orders, the oath of office of the President requires that he take action to give that protection. Failure to act in such a case would be tantamount to acquiescence in anarchy and the dissolution of the Union."

It was bitterly ironical to hear all the arguments of pro-slavery days trotted out to prevent black children from mixing with whites in classrooms, or even against qualified men and women of that race entering professional schools. Blacks for the most part followed the Reverend Martin Luther King, Jr., who, borrowing the tactics of Gandhi which won independence for India, schooled his people to non-violence and patience, starting with a bus boycott in Montgomery, Alabama.

In several cities, blacks demonstrated successfully against segregation in streetcars and buses. In the spring of 1960 they began to "sit in" at lunch counters in drug and department stores, it being one of the peculiar tenets of jim crow philosophy that a black could buy goods in a white man's store, but must admit his inferiority by going humbly to the back door to get a sandwich. Yet, in nearby air force bases, integrated by the President's order, white and colored worked side by side and shared the same facilities. Within a few weeks the sit-in movement had swept the South, whose authorities retaliated by wholesale arrests. The Supreme Court, in *Garner* v. *Louisiana*, voided these arrests on the ground that merely to sit unserved at a lunch counter was no breach of the peace. The sit-in movement served notice that blacks intended to claim their legal rights, and that they were prepared to use economic and political as well as legal weapons in that struggle. Presently, to the joy of the white South and discomfiture of Northern liberals, they would extend their agitation to Northern cities in search of better housing, schools, and status.

It was all very well for President Eisenhower to declare, "There must be no second-class citizens in this country"—there were, and still are. The traditional American remedy for injustice is political power. The black had lost his right to vote, as we have seen, in the reaction against Reconstruction; it was now felt that if he regained it, and could be elected to at least minor offices, he could improve his status and force local politicians to respect his wishes. Accordingly, in 1957 Congress after sixty-three days of debate passed a new civil rights law, first since 1870, to protect the blacks' right to vote by removing some of the obstacles imposed by state and local officials. Federal judges were empowered to enjoin state officials from refusing to register qualified persons, and to fine or even imprison them for recalcitrance. This law, of benign intent, proved far too weak to surmount the numerous tricks resorted to by dominant Southern whites. Eisenhower did complete desegregation in the armed forces, begun under F. D. Roosevelt. In other directions integration spread. TVA had desegregated all its waterside parks by 1957, and has been increasing the employment of blacks at all levels, including the scientific staff. Between 1940 and 1957 the number of black professional men and women more than doubled, the number of skilled workers increased by 181 per cent, and the number of black clerks and salesmen more than tripled.

In other ways, Eisenhower proved himself a humanitarian and a man of peace. He played a vigorous part in obtaining, against opposition by isolationist leaders of both parties, the Refugee Relief Act of 1953, allowing him to admit during the next three years 215,000 Europeans, mostly refugees from communism, over and above the immigration quotas. These quotas had become even more restrictive under the McCarran-Walter Act of 1952, passed by Congress over President Truman's veto. Highly praiseworthy is his "Atoms for Peace" proposal to the United Nations on 8 December 1953. The idea, Eisenhower's own, was for the United States and Soviet Russia to make joint contributions from their uranium stockpiles to the United Nations. This would be administered and allocated by a UN atomic energy agency "to serve the peaceful pursuits of mankind"; especially "to provide abundant electrical energy in the power-starved areas of the world." And, in an eloquent peroration, he pledged for his country a "determination to solve the fearful atomic dilemma," to find some way to consecrate "the miraculous inventiveness of man" to his life, not his destruction. But this sincere proposal was met by the Soviet government with surly contempt. Eisenhower nevertheless promoted a unilateral development of "atoms for peace," and the world's first non-military atomic power plant was started at Shippingport, Pennsylvania, on Labor Day 1954.

Although the President's life had been despaired of for a time in 1955, he made a good recovery and decided to run for a second term in 1956. The Eisenhower and Nixon team was nominated on the first ballot at the Republican convention in San Francisco. The Democrats, meeting in Chicago, renominated Stevenson with Kefauver, despite the open opposition of Harry Truman who wanted Averell Harriman and predicted that Adlai could not win more than the nine states he carried in 1952. Actually he carried only seven states, all in the South, with 73 electoral votes; Eisenhower carried the other 41 states with 457 electoral votes. The popular vote was 35.6 to 26 million. This, the biggest plurality in twenty years, was a magnificent endorsement.

Eisenhower proved to be a better leader during his second than his first term, especially after losing his administrative assistant Adams through the Goldfine affair, and Secretary Dulles by death in May 1959. Christian Herter, former governor of

Massachusetts and assistant secretary of state who succeeded Dulles, did not enjoy robust health, and the President assumed direction of foreign policy as well as making "good will tours" as far afield as India, Morocco, and Chile. He was received with enthusiasm everywhere.

Among the achievements of the second administration were a new Atomic Energy Act permitting exchange of information and co-operation in atomic research with trustworthy allies, the creation of an Aeronautics and Space Administration to direct space research, an educational act (spurred by Russia's "sputnik" achievement) providing millions for the support of teaching languages and science, and loans to students; and the overdue admission of Alaska and Hawaii to statehood. The people "liked Ike" as much in December as they did in May; but they were becoming increasingly tired of the G.O.P., as evidenced by the fact that they returned Democratic majorities to the last three congresses of Eisenhower's two terms and increased the majority in 1958. And a number of Republican state governors and United States senators were defeated the same year, portending a Democratic comeback.

2. Foreign Relations

During the Truman administration a new situation had been developing in Asia and Africa, the liquidation of all colonial empires. Adding more than fifty new independent nations to those which formed the UN in 1945, this movement constituted as great a revolution in world affairs as the spread of communism.

Starting with the rediscovery of West Africa and India by the Portuguese, and the discovery of America by Columbus, Spain, England, France, the Netherlands, and Portugal had built up world-wide empires. Between 1775 and 1810 there occurred a series of revolutions by overseas colonists of the same language and race as the mother country—the American Revolution and the successive Latin-American revolutions. But the revolutions of 1945–65 were of entirely different character—revolts of the *indigènes*, the colored natives, not only against the colonizing nation but against the white officials, traders, and entrepreneurs who had come from the mother country to bring law and order and to develop or exploit natural resources with native labor.

The Philippines, already promised independence by the United States before the war began, achieved it on 4 July 1946 and remained our good friends. The subcontinent of India, to which Britain had brought peace and justice, broke up into four independent states—India, Pakistan, Ceylon, and Burma. French Indochina, of which more anon, relapsed into four turbulent little states, Laos, Cambodia, North and South Vietnam. The Netherlands East Indies, which the Allies had culpably neglected to occupy immediately after World War II, threw off Dutch rule and emerged as the Republic of Indonesia under Sukarno; a child of revolution who, like others before him, stayed in power only by demanding more and more territory, and got it. These nationalist revolutions of the 1940's were followed by another series in Central and South Africa against England, France, and Belgium, leaving only the Portuguese colonies and the Union of South Africa, where a minority of white Africans, descendants of seventeenth-century Dutch colonists, clamped a tight lid on millions of native blacks.

Next there came to a head three revolutions in North Africa. The old Barbary states, whose piratical activities had caused so much trouble to Presidents Washington and Jefferson, had been occupied, pacified, and colonized by France and Spain since 1830. Now they, too, threw off the foreign yoke; Morocco, Algeria, and Tunisia recovered their independence, and the native Moslems either expelled or squeezed out millions of European *colons*. General Charles de Gaulle, summoned to power to preserve *Algérie française*, was forced to acquiesce. It was as if the Tecumseh Confederacy of 1811 had succeeded in forcing all white North Americans to return to Britain. And in Egypt, to which Britain had brought peace and the rule of law in the nineteenth century, fat but friendly King Farouk was thrown out by a military junto from which emerged clever, ruthless Gamal Abdel Nasser. In the late 1950's the British West Indies began severing their imperial ties to set up little insular republics, with the consent and aid of the British government.

Beginning in the Roosevelt era and extending into the Eisenhower regime, the United States adopted a very benevolent policy toward these nationalist revolutions, partly because of popular prejudice for independence and against "colonialism," but mostly to compete with Russia for their friendship and their votes in the United Nations, and to prevent communist take-overs. Russia and Red China, however, have been strong competitors though disappointed by the results. According to the Marxian gospel, capitalism had maintained itself only through colonial expansion; but these revolutions, it turned out, saved the mother countries a great deal of trouble and expense in administration without significantly diminishing their trade. Nonetheless, the colonial breakdown lessened the world-wide power of Britain, France, and the Netherlands. The Indian army, formerly a major stabilizing power factor in Asia, has deteriorated since the British withdrew, and the British navy no longer has the force to patrol the Indian Ocean. The French can no longer draw on Africa for some of their best troops—the Zouaves, whose exploits and uniforms so impressed our Civil War ancestors; the *tirailleurs marocains,* and the *sénégalais,* who were terrors to the Germans in both world wars. Nor can Holland recruit Javanese for her navy.

Coincident with these nationalist explosions came the terrifying development of thermonuclear weapons: first the "A" atomic bomb, then the "H" hydrogen bomb, then the guided missile, land- or ship-based, with intercontinental range and warheads a hundred times more powerful than the bomb which wiped out Hiroshima.

Thus Eisenhower, like Truman, was faced almost daily by issues such as had formerly arisen only in time of war. He was buffeted from one crisis to another, on four continents. The United States could not act, or even be strong, everywhere. Which troubled theater should have priority—Central Europe, Middle East, India, Southeast Asia, Africa? And, before long, Latin America would be shouting for attention. The President was beset by differing estimates and demands by the service chiefs for concentration on this or that weapon or arm; should we go all out for very long range bombers, or rely on shorter ones, based on fields in Turkey, Morocco, Spain, and western Europe, which we held at sufferance of the several sovereign states? Should the navy be developed as an anti-submarine force (since it was known that Russia was building up a mighty submarine fleet), or a striking force for limited war, or as floating bases for launching ballistic missiles?

Russia, by boasting that she was building a great bomber fleet, goaded North America into setting up an expensive radar-warning grid across northern Canada, to detect any possible hostile flight over the North Pole. But Russia never built those bombers; instead she developed enormously powerful rockets to propel guided missiles, and in 1957 shocked the American public, as it had not been since Pearl Harbor, by launching the first satellite "Sputnik" into outer space. That exploit sparked off a feverish effort to develop bigger and better rockets and missiles here; and one of these efforts, the fleet of Polaris-equipped nuclear-powered submarines which are capable of carrying war against an enemy even if America is devastated, has probably been the major deterrent of our time. The first of this fleet, U.S.S. *Nautilus* (Commander William R. Anderson), submerged on 1 August 1958 north of Alaska, steamed for

1800 miles under the polar ice cap, emerging four days later on the European side of the Pole. The second, U.S.S. *Triton* (Captain Edward L. Beach), circumnavigated the globe under water between 16 February and 10 May 1960, broaching only twice in 84 days—to land a sick seaman at Montevideo and at Cadiz to honor the memory of Magellan, whose course she followed.

During the presidential campaign of 1952, the Republicans had made brave noises about "liberation" of captive nations. But, to do that, as General Ridgway observed, America must be able to apply air, sea, or land power, or all three, to influence any particular situation. Yet, as soon as the Korean War appeared to be about over, Wilson and Humphrey, the secretaries of defense and the treasury, insisted on cutting armed forces appropriations by some $5 billion. That basic situation, which existed through the Eisenhower regime, forced Dulles to reconsider foreign policy. As he announced it on 12 January 1954, the country would depend for its security in the future on "the deterrent of massive retaliatory power." President Eisenhower veered between the two points of view, seldom taking a strong line, but generally favoring the civilians. He undertook to play world policeman with no big stick—only the big bang of the A and H bombs which he dared not use, well knowing that they would spark off mutual destruction.

The Korean truce was signed in July 1953 after Eisenhower had been President for six months. The Joint Chiefs of Staff anticipated that Mao, defeated here, would probe elsewhere; and before the end of the year he did so in Indochina, where the French government, unwisely refusing to follow the British example of granting immediate independence to India, fiddled around fruitlessly with attempts to set up protectorates under native princes. Here the upsetting force was the Viet Minh—a guerrilla army recruited in China and from the bordering peasants in Vietnam. The French garrison under the war hero De Lattre de Tassigny had been driven into a stockade at Dien Bien Phu in North Vietnam and, if not shortly relieved, could not hold out. Certain military advisers of President Eisenhower, notably Admiral Arthur W. Radford, chairman of the Joint Chiefs of Staff, were in favor of our intervening militarily in Indochina as we had in Korea. But army chief of staff General Ridgway, who knew the terrain and predicted a struggle as tough as in Korea, and Secretary Dulles, opposed intervention as beyond the power of our reduced military establishment. While Washington debated, Dien Bien Phu fell (7 May 1954). The diplomats now took over, and the President followed their advice at the Geneva conference that summer. By agreement with Russia and Red China (20 July 1954), their followers retained control of North Vietnam but they recognized and promised to respect the independence of non-communist South Vietnam, Laos, and Cambodia. This decision created three more weak succession states to be supported by financial, economic, and military aid against attack or subversion. In the hope of preserving the status quo in this part of the world, Dulles and other members of the Geneva conference set up the Southeast Asia Treaty Organization (SEATO) between the United States, Australia, New Zealand, the United Kingdom, France, Pakistan, Thailand, and the Philippines, signing the treaty at Manila on 8 September 1954. It obliges all signatory powers to help any one of them against aggression by an outside power. When it came to a showdown in 1963, SEATO proved to be a weak reed—and only Australia helped the United States defend the three non-communist states against attacks by the Viet Minh.

No sooner was the fate of Indochina handed over to the diplomats than Mao's Chinese government started to bombard two small island groups off the China coast, Quemoy and Matsu, which were still under Chiang's government in Formosa. Dulles, like Acheson before him, refused to tie his hands by signing an offensive-defensive alliance with Chiang's government in Formosa, but Congress had already given the President authority to use force if necessary to defend this territory. Should Quemoy and Matsu be considered part of Formosa? The British were very keen to put pressure on Chiang to cede the little islands to Mao in return for a Chinese pledge to settle the Formosa question peacefully. Dulles rightly prevented this, pointing out that it would smell of Munich. Mao, not caring at this point to risk war with the United States, caused the cannonade to cease, and that neck of the woods was relatively quiet for four years.

The Matsu-Quemoy business erupted again in August 1958 when the Chinese reopened their artillery bombardment. The fainthearted argued that America should keep out of this fight and let the Reds take the islands. It was pointed out that Quemoy and Matsu were as close to China as Vancouver Island is to British Columbia, or Staten Island to New York. Should we risk an all-out war for little offshore islands which Chiang ought to evacuate anyway? All Asia was watching to see what we would do; it was a test case. The Eisenhower administration stood firm. Both navy and air force helped Chiang to reinforce and support the islands and to evacuate civilians; and the communists, lacking naval control of the Formosa strait, dared not launch an amphibious attack. The result was that they knocked off in October, and the United States gained face in the Far East.

Between the two Matsu-Quemoy crises came a much more serious one, over the Suez Canal. In 1952 King Farouk of Egypt was dethroned by an army officers' rebellion, and the Naguib-Nasser group took over. A friendly and helpful policy by the United States toward Egypt was inherited by Secretary Dulles from Secretary Acheson. But the Eisenhower-Dulles team handled the situation with incredible gaucherie and stupidity. As a starter, President Eisenhower presented General Naguib—then Nasser's partner—with a pearl-handled revolver on the day after he had denounced Britain as "the enemy." This gesture meant to the Arabs that America was on their side, to force the European nations out of Suez. After that "blooper" Eisenhower left the Suez affair completely in the hands of Dulles, who approached the subject as if he had been a Wall Street lawyer reorganizing a corporation in trouble. Dulles's hold over Eisenhower is explained by his encyclopedic knowledge of international relations, and by the fact that he appeared to have all the answers.

The Suez Canal from Port Said to the Red Sea was built by Ferdinand de Lesseps's *Compagnie Universelle* between 1859 and 1869, at a cost of about $87 million, most of which was subscribed by European governments. In 1888 an international convention between nine nations including Turkey (of which Egypt was then a part) declared the canal a neutral zone. The British government, which by 1950 had become the company's largest shareholder, maintained a small military base at Suez, by treaty with Egypt. Nobody questioned that the canal had been well and fairly managed by the company, whose board of directors included five Egyptians, or that Egyptian sovereignty had been respected. Its importance for world trade was vital; 14,555 ships passed through in 1955. The Convention of 1888 required the canal to be open to ships of all nations in war as in peace. Hitherto this stipulation had been respected; but it did not suit the Arab nations of which Nasser now became leader. In their implacable hostility to Israel they denied the canal to her ships. In 1951 the Security Council of the United Nations ordered Egypt to end this illegal prohibition, but Egypt refused to comply.

It took Dulles a long time to realize that Gamal Abdel Nasser was not a "reasonable" dictator like Tito[1] but an Arab Mussolini—the same rolling eyes, calculated rages, lust for power, and contemptuous disregard for treaty obligations or international law. Owing to pressure from Nasser, which Dulles supported, the British government agreed on 27 July 1954 to evacuate its Suez base by 1958, and did so two years earlier. It was expected, if not promised, that when this "thorn in Egypt's sovereignty" was removed, Nasser would respect the treaty of 1888.

The bait of the Western Powers to keep Nasser in line was his need for help in financing an immense dam at Aswan, to irrigate millions of acres and improve the lot of his wretched subjects; it was to cost between $1.3 and $2 billion. Negotiations between the state department, the British foreign office, and the World Bank to foot the initial bill of $70 million ($14 million from Britain, the rest from the United States), and finance the balance by loans, were complete before the end of 1955. Dulles, however, became increasingly irritated by Nasser's truculence and by his mortgaging Egypt's stocks of cotton to buy $200 million in arms from iron curtain countries. Finally, learning that he was dickering with Russia for a better financial deal for the dam, Dulles on 19 July 1956, without warning, canceled the American offer to participate in the loan. England, perforce, followed suit. This was the worst way to handle a sensitive and arrogant dictator, who could easily have been kept guessing for months. Nasser retaliated promptly. On 26 July he seized the offices and physical plant of the Suez Canal, expelled the company's employees, and began collecting the tolls for his own treasury.

Dulles, profoundly shocked by this breach of international obligations, made the mistake of imagining that Nasser could be persuaded to backtrack by diplomacy and world public opinion. He initiated two London conferences of the principal nations which used the Suez Canal. They presented to Nasser two moderate and reasonable schemes as a basis for negotiation, which he rejected with contempt. Sir Anthony Eden, the British premier, and Christian Pineau, the French foreign minister, repeatedly pointed out that force must be used to recover the canal if Nasser declined to negotiate. Dulles, who detested Eden and feared that Britain was aiming to recover her prewar position in the Middle East, refused to commit himself, but President Eisenhower, at a news conference on 31 August, did so in the worst way. He said, "We are committed to a peaceful

---

[1] Robert Murphy of the state department, conferring with Tito, and Ambassador Clare Booth Luce conferring with the Italian government, achieved an accord on the thorny subject of Trieste in September 1954.

settlement of this dispute, *nothing else.*" And that came just at a moment when Robert Menzies of Australia, representing the London Conference, had persuaded Nasser to negotiate.

Nasser now felt that he had the Western Allies "over the barrel," especially since Khrushchev had assured him of Russia's support. But Britain and France were not through. Military preparations to invade the canal zone had already been started. Dulles knew about this; had been informed at least as early as 1 September. Israel, at that time suffering from raids by Nasser-supported Arab guerrillas, started hostilities by sending a military column into the Sinai peninsula of Egypt on 29 October 1956, administering a sound beating to an Egyptian army of 45,000, and in four days reaching the banks of the canal. Eden informed Eisenhower next day that England and France were about to render Israel military support. This decision was a bad diplomatic error which Eden and Pineau compounded by a confused and ineffective military action. Dulles was furious; and the President, according to Sir John Slessor (first person to talk with him after he had read Eden's note), expressed "amazed stupefaction" with the conduct of our major ally.

Nasser promptly blocked the Suez Canal by sinking ships across the channel. The communist bloc denounced the action of England, France, and Israel as "imperialist aggression," threatened to join Egypt unless there were an immediate cease-fire, and hinted at dropping atomic bombs on England and France. It was reasonable to expect that the United States would ignore these threats and give at least moral support both to Israel and the Anglo-French, who had law and right on their side. On the contrary, President Eisenhower instructed Henry Cabot Lodge, his representative at the United Nations, to support an Afro-Asian resolution meeting Russian demands and calling for an immediate cease-fire. England and France vetoed the resolution; but, faced with UN disapproval, threatened by Russia, helpless without American support, slow and bumbling in their attempts to occupy Port Said and Suez, they announced a cease-fire on 6 November and withdrew their armed forces. Israel followed early next year after the state department had threatened to stop financial aid and to invoke UN sanctions against her. Thus Israel was robbed of her well-earned military victory, and to this time—(1971) no Israeli ship has been allowed to use the Suez Canal.

As a result of the diplomacy of Eisenhower and Dulles, Russia was able to pose as Africa's great and good friend who had forced England, France, Israel—and the United States!— to yield; the NATO alliance was strained, Nasser kept and operated the canal which he had illegally seized, collected 100 per cent of the tolls, and went on to fresh trouble-making in the Middle East. The Eisenhower administration piously proclaimed that it had prevented the outbreak of a world war, but Russia's threat to start a war on this issue was a mere bluff which nobody dared call on the eve of a presidential election.

In the same October of 1956, while these events were breaking in the Middle East, Hungary revolted against her Russian masters and, for a brief period, the new government at Budapest drove out the Russian garrison. Here again was opportunity for resolute action to support freedom and justice; again both the UN and its members muffed it. The UN merely passed resolutions of protest and Eisenhower did no more than declare, "The heart of America goes out to the people of Hungary." The heart of America was not enough. On 4 November 1956 the Russian army re-entered Hungary, stamped out the revolt, and set up a communist regime. Almost 200,000 Hungarians became refugees and many eventually reached America.

As Robert Murphy, the state department's trouble-shooter since 1939, remarks in his memoirs, "American policy of promoting the liberation of captive nations always stopped short of war, and this was well known."

Possibly a feeling of shame over Suez and Hungary is the reason why Eisenhower and Dulles applied force vigorously in 1958 when Nasser's United Arab Republic, having absorbed Syria, pulled off a coup d'état in Iraq, killing King Faisal and his family. It was preparing a similar fate for Jordan, and beginning to subvert neighboring Lebanon, whose president appealed to the UN for help. While they were debating, he turned to the United States; and Eisenhower (14 July) responded promptly by ordering Sixth Fleet (Vice Admiral J. L. Holloway) to demonstrate off the coast of Palestine, and sending all available marines and a group of the 187th Infantry (airborne) to land at Beirut. This was neatly accomplished within a week, during which Robert Murphy, and Robert McClintock the American ambassador to Lebanon, managed to dissuade pro-Nasser elements from firing on the marines. At the same time Britain landed 2500 paratroops in Jordan. There is no doubt that this display of strength saved Lebanon and Jordan from subversion and threw Nasser for a loss; and, strangest of all, silenced momentarily the Soviet threats. As the President well said, the Lebanon incident demonstrated "in a truly practical way that the United States was capable of supporting its friends." And the operation also proved the value of having conventional military forces trained and readied for any emergency.

Immediately after the Lebanon crisis ended by the American armed forces' withdrawal in October 1958, a new one flared, directly with Russia. Premier Khrushchev announced that if the Western powers did not get out of Berlin within six months he would turn it over to communist East Germany. This threat was removed, and a slight détente accomplished, by Khrushchev's visiting the United States in September 1959 and staying with President Eisenhower at Camp David. Arrangements were there begun for a "summit meeting" in the summer between the premiers or presidents of the United States, Britain, France, and Russia, to try to resolve the Berlin and other disputes. Unfortunately, just before the conference was to meet, the Russians shot down a U-2 high-altitude photographic plane of the United States Air Force some 1200 miles within Russia. This crisis could not have been handled worse in Washington. First, a routine statement was given out that the U-2 had simply lost its way when studying the weather, and that no photographic flights deep within Russian territory had been authorized. Then the President admitted that the Russian story was correct and that these planes had been taking photographs in order to spot Russian nuclear activities. The President's order to discontinue such flights was first announced, then denied, then confirmed. The net result was to put the United States in the wrong, to enable Khrushchev to pillory Eisenhower as an aggressor, and to break up the summit conference—as Khrushchev probably intended anyway—without accomplishing anything.

As if there were not enough old-world crises to keep the administration busy and worried, the cold war spread to the Western Hemisphere in 1954. Both postwar administrations tended to take for granted Latin American friendship, so well cultivated by F.D.R., and assumed that our sister republics were getting along all right. Canada, which had suffered more from the war than the United States, asked for nothing; why, then, should the Latin American nations need anything? Accordingly, during the seven years 1945–52, when the United States granted $44.8 billion in Marshall Plan and other foreign aid to Western Europe, all Latin America got only $6.8 billion, less than the total dispensed to Turkey and Greece ($7.3 billion), and only half again as much as the $4.4 billion largess poured into the bottomless pit of Chiang's Formosa. It was also assumed in Washington that communism was no danger to Latin America—did not the *latinos* have democratic institutions and the Roman Catholic church to keep it out? Washington was wrong again.

Latin America was suffering from a lopsided economy based on the export of minerals and products of the soil; most of the countries were too small and too hedged about with tariff restrictions to build up successful manufactures of consumer goods. And the Communist parties in Russia and China were paying court to the Americas. They did not bother with the submerged Indians, but infiltrated labor in countries like Mexico, Brazil, and Chile where the unions were strong, and also cultivated college students. These, too numerous to be absorbed in the backward economy and limited professions of their respective countries, offered fertile seedbeds for subversive movements planned in Moscow and Peking. Working in their favor was the fact that Latin American intellectuals had long regarded the "Colossus of the North" with fear, tinged by envy. Puerto Rico, having been granted commonwealth status and profiting from New Deal bounty, was an exception and a showcase of what a small, poor country could do under good government and free trade with the United States; but even Puerto Rico had a small terrorist party, which tried to assassinate President Truman, and fired pistol shots into the House of Representatives.

One strong talking point of the South American radicals was North America's alleged support of dictators. According to the non-intervention policy which began even before Roosevelt, the United States had to recognize a dictator even though his regime smelled to high heaven. President Truman burned his fingers trying to get rid of the highly unsavory dictator Perón, in powerful Argentina. During the Argentinian presidential election of 1945, the American ambassador Spruille Braden, a Yale graduate married to a Chilean lady, attempted to discredit Perón. But his efforts only served to re-elect the dictator, who lasted another ten years. Eisenhower and Dulles, however, helped pull off a successful revolt in 1954 against Jacobo Arbenz, dictator of Guatemala, who allowed communists to control his government, and imported arms from Poland to support his power. Basing his policy on a resolution of the Organization of American States that "dominion or control of the political institutions of any American state by the international communist movement must be resisted," Dulles saw to it that Guatemalan exile groups obtained arms from the United States. They mounted an invasion, ousted Arbenz, and set up a conservative, constitutional government. Among the communists who fled was an Argentine physician, Ernesto ("Che") Guevara, who later reappeared in Cuba as Fidel Castro's mentor. This indirect intervention by the United

States provoked a frenzy of rage and agitation among students throughout the continent and was partly responsible for the disgraceful mobbing of Vice President and Mrs. Nixon when they visited Lima and Caracas in 1958. President Eisenhower threatened to send the Marine Corps into Venezuela if necessary, to get the Nixons out alive; but the Venezuelan government managed to protect its guests.

Eisenhower now adopted a policy of financial help to South America, in hope of exorcising the bitter hatred which the Nixon episode revealed. It took the form of increasing Latin America's slice of the foreign aid pie, setting up an Inter-American Development Bank with a capital of $1 billion to make loans repayable in local currencies rather than dollars, and an extended tour by Eisenhower himself, in 1960, of South America. "We are not saints," he said at Santiago de Chile, "but our heart is in the right place."

But the beloved if misunderstood "Ike" was not to leave office before having a new and apparently insoluble problem dumped on his back doorstep—Fidel Castro and communist Cuba. For years the "Pearl of the Antilles" had groaned under an unusually cruel, corrupt, and ruthless dictator, Fulgencio Batista. He stopped at nothing—confiscation, blackmail, torture, murder—to stay in power; and the United States, warned by what had happened in Argentina, made no effort to oust him. In 1956 an able young revolutionary fanatic named Fidel Castro landed in Oriente Province with a tiny band of bearded guerrillas, increased his following, forced Batista to flee the country on New Year's Day 1959, entered Havana in triumph, and made himself dictator. Castro then enjoyed the support of most professional and bourgeois elements in his own country and in the United States. Herbert L. Matthews of the *New York Times*, who had visited his camp in the mountains, played him up as a democratic liberator; and when Castro visited the United States in April 1959, he received thunderous ovations at the leading universities and was offered liberal foreign aid for schools and welfare by the state department. But Fidel had other ideas. Shrewdly estimating that his share of North American financial assistance would be small, and influenced by Guevara and his communist brother Raúl, he decided that it would be more profitable for Cuba to become the first American satellite to Russia, even at the risk of breaking off her subsidized sugar trade with the United States. He expropriated all banks, sugar plantations, and major industries, threw everyone who objected into jail, closed churches, and forced at least 250,000 Cubans into exile. Khrushchev's deputy premier,

Mikoyan, made Castro a state visit in 1960, extended generous credit, promised to buy the entire sugar crop, and provided enough rifles and machine guns for Castro to arm practically the entire population. This bearded revolutionary had done what Sandino had failed to do thirty years earlier—he had established a communist-supported state in the Caribbean.

Here was a crisis in foreign intervention similar to that which had provoked the declaration of the Monroe Doctrine. Eisenhower protested, broke off diplomatic relations, and forbade Americans to trade with Cuba; but he was unable to obtain the unanimous support of the Organization of American States, or of Canada or the United Nations, for a policy of economic isolation. Castro became a hero to the militant Latin American students, and afforded no end of pleasure to noncommunist elements who enjoyed seeing Uncle Sam jump up and down in futile rage. And Cuba became a rallying point and breeding place for communist organizers and guerrilla specialists from the Rio Grande to Tierra del Fuego.

Secretary Dulles, who died before Castro's sun rose in Oriente, made an extraordinary defense of his and Eisenhower's foreign policy in *Life* magazine in January 1956: "The ability to get to the verge without getting into the war is the necessary art. If you cannot master it, you inevitably get into war. If you try to run away from it, if you are scared to go to the brink, you are lost. We've had to look it square in the face—on the question of enlarging the Korean War, on the question of getting into the Indochina war, on the question of Formosa. We walked to the brink and we looked it in the face. We took strong action."

The trouble with this statement is that in few instances did the Eisenhower administration act boldly. It did nothing about Castro, refused to enlarge the Korean War (as General MacArthur again urged in 1953), dropped Indochina into the Lake of Geneva, let our allies down and flinched from Russian threats over Suez, ran away from Hungary, and apologized for the U-2. The administration was demonstrably right in refusing to risk world war on these issues, especially in view of the drastic cuts in defense that the President had accepted and Congress approved; but it takes two to make a war, and it is possible that the communist powers were more scared of a nuclear war than we were. "Brinkmanship," as Dulles critics derisively called his policy, was far short of heroic. America's relation to the world situation was comparable to that of 1905–41. At that time we had commitments to the Philippines and China; in this era, to every western European country, to the SEATO nations, and to Japan and Formosa; but in neither era were we sufficiently powerful or resolute to implement these commitments when it came to a showdown. Excepting, however, in the Quemoy-Matsu crisis.

3. *The New Free Enterprise*

Many and dire were the prophecies that New Deal, Fair Deal, and especially the TVA marked the beginning of the end to free enterprise, that "creeping socialism" would smother the American Way of Life. Republican orators played this theme in elections and in Congress, and they found support from three eminent economists, F. A. Hayek, John Jewkes, and Joseph Schumpeter who, like the three witches in *Macbeth*, prophesied that each deviation from economic truth would propel a nation irresistibly into socialism, and from socialism to some form of police state. Many years have elapsed since the first of these three weird sisters uttered his gloomy prophecy on the barren heath of the dismal science; yet our economic Macbeth is still Thane of Glamis. Postwar developments, especially those under Eisenhower, justify the quip of Adolf Berle that instead of creeping socialism, galloping capitalism emerged from the New Deal and the war.

What the New Deal and the Great Depression really did— as the economist Arthur R. Burns pointed out back in 1936— was to impel the United States, Canada, and Britain into a new and different form of capitalism, the development of which continued rapidly during the postwar years. Pricing, sales, and investment no longer depend on the "verdict of the market" as in laissez-faire days. Transportation services, public utilities, and fuels are now under so much public regulation in the United States, or nationalized in Canada, that pricing is often done by administrative decision, not by what business men think the market will take. Free venture capital has diminished, owing to high income taxes and social pressure to spend rather than save, so that most big corporations are financing changes and expansion by plowing in their own profits rather than by borrowing, or issuing new stock. The First National City Bank of New York estimated that in eight years 64 per cent of the $150 billion invested in the United States to enlarge and modernize plant and equipment came out of retained earnings and reserves of the industries themselves. Most major corporations today do not seek new capital; they form it themselves out of earnings. Despite the row about "government planning" in the Roosevelt administrations, big corporate executives then and ever since have been seeking nation-wide central planning nuclei. The Interstate Oil Compact of 1935 provided for the adjustment of crude oil production to estimated demand, and was enforced by the Connally "Hot Oil Act" of 1935, which forbids the shipment of petroleum from one state to another without a certificate proving that it was produced in accordance with the controls. What a drag on free enterprise! Yet even the Texas oil industry demanded it and has worked it successfully. The American aircraft industry is in private hands, but since the United States government buys about 95 per cent of its products, government dictation as to specifications, prices, wages, and hours is complete and continuous. Electronics are in much the same situation.

In no really big American industry is competition permitted to carry through to its logical end. Whenever things get out of hand, and competition threatens to become ruinous, as when Texas oil gushers were inundating the refiners with crude oil, government is asked to step in and referee a plan to control the entire industry. Or, if the industry is international in character, an international compact is formed. That is the modern pattern. By 1956, 135 corporate Goliaths owned 45 per cent of all industrial assets of the United States and were able to finance their own growth and research. Hence, corporate Davids are becoming scarce. And the social effects are no less important than the economic. Major industries in 1910 did not want college graduates; now they send personnel experts to colleges and technical schools to recruit college graduates.

The big concentrates, as the super-corporations are called, set and maintain prices by agreement or collusion. The recession of 1957–58 was the first slump in our history in which prices of manufactured products, and of raw materials such as copper, which the concentrates controlled, were not reduced. The concentrates simply agreed to cut production and create an artificial scarcity. Nobody in big industry really wants free competition nowadays. The thrills of the old cutthroat wars between railway and steamship companies, and Standard Oil and its competitors, are now regarded as childish. From top executive to lowliest stevedore, everyone wants a steady job, producing predictable goods at a predictable cost, to be sold at a predictable price. That is what the country now means by security, not the guarantee of liberty that it meant in the eighteenth century.

Nevertheless, competition continues in other forms, especially by advertising and salesmanship for new products. And there is competition between alternate products. For instance, anthracite coal has priced itself out of the domestic fuel market in favor of oil, and natural gas is running oil a hard race. Nylon, dacron, and other chemically produced fabrics have absorbed most of the market formerly monopolized by cotton, just as cotton in the nineteenth century replaced linen and wool. Plastics and aluminum have reduced the peacetime market for iron and steel. There is even competition from communist Russia. In April 1958 Aluminium Ltd. of Canada initiated its first price cut since 1941, and the United States aluminum industry followed. The reason, it turned out, was that Russia was undercutting the Canadian company in the British market.

The highlight of the economic picture in the Eisenhower era is the concentrate. In the manufacture of automobiles, radios, and other electrical appliances, in oil refining, meat packing, and iron and steel, a few mammoth concentrates share from one-half to three-fifths of these respective industries in the United States. The remaining half to two-fifths is shared by several competitors, so that there is no monopoly; but the pricing, production, and sales policies of the concentrates set the pace for the little fellows. Privately owned concentrates have grown by leaps and bounds since World War II.

These giant American and Canadian concentrates, either alone or in partnership with European counterparts, have been effecting an economic revolution which has become a lusty rival to the communist revolution. These are no longer mere corporations but institutions; and in spite of the governmental regulation to which they are subjected—usually by their own desire—they are free units in a free world. They still produce for profit, bargain with labor, compete with other products in the market, reward skill and initiative, and, except for the fixing of prices, satisfy every test of a free enterprise.

The power that these concentrates wield is terrific, their ability to affect people's lives is frightening, and their lack of a guiding principle or philosophy is appalling. Who will regulate these giant concerns which control such immense segments of the economy? John K. Galbraith hopefully asserts that they are being automatically regulated by the "countervailing power" of labor unions and of buyers. Some of the principal purchasers of consumer goods are department and chain stores which are concentrates themselves. But what of the automobile industry, which sells directly to the public through agents? Or the building industry, before which the individual home builder is helpless? The fabulous R. Buckminster Fuller has some of the answers with his dymaxion three-wheeled car and his dymaxion steel igloo; but "Bucky" is a generation or more ahead of his time.

In the midst of the New Deal it was freely predicted by financiers and economists that the United States could not stand a national debt of more than $100 billion. The debt rose to $258.7 in 1945; Truman reduced it by a few billion before the Korean War, when it started to rise again, and throughout the Eisenhower administration it continued to rise, reaching $289 billion in 1961; but that was the lowest debt per capita since 1944. We still seem to be happily borrowing along; the debt stood at $316.3 billion in November 1964, and by April 1971 it amounted to $404.56 billion.

Prophets of doom were also worried about the growing press of people on the payroll of the federal government. The number of paid federal employees, which never exceeded a million before the Great Depression, rose to 2.9 million in 1946; and the Eisenhower administration succeeded in reducing it only by half a million. By 1963 it had risen again to 2.5 million and in mid-1971 there were 2.6 million people "feeding at the public crib," and this figure does not include state or municipal employees, who would account for a couple of million more; yet the economy seems to be able to support them. "Wolf!" has been cried so often that people have come to believe that there is no wolf, but this cannot go on indefinitely. There must be a halt short of every American adult being on a government payroll, as happened in Newfoundland before it went bankrupt.

4. Labor, Automation, and Antarctica

Of all the forces which check the former freedom of capitalists to pay the market wages and charge "all the traffic will bear," the great federations of union labor have probably been stronger than the government. C.I.O. and A. F. of L. merged in 1955, with a total membership of 17 million. Nevertheless, considering the enormous gains that organized labor has made since 1933, not only in higher wages and shorter hours but all manner of "fringe" benefits, union labor's feeling of responsibility for helping to maintain the economy on an even keel is still spotty. George Meany, head of the combined A. F. of L. and C.I.O., and Walter P. Reuther of the United Automobile, Aircraft and Agricultural Workers, responsible labor statesmen, have expelled the communist influences which had infiltrated their federations, and recognized the responsibility of the unions to promote a stable economy, full employment, and racial integration. A few others, like "Jimmy" Hoffa of the Teamsters, are rough, tough, and corrupt, accepting bribes to call off threatened strikes, borrowing money from union funds for their own purposes, living like millionaires of the 1890's, and maintaining power over their members by strong-arm methods. So many and serious were the abuses within unions that in 1959 Congress passed a new Labor Act which set up codes of ethical practice for them and extended federal supervision to their internal affairs. On the other hand, the so-called managerial revolution, the result of studies by sociologists of human relations in industry, has brought about a better understanding of worker psychology and eased many points of friction. In the 1920's Englishmen visiting America were surprised to see workmen's automobiles parked outside factories —operatives, in their opinion, should walk to work or ride bicycles. Jan Strzelecki, a Polish communist who visited America forty years later, found dock workers in San Francisco going to work in Cadillacs, and was shocked to hear that they did not want their union newspaper mailed to their home addresses, as it might injure their middle-class status with the neighbors. Which only confirms a fact that has puzzled socialists and communists for a century:—the American workman is an expectant capitalist, not a class-conscious proletarian.

This is not to say that American labor lacks problems. The first is to complete the eradication of thugs and hoodlums from union officialdom, and the second and more serious is how to deal with technological unemployment caused by the spread of automation. That movement, so far, has fallen more heavily on the clerks and sales people, the "white-collar" employees, than on the "blue-collar" workers. In 1954, when General Electric bought its first Universal Automatic Computer (UNIVAC) from Remington Rand, the *Harvard Business Review* announced, "The revolution starts this summer. Computers are taking over tasks that used to be the sole prerogative of management, and which had formerly been considered beyond the capability of machines." In UNIVAC, big business found the means to cope with the rising flood of paper work. Computers are also taking over the calculating part of the stockbroker and banking industry. "We're working toward the day when most of our employees spend their days smiling at the customers," is the way one of the big bankers put it. This means a painful dislocation of employment in the clerical branches of labor.

Automation, or mechanization as it is often called, has impoverished entire communities such as the West Virginia coal mining districts, and is seriously affecting others. Walter Reuther, in September 1963, pointed out that in the past fifteen years the automobile industry had eliminated 68,000 jobs while increasing its annual output by more than 3 million units. Estimates of the number of workers annually displaced by automation range from two to three million. This explains the anxiety of recent Presidents to speed up economic growth, the only way, it seems, to take care of the burgeoning population.

Labor, like everyone else, has benefited from the built-in safeguards to the economy, such as government control of credit and currency, unemployment and social insurance which flatten the peaks and fill in the valleys of the business cycle, and which prevented the usual postwar depression. We cannot yet appreciate what several years of continuously good employment did for the morale of the Western world, or how profoundly disappointed the Russians were at this outcome. Their diplomacy in the Stalin era was based on the expectation that American economy would go into a tailspin, followed by American withdrawal from Europe. In the United States and Canada, owing to new methods of using old materials such as oil, iron ore, and uranium; to newly invented products such as plastics, nylon, and dacron; to new gadgets for the home and for amusement; and to the extension of electric power, opportunities increased faster than population. But the problem remains of what to do with those left without jobs by automation.

Owing largely to the efforts of Admiral Richard E. Byrd, the polar explorer, a notable gain for international co-operation was made in the Antarctic during those postwar years. Byrd had long been devoted to the cause of world peace; he brooded over it during his five months' isolation in the Antarctic wastes in 1935, and seldom failed to conclude a lecture without a plea that this almost undiscovered continent, whose strategic value had been revealed by air power, might not become, like Asia and Africa, a fresh theater of discord and war between the nations.

The prospect did not seem bright in 1945, when at least six nations laid claim to the whole or part of Antarctica by right of proximity or discovery. Admiral Byrd conducted a third Antarctic expedition (Operation "High-jump") in 1946–47, significantly dropped flags of the UN over the South Pole, and then, in co-operation with scientists of several European and American nations and New Zealand, furthered the movement to establish an International Geophysical Year in 1957–58. Out of this he hoped the world might agree to make Antarctica, in his phrase, "The Great White Continent of Peace." In preparation, as commander of the American Operation "Deep-Freeze," he established seven more Antarctic bases for scientific research, invited other nations to do the same, and some eleven of them responded, establishing bases of their own or in conjunction with others. And, in this far-off corner of the world, the best of human nature triumphed over rival races, nations and ideology; American and Russian scientists and workers, for instance, became the best of friends.

Together and severally the workers in these bases have unlocked many secrets of the earth's most fertile untouched field for scientific research. Out of this co-operation came the Antarctic Treaty, signed by thirteen countries, including Russia, on 1 December 1959, and ratified unanimously the following August by the United States Senate. This significant agreement outlaws nuclear warfare in the Antarctic, adopts a workable mutual inspection system, and provides for a free exchange of scientific data and discoveries made in the southern continent.

Unfortunately the gallant Byrd died in 1957 before the International Geophysical Year began. But the Antarctic Treaty which he had worked for years to bring about, to make the Antarctic "shine forth as a continent of peace," is none the less his monument. He might well have said, like the hero in Heredia's sonnet *Plus Ultra,* "The waves of an ocean hitherto silent for all men will for me utter an imperishable murmur of glory."

President Eisenhower called the personal story of his first administration, *Mandate for Change.* The historian is entitled to ask, "What change, except in men?" There was little change in domestic affairs, apart from sniping at TVA and other New Deal institutions; all basic New Deal measures were continued and even enlarged upon. The economic developments that we have just described began before 1952, and were largely independent of government. In foreign affairs there was the same cold war challenge, which President Eisenhower and Secretary Dulles attempted to meet. No positive initiative in foreign affairs can be credited to the Eisenhower-Dulles team; Russia, China, and Egypt called the tunes to which they responded as best they could. Nevertheless, they led their country through the most critical period of the cold war and the intensified atomic race without an international disaster, which might easily have been touched off in a moment of impatience or carelessness.

So, let us not be too critical of President Eisenhower. At a relatively advanced age, devoid of political experience, he was elected largely as a symbol of what Americans admired, and he retained their confidence to the end. He took over the presidency at a time of malaise and hysteria; he left it with the country's morale restored and prosperity assured. These intangibles, apart from any positive accomplishments, make Eisenhower's eight years in the presidency memorable.

XVIII

The Kennedy Administration

1961-1963

1. *The Election of 1960*

IF THE REPUBLICANS had not tied their own hands by pushing through Amendment XXII limiting presidential terms to two, Eisenhower could easily have won a third; and the improvement that he showed during his last two years, as well as the vigor that he has exhibited since his retirement, suggest that it would have been his best term. Since the Republicans could not renominate "Ike," they would have been wise to have chosen Nelson Rockefeller, governor of New York, who had been in and out of the federal government since the war. He had plenty of experience, an attractive personality, and had not yet (as one politician remarked) alienated every married woman over forty by swapping wives in midstream.

Nevertheless, political considerations decreed that Vice President Richard M. Nixon had to have it, and he got it on the first ballot. Nixon had been "groomed" for the presidency for eight years. He had sat in cabinet meetings, gone on difficult and dangerous missions for the President, and behaved with good taste and circumspection when Eisenhower's illness suggested that he was only "a heartbeat" from being called upon to take over the presidency. Yet, Eisenhower's attitude toward him was ambiguous. He called him "my boy" in 1952, but he seems to have shared to some extent the jealousy that monarchs of the House of Hanover felt toward heirs apparent. The President did little or nothing to help Nixon's campaign, and when asked by an interviewer to indicate which policies or acts of his administration had been helped by the Vice President, replied that he could not recall any! Nixon, too, was a young man for a presidential candidate, only four years older than Kennedy; but his public appearances suggested someone well over fifty and his oratory was ponderous. Nevertheless, enough of "Ike's" popularity might have rubbed off on "Dick" to ensure victory but for John Fitzgerald Kennedy.

Here was something new in national politics: a young (aged forty-three) and attractive senator with a younger and even more attractive wife, as Irish and Catholic as Al Smith of "The Sidewalks of New York," but two generations removed from the Irish ghettos of South and East Boston. His great-grand-parents came over from Ireland in mid-nineteenth century. Both his grandfathers were run-of-the-mine Boston Irish politicians; more honest than Jim Curley, less successful in reaching high office than Al Smith. His father, Joseph P. Kennedy, determined to break loose from the Boston Irish pattern. Joe graduated from Harvard, went into banking and investment, and became a millionaire at the age of thirty; by the time his son became a candidate, he was one of the richest men in the United States. And he took care to send his boys to leading preparatory schools instead of public or parochial schools, and to Harvard University. We have already noted the circumstances under which the elder Kennedy came to the favorable notice of President Roosevelt, who made him chairman of the Securities and Exchange Commission, and ambassador to Great Britain. During World War II his eldest son Lieutenant Commander Joseph P. Kennedy, Jr., whom he had designated as the family politician, was killed on a bombing mission for which he had volunteered, and the next younger, John F. Kennedy, was badly injured when his PT boat was knifed by a Japanese destroyer in the Solomons. But Jack showed such courage and resourcefulness in rescuing survivors of the crew that he emerged a war hero.

Financed by his father, Jack entered politics by running for Congress in 1946 from one of the Boston city districts. Old-line Boston Democrats snorted, "What has he ever done to be elected? Has he ever got a man a job, or given a poor family a bag o' coal or a basket o' groceries?" Such was the old Tammany system; but, as one of the characters in Edwin O'Connor's *Last Hurrah* points out, the New Deal made that sort of thing obsolete; and the Boston Irish, far from being annoyed by Jack's wearing good clothes and never talking down to them, were complimented that one of theirs looked and acted like a thoroughbred. Jack was elected largely on the strength of his personality. After two terms in the House, the Massachusetts Democrats nominated him for the Senate in 1952 in opposition to the incumbent, Henry Cabot Lodge; and in the election that fall, when the Bay State went heavily for Eisenhower and elected a Republican governor, she chose Kennedy for the Senate.

Kennedy did not particularly distinguish himself in the Senate. Elder statesmen told him, "The way to get along is to go along," and for about two years he did. On McCarthy, for instance, his attitude was equivocal, possibly because his father supported Joe, probably because he feared to offend his Irish Catholic constituents who regarded McCarthy as a hero. In any case, an operation and a long convalescence in 1954 raised Kennedy's sights and gave him time to write *Profiles in Courage,* a series of thumbnail sketches of politicians from John Quincy Adams to Robert A. Taft who had exhibited that rare quality. And it is possible that Theodore Sorensen, the Unitarian from Nebraska who became Kennedy's intimate friend and private secretary, indoctrinated him with the views of the Middle-West farm belt and the idealism of George W. Norris. Kennedy's victory over Lodge made him "presidential timber," and his appearance and personality were enhanced by his marriage to Jacqueline Bouvier who belonged to the highest social circles of New York and Newport.

In the Democratic convention of 1956, Senator Kennedy was a candidate for the vice-presidential nomination but, fortunately for himself, did not get it. In 1960 he became an avowed candidate for the presidential nomination of his party, and hard he worked to get it. Adlai Stevenson, still a candidate, had kept in the public eye by traveling world-wide, making speeches, and writing articles, all very intelligent and understanding of the world situation; but the burden of two successive defeats was too much for a party that remembered Bryan. Senator Hubert Humphrey of Minnesota stood well to the left. Senator Lyndon B. Johnson of Texas, leader of the Democrats in the Senate for several years, a one-time protégé of Franklin D. Roosevelt, representing the moderate rather than the "Dixiecrat" South, and with an abundance of friends in the North as well, looked like the logical candidate. But Kennedy, liberally subsidized by his wealthy father, supported in the hustings by his pretty sisters and handsome brothers— for the Kennedys were not merely a family but a clan—entered the Democratic primaries of seven widely separated states and handily won them all. That sort of thing leads to high national office. Many politicians, remembering how Al Smith had been snowed under, were loath to risk another Catholic candidate; but Kennedy's replies to leading questions on church-state relations satisfied most of the Protestants that, if elected, he would not invite the Pope to Washington. And his youth, candor, quick wit, and grasp of political realities overcame religious prejudice. He was nominated for the presidency on the first ballot. Characteristically, he persuaded the convention to nominate for second place his chief rival Senator Johnson; and Johnson, at his earnest request, accepted.

Kennedy made an ideal candidate. His "Harvard accent" may have offended some, but his fine presence, youthful vigor, words well chosen and phrased, delivered in a strong, virile voice, appealed to voters who cared little for religion and programs but appreciated personality and character. The election, as far as issues were concerned, was not exciting, as both candidates promised about the same things—peace from strength, continuation of welfare, streamlining the federal government, etc. The most interesting feature was a TV debate between Nixon and Kennedy, in which nimble Jack ran circles around somber, jowly Dick. The popular vote, heaviest ever cast, was very close—34.2 million for Kennedy, 34.1 million for Nixon; had New York's 45 electoral votes gone the other way, Nixon would have won. Kennedy took 303 electors to Nixon's 219. In addition, 14 "Dixiecrat" electors from the lower South voted for Senator Harry F. Byrd of Virginia, and one Oklahoma Republican who hated Nixon "crossed over" and did likewise. The religious aspect was by no means absent from the campaign: Maria Monk and all the old standbys were trotted out once more, and countercharges were directed against "Protestant bigots"; but how this actually affected the vote nobody knows. Probably about as many Protestant Democrats voted against Kennedy as the Catholic Republicans who voted for him. In any case, there was a big switch of voting habits. Other political experts believe that Kennedy and Johnson were put over by the young; for they were the first presidential team to have been born in the twentieth century. Nixon thought he had been defeated by a recession in the fall of 1960, which he and one of the economists on Eisenhower's staff predicted, but were unable to persuade the President to enlist federal credit control and public-works spending to stop.

Whatever the cause, here was something fresh and new, yet in the pattern of tradition. Millions of spectators and TV viewers felt just that on 20 January 1961 when they saw and heard venerable, white-haired Robert Frost read "The Gift Outright," and the young President—just half the age of the poet—fling out a challenging inaugural address. He opened with a promise that his administration meant "renewal" as well as change. In a very different world that confronted us from the one that confronted Washington when he took the same oath of office in 1789, "the same revolutionary beliefs for which our forebears fought are still at issue around the globe—the belief that the rights of man come not from the generosity of the state but from the hand of God."

"We dare not forget today that we are the heirs of that first revolution. Let the word go forth from this time and place, to friend and foe alike, that the torch has been passed to a new generation of Americans—born in this century, tempered by war, disciplined by a hard and bitter peace, proud of our ancient heritage—and unwilling to witness or permit the slow undoing of those human rights to which this nation has always been committed, and to which we are committed today at home and around the world."

He pledged our allies "the loyalty of faithful friends," to the poor everywhere "our best efforts to help them help themselves," to "our sister republics south of our border . . . to convert our good words into good deeds—in a new alliance for progress," to the United Nations, support and strength, to "those nations who would make themselves our adversary . . . that both sides may begin anew the quest for peace," to get away from "that uncertain balance of terror that stays the hand of mankind's final war."

"So let us begin anew—remembering on both sides that civility is not a sign of weakness, and sincerity is always subject to proof. Let us never negotiate out of fear. But let us never fear to negotiate."

Addressing again his compatriots, he said, "Now the trumpet summons us again—not as a call to bear arms, though arms we need—not as a call to battle, though embattled we are—but a call to bear the burden of a long twilight struggle year in and year out, 'rejoicing in hope, patient in tribulation'[1] —a struggle against the common enemies of man: tyranny, poverty, disease and war itself. . . . And so, my fellow Americans, ask not what your country can do for you—ask what you can do for your country."

There had been no inaugural address like this since Lincoln's second. Note the recurrent theme—new, anew, renewal,

[1] Romans xii.12.

recalling the motto on our Great Seal, *Novus Ordo Seclorum*, and Shelley's: "The world's great age begins anew, . . ."

But observe, also, the solemn warning of "the long twilight struggle year in and year out." And that was the note on which his life closed; in his last speech at Fort Worth, Texas, on 21 November 1963, President Kennedy said, "This is a dangerous and uncertain world. . . . No one expects our lives to be easy —not in this decade, not in this century."

2. *The Cabinet and Domestic Policy*

Kennedy followed Eisenhower's principle of cabinet appointments, but with greater success in the selection. Whilst "Ike" for defense secretary chose the head of General Motors, "Jack" selected Robert S. McNamara, graduate of the University of California, president of Ford Motor Company, and a Republican; and McNamara made so acceptable a defense secretary that he was continued in office by President Johnson. C. Douglas Dillon, chairman of the board of Dillon, Reed, Eisenhower's undersecretary of state when Christian Herter was promoted, became secretary of the treasury. Dean Rusk of Georgia, a former Rhodes Scholar at Oxford, and in subordinate positions of state and war departments since 1946, became secretary of state. Arthur J. Goldberg of Chicago, a leading labor lawyer, became secretary of labor; J. Edward Day, a California insurance man, postmaster general. These major appointments were generally approved throughout the country, but there were some misgivings when the President made his fellow Harvardian, thirty-five-year-old brother Robert F., attorney general. Bob Kennedy, however, had plenty of experience, as he had practised in Washington and had been counsel to the Senate investigation of the labor rackets which exposed Jimmy Hoffa of the Teamster's Union. For special assistants, undersecretaries, and diplomats the President called to Washington any number of the despised "eggheads," drawing so heavily on members of the Harvard faculties, such as McGeorge Bundy, Arthur Schlesinger, Jr., Archibald Cox, and others, that the newspapers were inquiring, "Who is left in Cambridge to teach the students?"

There was no "gray eminence" in the Kennedy administration. He abolished the position of Assistant to the President, which Sherman Adams had held. He also abolished the staff system that President Eisenhower had installed in the White House. Instead of plans and programs being worked out by the staff and reaching the President on one sheet of paper for his approval or disapproval, Kennedy worked directly with his staff. He took an active part in the hour-by-hour work of the White House on almost every subject, and often talked on the telephone to subordinates in the departments who had never before heard a presidential voice. Although this did make the executive department seem disorderly, as in the Roosevelt administration, it enabled the President to exert his power of decision all along the line, and made him extraordinarily well informed as to what was going on. His display in his press conferences of being well informed was a most important political asset.

There had never been such youthful euphoria in Washington since the early days of the New Deal. Kennedy's theory of the presidency was a dynamic leadership, like Roosevelt's, rather than the "Laodicean drift" (as Allan Nevins calls it) of Eisenhower. He hoped to re-create the spirit of the Hundred Days and push through Congress a series of reform measures which he called the New Frontier, similar to those of March-June 1933. To the first session of the new Congress, Kennedy sent no fewer than twenty-five messages directed toward economic recovery, stepped-up national defense and foreign aid, conservation of natural resources, federal aid for housing and schools. Comparatively few of these measures reached enactment because neither Congress nor the public felt any sense of urgency, as they had in 1933. The country was prosperous, there had been an apparent thawing of the cold war, and despite Democratic majorities in both houses, the coalition of Southern Democrats and conservative Northern Republicans which existed during the second Eisenhower administration still held firm. Only about 180 out of 260 Democrats in the House could be depended upon to vote for New Frontier measures, and a similar number to vote against them. It became blatantly evident in the Kennedy administration what had been adumbrated in the less demanding Eisenhower administration, that the two-party system had broken down, so far as Congress was concerned. The two ends of both parties, liberal and conservative, were closer together than the parties themselves; and the committee system, by putting senior members of each party on key committees like rules, and ways and means, enabled the conservatives to kill presidential proposals before they even came to a vote. As Walter Lippmann wrote in January 1964, "Congress is using a procedure of smothering and strangling, rather than of debating and voting, which violates the basic principles of representative government." Since the principal point where presidential proposals were done to death was the rules committee, presided over by Howard W. Smith of Virginia, a member since 1931 who hated the New Deal and all welfare legislation, Speaker Rayburn got through a bill increasing the membership of the rules committee from 12 to 15. That helped a little, but not much: a federal aid to education bill finally emerged from the rules committee in 1963, but the civil rights bill on which Kennedy had set his heart—"this nefarious bill" as Smith called it—remained bottled up until after Kennedy's death.

Kennedy was keenly sensitive to the "black revolution" that was going on, and eager to help colored citizens to secure their political rights and realize their potentialities through education. The great crisis in that revolution during his term arose over the efforts of one black to enroll in the hitherto lily-white University of Mississippi. The man was enrolled despite cowardly mob efforts to intimidate him, and the President continued to protect him within the university with federal marshals. He felt intensely the injustice of excluding a qualified citizen from an American university on account of his race.

The President used patronage and personal talks to win support of the middle-of-the-road group in Congress. He exhibited the tact and patience of an old campaigner, but had to be content with somewhat less than half a loaf. A new minimum wage law raised the hourly rate from $1 to $1.25 and covered some 3.6 million more people than the old one. A housing act allotted $4.9 billion in grants or loans, for four years, to develop local transportation systems and build middle-income housing. "Medicare" for the aged failed, federal aid to education and school-building failed when it became clear that no such bill would pass unless it excluded parochial and non-integrated public schools from its benefits. Sam Rayburn, speaker for seventeen years but a friend to progressive legislation, died before Kennedy had been President a year. The new speaker, John W. McCormack, a septuagenarian who had served in Congress since 1927, came from the same background as the Kennedys and, bound to Jack by all manner of ties, used his shrewd knowledge of parliamentary law to further the presidential program. But not much grist emerged from the congressional hopper. The Southern Bourbon-Northern Republican alliance was too strong.

Kennedy entered office on the upswing from a mild slump, but the economy was sluggish; GNP (Gross National Product, that mysterious sum computed by anonymous statisticians which politicians watch as they once did the market) was not rising as fast as in several European countries. One of the President's economic advisers, Paul A. Samuelson from M.I.T., recommended more government spending, lower interest rates to stimulate building, aid to depressed areas, and a tax cut as ace-in-hole. The President did not ask for the first and the last of these, but he got most of those in between; and Khrushchev indirectly helped the American economy by resuming nuclear weapons testing, which he had promised Eisenhower not to do. This induced Congress to add another $4 billion to the defense budget. Unemployment remained fairly constant—4.4 million or 5 per cent of the civilian working force, in March 1962. About half of it was due to automation in textiles, coal mining, motor cars, and aircraft. Kennedy tried to fill this gap by establishing new industries in chronically depressed areas and retraining the workmen replaced by machines; but very little was accomplished.

On the conservative side, Kennedy's leadership succeeded in checking the inflation which had continued, despite Republican promises, throughout the previous administration. The only time he lost his temper was in April 1962 when United States Steel and other companies announced a 3.5 per cent increase in prices after the President had persuaded striking unions to accept an infinitesimal wage increase. Steel backed down and rescinded the price raise. Big business, which had regarded Kennedy with a somewhat tolerant mistrust since his inauguration, now decided that it had an enemy to deal with like "that man in the White House." Nevertheless, at the New Year the President came out for a $13.5 billion cut in income taxes over three years, hoping that this would produce more venture capital and more jobs. The Republicans said in effect, O.K., if the budget be reduced at least $10 billion. Kennedy retorted that this could not be done, unless by weakening national defense. So nothing was done.

3. Defense and Foreign Policy

Kennedy was no less determined than Truman and Eisenhower to keep civilian control over the military establishment, which at the time of his accession consumed half the federal budget, almost 10 per cent of GNP, and employed 3.5 million people. Secretary McNamara asserted firm control over the Joint Chiefs of Staff and the complicated defense forces. He even brought in computers and cost-analysis techniques to plot policy changes.

The main difference between the Kennedy and Eisenhower defense policies was a transition from an all-out "strategic" deterrent by bombers and missiles to a "balanced" build-up of navy, Marine Corps, and ground forces to cope with limited wars. The number of combat divisions was raised from 11 to

16, the air force "tactical" wings were increased in number.[1]

[1] Since World War II the terms "strategic" and "tactical" had acquired new connotations. "Strategic" now meant an independent, intercontinental nuclear-bombing force; "tactical" meant shorter-range bombers and fighters which co-operated with the army.

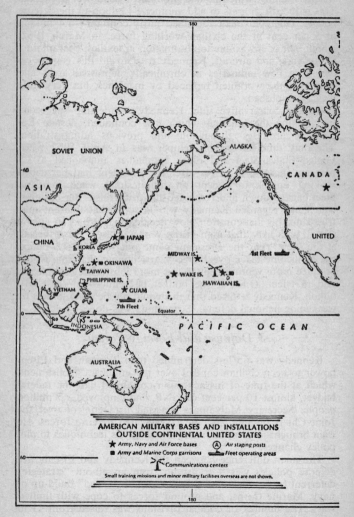

AMERICAN MILITARY BASES AND INSTALLATIONS
OUTSIDE CONTINENTAL UNITED STATES
★ Army, Navy and Air Force bases   Ⓐ Air staging posts
■ Army and Marine Corps garrisons   ⚓ Fleet operating areas
🛩 Communications centers

Small training missions and minor military facilities overseas are not shown.

And, profiting by experience in Indochina, a substantial contingent of the army was trained to fight guerrillas.

During the 1960 campaign it was charged, and generally assumed, that the United States was at the short end of the missile competition. In February 1961, Secretary McNamara

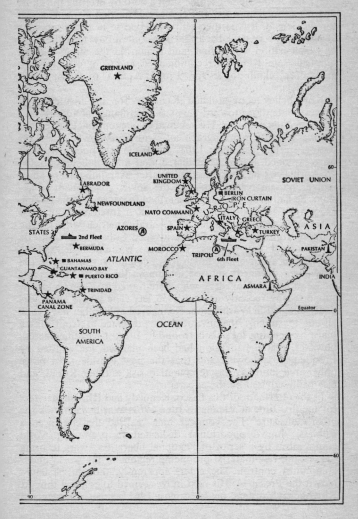

let it be known that in his opinion there was no "missile gap." The public, however, was more interested in the lunar race with the Soviets. Russia won the first round by the 1957 Sputnik and the second by sending an astronaut around the globe in April 1961. Alan Shepard, American, went up into space in May; and John Glenn became such a hero by orbiting the globe thrice in five hours on 20 February 1962 that he almost ran for the Senate. Russia then sent a satellite so near the moon as to photograph its dark backside. The contest now took the form of which nation would first land a man on the moon and get him back safe. Kennedy recommended, and Congress appropriated, a few billion dollars for "Project Apollo" to compete with the Soviets.

Khrushchev congratulated Kennedy for his assurance of peaceful intentions toward Russia in the inaugural address, but continued the cold war. His renewal of open-air nuclear testing, despite a "gentleman's agreement" with Eisenhower to call off testing, started in August 1961, and some fifty nuclear devices were exploded. Kennedy retaliated after much deliberation. On 25 April 1962 he announced that, after examining every alternative and, unable to persuade the Soviet government to abstain, he had ordered America's armed forces to resume testing.

In April 1961 Cuba flared up again. A force of about 1500 anti-Castro Cubans, trained in Central America with logistic support from the United States, invaded Cuba at the Golfo de Cochinos, or Bay of Pigs. This force was not nearly strong enough for an invasion, much less a counter-revolution. In the showdown, Kennedy refused to commit the United States Air Force to help the invaders, who were routed by Castro's forces, supported by recently arrived T-33 jets. The whole affair was badly bungled in Washington. Kennedy should either have gone all-out to support the invasion, or prevented it from taking place by denying the rebels troop-lift. It must be remembered, however, that the invasion had been planned and assisted by President Eisenhower, and that the new President, in office only three months, was reluctant to risk another Korea, and was badly advised by the experts.

In the aftermath of this fiasco, Kennedy and Khrushchev met for the first time at Vienna in June 1961. Warily each took the other's measure. The younger man realized that he faced a ruthless, shrewd opportunist dedicated to promoting world communism by a series of "national liberation" wars to bring the leading raw-material-producing regions of the world under communist control. The elder, apparently, thought he could outwit the President. His next move seemed to confirm this. At Khrushchev's orders, on 13 August 1961 a great concrete and barbed-wire wall began knifing through Berlin between the Eastern and Western zones. Khrushchev's object, to stop the flight of Germans from communism, was attained by breaking all prior agreements to preserve free access through partitioned Berlin. Once again the Russians had called the tune, and the Western powers, balancing fears of an all-out nuclear war against the risk of appeasement, did nought but protest, protest, protest.

Khrushchev took heart and tried another aggressive move. In July-August 1962, while the United States was trying to tighten her economic blockade of Cuba, some thirty Russian ships, laden with technicians, fighter planes, and ballistic missiles, landed their cargoes on Castro's shores. President Kennedy authorized high-level photographic flights to find out what was going on. On 14 October a U-2 plane brought back evidence that new missile sites were being constructed, and photographs made on succeeding days showed that this was being done faster than anything ever before accomplished in Cuba. The photos revealed short-range missiles which could have hit anywhere within an arc from Washington to Panama, and medium-range missiles with a range north to Hudson Bay and south to Lima. On 18 October, Russian foreign minister Gromyko assured Kennedy that the installations were "purely defensive," but photographs proved that he lied. Kennedy called in his principal military and civilian advisers to discuss the situation. They recommended a tight blockade. On the 22nd the President, after briefing leaders of Congress and calling a meeting of the Organization of American States, presented over television the convincing photographic evidence of the missiles on their recently prepared sites, and announced that this "deliberately provocative and unjustified change in the status quo . . . cannot be accepted by this country." Several days of acute tension followed. Army, navy, and marine corps were mobilized in Florida and several Gulf ports. The Council of the Organization of American States on 23 October approved the blockade unanimously. The United States Navy threw an armed ring about Cuba, air force and carrier-based planes patrolled its shores; 12,000 marines stood ready, the strategic air command had nuclear-armed B-52s in the air ready to bomb, 156 ICBMs were in readiness, as well as Polaris missiles from submarines. Everything was set for an all-out invasion of Cuba and an equally massive nuclear attack on Russia if Khrushchev chose to make Castro's cause his.

Then Khrushchev crawled. On 26 October he offered to evacuate the missiles if Kennedy would promise not to invade Cuba, and Kennedy accepted. He also turned back Russian ships which were approaching Cuba. The crisis was over. By the clarity and boldness of his policy Kennedy had seized the advantage, but he was careful not to put Khrushchev in a position from which withdrawal would have been impossible. And the risk of millions of American lives was incommensurate with the advantage of ousting a dictator from Cuba. The country breathed a sigh of relief, the Russians did remove their missiles, much to Castro's rage and disappointment, and the President reached a peak of popularity at home and abroad.

Simultaneously with the Cuban crisis, Red China again made trouble, launching a series of surprise invasions over the northern Indian frontier. This was a serious blow to Jawaharlal Nehru who, ever since World War II, had followed a neutralist policy between the Western and Eastern power blocs. Nehru was a particularly irritating ruler to deal with because of his constant assumption that India's superior spiritual qualities would protect her, and that the United States was hopelessly materialistic and aggressive. And, as an alleged man of peace, Nehru was a humbug. He prevented settlement of the Kashmir border province dispute with Pakistan by a UN-supervised plebiscite; he gobbled up Portuguese Goa, whose people wished to stay Portuguese. Nehru fancied that he could mediate peace in Asia and please the Chinese by letting his defense minister Menon vilify the United States on every possible occasion. When any Westerner pointed out to a leading Indian the menace of his northern neighbor, who had already grabbed Tibet, the Indian would answer with a superior smile, *"Hindi Chini bhai bhai"*—"Indians and Chinese are buddies." Now, in September 1962, Mao's army, with neither provocation nor warning, advanced across India's northern border. Nehru screamed for help from the UN and the United States, and Indian public opinion forced him to dismiss Menon. The United States promptly responded. Within a few days, air force transport planes were ferrying weapons and supplies to the Indians on the Himalayan front. China announced a truce, and Nehru went so far as to thank the "deep sympathy and practical support received from the United States," and to admit, "There is much in common between us on essentials."

One crack made by Khrushchev in 1968 really stung: "America has stumbled into a bog in South Vietnam, and will be mired down there for a long time." It still is, as I write in mid-1971.

The successive steps by which the United States became involved in an undeclared war, in which it had lost 45,275 men by mid-June 1971, were: (1) in 1950, the Truman administration granted $10 million credit to help French and South

Vietnamese efforts to protect themselves against North Vietnam and its communist-supported guerrillas; (2) in 1954, the Eisenhower administration increased credit and sent a substantial number of "advisers" and "observers" to the South Vietnam government, but rejected the proposal of a direct declared war.

When Kennedy became President, there were (according to the "Pentagon documents" published in 1971) 685 American military personnel in South Vietnam. Warned by his military and diplomatic advisers that the South Vietnam government (then under Diem) was too inefficient and corrupt to defend its country against the communists, Kennedy beefed up this force to about 16,000 and gave orders that the American troops need not limit their activities to advice and training, but could fight with the South Vietnamese. And that they did, probably saving South Vietnam from a complete collapse in 1961. The American public was given no inkling of how seriously their country was committed. And as we poured men, money, and munitions into South Vietnam, Russia and China did the same to North Vietnam. Thus President Kennedy, more than President Eisenhower but less than President Johnson, involved us in a war which was never declared, and which many sensible people predicted would be well-nigh impossible to win, even with the half-million troops committed under President Johnson. Kennedy seems to have been sold the Department of State "domino" theory that if one Southeast Asia state went communist, it would knock down all the rest—Laos, Thailand, Cambodia, Indonesia, and the Philippines would topple into the Red camp.

Foreign aid to undeveloped countries continued through an Agency of International Development (AID), promoted by the President. Some AID projects were sheer waste; others, such as the expenditiure of $43,000 in Greece under the direction of a California soil reclamation expert, were a spectacular success. Greece, a rice-importing nation, was soon supplying her own needs and exporting a surplus valued at $5 million. The Alliance for Progress in Latin America encountered many snags from the Latins themselves; and in 1963 Senator Hubert Humphrey well said, "In terms of where it was a year ago, the *Alianza para el Progreso* has taken a giant leap forward. In terms of where it has yet to go, it has taken only a short, faltering step."

More successful and far less expensive was the Peace Corps organized by President Kennedy's brother-in-law Sargent Shriver. It trained and sent abroad thousands of young men and women to help undeveloped peoples to realize their potentialities. In South America, in the emerging nationalities of

Africa, in the Philippines, and in Asia, these youths turned-to and helped the people build schools, roads, sanitary systems, hospitals; taught in their schools and marketed their handicraft. The Peace Corps was the best thing done in the Kennedy administration to restore the old beneficent image of the United States, after its successive blackenings by enemies abroad and extremists at home.

So many fruitless attempts to lay a basis for permanent world peace have been made by so many Presidents that one hesitates to give unqualified approval to John F. Kennedy's principal effort in that direction, the nuclear test-ban treaty with Russia. But that treaty certainly inaugurated a thaw in the cold war, and if it is succeeded by really amicable relations between the Soviet Union and the West, it may eventually be regarded as the dawn of a better day. Kennedy, at the same time, smoothed matters by approving the sale of 250 million dollars' worth of American wheat to Russia.

In the nuclear sphere the President and Dean Rusk shrewdly profited by the growing tension between Russia and China to renew a search for solution, which Presidents Truman and Eisenhower had sought in vain. Few thought success possible, so shortly after the hullabaloo over a U-2 being shot down over Russian territory. As the negotiation drew to a close, on 10 June 1963 the President made a notable public address in Washington. He rejected the concept of a peace imposed on the world by his own country, or by Russia. He recognized the necessity for living together in diversity: "Let us not be blind to our differences, but let us also direct attention to our common interests and the means by which these differences can be resolved. And if we cannot end our differences, at least we can help make the world safe for diversity."

After many conferences between British, American, and Russian scientists, Khrushchev was convinced by his experts that he had more to gain than lose by mutual renunciation. The troublesome inspection issue was shelved because any country could now be photographed, and nuclear testing detected, from unmanned satellites. Finally, on 5 August 1963, the nuclear test-ban treaty was signed by Russia, Great Britain, and the United States at a ceremony in the Kremlin. The signatory nations agreed to hold no more open-air or underwater tests of nuclear explosives. Next day President Kennedy announced: "Yesterday, a shaft of light cut into the darkness. . . . For the first time an agreement has been reached on bringing the forces of nuclear destruction under international control. . . . It offers to all the world a welcome sign of hope. It is not a victory for one side—it is a victory for mankind.

It ended the tests which befouled the air of all men and all nations."

The United States Senate gave its advice and consent to this treaty by the emphatic vote of 80 to 19, and it went into effect on 10 October. Almost every member of the United Nations has since adhered.

4. The New Picture and the End

President Kennedy was remarkable not only for his courage and wisdom in meeting the challenges of our day; he chose to take the most important steps ever made by a President of the United States to foster literature and the arts. His admiration for accomplishment in every field led by him to cultivate artists and writers. He did his best to impart to the public his respect for excellence and dislike of mediocrity. He made a good beginning of what J. Q. Adams tried and failed, the transplanting of high cultural values to the federal city. To a newly created post, special consultant on the arts, he appointed August Hecksher. Mrs. Jacqueline Kennedy, the President's fair partner in these enterprises, by her excellent taste and boundless energy, and through persuading collectors to give appropriate pieces of furniture, transformed the White House into a residence worthy of the chief magistrate of a great republic. They were the first presidential couple within the memory of White House gardeners to care about the flower gardens. They invited Pablo Casals from Puerto Rico to give a 'cello recital at the White House, his first visit to Washington since Theodore Roosevelt's time. Not only did the Kennedys by their example enhance public respect for the arts, they surrounded themselves with gay, active, intelligent people who imparted a verve and style to Washington society that it had not known in fifty years. At the same time they were an image of the typical American family, frolicking with their children and taking pleasure trips to the country or New York. American winners of Nobel prizes, never before given official recognition in Washington, together with writers, scholars, and artists of many races, were given a dinner and reception in the White House, conducted with a good taste that no European court could have surpassed; and it was typical of the President that instead of greeting his guests with a solemn address, he set a gay note by announcing, "This is the most extraordinary collection of talent . . . that has ever been gathered together at the White House—with the possible exception of when Thomas Jefferson dined alone!"

It is to Kennedy's credit that he aroused the enmity of racial, religious, and political bigots. He gave no aid and comfort to the superpatriots who wanted to get out of the United Nations, or the left-wingers who followed the Soviet party line. But, by and large, the country, and the young and perceptive people in every country, adored the presidential couple and their little children Caroline and "John-John," as the President called his son. Everything that the Kennedys did was done with grace, elegance, and style, and it all seemed natural, not forced; this was what Washington and the White House should always have been but almost never had been. Through all the crises and complexities of his short career, President Kennedy managed to seem relaxed, unhurried, confident.

In November 1963, a few months after his forty-sixth birthday, the President decided to visit first Florida and then Texas, to court votes for the election of 1964. Florida had voted against him in 1960; and Texas, though carried through the exertions of Vice President Johnson, was a stronghold of the ignorant but affluent "extreme right," which hated his policies. His visit to Florida was a continual ovation. Thence he flew to Fort Worth, where he delivered his last speech and perfected the one that he was to have given next day. In it he begged his countrymen to exercise their strength "with wisdom and restraint—that we may achieve in our time and for all time the ancient vision of 'Peace on Earth, Good Will toward men.' " For, "As was written long ago, 'Except the Lord keep the city, the watchman waketh but in vain.' "[1] American policy, he wrote, must be guided by learning and reason, "Or else those who confuse rhetoric with reality, and the plausible with the possible, will gain the popular ascendancy with their swift and simple solutions to every world problem. . . . We cannot expect that everyone . . . will 'talk sense' to the American people, but we can hope that fewer people will listen to nonsense. And the notion that this nation is headed for defeat through deficit, or that strength is but a matter of slogans, is nothing but *just plain nonsense*."

Friday, 22 November 1963, *dies irae* for America and the free world, dawned. The President and his wife made the short flight from Fort Worth to Dallas, arriving at 11:40. From the airport, accompanied by Governor Connally of Texas, they drove toward the center of the city in an open car. At 12:30 p.m. shots rang out. A wretched young man, a returned expatriate from Russia, firing a rifle from a sixth-floor window overlooking the presidential route, hit the President in the neck and the back of his head, and wounded the Governor. Jack Kennedy, his head cradled in the lap of his indomitable wife,

[1] Psalm 127:1.

was rushed to a hospital where he was pronounced dead one hour after noon.

Vice President Johnson, fortunately, was on hand. Not knowing whether the assassination was an isolated act or part of a conspiracy to wipe out the federal government, he insisted on accompanying Kennedy's body promptly to the presidential plane at Dallas airport, and taking off for Washington.

In that plane, in the presence of Mrs. Kennedy, still wearing her blood-stained suit, Lyndon B. Johnson at 2:38 p.m., 22 November 1963, took the oath of office as President of the United States.

"Let us continue!" was the theme of President Johnson's first message to Congress five days later.

CAMELOT

Ask ev' - ry per - son if he's heard the sto - ry;

And tell it strong and clear if he has not:

That once there was a fleet - ing wisp of glo - ry

called Cam - e - lot. Don't let it be for-

got That once there was a spot For one brief shin - ing

mo - ment that was known As Cam - e - lot.

With the death of John Fitzgerald Kennedy something seemed to die in each one of us. Yet the memory of that bright, vivid personality, that great gentleman whose every act and appearance appealed to our pride and gave us fresh confidence in ourselves and our country, will live in us for a long, long time.

INDEX

A

Acheson, Dean, 415, 416, 433, 438, 439, 440, 442, 464, 465
Adams, Brooks, 133, 163, 173
Adams, Charles F., 33, 34
Adams, Henry, 43, 96, 167, 251; *quoted,* 34
Adams, John Quincy, 483, 497
Adams, Sherman, 452, 459, 486
Addams, Jane, 97
Adler, Dankmar, *quoted,* 91
Advertising: advent and growth, 227–9; politics, 325
Agriculture Adjustment Act, 306–7; 321
Agriculture
   PRODUCTION (U.S.), Far West, 64–7; Midwest and prairies, 55; general, 72–3; control of: AAA, 306–7, 321; Soil Conservation Act, 315; Soil Bank, 455;
   PRICES AND INCOME: 19th century, 55, 104–6; 20th century, 286–7; Depression, 306–7; AAA, 306–7, 321;
   CONSERVATION, 142, 303–4, 315, 455; TVA, 309–15;
   MECHANIZATION, 55, 72–3, 255–6;
   SYSTEMS: share cropping, 105 *see also* Cattle; Conservation; Corn; Cotton; Farms and Farming; Sugar; Tobacco; Wheat
Alaska: purchase, 30, 32; gold strike in, 158; organized as Territory, 157; statehood, 460
Albania, 344
Aldrich, Nelson W., 36, 143, 155
Aleutian Islands, 371, 378
Algeria, 377–8, 461
Alien and Sedition Acts, 416
Allen, James Lane, 96
Alliance for Progress, 495
Allison, William B., 35, 143
Almond, Gen. Edward M., 436
Altgeld, Gov. John P., 82, 113
America First, 353
American Federation of Labor

(A.F. of L.), 82–6, 113, 165, 330; merges with C.I.O. 476–7
American Liberty League, 319, 342
Anderson, Sherwood, 72, 250
Angell, Norman, 174
Antarctica, 256–8, 478–9
Anthony, Katherine, 246
Anthony, Susan B., 237
Anti-Semitism: in U.S., 107, 218, 322, 325, 353; in Germany, 343, 344, 403; in Arab countries, 425
Apache Indians, 59, 61
Appomattox, 29, 361
Arapaho Indians, 59
Architecture: *1870–1900,* 89–91
Argentina, 470
Arizona: statehood, 157; Indians denied vote, 337
Arkansas: Little Rock, 457
Arnold, Gen. H. H., 364
Arthur, Pres. Chester A., 40–2; 43, 62
Arthur, Julia, 94
Astor, William, 100
Astin, Allen, 452
Aswan Dam, 466
Atlantic Charter, 356
Atomic Energy: weapons, 214, 406, 407–8, 412, 422, 437, 462, 493; development, 253, 314, 307; used, 407–8; in peace, 422, 455–6, 459; Commission, U.S., 455; U.N., 422; Atomic Energy Act, 460; test-ban treaties, 496–7
Atoms for Peace, 459
Attlee, Clement, 413, 416
Auchinleck, Gen. C., 378
Australia, 361, 369, 464
Austria, 175, 191, 204–5, 209, 212, 402, 421
Automation, 477–8
Automobiles, 223–8; and farmer, 225; railroads and, 234; social revolution, 245
Aviation and Air Power: development, 229–34; WW I, 194–5, 199; women in, 233; WW II, 359–61, 366, 383–8, 389–90,

397–8, 404–6, 407–8; Korea, 433, 435

B

Babcock, Gen. Orville E., 35
Baker, Joseph, 92
Baker, Newton D., 294; sec. of war, 181, 202, 205; and army in WW I, 196–200
Baker, Ray Stannard, 135
Balfour, Arthur J., 119, 265, 425
Ball, Thomas, 92
Ballinger, Richard A., 156
Baltimore, Md., 89
Banking Bill, Emergency, 303
Banks and Banking
  PRIVATE: growth, 104, 138–9, 177; panic of 1907, 151; Fed. Reserve System, 168–9; boom and, 281–2, 285; Depression, 287, 290, 292–3, 296; New Deal legislation, 302, 303, 304, 308–9; WW II, 369;
  CENTRAL: credit control, 169, 282, 307, 309; Fed. Reserve System, 168–9;
  INTERNATIONAL, 422; see also Money and Currency
Barbey, Adm. Dan, 387, 406
Barton, Rev. James L., 264–5
Baruch, Bernard, 205, 207, 216, 305, 422
Bataan, 361, 396
Batista, Fulgencio, 471
Bay of Pigs, 492
Bayard, Thomas F., 45
Beard, Charles A., 414
Beecher, Henry W., 88
Belasco, David, 94
Belgium, 461; WW I, 175, 182; WW II, 349, 394, 400
Belknap, Gen. Wm. W., 35
Bell, Alexander Graham, 69n., 229
Bellamy, Edward, 96
Belleau Wood, Battle of, 203
Bellinger, Adm. P. N. L., 94, 358
Benét, Stephen Vincent, 251
Bennett, Richard B., 333–5
Benson, Ezra T., 451–2, 453, 455
Benson, Adm. William S., 192, 200
Bering Strait, 158
Berle, Adolf, 473
Beveridge, Sen. Albert J., 156, 166, 251
Biddle, George, 252, 306
Big Navy Act, 181, 262–3
Bikini Atoll, 422
Bismarck Archipelago, 385–6

Black, Justice Hugo, 321, 331
Blackfoot Indians, 59, 61
Blacks,
  U.S.: equality not sought, 108; Jim Crow, 106–11; cultural contributions, 252; in literature, 96, 108, 109–1, 252; lynching, 110–1; segregation and, 107–9; politics, Populists, 106–7, 164, 239, Democrats, 239, 338–9, communists, 339;
  MILITARY SERVICE: integration of forces, 338, 458;
  VOTING AND CIVIL RIGHTS: disfranchised, 107–8; New Deal, 338–9; Rights Bill, 419, 458, 488; EDUCATION, 108; school decision, 456–7;
  ECONOMIC STATUS: New Deal, 458–9;
  EMPLOYMENT: labor movement and, 86, 236, 339; in North, 219; Fed. govt., 173, 338–9, 457–8; professions, 459
Blaine, Sen. James G., 35–6, 37, 40, 43–4, 47–8, 77, 110
Blease, Sen. Coleman L., 107
Bliss, Gen. Tasker H., 210
Bolivia, 42; see also Latin America
Bonaparte, Napoleon, 368, 415
Bonnet, Georges, 304
Booth, Edwin, 94
Borah, Sen. William E., 215, 261, 348
Borden, Sir Robert, 159, 272
Boston: police strike in, 219, 277, 445
Bougainville, 385, 387
Bradley, Gen. Omar, 379, 392, 400, 437, 439
Brandeis, Justice Louis, 132, 156, 182, 320
Brazil, 364, 470
Brest-Litovsk, Treaty, 190, 202
British North America Act, 76, 124
British West Indian Federation, 461
Brooke, Gen. Sir Alan, 382, 403
Brooks, Rev. Phillips, 88
Browder, Earl, 328, 413
Brownell, Herbert, 452
Bryan, William Jennings, 48, 164, 483; Scopes trial, 88; 1896 election, 115–7; 1900 election, 127–8; big government, 132; 1908 election, 152, 154; Wilson nomination, 165; sec. of state,

167; Mexico, 170–1; neutral rights, 177; resignation, 179; Prohibition, 238
Bryce, James, 42, 98
Buckner, Gen. Simon B., 405
Budget, Bureau of the, 455
Bulganin, Nikolai, 448
Bulge, Battle of the, 401–2, 412
Bull Moose Party, 164, 166, 183, 259, 300, 302
Bunche, Ralph, 323
Burke, Capt. Arleigh, 386
Burma, 344, 461; WW II, 361, 406
Burroughs, John, 137
Bush, Vannevar, 351–2
Butler, Gen. Benjamin F., 35, 44
Butler, Major S. D., 160
Butler, Nicholas Murray, 220
Butler, Sen. Hugh, 444
Byrd, Sen. Harry F., 295, 484
Byrd, Rear Adm. Richard, 194, 232, 257–8, 478–9
Byrnes, James F., 321, 421

C

Cable, George W., 109
Calhoun, John C., 36, 312, 457
California: growth and population, 53
Callaghan, Adm. D. J., 375
Calles, Plutarco, 267–8
Canada
  AS DOMINION: government, 31–2; 1870–1900, 76–9; Riel Rebellion, 76–7, 78, 159; post-WW I, 270–6; 1930's, 332–5; post-WW II, 476;
  INTERNAL CONDITIONS: population and settlement, 76–7, 270–1; and immigration, 271; French influence, 76–7, 78, 159, 335; church influence, Catholic, 78; economic conditions, 77, 271, 469; in Depression, 332–5; agriculture and trade, 159, 270–1, 332–3; price support, 273; in Depression, 332–3; railroads, 77–8, 271; in WW I, 175, 199n., 270; in WW II, 352, 381, 383, 400; farm parties, 271, 272–3, 333, 334; social welfare, 333–4
  U.S. RELATIONS WITH: annexation proposals, 31; tariffs, 77, 159, 274–5, 335; Fenian invasion, 30–1; Treaty of Washington, 32–3; Alaska, 158–9; St. Lawrence Seaway, 275; defense pact, 352; see also Fishing; France

Cannon, Joseph G., 155
Cape St. George, Battle, 386
Caporetto, Battle of, 200
Cardenas, Lázaro, 268, 318
Cardozo, Justice Benjamin J., 320
Carnegie, Andrew, 85, 127, 138, 160
Carpenter, John Alden, 252
Carranza, Gen. Venustiano, 171–2, 187, 267
Carroll, Dr. James, 127
Carter, Hodding, 106
Casablanca, 377–8
Castlereagh, Visc., 184
Castro, Fidel, 269, 471–2, 493–4
Cather, Willa, 71
Catholic Church and Catholics; political office, 280, 482–3, 484; growth in U.S., 86–7, 103; persecution, 107, 218; immigrants, 86–7; schools and colleges, 86; papal relations, 86–7; in Mexico, 161; sexual upheaval, 243; Latin America, 469
Catt, Carrie Chapman, 237
Cattle: brought by Spanish, 65; U.S. dairy, 55; beef, 64–7; breeding, control, AAA, 307
Central America, 145–8, 268–70; treaties, 147–8, 170
Ceylon, 461
Chamberlain, Joseph, 79
Chamberlain, Neville, 350; at Munich, 344; and Japan, 347
Channing, William E., 299n.
Chanute, Ocatve, 90, 230
Chase, Salmon P., election of 1872, 34
Château-Thierry, Battle of, 203
Cherokee Indians, 336
Chiang Kai-shek, 351, 426–9; and Japanese, 356–7; meets with Allies, 364; and Formosa base, 428, 438, 464–5; see also China
Chicago, 73, 89; beef center, 66, 67; Haymarket Square riot, 82; architecture, 89–90; Pullman strike, 112–3; race riots, 219; gang wars, 239
Chickasaw Indians, 64
Chile, 42; communism, 470; Eisenhower in, 471
China: breakup of, 123, 125–6; 266–7; Boxer Rebellion, 125–6, 145; "Open Door Policy," 125–6, 150, loan to, 170; Japanese aggression against, and U.S. policy, 266–7, 318, 342, 344–6, 347,

356–7, 370; and WW II, 364, 385, 409, 426–9; and U.N., 420

China (Communist): and Korean War, 432–42; and Tibet, 437; in S. Vietnam, 463; Quemoy and Matsu, 464–5; and Latin America, 469–72; India and Russia, 494–7

Chinese, immigrants and exclusion acts, 43, 81, 235; *see also* Immigration

Christian Scientists, 88

Choctaw Indians, punished, 64; citizenship of, 64; *see also* Indians

Churchill, Sir Winston, 301, 304, 305, 348, 351; directs the Combined Chiefs of Staff, 364; capabilities, 365; Allied offensive in Europe, 376–8; Darlan deal, 377–8; Casablanca meeting, 378–9; Italian campaign, 382–3; opposes invasion of southern France, 394; Potsdam meeting and Japanese surrender, 407; China, 426; Korea, 437; MacArthur, 439; *quoted*, 309, 350, 389

Civil Liberties: Espionage & Sedition Acts (*1917*), 206; McCarthy, 442–4, 453–4, 456

Civil Rights: Hayes election, 38; Jim Crow laws, provisions of, 108–9; conditions under, 107–11; legal sanctions (*1896*), 456; New Deal and, 338–9; Supreme Court and schools (*1954*), 456–7; Little Rock, 457; non-violent rights movement, 458; sit-ins ruled legal, 458; Civil Rights bills, 458, 488; Univ. of Mississippi, 488

Civil Service: Tenure of Office Act, 41; scandals, 33–6; reform, 34; extension, under Hayes, Cleveland, Wilson, and New Deal, 39, 41–2; morale, 152–3; workmen's compensation, 169, 182; Negroes in, 173, 338–9, 458; increase in, 476

Civilian Conservation Corps, 303–4

Clark, Champ, 155, 159, 165

Clark, Grenville, 180

Clark, Gen. Mark W., 382, 383, 404

Clarke, Rev. James Freeman, 88

Clay, Henry, 36

Clay, Gen. Lucius D., 425

Clayton Anti-Trust Act (*1914*), 144, 169

Clayton-Bulwer Treaty (*1850*), 146

Clemenceau, Georges, 192, 197, 209–10, 212, 214

Cleveland, Grover: extension of civil service, 41–2; elected President (*1884*), 45; character and ability, 45; defeated, 46; re-elected, 48; conservation, 54; Chicago Pullman Strike, 112–3; and Cuba, 117; *1900* election, 127; labor, 140

Coercive or Intolerable Act (*1774*), 76

Cohen, Benjamin, 301, 308

Cold War, 406, 413, 424, 469, 479, 492

Coletti, Joseph, 252

Colfax, Schuyler, 35

Collier, John, 337–8

Collins, Seward, 322

Colombia: Panama Canal, 145–8

Colonialism: U.S., 122–7; end of, 460–1

Colorado, 53; railroads and settlement, 53

Communism: and McCarthy, 442–4, 453–4; newly independent countries, 460–4; in Latin America, 469–72; Khrushchev, 492–4

Communist Party in America: and Socialists, 134, 323; line, 134, 323, 413; votes polled, *1924*, 279, *1932*, 296, *1936*, 328, *1940*, 354; and labor unions, 323, 419, 476; front organizations, 323–4

Concentration Camps: Cuba, 117; Europe, 403

Congress of Industrial Organizations (C.I.O.), 331

Connally, Gov. John, 498

Conscription: WW I, 197; WW II, 352, 355, 366

Conservation: national parks and forests, 53–4; reclamation services, 141; irrigation, 141, 309–17, 339; mineral resources, Bureau of Mines, 156–7; flood control and soil conservation, 303–4, 306, 309–17, 455, 456; reforestation, 303–4, 315, 339, 455; Shipstead-Nolan, Wilderness, and Humphrey Acts, 317; New Deal, 317, 339; Eisenhower, 355–6; Kennedy, 487

Constitutional Amendments: XIV, confiscation of property, 84; XV, right to vote, 38; XVI, federal income tax, 112, 157, 168; XVII, election of Senate by people, 157; XVIII, Prohibition, 237; XIX, women's suffrage, 237; XX, alters beginning of presidential administration, 296; XXII, limits presidential term, 446, 481

Cooke, Morris Llewellyn, 316

Coolidge, Calvin, 278–9, 455; and *1920* election, 219, 259–60; succeeds Harding as President (*1923*), 276–7; Mexico, 268; civil war in Nicaragua, 268–70; the Philippines, 270; Canadian tariffs, 274–5; character and ability, 277–8; speculation, 278, 282; *1928* election, 280–1; Muscle Shoals, 312

Copland, Aaron, 252

Coral Sea, Battle of, 371

Corcoran, Thos. C., 301, 308

Corn: 55; prices, 105, 286, 307

Corregidor, 361

Cotton: as King, 55; controls, AAA, prices, 286, 307

Coughlin, Rev. Charles E., 304, 324–5, 327, 354

Cox, Gov. James A., 219, 260, 294

Crane, Stephen, 96

Crawford, F. Marion, 96

Crawford, Thomas, 96

Credit, *see* Banks and Banking; Farms and Farming; Securities and Stock Market

Credit Mobilier Scandal, 35

Creek Indians, citizenship, 64; assimiliation, 336

Creel, George, 205, 220

Croly, Herbert, 132, 133, 176

Cuba, insurrections, 113, 117; *Maine* incident, 117–8; war with U.S., 118–22, 126; as republic, 127; Guantanamo naval base, 127; Platt Amendment, 127, 145, 318; communism, 471–2; Bay of Pigs and missile crises, 492–4

Culture and Society: "Gilded Age," 33–7; Wild West, 64–9; farm life, 69–72; *1870–90*, 86–106; automobile age, 223–9; bootlegging and sports, 237–43; arts, sciences (20th cent.), 249–58

Cummings, E. E., 250

Cunningham, Adm. Sir Andrews, 377

Curley, J. M., 445, 482

Curtis, Charles, 281, 336

Curtis, George W., 44

Curtiss, Glenn, 231, 233

Custer, Col. George A., 60–1

Czechoslovakia, 212, 343–4, 347, 402, 423

D

Daniels, Josephus, 109, 181, 294; sec. of navy, 186, 193; and England, 193–4; and Wilson, 200

Darlan, Adm. J. L., 377

Darwin, Charles, 83, 88–9

Daugherty, Harry, 260, 261, 262, 277

Davies, Joseph, 410

Davis, James J., *quoted*, 291

Dawes Act (*1887*), 46, 62–4, 336

Dawes, Charles G., 266, 274

Debs, Eugene V., 113, 134, 165, 220, 262

Decker, Adm. B. W., 431

De Gaulle, Gen. Charles, 378, 394, 461

De Koven, Reginald, 93

Depew, Chauncey, 35

Depression, 228, 235, 251, 258, 265, 278, 284, 286–93, 299, 304, 473, 476; conditions caused by, 290–3; RFC, 292–3; New Deal, 299–341; deviationists, 322–7; Canada, 332–5; Negroes, 338–9; *see also* Financial Panics; New Deal; F.D.R.

DeVoto, Bernard, 54

Dewey, Adm. George, 120–2

Dewey, John, 250

Dewey, Thos. E., 353, 399–400, 419, 438*n.*, 445, 452

Díaz, Porfirio, 161, 170

Dickinson, Emily, 95

Diefenbaker, John, 273

Dillon, C. Douglas, 486

Disarmament Agreements: naval, 262–3; German, Versailles Treaty, 212; Hitler renounces, 342; test-ban treaties, 496–7

District of Columbia, 108

Dixiecrat Party, 419, 483–4

Dixon, Thomas, 109

Dodge, Thomas M., 430, 451

Doenitz, Adm. Karl, 362, 364, 380, 404

Doheny, Edward L., 276–7

Dominican Republic, 149, 170

Donnelly, Ignatius, 106
Doolittle, Col. James H., 369–70
Dos Passos, John, 220, 251
Douglas, Donald, 233
Douglas, Paul H., 133
Douglas, Justice W. O., 321
Dreiser, Theodore, 250, 325
Dulles, John Foster, 432, 438*n.*; sec. of state, 449; character and ability, 450; and McCarthy, 453; massive retaliation policy, 463; Suez Canal, 465–8; death, 459; *quoted*, 472
Dunne, Finley Peter, 249
Durkin, Martin, 452
Dwight, John Sullivan, 94

E

Eads, James B., 90
Eakins, Thomas, 91
Eames, Emma, 94
Earhart, Amelia, 233
Early, Gen. Jubal A., 401
Eddy, Mary Baker, 88
Eden, Sir Anthony, 466–7
Edison, Thomas A., 69*n.*, 98
Education
    GENERAL: immigrants and, 97; adult, 97; private, 97;
    COLLEGES AND UNIVERSITIES: endowment, 97, 253; professional, 97–8; Red scares in, 249; medical, 254–6;
    FUNDS FOR: endowments, 97; G.I. Bill of Rights and Fulbright scholarships, 417–8
Egypt, 378, 461, 465–8, 479
Eichelberger, Gen. R. L., 376, 406
Einstein, Albert, 253, 407
Eisenhower, Dwight D., 147*n.*, 413, 449–51, 479–80, 487; in North Africa, 377–8; invasion of Italy, 381–3; Normandy invasion, 389–94; southern France, 394; victory in Europe, 400–4; Supreme Commander of NATO, 426; President (*1953–61*), 448–80; welfare measures, 454–9; foreign affairs, 460–73; U-2 incident, 469; *1960* election, 482; defense policies, 489
El Alamein, Battle of, 377
"Electrics," 55–6
Eliot, Chas. W., 97–8, 127
Eliot, T. S., 249, 250, 261
Elliott, Maxine, 94
Emerson, Ralph Waldo, 95, 326
Endicott, William C., 45

Espionage Act (*1917*), 206
Espiritu, Santo, 374, 375
Estonia, 348
Ethiopia, 342
European Common Market, 79
Evarts, William M., 39
Evolution, theory of, 88

F

Fair Labor Standards Act (*1938*), 331–2
Fair Trade Laws, 227
Falaise Gap, Battle, 394
Fall, Albert Bacon, 260, 262, 276–7, 336
Farley, James A., 295, 300, 320, 328, 352, 354
Farms and Farming: post-Civil War, 39, 104–6; Rural Credit Act, 182; McNary-Haugen bill, 278; RFC, 292–3; Emergency Farm Mortgage Act, 307;
    LABOR: 71, 165;
    LIFE: West, 64–7, 68–9; North, 69–72; automobile, 255; rural electrification, 316; postwar prosperity, 417;
    MOVEMENTS: Greenback party, 39; Populist movement, 104–6; Progressives, 130, 132, 134; Farm Labor party, 323; Long, Lemke, and Union Party, 326–7;
    STATISTICS, 72, 286, 293
Farrell, James T., 247
Fascism, in America, 293, 302, 322–3; 324, 340
Faulkner, William, 110, 247
Federal Emergency Relief Act, 305
Federal Reserve Act & Board, 168–9, 282, 308, 451
Federal Surplus Relief Corp., 307
Federal Trade Commission, 169, 282, 452
Ferber, Edna, 64
Fermi, Enrico, 253, 407
Fijis, 370, 374
Finance
    GOVERNMENT: deficit financing and debt management, Civil War, 39; WW I, 207; WW II, 369; post-WW II, 369, 451, 476; *see also* Taxation
Financial Panics: *1873*, 37; *1893*, 104–6, 111–3; *1907*, 151–2; *see also* Depression
Finlay, Dr. Carlos, 127, 148
Fish, Hamilton, 30, 32–3

Fishing: Newfoundland rights, 33, 158; West Coast, 158; sport, 242

Fisk, Jim, 33, 36

Fiske, Minnie Maddern, 94

Fitzgerald, F. Scott, 247

Five Civilized Tribes, see Indians

Fletcher, Adm. Frank Jack, 371–4

Flood Control, see Conservation

Foch, Marshal Ferdinard, 199–200, 202–5, 208

Ford, Henry, 71, 176, 218, 225, 227, 312

Formosa, 359, 428–9; Quemoy-Matsu, 464–5

Forrestal, James V., 283–4, 308, 365

Fort Sumter, 174, 358

Foster, John W., 450

Foster, William Z., 279, 413

Fox hunting, 102

France:
U.S. RELATIONS WITH: arbitration treaties, 160; and WW I, 175, 177, 180, 181–2, 184–214; naval limitations, 263; fall of, 348–50; liberation, 393–5; See also Canada

Franco, Gen. F., 342, 343

Frankfurter, Justice Felix, 307, 321

Fredericksburg, Battle of, 198

Freeman, Mary E. W., 71

French, D. C., 92, 252

French Indochina, 344, 472; Japanese protectorate, 356–7; Viet-Minh revolt, 437; divided up, 461; Geneva Conf., 463–4

Freud, Sigmund, 246, 248

Frost, Robert, 71, 250, 485

Fuchs, Klaus, 442

Fulbright, J. W., 417–8, 445

Fuller, Chief Justice M., 456

G

Gage, Lyman J., 117

Galbraith, John K., 475

Gandhi, Mahatma, 458

Garfield, Harry A., 207

Garfield, James A., elected President (1880), 40; assassinated, 41

Garland, Hamlin, 71

Garner, John N., 294–5, 354

Garrison, Lindley M., 167

Gates, Lieut. A. L., 194

Gates, Thomas S., Jr., 451

George III, 206

Germans: immigrants, 86, 133–4; political attitudes, 160, 239; in WW I, 176, 184, 215

Germany: blockade of Venezuela, 149; and Morocco, 151; naval build-up, 158; Mexico, 171; WORLD WAR I, 175; conduct of war, 177–87; U.S. declares war on, 188–90; naval and air operations, 191–6; land operations, 196–205; Armistice signed, 204–5, 208; Treaty of Versailles, 212–3; Kellogg-Briand Peace Pact, 264; war debts and inflation, 265–6; recovery, 282; Hitler's rise, 293n., 302; pre-war aggressions, 342–8;
WORLD WAR II: European phase, 348–50; "short of war" phase, 350–8; declares war on U.S., 360; U-boat offensive, 362–4; North Africa, 376–9; in Atlantic, 378–80; Italian campaign, 381–3; Allied bombings, 389–90; Normandy invasion, 393–5; Battle of the Bulge, 401–2; unconditional surrender, 404; Nuremberg trials, 421; and Berlin blockade, 425; West, and NATO, 426; Berlin Wall, 402–3

Gershwin, George, 252

Gettysburg, Battle of, 375

Gilbert Is., 360, 383–8

Gildersleeve, Basil, 98

Gilman, Daniel Coit, 97

Gladden, Washington, 105

Gladstone, William E., 33

Glass-Steagall Banking Act (1933), 303, 309

Glenn, John, 492

Goethals, Col. George W., 148

Gold: South Dakota, 60; Idaho, 61; Yukon, 158; standard, 111–2, 115–7, 303–5; see also Banks and Banking; Money and Currency

Goldberg, Arthur J., 486

Goldwater, Sen. Barry, 131

Gompers, Samuel, 82, 83, 84, 85, 86, 113, 169, 331

Good Neighbor Policy, 318

Gould, Jay, 33, 36, 82

Grant, Ulysses S., 29, 30, 38–9, 283, 378; and Canada, 31; scandals, 33–7; 1876 election, 37–9

Great Britain: 19th century, 29–33, 83, 114, 119–20; 20th century, 145–6, 158–60, 170, 177, 178, 262–3, 304–5, 425, 437; see also Canada; World Wars I and II

Greece: hostilities with Turkey, and U.S. aid, 264–5; Marshall Plan, 424–5, 469; civil war, 424–5; soil reclamation in, 495

Greely, Horace, 34

Greenland, 355

Grimes, Sen. J. W., 34

Groves, Gen. W. S., 407

Guadalcanal, Battle of, 371, 374–6, 383

Guam, 124, 263, 359, 360, 387, 388

Guantanamo Naval Base, 127

Guatemala, 172, 470

Guevara, Ernesto ("Che"), 470–1

H

Hague, The Tribunal, 145, 149, 160; Conventions, 174, 450; Court of International Justice, 213

Haig, Gen. D., 200, 202

Haiti: U.S. relations, 149, 170, 318

Halsey, Adm. William F., 369, 374, 395–8

Hamilton, Alexander, 341

Hampton, Gov. Wade, 39

Hancock, Gen. Winfield S., 40

Hanna, Marcus (Mark), 35, 115, 116, 118, 129, 142; quoted, 129

Harding, Warren G., 33; elected President (1920), 219–20, 260; character, 260–1; Naval Disarmament, 262–3; scandals, 273, 276–7; death, 276

Harlan, Justice J. M., 456

Harper, William R., 97

Harriman, E. H., 139, 141

Harriman, W. Averell, 308, 411, 413, 439, 446, 459

Harris, Roy E., 252

Harrison, Benjamin: elected President (1888), 46; renominated, 48

Harrison, F. Burton, 270

Hart, Adm. Thomas C., 361

Harvey, George, 164

Hawaii: annexation by U.S., 113, 126; Pearl Harbor attack, 357–61; defense of, 369, 371–4; base for Pacific fleet, 374; state, 460

Hawthorne, Nathaniel, 247

Hay, John, 118, 125–6, 139, 145–8, 150

Hayden, Ferdinand V., 54

Hayek, F. A., 473

Hayes, Rutherford B., elected President (1876), 38; civil rights, 38; cabinet, 39; institutes civil service reforms, 39

Haymarket Riot, 82

Hearst, William Randolph, 117, 164–5, 176, 283, 295, 322, 353, 399

Hecker, Isaac, 87

Hemingway, Ernest, 200, 220, 251, 343

Herreshoff, Nathaniel G., 101

Herridge, William D., 334

Herring, Augustus M., 230

Herter, Christian, 459–60, 486

Hewitt, Adm. H. Kent., 377

Hickok, "Wild Bill," 60

Higginson, Henry L., 93

Hill, David B., 35

Hill, Adm. Harry, 386

Hill, James J., 52–3, 74, 78, 141

Hindemith, Paul, 253

Hindenburg, Field Marshal, 178, 184, 204, 208

Hirohito, Emperor, 344, 408, 429, 432

Hiroshima, 408, 422, 462

Hispaniola, see Haiti & Dominican Rep.

Hiss, Alger, 324, 443, 445

Hitchcock, Sen. Gilbert M., 216

Hitler, Adolf, 317, 322–3, 352–3, 355, 403, 411; Rome-Berlin Axis, 342; period of conquests, 343–9; and Vichy, 349, 351; break with Russia, 355; plot against, 393; Rommel killed, 393; Ardennes forest, 401; suicide, 404

Hobby, Mrs. Oveta C., 452

Hodge, Gen. John R., 432

Hodges, Gen. Courtney H., 394, 400, 402

Hoffa, Jimmy, 476, 486

Holmes, Dr. Oliver W., 55, 70, 98

Holmes, Justice Oliver Wendell, 83, 85, 158, 162

Homer, Winslow, 91, 92, 101

Honduras, 149

Hoover, Herbert C., 259, 438, 449, 456; war relief, 206–7, 264, 265; elected President (1928), 220, term, 280–98; Prohibition, 239–40; as sec. of comm. 280; and Depression, 290–3; last campaign, 295–6; quoted, 290, 291

Hopkins, Harry, 278, 301, 452; head of Emergency Relief Act, and CWA, 305; WPA, 306; assists F.D.R., 366

Horses, 102

House, Col. Edward M., 164, 167, 170, 175, 210–1, 278

Houseman, John, 306

Howe, Edgar, 71

Howells, William Dean, 96

Hudson River School of Painting, 91

Hudson's Bay Co., 32

Huerta, Gen. Victoriano, 145, 161, 170–1, 187

Hughes, Chief Justice Chas. Evans, 135, 183–4, 210, 214, 218, 220, 238, 260, 262, 263, 265, 266, 320, 321, 330

Hull, Cordell: sec. of state, 300, 365; fiscal policies, 305; conservation, 317; reciprocity agreements with Latin America, 318; Canada, 335; Japanese evacuation of China and Indochina, 357; U.N., 420

Humphrey, George M., 451, 463

Humphrey, Sen. Hubert H., 483; quoted, 495

Hungary, 402, 472; 1956 revolt, 468

Hunt, Richard M., 89, 90

Hunt, William Morris, 91

Huntington, Anna Hyatt, 252

Huntington, Collis P., 36, 57–8, 75

Huxley, Thomas, 83, 88

I

Ickes, Harold L., sec. of interior, 300–1; conservation, 317; Indian affairs, 338; and Negroes, 338; resignation, 419

Idaho: statehood, 48n., population expansion, 53; discovery of gold, 61

Immigrants: national origins, 80, 133–4, 150, 234–5; attitude of native Americans toward, 234–5; labor supply, 52, 80, 133–4; social and religious backgrounds, 243–4; attitudes of, abolition, wage rates, impact on, 80, 133, 234–5; social life, impact on, 235–6

Immigration, 234–7; English in West, 68–9; 1870–1900, 80–1; 1900's 325; Puerto Ricans, 235; restrictions, 81, 134, 150, 234–5; McCarran-Walter Act, 459; Refugee Relief Act, 459

India, 344, 437, 460, 461, 494

Indians, American

FIVE CIVILIZED TRIBES: land take-over, 64; punishment for support of Confederacy, 64; indemnities and Dawes Act allotments, 64; culture of, 336;

PLAINS AND WESTERN: in reservations, 53; hunting grounds destroyed, 58–61; wars, 59–61; breakup of reservations, 62–3; Meriam report, 337;

SOUTHWEST, 336, 337; see also individual tribes

Indochina, French, see French Indochina

Indonesia, 344, 461

Insull, Samuel E., 284–5

Integration, Schools, see School Integration

Inter-American Development Bank, 471

International Geophysical Year, 478–9

Interstate Commerce: Act and Commission, 46, 75; powers increased, 141–2, 144, 157; see also Labor; Manufacturing and Industry; Railroads; Trusts

Interstate Commerce Act, 46

Interstate Oil Compact, 474

Irish: in politics, 164, 280, 482–3, 484; Fenians, 30–1; Molly Maguires, 81; and Cahensly movement, 86; anti-English, 160, 181–2, 215; in WW I, 176; and Prohibition, 239

Iron Curtain, the, 410–5

Isolationism, 166, 176, 191, 205, 214–5, 221, 258, 260, 264, 345–6, 353, 354, 355, 360, 399, 420

Israel, 425, 465–8

Italians: as immigrants, 86, 103, 133; in WW I, 215; crime and restriction of, 234–5; and Prohibition, 239

Italy, 202; in WW I, 191, 200, 204; and peace conference, 207–14; and Kellogg-Briand Peace Pact, 263, 264; invasions, 342, 344; Rome-Berlin axis, 342; declares war on France, 349; and U.S., 360; Allied campaigns in, 378–83; Allied advance, 383, 395; Mussolini killed, 404; communism, 411; economy, 423; NATO, 426

Iwo Jima, 404

J

Jackson, Andrew, 135, 340

Jackson, Robert H., 352
Jacobinism, 87
James, Henry, 96
James, William, 127; *quoted*, 228
Japan, 145, 473;
    WORLD WAR I: China, 125–6;
    Russo-Japanese War, 150; Root-
    Takahira agreement, 150; treaty
    with England and France, 191;
    U.S. fleet, 192; invades Siberia,
    211; Paris Peace Conference,
    212; Naval Disarmament Con-
    ference, 262–3;
    WORLD WAR II: militarism, 266–
    7; invasion of China, 267, 342,
    344–5; and U.S., 318, 356; East
    Asian empire, 344–5, 361–2;
    Indochina, 356; Pearl Harbor,
    357–60; Pacific offensive and
    strategy, 359–61, 369–74; Mid-
    way, 371–4; Guadalcanal and
    Pacific losses, 375–6, 381–8;
    Leyte Gulf battle, 396–7; Oki-
    nawa, 405–6; atomic attack,
    407–8; surrender, 408–9; Allied
    occupation, 427
Japanese: in America, 150; im-
    migration quotas, 150, 235; *see
    also* Immigration
Jefferson, Joseph, 94
Jefferson, Thomas, 343, 416, 497
Jewett, Sarah Orne, 247
Jews: as immigrants, 235; in Ger-
    many, 343, 344, 403; in Israel,
    425; *see also* Anti-Semitism
Joffre, Marshal, 178, 202
John XXIII, Pope, 87
Johnson, Andrew, 416; and Can-
    ada, 30, 31
Johnson, Gov. Hiram, 135, 183,
    215
Johnson, Lyndon B., 483; Vice
    President, 484, 499; President,
    499
Johnson, Thomas L., 134
Jones, Jesse, 352
Joy, Adm. C. T., 431, 436
Joyce, James, 248
Juárez, Benito, 161
Judiciary, *see* Supreme Court
Jung, Carl, 246
Jutland, Battle of, 182

K

Kaltenbach, Fred, 323
Kansas, deflation and drought,
    105; migration from, 105
Kashmir, 494

Kauffman, R. W., 244
Kefauver, Estes, 446, 459
Kellogg, Frank B., 263–4, 266, 268,
    274
Kellogg-Briand Pact, 264, 347
Kennan, George, 411, 423
Kennedy, John F., 132, 147n., 152,
    315, 444; PT. boat service, 482;
    Senator, 483; Catholicism and
    Nixon debate, 484; elected Presi-
    dent (*1960*), 484; and defense,
    489–92; meets Khrushchev, 492;
    test-ban treaty, 496; and the arts,
    497; assassination, 498–500;
    quoted, 485, 496, 497
Kennedy, Joseph P., 283, 295; and
    SEC, 308, 482; Ambassador to
    England, 308, 482
Kennedy, Robert F., 486
Kerensky, Alexander, 201, 318
Kesselring, Marshal Albert, 382–3,
    400
Keynes, John M., 213n., 305
Khrushchev, Nikita, 467, 489; U-2
    incident, 469; Berlin wall, 469,
    492–3; Cuba, 471–2; test-ban
    treaty, 489, 496; Cuban missile
    sites, 493–4
King, Clarence, 53
King, Adm. Ernest J., 194, 363,
    364, 369, 375
King, Rev. Martin Luther, Jr., 458
King, Richard, 66
King, William Lyon Mackenzie,
    271–5, 333–5, 352; *quoted*, 442n.
Kinkaid, Adm. Thomas C., 387,
    396, 406
Kipling, Rudyard, 56, 122, 159, 177
Kirk, Adm. Alan, 392
Knox, Frank, 352, 365
Knox, Philander C., 160, 163, 170,
    215
Korea, 125, 150, 367, 432–41, 448,
    463, 472, 471
Korean War, 367, 448, 472, 476;
    background of, 432–3; battles
    and strategy of, 433–41; casu-
    alties in, 441n.–2n.; and truce,
    441, 463
Kreuger, Ivar, 284–5
Krueger, Gen. Walter, 396
Ku Klux Klan, revival of, 218

L

Labor
    U.S.: legislation, 83–4, 169, 306;
    immigration, 80, 133–4, 235–6;
    legislation, 81, 133–4, 234–5;

movement, and radicals, 80–1, 82–3; Negroes, 85–6, 339; politics, 83, Progressives, 130–4, Socialist party, 134, 165, Prohibition, 237, communist infiltration, 323, 419, 476; automation, 447–8, 489

Labor Unions: membership, *1886*, 82, *1920*'s, 235–6, *1936*, 330, *1955*, 476; Knights of Labor, 81–2; Black International, 82; A.F. of L., 82–3, 330; I.W.W., 165; C.I.O. and A.F. of L., 331, 476; statesmanship and abuses in, 476–7; regulation of, 418–9, 454–5, 477;

STRIKES AND REGULATION OF: legality of, 112–3; Molly Maguires, 81; rail, *1884*, 81; Haymarket, 82; Pullman, 113; coal, *1902*, 140; I.W.W., 165; Clayton Act, 169; NRA, 330; sitdown, 331; post-World War II, 418–9; Taft-Hartley, 418–9, 445;

WAGES AND HOURS: working conditions, steel, 72; *1890–1914*, 133; "real," 157, 418; textile industry, 165; *1920*'s, 235–6; legislation, Massachusetts, 84, New York, 84; Seamen's Act, 169; Workmen's Compensation for Federal Employees, 169, 182, Adamson Act, 183, Ford and, 225, NRA, 306, Fair Labor Standards Act, 331–2, minimum wage laws, 454, 488; courts and, 85, 320, 321–2, 330;

COLLECTIVE BARGAINING: NRA, 306, 330; Wagner Act, 321, 330; NLRB, 330; Taft-Hartley, 418–9

La Farge, John, 91

La Follette, Sen. Robt., 135, 141, 156, 162, 180, 187, 215, 279

La Follette, Sen. Robt., Jr., 292, 443

La Guardia, Fiorello H., 199, 421

Lamar, Lucius Q. C., 36, 45

Land, Land Systems

U.S.: land speculation, 105; sharecropping, 105; railroads, 52–3

Landis, James M., 307, 308

Landon, Gov. Alfred M., 305–6, 328

Lane, Franklin K., 167

Langley, Sam. P., 229, 230

Lanier, Sidney, 37, 95

Lansing, Robert, 171, 181, 210, 216, 450

Latin America, Monroe Doctrine, and English rivalry, 113–4; War of Pacific, 42; Pan American Congress, 48; McKinley tariff, 48; and Theodore Roosevelt, 145–9; "dollar diplomacy," 160, 170; and WW I, 182; U.S. Intervention, 267–70; Good Neighbor Policy, 318; Act of Havana, 352; declares war on axis, 364; and F.D.R., 365; economy, 469–70; dictatorships, 470; Inter-American Development Bank, 471; Organization of American States, 470, 472, 493; communism, 470–2; Alliance for Progress, 495; *see also individual countries*

Latter-Day Saints, *see* Mormons

Laurier, Sir Wilfred, 78–9, 158–9, 271, 274

League of Nations, 206, 207–14, 238, 249, 266; Court of International Justice, 213; U.S. controversy over, 214–7, 220; Japanese aggression, 267; Canada and, 272; rise of dictators, 342; Italy and, 342

Lee, Gen. Fitzhugh, 120

Lehman, Sen. Herbert H., 421

Lemke, William, 327, 328

Lend-Lease Act (*1941*), 354–5, 368

Lenin, Nikolai, 201–2, 211, 264

Leo XIII, Pope, 87

Lewis, John L., 312, 331, 418

Lewis, Sinclair, 55, 71, 250

Leyte Gulf, Battle of, 395–9, 404

Lilienthal, David E., 313

Lincoln, Abraham, 110, 200, 299, 329, 338, 341, 365, 485

Lindbergh, Charles A., 232, 268, 274, 353

Lindsay, Vachel, 116n.; *quoted*, 103

Lippmann, Walter, 133, 220, 282; *quoted*, 220, 448, 487

Literature: *1865–1900*, 36–7, 43, 71–2, 95–6; post-*1900*, 110, 243–4, 247, 249–51

Little Rock, 457

Lloyd, George, D., 132, 193, 209–12, 214, 263

Lodge, Henry Cabot, 44, 118, 158, 163, 214, 216

Lodge, Henry Cabot, Jr., 438n., 467, 483

Long, Sen. Huey P., 326–7, 341, 443
Longfellow, H. William W., *quoted*, 37
Louis XVI, 133
Louisiana: Reconstruction, 39, 107
Lowden, Gov. Frank, 219
Lowell, James Russell, 37, 95
Luce, Clare Booth, 352, 466*n*.
Ludendorff, Gen. Erich F. W., 178, 202–4
Lusitania, 179, 180
Lyell, Charles, 88
Lynching, 110–1

M

MacArthur, Gen. Arthur, 124
MacArthur, Gen. Douglas, 124, 152, 196; Far East command, 356; Pearl Harbor and Manila, 359–61; strategy, 374–5, 383–6; return to Philippines, 395–8, 406; and politics, 399, 444–5, 447; Japanese surrender and occupation, 408–9, 429–32; China, 411, 427; Korean War, 433–41, 472; *quoted*, 204, 409, 432
MacDonald, Sir John, 31, 76, 78
Macdonald, Ramsay, 263, 274
MacDowell, Edward, 94
MacKay, Douglas, 451
Madison, James, 177, 340
Mahan, Adm. Alfred T., 35, 361
Maine: shipbuilding, 58; political offices, 47–8
Malay Peninsula, 356, 357, 359, 360, 437
Manila Bay, Battle of, 120; in WW II, 359, 360–1, 406
Mann Act, 244
Manufacturing and Industry: industrial economy, 72–6, 103; big business, abuses, and regulation, 73–6, 138–42; in WW I, 207; automobile and mass production, 225, 227; advertising, 227–8; Depression, 290, 291, 292, 293; New Deal, 306, 319–21, 329–32, 340–1; "New Free Enterprise," 373–6; automation, 476–8, 489; Kennedy, 488–9; *see also individual industries*
Mao Tse-tung, 345, 415, 428, 433, 436–41, 464
Marianas Is., 387, 388, 395
Marne, Battles of, 176, 203

Marshall, Chief Justice John, 166, 338
Marshall, Gen. George C., 203, 364, 403, 416, 417, 442; Marshall Plan, 423–4, 469; Communist China, 428; McCarthy, 444
Marshall Is., 126, 383, 385, 386, 422
Marx, Karl, 81, 82, 246, 413
Massachusetts: labor, 83–4; *see also* New England
Mayo, Adm. H. T., 192, 194
McAdoo, William G., 167, 219, 239, 278, 294
McAuliffe, Gen. Anthony, 402
McCarran-Walter Act (*1952*), 459
McCarthy, Sen. Joseph, 217, 416, 439, 442–4, 453–4
McClellan, Gen. George B., 41, 416
McKay, Donald, 58
McKinley, William: conservation, 54; elected President (*1896*), 115–6; Spanish-American War, 117–29; 2nd term, 128–9; assassination, 128–9; Panama Canal, 146
McNamara, Robert S., 486, 489
Meany, George, 476
Medicine and Health
HEALTH AND MEDICAL CARE: Indians, 336, 337; Spanish-American War, 122; yellow fever, 126–7; Pure Food and Drug Act, 140–1; venereal disease, 244; revolution in, 254–6; quackery, 256; in WW II, 366–7; medicare, 488
EDUCATION: reform, 97–8; revolution in, 254–6
Mencken, H. L., 249–50; *quoted*, 110, 243-4, 256, 327–8
Menzies, Robert, 467
Meriam, Lewis, 337
Meuse-Argonne, Battle, 204
Mexicans, in U.S., 235
Mexico, 145, 173, 267–8, 269, 270; under Díaz and Madero, 161; revolutions, 161, 170–2; Zimmerman note, 187; constitution of, 172; policies under, 172, 268, 318–9; communist influence, 268, 470
Midway, Battle of, 371–4
Millay, Edna St. Vincent, 250, 251, 346
Mississippi, school integration, 488

Mitscher, Adm. Marc, 386, 397–8

Moley, Raymond, 301, 305

Money and Currency
  CONTROL OF: federal, 168–9, 304–5; international, 304–5; 421–2, 469;
  GOLD: standard prices and drain, 39, 111–2, 151, 207, 281, 303, 308–9; corner, 33–4; off standard, 304–5;
  BIMETALLISM, free silver, 39, 47, 106, 111–2, 115–6, 128;
  GREENBACKS: 39

Monroe Doctrine, 31, 113–4, 215, 318

Monte Cassino, 383

Montgomery, Gen. Bernard, 377, 379, 394, 395, 403

Morgan, J. Pierpont, 100, 112, 139, 141

Morgenthau, Henry, Jr., 305, 317

Morison, George S., 90

Mormons: culture, 88

Morocco, 377–8, 461

Morrow, Dwight W., 268

Morse, Samuel F. B., 91

Muir, John, 54, 137

Muñoz-Marin, Gov. Luis, 127

Murphy, Justice Frank, 321, 331

Murphy, Robert, 466n., 468

Muscle Shoals, 312, 315

Music: 1870–1900, 37, 93–4; post-1900, 245, 352–3, 369

Mussolini, Benito, 209, 253, 351, 378, 415; Ethiopia, 342; Rome-Berlin Axis, 342, 343–7; North Africa, 378; killed, 404

N

Nagaski, 408, 422

Nasser, Gamal, 461, 465–8

National Aeronautics and Space Administration, 460; space race, 491–2

National Association for the Advancement of Colored People (NAACP), 338

National Defense Research Committee, 351

National Health Service, 337; see also Medicine & Health

National Industry Recovery Act (NRA), 306, 320–1

National Labor Relations Act 321; Board, 330–1

National Resources Planning Board, 340

Nazi Party: U.S., 322–3, 324; Germany, 267, 342–3, 344, 403

Near East Relief, 264–5

Nebraska: settlement, 51–3; Indian lands, 63; see also Kansas

Negroes, see Blacks

Nehru, Jawaharlal, 437, 494

Netherlands
  EMPIRE, 460; East Indies, 461; South Africa, 461

New Deal, 287, 295, 296, 299–328, 455, 470, 473, 476, 482, 487, 488; emergency measures, 303–9; and business community, 319–21; Supreme Court, 321–2; 1936 election, 327–8; labor, 329–32; new role of government, 339–41; salvation of capitalism, 295–6, 302, 341; 1940 election, 353–4; see also Depression

New England
  ECONOMY: textile, 165; shipbuilding, 58;
  TRADE: shipping, 56–8

New Frontier, 487

New Guinea, 374, 375, 376, 383, 387, 395; see also Coral Sea

New Mexico: statehood, 157; Pueblo steal, 336–7

New York City: Tammany Hall, 44, 165; architecture, 89–90

New Zealand, 369, 464

Newfoundland: Crown colony, 32; fishing rights, U.S., 33, 158; U.S. bases, 352

Newspapers: yellow journalism, 117; and T. Roosevelt, 142, 151, 152; in WW I, 176, 206; and boom, 285; in WW II, 353, 399

Nicaragua, 146, 149, 160, 170, 268–70; see also Latin America

Nimitz, Adm. Chester W., 396, 371, 374, 385, 387–8, 395, 396, 427

Nixon, Richard M., 439, 445, 447, 471, 481–2

Norris, Frank, 75

Norris, Sen. George W., 155, 187, 261, 310–4, 316, 317, 483

North Atlantic Treaty Organization (NATO), 214, 426, 467

North Vietnam, 461, 463–4

Norton, Charles Eliot, 91, 98, 127

Norway, 348, 352

Nullification: South, school integration, 457

O

Oak Ridge Atomic Center, 314, 407

Obregón, Gen. Álvaro, 172, 267, 268

O'Connor, Edwin, 482

Oil Industry: Standard Oil Trust, 73, 144; Teapot Dome, 156, 268, 276–7, 336; automobile industry, 229; Mexico, 267–8, 318–9; govt. control, 419, 474; large corporations, 475

Okinawa, 405–6, 412, 433

Oklahoma, 53; "boomers" and "sooners," 64; statehood, 64, 157

Old-Age Security, 302, 309

Oldendorf, Adm. Jesse, 396–7

Olmsted, Frederick Law, 91

O'Neill, Eugene, 251

Oppenheimer, J. R., 407

Oregon country, divided into states, 53

Organization of American States, 470, 472, 493

Osage Indians, 62, 64, 336

Ozawa, Adm. J., 387–8, 396–8

P

Page, Walter H., 42, 109, 192; quoted, 175

Paine, Thomas, quoted, 83

Painting and Sculpture: 1870–1900, 91–2; post-1900, 251–2

Pakistan, 461, 464, 494

Palmer, A. Mitchell, 217–9

Pan American Union, 48

Panama, 170, 191; government, 147–8

Panama Canal, 145–8, 170, 192; 318; rent raised, 147n.

Panics, see Financial Panics

Parkman, Francis, 96

Patch, Gen. Alex. C., 394, 401, 403, 404

Patterson, Robert, 365

Patton, Gen. George S., 366, 377, 381, 392, 393–5, 401–2, 403, 413

Paul VI, Pope, 87

Pauncefote, Sir Julian, 119, 146

Payne, Henry C., 155

Payne-Aldrich Tariff, 155–6, 157, 165

Peace Corps, 495–6

Pearl Harbor, 357–60, 368, 397

Peary, Adm. Robert E., 256

Pecora, Justice Ferdinand, 284, 308–9

Pelley, William D., 322

Pendergast, Jim, 416

Pendleton, George, 41

Periodicals: reform and, 42, 164; 20th century, 247, 249–50, 285; rightist, 322

Perkins, Frances, 301

Perón, Juan, 470

Perry, Commo. Matthew C., 405

Pershing, Gen. John J., 172, 183, 196, 199–200, 202–3, 204, 208

Peru, 42

Pétain, Marshal Henri, 182; collaboration, 349; Darlan deal, 377–8

Petersburg, Battle of, 178

Philippine Sea, Battle of, 387–8

Philippines, 399, 412, 437, 472; Spain in, 119; blockade and annexation, 122–5, 126; and tariffs, 156; Stimson mission, 270; in WW II, 356–61, 395–9; liberation (map), 398; Republic 406, 450, 460, 464

Phillips, William, 273, 274, 275

Pierce, Franklin, 219, 277

Pinchot, Gifford, 141, 156, 162

Piston, Walter, 253

Pius X, Pope, 87

Platt, Orville H., 143

Platt, Sen. Thomas C., 35, 129

Plessy v. Ferguson, 108, 456

Poland, 182, 212; invaded, 347–8, 395; Russia, 412

Polk, James K., treaty with Colombia, 148

Population: U.S. (1869–99), 72; trend (1860–1900), 72, 103; Far West (1880–1960), 53; U.S. (1960), 236–7; see also Indians; individual cities, countries, states; Blacks

Populist Party, 106, 112, 333; formation and platform, 106; anti-Negro stand, 107; election of 1894, 114; free silver, 115; reform groups, 135

Portugal, 461

Potsdam Conference, 407, 410, 413–4, 421, 433

Pound, Ezra, 250, 323

Press, Freedom of, and Espionage Act of WW I, 206

Progressive Party, see Bull Moose

Prohibition, 234; state, 45, 237; party, 45, 128, 142; federal, 237; social effects, 237–40, 273; repeal, 240, 295

Propaganda, 175, 176, 177; in U.S. during WW I, 205–6, 220; Russian, 318; Nazi, 348; France, 348–9

Protestants and Protestantism: science, 88–9; sexual upheaval, 243–5

Public Utilities, 144; power, early, 74; local regulation, 74; tel. and tel., fed. regulations, 141; holding companies, 283, 284; Insull, 284–5; Holding Co. Act, 309; SEC control, 308; TVA, 309–17; REA, 316; Dixon-Yates, 455–6

Pueblo Indians, 336–7, 338

Puerto Ricans, as immigrants, 235

Puerto Rico: ceded to U.S., 122, 123–4, 125, 127; economic problems, 127, 362; government, 470; immigration to U.S., 235

Pulitzer, Joseph, 117

Pure Food and Drugs Act (1906), 99, 141

Pyle, Ernie, quoted, 382

Q

Quebec (province and city): incorporated in Dominion, 31; Riel Rebellion, 76–7; influence in politics, 78–9, 159, 335; economy and culture, 159; see also Canada

Quebec Act (1774), 76

R

Rabaul, 375, 385–7

Race Prejudice
SOUTH, middle-class and poor white, 106–11, 456–8;
NORTH, 86; workers, 218–9;
VIOLENCE: Ku Klux Klan, 218; lynchings, 110–1

Radford, Adm. Arthur W., 450n., 463

Railroads: Canada, 77–8, 271; West, 50–3; impact on agriculture, 52, 55, 66; automobiles, 234; RFC and, 293;
FINANCIAL ABUSES, 35, 36, 44;
TRUSTS, 52–3, 74–5, 139; ICC, 75; Sherman Anti-Trust Act, 75, 139; Clayton Act, 144;
RATES, 74–5; regulation: ICC, 75, Act of 1903 and Hepburn Act, 141–2, Transportation Act, 144;
LABOR RELATIONS: strikes, 81, 82,

112–3; Railway Labor Board, 144; Adamson Act, 183; Truman and, 418

Rayburn, Sam, 308, 488

Reconstruction Finance Corp., 292–3, 445–6

Recreation: 1870–1900, farm, 69–71; general, 99–103; shorter working day, 99; "joining," 103; 20th century, 237, 240–3; and leisure, 240; sexual revolution, 245; broadcasting, 253; baseball, 79, 241; boxing, 102–3, 241; horseracing, 101–2, 241–2; yatching, 100–1

Reed, Thomas B., 47–8, 115, 117, 119, 127, 155

Reed, Dr. Walter, 127, 148

Refugee Relief Act, 459

Reid, Whitelaw, 35

Religion: science and, 87–9; sexual upheaval and, 243–8; persecution: of Catholics, 107, 218; elective office, 280, 481–4

Remington, Frederic, 68–91

Reuther, Walter P., 476, 477

Reynaud, Paul, 349

Richardson, H. H., 89

Richmond, Va., 55

Ridgway, Gen. Matthew B., 438–9, 441, 451, 463

Riley, James Whitcomb, 71, 95

Roberts, Kenneth, 234

Roberts, Owen J., 321

Robinson, E. A., 152

Rockefeller, John D., 36, 73, 139, 272, 291

Rockefeller, Nelson A., 452, 481

Roebling, John, 90

Rogers, Will, 249, 268, 277, 336; quoted, 281, 293, 296, 298, 303

Rolland, Romain, 88, 323

Romania, 212, 347, 348

Rommel, Field Marshal, 377, 378–9, 393

Roosevelt, Eleanor, 294, 300, 338

Roosevelt, Franklin D.: civil service extension, 41–2; asst. sec. of navy, 186, 192, 294, 300; 1928 election, 281; background, 294; governor of New York, 294, 300; elected President (1932), 295–6; cabinet and "Brain Trust," 300–1; passes emergency measures, 303–9; foreign affairs, 317–9; opposition to, 319–21; Supreme Court, 321–2; 340; and deviationists, 322–4; 1936 election, 327–8; labor legislation, 329–32; and Mackenzie King, 335; Indian affairs, 338; the Negro, 338–9; neutrality legislation, 346–7; French appeal for help, 349; "short of war" policy, 350–6; *1940* election, 351, 353–4; signs naval expansion bill, 351; "Four Freedoms" and Lend-Lease, 354–5; Atlantic Charter, 356; strategy, 364–9; as leader, 365–6; plans Allied offensive, 376–9; *1944* election, 399–400; Stalin, 410; U.N., 420; death, 403–4; *quoted*, 297, 346, 350

Roosevelt, Theodore, 42; civil service, 41–2, 47; *1884* election, 44; conservation, 54, 141; the West, 68; Rough Riders, 68, 120, 128; Supreme Court, 85; Spanish-American War, 120–2; elected Vice President (*1900*), 128; becomes President (*1901*), 129; economic policy, 130–2; character and ability, 135–8, 152; and labor, 140; interstate commerce, 140; re-elected (*1904*), 142; trusts, 140, 143–4; army and navy build-up, 145; foreign affairs, 145–53; Panama Canal, 145–8; Monroe Doctrine, 149; Japan, 150; no second term, 151–3; Bull Moose party, 163–6, 302; WW I, 175, 179, 197; *1916* election, 183; League of Nations, 214; Prohibition, 238; *quoted*, 75–6, 159, 162

Root, Elihu, 210, 214, 265; sec. of war, 139; Alaska-Canadian dispute, 158; Central America, 160; alienation from T. Roosevelt, 163; *quoted*, 130–1

Ruhr, Battle of the, 402–3

Runstedt, Gen., 400–2

Rural Credit Act, 182

Rural Electrification Administration (*1936*), 316

Rusk, Dean, 486, 496

Russell, Lord John, 30

Russell, Sen. Richard, 457

Russia: Alaska, 30; Russo-Japanese War, 150, 174; Anglo-Russian Treaty, 158; and WW I, 175, 177, 178, 182, 191; Revolution, 179, 187–8, 200–2, 211–2; Treaty of Brest-Litovsk, 202; Paris Peace Conf., 211–2; Hungary, 211, 468; starvation, 264, 265; recognizes Soviet Govt., 318; religious freedom, 318; purges, executions, and famine, 324; Hitler pact, 347–8; invaded by Germany, 355; and Allies, 355, 363–4, 378, 379, 410–5; second front, 376–7; Stalingrad, 378; Yalta, Teheran, and Potsdam, 410–5; UN, 420; atomic stockpiles, 422; rejects Marshall Plan, 423; competes with U.S., 461; South Vietnam, 464; Egypt, 466; Berlin wall, 469, 492–3; U-2 incident, 469; Latin America, 469–72; space race, 491–2; nuclear tests, 492, 496; Cuban missiles, 493–4; U.S. wheat, 496; and Red China, 496

Russo-Japanese War, 150, 167, 174

S

Sacco-Vanzetti Case, 82, 218

Saint-Gaudens, Augustus, 92, **137**

St. Lawrence Seaway, 275

Saint-Mihiel, Battle of, 204

Saipan, 387, 388, 404

Salerno, Battle of, 382

Salisbury, Lord, 114, 119

Sampson, Adm. W. T., 122

Sandino, Augusto, 269–70

Sargent, John Singer, 92

Scandinavians, as immigrants, 133–4

Schlesinger, Arthur, Jr., 486

School Integration: segregation upheld: Negroes, 108, Jim Crow laws, 108, by Supreme Court (*1896*), 108; school decision (*1954*), 456–7; progress, 457–8; Little Rock, 457, Mississippi, 488

Schurz, Carl, 39, 44, 62

Science and Technology

APPLIED SCIENCES: construction, 51, 55–6, 66, 90–1, 223–5, 229–34; electricity and communications, 69n.; farming and food processing, 50, 55, 66; industrial machinery and power, 50, 229; and computer, 477–8; transport, 50, 56; automobile, 223–5, aviation, 229–34;

NATURAL AND PHYSICAL SCIENCES: 20th century, 253

Scott, Gen. Hugh L., 186, 197

Sculpture, *see* Painting and Sculpture

Sea Power

ENGLISH: WW I, 177–8; 209, 262–4;

ROLE OF: in Spanish-American War, 119, 120; in WW I, 169, 177–81, 191–6, 205; limitations, 323; in WW II, 359–64, 369–74, 374–6, 379–80, 383–8, 395–9, 406

Securities and Exchange Commission, 308, 452, 482

Securities and Stock Market: speculation, gold corner, 33–4, Credit Mobilier, 35; railroad finance 36, 52–3, 144; panics of *1873* and *1893*, 73, of *1907*, 151–2; "Trusts," 73, 74, 138–9; Federal Reserve Board, 169, 282, 308; WW I, 207; foreign bonds, 265, 266; boom, 281–6; crash, 286–90; regulation, 307–8; Truth-in-Securities Act, 307–8; SEC, 308; Glass-Steagall Act, 309; Public Utilities Holding Co. Act, 309; Pecora investigation, 308–9

Sedition Act (*1918*), 206

Seward, William H., sale of Alaska, 30; and Canada, 31

Shaw, George Bernard, 95

Shays, Daniel: Rebellion, 96

Shelley, Percy Bysshe, *quoted*, 486

Sheridan, Gen. Philip, 37, 60

Sherman Anti-Trust Act (*1890*), 138, 139, 143, 144, 157

Sherman, Sen. John, 39, 117

Sherman, Gen. William T., 60

Ships and Shipping, 278; post-Civil War, 55, 56–8; in WW I, 181, 195–6; in WW II, 367–8, 379–89; *see also* Trade

Sicily, 378, 381, 400

Silver Purchase Act (*1890*), 47, 111–2

Sims, Adm. William S., 192–3, 200

Sinclair, Harry F., 276–7

Sinclair, Upton, 134, 140, 325

Sioux Indians, 59, 60, 61; *see also* Indians

Slossan, Edwin D., 251

Smith, Gov. Alfred E., 274, 294, 295, 482, 484; Prohibition, 239, 281; *1924* election, 239, *1928*, 280–1; New Deal, 295, 319

Smith, Bessie, 252

Smith, Gerald L. K., 354

Smith, Gen. H. M., 386

Smith, Jess, 261, 276

Smith, Joseph, 88

Smith, Gen. Oliver, 437–8

Smithsonian Institution, 43

Social Security Act, 309, 321

Socialism, 81, 107, 113, 134, **165**, 302, 314, 473, 475

Socialist Party, 128, 134, 142, 165, 184, 206, 217, 220, 296, 328

Soil Conservation Act (*1936*), 315

Solomon Islands, 375, 376, 385, 482

Somme, Battle of, 203

Sousa, John Philip, 93, 120

South Africa, Union of, 114, 461

South Vietnam, 461, 463–4

Southeast Asia Treaty Organization (SEATO), 464, 473

Spaatz, Gen. Carl, 199, 389

Spain: U.S. relations, 117–29; civil war, 300, 342, 343; loses colonial power, 461

Spanish-American War 54, 117–29

Spellman, Francis Cardinal, 444

Spencer, Herbert, 83, 84, 88, 89, 132

Sports, *see* Recreation

Sprague, Adm. Clifton, 397

Spruance, Adm. Raymond A., 371–3, 386, 387–8, 405

Stalin, Josef, 201–2, 318, 410–1, 425; pact with Hitler, 347–8; meets with Allies, 364, 410; objectives, 411; U.N., 420; Chinese Communists and Korea, 428, 432–4

Stalingrad, Battle of, 378

Stanford, Leland, 75

Stark, Adm. Harold R., 193, 351

Stassen, Harold, 438*n.*, 445

States' Rights and Sovereignty SOCIAL COMPACT THEORY, school integration, 456–7;
MOVEMENTS: Dixiecrats, 419; school integration, 456–7; *see also* Nullification

Steel Industry: growth, 72; U.S. supremacy, 103; trusts, 144; 20th century, big business, 144, 475; sit-down strikes, 331; and Kennedy, 489

Steffens, Lincoln, 134, 282

Stephen, George, 52, 77

Stevens, Robert, 454

Stevenson, Adlai E. (I), 128; (II), 446–7, 459, 483; *quoted*, 451

Stilwell, Gen. Joseph W., 427

Stimson, Henry L., 266, 269, 352; sec. of war, 155, 365; Philippines, 269–70

Stone, Chief Justice Harlan F., 319, 320, 321

Story, Justice Joseph, 37
Suez Canal, 146, 379, 465
Sugar: production, 127
Sukarno, Achmed, 461
Sullivan, John L., 103, 241
Sullivan, Louis H., 89, 90, 91
Sumner, Sen. Charles, 31
Sumner, William G., 85n., 132
Supreme Court: *Plessy* v. *Ferguson*, 108; income tax, 112; trusts, 138–9; NRA, 306, 320–1, 330, 340; AAA, 321; civil rights, 456–8
Surigao Strait, Battle of, 397
Swedes, 133–4; *see also* Immigration

T

Taft-Hartley Act, 418–9, 445
Taft, Sen. Robert A., 353, 418, 423, 424, 438, 445, 453, 483
Taft, William H., 124, 130, 210, 214, 220, 265; Supreme Court and, 85, 162; sec. of war, 147–8; elected President (*1908*), 152; character and ability, 154–5; domestic policies, 154–7; Mexico and Nicaragua, 160–1, 268; and Theodore Roosevelt, 162–3; *1912* election, 162–6; Chief Justice, 166; "dollar diplomacy," 160; Prohibition, 238; *quoted*, 147–8
Talleyrand, Charles M. de, 184
Tammany Hall, 165, 482; Cleveland and, 44
Tarawa, 203, 386
Tarbell, Ida, 135
Tariffs
 u.s.: Civil War, 34, 46; McKinley Tariff Act, 48; Wilson, 112; Dingley, 117, 155; insular levies, 124; Payne-Aldrich, 155–6, 157; reciprocity with Canada, 159; Underwood, 168; Fordney-McCumber, 265; Smoot-Hawley, 275; Reciprocal Trade Agreements, 295, 317–8; post-WW II reductions, 421
Taxation
 u.s.: "Whisky Ring," 35; trusts and, 75, 143; income, 112; XVI Amendment, 157; WW I, 207; in *1920*'s, 278; New Deal and taxing power, 302, 320, 321; WW II, 369; venture capital, 473; reduction, 489
Taylor, Gen. Maxwell D., 451

Teapot Dome, 156, 268, 276–7, 336
Tennessee: evolution controversy, 88
Tennessee Valley Authority, 309–17, 473, 476; Dixon-Yates, 455–6
Tenure of Office Act, 41, 45
Terry, Gen. Alfred H., 60
Texas: *1880–1960*, 53; ranching, 64–6; oil industry, 229, 474; extreme right, 498
Thailand, 357, 360, 464
Theater: *1870–1900*, 93, 94–5; post-*1900*, 245, 252
Thomas, Norman, 134, 328
Thomas, Theodore, 37, 93
Thurmond, Gov. Strom, 419
Tilden, Gov. Samuel J., 38
Tillman, Benjamin R., 107, 116
Tobacco: New Deal and AAA, 307
Tojo, Gen. Hideki, 351, 357, 385, 431
Townsend, Dr. Francis E., 325, 326, 327
Toyoda, Adm. S., 387, 396
Trade: post-Civil War, 56–8, 66; dumping, 145; WW I, 207; post-war, 282; New Deal, 304–5; Atlantic Charter and, 356
Transportation: roads and highways, 225–6, 455; water (inland), 226–7; post-Civil War, 50–8; autos, 223–8, 234; commercial aviation, 229–34; *see also* Railroads; Ships and Shipping
Trotsky, Leon, 201–2, 211
Trujillo, Rafael, 170
Truman, Harry S, 132, 226, 460, 470, 476, 496; as Senator, 320; as Vice President, 400; becomes President (*1945*), 404; Potsdam, 407; atom bomb, 407–8; Russia, 410–5; nuclear weapons research, 415; character and ability, 415–7, 447; labor, 418–9; civil rights, 419; Marshall Plan, 423–4; Truman Doctrine, 424; founds NATO, 426; China, 426–9; Korea, 432–41; U.N., 434–5; *1952* election, 442–7; vetoes McCarran-Walter Act, 459; Dulles, 453, *quoted*, 416, 442
Trumbull, Sen. Lyman, 34, 36
Trusts and Concentration:
 rise of and abuses, 73–6; general, 73–6, 138–44; Progressives'

view of, 130–5; exposés, 134–5; mergers and holding companies, 138–9, 141; impact on labor and consumers, 138–9; concentration competition and New Free Enterprise, 473–6; regulation, 77; ICC and Sherman Acts, 75; Supreme Court and pools, 138; holding companies, 141; Act of *1903*, Hepburn Act, and ICC powers, 141–2; Standard Oil case and "rule of reason," 144; Clayton Act, Federal Trade Commission, and Transportation Act, 144; Public Utilities Holding Co. Act, 309; *see also* Conservation; Oil Industry; Railroads; Securities and Stock Market; Steel Industry

Truth-in-Securities Act (*1933*), 307–8, 309

Tugwell, Rexford G., 301

Tunisia, 378, 461

Turgot, Robert, 133, 341

Turkey, 191, 204, 265, 423–5, 469

Turner, Adm. R. Kelly, 386–7, 404

Twain, Mark, 36, 43, 96, 127

Tweed, William M. ("Boss"), 36, 38

Tydings, Sen. Millard, 443–4

Tyler, John, 296

U

U-2 Incident, 469, 472, 496

Un-American Activities Committee, 442–5

Unemployment: *1887*, 81; *1893*, 112, 290; *1930*'s, 290, 292, 297; New Deal measures, 303–4, 305–6, 309; *1936* election, 327–8; *1937* recession, 339; federal responsibility for, 339; demagogues and, 341; WW II, 368; compensation, 454; automation, 477–8, 489

Unitarian Church: evolution theory, 88

United Arab Republic, 468; hostility to Israel, 425, 465–8; Nasser, 465–6

United Mine Workers Union, 312, 331

United Nations, 214, 413, 450, 485, 497; UNESCO and UNRRA, 420–1; and atomic energy commissions, 422; and Israel, 425; Korea, 433, 434–5,

437; "Atoms for Peace," 459; new nations in, 461; Suez Canal crisis, 465; and Hungary, 468; Kashmir-Pakistan dispute, 494

Uruguay, 172

U.S. Air Force: in WW I, 194–5, 199; in WW II, specialization of, 366; research in, 366

U.S. Army, reduction, 463; WW I, 196–200; WW II, peacetime conscription, 352, 355; training, 356, 366; jungle warfare, 376; North African campaign, 376–9; Italy and Normandy invasion, 381–3; demobilization, 417; desegregation, 458; build-up under Kennedy, 489–90; *see also* World Wars I and II

U.S. Marines, WW I, 203; Haiti, 170; Nicaragua, 268–70; WW II, Battle of Midway, 371–3; Guadalcanal, 374–7; Korea, 435–6; 437–8; build-up under Kennedy, 489

U.S. Merchant Marine:
World War I build-up, 181, 195, arming of ships, 181, 187; ships sunk before WW II, 355; building program, 366–7

U.S. Navy:
WORLD WAR I: Big Navy Act, 181, 262–3; operations, 191–6; aviation, 194–5;
WORLD WAR II: two-ocean war, 351, 356; Germany, 355; Pearl Harbor, 357–60, convoys, 362; Battle of Atlantic, 362–3, 379–80; Kamikaze, 367, 405; special forces, 366–7; Coral Sea and Midway battles, 371–4; Guadalcanal, 371, 374–6; new techniques, 376; Casablanca, 378–81; amphibious campaigns, 386–8; Leyte Gulf battle, 395–9; Okinawa, 405–6;
POSTWAR: Korea, 435; cold war, 462–3; build-up under Kennedy, 489

V

Vandenberg, Sen. Arthur H., 309, 353, 360, 420, 423

Vanderbilt, Commo. Cornelius, 36

Vaughan, Gen. Harry, 445

Venezuela, 114, 148–9, 368

Versailles Treaty (*1919*), 212–5, 216–7, 342

Victoria, Queen, 31, 119–20

Villa, Pancho, 171–2, 183, 196
Virginia: "interposition," 457
Volstead Act (*1919*), 237–8

W

Wagner-Connery Act (*1935*), 330
Wainwright, Gen. Jonathan M., 361
Wake Island, 360
Walker, Gen. Walton H., 436
Wallace, Henry A.: sec. of agriculture, 300; Agricultural Adjustment Act, 306–7; Vice President, 354; *1944* election, 400; forms Progressive party, 414, 419; soil bank, 455
Wallace, Henry C., 301
Wallas, Graham, 132–3, 137
Walsh, Sen. Thomas J., 276
War Crimes Trials: Nuremberg, 264, 403, 421; Japan, 431–2
War of *1812*, 177
War of the Pacific, 42, 44
War Production Board, 368
Warren, Chief Justice Earl, 456–7
Washington, Booker T., 107, 164
Washington, D.C., *see* District of Columbia
Watson, Tom, *quoted*, 107
Weaver, Gen. James B., 40, 48, 106
Wedemeyer, Gen. Albert C., 427
Welles, Sumner, 170, 365
West, American
  U.S. ACQUISITIONS: Alaska, 30, 32; WESTWARD MOVEMENT: Far West, 51–54, 58–69, 104–6; railroads, 50–55
  GOLD RUSH, 60, 61
Wharton, Edith, 250
Wheat: production, rise in, 55; new Wheat Belt, 55, 72; prices, 105; control of, 307; Depression, 307
Wheeler, Burton K., 355
Wheeler, Gen. Jos., 120
Wheelock, John H., 250
Whisky Ring, 35
Whistler, James McNeill, 92
White, William Allen, 353
Whitehead, Alfred North, 329
Whitman, Walt, 95; *quoted*, 232
Wilderness Act, *see* Conservation
Wilhelm II, Kaiser, 114, 119, 123, 151, 176, 184, 205, 206, 208, 349
Wilkinson, Adm. Theodore S., 385
Willkie, Wendell, 309, 444; *1940* election, 353–4; *1944*, 399; "One

World," 399; and Russian regime, 411
Wilson, Charles E., 450, 463
Wilson, Gen. Sir Henry, 382
Wilson, Woodrow: background, 164; civil service, 41–2; Supreme Court, 85; segregation, 108; tariffs, 112, 168; "dollar diplomacy," 160, 170; Mexican revolution, 170–3; governor of New Jersey, 164; elected President (*1912*), 164–6; Federal Reserve Act, 168–9; neutrality, 175–177; Navy Act, 181, 262–3; mediation efforts, 182; *1916* election, 182–4; declaration of war (*1917*), 188–9; Fourteen Points, 192*n*., 208; Paris Peace Conference, 207–14; League of Nations, 208–17; illness, 216; evaluation of, 221–2; Prohibition, 238
Wine & Liquor, 237; *see also* Prohibition
Wister, Owen, 68–9
Women: suffrage, 135, 237, 239, 243; employment, 84, 85, 97, 236; Prohibition and, 237; in higher education, 97; labor legislation and, 83–5; in aviation, 233; emancipated, 243–8; in military service, 366
Wood, Gen. Leonard, 126–7, 180, 219, 270
Woodin, William H., 300–1, 305, 317
Woodward, William E., 249
Work, Hubert, 337
Works Project Administration (*1933*), 306
World War I
  outbreak and neutrality policy, 174–80; preparedness, 180–4; peace efforts, 182, 184–5; war declared, 189; forces: navy, 191–6; army, 196–200; air forces, 194–5, 199; casualties, 199*n*.; *1918* offensive, 200–5; internal attitudes, 174–7, 180–1, 182–3; and propaganda, 205–6; Espionage & Sedition Acts, 206; production and price control, 206–7; finance, 207; lessons of, 346, 355, 364
World War II, 342–409; background, Europe and Asia, 342–50; Neutrality Acts, 346; "short of war" policy and Lend-Lease, 350–5; negotiations with Japan,

356–7; Pearl Harbor, 357–8; U.S. in, military preparations, 351–3, 355, 366–9; joint Allied strategy, 364–6, 376–9, 389–93, 407–9; Battle for the Atlantic, 362–4, 379–80; Africa, 376–9; Sicily and Italy, 381–3; France and Germany, 389–95, 400–4; Pacific. 359–61, 369–76, 383–8, 395–8, 404–9; surrender, 404, 409, internal attitudes, 345, 350–1, 352–3, 399–400; production and controls, 368–9; finance, 369

Wright, Frank Lloyd, 71, 90
Wright, Orville & Wilbur, 230–1

Y

Yalta Conference, 404, 410, 412–414
Yamamoto, Adm. Isoroku, 370, 371–74, 387
Ypres, Third Battle of, 200

Z

Zapata, Emiliano, 171–2
Zimmerman Note, 187

NOTES